THE WARS OF RELIGION
IN FRANCE
1559-1576

VIEW OF PARIS

From a sketch by Jacques Callot (1592-1635).

The Wars of Religion in France

1559 - 1576

THE HUGUENOTS
CATHERINE DE MEDICI
PHILIP II

BY

JAMES WESTFALL THOMPSON

FREDERICK UNGAR PUBLISHING CO.

New York

Library of Congress Catalog Card Number 58-7725

TO
MARY HAWES WILMARTH
THE LARGESS OF WHOSE SPIRIT HAS MADE THE
WORLD RICHER AND LIFE NOBLER

PREFACE

No one acquainted with the history of historical writing can have failed to observe how transitory are its achievements. Mark Pattison's aphorism that "history is one of the most ephemeral forms of literature" has much of truth in it. The reasons of this are not far to seek. In the first place, the most laborious historian is doomed to be superseded in course of time by the accumulation of new material. In the second place, the point of view and the interpretation of one generation varies from that which preceded it, so that each generation requires a rewriting of history in terms of its own interest.

These reasons must be my excuse for venturing to write a new book upon an old subject. It is now nearly thirty years since the appearance of the late Professor Henry M. Baird's excellent work, *The Rise of the Huguenots* (New York, 1879), and little that is comprehensive has since been written upon the subject in English, with the exception of Mr. A. W. Whitehead's admirable *Gaspard de Coligny, Admiral of France* (London, 1904). But the limitations imposed by biographical history compel an author inevitably to ignore movements or events not germane to his immediate subject, which, nevertheless, may be of great importance for general history. Moreover, a biography is limited by the term of life of the hero, and his death may not by any means terminate the issue in which he was a factor—as indeed was the case with Coligny.

An enumeration of the notable works—sources and authorities—which have been published since the appearance of Professor Baird's work may serve to justify the present volume. First and foremost must be mentioned the notable *Lettres de Catherine de Médicis*, the lack of which Ranke deplored, edited by the late Count Hector de la Ferrière and M. Baguenault de la Puchesse (9 vols.), the initial volume of which appeared in 1880. Of diplomatic correspondence we have the *Ambassade en Espagne de Jean Ebrard*,

seigneur de St. Sulpice de 1562 à 1565 (Paris, 1902), edited by
M. Edmond Cabié, and the *Dépêches de M. Fourquevaux, ambassadeur du roi Charles IX en Espagne, 1565-72*, in three volumes,
edited by the Abbé Douais (Paris, 1896). Other sources which
have seen the light within the last three decades are M. Delaborde's
Vie de Coligny (3 vols., 1877-), the title of which is somewhat mis-
leading, for it is really a collection of Coligny's letters strung upon
the thread of his career; the Baron Alphonse de Ruble's *Antoine
de Bourbon et Jeanne d'Albret* (4 vols., 1881); M. Ludovic Lalanne's new annotated edition of *D'Aubigné* (1886), and the new
edition of Beza's *Histoire ecclésiastique* (ed. of Baum, 1883).
Finally, among sources should be included many volumes in the
"Calendar of State Papers." Professor Baird has rightly said that
"Too much weight can scarcely be given to this source of
information and illustration." His praise would probably have
been even greater if he could have used the correspondence of Dale
and Smith as freely as he did that of Throckmorton and Norris.

When we pass from sources to authorities the list of notable
works is even longer. La Ferrière's *Le XVIᵉ siècle et les Valois*
—the fruit of researches in the Record Office in London—appeared
in 1879; M. Forneron's *Histoire de Philippe II* (4 vols.) was
published in 1887, and is even more valuable than his earlier
Histoire des ducs de Guise (1877). Besides these, in the decade of
the 80's, are Durier's *Les Huguenots en Bigorre* (1884); Communay's *Les Huguenots dans le Béarn et la Navarre* (1886); Lettenhove's *Les Huguenots et les Gueux* (1885); the baron de Ruble's
Le traité de Cateau-Cambrésis (1889), and the abbé Marchand's
Charles de Cossé, Comte de Brissac (1889). M. de Crue's notable
Anne, duc de Montmorency appeared in the same year and his
no less scholarly *Le parti des politiques au lendemain de Saint Barthélemy* three years later. M. Marlet's *Le comte de Montgomery*
was published in 1890; M. Georges Weill's *Les théories sur le
pouvoir royal en France pendant les guerres de religion*, in 1891;
M. Henri Hauser's *François de La Noue* in 1892; M. Bernard de
Lacombe's *Catherine de Médicis entre Guise et Condé* in 1899, and,
most recently of all, M. Courteault's *Blaise de Montluc* (1908).

Many contributions in the *Revue historique*, the *Revue des questions historiques*, the *English Historical Review*, the *Revue d'histoire diplomatique*, the *Revue des deux mondes*, and one article in the *American Historical Review*, January, 1903, by M. Hauser, "The Reformation and the Popular Classes in the Sixteenth Century," are equally valuable, as the notes will show. I have also consulted many articles in the proceedings of various local or provincial historical societies, as the Société de Paris et de l'Ile de France; the Société de l'histoire de Normandie, the Société d'histoire et d'archéologie de Genève, etc., and the admirable series known as the *Bulletin de la Société d protestantisme français*, which is a mine of historical lore.

While the present work falls in the epoch of the French Reformation, no attempt has been made to treat that subject in so far as the Reformation is assumed primarily to have been a religious manifestation. Doctrine, save when it involved polity, has been ignored. But into the political, diplomatic, and economic activities of the period I have tried to go at some length. As to the last feature, it is not too much to say that our interpretation of the sixteenth century has been profoundly changed within the last twenty years by the progress made in economic history. Such works as Weiss's *La chambro ardonto* and Hauser's *Ouvriers du temps passé* have revolutionized the treatment of this subject.

Such an interpretation is merely a reflection of our own present-day interest in economic and social problems. In this particular it is the writer's belief that he is the first to present some of the results of recent research into the economic history of sixteenth-century France to English readers. My indebtedness to M. Hauser is especially great for the help and suggestion he has given me in the matter of industrial history. But I have tried to widen the subject and attempted to show the bearing of changes in the agricultural régime, the influence of the failure of crops owing to adverse weather conditions, and the disintegration of society as the result of incessant war and the plague, upon the progress of the Huguenot movement. In an agricultural country like France in the sixteenth century, the distress of the provinces through the failure of the harvests was sometimes nearly universal, and the retroactive effect of such conditions in promoting popular discontent had a marked influence upon the religious and political issues.

It has been pointed out that "the religious wars of France furnish the most complete instance of the constant intersection of native and foreign influences."[1] The bearing of the Huguenot movement upon Spanish and Dutch history was intimate and marked, and this I have also attempted to set forth. In so doing the fact that has impressed me most of all is the development and activity of the provincial Catholic leagues and their close connection with Spain's great Catholic machine in France, the Holy League.

The history of the Holy League in France is usually represented as having extended from 1576 to 1594. This time was the period of its greatest activity and of its greatest power. But institutions do not spring to life full armed in a moment, like Athené from the head of Zeus. "The roots of the present lie deep in the past," as Bishop Stubbs observed. Institutions are a growth, a development. The Holy League was a movement of slow growth and development, although it has not been thus represented, and resulted from the combination of various acts and forces—political, diplomatic, religious, economic, social, even psychological—working simultaneously both within and without France during the civil wars. I have tried to set forth the nature and extent of these forces; to show how they originated; how they operated; and how they ultimately were combined to form the Holy League. Certain individual features of the history here covered have been treated in an isolated way by some writers. The late baron de Ruble and M. Forneron have disclosed the treasonable negotiations of Montluc with Philip II. M. Bouillé and more recently M. Forneron have followed the tortuous thread of the cardinal of Lorraine's secret negotiations with Spain. Various historians, chiefly in provincial histories or biographies like Pingaud's *Les Saulx-Tavannes*, have noticed the local work of some of the provincial Catholic associations. But the relation of all these

[1] *The Wars of Religion* ("The Cambridge Modern History," Preface).

various movements, one to the other, and their ultimate fusion into a single united movement has not yet been fully brought out. What was the number and form of organization of these local Catholic leagues? What influenced their combination? What bearing did they have upon the course of Montluc and the cardinal of Lorraine? Or upon Philip II's policy? How did the great feud between the Guises and the Montmorencys influence the formation of the Holy League and its hostile counterpart—the Association of the Huguenots and the Politiques? These questions I have tried to answer and in so doing two or three new facts have been brought to light. For example, an undiscovered link in the history of the Guises' early secret intercourse with Philip II has been found in the conduct of L'Aubespine, the French ambassador in Spain in 1561; the treasonable course of the cardinal of Lorraine, it is shown, began in 1565 instead of 1566, a fact which makes the petty conflict known as the "Cardinal's War" of new importance; the history of the Catholic associations in the provinces, hitherto isolated in many separate volumes, has been woven into the whole and some new information established regarding them.[1]

The notes, it is hoped, will sufficiently indicate the sources used and enable the reader to test the treatment of the subject, or guide him to sources by which he may form his own judgment if desired.

In the matter of maps, the very complete apparatus of maps in Mr. Whitehead's *Gaspard de Coligny, Admiral of France*, has greatly lightened my task, and I express my cordial thanks to Mr. Whitehead and Messrs. Methuen & Co., his publishers, for permission to reproduce those in that work. My thanks are also due to M. Ch. de Coynart and MM. Firmin Didot et Cie for permission to reproduce the map illustrating the battle of Dreux from the late Commandant de Coynart's work entitled *L'Année 1562 et la bataille de Dreux;* and to M. Steph. C. Gigon, author of *La bataille de Jarnac et la campagne de 1569 en Angoumois,* for

---

[1] In the appendix I have published the constitution of two of these provincial leagues hitherto unknown.

permission to use his two charts of the battle of Jarnac. Those illustrating the Tour of the Provinces in 1564–66, the march of the duke of Alva and Montgomery's great raid in Gascony are my own. Some lesser maps and illustrations are from old prints which I have gathered together, in the course of years, except that illustrating the siege of Havre-de-Grace and the large picture of the battle of St. Denis, which have been photographed from the originals in the Record Office.

During the preparation of this volume, which has entailed two prolonged visits to Paris and other parts of France, and to London, I have become the debtor to many persons. Among those of whose courtesy and assistance I would make special acknowledgment are the following: His Excellency, M. Jean-Jules Jusserand, French ambassador at Washington; M. Henri Vignaud, chargé d'affaires of the American legation in Paris; MM. Charles de la Roncière and Viennot of the Bibliothèque Nationale; MM. Le Grand and Viard of the Archives Nationales, where I chiefly worked in the K. Collection. At the Record Office, Mr. Hubert Hall and his assistant, Miss Mary Trice Martin, were unfailing in the aid given me. For the transcript of the "Discorso sopra gli humori del Regno di Francia," from the Barberini Library in Rome, I am indebted to P. Franz Ehrle, prefect of the Vatican archives. I also hold in grateful memory the friendship and assistance of the late Woodbury Lowery, author of *The Spanish Settlements within the Present Limits of the United States: Florida* (1562–74), New York, 1905, with whom I was a fellow worker at the Archives Nationales in the spring and early summer of 1903.

Finally, I owe much to the suggestive criticism of my friend and colleague, Professor Ferdinand Schevill, and my friends, Professor Herbert Darling Foster, of Dartmouth College, and Professor Roger B. Merriman, of Harvard University, each of whom has read much of the manuscript.

JAMES WESTFALL THOMPSON

THE UNIVERSITY OF CHICAGO
January 1909

CONTENTS

xiii

LIST OF MAPS AND PLATES

CHAPTER I

THE BEGINNING OF THE HUGUENOT REVOLT. THE CON-SPIRACY OF AMBOISE

The last day of June, 1559, was a gala day in Paris. The marriages of Philip II of Spain with Elizabeth of France, daughter of King Henry II and Catherine de Medici, and that of the French King's sister, Marguerite with Emanuel Philibert, duke of Savoy, were to be celebrated. But "the torches of joy became funeral tapers"[1] before nightfall, for Henry II was mortally wounded in the tournament given in honor of the occasion.[2] It was the rule that challengers, in this case the King, should run three courses and their opponents one. The third contestant of the King had been Gabriel, sieur de Lorges, better known as the count of Montgomery, captain of the Scotch Guard,[3] a young man, "grand et roidde," whom Henry rechallenged because his pride was hurt that he had not better kept his seat in the saddle in the first running. Montgomery tried to refuse, but the King silenced his objections

---

[1] *Mém. de Tavannes*, 239.

[2] The constable Montmorency, in a letter to Queen Elizabeth dated June 30, 1559, says that the accident happened "yesterday," i. e., June 29.—*C. S . P. Eng. For.*, No. 698. Almost all the sources, however, give June 30. Cf. Castelnau, Book I, chap. i. Throckmorton gives June 30. See p. 3, note 1.

[3] The origin of the Scotch Guard goes back to the Hundred Years' War. In 1420, five years after the battle of Agincourt, when Henry V was in possession of all of northern France, the dauphin, Charles VII, sent the count of Vendôme to Scotland to ask for assistance in virtue of the ancient league between the two nations. In 1421 a body of 1,000 Scots arrived in France under the earl of Buchan. They fought at Baugé in Anjou in that year, but were almost all destroyed in 1424 in the furious battle of Verneuil. The remnant, in honor of their services, became the king's own guard. See Skene, *The Book of Pluscarden*, II, xix–xxi, xxvi–xxix; Houston, *L'Escosse françois* (Discours des alliances commencées depuis l'an sept cents septante, et continuées jusques à present, entre les couronnes de France et d'Escosse), Paris, 1608; Forbes Leith, *The Scots Men-at-Arms and Life Guards in France, from Their Formation until Their Final Dissolution*, 2 vols., 1882. The Guard consisted of the principal captain, the lieutenant, and the ensign, the maréchal-de-loges, three commis, eighty archers of the guard, twenty-four archers of the corps; the pay of whom amounted annually to 51,800 francs, or 6,475 pounds sterling.—*C. S. P. For.*, No. 544, December, 1559.

with a command and reluctantly[1] Montgomery resumed his place. But this time the Scotch guardsman failed to cast away the trunk of the splintered lance as he should have done at the moment of

MONTGOMERY IN TOURNAMENT COSTUME
(Bib. Nat., Estampes, *Hist. de France*, reg. Q. b. 19)

the shock, and the fatal accident followed. The jagged point crashed through the King's visor into the right eye.[2]   For a minute

[1] Claude Haton, whose Catholic prejudice was strong, believed this reluctance to be feigned (*Mémoires*, I, 107).

[2] D'Aubigné, Book II, chap. xiv, says the blow raised the King's visor, and that the end of the lance, which was bound with a *morne*, or ring, to dull the point, crashed through the helmet like a bludgeon.   Tavannes, chap. xiv, says that the King had failed to take the precaution to fasten his visor down.

Henry reeled in his saddle, but by throwing his arms around the neck of his horse, managed to keep his seat. The King's armor was stripped from him at once and "a splint taken out of good bigness."[1] He moved neither hand nor foot, and lay as if benumbed or paralyzed,[2] and so was carried to his chamber in the Tournelles,[3] entrance being denied to all save physicians, apothecaries, and those valets-de-chambre who were on duty. None were permitted for a great distance to come near until late in the day, when the duke of Alva, who was to be proxy for his sovereign at the marriage, the duke of Savoy, the prince of Orange, the cardinal of Lorraine, and the constable were admitted.[4]

After the first moment of consternation was past, it was thought that the King would recover, though losing the sight of his eye,[5] since on the fourth day Henry recovered his senses and his fever was abated. Meanwhile five or six of the ablest physicians in France had been diligently experimenting upon the heads of four criminals who were decapitated for the purpose in the Conciergerie and the prisons of the Châtelet. On the eighth day Vesalius, Philip II's physician, who had long been with the emperor Charles V, and who enjoyed a European reputation, arrived and took special charge of the royal patient.[6] In the interval of consciousness Henry commanded that the interrupted marriages be solemnized. Before they were celebrated the King had lost the use of

[1] Throckmorton to the Lords in Council, *C. S. P. For.*, June 30, 1559.

[2] D'Aubigné, *loc. cit.* La Place, 20, says that the King spoke to the cardinal of Lorraine. De Thou, Book II, 674, on the authority of Brantôme, doubts it.

[3] The Palais des Tournelles stood in the present Place Royale. It was torn down in 1575.

[4] Throckmorton, *loc. cit.*

[5] The constable Montmorency to Queen Elizabeth, *C. S. P. For.*, No. 898, June 30, 1559. Throckmorton, *ibid.*, No. 928, July 4, "doubted the King would lose his eye." •

[6] *C. S. P. For.*, No. 950, July 8, 1559. De Ruble, *Antoine de Bourbon et Jeanne d'Albret* I, 432, has published Vesalius' official report. Henry II had a body-physician who also enjoyed a European reputation. This was Fernal. He was the author of a Latin work upon pathology which was translated into French in 1660 under the title: *La pathologie de Jean Fernal, premier medicin de Henry II, roy de France, ouvrage très-utile à tous ceux qui s'appliquent à la connoissance du corps humain.*

speech and lapsed into unconsciousness, and on the morrow of
the marriages he died (July 10, 1559).   On August 13 the corpse
was interred at St. Denis.[1]   When the ceremony was ended the
king of arms stood up, and after twice pronouncing the words
"Le roi est mort," he turned around toward the assembly, and
the third time cried out: "Vive le roi, très-chretien François le

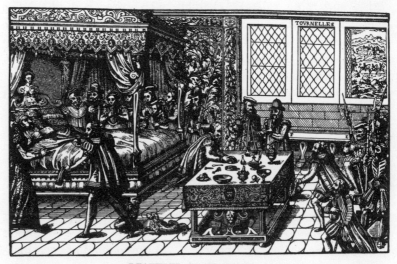

DEATHBED OF HENRY II

A. Catherine de Medici   D. Couriers
B. Cardinal of Lorraine   E. Courtiers
C. Constable Montmorency   F. Physicians

deuzième de ce nom, par la grace de Dieu, roi de France."   Thereupon the trumpets sounded and the interment was ended.[2]   A
month later, on September 18, Francis II was crowned at Rheims.
Already Montgomery had been deprived of the captaincy of the
Scotch Guard and his post given to "a mere Frenchman," much
to the indignation of the members of the Guard.[3]

[1] There is an account of the funeral in *Arch. cur.*, III, 309–48.   The MS
account of the funeral expenses is in the Phillipps Collection, 2,995.   Compare
Galembert, *Funerailles du roy Henri II, Roole des parties et somme de deniers
pour le faict des dits obsèques et pompes funèbres.*   Publié avec une introduction.
Paris, Fontaine, 1869.

[2] See the description of Throckmorton, written to Queen Elizabeth, *C. S. P.
For.*, No. 1,190, August 15, 1559.

[3] *C. S. P. For.*, No. 1,242, August 25, 1559.

The reign of Henry II had not been a popular one. He had neither the mind nor the application necessary in public affairs.[1] On the very day of the accident the English ambassador wrote to Cecil: "It is a marvel to see how the noblemen, gentlemen, and ladies do lament this misfortune, and contrary-wise, how the townsmen and people do rejoice."[2] The wars of Henry II in Italy and in the Low Countries had drained France of blood and treasure, so that the purses of the people were depleted by an infinity of exactions and confiscations; offices and benefices had been bartered, even those of justice, and to make the feeling of the people worse, Henry II was prodigal to his favorites.[3] Finally the treaty of Cateau Cambrésis (1559) was regarded as not less disadvantageous than dishonorable.[4]

Meanwhile much politics had been in progress.[5] The new king was not yet sixteen years of age.[6] He was of frail health and insignificant intellect, being quite unlike his wife, the beautiful and brilliant Mary Stuart, who was a niece of the Guises, Francis, duke of Guise, and his brother Charles, cardinal of Lorraine, who had been in no small favor under Henry II. Even in the king's lifetime the ambition of the Guises had been a thing of wonderment

[1] *Rel. vén.*, I, 195. "De fort petit sens," says La Planche, 202.

[2] Throckmorton to Cecil, June 30, 1559, *C. S. P. For.*, 899.

[3] And yet the evil nature of Henry II's reign may be exaggerated. An extended and critical history of his reign is still to be written. Claude Haton, no mean observer of economic conditions says: "En ce temps et par tout le règne du dit feu roy, faisoit bon vivre en France, et estoient toutes denrées et marchandises à bon marché, excepté le grain et le vin, qui enchérissoient certaines années plus que d'aultres, selon la stérilité, et toutesfois esdittes treize années de son règne n'ont esté que trois ans de cherté de grain et de vin, et n'a valu le blé froment, en la plus chère des dittes trois années, que 14 et 15. s. t. le bichet (à la mesure de Provins), et les aultres grains au prix le prix, et ne duroit telle cherté que trois moys pour le plus." A valuable table of prices of food stuffs follows.—Claude Haton, I, 112, 113.

[4] See De Ruble, "Le traité de Cateau-Cambrésis," *Revue d'hist. diplomatique* (1887), 385, and the more extensive work (1889) with the same title by this author.

[5] On the general situation between the wounding and the death of Henry II see *Nég. Tosc.*, III, 400.

[6] Castelnau, Book I, chap. i. He was sixteen on January 19, 1560. Cf. Castan, "La naissance des enfans du roi Henri de Valois," *Revue des savants*, 6me sér., III.

and his unexpected death opened before them the prospect of new and prolonged power. Henry II had scarcely closed his eyes when the duke of Guise and the cardinal of Lorraine took possession of the person of Francis II and conducted him to the Louvre, in company with the queen-mother, ignoring the princes of the blood, the marshals, the admiral of France, and "many Knights of the Order, or grand seigneurs who were not of their retinue." There they deliberated without permitting anyone to approach, still less to speak to the King except in the presence of one of them. Francis II gave out that his uncles were to manage his affairs.[1] In order to give color to this assumption of authority, as if their intention was to restore everything to good estate again, the Guises recalled the chancellor Olivier, who had been driven from office by Diane de Poitiers, Henry II's mistress.[2]

Even before these events the Guises had shown their hand, for on the day of Henry II's decease the constable, the cardinal Châtillon and his brother, the admiral Coligny, had been appointed to attend upon the royal corse at the Tournelles, by which maneuver they were excluded from all active work and the way was cleared for the unhampered rule of the King's uncles. Rumor prevailed that D'Andelot, the third of the famous Châtillon brothers, was to be dismissed from the command of the footmen and the place be given to the count de Rochefoucauld.[3] Before the end of the month the duke of Guise was given charge of the war office and the cardinal of Lorraine that of finance and matters

[1] Throckmorton to the queen, July 18, 1559, C. S. P. For., No. 1,009. This information was given to the council and a deputation of the Parlement, but no official proclamation was made.—D'Aubigné, I, 243, n. 1.

[2] Claude Haton, I, 106; Tavannes, 245. The deposed beauty surrendered the keys of the royal cabinets and some bags of precious jewels to the new queen, La Planche, 204; Baschet, 494, dispatch of the Venetian ambassador, July 12, 1559. Cf. Guiffrey, Lettres inédites de Diane de Poitiers, 1866; Imbart de St. Amand, Revue des deux mondes, August 15, 1866, p. 984. For light upon her extravagance see Chevalier, Archives royales de Chenonceau: Comptes des recettes et despences faites en la Chastellenie de Chenonceau, par Diane de Poitiers, duchesse de Valentinois, dame de Chenonceau et autres lieux (Techener, 1864). Hay, Diane de Poitiers, la grande sénéschale de Normandie, duchesse de Valentinois, is a sumptuously illustrated history.

[3] C. S. P. For., No. 1,024, July 19, 1559.

of state.[1]   At the same time, on various pretexts, the princes of the blood were sent away,[2] the prince of Condé to Flanders, ostensibly to confer with Philip II regarding the peace of Cateau-Cambrésis,[3] the prince of La Roche-sur-Yon and the cardinal Bourbon to conduct Elizabeth of France into Spain, so that by November "there remained no more princes with the King save those of Guise,"[4] who had influential agents in the two marshals, St. André[5] and Brissac.[6]

[1] Castelnau, Book I, chap. ii; C. S. P. For., No. 972, July 11, 1559; No. 1,080, July 27, 1559.

[2] La Planche, 208; Claude Haton, I, 108; Paulin Paris, Négociations, 108, note.

[3] Tavannes, 245; Paris, Négociations relatives au règne de François II, 61, 76, 80, 83, 86; La Planche, 207; C. S. P. For., No. 1,121, August 4, 1559; ibid., August 1, 1559, No. 1,101, Throckmorton to the Queen: "The French . . . . are in fear because of the king of Spain, who has not as yet restored S. Quentin's, Ham nor Chastelet, the Spanish garrisons of which daily make courses into the country as far as Noyon, about which the governor of Compegny has written to the King, adding that it were as good to have war as such a peace." C. S. P. For., July 13, 1559, No. 985, Throckmorton to the Queen: "It is thought that the treaty already made is void by the French King's death; . . . . that the king of Spain, seeing his advantage and knowing the state of France better than he did when he made that peace, will either make new demands, or constrain France to do as he will have them, who would be loath to break with him again."

[4] Tavannes, op. cit.

[5] Jacques d'Alban de St. André, born in the Lyonnais, marshal 1547, favorite of Henry II. He was taken prisoner at the battle of St. Quentin. After the death of Henry II, fearing prosecution for his enormous stealings in office, he became the tool of the Guises. See La Planche, 205, 206; Livre des marchands, 438, 439; and especially Boyvin du Villars, 904 ff., on his administration in Provence.

[6] Brissac was governor of Piedmont under Henry II, where he sustained the interests of France so energetically that Philip hated him. The Guises made great efforts to attach him to their party, with the hope of playing him against the Bourbons and Montmorencys (Paris, Négociations, 73, note). After the peace of Cateau-Cambrésis, the fortresses of the duke of Savoy were dismantled, to the intense anger of the latter. Cf. Fillon Collection, 2,654: Letter of July 16, 1560, to the duchess of Mantua, complaining that the people of Caluz have revolted against the authority of the marshal Brissac. This hard feeling probably explains Brissac's transfer to the government of Picardy, in January, 1560, to the chagrin of the prince of Condé, who asked for the place (Varillas, Hist. de François II, II, 35; De Thou, Book XXV, 518) after the marriage of Emanuel Philibert to the sister of Henry II. See Marchand, Charles I de Cossé, comte de Brissac, Paris, 1889, chap. xvi.

Much depended upon the attitude of Antoine of Bourbon, sieur de Vendôme and king of Navarre, who was first prince of the blood, and the person to whom the direction of affairs would naturally fall. At the time of Henry II's death he was in Béarn, whither La Mare, the King's valet-de-chambre, was sent to notify him,[1] the Guises having shrewdly arranged to have the ground cleared of the opposition of the Bourbons and Châtillons when he should arrive.[2]

But not all the opposition had been overcome. While Henry II had been generous to the Guises, he had been even fonder of the constable Montmorency, a bluff, hearty man of war, who became the royal favorite upon the fall of the admiral Hennebault, after the death of Francis I.[3] Montmorency was the uncle of the three Châtillons, Odet, the cardinal-bishop of Beauvais, Gaspard, the admiral Coligny, and François de Châtillon, sieur d'Andelot, and the King was openly accused of having made a disadvanta- geous peace in order to protect the constable and secure the ran- som of Coligny, who was captured at the battle of St. Quentin.[4] In order to prevent the constable and the king of Navarre from meeting one another and concerting an arrangement, the Guises contrived Montmorency's summary dismissal from court,[5] Francis II at their instigation sending him word to retire at once (August 15). The old war-dog[6] took the affront gallantly, and like an artful

[1] La Place, 26.

[2] C. S. P. For., Nos. 1,121, 1,149, August 4 and August 8, 1559.

[3] C. S. P. For., No. 972, July 11, 1559.

[4] Tavannes, 244. In Spain it was the prevailing belief that France had been compelled to make the peace of Cateau-Cambrésis more through the troubles caused by the affairs of religion than from any other necessity; cf. C. S. P. Ven., No. 57, 1559. This suspicion is confirmed by Tavannes, who says that the set- tlement of matters still pending under the terms of the treaty was hastened by the Guises through knowledge that the state of affairs in France was exceed- ingly unsatisfactory to many of the nobles and fear that their power would be openly rebelled against (Tavannes, 245; C. S. P. For., No. 590, January 18, 1560, and No. 26, October 5, 1559).

[5] The pretext was Montmorency's complaint because his son Damville was not given the government of Provence, which St. André had held (Rel. vén., I, 435; cf. Nég. Tosc., III, 401).

[6] "Vieil routier."—La Planche, 207.

courtier said that he was glad to be relieved of active duties on account of his age.[1] In the absence of the princes of the blood, the opposition to the Guises gathered around Montmorency and the Châtillons, the faction for a short time taking its name from the constable's title, being known as "connestablistes."[2] The political line of division was drawn very sharply, and the growing influence of Huguenot teachings gave it a religious accentuation as well. The less significant portion of the noblesse was inclined to repose after the long wars and was indifferent to politics; but the upper nobility were eager partisans, either having hopes of preferment or being, in principle, opposed both to the usurpation and the religious intolerance of the Guises.[3]

As to the clergy, its members almost without exception were supporters of the faith and the government of the Guises. The mass of the people as yet were disregarded by both factions, but were soon to come forward into prominence for financial and other reasons.[4] Henry II, unlike his father, had never suffered French Protestantism to flourish,[5] but, on the contrary, had under-

[1] "Le connestable . . . . resigna bien d'estat de grand-maistre entre les mains du roy, mais purement et simplement, et non en faveur du dict de Guyse, déclarant assez qu'il ne cédoit en rien à son adversaire."—La Planche, 216. Cf. D'Aubigné, I, 245, Book II, chap. xiv; *Rel. vén.*, I, 393; Tavannes, 245; Castlenau, Book I, chap. ii, Daschel, *La diplomatie vénétienne*, 495. La Place, 26, is in error. An attempt was made to soften Montmorency's fall by making his eldest son a marshal of France; Tavannes, 245; *C. S. P. For.*, No. 376, December 5, 1559.

[2] La Planche, 203.

[3] Castelnau, Book I, chap. iii.

[4] See the interesting analysis of public opinion by La Planche, 203. On p. 208 he gives a highly drawn picture of the venality of the parlements, whose "ancienne splendeur estoit desja esvannoye peu à peu," while they were frequented by "les soliciteurs des courtisans, et les advocats favoris des grands," in whose precincts justice was not possible for simple, honest folk. He is as bitter in speaking of the *conseil des affaires* and the *conseil privé*, but it must be remembered that the author was a Protestant and imbued with hatred against the government because of its persecution of the Huguenots. See Tavannes' (p. 243) eulogy of the French bar which is nearer the truth.

[5] For Henry II's policy toward Protestantism see De Crue, *Anne de Montmorency*, 244–48; Weiss, *La chambre ardente*, Introd.; Hauser, "De l'humanisme et de la réforme en France," *Rev. hist.*, LXIV (1897), 258, minimizes the intellectual causes of the French Reformation.

taken rigorous repressive measures. The edicts of Paris (1549), of Fontainebleau (1550), and of Chateaubriand (1551), made the Huguenots[1] subject to both secular and ecclesiastical tribunals.

[1] The origin of this word has been much discussed. In the early period of the Reformation in France, all religious schismatics save the Vaudois, whose historical identity was different and familiar, were called "Lutherans." The Venetian ambassador so characterized the French Protestants in a dispatch to the signory in 1558 (*Relazione de Giovanni Sorano*, ed. Alberi, I, 2, 409). Boyvin du Villars (Book XII, 204) employs this same term in 1560.

The etymology of the word "Huguenot," most commonly accepted is that which derives it from the German word *Eidgenossen* (confederacy) which designated the Swiss Confederates (see *Papiers d'état du cardinal de Granvelle*, VII, 660). The word in Geneva was naturally not German but French or Savoyard.   It is variously spelled—Eydgenots, Eygenots, Eyguenots.   But this derivation, though the best supported, is opposed by the eminent philologist, Littré.   Grandmaison, *Bulletin Soc. hist. prot. franç.*, LI (January, 1902), argues against the German origin of the word and gives examples of its appearance as a French surname from the fourteenth century onward.   But how it came to be applied to the French Protestants he is unable to say. Cf. Weiss: "La dérivation du nom Huguenot," *Bull. Soc. hist. prot. franç.*, XLVIII, 12 (December, 1898).   A note by A. Mazel states that in Languedoc the word was pronounced "Duganau," which he conjectures to be a diminutive of "Fugou," the great owl.   If this is so, the origin of the word is akin to that of "Chouan" in the French Revolution.   The earliest use of the word "Huguenot" in Languedoc is in Devic and Vaisette, *Histoire du Languedoc*, XI, 342. It undoubtedly was a term of reproach, *ibid.*, XI, 374, note; cf. Claude Haton, I, 121.   Without attempting to pronounce upon the origin of the word, I subjoin some allusions which I have come upon.   Castelnau, Book II, chap. vii, says: " . . . . qui depuis s'appelèrent huguenots en France, dont l'étymologie fut prise à la conjuration d'Amboise, lors que ceux qui devoient présenter la requeste, comme éperdus de crainte, fuyoient de tous costés.   Quelques femmes des villages dirent que c'estoient pauvres gens, qui ne valloient pas des huguenots, qui estoient une forte petite monnoye, encore pire que des mailles, du temps de Hugues Capet d'où vint en usage que par moquerie l'on les appelloit huguenots." Henri Estienne and La Place, 34, say the word arose from the circumstance that the Calvinists of Tours used to go outside of the Porte du roy Huguon to worship. La Planche's derivation is a study in folklore (p. 262, col. i).

The Venetian ambassador wrote in 1563: "In quel tempo medesimo fu tra questi principalmente, che cercorno di seminar la false dottrina un predicator della regina di Navarra, madre del presente re di Navarra, nominate Ugo, il quale alienò prima l' animo di quella regina dalla religion cattolica, e poi cercò d' alienare e di corromper, come fece, infiniti altri uomini e donne delli più grandi."—*Rel. vén.*, II, 50.   A unique explanation, which I have not found noticed elsewhere is preserved by Jean de Gaufreton, *Chronique bordelaise* (1877), I, 92: "En cette année les catholiques commencèrent d'appeller les Luthériens et protestants 'Huguenots,' et les autres nomèrent les catholicques papistes à cause, qu'ils tenoyent le parti du pape, et qu'ils soustenoyent son authorité.   Mais la raison pourquoy les Luthériens

The Protestant issue was both a religious and a political one, for to many men it seemed impossible to alter the religious beliefs of the time without destruction of the state. Francis I recognized this state of things in the rhymed aphorism:

Un roi
Une loi
Une foi

and his son rigidly sustained the dictum. The Edict of Compiègne, of July 24, 1557[1] imposed the death penalty upon those who publicly or secretly professed a religion other than the Catholic apostolic faith; the preamble declaring that "to us alone who have received from the hand of God the administration of the public affairs of our realm," clearly shows the intimate relation of the French state and the French church. It is significant that the *Chambre ardente* was established to prosecute the Huguenots in Henry II's reign.[2]

furent appellées Huguenots procède de ce que les princes protestants d'Allemagne et Luthériens ayant envoyé une solemnelle ambassade au roy, à la requête des Luthériens et protestants de France pour demander libre exercice du Luthéranisme en son royaume, en faveur des dits Luthériens français, comme le chef de cette ambasse voulut en sa première audience parler latin devant le roy, assisté des messieurs de son conseil, il ne put jamais dire que les deux mots à sçavait 'huc nos' et s'arresta tout court. Despuis les courtisans appellèrent les Luthériens françois 'huc nos,' et en suite 'Huguenots.' "

[1] Isambert, XIII, 494.

[2] Weiss, *La chambre ardente*, Paris, 1889, a study of liberty of conscience under Henry II, based upon about five hundred *arrêts* rendered by the Parlement of Paris between May, 1547, and March, 1550. Before its creation heresy was dealt with by the regular courts. In *Bulletin des comités historiques* (1850), 173 ("Inventaire des lettres relatives à l'histoire de France aux archives de Bâle"), there is noted a letter of the King written in 1552 to the effect that those who have been arrested for heresy at Lyons shall not be dealt with unjustly; but the King reiterates his determination not to permit any new religious doctrine to obtain. In the very month before his death, in June, 1559, the edict of Ecouan prescribed the death penalty for all heretics, without the least limitation or restriction, and with injunctions to the judges not to mitigate the punishment, as they had done for some years (Castelnau, Book I, chap. iii). The Huguenots regarded Henry II's death as a judgment of God.—*C. S. P. For.*, No. 899, June 30, 1559: "They let not openly to say the King's dissolute life and his tyranny to the professors of the gospel hath procured God's vengeance." A letter of Diane de Poitiers in the *Catalogue de la collection Trémont*, No. 424, proves that some of the property confiscated from the Huguenots was given by the King to his favorite.

Ever since the duke of Alva had been in Paris the impression had prevailed that Henry II and Philip II purposed to establish the Inquisition in France,[1] and that the project had been foiled by the French king's sudden death. The Huguenots were convinced of it and keen politicians like the prince of Orange and Count Egmont taxed Granvella with the purpose in 1561.[2] What the government did do has been carefully stated by another:

The Government largely increased the powers of the Ecclesiastical Courts, and, *pari passu*, detracted from those of the regular Law Courts called the Parlements. The Parlement of Paris protested not only against the infringement of its privileges, but against conversion by persecution, and the same feelings existed at Rouen, where several members had to be excluded for heretical opinions. The introduction of the Spanish form of inquisition, under a bull of Paul IV, in 1557, still further exasperated the profession. The Inquisitors were directed to appoint diocesan tribunals, which should decide without appeal. The Parlement of Paris flatly refused to register the royal edict, and continued to receive appeals. The finale was the celebrated Wednesday meeting of the assembled chambers, the Mercuriale, where the King in person interfered with the constitutional freedom of speech, and ordered the arrest of the five members, thus giving his verdict for the ultra-Catholic minority of Parlement against the moderate majority. Marshal Vieilleville, himself a sound Catholic, strongly dissuaded this course of action. Its result was that one of the most influential elements of the State was not indeed brought into connection with Reform, but as placed in an attitude of hostility to the Government, and as the grievance was the consequence of the religious policy of the Crown, it had at all events a tendency to bring about a *rapprochement* between the Reformers and the judicial classes.[3]

Five of the advocates of the Parlement of Paris, of whom Du Bourg and Du Four were the most prominent, protested against this action, both because of its intolerance and because they believed it to be a political measure, at least in part, and were put under arrest for this manifestation of courage. Men reasoned very differently regarding this edict. The politicians and intense Catholics

[1] Vargas, *Histoire de François II*, 314.

[2] Granvella to Philip II, June 14, 1561—*Papiers d'état du cardinal de Granvelle*, VI, 569.

[3] Armstrong, *Wars of Religion in France*, 4, 5. Cf. De Crue, *Anne de Montmorency*, 246. The establishment of the Jesuits was not approved in France until after the death of Henry II, owing to the resistance of the mendicant orders and the Sorbonne.—Claude Haton, II, 636.

regarded it as necessary, both to preserve the church and in order to suppress those seditious spirits, who, under color of religion, aimed to alter or subvert the government.   Others, who had no regard either for policy or religion, likewise approved of it, not as tending to extirpate the Protestants, for they believed it would rather increase their numbers, but because they hoped to be enriched by confiscations and that the King might thereby be enabled to pay his debts, amounting to forty-two millions, according to

EXECUTION OF DU BOURG
(Tortorel and Perissin)

Castelnau, and thus restore his finances.[1]   The trial of the parliamentary councilors was postponed for some time on account of Henry II's death, but soon afterward they were brought before "the bishops and Sorbonnists."[2]   Du Four, upon retraction, was suspended from office for five years;[3] three others were fined and ignominiously punished; but Du Bourg[4] was condemned and executed on December 23, 1559, in spite of the solicitations of

[1] Castelnau, Book I, chap. iii.

[2] *C. S. P. For.*, No. 950, July 8, 1559.   [3] *Mém. de Condé*, I, 264.

[4] He had been converted by Hotman, the famous Huguenot pamphleteer.—Weiss, 31.

Marguerite, wife of the duke of Savoy, and the count palatine who wrote to the King for his life.[1]

At the same time the measures of the government were redoubled. In November, 1559, a new edict ordained that all who went to conventicles, or assisted at any private assemblies, should be put to death, and their houses be pulled down and never rebuilt. By special decree the provost of the city was authorized, because Huguenot sessions were more frequent in Paris and its suburbs than elsewhere, to proclaim with the trumpet that all people who had information of Protestant assemblies should notify the magistrates, on pain of incurring the same punishment; and promise of pardon and a reward of five hundred livres was to be given to every informer. The *commissaires des quartiers* of Paris were enjoined to be diligent in seeking out offenders and to search the houses of those under suspicion from time to time using the *archers de la ville* for that purpose. Letters-patent were also given to the lieutenant-criminal of the Châtelet and certain other judges chosen by the cardinal of Lorraine to judge without appeal. The curés and vicars in the parishes were to excommunicate all those who had knowledge of Protestant doings and failed to report them.[2] In order to discover those who were Calvinists, priests bore the host (*corpus Domini*) through the streets and images of the Virgin were set up at the street corners, and all who refused to bow the head and bend the knee in adoration were arrested.[3] Similar measures were adopted in Poitou, at Toulouse, and at Aix in Provence where the double enginery of state and church was brought to bear in the suppression of heresy.[4] So great was the volume of judicial business as a result of these new measures that four criminal chambers were established at the end of the year, one to try offenses carrying the death penalty, the second for trial of those who might be condemned to make *amende honorable*, the third to judge those who

---

[1] Weiss, *op. cit.;* Castelnau, Book I, chap. iii. La Planche, 209–12 and 235, 236, gives an account of his sufferings and death. The *Mém. de Condé*, I, 217 ff., contain part of the trial.

[2] Castelnau, Book I, chap. v, and especially La Planche, 220–22.

[3] La Planche, 237.　　　　[4] *Ibid.*, 226.

might be publicly burned, the last to punish various other offenses.[1] The saner Catholic opinion, as, for example, that of Tavannes, the brilliant cavalry leader, reprobated this recourse to extraordinary tribunals on the ground that the judging of criminals by special commissioners, who were persons chosen according to the passion of the ruler, was bound to be unjust or tyrannical, and that those counselors who were drawn from the courts of the parlements to be so employed offended their consciences and mingled in that which did not pertain to them. Tavannes justified his contention, legally as well as morally, on the ground that the King, being a party in the cause could not justly change the ordinary judges.[2]

The assassination of Minard, vice-president of the Grand Chamber of the Parlement of Paris, and one of the judges, who was shot in his coach[3] on the night of December 18, the same day that Du Bourg was degraded, was the protest against this order of things.[4] The murder was committed in such a way that the author of it could never be discovered.[5] This was followed by that of Julien Frène, a messenger of the Parlement, while bearing some papers and instructions relating to the prosecution of certain Protestants. These two crimes undoubtedly hardened the govern-

---

[1] La Place, 28.

[2] Upon the patriotism and loyalty of the French magistracy see the notable extract from a letter of the Spanish ambassador, April 29, 1560, in *Rev. hist.*, XIV, 78. Cf. the address of M. Alfred Levesque, "Le barreau et la liberté sous les Valois: discours prononcé à la séance d'ouverture des conférences de l'ordre des avocats," November 28, 1846.

[3] *C. S. P. For.*, No. 451, December 21, 1559. Carriages came into use in the sixteenth century, the practice being borrowed from Italy. Catherine de Medici was the first queen who possessed one. For interesting information on this subject see Burgon, *Life and Times of Sir Thomas Gresham*, I, 242, 305, 383, 486, 487; Ellis, *Letters*, Series II, I, 253; Strutt, *Dresses*, II, 90, and a paper in *Archeologia*, XX, 426 ff.

[4] Castelnau, Book I, chap. v; La Planche, 232–34.

[5] Robert Stuart, who claimed to be a relative of Mary Stuart, was suspected of the murder. It was he who killed the constable Montmorency at the battle of St. Denis in 1567.—D'Aubigné, I, 255. Another upon whom suspicion rested was the natural son of the cardinal of Meudon, whom Minard had persuaded to leave all his property to the poor.—*Nég. Tosc.*, III, 407.

ment[1] and hastened the prosecution of Du Bourg, who was put to death just a week later, on December 23, and led to some new regulations. In order to protect the Parlement, it was commanded to adjourn before four o'clock, from St. Martin's Eve (November 10) until Easter; a general police order forbade the carrying of any firearms whatsoever[2] and in order to prevent their conceal-ment, the wearing of long mantles or large hunting-capes was forbidden.[3]

It is to be observed that the Huguenots were concerted not only for religious, but for political interests. The distinction was fully appreciated at the time, the former being called "Huguenots of religion" and the latter "Huguenots of state."[4] The former were Calvinists who were resolved no longer to endure the cruelties of religious oppression; the latter—mostly nobles—those opposed to the monopoly of power enjoyed by the Guises.[5] The weight

[1] D'Aubigné, I, 255, II, chap. xvi. Two edicts were issued on December 17 from Chambord. See Isambert, XIV, 12.

[2] La Place, 28.   [3] La Planche, 209.

[4] La Place, 41; Tavannes, 241. "There be two kinds of the people whom the Papists term Huguenots, viz., Huguenots of religion, and Huguenots of State. The one of these perceiving that the cardinal works to ruin them, and their own peculiar force not sufficient to withstand his malice, have shown appearance that they will join with the other, who seeing themselves excluded from all government, and those of Guise to usurp the whole authority, presently practise a firm faction and league between themselves, either part promising to support the other."— C. S. P. For., No. 2,235, May 31, 0568.

[5] Rel. vén., I, 523–25; II, 57; Davila, VI, 359. Claude Haton emphatically asserts the feudal purposes of the Huguenot noblesse: "Les grand seigneurs de la ligue condéienne et cause huguenoticque s'atendoient d'estre haults eslevez, non és offices royaux, mais au partage du royaume qu'ilz espéroient faire entre. eux en le contonnant par provinces, desquelles ilz prétendoient d'estre seigneurs souverains, sans recognoistre roy ni aultre personne par dessus eux."—I, 291. Tavannes characterizes the Huguenot association in 1572 as "demi-democratique et demi-aristocratique" (Panth. lit., 413). The identification of Calvinism with the political purposes of the nobles is shown in the following letter of the cardinal de Tournon to King Henri II, written "De Bains de Lucques, 9 juillet 1559": "L'une des principal ruses de ces malheureux est de commencer, s'ils peuvent, à semer leur venin et mauvaise doctrine par les plus Grands, les attirer et gaigner à eux, afin de pouvoir après tout plus aisément & sans punition, infecter & gaster le reste & s'aider à un besoin de leur force & authorité."—Ribier, II, 807.

The cardinal Tournon and the admiral Hennebault had been trusted with the

of evidence is increasingly in favor of the view that the causes of the Huguenot movement were as much if not more political and economic than religious.

It was only in the general dislocation and *désœuvrement* of society that followed the cessation of the foreign wars that the French began to realize the weight of the burdens which their governmental system laid upon them. . . . . Until . . . . the religious sense gave a voice to the dumb discontent, social or political, first in the Huguenot rising and afterward in the outbreak of the League, there was little to show the real force of the opposition to the established order.[1]

Abstractly considered, the religious Huguenots were not very dangerous to the state so long as they confined their activity to the discussion of doctrine. This could not easily be done, however, nor did the opponents of the church so desire; for the church was a social and political fabric, as well as a spiritual institution, and to challenge or deny its spiritual sovereignty meant also to invalidate its social and political claims, so that the whole structure was compromised. Thus the issue of religion raised by the Huguenots merged imperceptibly into that of the political Huguenots, who not only wanted to alter the foundations of belief, but to change the institutional order of things, and who used the religious opposition as a means to attack the authority of the crown. The most active of this class were the nobles, possessed of lands or bred to the profession of arms, whom a species of political atavism actuated to endeavor to recover that feudal power which the noblesse had enjoyed before the powerful kings like Louis IX and Philip IV coerced the baronage; before the Hundred-Years' War ruined them; before Louis XI throttled the League of the Public Weal in 1465. The weakness of Francis II, the minority of the crown

duties of affairs of state after the fall of the constable Montmorency in 1541. When Henry II came to the throne Montmorency was restored to office and Tournon fell. After the death of Henry II the queen mother proposed the return of Cardinal Tournon. The Guises at first hesitated, but soon yielded, first because the cardinal was the personal enemy of the constable, and second, because he was very hostile to the reformed religion (*Rev. hist.*, XIV, 72, 73).

[1] From an admirable article by E. Armstrong, "The Political Theory of the Huguenots," *Eng. Hist. Rev.*, IV, 13 ff Cf. Weill, *Les théories sur le pouvoir royal en France pendant les guerres de religion*, Paris, 1891.

under Charles IX, and, above all, the dissatisfaction of the princes of the blood and the old aristocracy, like the Montmorencys, with the upstart pretensions and power of the Guises—these causes united to make the Huguenots of state a formidable political party. Religion and politics together provoked the long series of civil wars whose termination was not until Henry IV brought peace and prosperity to France again in 1598.[1]

It is necessary to picture the state of France at this time. The French were not essentially an industrial or commercial nation in the sixteenth century. France had almost no maritime power and its external commerce was not great. The great majority of the French people was composed of peasants, small proprietors, artisans, and officials. If we analyze city society, we find first some artisans and small merchants—the bourgeois and the *gens-de-robe* forming the upper class. The towns had long since ceased to govern themselves. Society was aristocratic and controlled by the clergy and nobility. The upper clergy was very rich. High prelates were all grand seigneurs, while the lower clergy was very dependent. Monks abounded in the towns, and the curates possessed a certain influence. The most powerful class was the nobles, seigneurs, and gentlemen, who possessed a great portion of the rural properties, and still had fortified castles. They were wholly employed either at court or in war, or held appointments as governors of provinces and captains of strongholds. The nobles alone constituted the regular companies of cavalry, that is to say, the dominant element of the army. This class was therefore of influence in the state and the most material force in society.

The government was an absolute monarchy. The king was theoretically uncontested master and obeyed by all; he exercised an arbitrary and uncontrolled power, and could decide according to his pleasure, with reference to taxes, laws, and affairs both of the state and of the church, save in matters of faith. He named and revoked the commissions of all the governors and acted under the advice of a council composed of the princes of the blood and favorites. But this absolute authority was still personal. The

[1] See the observations of La Place, 41–45.

king was only obeyed upon condition of giving the orders himself. There was no conception of an abstract kingship. If the king abandoned the power to a favorite, the other great personages of the court would refuse to obey, and declare that the sovereign was a prisoner. Everything depended upon a single person. No one thought of resisting Francis I or Henry II because they were men grown at their accession. But after 1559 we find a series of royal infants or an indolent monarch like Henry III. Then began the famous rivalries between the great nobles, rivalries out of which were born the political parties of the times, in which the Guises, the Montmorencys, and the famous Châtillon brothers figure so prominently.

Fundamentally speaking, the aims of both classes of Huguenots were revolutionary, and were directed, the one against the authority of the mediaeval church, the other against the authority of the French monarchy. The latter was a feudal manifestation, not yet republican. The republican nature of early political Huguenotism has been exaggerated. There was no such feeling at all as nearly as 1560,[1] and even at the height of Huguenot activity and power in 1570–72, most men still felt that the state of France was *vrayement monarchique*,[2] and that the structure of society and the genius of the people was strongly inclined to the form of government which eight centuries of development had evolved; that it was searching for false liberty by perilous methods to seek fundamentally to alter the state.[3] In a word, most political Huguenots in 1560 were reformers, not revolutionists; the extremists were Calvinist zealots and those of selfish purposes who were working for their own ends. For in every great movement there are always those who seek to exploit the cause. Mixed with both classes of Huguenots were those who sought to fish in troubled waters, who, under the guise of religion or the public good, took occasion to

---

[1] It is true that De Thou so says: "et établir en France une république semblable à celle des Suisses," Book XXV, 501, but it is to be remembered that De Thou was writing late in the reign of Henry IV, and read back into the past the republicanism of 1572.

[2] See the eminently sane remarks of Tavannes, 260.

[3] Cf. Castelnau, Book I, chap. vi.

pillage and rob all persons, of whatever degree or quality; who plundered cities, pulled down churches, carried off relics, burnt towns, destroyed castles, seized the revenues of the church and the king, informed for the sake of reward, and enriched themselves by the confiscated property of others. Similar things are not less true of the Catholics. For there were zealots and fanatics among them also, who under pretext of religion and patriotism were guilty of great iniquity and heaped up much ill-gotten wealth.[1]

The ascendency of the Guises quite as much as the suppressive measures of the government against Calvinism served to bring this disaffection to a head. The issues, either way, cannot be separated. The practical aims of the Guises were large enough to create dismay without it being necessary to believe that as early as 1560 they aimed to secure the crown by deposing the house of Valois. It was unreasonable to suppose, though it proved to be so in the end, that the four sons of Henry II would all die heirless, and even in the event of that possibility, the house of Bourbon still remained to sustain the principle of primogeniture.

The Guises came from Lorraine, their father having been brother of the old duke of Lorraine; and through their mother they were related to the house of Bourbon. They were thus cousins-german of the king of Navarre and the prince of Condé and related to the King and the princes of the blood. Their income, counting their patrimony, church property, pensions and benefits received from the king, amounted to 600,000 francs (nearly $500,000 today), the cardinal of Lorraine alone having the disposal of half that sum. This wealth, united with the splendor of their house, their religious zeal, the popularity of the duke of Guise, and the concord which prevailed among them, put them ahead of all the nobles of the realm. The provincial governments

---

[1] The avarice and dishonesty of the cardinal, it is said, even went so far as to force Catherine de Medici to divide with him the fees arising from the confirmation of offices and the privileges accorded towns and municipal corporations in the time of Henry II, which sums lawfully went to her; and even then he is said to have fraudulently estimated them in *livres* instead of *écus d'or*.—La Planche, 208. The *écu d'or* was worth two *livres tournois* in the reign of Francis I, so that the cardinal's little trick cut the sum in half.

and the principal offices were in their hands or those of their partisans.

The cardinal, who was the head of the house, was in the early prime of life. He was gifted with great insight which enabled him to see in a flash the intention of those who came in contact with him; he had an astonishing memory; a striking figure; an eloquence which he was not loath to display, especially in politics; he knew Greek, Latin, and Italian, speaking the last with a facility that astonished even Italians themselves; he was trained in theology; outwardly his life was very dignified and correct, but, like many churchmen of the time he was licentious. His chief fault was avarice, and for this he was execrated. His cupidity went to criminal limits, and coupled with it was a duplicity so great that he seemed almost never to tell the truth. He was quick to take offense, vindictive, envious. His death would have been as popular as that of Henry II.[1]

On the other hand, the duke of Guise was a man of war, famed as the recoverer of Calais and the captor of Metz. He was as popular as his brother was otherwise. But, like him, he was avaricious stealing even from his own soldiers.[2] According to their opponents the ambition of the Guises was not to be content with the throne of France merely. The throne of St Peter and the crown of Naples were also believed to be goals of their ambition, the cardinal of Lorraine aspiring to the first and his brother, the duke, aspiring to the other in virtue of the relationship of the Guises to the house of Anjou, one-time occupants of the Neapolitan throne.[3] Even this programme was to be excelled. Their enterprises in Scotland in favor of Mary Stuart[4] are known to every student of English history; and after having vanquished Scotland many of the German princes feared that they might move their forces into Denmark in order to put the duke of Lorraine, their relative and the brother-in-law of the king of Denmark, into possession of the kingdom.[5]

[1] See the character sketch in *Rel. vén.*, I, 437–39.

[2] Cf. La Place, 28.   [3] Baschet, 497, 498.

[4] See *C. S. P. For.*, 1559–61, *passim*.

[5] *Ibid.*, No. 405, December 12, 1559. The duchess of Lorraine was a daughter of Christian II, the exiled ruler of Denmark. On this question see the

"La tyrannie guisienne"[1] was a practical ascendency, not a mere fiction of their opponents. As uncles of Francis II, destined morally to be a minor always, owing to his weakness of will and mediocre ability, having in their hands the chief offices of state, the Guises proceeded to build up a system of government wholly their own, not only in central but in provincial affairs, to compass which the removal of the constable and the princes of the blood from the vicinity of the King was the first step. Then followed an attempt to acquire control of the provincial governments. Montmorency, the late constable, was deprived of the government of Languedoc;[2] the governments of Touraine and Orleans, in the very heart of France, were given to the duke of Montpensier and the prince de la Roche-sur-Yon. Trouble arose, though, in January, 1560, when the Guises excluded the prince of Condé from the government of Picardy and gave it to the marshal Brissac, although "the office had been faithfully administered by his predecessors."[3]

The cardinal of Lorraine's position with reference to the finances enabled him to provide the Guise faction with the resources necessary to back up its political intentions.[4] The onerous taxation of Francis I had been increased by Henry II, both the taille and the gabelle, the collection of which had caused a fierce outbreak at Bordeaux in the middle of the last reign; loans were resorted to, "not without great suspicion of their being applied to the King's finances;" and the wages of the soldiers in garrisons and officers withheld.[5] This condition of things naturally drew

long note (with references appended) in Poulet, I, 126. Cf. *Arch. de la maison d'Orange-Nassau*, I, 132. There is little doubt that Philip II and the Guises contemplated such a move (Languet, *Epist., secr.*, II, 22, 30, 34). The war going on between Denmark and Sweden favored the project. This war lasted for seven years (*Arch. de la maison d'Orange-Nassau*, I, 103, 104; Raumer, II, 211).

[1] La Planche, 273.   [2] *C. S. P. For.*, No. 451, December 5, 1559.

[3] Tavannes, 245; La Place, 27, 51; La Planche, 216; *C. S. P. Ven.*, No. 272, 1506.

[4] La Planche, 212. "Il Cardinale di Lorraine è quà Papa e re," *Nég. Tosc.*, III, 404, August 27, 1559.

[5] La Planche, 212; La Place, 28; *Rev. hist.*, XIV, 67, 68. On the economic discontent due to the extravagance of Henry II, see *Rev. hist.*, XIV, 71. Claude Haton, I, 110–12 gives a favorable contemporary judgment.

the constable[1] and his partisans toward the prince of Condé, who vainly endeavored to persuade the king of Navarre, as first prince of the blood, and therefore the natural supporter of the crown instead of the Guises, to take a firm stand, Condé especially representing to him how great a humiliation it was to the crown that the administration of the kingdom should fall so completely into the hands of the "foreigners" of Lorraine; that, considering the weakness of the King, the fact that the provincial governorships and those of the frontier fortresses and the control of finances (which enabled the Guises to subject the judiciary to their devotion) were in their hands, foreboded ill to France.

Antoine of Bourbon listened to the complaints against the the Guises, but did little. At this time he was forty-two years of age. He was tall of stature, well-knit, robust; affable to everybody without affectation or display. His manners were open and frank, and his generosity was so great that he was always in debt. By the two merits of urbanity and generosity he made a superficial impression that did not last. In speech he was vain, and imprudent and inconstant in word and deed, not having the strength of will to adhere to a fixed purpose. He was suspected of indifference to religion and even of impiety at this time because he renounced the mass, though it was generally thought that this was with the purpose of making himself chief of the Huguenot party and not for religious zeal. The Protestants themselves called him a hypocrite.[2] Antoine would not make common cause with the constable partly from natural vacillation of character, partly because he believed that the constable had not supported his claims to the kingdom of Navarre, which he had been in hopes of recovering during the late negotiations at Cateau-Cambrésis.[3] With the conceit of a weak man in a prominent position, the king of Navarre entertained schemes of his own, which he proceeded to develop. His purpose was to play Spain and

---

[1] The act revoking many of the alienations of the royal domain fell hardest upon the followers of the constable and of Diane de Poitiers (*Rev. hist.*, XIV, 71, 72).

[2] *Rel. vén.*, I, 431. See the character-sketch by Suriano in *Rel. vén.*, II, 47; *C. S. P. Ven.*, No. 272, 1561.

[3] La Planche, 212.

England against one another, in the hope that he either might persuade Philip II to restore the kingdom of Navarre to him by a firm advocacy of Catholicism in France, which, of course, prevented him from affiliating with the Huguenot party to which Condé and the Châtillons were attached; or, in the event of failure in this, to side with the Huguenots and enlist English support. Accordingly, shortly after his arrival at the court from Béarn, on August 23, 1559, Antoine sent a gentleman to Throckmorton, the English ambassador in France, desiring him to meet him "in cape" in the cloister of the Augustine Friars on that night. When they met, after a long declaration of his affection for Elizabeth, he said that he would write to her with his own hand, since he would trust no one except himself, for if either the Guises or the Spanish ambassador knew of it, "it would be dangerous to both and hinder their good enterprise."[1]

In the interval, while waiting to hear from the English queen, Antoine of Bourbon, who had been coldly received at court, found that there was no room for a third party between those of the constable and the Guises.[2] At the same time the latter were made fully aware of his doings through the treachery of D'Escars, his chamberlain and special favorite,[3] and shrewdly schemed to rid themselves of his presence by sending him to Spain as escort for Elizabeth, the celebration of whose marriage (by proxy) to the King of Spain had come to such a fatal termination, and whose departure had been necessarily delayed by her father's death.[4]   In

---

[1] Throckmorton to the Queen, C. S. P. Eng. For., No. 1,244, August 25, 1559.

[2] La Planche, 216.   [3] Ibid., 212, 216.

[4] Weiss, L'Espagne sous Philippe II, I, 115, 16. The queen of Spain, in company with Antoine of Navarre and Jeanne d'Albret, arrived at Pau on December 21, having proceeded from Bordeaux. Great preparations were made for her reception and she was nobly entertained. The king and queen of Navarre did their part with great magnificence. The maître des postes of Spain arrived at Pau the same day as Her Majesty did, with instructions how she was to conduct herself toward the Spanish nobles by whom she was to be met on her arrival in Spain.—"Extraict," written in a French hand, indorsed "My Lord Ambassador," C. S. P. For., II, No. 469, December 21, 1559. The king and queen of Navarre and the cardinal Bourbon conducted her to the frontiers and then returned; the prince of Roche-sur-Yon went through with her to Guadalajara and carried

order to bait the hook the Guises represented to the beguiled
king of Navarre that the opportunity was a most excellent one to
urge his claims to his lost kingdom, and called in Chantonnay,
the Spanish ambassador in France, to enforce this argument.[1]

to Philip the order of St. Michael (C. S. P. For., No. 337, November 29, 1559:
Killigrew and Jones to the Queen). Philip II planned to meet his spouse at
Guadalajara and thence go to Toledo, where the marriage festivities were to be
celebrated until Shrovetide (C. S. P. For., No. 354: Challoner to Cecil from Brus-
sels). At the celebration, the duke of Infantado, whose guest the King was at
Guadalajara, had sixty shepherds clad in cloth-of-gold (C. S. P. For., No. 540,
January 24, 1560). The marriage was accomplished on January 20, 1560 (C. S. P.
For., No. 540, January 24, 1560: statement of Granvella to Challoner). The
French were offended because, at the receiving of the Queen-Catholic at Guadalajara, the verse of the forty-fifth Psalm was sung, "Audi, filia, et vide, etc.," which
the French disliked much, "concluding that they did not have altogether that which
they looked for at King Philip's hands by means of his wife" (C. S. P. For., No.
591, January 18, 1560: Killigrew and Jones to Cecil).

[1] See a letter of Francis II to the bishop of Limoges, May 21, 1506, "De
l'ambassadeur espagnol, Perrenot de Chantonnay, et de ses intrigues," in Paris,
Négociations, 584. Thomas Perrenot, sieur de Chantonnay, was a younger
brother of the cardinal Granvella and was a native of Besançon. He was named
Spanish ambassador in France after the treaty of Cateau-Cambrésis (Paris, Nég.
relatives au règne de François II, 56-60). His official correspondence is in the Archives
nationales at Paris, K. 1,492 ff. Quite as valuable is the private correspondence
he maintained with his brother and Margaret of Parma, transcripts of which are
in the Brussels archives. The originals are divided between Besançon and Vienna.
M. Paris pertinently says of him: "On ne sait pas assez toutes des manœuvres de
ce personnage."—Négociations relatives au règne de François II, 56, note. A history
of his public career would be a cross-section of the history of the times. He spoke
French and German fluently and had a knowledge of Spanish and Italian. Catherine de Medici feared and hated him and in August, 1560, demanded his recall
in vain.—Paris, Négociations, etc., 873. In 1564 he was transferred to Vienna
(R. Q. H., January, 1879, 19, 20) and was succeeded by Alava. All the official
correspondence of the epoch abounds with allusions to him. See Papiers d'état
du cardinal de Granvelle, VII, 393, 400, 402, 518, 592; VIII, 353, 383, 387, 457, 513,
523, 557, 568, 574, 594, 679; IX, 1, 36, 65, 94-102, 136, 154, 166, 169, 177, 182-
98, 225, 421, 264, 345-52, 358, 361, 377-81, 394, 415, 430, 434-37, 446, 452, 461,
468, 482, 489, 510, 514, 522, 538, 540-43, 549-52, 556-58, 562-64, 567, 568, 581-
89, 602-9, 615, 625, 628, 654, 668, 671; Gachard, Correspondance de Philippe II,
II, 27, 48, 89, 108, 121, 163, 171-74; Poulet, Correspondance du cardinal de Granvelle, I, 565, note; R. Q. H., January, 1879, 10-12. Some of his letters which
were intercepted by the Huguenots are published in the Mémoires de Condé. M.
Paillard has printed a portion of those relating to the conspiracy of Amboise in
the Rev. hist., XIV; at pp. 64, 65 is a brief sketch of the ambassador's life. See
also Weiss's introduction to edition of Papiers d'état du cardinal de Granvelle, I.

The spirit of unrest in France, both political and religious, was so great that only a head was wanting, not members, in order to bring things to a focus. The whole of Aquitaine and Normandy was reported, in December, 1559, to be in such "good heart" as to be easily excited to action if they perceived any movement elsewhere;[1] in February, 1560, the turbulence in Paris was so great that Coligny was appointed to go thither in advance of the King's entrance "for the appeasing of the garboil there."[2]   In order to repress this spirit of rebellion the government diligently prosecuted the Huguenots.[3]   The Guises hoped that the severity exercised during the last few months in Paris and many other cities against persons condemned for their religion, of whom very great numbers were burnt alive,[4] would terrify the Calvinists and

[1] C. S. P. For., No. 543.

[2] Ibid., No. 508, December 27.   Throckmorton wrote to the council on February 4, 1560: "At present the French have to bestir themselves for the good and quiet of their own country, as factions in religion are springing up everywhere."—Ibid., No. 685.   Indeed, the chancellor at this time for three days refused to sign an order necessary for the prosecution of the war in Scotland, on the ground of the dangers at home and the necessity of harboring the government's resources (ibid., No. 292, November 18, 1559: Killigrew and Jones to Cecil).   Among the financial expedients resorted to at this time was an order in December, 1559, that all posts and postmasters should henceforth be deprived of the fees which they enjoyed which amounted to 100,000 crowns yearly, and for compensation to them the price of letters was increased a fourth part (ibid., No. 508, December, 1559).   On May 29, 1560, a royal ordinance abolished the King's support of the post entirely and some new ordinances of Parlement were calculated to increase the revenue by 2,000,000 francs (ibid., No. 550, January 6, 1560).   In February the King raised a loan of 7,000 francs at 8 per cent. from the Parisians (ibid., No. 750, February 20, 1560: Throckmorton to the Queen).

[3] "Six score commissions are sent forth for the persecution for religion."—Ibid., No. 451: Killigrew and Jones to the Queen, December 18, 1559.   This was just after the murder of the president Minard.   "The Cardinal of Lorraine lately sent . . . . a bag full of commissions for persecution to be done about Poitiers and certain letters which he carried apart in his bosom; the messenger was met and the letters taken from him."—Ibid., No. 590, January 18, 1560.   One of these— "Lettre de roi à tous les évêques de son royaume"—is preserved in K. 1,494, fol. 4.   It is dated January 28, 1560.

[4] Nég. Tosc., III, 408, January 22, 1560.   On January 29 a poor man, a binder of books, was condemned to be burned for heresy at Rouen.   While riding in a cart between two friars to be burned, a quarrel was made with a sergeant who

the political Huguenots into obedience. But on the contrary, local rebellion increased. At Rouen, at Bordeaux, and between Blois and Orleans, Huguenots arrested by the King's officers were rescued by armed bands, in some cases the officers being killed. Indeed, so common did these practices become that they were at last heard of without surprise.[1]

Imagine a young king [wrote the Venetian ambassador] without experience and without authority; a council rent by discord; the royal authority in the hands of a woman alternately wise, timid, and irresolute, and always a woman; the people divided into factions and the prey of insolent agitators who under pretense of religious zeal trouble the public repose, corrupt manners, disparage the law, check the administration of justice, and imperil the royal authority.[2]

The interests of the religious Huguenots and the political Huguenot's continued to approach during the autumn and winter of 1559–60. In order to make head against the usurpation of the Guises,[3] which they represented as a foreign domination, the latter contended that it was necessary to call the estates of France in order to interpret the laws, just as the Calvinists contended for an inter-

convoyed him and he was unhorsed, the poor man was taken out of the cart, his hands were loosed, and a cloak was thrown over him, and he was conveyed out of the hands of his enemies. The justices and the governors, having knowledge of this, commanded the gates to be shut, and, making a search that night, found him again and burned him next day. And at his burning were three hundred men-at-arms, for fear of the people (*C. S. P. For.*, No. 708, February 8, 1560).

[1] *C. S. P. For.*, No. 256, November 14, 1559; *ibid.*, *Ven.*, No. 132, March 6, 1560.

[2] Baschet, I, 559; cf. *Nég. Tosc.*, III, 310, January, 1560.

[3] The fear of attempts being made to assassinate them or the King haunted the cardinal and his brother. In November the French King, while out hunting near Blois, became so terrified, that he returned to court, and orders were given to the Scotch Guard to wear jack and mail and pistols (*C. S. P. For.*, No. 166, November 15, 1559); in December rumors reached the cardinal's ears that his own death and that of the duke of Guise was sworn (*ibid.*, No. 528); in January the use of *tabourins* and masks in court pleasures was forbidden on account of the fear which the cardinal of Lorraine had of being assassinated (*ibid.*, No. 658, January 28, 1559). De Thou says the cardinal was "natura timidus."—Book XXV. The wearing of pistols and firearms was prohibited by two edicts, the one of July 3, 1559, the other of December 17, 1559. The law also forbade the wearing of long sleeves or cloaks or even top boots, in which a pistol or a poignard might be concealed. Both measures were attributed with good reason to the timidity of the cardinal of Lorraine.

pretation of the Scriptures. The contentions of the Huguenots, the
tyrannical conduct of the Guises, the menaces which they did not
hesitate to utter against the high nobles of the realm, the retirement
into which they had driven the constable, the removal of the princes
of the blood which they had brought about upon one pretext or
another, the contempt they expressed for the States-General, the
corruption of justice, their exorbitant financial policy, the disposal
of offices and benefices which they practiced—all these causes,
united with religious persecutions, constituted a body of grievances
for which redress inevitably would be demanded. The question
was, How? The leaders of the Huguenots—and the term is used
even more in a political sense than in a religious one—were not
ignorant of the history of the Reformation in Germany, nor unaware of the fact that politics had been commingled with religion
there.[1] The question of ways and means being laid before the
legists of the Reformation and other men of renown in both France
and Germany, it was answered that the government of the Guises
could be *legally* opposed and recourse made to force of arms, provided that the princes of the blood, who, in such case had legitimate
right to bear rule in virtue of their birth, or any one of their number,
could be persuaded to endeavor to do so.[2] But the attempt necessarily would have to be of the nature of a *coup de main*, for the
reason that the King was in the hands of the Guises and the council
composed of them and their partisans. After long deliberation
it was planned, under pretext of presenting a petition to the King,
to seize the cardinal of Lorraine and the duke of Guise, then to
assemble the States-General for the purpose of inquiring into their
administration, and before them to prosecute the ministers for
high treason.[3] Three classes of men found themselves consorting
together in this movement: those actuated by a sentiment of

[1] "Les protestans de France se mettans devant les yeux l'example de leurs
voisins."—Castelnau, Book I, chap. vii.

[2] La Planche, 237.

[3] *Ibid.;* Castelnau, Book I, chap. viii. The Huguenots did not intend to take
up arms against the person of the King or to force Francis II to change the
religion of the state. The assertion that these were their purposes was an adroit
stroke of the Guises (*Rev. hist.*, XIV, 85, 101).

patriotism, conceiving this to be the right way to serve their prince and their country; second, those moved by ambition and fond of change; finally, zealots who were filled with religious enthusiasm and a wish to avenge the intolerance and persecution which they and theirs had suffered.[1]   For such an enterprise Louis of Bourbon, the prince of Condé, was the logical leader, both because of his position as a prince of the blood and on account of his resentment toward the Guises for having been excluded from the government of Picardy.   But the prince, when besought to attempt the overthrow of the Guises for the deliverance of the King and the state, in view of the dubious conduct of his brother, concluded that it would be too perilous to the cause for him to be overtly compromised, in event of failure.[2]   Montmorency was not possible as a leader, for his religious leanings were in no sense Calvinistic; he was not a prince of the blood, and therefore his contentions could not politically have the weight of Condé's; and finally, his grievance was more a personal than a party one.[3]

[1] *Rel. vén.*, I, 525.

[2] Volrad of Mansfeldt and Grumbach, counselor of the elector palatine, but personal enemies of the cardinal of Lorraine, had been drawn by sympathy into the plan, and on March 4, through their influence, Hotman was received by the elector at Heidelberg, who gave Hotman a letter of credit to the king of Navarre and the prince of Conde. See Dareste, "Extraits de la correspondance inédite de François Hotman," *Mém. de l'Academie des sciences morales et politiques*, CIV (1897), 649.

[3] After the failure of the conspiracy, during the course of the investigation set on foot by the government, the constable was accused of complicity in the affair but vigorously denied it in a remonstrance laid before the Parlement (La Place, 37, gives a part of the text; Castelnau, Book II, chap. xi), and while condemning the conspiracy artfully contrived to imply that the Guises were to be blamed for much (La Planche, 269). De Thou, II, 778, perhaps reproduces the actual language of the constable before the Parlement, his father having been president of the body at this time.   But in the early winter Montmorency had visited his lands in Poitou and Angoumois, and his daughter, Madame de la Tremouille, having quitted his usual place of residence at Chantilly, and traveled in those quarters of France which, it will be observed, are identical with those wherein the conspiracy of Amboise was hatched (La Place, 32).   Is it reasonable to believe that a man of his political acumen and state of feeling at the time toward the Guises could have been unaware of at least something of what was in preparation?   The strongest evidence in favor of the innocence of the constable is the fact that his two nephews, the cardinal de Châtillon and the admiral Coligny were undoubtedly without knowledge of the plot.   See the

The conspirators found a leader in the person of a gentleman of Limousin or Périgord, one Godfrey de Barry, sieur de la Renaudie,[1] who had been imprisoned at Dijon, escaped and found refuge in Switzerland;[2] he had a special grievance against the Guises, who had lately (September 4, 1558) put his brother-in-law, Gaspard de Heu, sieur de Buy, to death.[3]

The active participants were, in the main, recruited from the Breton border, Anjou, Saintonge, and Poitou, with individual captains from Picardy, Normandy, Guyenne, Provence, and Languedoc.[4]   Their rendezvous was at Nantes, in a house owned, it is said, by D'Andelot.[5]   But the author of the whole daring project was the famous François Hotman, a French refugee at Geneva, and the real inspiration of the movement came from Switzerland, for the unexpected death of Henry II seemed to the French exiles in Switzerland to open the door of the mother country again to them.[6]

proofs in Delaborde, *Vie de Coligny*, I, 391–414; D'Aubigné, ed. De Ruble, I, 263, n. 6; Paillard, "Additions critiques à l'histoire de la conjuration d'Amboise," *Rev. hist.*, XIV (1880), 70. 71. It is hard, however, to believe that the constable had no information at all of what was on foot, considering his politics and his movements during the winter.

[1] La Place, 33; Le Laboureur, I, 386, says his first name was Jean.

[2] *C. S. P. Ven.*, No. 137. He had been imprisoned for devising false evidence in a process of law (D'Aubigné, ed. De Ruble, I, 258, n. 3). La Renaudie is said even to have gone to England to see Queen Elizabeth (Haag, *La France protestante*, I, 259). No reference is given, but from Hotman's correspondence (*Acad. des sc. moral. et polit.*, CIV [1877], 645) it is evident some one was so sent. The further fact that Mundt was approached in Strasburg and French proclamations printed in England were circulated in Normandy (*C. S. P. For.*, 954, April 6, 1560) seems to sustain this view.

[3] La Place, 41; Castelnau, Book I, chap. viii.

[4] D'Aubigné, Book II, chap. xvii; I, 259–61 gives the names of the provincial captains.

[5] La Planche, 239.

[6] Mundt, Elizabeth's agent in Strasburg (he was also agent of the landgrave Philip of Hesse), was applied to and "thought that the Queen would not be wanting in kind offices. Already it is whispered," he wrote, "that there is a great agreement among the nobility and others throughout France, who will no longer endure the haughty and adulterous rule of the Guises, and that some of the first rank in France are cognizant of the conspiracy who remain quiet; the rest will rise in arms

The whole plot was concerted in a meeting held at Nantes on February 1, 1560,[1] which was chosen partly because of its remoteness, partly because the Parlement of Brittany being in session, the conspirators could conceal their purpose by pretending to be there on legal business. A marriage festival also helped to disguise their true purpose; and for the sake of greater caution, the principals were careful not to recognize one another in public.[2] It was determined to muster two hundred cavalry from each town in the provinces of Guyenne, Gascony, Périgord, Limousin, and Agenois. For the maintenance of this force they intended to avail themselves of the revenues and effects of the abbeys and monasteries of each province, taxing them arbitrarily and using force if unable to obtain payment in any other way.[3] The initiative was to have been taken on March 6,[4] under the form of presenting a

against the Guises."—C. S. P. For., No. 779, February 27, 1560. Cf. Nég. Tosc., III, 409.

An added element of adventure was the participation of a certain nobleman of wealth who seems to have financially supported the conspiracy for self-advantage. This man imagined that the movement might be converted into a movement for the recovery of Metz from the French (letter of Hotman to Calvin, September 19, 1559). In Hotman's eyes, to restore Metz to Germany was to restore it to Protestantism, but Calvin was cautious, for his sound policy distinguished between rebellion and constitutional restriction of tyranny. He sent Beza to Strasburg to attempt to prevent such an action. But the Senate of Strasburg seized upon the project, demanded liberty for the Protestants of Metz and Trèves, abolished the Interim, interdicted the Catholic religion, and even expelled the Anabaptists from the city, to the jubilation of radical Protestants, who looked upon it as just reprisal for the repressive policy of the Guises in France.

[1] La Planche, 238.

[2] La Place, 23; La Planche, 238. Some thirty captains were party to it, who were to be put in command of some companies of German lansquenets (La Place, 33). "Upward of sixty men, part foreigners and part native Frenchmen" came to aid the plot (C. S. P. Ven., No. 134, March 15, 1560).

[3] C. S. P. Ven., No. 125, March 16, 1560. The correspondence of the Spanish ambassador testifies to the fact that the Protestant soldiery was well paid, the money having been procured by spoliation of the churches. They gave to each footman 14 francs per month and to each horseman 16 sous per day.—Rev. hist., XIV, 104. The Venetian ambassador says the horsemen got 18 soldi, the footmen 10 daily (C. S. P. Ven., March 17, 1560).

[4] The Spanish Ambassador puts it upon the 6th. La Planche, Beza, Castelnau, De Thou, D'Aubigné, La Popelinière, Le Laboureur make March 10 the day. The

petition to the King against the usurpation of the Guises.[1] Unfortunately for the success of the enterprise, it was too long in preparation and too widely spread to keep secret.[2] The magnitude of the plot alarmed the Guises, in spite of the full warning they had received.[3] Aside from outside sources of information, the conspiracy was revealed by one of those in it, an advocate of the

discrepancy perhaps is to be accounted for by the circumstance that Avenelles had said that March 6 was the day designated, but the unexpected removal of the court from Blois to Amboise (La Place, 33; La Planche, 346) postponed the date of action. Cf. *Rev. hist.*, XIV, 66, 85.

[1] Castelnau, *ibid.;* La Planche, 239, 246. The statement is confirmed by La Place, 33, 34, and La Planche, 255 who say that the petition was written in invisible ink and intrusted to one Bigne, a servant of La Renaudie, who having been captured after the death of his master, in order to save his life, revealed the secret of the document. The first article was couched in these terms: "Protestation faicte par le chef et tous les ceux du conseil de n'attenter aucune autre chose contre la Majestie du roy et les princes de son sang. Et estoit le but aussi de la dicte entreprise de faire observer d'ancienne coustume de la France par une legitime assemblée des estats."—Tavannes, 247. Tavannes says Bigne directly said that Condé and Coligny were implicated. Other incriminating papers were found in the boots of the baron Castelnau (*Rev. hist.*, XIV, 99, 100; La Planche, 254, 255).

[2] Castelnau, Book I, chap. xi. De Croze, *Les Guises, les Valois et Philippe II*, I, 60–70 (2 vols., Paris, 1866), shows admirably that there is no doubt of the formidable nature of the conspiracy of Amboise.

[3] It is said that the cardinal and his brother received intimations of danger from Spain, Italy, Savoy, Germany, and Flanders (La Place 32; Castelnau, Book I, chap. viii) and it is certain that the cardinal Granvella, Philip's representative in the Netherlands, warned them. De Thou says that warnings came from Germany, Spain, Italy, and France. Paillard in *Rev. hist.*, XIV, 81, is dubious about an Italian source, but it is confirmed by *C. S. P. Ven.*, 137, March 6, 1560. He thinks that any Spanish source of information was impossible, for the reason that Philip II learned everything from Chantonnay. Granvella's warning is acknowledged by Chantonnay in a letter of March 3, 1560, to his brother. He was expressly told that the aim of the conspiracy was to make away with the cardinal of Lorraine and all those of the house of Guise (*Rev. hist.*, XIV, 80, 81). This is supported by the testimony of the constable and the Venetian ambassador (D'Aubigné, I, 263, n. 3). It seems certain that this information was conveyed to the Guises by February 12 (*Rev. hist.*, XIV, 83; *Mém. de Condé*, I, 387; D'Aubigné, Book II, chap. xvii). Dareste, "Francois Hotman et la conspiration d'Amboise," *Bibliothèque de l'Ecole des Chartes*, sér. III, V, 361, thinks that Hotman's own indiscreet boasting at Strasburg was responsible, at least in part, for the discovery of the plot.

The duke of Guise and his brother were in such fear that they wore shirts of chain mail underneath their vestments, and at night were guarded by pistoleers and men-at-arms. On the night of March 6, while at Blois, the alarm was so great that the duke, the cardinal, the grand-prior, and all the knights of the order there, watched all night long in the courtyard (*C. S. P. For.*, No. 837, March 7, 1560).

Parlement named Avenelles, whose courage failed him at the critical moment.[1]   Thereupon, for precaution's sake, the court moved from Blois to the castle of Amboise, which the duke, having the King's authority to support him, immediately set about fortifying.   He likewise secured the garrison and townspeople, and found a plausible pretext to watch the prince of Condé, by giving

CONSPIRACY OF AMBOISE
SURRENDER OF THE CHÂTEAU DE NOIZAY
(Tortorel and Perissin)

him one of the gates to defend, but, at the same time, sent his brother, the grand prior along with a company of men-at-arms of assured fidelity.   In view of alarming rumors a posse was sent on March 11 under command of the count of Sancerre to Tours, where some ten or twelve of those in the plot, notably the baron

[1] Castelnau, Book I, chap. viii; La Planche, 246, 247. He received one hundred écus and a judicial post in Lorraine (De Thou, II, 774, ed. 1740).

de Castelnau, the captain Mazères, and a gentleman named Renay were already awaiting the money which was to be distributed among companies of theirs secretly stationed in the neighboring villages.[1] Twenty-five of the conspirators were arrested without opposition, whilst incautiously walking outside the Château de Noizay, between three and four leagues from Amboise, which belonged to the wife of Renay, and the whole number of them, with five others arrested at Tours by the count de Sancerre, were taken to Amboise. Immediate examination, though, showed that some of them had risen in arms, partly from friendship for certain captains under whom they had served, while others had been tempted by a trifle of earnest money in lieu of pay, as usual when soldiers were raised for companies, without knowing the place of their service, or its purpose. They were all dismissed, with the exception of one or two who remained prisoners, the chancellor Olivier having admonished them and told them that though they deserved to die the king of his clemency, for this once granted them their lives.[2] To enable them to return home, the King had a crown (teston = 10 to 11 sous) given to each man. But the alarm was not yet ended. That night (March 14) several couriers arrived at the court bringing new advices. The next morning at daybreak there was greater commotion than ever before the castle, for two hundred cavalry made their appearance in the town. They thought themselves almost sure of not finding any sort of resistance and that

[1] "Among the prisoners was a Gascon gentleman, one baron de Castelnau, who considering himself ill-used by the cardinal and the duke of Guise, with many other captains and soldiers, dissatisfied on account of non-payment of their arrears and because they had been dismissed from the Court, finding themselves without salary or any other means, and being half desperate, joined the other insurgents about religion and conspired against the cardinal and the duke of Guise."—C. S. P. Ven., No. 135, March 16, 1560. Sancerre had known Castelnau during the late war, and when he sought to arrest him and his companions, they resisted. Although the city of Tours took up arms in the king's name against them, they made their escape into the château de Noizay (Indre-et-Loire), between three and four leagues from Amboise, which belonged to the wife of Renay (La Place, 33. She had been maid of honor to Jeanne d'Albret, C. S. P. Ven., No. 135, March 16, 1560). Cf. C. S. P. For., March 21, 1560, and note, on p. 462—the account of Throckmorton. The two versions substantially agree.

[2] C. S. P. Ven. For., March 16, 1560.

they consequently would be able to effect their purpose, as all the princes and lords, like all the rest of the court, had no sort of defensive armour except some coats of mail, and very few even of those, while their offensive weapons were merely swords and daggers, with a few pistols, whereas, on the contrary, the insurgents were well armed with both kinds of weapons and were for the most part well horsed. Some boatmen saw the insurgents following the course of the Loire, and their shouts aroused the castle. One or two were killed, whereupon the rest took to flight toward the

THE EXECUTION OF AMBOISE, DEATH OF CASTELNAU
(Tortorel and Perissin)

country. But several were captured and two of them having been recognized as among the company who had been pardoned on the evening before, they were instantly hanged, with two others taken on the preceding day, on the battlements over the castle gate.

As a result of the new alarm there was a general scattering of bands of arrest on the next day (March 15). The marshal St. André was dispatched to Tours with nearly two hundred horse, with orders to take five companies of men-at-arms from the garrison in the immediate neighborhood. He was followed by Claude of Guise, the duke d'Aumale, the duke de Nemours and the prince of Condé.[1] Marshal Termes was sent to Blois; the marshal Vieilleville to Orleans; the duke of Montpensier to Angers; La Rochefoucault to Bourges; Burie to Poitiers.[2] During the day some forty others were taken. Fifteen of those pursued retreated into a house and defended themselves most obstinately, wounding many of their assailants who surrounded it, so that the house was set on fire: one of them, rather than surrender, burned himself alive by throwing himself into the flames. Toward nightfall six or seven more of them were hanged. The duke of Guise, whom the King in the exigency of the moment, made lieutenant-general on March 17,[3] did not fail to take every precaution; he appointed two princes and two knights of St. Michael for each quarter of Amboise, keeping sentries there and sending out scouts as if the town were besieged. The most exposed parts of the castle were repaired and supplied with food, and above all with money, weapons, and artillery. The most useful remedy, however, was the publication and transmission for publication to all the towns and places in France of a general pardon for all the insurgents who within twenty-four hours after its notification should return to their homes, or otherwise they would be proclaimed rebels and traitors, and license would be given to all persons to slay them and inherit their property; but assuring the insurgents, nevertheless, that if they wished to say anything, or to present any request to the King they would be heard willingly, without hurt, provided they made their appearance as loyal subjects.[4]

The prisoners confessed that in all the neighboring towns, viz., Blois, Orleans, Chartres, Chateaudun, and others, a great

[1] C. S. P. For., No. 859, March 15, 1560; ibid., Ven., No. 135, March 16.

[2] Rev. hist., XIV, 102; La Planche, 247; Arch. de la Gironde, XXIX, 8. Vieilleville was sent to pacify the Beauce and M. de Vassey, another knight of the order, to Maune, near Angers, to subdue a commotion there (C. S. P. For., 902, March 26, 1560).

[3] His orders at this hour are printed in the Mém.-journ. du duc de Guise, 457; Mém. de Condé, I, 342; La Popelinière, I, 166; cf. La Planche, 225, who gives the gist of them.

[4] Lettres-patentes du Roi Francois II au sénéschal de Lyon "concernans la revelacion de grace que sa Mate veult faire à ceulx qui avaient conspiré contre l'estat de la religion et son royaume," March 17, 1560.

supply of arms had been made in secret, most especially of arquebuses, one of the men who were hanged having revealed that in
one single house at Blois there were six large chests full of these.
During the next three days nothing was attended to but fortifying
the castle, repairing the weakest places around it, and making a
trench in front of the principal gate, which opened on the country,
in which some arquebuses and three or four small pieces of artil-

DEATH OF LA RENAUDIE
(Tortorel and Perissin)

lery found accidentally and brought there from neighboring places,
were fixed. Round the town, besides cutting the bridges which
were at its gates, except the principal bridge over the Loire, the
moats were cleansed and restored, leaving but one gate open.[1]
Scouting parties were daily sent out, and on March 19 a company
of five fell in with an equal number of insurgents; after a long and
stout fight the posse at length killed their commander and two of

[1] See the extended account in *C. S. P. Ven.*, March 20, 1560; *Nég. Tosc.*, III
412–15.

his men and made the other two prisoners.   One of those killed proved to be La Renaudie.[1]

But the Guises did not stop with these acts of punishment near by.   Besides sending letters of authority to all bailiffs and seneschals ordering the arrest of all men, whether on foot or on horseback, to be found in the country surrounding Amboise,[2] Tavannes, on April 12, 1560, was ordered to do the like in Dauphiné, being actually armed with *lettres de cachet* issued in blank.[3]

Few other disturbances developed except at Lyons, and in Provence and Dauphiné[4] but the government was anxious with regard to Gascony and Normandy, "their populations being much more daring."[5]   "The whole of Normandy is filled with Huguenotism," wrote the Venetian ambassador, "the people by thousands sing every night until ten o'clock the Psalms of David and the

[1] His corpse was hanged March 20, 1560, upon a gibbet before the court gate, and left there for two whole days, with an inscription at his feet running: "C'est La Renaudie dict la Forest, capitaine des rebelles, chef et autheur de la sedition" (La Place, 35; D'Aubigné, I, 268, Book II, chap. xvii; C. S. P. For., 463, note, March 23, 1560).

[2] The sentencing to death of prisoners continued daily, several being sent for execution to Blois, Tours, Orleans, and other places, "that these acts of justice might be witnessed universally and be better known."

[3] The instructions of the King are a curious witness of the fury of the Guises: "Je vous prye, y estant arrivé, faire si bonne dilligence que vous les puissiez chastier comme ils méritent, sans avoir aucune pitié ny compassion d'eux. . . . . Aussy je vous envoye des lettres *dont le nom est en blanc* et lesquelles vous ferez remplir à votre fantaisie, que j'escrips aux principaux seigneurs et gentilshommes dudit païs à ce qu'ils ayent *à assembler leur voysins et vous accompaigner* en ceste entreprinse."—*Négociations relatives au règne de François II*, 342, 343.

[4] Throckmorton wrote on February 27, 1560: "It is reported that the idols have been cast out of the churches throughout Aquitaine and that the same would speedily be done in Provence."—C. S. P. For., No. 779.   Later, on April 14, the Venetian ambassador reports that the insurgents in Provence "have stripped the churches, and mutilated the images."—*Ibid., Ven.*, No. 146.   In Dauphiné the achievements of Montbrun made him famous; see De Thou, Book XXV, 548 ff.

[5] Chantonnay to the duke of Sessa, March 24, 1560, K. 1,493, No. 45.   At St. Malo the insurgents killed certain public officials and prevented an execution. On March 25 the cardinal of Bourbon went to Rouen; and on the same day there was a sermon in a wood without the town to above two thousand people.   A priest and a clerk called them Lutherans and cast stones at them, and a riot ensued. Two days after the preacher was taken and burned (C. S. P. For., 930, March 30, 1560).

men-at-arms dare not touch them.   The people of Dieppe every night in the market-place sing psalms and some days have sermons preached to them in the fields; in most towns in Normandy and many other places they do the same thing."[1] In consequence of this state of things, the marshal de Termes was appointed with royal authority and full and absolute powers throughout the province summarily to confiscate, imprison, condemn and put to death whomsoever he pleased.[2]

In the end the government sent 1,200 of those implicated in the conspiracy of Amboise or under suspicion to execution.   A morbid desire to witness the shedding of blood seized upon society, and it became a customary thing for the ladies and gentlemen of the court to witness the torture of those condemned after the manner of the *auto da fé* in Spain.[3]   D'Aubigné[4] the eminent historian of the French Reformation, was an eye-witness of such incidents, and though but ten years of age, swore like young Hannibal before his father, to devote his life to vengeance of such atrocities.[5]

[1] *C. S. P. Ven.*, No. 142, March 26, 1560.

[2] *Ibid.*, No. 146, April 4, 1560; *ibid.*, *For.*, 952, April 6.   The cardinal of Lorraine justified the drastic policy of the government, saying: "It will be more than necessary to apply violent remedies and proceed to fire and sword, as otherwise, unless provision be made, the alienation of this kingdom, coupled with that of Germany and England and Scotland, would by force draw Spain and Italy and the rest of Christendom to the same result."—*Ibid.*, *Ven.*, No. 142, March 28, 1560.

[3] The court attended the spectacle of these executions "comme s'il eût été question de voir jouer quelque momerie."—La Planche, 263.

[4] Monod, "La jeunesse d'Agrippa d'Aubigné," *Mém. de l'Acad. . . . . de Caen*, 1884.

[5] *C. S. P. For.*, 1560, Introd.   Hotman vented his disappointment at the failure of the conspiracy and his wrath because of the cruel policy of the Guises in a famous pamphlet directed against the cardinal of Lorraine.   It bore the significant title "Le Tigre." See De Thou, Book XXV, 512; Weill, 40, 98, Asse, "Un pamphlet en 1560," *Revue de France*, January 1876, and Dareste, *Mém. de l'Acad. des sc. moral. et polit.*, CIV (1877), 605.   Hotman's authorship of it remained undiscovered for years.   A counselor named Du Lyon, believed to be the author of it, a printer named Martin, and a merchant of Rouen, who had sponsored it, were hanged in the Place Maubert (Castelnau, Book I, chap. xi; La Planche, 312, 313; La Place, 76, 77).

In 1875 M. Charles Read published this famous pamphlet in facsimile from the only existing copy which was rescued from the burning of the Hôtel-de-Ville in 1871.   The text is accompanied with historical, literary, and bibliographical notes.

CHAPTER II

CATHERINE DE MEDICI BETWEEN GUISE AND CONDÉ. PROJECT OF A NATIONAL COUNCIL

The insurrection of Amboise was not wholly displeasing to many even in the court. Huguenot dissidence and the discontent of many persons with the government gave the cardinal and the duke of Guise many troubled thoughts even after every external sign of disquiet had ceased. Strong suspicion rested upon the prince of Condé[1] who was forbidden to leave the court and so closely watched that he was afraid to speak to any of his friends. The Guises were in a dilemma, not having the courage to shed the blood royal,[2] yet, on the other hand, they feared lest, by letting their suspicion pass in silence, the prince might be rendered more daring and confident for the future.

So pointed did the accusation become that Condé finally demanded a hearing before the Council, where he cast down the gauntlet to the Guises, declaring that "whoever should say that he had any hand in conspiring against the King's person or government was a liar and would lie as often as he said so;" he then offered to waive his privilege as a prince of the blood in order to have personal satisfaction and withdrew. But the cardinal of Lorraine, instead of accepting the challenge, made a sign to the King to break up the session.[3]

Antoine of Navarre had been in the south of France during these évents but, nevertheless, he also did not escape suspicion;

[1] The baggage of the prince of Condé was opened, it being expected to find therein letters or other writings relating to the conspiracy, and although excuses were made after the search, attributing it to thieves, yet as none of the contents were missing, the belief greatly prevailed of the search having been made for that purpose (*C. S. P. Ven.*, No. 178, 1560).

On March 22 the prince of Condé was confronted with one of the condemned conspirators, but to the discomfiture of his enemies, no evidence against the prince could be elicited (*C. S. P. For.*, No. 919, March 29 1560).

[2] La Planche, 267.

[3] Castelnau, Book I, chap. xi.

a secretary of his who was staying in Paris to look after his affairs was searched and all the furniture of his house ransacked to discover incriminating papers, if possible.[1] The Bourbon prince was doubly alarmed at the suspicion of guilt because his name was associated with that of the English queen.[2] The king of Navarre may have had imperfect knowledge that something was in the wind when he left the court to visit his dominions in the south, but he was no party to the conspiracy.[3] Of Queen Elizabeth's indirect participation there is no doubt at all. The belief prevailed in Paris that great offers had been made to the earl of Arran by Gascony, Poitou, Brittany, and Normandy, if he would lead an English descent into those parts,[4] and in the two last-named provinces English merchants and sailors animated the people to rebellion against the house of Guise by means of proclamations in the French language *printed in England.*[5] But if the Guises shrank from shedding the blood of the princes, they struck as near to them as they dared, by urging the pursuit of Visières, a former lieutenant of Montgomery, for whose apprehension, dead or alive, a reward of 2,000 crowns was offered,[6] and Maligny, a lieutenant of the prince of Condé.

[1] La Planche, 268.

[2] May 6, 1560, Navarre to Throckmorton: "Has received a letter . . . . enclosing a proclamation of the Queen in which he sees it intimated that the princes and estates of France are to call her to their aid. As first prince of the blood he repudiates this, and . . . . hopes she will not mention him or the others in her proclamations again, as it will only injure them with the King" (written from Pau).—*C. S. P. For.*, No. 40.

[3] *Mém. de Condé*, I, 398; La Popelinière, I, 170.

[4] *C. S. P. For.*, No. 992, April 12, 1560.

[5] *Ibid.*, No. 954, April 6, 1560; Chantonnay wrote to the duchess of Parma that Elizabeth was privy to the conspiracy (Ruble, *Antoine de Bourbon et Jeanne d'Albret*, II, 142).

[6] *C. S. P. For.*, No. 992, April 12, 1560. The unfortunate baron Castelnau, in view of the fact that he was a knight of the order, was at first sentenced to the galleys for three years, but later, at the instance of the Guises, was condemned to die and was beheaded on March 29, along with the captain Mazères, the duke of Nemours, the baron's captor, being absolved from keeping his promise to spare his life (*C. S. P. For.*, No. 952, April 6, 1560; La Planche, 264, 265; La Place, 34; D'Aubigné, 268–70, Book II, chap. xvii). One of the most prominent of those arrested was the Scotchman, Robert Stuart, who had already been suspected of the

Although the initial purpose of the conspiracy had failed, namely to take the King and drive out the Guises,[1] Condé and his followers did not fail to perceive that things were not entirely unfavorable.[2] Catherine de Medici, who while jealous of the position of the Guises in a place which naturally, and by tradition, if the regencies of Blanche of Castille and Anne of Beaujeu counted as precedents, belonged to her, had nevertheless sustained the drastic policy followed out after the execution of Du Bourg, in spite of the arguments of the admiral.[3]   Now, however, she saw her opportunity to make head against the cardinal and his brother and played into the hands of Coligny and Condé.[4]   She prevailed upon the King to send the

murder of President Minard, and who claimed to be a relative of Mary Stuart. He was imprisoned in the Conciergerie and put to torture, but would admit nothing. It was he who shot the constable Montmorency on the battlefield of St. Denis. Stuart had the reputation of being able to make bullets, called Stuardes, which would pierce a cuirass.   He himself was killed in turn at the battle of Jarnac by the marquis of Villars, count of Tende, who stabbed him with a dagger (*Rev. hist.*, XIV, 93; Forneron, *Histoire des ducs de Guise*, II, 92).

[1] "A conspiracy to kill them both and then to take the King and give him masters and governors to bring him up in this wretched doctrine," is the way the cardinal of Lorraine and his brother described it to the dowager queen of Scotland in a letter of March 20, 1560 (*C. S. P. For.*, No. 870).

The King's circular letter to the Parlements, bailiffs, and seneschals of the kingdom on March 30 declared that the conspirators "s'estoyent aidés de certains predicans venus de Genève."—*Mém. de Condé*, I, 398.

[2] "It had been well if the Guises had not been so particularly named as the occasion of these unquietnesses, but that it had run in general terms," wrote Throckmorton to Cecil (*C. S. P. For.*, No. 954, April 6, 1560).   Chantonnay advised the queen mother that, in order to avoid further difficulty, it was expedient for the Guises to retire from court for a season (La Place, 38).

[3] La Planche, 219, 20.

[4] Tavannes actually says she was privy to the conspiracy of Amboise, p. 247. During the reign of Henry II, Catherine de Medici had had no political influence. She was hated as an Italian (*Rel. vén.*, I, 105).   On one occasion only did she assert herself; "En 1557, à la nouvelle du désastre de Saint-Quentin, qui ouvrait à l'Espagne les portes de la France, il y eut un moment d'indicible panique.   Hommes d'état, hommes de guerre, tous avaient perdu la tête.   Par un hasard heureux, Catherine se trouvait à Paris; seule elle conserva son sang-froid, et, de sa propre initiative, courant en l'hôtel-de-ville et au parlement, et s'y montrant si éloquente et énergetique, elle arracha aux échevins et aux membres du parlement un large subside et rendit du cœur à la grande ville."—La Ferrière "L'entrevue de Bayonne," *R. Q. H.*, XXXIV, 457.

admiral upon a special mission to Normandy late in July, where he was expected to take the edge off the Marshal Termes' conduct, and secretly abetted the faction of the constable.[1] The opportunity was the better to do these things owing to the death of the chancellor Olivier on March 27,[2] who had been an instrument of the Guises, and the queen mother was quick to seize it. The famous Michel de l'Hôpital[3] was immediately appointed to the vacancy. He was a man of great knowledge in the law and of great culture; at the moment he was president of the *chambre des comptes* and had been chancellor to Madame Marguerite of France, the duchess of Savoy (who had Protestant leanings, and had interceded for Du Bourg), and was a member of the *conseil privé* of the King. L'Hôpital's accession was followed by the proclamation of letters of pardon to all recent offenders, provided they lived as good Catholics, the King declaring that he was unwilling to have the first year of his reign made notorious to posterity for its bloody atrocities and the sufferings of his people.[4] This was followed in May, 1560, by the royal edict of Romorantin, whereby the jurisdiction of legal processes relating to religion was completely taken away from the courts of parlement and from lay judges who had power to pass summary judgments, and was remitted to the ecclesiastical judges; which was interpreted as an assurance to

---

[1] "Ut exorientes tumultus reprimeret," Raynaldus, XXXIV, 72, col. 1; Chantonnay to Philip II, August 31, 1560, K. 1,493, No. 76; D'Aubigné, I, 27; La Planche, 269. Shortly before the death of Henry II, Coligny had sought to resign his government, wishing to retain only his office of admiral but Henry refused to accept the resignation (Delaborde, I, 362). Coligny then endeavored to have his government of Picardy given to his nephew, the prince of Condé (*Rev. hist.*, XIV, 74). Meanwhile he continued to hold the office of governor to prevent the Guises getting control of it (La Planche, 216). Finally in January, 1560, the admiral again went to court to present his resignation, and at the same time to urge the appointment of his nephew. This time it was accepted, and the prince of Condé was appointed to the post (La Planche, 217; *Rev. hist.*, XIV, 74, 75).

[2] La Place, 36; *C. S. P. For.*, No. 952.

[3] La Place, 38. On L'Hôpital see Dupré-Lasale, *Michel de l'Hôpital avant son elévation au poste de chancellier de France*, 2 vols., 1875; Amphoux, *Michel de l'Hôpital et la liberté de conscience au XVIe siècle;* Guer, *Die Kirchenpolitik d. Kanzlers Michel de l'Hôpital*, 1877; Shaw, *Michel de l'Hôpital and His Policy.*

[4] La Place, 37.

accused persons that they needed no longer fear the penalty of
death, owing to the opportunity of delaying sentences by means
of appeals from the acts and sentences of bishops to archbishops
and from thence to Rome.[1]   In August a supplementary decree
ordered the bishops and all curates to reside at their churches, the
bishops being prohibited in the future from proceeding against
anyone in the matter of religion except the Calvinist preachers or
persons in whose houses Huguenot meetings were held, the government thus tacitly permitting others to live in their own way,
which was interpreted as a virtual "interim."[2]   The spirit of this
legislation, as well as the skilful use of the law made therein, is
certainly due to the heart and brain of the chancellor L'Hôpital,
although Coligny is not without credit for his influence.[3]

These changes had the double effect, first, of persuading the
queen to take the management of affairs upon herself and endeavor
to remove the house of Guise from court; and second, in giving
the Huguenots and their partisans the opportunity of strengthening
themselves. The leniency of the government drew back into
France numbers of those who had withdrawn, among them preachers from Geneva and England who gave new life to the party by
exhorting them to continue their assemblies and the exercise of

[1] Castelnau, Book I, chap. xi; *C. S. P. Ven.*, No. 174, 1560; Raynaldus,
XXXIV, 66, col. 2; D'Aubigné, I, 274, n. 3; La Planche, 305; La Place, 468, gives
the text. The edict was not published, though, until July 17 (K. 1,494, folio 6).

[2] *C. S. P. Ven.*, No. 193, August 30, 1560. The term "interim" was technically applied to a resolution of the sovereign, with or without the approbation of
the diet or the estates of the country. By such an edict religious affairs were regulated provisionally, pending a final settlement by a general council of the church.
The practice first obtained in Germany, where Charles V issued such a decree in
favor of the Lutherans in 1548. See *Rev. hist.*, XIV, 76, 77. "In modo che,
restando ciascuno d'allora in dietro assicurato dalla paura che avea per innanzi,
di poter esser inquisito, questo si può dir che fosse uno tacito *interim*."—*Rel.
vén.*, I, 414.

[3] "La reyne mère du roy, monstrant une bonne affection à l'admiral, le pria de
la conseiller et l'advertir par lettres, souvent, de tous les moyens qu'il sçauvoit et
pourroit apprendre d'appaiser les troubles et séditions du royaume."—Castelnau,
Book I, chap. xi. Those of the Council who were unwilling to consent to such
changes absented themselves. The marshals Brissac and St. André did so, the
one alleging ill health as his excuse, the other hatred of the king of Navarre
(*Rel. vén.*, I, 549).

their religion.[1]   There was fear that the "interim" would be used by the Huguenots like the edge of a wedge to open the way to possess churches of their own, and such a demand was shortly to be made openly in the King's council at Fontainebleau in August, 1560.

It was apparent that there was not a province which was not affected, and there were many in which the new religion was even spreading into the country, as in Normandy, Brittany, almost all Touraine, Poitou, Guyenne, Gascony, the great part of Languedoc, Dauphiné, Provence, and Champagne.[2]   The "religion of Geneva" extended to all classes, even to the clergy—priests, monks, nuns, whole convents almost, bishops, and many of the chief prelates.   The movement seemed to be widest among the common people, who had little to lose, now that life seemed safe.   Those who feared to lose their property were less moved.   But nevertheless all classes of society seemed deeply pervaded.   While the "interim" lasted only those were punished who were actually preaching and holding public assemblies.   The prisons of Paris and other towns were emptied, and in consequence there was a great number of persons throughout the kingdom who went around glorying in the victory over the "papists," the name which they give their adversaries.   To add to the discomfiture of the Guises, the breach between them and Montmorency was widened.[3]   The duke of Guise had purchased the right of the sieur de Rambures to the county of Dammartin, not far from Paris, and adjacent to that of Nanteuil,[4] which the duke had shortly before acquired, the lower court of which was held in relief of Dammartin.   In order to do so the duke of Guise had persuaded Philippe de Bou-

[1] Castelnau, Book I, chap. xi; Rel. vén. I, 415 and n. 2.

[2] Davila, I, 295; Rel. vén., I, 413.   "In the rural portions of Normandy, for unknown reasons, 'Lutheranism' had spread so much that to one district of that province was given the name of 'Little Germany.'"—Hauser, American Hist. Rev., January, 1899, 225.

[3] The Tuscan ambassador, as early as April, 1560, advised his government of the likelihood of this feud (Nég. dip. de la France avec la Toscane, III, 415–17 Rev. hist., XIV, 74).

[4] Nanteuil, near La Fère (Aisne).

lainvilliers, who had lately sold the property to the constable, to rescind the contract which had been made, and sell it to him.[1] But the duke met with a straight rebuff, for when he sent word of the transaction, the constable answered by Damville, his son, that "as he had bought it, so would he keep it."[2] The feud between the Guises and Montmorency naturally threw the "connestablistes" more than ever to the side of Condé. Damville was sent to the King and the queen mother, who were staying at Chateaudun, to inform them that the Guises were his declared adversaries, and then went to confer with the prince of Condé, whom he met, "environ le jour appelé la feste de Dieu au mois de Mai,"[3] between Etampes and Chartres, near Montlhéry, when on his way to Guyenne, to see his brother of Navarre. The Guises, who had information of the interview, enlarged upon the dangerous conduct of Condé and pushed the suit for the lands of Dammartin in the courts.[4]

Catholic zealots made much of the events of Amboise to enlarge the reputation of the Guises. "During the whole of this Passion week," wrote the Venetian ambassador, "nothing has been attended to but the sermons of the cardinal of Lorraine, which gathered very great congregations, not only to his praise, but to the universal astonishment and admiration, both on account of his doctrines and by reason of his very fine gesticulation, and incomparable eloquence and mode of utterance."[5]

On the other hand, those who abhorred him on account of religion and for other causes did not fail to defame him by libels and writings placarded publicly in several places in Paris, where they were seen and read by everyone who wished.[6] Scarcely a day passed without finding in the chambers and halls of the King's own palace notes and writings of a defamatory nature abusing

---

[1] La Place, 38.

[2] C. S. P. For., No. 232, June 24, 1560; D'Aubigné, I, 276; Mém. de Condé, I, 151.

[3] La Place, 41; D'Aubigné, I, 277.

[4] La Place, 41.   [5] C. S. P. Ven., No. 149, 1,560.

[6] Rel. vén., II, 139; Nég. Tosc. III 417. La Planche, 217, gives a sample ampoon.

the cardinal of Lorraine.   In Paris the Palais de Cluny, belonging
to the Guise family, full of furniture of great value, was nearly
burnt by a mob.[1]   In several places the cardinal's painted effigy,
in his cardinal's robes, was to be seen, at one time hanging by the
feet, at another with the head severed and the body divided into
four quarters, as was done to those who were condemned.   In the
Place Maubert he was hanged in effigy and burnt with squibs.[2]

But worse disturbances than violent manifestoes disquieted the
government.   On June 1, 1560, the day of the Corpus Domini at
Rouen, when the procession passed through the city with the
customary solemnities, it was remarked that in front of a certain
house before which the procession passed no tapestry or any other
decoration had been placed.   Villebonne, the King's officer, "who
on account of these disturbances about religion remained there,"
perceived the omission and being suspicious of some clandestine
meeting of the Huguenots, chose to verify the fact instantly.   He
attempted to enter the house by force, but met with such stout
resistance on the part of its inmates that the procession was interrupted, and a great tumult arose, both sides having recourse to
arms.   After much fighting, each party having several wounded,
at length with the death of some defenders of the house and after
very great effort, the authorities quieted the uproar as well as they
could.   Next morning upward of 2,000 persons appeared before
the royal magistrates, not only very vehemently to demand justice
and satisfaction for the death of those persons who had been killed,
but to present also the "Confession" of what they believed and
the mode in which they intended it should be allowed them to live,
demanding that the "Confession" should be sent to the King that
it might be granted, and protesting that if on that account his

[1] C. S. P. Ven., No. 151.

[2] Ibid., For., No. 992, April 12, 1560.   On one occasion the police of Paris,
when pursuing a murderer, entered a house at a venture, into which they thought the
culprit had made his escape, where they found and arrested the man who printed
and placarded over the walls of Paris the writings against the Guise family and
against the cardinal (ibid., Ven., No. 178, 1560; Nég. Tosc., III, 417, 418).
The offending printer was hanged and then quartered (C. S. P. Ven., No. 186,
July, 1560).

ministers proceeded against any of them by arrest or capital punishment or other penalty, they would put to death an equal number
of Catholic officials of the government. The president and four
councilors of the Parlement of Rouen journeyed to Paris to present
the "Confession." They assured the King that the whole of Normandy was of the same opinion as those who declared themselves.
In its quandary the government blamed Villebonne, accusing him
of too much zeal and inquisitiveness. Moreover, fresh commotions
were heard of daily, and the government plainly feared some
sudden attack like that of Amboise.[1]

The Guises plucked courage, however, from the fact that under
the pretext of still preparing for the war in Scotland in support of
Mary Stuart,[2] they could fill France with soldiery.[3] Months
before the outbreak of the conspiracy of Amboise their agents had
been at work in Germany, using French gold for the purchase of
arms, ammunition, and above all, men, for Germany was filled
with small nobles of broken fortune, vagabond soldiers,[4] and
lansquenets ready to serve wherever the pay was sure and the
chance for excitement and plunder good.[5]

[1] *C. S. P. Ven.*; No. 174; *ibid., For.,* No. 232, June, 1560; No. 234, June 24,
1560; La Planche, 261. Francis II, during the course of this investigation, stayed
at Maillebois, a house of D'O, the captain of the Scotch Guard, on the edge of
Normandy (*C. S. P. For.,* No. 233, June 24, 1560).

[2] D'Andelot and Coligny refused to make war upon the Scotch Calvinists
(*C. S. P. For.,* No. 168, June 7, 1560).

[3] "Rapport indiquant les preparatifs faits pour l'enterprise sur l'Ecosse, à
Rouen, au Hâvre et à Dieppe," K. 1,495, No. 2, 11 juillet 1560.

"The embarkment for Scotland hastens. Soldiers arrive daily from Dieppe
and New Haven. . . . . At Caudebec, Harfleur, and New Haven there is exceeding great store of provision and munitions, sufficient for 25,000 men for six months."
—*C. S. P. For.,* No. 233, June 24, 1560.

[4] Mundt to Cecil, from Strasburg, *ibid.,* No. 52, May 7, 1560.

[5] Gresham to Cecil, *ibid.,* No. 617, January 22, 1560: "The French king
brings at least 20,000 footmen in Germany and he has taken up at Lyons as much
money at interest as he can get."

The count of Mansfeldt to the Queen, *ibid.,* No. 33, May 5, 1560: "The
French continue to raise troops and to buy horses and ammunition. . . . . Possibly
these preparations are being made against the insurgents of France, but it is doubtful whether under pretense of invading Scotland. . . . . "

After the conspiracy of Amboise the duke of Ferrara sent 1,000 harquebusiers
and the Pope 4,000 Italians (*ibid.,* No. 952, April 6, 1560).

On March 30, 1560, Guido Giannetti, Elizabeth's secret agent at Venice, wrote to Cecil, "France will have enough to do in her religious wars that have just sprung up, which will be worse than the civil war of the League of the Public Weal, in 1465 under Louis XI."[1] The prophecy soon became true. In spite of the formidable preparations made to continue the war in Scotland,[2] the more necessary since the death of the queen dowager of Scotland, news of which reached France on June 18,[3] France—or rather the French party in Scotland—on July 6, 1560, signed the treaty of Edinburgh, which, so far as the Guises were concerned, was the renunciation on their part of aggression abroad.[4] Nothing but the grave state of home politics could have induced the Guises so to yield the cause of their niece in Scotland.[5]

The Huguenot issue promised to come to a climax during the summer of 1560.[6] From all over France came reports of sedition and insurrection. The Protestants were masters of Provence.[7]

[1] *C. S. P. Eng.*, No. 931. The clever Italian, in this case, had more discernment than Cecil, who thought that the French would rather "yield in some part than to lose their outward things by inward contentions."—Cecil to Elizabeth, June 21, 1560; *ibid.*, 1560-61, No. 152, n.; Keith, 414; Wright, I, 30.

[2] See letter of the cardinal of Lorraine and duke of Guise, Appendix I.

[3] *C. S. P. For.*, No. 255, June 30, 1560. The news was concealed from Mary Stuart for ten days.

[4] *Précis d'articles arrêtées conclus entre le commissionaire d'Angleterre et de la France: Affaires d'Ecosse* (summary), K. 1493, No. 59, 6 juillet 1560.

Montluc, the bishop of Valence, the bishop of Amiens, and MM. de la Brose, d'Oysel, and Randau were the French ambassadors who accepted the terms offered by Cecil. Their commission was issued from Chenonceaux May 2, 1560. Montluc and Randau signed the instrument, an abstract of which is in *C. S. P. For.*, No. 281, July 6, 1560. Castelnau, Book II, chaps. i-vi, gives an account of the Anglo-Scotch war. See the memoir of Montluc upon his mission, in Paulin Paris, *Négociations*, etc., 392; and Schickler, *Hist. de France dans les archives privées de la Grande Bretagne*, 6. The treaty may be found in Rymer, XV, 593; Keith, I, 291; Lesley, *Hist. of Scotland* (1828), 291.

[5] "The late peace was forced upon the French rather by necessity occasioned by their internal discord than from their desire for concord."—Mundt to Cecil from Strasburg, August, 13, 1560, *C. S. P. For.*, No. 416.

[6] Chantonnay to Philip II, June 27, 1560, K. 1493, 68c.

[7] *Nég. Tosc.*, III, 419, 420, May, 1560. Biragues, king's lieutenant in Saluzzo, to the duke of Anjou, March 1, 1560, Collection Montigny, No. 298.

The cardinal Tournon, returning from Rome, dared not bring
with him the cross of the legation, for fear of its meeting with dis-
respect by the people of the places through which he would have
to pass.[1] From another source came the report that "very free
sermons have been delivered in the churches of Bayonne."[2] The
bishop of Agen wrote the council that all the inhabitants of that
city were in a state of furious insurrection; that they went to the
churches, destroyed all the images, and maltreated certain priests.
The queen mother was mysteriously warned that unless she released certain preachers imprisoned at Troyes she would become
the most unhappy princess living.[3] The Pope's legate left
Avignon in disgust at the license of the "Lutherans,"[4] and when
the pontiff proposed to send thither the cardinal Farnese, who
was willing to go provided a suitable escort of Italian and Swiss
infantry was furnished, France refused to consent, being unwilling to allow a foreign prince to enter the kingdom on such a
warlike footing.[5]

At the same time the personal attack upon the Guises became more venomous.[6] The enmity between the Guises and
the house of Montmorency had become so open and proceeded
so far, owing to the dispute about Dammartin, that it was expected they would take up arms. To crown all, the government received information through several channels of a design
against the King and his ministers of worse quality than the
recent Amboise conspiracy.[7] The information that came to light
caused the greatest anxiety because this time the evidence seemed

[1] C. S. P. For., No. 386, August 3, 1560. Throckmorton was told that "all
in this country (Picardy) seem marvellously bent to the new religion."—Ibid., No.
405, August 7, 1560.

[2] Ibid., No. 416, August 13, 1560.

[3] Ibid., Ven., No. 188, July 30, 1560.

[4] Ibid., For., No. 416, August 13, 1560.

[5] Ibid., No. 494, September 7, 1560.

[6] A pamphlet, issued in the nature of a petition and addressed to the king of
Navarre and the princes of the blood, abounded in invective against them.—Castelnau, Book II, chap. vii; C. S. P. For., No. 168, June 7, 1560.

[7] C. S. P. Ven., No. 188, July 30, 1560.

strongly to compromise the vidame de Chartres,[1] and the prince of Condé.[2]

Although the war in Scotland was practically at an end, the

[1] A vidame is a baron holding of a bishop. The vidame of Chartres was cousin-german of Maligny, suspected in the Amboise conspiracy. The vidame not having any children, Maligny and his brother were his sole heirs. The comte de Bastard has written a biography of him, *Vie de Jean de Ferrières, vidame de Chartres*, Auxerre, 1885.

[2] *C. S. P. Ven.*, No. 193, August 30, 1560.
The prince of Condé, during this summer, had repaired to Guyenne to see his brother, the king of Navarre, at Bordeaux where he protested against the Catholic policy of Antoine (La Planche, 276; La Place, 35). The brothers met on June 25 (Rochambeau, *Lettres d'Antoine de Bourbon et de Jeanne d'Albret*, 202). In his journey he inveighed against the usurpation of the Guises, and found a hearing from the noblesse and gentlemen of the south, who urged him and his brother to assume the place to which their rank entitled them. The Guises were kept informed of this journey of the prince by the marshal St. André, who, under pretense of visiting his brothers, kept watch of Condé (La Planche, 314, 315; La Place, 53). The discovery of the plot was owing to the suspicious vigilance of the duke of Guise, who marked a Basque gentleman who appeared in Paris as a stranger bent on important business, and surmised that he had been sent by the king of Navarre. It was noticed that he had conferred with the vidame of Chartres, and so, "as he was returning . . . . to . . . . Navarre, the duke of Guise had him and his valises, with (his) letters and writings, seized at Etampes. . . . . In the valise many letters were found, said to have been addressed both to the king of Navarre and to his brother, the prince of Condé. Among them were letters of the constable and his son, Montmorency, though they were merely letters of ceremony; but those of importance were what the vidame wrote to the prince, part in cipher and part without."—*C. S. P. Ven.*, No. 193, Aug. 30, 1560. Cf. La Planche, 355–58; De Thou, III, 357; *Négociations relatives au règne de François II*, 367; De Crue, 277, 278. The vidame of Chartres was arrested on August 29, 1560, by the provost-marshal and the lieutenant-criminal, at his lodgings in Paris, and carried through the streets upon a mule, "with a great rout of armed men to the Bastille."—*C. S. P. For.*, No. 483, September 3, 1560. Castelnau, Book II, chap. vii, says that the letters promised to assist the prince of Condé against all persons whatsoever except the King and the royal family. The Venetian ambassador says that there was enough in them "clearly to indicate that for many months there had been an intrigue."—*Ibid.*, Ven., No. 193, August 30, 1560. On the other hand, Throckmorton asserts that "the substance of the letter sent by the vidame to the king of Navarre is said to be so wisely written that it is thought that nothing can be laid to his charge."—*Ibid.*, For., No. 502, September 8, 1560. He was examined by the archbishop of Vienne and the president De Thou. Upon his arrest the vidame said "he was glad of it, for now the King would know of his innocence."—*Ibid.*, No. 502; La Place, 70.

Guises had not relaxed their efforts to raise men and money.[1] Philip II, knowing what was in progress, seems to have made a partial offer of assistance. In July fifteen German captains were dispatched beyond the Rhine, each commissioned to bring back three hundred pistoleers for the King's service;[2] letters were sent to the Rhinegrave and Duke John William of Saxony, urging them to form a league of the German princes and procure forces in case there should be need of them.[3]   La Mothe Gondrin was sent into Provence and Dauphiné, and another agent into Champagne, on similar errands.[4]   Fifteen hundred men with armor and munitions were sent to the castle of Guise.[5]   The Guises even endeavored to effect a reconciliation with the constable through the mediation of the marshal Brissac.[6]

The prevailing alarm was not allayed by the admiral, Gaspard de Coligny, who at a full council meeting held at Fontainebleau, on August 20, 1560, presented two petitions,[7] one for the King, the other for his mother, asking the King, in the matter of religion, to concede the petitioners two places of worship in two parts of the kingdom for greater convenience, that they might there exercise their rites and ceremonies as private congregations, without being

---

[1] The treaty of Edinburgh between Scotland and England was signed on July 6, 1560 (*C. S. P. Scot.*, IV, 42).

On July 28, 1560, Francis II, writing to the bishop of Limoges, says it is unnecessary to do more than inform the king of Spain that he has made peace with Scotland, which will leave him leisure to attend to the internal affairs of the realm and to thank him for his good offices (Teulet, I, 606); cf. *C. S. P. For.*, July 28, 1560, 194, n.

[2] *C. S. P. For.*, No. 345, July 19, 1560.

[3] Castelnau, Book II, chap. vii; *C. S. P. For.*, No. 416, August 13, 1560, from Strasburg.

[4] *C. S. P. For.*, No. 502, September 8, 1560.

[5] *Ibid.*, No. 354, July 19, 1560.

[6] *Ibid.*, No. 317, July 8, 1560; *Nég. Tosc.*, III, 421–23, June, 1560.

[7] At the assembly at Fontainebleau the King proposed four points for deliberation: (1) religion; (2) justice; (3) the debts of the crown; (4) means to relieve the people (*Nég. Tosc.*, III, 424, August 25, 1560). *C. S. P. For.*, No. 442; August 20, 1560; La Place 53; La Planche, 351; Castelnau, Book II, chap. viii, give the names of those present.   The petitions are printed in *Mém. de Condé*, II, 645.   Picot, *Hist des états généraux*, II, 14, erroneously gives the date as August 23.

molested by anyone, arguing that meetings in private residences would thus be obviated.[1]   Coligny claimed to speak with authority, having been officially sent into Normandy by the queen mother to inquire into the cause of the disturbances there.   A hot altercation ensued between the admiral and the cardinal of Lorraine. Coligny had prudently omitted signatures to the petition, but declared that he "could get 50,000 persons in Normandy to sign it," to which the cardinal retorted that "the King could get a million of his own religion to sign the contrary."[2]   L'Hôpital, the chancellor, however, deftly diverted the discussion into a political channel by a long discourse[3] upon the condition of the realm, comparing it to a sick man, asserting that the estates were troubled and corrupt, that religious dissidence existed, that the nobility were dissatisfied, and concluded by saying that if the source and root of all the calamities visiting France could be discovered, the remedy would be easy.[4]   In reply the cardinal of Lorraine offered to answer publicly for the administration of the finances and showed by an abstract of the government accounts that the ordinary expenses exceeded the revenue by 2,500,000 livres (over seven and one-half million dollars); his brother, the duke of Guise, as lieutenant-general, laid papers upon the table with reference to the army and forces of the kingdom.[5]   An adjournment was then taken until August 23, when, upon reassembling, each member of the Council was provided with a memorandum containing a list of the topics which the crown wished to have debated.[6]

Montluc, the bishop of Valence,[7] as the youngest privy-coun-

---

[1] C. S. P. Ven., No. 195, August 30, 1560; Castelnau, Book II, chap. viii, gives an abstract of the speech, in the third person.   Cf. La Place, 54, 55.

[2] Castelnau, loc. cit.

[3] "En termes prolixes."— De Thou, Book XXV, 525.   It is printed in Œuvres complètes de L'Hôpital, ed. Dufey, I, 335.

[4] "They might see all states troubled and corrupted, religion, justice, and the nobility, every one of them ill-content, the people impoverished and greatly waxed cold in the zeal and good will they were wont to bear to their prince and his ministers."—C. S. P. For., No. 442.

[5] La Planche, 352; Castelnau, Book II, chap. viii; the statement of the debt given by La Planche agrees exactly with C. S. P. For., 442.

[6] Castelnau, loc. cit.; La Planche, 352.

[7] See Reynaud, Jean de Montluc, evêque de Valence, 1893.

cilor, began the discussion when the Council reconvened.[1] But the speech of the occasion was that of Marillac, the liberal archbishop of Vienne, who, taking his cue from the chancellor, in a long discourse[2] enlarged upon the religious, political, and economic distress of France. His address is a complete statement of the Huguenot programme in church and state. He began by saying that the true "ancient and customary" remedy was a general council, but failing that, recourse must be had to a national council, and then proceeded to enumerate the things to be considered therein; first, the intrusion of foreign prelates—chiefly Italians—into French ecclesiastical offices,[3] "who fill a third portion of the benefices of the kingdom, who have an infinite number of pensions, who suck our blood like leeches, and who in their hearts, laugh at us for being so stupid as not to see that we are being abused;" secondly, he demanded that the clergy of France show by some notable act that they were sincerely bent upon reform and not merely seeking to fortify their prerogatives and privileges under the pretension of reform; and to this end the illicit use of money— "that great Babylonian beast, which is avarice, in whose path follow so many superstitions and abominations"—must be guarded against; thirdly, the wicked must make sincere repentance; fourthly, for the adjustment of the political and economic questions vexing the people the States-General must be convened. Then followed a statement of conditions: that the king must live upon the income of the royal domains, the spoliation of which should cease; that his wars be supported by the old feudal aids and not by recourse to extraordinary taxes.

This speech highly pleased the admiral, who added three points,

[1] "Les derniers et plus jeunes conseillers opinent les premiers, afin que la liberté des advis ne soit diminuée ou retranchée par l'authorité des princes ou premiers conseillers et seigneurs."—Castelnau, Book II, chap. viii. He made a typically episcopal, not to say unctuous, address. Cf. La Place, 54; La Planche, 352; printed in *Mém. de Condé*, I, 555; La Popelinière, I, 192.

[2] La Planche, 352–61; La Place, 53–65.

[3] Reform in the collation of benefices was one of the important deliberations of the Council of Trent (Baguenault de la Puchesse, "Le Concile de Trente," *R. Q. H.* October, 1869, 339).

namely, that, a religious "interim" be officially granted until the findings of the Council of Trent, which the Pope was to be asked to reconvene; that in event of refusal to do so, a national council of the clergy of France be called in which the Huguenots should have a representation;[1] and that the number of guards around the court, "which were very expensive and only served to infuse fears and jealousies into the people's minds" be reduced.[2]

The upshot of the conference was the resolution to call a meeting of the States-General for December 10 at Meaux (later changed to Orleans), and in default of the convening of a general church council, to convene a national body of the clergy at Paris on January 10, 1561, the long interval being allowed in order to permit the Pope to act.[3] In the meantime the *status quo* was maintained with reference to the worship of the Protestants, but for the sake of precaution, an edict was issued by which all subjects of the realm, whether princes or no, were prohibited from making any levy of men, arms, armor, horses, or moneys, on pain of being declared rebels against his majesty.[4]

There is no doubt that the resolution of the Council of Fontainebleau conformed to the conviction of a large element in France, the religious troubles having stirred up a strong demand for another general council of the church (the second session of the Council of Trent having been interrupted by the defeat of the emperor Charles V in the Smalkald war), or a national council, if the convocation of the former proved impossible.[5] Even the cardinal

[1] *Nég. Tosc.*, III, 424, August 29, 1560.

[2] Castelnau, Book II, chap. viii; La Planche, 361.

[3] *C. S. P. For.*, No. 193, August 30, 1560; Paris, *Négociations relatives au règne de François II*, 481; *Correspondance de Catherine de Médicis*, I, 149, n.; La Place, 68; La Planche, 363. "The government seems determined not to await the meeting of a council general, the decision of which will be tardy, but to convene a national one, assembling in a synod all bishops and other leading and intelligent churchmen of the kingdom, to consult and provide for the urgent need of France in matters of religion which admit of no delay."—*C. S. P. Ven.*, No. 142, 1560.

[4] La Place, 70.

[5] In Tours as early as April, 1560, a letter was published to all the governors and ministerial officials of the cities and provinces of the kingdom concerning the reformation of the church by means of a congregation of the prelates of the Gallican church to be assembled for a national council (*C. S. P. Ven.*, No. 151, 1560).

of Lorraine, desirous of acquiring fame by reforming the church
of France, urged the course, though it was hostile to the interest
of the Holy See, until the development of events at home persuaded him to change his tactics.[1]

The project of a national council was not pleasing to the Pope,
who cherished the hope of reconvoking the Council of Trent,[2]
either in France, Spain, or Germany.[3] When the cardinal of
Lorraine urged it, the Pope's rejoinder was that he would not divide
Christ's garment.[4] The Holy Father was in a quandary, being
unable with safety to grant a free council, or to refuse the general
one. He wanted to regard the prospective council as a *continuation* of the Council of Trent, and not as a new council.[5] But there
were political difficulties in the way of so doing, for not all the German princes were in favor of the decrees of Trent, and the Emperor
was bound by his oath not to attempt execution of the decrees lest
the princes of the Confession of Augsburg become alarmed for
fear that the Emperor, His Catholic Majesty and the Most Christian King had formed a Catholic concert.[6] The Kings of Spain

[1] The ultra-Catholic party at Trent accused the cardinal of wanting to create
an independent patriarchate out of the Gallican church. Desjardins. *Nég. de
la France dans le Levant*,.II, 728.
   As a matter of fact, at this season, the cardinal was disposed to favor the project of a national council, as he hoped thereby to enlarge the power and dignity
of his office as primate of France. His ambition was to become a sort of French
pope, so that "he would not have thought it wrong had all obedience to the pontiff
ceased."—*Despatches of Suriano* (Huguenot Society), September 23, 1560.

[2] Maynier, *Etude historique sur le concile de Trente (1545–62)*, 1874; *Journal
du concile de Trente, redigé par un secrétaire vénitien présent aux sessions de 1562 à
1563, et publié par Armand Baschet, avec d'autres documents diplomatiques relatifs
à la mission des Ambassadeurs de France au concile;* Desjardins, *Le pouvoir civil au
concile de Trente*, Paris, 1869; Baguenault de la Puchesse, "Le concile de Trente,"
R. Q. H., October, 1869.

[3] *C. S. P. Ven.*, No. 161, 1560.

[4] *Ibid., For.*, No. 232, June 24, 1560. When the Pope showed anger at the
determination of France, the cardinal of Lorraine actually apologized for himself
by saying that it was neither by his orders nor with his consent, but that the printers
took the liberty to give the name of National Council to the "Congregation" which
the King intended to convoke! (*ibid.*, No. 174, 1560).

[5] *Ibid.*, No. 569, September 8, 1560.

[6] *Ibid.*, No. 615, October 8, 1560. The demands of the Protestants were
as follows: (1) That the Council be convened in a free city of Germany; (2) that
summons be not by a papal bull, but by the Emperor, who should provide them
with safe-conducts; (3) that the Pope be subordinated to the Council; (4) that those

and France, moreover, although in favor of the general council, had reservations of their own regarding the application of the Tridentine decrees.[1]

The matter of the council was of much importance to every ruler in Europe. France, although resolved to convene the national clergy if the Pope protracted things, nevertheless urged the latter to hasten to grant a free and general council, not only by means of the bishop of Angoulême, the French ambassador in Rome, and the cardinals, but also through Bochetel, the bishop of Rennes, ambassador to the Emperor, and Sebastian de l'Aubespine, the bishop of Limoges, ambassador to Philip II. The Venetian senate, too, was importuned to use its influence. But the Pope hesitated for a long time, because the secular governments and himself were divided upon the question as to whether such a council should be regarded as a continuation of the Council of Trent (as the Pope wished), or as a council *de novo*. The Pope was fearful of compromising the papal authority by admitting the French contention of an authority superior to himself, for this he could never grant, taking the ground that, whether present or absent, he was always the head of and superior to all councils. Finally, Pius IV, alarmed by the resolution of the French government to assemble a national council if the general council should not be held, both because it would diminish his authority and because, even though nothing should be resolved on in opposition to the see of Rome, yet the assembling of a council by France without its consent would be prejudicial, and might be made a precedent by other states, came to the conclusion that further delay was dangerous, and convoked the general council for Easter, 1561,

---

of the Confession of Augsburg have a vote equally with the Catholics; (5) that the judgment be according to the Holy Scriptures, and not according to the decrees of the Pope; (6) that the prelates of the Council be absolved from the oath by which they are bound to the Pope and the Church of Rome; (7) that the acts of the Council of Trent be annulled (cf. *C. S. P. For.*, No. 782, sec. 14).

[1] "A general council is necessary for abolishing these heresies; but . . . . especial care must be taken with the Emperor and the kings of France and Spain to decide what shall be settled therein."—*C. S. P. For.*, No. 416, August 13, 1560, from Strasburg.

at Trent, "to extirpate heresy and schism and to correct manners,"[1] declaring that the canons of the church could permit of no other course.

The resolution of the French government had forced the hand of the Pontiff, who, however, consoled himself by the thought that either the national council would not now take place, or that the Guises would prevail in the States-General, so that the national council could be silenced, if held.[2]   The Pope figured that he would force the Catholic princes to side with him, lest by hazarding a

[1] The Vatican understanding was that the former Council of Trent was to be *continued*; although in the bull the word continuation was not made use of, as in that of the jubilee, a show of deference thereby being made to the Emperor and the French King, who had demanded a new council.   But the French government although it allowed the place, did not allow the continuation of the former Council of Trent convened by Paul III.   For if it accepted the council as it was published by the bull, it would have had to accept all the articles which had been concluded in the former council.   When it was argued that Philip II was satisfied with the continuation, Francis II replied that although continuation might suffice for the needs of his dominions, it would not do for France, the more so because Henry II of France having caused protest to be made in Trent of the nullity of that council, from its not having been free, his son could not think well of the continuation.   (The reply of Francis II to Philip II, October, 1560, is in Paris, *Négociations*, 615–22. Cf. also the luminous accounts of Elizabeth's agent in Venice, Guido Gianetti, *C. S. P. For.*, No. 782, December 7, 1560; No. 815, December 21, 1560; and the dispatch of Throckmorton to the queen, of December 31, 1560, giving an account of a conversation with the king of Navarre, No. 832, §7.)   In the reply made to Philip in October, 1560, the French King declared that, by the advice of his council, he had resolved upon an assembly of his prelates, from which nothing was to be feared for the apostolic see, it being intended only to provide the necessary remedies, and that it would not be a hindrance but rather an aid to the General Council, for when it came to open, the French prelates would be already assembled and "well informed as well of the evil as of the remedy," and that when the Council at Trent should have once begun, it would put an end to the lesser assembly.   As to the place of the council, the French at first preferred to have it meet in one of the Rhenish towns between Constance and Cologne, or at Besançon in Burgundy, which belonged to Philip II; later, in the answer to Don Antonio and in his letters to Rome, Francis II agreed to accept whatever place the Emperor and the Pope decided upon.

The new session of the Council of Trent was to be preceded by a general jubilee, giving power to confessors to absolve from all sins, *even from that of having read prohibited books*.   The bull warmly exhorted the extirpation of heresy.   This jubilee was first celebrated at Rome, on Sunday, November 24, 1560, by a procession, with the Pope walking at its head (*C. S. P. For.*, No. 782, §§15, 16).

[2] La Place, 114; *C. S. P. For.*, No. 630, October 12, 1560, from Venice.

change of religion in a national council they would also endanger their kingdoms. Philip II concurred in this belief. A king so orthodox as he had not failed to watch the course of the movement in France upon the ground of religious interests. But the Spanish King had also a political interest in France. His own Flemish and Dutch provinces were turbulent with revolt, and Granvella wrote truly when he said that it was a miracle that with the bad example of France, things were no worse in the Low Countries.[1] Accordingly, Philip II sent Don Antonio de Toledo into France to divert the French King from the idea of a national council.[2] The means of persuasion were readily at hand, for the French King was already far too compromised with Philip II to refuse his request. After the arrest of the vidame of Chartres, Francis II, in a long ciphered letter of August 31, 1560, to his ambassador in Spain, had besought the Spanish king to be prepared to assist him, in case it should be necessary.[3] To forefend the proposed national council, Philip II now offered at his own expense to give the French aid in suppressing all rebellion and schism.[4]

---

[1] Gachard, *Correspondance de Philippe II*, I, 191, Granvella to Antonio Perez from Brussels, August 9, 1560.

[2] Paris, *Négociations*, etc., 615–22; *Papiers d'état du cardinal de Granvelle*, VI, 137, 149. Don Antonio arrived at the French court on September 23, and departed four days later (*C. S. P. For.*, 619, Oct. 10, 1560). Philip II took the ground that any discussion looking toward the reformation of religion would not only imperil the faith, but prejudice his policy in Spain and the Netherlands; for if France should alter anything, he feared it would cause a schism universally (*ibid.*, No. 619, Oct. 10, 1560). The growth of the reformation in Spain alone was already quite great enough to alarm him. In the early autumn of 1559, Miranda, the archbishop of Toledo, the archbishop of Seville, and twelve of "the most famous and best-learned religious men" in Spain had been arrested for heresy (*ibid.*, No. 133, October 25, 1559), and at this time the inquisitors had just laid their hands on the brother of the admiral of Spain (*ibid.*, No. 619, October 10, 1560). On this whole subject see Weiss, *The Spanish Reformers*, and Wiffen, *Life and Writings of Juan de Valdés*, 1865. Montluc accused Jeanne d'Albret of printing Calvinist catechisms and the New Testament in Spanish, in Basque, and in Béarnais, and of secretly distributing them in Spain by colporteurs (La Ferrière, *Blaise de Montluc*, 61).

[3] Paris, *Négociations*, 495; Forneron, *Histoire de Philippe II*, I, 225. The Venetian ambassador learned the news within less than a month (*C. S. P. Ven.*, No. 199, September 28, 1560).

[4] This important offer was Philip's answer to Francis II's letter of August 31 and was made to L'Aubespine, the French ambassador in Spain, on September

Warlike preparations accordingly went forward under cover
of a proposed intervention in Scotland,[1] which the uncertainty
regarding Condé and Antoine of Bourbon facilitated, for it was
currently believed that both the king of Navarre and the prince
absented themselves from court on purpose.[2] At the court the
rumor prevailed that both were plotting recourse to arms, so much
so that on September 2 the cardinal Bourbon was sent to them,
desiring them in the name of the King to repair to the court, which,
on the next day, was moved from Fontainebleau to St. Germain.[3]
The marshal Brissac was transferred from the government of
Picardy to that of Normandy, and Du Bois, master of the footmen, was instructed to conduct all the footmen he could levy
with great secrecy into Normandy, while all the men in the
ordinary garrison of Picardy and other frontier points were drawn
in toward Orleans.[4] At the same time the Rhinegrave was notified
to come, but met unexpected opposition.[5]

13, 1560, as appears from the minutes of the Spanish chancellery in K. 1,493, No. 84.
After the departure of Don Antonio, Catherine wrote a letter to Philip II, thanking
him for the offer (*Correspondance de Catherine de Médicis*, I, 149).

The Venetian ambassador is particular and says he offered to put 3,500 troops
in Flanders at the disposal of France, to place 2,000 infantry near Narbonne, and
another 4,000 near Bayonne, besides "a large body of Spanish cavalry."—*C. S. P.
Ven.*, No. 199, September 28, 1560. Throckmorton's figures are 3,000 Spaniards
from the Low Countries; 500 men-at-arms and 2,000 footmen, who would enter
by way of Narbonne; and 3,000 through Navarre with 500 horses of that country
(*ibid., For.*, No. 619, §13, October 10, 1560).

[1] *C. S. P. Eng.*, No. 620, October 10, 1560.

[2] *Ibid., For.*, No. 411, August 9, 1560.

[3] *Ibid.*, No. 502, September 8, 1560; Chantonnay of Philip II, same date, K.
1,493, No. 83.

[4] *Ibid.*, No. 619, §§13, 15, October 10, 1560. The gendarmerie is appointed
to remain in divers countries according to an edict. Has been informed that
there is a league in hand between him (the king of France) and the king of
Spain. On the 16th there departed out of Paris ten cartloads of munitions and
artillery, but whither it is to be conveyed and how it is to be employed he cannot

[5] "From Strasburg: Frequent negotiations between the French King and the
German princes. The Rhinegrave has departed into Hesse . . . . with Count
John of Salm, who is also a French pensioner; where, by the landgrave's permission
and the dissimulation of the Saxon duke of Weimar, they have levied 2,000 cavalry
to take into France, which they have partly collected in the territories of the abbot

Parallel with these military preparations new financial measures were taken. On October 11, 1560, the King demanded 100,000 crowns (testons—a silver coin valued at ten or eleven sous; the amount was between $750,000 and $775,000) from the members of the Parlement, the provost, the chief merchants of Paris,[1] and "certain learned men of the Sorbonne."[2] The Parisians murmured because they thought the military display was meant to intimidate them. In November the crown imposed 10,000 francs (approximately $7,500) upon Orleans and demanded 100,000 more to pay the troops.[3] Lyons furnished a loan[4] and money was also secured by confiscations from the Huguenots on the part of the local authorities in many places.[5]

In the provinces disturbances continued to take place.[6] In Amboise and Tours the people stormed the prisons and released all those who had been confined as agitators on account of religion.[7]

learn (*C. S. P. For.*, No. 655, October 22, 1560). On the 30th Du Bois passed bringing with him out of the places and forts in Picardy 1,000 footmen, who marched between this town and Rouen toward Anjou; but where they shall go is only known to himself and the duke of Guise. They keep together strong, as if they were in an enemy's country. After them come 500 more (*ibid.*, No. 692, Oct. 31, 1360). The Tuscan ambassador notices the ardor of Paris to contribute blood and treasure (*Nég. Tosc.*, III, 436).

of Fulda on the boundaries of Hesse. The prefect of the Rhenish Circle, the count of Salm, being informed of this preparation of cavalry, assembled his captains at Worms, where it was decided that they would not be permitted to transport their cavalry into France. For a warning had been given in the Imperial Diet that no assembling or travelling of soldiers would be allowed unless by the express permission of the Emperor; for wherever they went they did great damage to the inhabitants."
—*Ibid.*, No. 736, November 26, 1560.

[1] For the organization of Paris at this time see *Livre des marchands*, 423, 440–43.

[2] *C. S. P. For.*, No. 665, October 22, 1560. The Venetian ambassador says 400,000 francs—twice the amount given by Throckmorton (*C. S. P. Ven.*, 220, October 15, 1560).

[3] *Ibid.*, No. 726, November 18, 1560.   [4] *Ibid.*, No. 619, October 10, 1560.

[5] "The goods of divers Protestants have been seized and divers men dispatched by night and sent by water in sacks to seek heaven."—*Ibid.*, No. 726, November 18, 1560. Cf. La Planche, 226, 227, 233.

[6] D'Aubigné, Book II, chap. xx; *Nég. Tosc.*, III, 424; for details see La Planche, 366–73.

[7] *C. S. P. Ven.*, No. 200, October 15, 1560.

The valley of the Loire seems to have been the storm center of these provincial uprisings, and in the middle of October[1] the king came hastily to Orleans with three companies of veteran infantry from the garrisons of Picardy.[2]   It was now decided to convene the States-General at Orleans instead of Meaux.[3]   On October 30 the prince of Condé, who all along had borne himself as if innocent and who came with his brother to Orleans, was arrested,[4] and the vidame of Chartres, who had been incarcerated in the Bastille, was sent for from Paris that he might be examined face to face with Condé.[5]   Besides being accused of implication in the conspiracy of Amboise, he was accused of being the author of the recent insurrection at Lyons.[6]

A significant change was made in the provincial administration at this time.   The Guises, having observed the dissatisfaction that prevailed because so many offices, dignities, and commissions had been distributed among them, in order to fling a sop to the princes of the blood and their faction, advised the King to create

[1] On October 18 (La Planche, 378).

[2] "Very well armed and numbering more than 300 men in each company and several pieces of cannon."—C. S. P. For., No. 665, October 25, 1560.

The people of Orleans were completely disarmed, even to knives, by an edict which required all arms to be deposited in the Hôtel-de-Ville (Despatches of Suriano [Huguenot Society], November 1, 1560).

[3] Paris, Négociations, etc., 486. Castelnau, Book II, chap. x, says the change was made because the Huguenots were numerous around Meaux (but so were they also around Orleans), and fear lest another conspiracy might be formed by having the place known so long in advance.   A rumor was current that the Huguenots were planning to surprise it.   I believe the real reason to be the more central location of Orleans.

[4] "On his arrival with his brethren, the cardinal of Bourbon and the prince of Condé, the prince was taken before the Council who committed him prisoner to MM. de Bressey and Chauverey, two captains, with 200 archers. . . . . The king of Navarre goes at liberty but is as it were a prisoner."—C. S. P. For., No. 716, §18, November 17, 1560; La Place, 73; Castelnau, Book II, chap. x; Nég. Tosc., III, 425.   La Planche, 381, describes the method of his imprisonment.

[5] La Planche, 380; C. S. P. For., No. 725, November 18, 1560; Nég. Tosc., III, 425, 426.

[6] "Qu'il avoit faict et faisoit plusieurs entreprises contre luy (le roi) et l'estat de bon royaume."—La Planche, 380; Despatches of Suriano (Huguenot Society), November 10, 1560.

two new governments in the middle of the kingdom in favor of the duke of Montpensier and his brother, the prince de la Roche-sur-Yon. In compliance with this suggestion the government of Touraine, to which province was added the duchies of Anjou and Vendôme and the counties of Maine, Blois, and Dunois, was created in favor of the former, and the government of Orleans, to which was added the duchies of Berry, the *pays* Chartrain, the Beauce, Montargis, and adjacent places, in favor of the latter. But the new office was reduced to a shadowy power by the revolutionary step of appointing provincial lieutenants over the governors, who were responsible to the duke of Guise as lieutenant-general of the realm, in this case the sieur de Sipierre being lieutenant in the Orléannais and Savigny in Touraine, each of whom was a servitor of the Guises.[1]

There is little reason to doubt that the Huguenots would have made a formidable revolt at this early day if they had been certain of effective leadership. But the cowardice of Antoine of Navarre, the logical leader of the party, prevented them from so doing. The great influence he might have exerted as first prince of the blood was in singular contrast with his weak character.[2] His policy, which he flattered himself to be a skilful one of temporization, was looked upon with contempt by the Huguenots, who despised him for weakly suffering his brother to be so treated and then added to his pusillanimity by foregoing his governorship of Guyenne, which was given to the marshal Termes.[3] In vain the Huguenot leaders urged upon him their supplications and their remonstrances;[4] in vain they laid before him the details of their organiza

---

[1] La Place, 38; La Planche, 378; Castelnau, Book II, chap. x; *Rel. vén.*, I, 557; Brantôme, III, 278.

[2] Yet he was so carefully watched that he was practically a prisoner—"tanquam captivus," says Throckmorton to Lord Robert Dudley (*C. S. P. For.*, No. 721, 1560). Damville was also regarded with suspicion.

[3] *Ibid.*, No. 716, §18, November 17, 1560.

[4] Castelnau, Book II, chap. ix; La Planche, 318–38, gives the text of one, which is significant because it is almost wholly a *political* indictment of the Guises; next to nothing is said touching religion, conclusive evidence that the Huguenot party was much more political than religious.

tion; that six or seven thousand footmen throughout Gascony and Poitou were already enrolled under captains; that between three and four thousand, both foot and horse, would come from Provence and Languedoc; that from Normandy would come as many or even more, with a great number of cavalry; that with the aid of all these he would be able to seize Orleans (thus controlling the States-General), and Bourges, with Orleans the two most important towns in central France. They assured him that thousands were merely waiting for a successful stroke to declare themselves and that money was to be had in plenty; for every cavalryman and every footman was supplied with enough money for two months and that much more would be forthcoming, provided only the king of Navarre would declare himself the protector of the King and the realm and oppose the tyranny of the Guises.[1]

This was the moment chosen by Catherine de Medici to assert herself. Hitherto, there had been no room for her between the two parties, each of which aspired to absolute control of the King. The queen mother had no mind to see herself reduced to a simple guardian of the persons of her children, utterly dependent upon the action of the council, without political authority nor "control of a single denier,"[2] and perceived that she might now fish to advantage in the troubled waters; to change the figure, she determined to play each party against the other[3] in the hope of herself being able to hold the balance of power between them. This explains her double-dealing after the conspiracy of Amboise, when she represented to Coligny that she wished to be instructed in the Huguenot teachings in order, if possible, that she might be able to discover the "true source and origin of the troubles," and conferred with Chaudien, the Protestant pastor in Paris, and Duplessis, the Huguenot minister at Tours, at the same time also inquiring into the political claims of the Huguenots, having the cardinal of Lorraine concealed, like Polonius, behind the arras;[4]

[1] La Planche, 375, 376.   [2] Ibid., 318.

[3] "Qu'il seroit meilleur pour elle d'entretenir les choses en l'estat qu'elles estoyent, sans rien innover."—Ibid., 313.

[4] Ibid., 316, 317.

why, too, she used fair words at the conference at Fontainebleau and simultaneously saw Francis II write to Philip II asking for Spanish aid in the event of civil war.

The Venetian ambassador said truly that the famous Roman temporizer, Fabius Cunctator, would have recognized his daughter in this astute woman of Etruria.[1] For fear of being sent back to Italy or of staying in France without influence, she aimed to play the two parties against one another. She did not hesitate to hazard the crown in order to keep the government in her hands, although, as the Venetian ambassador said, "to wish to maintain peace by division is to wish to make white out of black."[2]

The time was a peculiarly propitious one. With the prince of Condé out of the way[3] she counted upon the vacillation and hesitancy of the king of Navarre to keep the Huguenots from overt action, while the prospect of the coming States-General, which had grown out of the assembly at Fontainebleau, as the bishop of Valence had predicted,[4] filled the Guises with dismay, so much so that when the demand for the summons of that body began to grow, they had endeavored to persuade the King to ordain that whoever spoke of their convocation should be declared guilty of lèse-majesté.[5] The reason of their alarm is not far to seek. The demand for the States-General was the voice of France, speaking through the noblesse and the bourgeoisie, crying out for a thorough inquiry into the administration of the Guises and reformation of the governmental system of both state and church; as such it was a menace to the cardinal and his brother and in alignment with the demands of the political Huguenots. The costly wars of Henry II, the extravagance of the court; the burdensome taxa-

[1] Baschet, La diplomatie vénitienne, 499.

[2] Rel. vén., II, 65.

[3] The more one considers the arrest of the prince of Condé, the more certain it seems that Catherine de Medici inspired it. The Venetian ambassador believed Catherine was at the bottom of his arrest; see Baschet, 500, 501.

[4] "The bishop of Valence says . . . . that the meeting of Fontainebleau would turn into a general assembly of the three estates of France."—C. S. P. For., No. 445, August 22, 1560.

[5] La Planche, 218.

tion; the venality of justice; the lawlessness and disorder prevailing everywhere; the impoverishment of many noble families, and the rise of new nobles out of the violence of the wars in Picardy and Italy, more prone to license and less softened by the social graces that characterized the old families;[1] the dilapidation of ancestral fortunes and the displacements of wealth; the religious unrest; the corruption of the church—all these grievances, none of which was wholly new, were piling up with a cumulative force, whose impending attack the Guises regarded with great apprehension.[2]

The administration of the cardinal of Lorraine and his ducal brother had not mended matters, but in justice to them it should be said that their ministry was quite as much the *occasion* as the *cause* of the popular outcry for reform. The evils of the former reign were reaching a climax which their haughtiness and ambition served to accentuate.[3] Misappropriation of public moneys, exorbitant taxation, denial of justice, spoliation of the crown lands, especially the forests, the dilapidation of church property, and the corruption of manners, were undoubtedly the deepest popular grievances. In the demand for redress of these grievances all honest men were united. In 1560 the cry of the Huguenots for freedom of worship was the voice of a minority of them only. Most Huguenots at this time were political and not religious Huguenots, who simply used the demand of the new religionists as a

[1] See the scathing comparison of the house of Guise with that of Montmorency: "La plus ancienne yssue du premier chrestien du premier du royaume de la chrestienté."—*Livre des marchands*, 428–30.

[2] "Messieurs de Guyse vouloyent venir aux armes pour effacer ceste poursuite des estats et réformation de l'église . . . . la poursuitte que nous avions si justement commencée de leur faire rendre compte de leurs dons excessifs, c'est-à-dire de leurs larcins, et de leur mainement des finances, ou plustost de leurs finesses."— *Ibid.*, 456.

The petition of the estates of Touraine, assembled at Tours on October 26, 1560, to the King, is a good example of this popular demand. The articles reflect the state of the times (*C. S. P. For.*, No. 681). In connection with this authentic petition compare the imaginary "discours du drapier" in a fancied meeting of the estates-general, as given in *Livre des marchands*, 427–40, the satirical forerunner of the greatest political satire of the sixteenth century, the *Satyre Menippée*.

[3] La Planche, 260.

vehicle of expression; this sentiment also accounts for local risings to rescue arrested Calvinists, the participants in many cases being actuated more by the desire to make a demonstration against the government than by sympathy with the Calvinist doctrines.[1]

The debts of the crown at the accession of Francis II aggregated forty-three millions of livres,[2] upon which interest had to be paid, without including pensions and salaries due to officers and servants of the royal household, and the gendarmerie, which were from two to five years in arrears,[3] a sum so great that if the entire revenue of the crown for a decade could have been devoted to its discharge, it would not have been possible to liquidate it. The result was the provinces abounded with poor men driven to live by violence and crime, while even the nobility, because of their reduced incomes, and the soldiery on account of arrears of wages, were driven to plunder the people.[4] Even members of the judiciary and the clergy had recourse to illicit practices.[5] The regular provincial administration was powerless to suppress evils so prevalent, whose roots were found in the condition of society. It was in vain that the crown announced that it was illegal to have recourse to arms for redress of injuries and commanded the governors in the provinces, the bailiffs, seneschals, and other similar officers to stay within their jurisdictions and vigilantly to sustain the provost-

---

[1] Cf. La Place, 47–49, 110–13; La Planche, 342; and especially the indictment in *Livre des marchands*, 436–58.

[2] To be exact, 43,700,000 lives (Isambert, XIV, 63). Part of it was held by the Swiss cantons: "The French King is conferring with the Swiss about paying his debts, and offers two-thirds with a quarter for interest, and to pay the whole within three years; which conditions they refuse, and desire him either to stand to his written promises or that the matter shall be discussed in some place appointed in Switzerland."—*C. S. P. For.*, No. 763, December 3, 1560, from Strasburg.

[3] "In so much as it was necessary for him to find the wherewithal to satisfy some of these obligations, the late king had abolished certain of them and reduced others; he had let 50,000 footmen be billeted upon the cities of the kingdom and caused money to be raised by the imposition of subsidies, so much so that he had found it necessary in some places to diminish the *taille*, the people having abandoned the county of Normandy."—*C. S. P. For.*, No. 658, January 28, 1560; cf. La Place, 47; *Livre des marchands*, 447, 448; *Nég. Tosc.*, III, 405 and 455.

[4] "The soldiers through necessity have begun to rob."—*C. S. P. For.*, *ibid.*

[5] La Place, 48.

marshals in suppressing sedition or illegal assemblies. Some
men thought the remedy lay in more drastic penalties and advocated the abolishment of appeal in criminal causes, as in Italy and
Flanders.[1] But history in many epochs shows that the social
maladies of a complex society cannot ·be so cured. Obviously
the true remedy lay in searching out the causes of the trouble and
destroying them, and this was the intent of the demand for the
States-General.

The summons of the States-General of Orleans and the further
act of the government in announcing that it would summon a national council of the French clergy to meet in Paris on January 10,
1561, unless the Council General was called in the meantime,
were equivalent to promises that reform would be undertaken
in both state and church. The double announcement was the
simultaneous recognition of one necessity—reformation.

[1] La Place, 49.

CHAPTER III

THE STATES–GENERAL OF ORLEANS

The prosecution of the prince of Condé and the· vidame of Chartres was pushed during the month of November in order to overcome any Huguenot activity in the coming States-General.[1] The Guises assured both the Pope and Spain that their intention was, after the execution of the prince, to send soldiery into the provinces under the command of the marshals St. André, Termes, Brissac, and Sipierre, whose Catholicism was of a notoriously militant type, and thus either to crush the Huguenots, or drive them out of the country.[2] Condé claimed, upon the advice of his counsel, the advocates Claudius Robert and Francis Marillac, that as a prince of the blood he had to give account to the King alcne and to judges suitable to his condition, as peers of France, denying the jurisdiction of the ordinary judges.[3] This the latter refused to allow, on the ground that there was no appeal from the King in council (which at least had been the practice of the crown since Francis I) because the judgment so given was an absolute declaration of the king's pleasure; whereupon Condé, after the example of Marchetas, when condemned by Philip of

[1] "Interrogatoire d'un des agens du prince de Condé," *Arch. cur.*, sér. I, IV, 35. Madame de Roye, Coligny's sister and mother-in-law of Louis of Condé, was also seized in the expectation of finding papers in her possession which would incriminate Condé, Lattoy, the advocate, and Bouchart, the king of Navarre's chancellor (Castelnau, Book II, chap. ix; La Planche, 381; Frederick, count palatine of the Rhine, to Elizabeth, from Heidelberg, *C. S. P. For.*, No. 721, November 17, 1560; No. 737, §8, November 28, 1560; No. 781, December 7, 1560; De Crue, *Anne de Montmorency*, 282 ff.).

[2] "MM. de Guise avoient asseuré le pape et le roi d'Espagne de chasser du royaume les huguenots; desseignent (après le procès du prince de Condé et luy executé) d'envoyer de la gendarmerie et de gens de pied sous la charge des sieurs de Sainct André, Termes, Brissac et Sipierre, leurs amis, pour chasser les hérétiques et faire obeyr le roy."—Tavannes, 257 (1560).

[3] *Mém. de Condé*, II, 379; Chantonnay to Philip II, November 28, K. 1,493, No. 108; *Despatches of Suriano* (Huguenot Society), November 22; Claude Haton, I, 130, 131.

Macedon, appealed from the King in bad council to the King in good council. The prince, however, adhered to his claim, until by a subterfuge he was made, in a way, to commit himself; for at last he signed an answer *to his counsel*, Robert, whereby the prosecution gained a point prejudicial to him, although good lawyers affirmed that a defendant's counsel could not be made his judge. Thereupon the government organized a court in which there was a sprinkling of peers, in order to seem to comply with the law.[1] Under such practices the judgment was a foregone conclusion, although even after being declared guilty, the general opinion was that the prince would not be put to death, but that the worst that could befall him would be imprisonment in the dungeons of Loches, where Ludovic Sforza died in the reign of Louis XII; or that he would be kept in confinement elsewhere pending greater age on the part of the king and new developments.[2]

What Condé's fate would have been still remains a problematical question, for Francis II died at Orleans on December 5, 1560, and his death put an end to all proceedings against the prince.[3] The prince of Condé was released on December 24, and imme-

[1] This action was a legal subterfuge, as Castelnau, Book II, chap. xii, no friend of Condé, is honest enough to admit, citing several precedents in favor of Condé. Cf. La Place, 73–75; La Planche, 400–2; D'Aubigné, I, 294, 295.

[2] *Despatches of Suriano* (Huguenot Society), November 25, 1560.

[3] Francis II, always had been of a frail constitution, and in his passion for hunting seems to have over-exerted himself. "The constitution of his body is such as the physicians do say he cannot be long lived, and thereunto he hath by this too timely and inordinate exercise now in his youth added an evil accident."—Throckmorton to Elizabeth, *C. S. P. For.*, No. 738, November 28, 1560; Chantonnay to Philip II, same date, K. 1,493, No. 108. He fell ill about November 20, seemingly with a catarrh (Suriano, November 20, 25), accompanied by headache and pain in the ear, of which he died on the night of December 5 at the eleventh hour, although the physicians, on December 1, "mistrusted no danger of his life" (*C. S. P. For.*, No. 758). Throckmorton elsewhere calls the King's disease "an impostume in the head."—*Ibid.*, No. 771, December 6, 1560; cf. La Planche, 413, 418; D'Aubigné, I, 299. Very probably the disease was *mastoiditis*—an affection of the mastoid bone back of the ear, induced by chronic catarrh which finally affected the brain. Suriano says: "Il corpo del morto Re è stato aperto et hanno trovato guasto tutto il cervello, in modo che per diligentia delli medici non si haveria potuto risanarlo" (December 8, 1560.)

diately went to La Fère in Picardy.[1]   The crown descended to the
dead king's younger brother, Charles IX, a boy ten years of age.
His accession was not an auspicious one.   Well might the Venetian
ambassador exclaim: "Vae tibi terra cujus rex puer est."[2]   The
execution of two Calvinists in Rouen on December 3 occasioned
a riot during which the gates of the city were shut,[3] and at Bordeaux
a serious insurrection of 1,200 persons had taken place in consequence of the arrest of Condé, so that the general pardon of religious offenders issued on January 3, 1561, was a wise step.[4]   All
the plans designed and prepared for execution at Orleans were
broken by the death of the King.   The Guises were furious.[5]

It was hoped that the new reign might be established tranquilly,
without an appeal to arms, but there was much misgiving owing
to "the bad spirit among the people on account of the religious
question, and of their dislike of the existing government."[6]   Many
had thought that in the event of the death of the king a general
uprising might result throughout the realm, for religious and

---

[1] D'Aubigné, I, 300, and n. 2.   The vidame of Chartres, who had been
confined in the Bastille, "though allowed to take the air" (C. S. P. For., No.
764, December 3, 1560), was released also, but died almost immediately (La
Place, 78–79, gives a eulogy of him).   See Lemoisne, "François de Vendôme,
vidame de Chartes," Positions de thèses de l'Ecole des Chartes, 1901, 89.   His
death enriched the house of Montmorency, for he left the lordship of Milly-en-
Gatinois, worth 3,000 crowns yearly, to Damville, the constable's second son
(C. S. P. For., No. 832, §10, December 31, 1560).   The will is printed in Bib.
de l'Ec. d. Chartes, 1849, 342; it is dated December 23.

[2] Rel. vén., I, 543. On the situation after death of Francis II see Weill, chap. ii.

[3] C. S. P. For., No. 764, December 3, 1560, Edwards to Cecil from Rouen.

[4] "Lettres-patentes du roi Charles IX; pardon-général au sujet des affaires
de religion."   The Spanish ambassador had been summoned to the court that he
might write to Philip II to stand ready to offer assistance in case of need.—Despatches
of Suriano [Huguenot Society], December 3, 1560; K. 1,493, No. 113, December
3, 1560.   Chantonnay's correspondence shows that the Spanish King was fully
informed of the progress of events in France, which is confirmed by Throckmorton.
"The King of Spain has given order to stay the five thousand Spaniards in the
Low Countries who were to go to Sicily . . . . the posts run apace and often
between the kings of France and Spain."—C. S. P. For., No. 737, November
28, 1560.

[5] La Place, 76; Claude Haton, I, 116.

[6] Despatches of Suriano (Huguenot Society), December 3, 1560.

administrative reform, since Charles IX, being a minor, would be placed under the guidance of the king of Navarre, the oldest and nearest prince of the blood, who by consenting to the demands of the Huguenots, either from inclination or from inability to repress them, would open the door to such a course. Others believed that the Guises would not be put down, but that with the military resources concentrated around Orleans, at their disposal, they would seek to overawe the opposition and retain their power, finding means, through papal dispensation, to marry Mary Stuart to the new king.[1] There was a third class who rightly surmised that the queen mother, if not able to establish the regency in her favor, would play the parties against each other in such a way as to be able to exercise large control herself. In pursuance of this double course, Catherine secretly incited the king of Navarre and the prince of Condé, giving out that the action lately taken against the latter had been by the advice of the Guises. At the same time she gave the Guises to understand that the hard feeling which the Bourbon princes felt for them was contrary to her wish and pleasure and that it was they who had sought to compel the Guises to render account of their administration.[2] As the constable seemed to command the balance of power, both the queen mother and the Guises began to compete for his favor,[3] Catherine

C. S. P. For., No. 773, December 6, 1560. "They have not only already good forces in this town at their devotion, but have sent for more men-at-arms to be here with all diligence . . . . so that if they cannot get it by good means, they see none other surety for themselves but to get it by such means as they can best devise . . . . if the Guise forces and party be best, they will not fail to betrap them all and to stand for it whatever it costs them."—C. S. P. For., No. 771, December 6, 1560. Catherine de Medici detested Mary Stuart. She called her "notre petite reinette écossaise."

[2] Claude Haton, I, 118, 119. The Guises wanted, above all, to prevent the undivided regency of Catherine de Medici and even cited the Salic law as a bar to such result (Chantonnay to Philip II, December 28, 1560; K. 1,494, No. 12). They favored the regency of the pliable Antoine of Bourbon, or a combination of the king of Navarre and the queen mother. In either event a galaxy of the Guises was to surround the throne, i. e., the cardinals of Tournon and Lorraine, the duke of Guise, the chancellor and the two marshals Brissac and St. André; cf. Nég. Tosc., III, 434, and De Crue, Anne de Montmorency, 288–90, a good brief statement.

[3] Catherine sent the sieur de Lansac at once to the constable at Etampes (cf. D'Aubigné, I, 299, and n. 2) who in turn went to consult with his son, Damville, at Chantilly, where he was kept by his wife's illness, those two in turn conferring with the princess of Condé (La Place, 76).

overcoming her old enmity on account of her fear of the Guises.[1] Between the Guises and Montmorency the enmity was too great for any *rapprochement*, so that the Guises endeavored to counter the coalition of Catherine de Medici and the constable by overtures to Antoine of Navarre, whose own pliant nature readily yielded to their blandishments, telling him that Philip II probably would be inclined to restore his lost kingdom of Navarre or give him an equivalent in Sardinia, in the event of the adoption of a strong Catholic policy on his part.[2]

Catherine de Medici, however, by the promptness of her action, and perhaps not a little owing to the unpopularity of the cardinal of Lorraine,[3] got the better of the Guises, the government being organized around the queen mother and the three Bourbon princes, the king of Navarre, the cardinal of Bourbon, the prince of Condé the constable, the three Châtillons—the admiral Coligny, the cardinal Odet, and D'Andelot—the duke de Montpensier and the prince de la Roche-sur-Yon.[4]   The duke of Aumale, the marquis of Elbœuf, the grand prior of France, and the cardinals of Lorraine and Guise, all brothers of the duke of Guise and the cardinal of Lorraine left the court at the same time,[5] but if the pride of the Guises was wounded, they did not show it.   They were followed

[1] *Despatches of Suriano* (Huguenot Society), December 18, 1560.

[2] How much Antoine yielded to the temptation the following report of an interview between Throckmorton and the king of Navarre shows: "Throckmorton said that there was a *bruit* that the Spaniards had passage given them by Bayonne and other forts of the French King. The king of Navarre said that it was true, and that he was about to verify the letters that are yet denied."—*C. S. P. For.*, No. 732, December 31, 1560, § 7.

On Sardinia see *Rel. vén.*, I, 555. Even the prospect of becoming emperor was held out to him (*ibid.*, I, 559; II, 76).

[3] "Although the duke of Guise is popular, above all with the nobility, yet everybody so detests the cardinal of Lorraine that if the matter depended upon universal suffrage, not only could he have no part in the government, but perhaps not in the world! It is cynically reported that his Right Reverend and Lordship took the precaution to send his favorite and precious effects early into Lorraine."— *C. S. P. Ven.*, No. 221, December 16, 1560.

[4] *Despatches of Suriano* (Huguenot Society), December 18, 1560; *Rel. vén.*, I, 433. "I found the court very much altered . . . . not one of the house of Guise."—*C. S. P. For.*, No. 832, December 31, 1560.

[5] Claude Haton, I, 11.

by all the companies of ordinance, both cavalry and infantry, which had been sent to Orleans.

But Catherine de Medici looked farther than the present order of things and schemed to have the coronation effected as soon as possible, thinking that it would remove many difficulties alleged of the King's minority[1] and make him of sufficient authority to appoint such governors as he pleased.[2] She found means to have it arranged in the Privy Council (March 27, 1561) that she and the king of Navarre, in the capacity of lieutenant-general, should rule jointly, the King's seal being in the custody of both and kept in a coffer to which each should carry a different key. This astute move gave Catherine exclusive guardianship of the person of Charles IX, and assured her at least an equal power in the regency.[3] At the same time orders were given for the ambassadors and others who wished for audience to ask it of the queen mother through the secretaries.[4] By this new arrangement it became unnecessary to give account of one's business first of all either to the cardinal of Lorraine or the constable, or to anyone else, as was usually done before; but at once to address the queen, who, should the matter need to be referred to the council, could propose it and give reply according to their decision. As not one of these

[1] The law of France, by ordinance of Charles V, had for generations provided that the king's majority was attained when he was fourteen years of age; but the King's uncles claimed that the meaning of the law was that the King's majority was not reached *until the end* of his fourteenth year, i. e., upon his *fifteenth* birthday, which, in the case of Charles IX, would not be until June 27, 1564. This ingenious argument was sustained by various authors subsidized by the Guises, who went farther and argued away the regency of the queen mother also, in spite of the precedents of Blanche of Castille and Anne of Beaujeu, on the ground of the Salic law (Chantonnay to Philip II, December 28, 1560; K. 1,494, No. 12).

[2] D'Aubigné, I, 302; *Correspondance de Catherine de Médicis*, I, 176; *Despatches of Suriano* (Huguenot Society), March 29, 1561; *C. S. P. For.*, No. 77, § 3, March 31, 1560; La Place, 120, 121; De Crue, *Anne de Montmorency*, 299.

[3] Cf. Viollet, *Inst. polit. de la France*, II, 95.

[4] The arrangement of executive offices at this time was very different from that of a modern government.   Instead of there being a single secretary for foreign affairs, there were individual secretaries *for each country*—one for Italy, one for Spain, one for Flanders, one for Germany, etc., and each one attended to his own business. This eliminated one more power in the government, exactly as Catherine wanted.

councilors was superior to another, the power was all in Catherine's hands. She had played her cards well and had won. The duke of Guise ceased to be of influence at court and the constable "was satisfied to lose his authority in order to damage his enemies."[1] France began to awaken to the fact that the queen who had led a life of retirement during her husband's reign, in that of her son was evincing that capacity for public affairs which was an hereditary possession in her family. In her quality as queen mother, she kept the King well in hand. She would not permit anyone but herself to sleep in his bed-chamber; she never left him alone. She governed as if she were king. She appointed to offices and to benefices; she granted pardon; she kept the seal; she had the last word to say in council; she opened the letters of the ambassadors and other ministers. Those who used to think she was a timid woman discovered that her courage was great; and that, like Leo X and all his house, she possessed the art of dissimulation.[2]

The Huguenots had hoped for much politically from the sudden revolution, and looked forward to organizing the States-General, while the Catholics hoped that the precautions taken during the elections had insured the election of men opposed to any novelty in the matter of religion.[3] The first session took place on December 13.[4] L'Hôpital, the chancellor, made an eloquent and earnest plea in favor of harmony among the members, endeavoring to draw them away from religious animosities by pointing out the great necessity of administrative and political reform, urging that the root of the present evils was to be found in the miscarriage of justice, the burdensome taxes, the corruption of office, etc.[5]

[1] *Despatches of Suriano* (Huguenot Society), March 29, 1561. "The King is young and the constable has now a great authority in the realm . . . . . But if they recover their authority, it is to be feared that they will use more extremity than they did before, and that therefore the queen cannot but fear his danger in this case."—*C. S. P. For.*, No. 1,030, February 26, 1561, § 6.

[2] See the remarkable character-sketch of the Venetian ambassador in *Rel. vén.*, I, 425–27.

[3] *Despatches of Suriano* (Huguenot Society), December 8, 1560. On the efforts of the Guises to control the States-General of 1560 see Weill, 40.

[4] D'Aubigné, I, 304; Paris, *Négociations*, 789.

[5] La Place, 85, 87.

He ascribed the religious inquietude to the degeneracy of the church and advocated thorough reform of it, saying that the clergy gave occasion for the introducing of a new religion, though he avoided entering into the matter of merit of its doctrines.[1] He pointed out the needs of France and the necessity for civil and religious concord, and, in the peroration pleaded for earnest, patriotic support of the boy-King, "for there never was a father, no matter of what estate or condition, who ever left a little orphan more involved, more in debt, more hampered than our young prince is by the death of the kings, his father and his brother. All the cost and expenses of twelve or thirteen years of long and continuous war have fallen upon him; three grand marriages are to to be paid for, and other things too long to tell of now; the domain, the aids, the salt storehouses, and part of the *taille* have been alienated."[2]

In spite of the efforts of the chancellor, however, to smooth the way, the ship of state encountered rough water at the very beginning. It was doubtful whether anything would come of the session, as the difficulties between the delegates were endless, partly from the diversity of their commissions and of the requests they had to make, partly from individual caprice. The commons and the clergy readily agreed to meet together, but many of the nobility made difficulty. Some of those of Guyenne and of some parts of Brittany, Normandy, and Champagne would not consent to treat with the government without a fresh commission, saying that their commission was to the late king, Francis II—an invention of those who were not satisfied with the present government

---

[1] Castelnau, Book III, chap. ii. In this connection the following observation is of interest: "A disputation has lately been at Rome among the cardinals, and the Pope has had the hearing of what is the cause that France is thus rebelled from them. The Romans would conclude that the dissolute living of the French cardinals, bishops and clergy, was the cause; but the French party and the bishop, who is ambassador there, say that nothing has wrought so much in France as of late the practice in Rome of divers of the nobility of France where they have seen such dissolute living of the clergymen as returning into France they have persuaded the rest that the clergy of Rome is of no religion."—C. S. P. For., No. 822, December 28, 1560.

[2] The address is printed *in extenso* in *Œuvres complètes de l'Hôpital*, I, 375 ff.

and disliked the queen's supremacy.[1] Perceiving this obstacle, the queen sent for the president of La Rochelle and told him to have an autograph list made of all those who dissented and to bring it to her. But no one dared to be the first to sign this list. This was admirable adroitness on Catherine's part. She was playing for a large stake, because if the estates treated with the new government, they would in a certain way approve its legitimacy by general consent.

Finally, after a week's delay, during which the *cahiers* of the delegates were handed in and classified, deliberations were resumed. The three chief questions before the estates of Orleans were religion, the finances, and the regulation of the courts of judicature. The three estates in order, beginning with the commons, presented each its cause. The orator of the third estate, an *avocat du roi* at Bordeaux, demanded a general council for the settlement of religious controversy; the discipline of the clergy, whom he denounced in scathing terms; their reformation in manners and morals; revision of justice, and alleviation of taxes.[2] As a whole, the commons seemed to wish for a general pardon for all the insurgents, and that everybody should be restored to favor; that the election of prelates should be regulated, so as to insure the nomination of fitting persons to reform the life and customs of the clergy; and that the revenues of the churches should be limited to persons appointed for that purpose.[3]

The spokesman of the noblesse, one Jacques de Silly, sieur de Rochefort, invoked biblical authority, besides Assyrian and classical history, to prove that the nobility had been ordained of God and recognized by men of all times as the pillar of the state. The harangue was a carefully worded assertion of the political interests and claims of the nobility. Even religion was subordinated to their political ends, a written memorial being presented by some

[1] Suriano, December 20; D'Aubigné, I, 303, 304; La Place, 88, 109. "The estates assembled on December 13, but have done little or nothing; divers of them will not put forth such things as they were instructed in, now the king is dead."— C. S. P. For., No. 832, December 31, 1560.

[2] La Planche, 389 96; D'Aubigné, I, 305, 306.

[3] Cf. C. S. P. Ven., No. 237, February 17, 1561.

of the nobles asking for leave for each great feudal proprietor to ordain what worship he might choose within his lands, after the manner of the settlement at Augsburg in 1555 (*cujus regio, ejus religio*).[1]

The clergy naturally were in conformity with the canons and the Catholic ritual. They were declared to be "the organ and mouth" of France, much history and doctrinal writing being cited to prove their supremacy. Liberty of election in the matter of

STATES-GENERAL OF ORLEANS
(Tortorel and Perissin)

church offices, abolition of the abuse of the *dîme*, which, it was complained, had been extorted from the church, not once, but four, five, six, and even nine times in a year, and prelates put in prison for failure to pay, to the destruction of worship in the churches; suppression of heresy (thus early stigmatized as *la prétendue réformation*), and royal support of the authority of the priest-class, were the four demands of the clerical order.[2] The sittings were rendered less tedious by a bold attack made upon the persecution of religion by a deputy who demanded that the

[1] La Place, 93.   [2] *Ibid.*, 93–109.

Huguenots be permitted to have their own church edifices—a plea which was reinforced by a hot protest of the admiral Coligny against an utterance of Quintin, the clerical orator.[1]

As to religion, grave questions arose. Would the toleration of religion occasion civil war? Would it cause an ultimate alteration of the faith of France? Would it, finally, alter the state, too? The States-General refused to enter deeply into these problems. The petition of the Protestants was not mentioned.[2] In the end it was determined to grant a general pardon to all throughout the kingdom, without obliging anyone to retract, or to make any other canonical recantation—a proposal which was quite at variance with the constitution of the church and was regarded by Rome as exceeding the bounds of the authority of the King and his Council, cognizance of matters of this nature appertaining to ecclesiastics and not to laymen.[3] The pressure of the third estate as well as the influence of Coligny, L'Hôpital, and others, is discernible in this measure. For it had been determined in the Privy Council that should the Council-General not be held before June, the National Council would assemble in France. This could not be denied to the estates who demanded it; and this concession apparently at first caused all the three estates to agree not to renounce the old religion. To this must be added another reason, viz., that although the greater part of the clergy, more especially the bishops, approved the old religion, yet many of the nobility approved the new one.[4]

[1] La Place, 109; La Planche, 397; D'Aubigné, I, 307.

[2] Castelnau, Book III, chap. ii.

[3] C. S. P. Ven., No. 237, February 17, 1561. The action practically flouted a papal bull of November 20, 1560, convening the Council at Trent, which was intended to anticipate and *prevent* any such action as this at Orleans (La Planche, 403).

[4] There was also a technical argument based on the fact that in the bull of the Council the words "*sublata suspensione*" were interpreted to mean that the Pope intended to continue the Council already commenced, and that the decrees already made were to be valid; which offended France. The cardinal of Lorraine was the one who raised these difficulties, though he tried to give the opposite impression; from him came the opposition to the words of the bull (C. S. P. Ven., No. 229, January 7, 1561; *Despatches of Suriano* (Huguenot Society), January 14, 1561).

Even more favorable action toward the Huguenots might have been taken if Catherine's caution and her fear of antagonizing the Guises too much had not acted as a restraint. The pardon of the government was theoretically not understood to be granted to those who *preached* the Calvinistic doctrine, nor to the King's judges who had authority in the cities and provinces of France who espoused it. But it was tacitly admitted that no one was to be prosecuted for heresy on this account. In Orleans the people worshiped in Huguenot form and in Paris—wonder of wonders—*Catholic* preachers were admonished to cease inveighing against "Lutherans" and Huguenots, and not to speak against their sects or their opinions—an order generally interpreted as consent from the Privy Council for all to follow such opinions about faith as most pleased their ideas.[1]

A corollary to the question of religion was that touching the government of the church. Several excellent ordinances were passed for reforming the abuses of the church, particularly for preventing the sale of benefices. The election of the bishops was taken out of the King's direct jurisdiction and remitted to the clergy, and to satisfy the people it was added that twelve noblemen and twelve commoners together with the governor and judges of the city in which a bishop was to be elected were to unite with the clergy in election, giving laymen the same authority as ecclesiastics. Another matter also was determined which was sure to displease the Pope, viz., that moneys should no longer be sent to Rome for the annates or for other compositions on account of benefices, on the ground that these charges drew large sums of money from the kingdom and were the cause of its poverty. Even the payment of the Peter's Pence was resented by some. The bishop of Vienne publicly asserted that it was with astonishment and sorrow that he observed the patience with which the French people endured these taxes "as if," said he, "the wax and lead of the King was not worth as much as the lead and the wax of Rome which cost so much."[2] As it would have seemed strange were

[1] *C. S. P. Ven.*, No. 237, January 23, 1561; La Place, 124–26, practically paraphrases the edicts.

[2] *Rel. vén.*, I, 443.

the Pope not first informed of it, the estates elected one of the presidents of the Parlement to go to Rome to give an account to the Pope of the matter, not so much to ask it as a favor from the Pope as merely to state the causes which moved the government thus to decide. The strong inclination of many in France whose catholicity could not be impugned, to diminish the papal authority and assert the old Gallican liberties, is noticeable. Pontifical authority would have been quite at an end if the estates had determined to lay hands on the church property, as was desired by many persons.

The two other questions before the estates were those of justice and finance. In the matter of the former nothing was done. For although there was universal dissatisfaction, the issue was too complicated, as all judicial offices were sold, and in order to displace those who had bought them it would have been necessary to reimburse the holders, which could not have been done then. The chances, accordingly, were that the administration of justice was likely to go from bad to worse.[1]

The main work of the estates of Orleans had to do with the reorganization of the finances of the kingdom, the administration of which was intimately connected with the future government. The crown was over forty million francs (exceeding eighteen million crowns) in debt.[2]

It may be well at this point to give a short survey of the financial policy of the French crown during the sixteenth century. Under Louis XII the *taille*, which was the principal tax, and which fell upon the peasant, was reduced to about six hundred thousand écus, a sum little superior to the amount originally fixed under Charles VII. It was raised by Francis I to two millions. In the time of Louis XII the total revenue amounted to barely two mil-

---

[1] *Despatches of Suriano* (Huguenot Society), February 17, 1561.

[2] Castelnau, Book III, chap. ii, says 42,000,000; Throckmorton put the figures at 43,000,000: *C. S. P. For.*, No. 1,032, February 26, 1561; cf. No. 988, February 12, 1561; Suriano, the Venetian ambassador, also gives the amount as eighteen million crowns (*ibid.*, *Ven.*, No. 237, February 17, 1561). This would approximate $75,000,000.

The debt of the King to the Genoese, Germans, Milanese, Florentines, and Lucca amounted to 644,287 ducats (*ibid.*, *For.*, No. 1,432, October 5, 1560).

lions; his successor brought it up to five, the *dîmes* of the clergy being included.[1] When the expenses of the government came to exceed the receipts, Francis I had recourse to extraordinary measures, that is to say, to augmentation of the taxes, to new loans, or to new forms of taxation. In 1539 he introduced the lottery from Italy. These extraordinary practices were not submitted to any process of approval, not even in the *pays d'état*. Foreigners were astonished at the ease with which the king of France procured money at his pleasure. Francis I quadrupled the *taille* upon land, and even had the effrontery to raise it to the fifth power. In general the people paid without murmuring, although in 1535 an insurrection broke out at Lyons on account of an alteration in the *aides* demanded by the crown; and in 1542 there was a serious outbreak at La Rochelle owing to burdensome imposition of the *gabelle*.

The author of the new financial measures of 1539 was the chancellor Poyet, a man of ability, who owed his advancement to the favor of Montmorency. Several very excellent measures are due to him, pre-eminently numerous ordinances relating to the inalienability of the royal domain, which he promulgated as a fundamental law of the monarchy, a law which the weak successors of Henry II repudiated. He also endeavored to suppress dishonest administration in the provinces. Thus he called to account both the marshal Montjean, whose exactions in the Lyonnais produced wide complaint, and Galiot de Genoullac, the sire d'Acir, whose stealings were enormous. These measures would have had a salutary effect if the administration of justice had been independent and honest in France. Unfortunately Poyet's reputation for integrity was not as great as it should have been in a minister, and his policy made him many enemies.

The incomes of Francis I, great as they were, did not suffice for Henry II, the renewal of the war continuing to increase his necessities. Under him the increase of the *gabelle* and the tithes and other special taxes brought the total of the revenues up to six and a half million écus, which did not yet save the King from

[1] Dareste, *Histoire de France*, III, 456, 457.

being reduced to the necessity of making alienations and loans, which reached on the day of his death fourteen millions of écus, about thirty-six millions of francs.[1]

The practice of the French government of making loans, a practice which has today become familiar to us on a colossal scale, both in Europe and America, antedates the Hundred Years' War. St. Louis contracted various loans with the Templars and Italian merchants for his crusades.[2] Philip the Fair borrowed from Italian merchants, from the Templars, and from his subjects.[3] His war with Edward I of England and his enterprises in Italy increased the amount, so that his sons inherited a considerable public debt. The Hundred Years' War enormously increased it. We have few means of knowing what rates of interest obtained upon most of the public loans of the fourteenth and fifteenth centuries, but they were probably high in most cases. Charles VIII in 1487 fixed the rate of interest upon a loan made in Normandy at twelve *deniers tournois* for each livre, which would not be over 5 per cent. Seven years later, when he was preparing for the Italian campaign, a rate of two sous per livre obtained, which would be approximately equivalent to 10 per cent.

In the time of the direct Valois kings, most of the government's loans were arranged in the provinces, as in Normandy and Languedoc. But, beginning with Francis I, the city of Paris became increasingly the place where the crown obtained financial aid, so much so indeed that the supervision of the *rentes* of the Hôtel-de-Ville became a separate administrative bureau of the royal treasury, although it must not be understood that the government's operations were henceforth exclusively confined to Paris; for loans continued to be made wherever possible with towns, corporations,

[1] Lorenzo Contarini in 1550 speaks with satisfaction of the even balance of the finances; Soranzo in 1556 speaks of their disorder (cf. Ranke, *Französische Geschichte*, Book VII, chap. iv, n. 2).

[2] An ordinance of 1270 authorized a loan of 100,000 *livres tournois* for the crusade that culminated in disaster before Tunis. Cf. G. Servois, "Emprunts de St. Louis en Palestine et en Afrique, *Bibliothèque de l'Ecole des Chartes*, sér. IV, IV, 117. Philip III borrowed of his great vassals and from the Flemish towns (Langlois, *Le règne de Philippe le Hardi*, chap. v).

[3] Boutaric, *La France sous Philippe le Bel*, 297.

the clergy, and private loan brokers and bankers. These *rentes* of the capital, it should be understood, were technically a substitution of the credit of the city of Paris for the somewhat dubious credit of the crown.[1] From that date (1522) forward in France, government loans took the form of perpetual annuities, payable at the Hôtel-de-Ville in Paris. But other cities, such as Orleans, Troyes, Toulouse, and Rouen, also furnished the King with money in the form of annuities.

Aside from Paris, the church of France was the grand pillar of the government's finances, and as the initiation of the *rentes* is due to Francis I, so to this king also is the second expedient to be ascribed. In 1516, on the occasion of the *concordat*, Leo X allowed Francis I to exact a new tenth, theoretically to be distinguished from the *dîme* of the clergy of France, the pretext being a war projected against the Turks. The new tithe was levied by the King's officers alone, on the basis of a grand survey of the property of the clergy (*Description générale du bien d'église*) made in this year. In this financial survey the tax or quota of each benefice and the total of the tithe in every diocese were indicated. Thenceforth it was easy for numerous tithes to be levied by the will of the King alone. However, in order to conceal the arbitrariness of this conduct, the crown sometimes indicated its purpose to Rome which issued the necessary validation, but more often the King addressed the clergy itself united in assemblies of the bishops at Paris and in provincial or diocesan assemblies. The consent of the clergy was nothing but a formality, for the royal authority fixed in advance the sum to be paid. The diocesan assembly had nothing to do but distribute the impost. This concession of the Pope was successively renewed, under different pretexts, for a number of years, under the name of a *don caratif*, and was equivalent to another tithe, the practice, prolonged year

[1] The preamble of the letters-patent of Francis I, bearing date of September 2, 1522, makes this fact clear; for in that document alienation is made by the government of the "aids, gabelles and impositions" of Paris, the fees of the "grand butchery of Beauvais," the rates upon the sale of wine, both wholesale and retail, and of fish, as security for the loan made. Cf. Vührer, *Histoire de la dette publique en France*, I, 15–26; Lavisse, *Histoire de France*, V, Part I, 241, 242.

after year, at last hardening into a permanent form of taxation required of the clergy, so much so that under Henry II receivers of the "gift" were established in every diocese.[1]

Wastefulness and bad management characterized the reign of Henry II from the very first. The treasury was soon completely exhausted. A reserve of four hundred thousand écus d'or, which Francis I had amassed to carry the war into Germany, with little owing save to the Swiss, payments to whom Francis I had continued in order to prolong his alliance with them, was dissipated within a few months, and the government had resort to increased taxation and the creation of new taxes. The *gabelle* upon salt, from which Poitou, Saintonge, and Guyenne had hitherto been exempt, and which was now introduced into those provinces, raised a terrible revolt which was not crushed until much violence had been done and much blood shed. The renewal of the war against Charles V and the invasion of Lorraine, added to the insatiable demands of the court, required new financial expedients. Not less than eighteen times during the twelve years of the reign of Henry II were the *échevins* of Paris called upon to supply the King with sums of money. Four millions and a half were thus demanded of the capital. In order to obtain these sums, which the people refused to advance gratuitously, the King was forced to humiliate himself exceedingly. Thus in 1550, in a general assembly of the sovereign courts of the clergy and of the bourgeois it was reported that "the King, being obliged to give money to the English, and not having any money in his treasury except mutilated and debased currency which could not be recoined, is under the necessity of offering this debased and mutilated coin as security for a public loan." As might be expected, this not very tempting offer did not entice the provost of the merchants, much to the chagrin of the King, who, however, consented to a short delay. But three years later Henry II was even less shameless. Although there was still just as much unwillingness on the part of the merchants of the city to take the King's notes, this little difficulty was easily overcome by the King's agents. If the money were not

[1] Esmein, *Histoire du droit français*, 631–34.

forthcoming, the sideboards of the wealthy bourgeois of Paris contained enough gold and silver plate to answer the purpose, and an edict of February 19, 1553, ordered certain specified persons to bring to the mint their vessels of gold and of silver, for which the government issued its notes.

But Paris was not the only city which was almost incessantly called upon to supply the King's needs. Each year, and even each month, was characterized by a new demand, and numbers of the cities of France were from time to time taxed for sums which were not secured, however, without resistance to the royal treasurers. Lyons, which was at this epoch the seat of a commerce greater even than that of Paris, was more often mulcted than any other in this way. Conduct so high-handed naturally resulted not only in creating bitterness against the government, but demoralized trade as well. The credit of the government depreciated to such an extent that the rate of interest rose as high as 14 per cent.[1] During the twelve years of Henry II's reign a greater amount in taxes had been imposed upon the people of France than in the fourscore years preceding, besides which many of the crown lands had been dissipated. Naturally "hard times" prevailed.[2]

[1] Vührer, *Histoire de la dette publique en France*, I, 22–25.

[2] Gold was at a premium, the payments for gold crowns and pistolets being above their valuation. All foreign coins were rated high: English "rose" nobles = 6 francs, 12 sous; "angels" = 4 francs, 6 sous; imperials and Phillipes were current at the same rate as "angels" (*C. S. P. For.*, No. 1,076, February 20, 1561). The gold crown was passable at 51 francs *tournois;* the pistolet gold and weight, 49 francs (*ibid.*, No. 886, January 17, 1561). Prices of commodities were also high. The duke of Bedford, who came over in February 1561 as a special envoy of Elizabeth, reports, February 26: "France is the dearest country I ever came in."— *Ibid.*, No. 1,031. Cf. the confession of Richard Sweete, an English fugitive in France, who was forced to return home on account of "hard times." "Within one month they came back from Paris, partly upon the death of the French king and partly for that victuals were there so dear that they could not live."—*Ibid.*, II, No. 36, October 5, 1559.

Without attempting to go at length into the intricate subject of the various kinds of money current in France in the sixteenth century, something yet is to be said upon the subject in order to make clear the working of these and other economic sources. In the sixteenth century, as during the Middle Ages, the standard of value was the *livre tournois*, divided into *sous* and *deniers* (1 livre = 20 sous; 1 sou = 12 deniers). The *livre tournois* was really a hypothetical coin and was merely

Some members of the States-General were for bringing the officers of finance to account and obliging them to submit the list of all the grants which had been made in favor of the great and influential at the court of Henry II. But the cooler element thought that this policy could not be followed out on account of the powerful position of those involved and that occasion for new

used as a unit of calculation. The French gold coin was the *écu d'or* which varied in value between 1 livre, 16 sous, and 2 livres, 5 sous. In 1561 it was equivalent to 2 livres in round numbers. The *teston* was a silver coin of a value of 10 or 11 sous and was sometimes called a crown or a franc by the English. The sou originally was made of an amalgam of silver and copper and the denier or penny of red copper.

The English during their long occupation of Normandy in the fifteenth century, and owing to their commercial communication with Flanders, introduced the pound sterling or "estrelin" (easterling) (Du Cange, *Glossarium, s. v.* "Esterlingus;" Ruding, *Annals of the Coinage*, I, 7; Le Blanc, *Traité historique des monnaies de France*, 82). Though much more stable than other coinage—except the Venetian ducat and the florin—it nevertheless slowly depreciated. Elizabeth in 1561 rechristened it the gold "sovereign." It was worth about 8 *livres tournois* in 1561 (Avenel, "La fortune mobilière dans l'histoire," *Revue des deux mondes*, July 15, 1892, 784, 785). The French peasantry still in certain parts of France estimate in terms of ancient coinage. The *pistole*, by origin a Spanish coin current in Flanders and the Milanais, was forbidden circulation as far back as Louis XIV. Yet the peasants of Lower Normandy at the cattle fairs today will estimate the price of their animals in ancient terms. Similarly the Breton peasantry talk of *réaux* (*real*), the last vestige of Brittany's commercial relations with Spain (Avenel, *op. cit.*, 783).

The actual value of these coins in modern terms has been much debated. M. de Wailly estimated the value of the *livre tournois* in 1561 at 3 francs, 78 centimes. The vicomte d'Avenel thinks these figures too high and has adopted 3 francs, 11 centimes as a mean value for the years between 1561 and 1572. M. Lavasseur prefers the round number of 3 francs. On the basis of the last estimate one sou would be equivalent to 15 centimes and 1 denier to 1.2 centimes in terms of modern French money. But these figures mean nothing until the purchasing power of money at this time is established. In this particular, estimates have varied all the way from 3 to 12 and even to 17 and 20. M. Lemmonier inclines to the ratio of 5 for the middle of the sixteenth century. For an admirably clear and succinct account of the value of French money in the sixteenth century, see Lavisse, *Histoire de France*, Vol. V, Part I, pp. 266–69. Larger references will be found in the bibliography appended to the chapter.

But whatever the ratio may have been, the decline in the purchasing power of money was great. Between 1492 and 1544 Europe imported 279 millions worth (in francs) of gold and silver. In the single year 1545, when the famous mines of Potosi were opened, 492,000,000 francs' worth were brought into Europe. The

commotions only would ensue.[1] Instead, retrenchment was resolved upon. The stipends of the gentlemen of the King's household and of the *gens de finance* were reduced one-half and all pensions were abridged one-third,[2] except in the case of foreigners in the King's service, who were supposed to have no other source of income. This last provision created an outcry, on the ground that foreigners could only be so employed in time of war, save in the case of the Scotch Guard.[3] Even this was cut down, one hundred men-at-arms and one hundred archers being dismissed. The royal stables and mews were also broken up and the horses and falcons sold.[4]

Something more constructive than mere economy, however, was necessary, and the burden of paying the King's debts fell heaviest upon the clergy. This was partly owing to the great wealth of the church; partly to the fact that the clergy had rushed in where others feared to tread, and, officiously asserting their superiority in matters of state as well as of church, had proceeded

purchasing power of money is estimated to have fallen one-quarter between 1520 and 1540 and one-half by the year 1600. After the peace of Cateau-Cambrésis when peaceful relations were renewed between France and Spain, France particularly felt the disturbing effect of the new conditions. According to the vicomte d'Avenel (*op. cit.*), from 1541–61 the *livre tournois* was valued at 3 francs, 34 centimes; from 1561–72 at 3 francs, 11 centimes; from 1575–79 at 2 francs, 88 centimes. "Un capital de 1,000 livres qui valait 22,000 francs en 1200, n'en valait plus intrinsèquement que 16,000 en 1300; 7,530 en 1400; 6,460 en 1500, et était tombé en 1600 à 2,570 francs."—*Revue des deux mondes*, July 15, 1892, 800.

One is astonished not to find greater complaints about the "hard times" in the chronicles and other sources of the period. To be sure, the misery did not reach its acutest stage until the time of the League, when the difference between the price of food stuffs and daily wages was outrageous. For example, since 1500 the wage of the laboring man had increased but 30 per cent., whereas the price of grain had increased 400 per cent. At the accession of Louis XII, wheat had cost four francs per hectolitre and the peasant earned sixteen centimes a day; at the accession of Henry IV (in 1590), wheat sold for twenty francs per hectolitre and the daily wage of the peasant was but seventy-eight centimes (Avenel, "Le pouvoir de l'argent," *Revue des deux mondes*, April 15, 1892, 838).

[1] Castelnau, Book III, chap. ii.

[2] La Planche, 112; *C. S. P. For.*, No. 990, February 12, 1561.

[3] La Planche, 113.

[4] *C. S. P. For.*, No. 889, January 16, 1561; No. 890, February 12, 1561.

to examine the royal accounts, which the nobles and the commons were too wary to inspect.[1] The nobles took the ground that they were not concerned in the matter of paying the King's debts, claiming that they paid their dues to the crown by personal service in war time.[2]

As far back as the assembly at Fontainebleau far-sighted councilors of the king had pointed out that the revenues of the church would have to be made to do duty for the government, and intercourse with Rome had been under way looking to such an arrangement.[3] The Pope was not as bitterly opposed to such a policy as one might at first be led to think, for he was thoroughly frightened at the prospect of a national council of the French clergy being convened in France and was disposed to be accommodating. But of course a roundabout method had to be resorted to, for the church would not have suffered a barefaced taxation of ecclesiastical revenues by the political authority. The resulting arrangement was in the nature of a political "deal." Upon the understanding that no French council should be convened, the French crown was permitted to appropriate three hundred and sixty thousand ducats *per annum* for five years from the incomes of the church,[4] the condition of the subsidy, theoretically, being that France was to maintain a fleet to serve against the Turks.[5]

When these things had been done and the King had received in writing the *doléances* and requests of the three orders, the States-General were prorogued[6] until the first of May, to meet at Pontoise

---

[1] *C. S. P. Ven.*, No. 237, February 17, 1561.   [2] La Place, 121.

[3] "They mean to levy the greatest subsidy that was ever granted in France. The chief burden rests with the clergy, who give eight-tenths; the lawyers, merchants, and common people are highly rated also. They reckon to levy 18,000,000 francs."—*C. S. P. For.*, No. 483, September 3, 1560.

[4] "The Pope has given faculty to the King to sell of the revenues of the church by the year, and has granted the like to the French King, *meaning to serve them to execute . . . . the order now to be taken at the General Council.*"—*Ibid.*, No. 777, December 7, 1560, from Toledo. A similar arrangement was made in Spain with Philip II, in order to restore his depleted finances.

[5] *Ibid.*, No. 850, January 1, 1561.

[6] The *ordonnance* of the King proroguing the estates did not appear until a month later, March 25, 1561.

in order to complete the settlement of affairs,[1] for time was necessary to make the arrangements with the church, since the prelates present had not been commissioned to enter into such a compact.

[1] La Place, 111; C. S. P. For., No. 938, February 12, 1561.   In a letter dated January 22, 1561, to Peter Martyr, Hotman gives an admirable account of the session of the States-General at Orleans.   See Dareste, "François Hotman," Mém. de l'Acad. des sc. moral. et polit., CIV, 654–56.

CHAPTER IV

THE FORMATION OF THE TRIUMVIRATE

The factional rivalry which had been engendered during the course of the session of the States-General at Orleans was so great that this discord, combined with the agitation prevailing on account of religion, seemed ominous of civil war, and "every accident was interpreted according to the passions of the persons concerned."[1] The affair of the custody of the seal created bitter feeling for a time between the duke of Guise and the king of Navarre, until the former out of policy and the latter either from policy or lack of courage, affected to become reconciled. The Guises realized that they had suffered a serious blow politically through the death of Francis II and Catherine was shrewd enough to know that while she controlled the seal, she was the keeper of the King's authority. The prince of Condé was a double source of friction. In the first place, his trial for treason was still pending before the Parlement of Paris.[2] The queen mother was anxious to have the cause settled out of court, for if condemned (which was unlikely) the whole Bourbon family would be disgraced as formerly through the treason of the constable Bourbon in 1527, and if acquitted, the prince would not rest until he had been avenged of his enemies. Accordingly, she caused a letter to be written in the King's name instructing the Parlement to dismiss the case. But the mettlesome spirit of the prince resented this process, and his discontent was increased to furious anger when the duke of Guise recommended that all the evidence be burned and prosecution be dropped, although his opinion was that legally Condé could not be acquitted as the trial so far had proved him to have been implicated in the revolt of Lyons.[3] To both parties Catherine de Medici steadily replied that she had written the letter in order to adjust the affairs of the prince of Condé to his honor and to the satisfaction of all,

[1] *Despatches of Suriano* (Huguenot Society), March 1, 1561.
[2] *C. S. P. For.*, No. 49, March 18, 1561.
[3] *Ibid., Ven.*, No. 242, March 3, 1561.

and that the seal was in her hands. On March 15 the prince was readmitted to the Privy Council; but the Parlement was not disposed to drop the case so easily and deliberated at length upon the matter, finally on June 13, going on record, in a delicately balanced pronouncement which was intended to please all parties concerned and satisfied none.[1]

A new source of friction was the vacant government of Champagne which the queen gave to the duke of Nemours. This offended Antoine of Navarre, because he wanted to have it conferred upon the prince of Condé.[2] To these dissensions, finally, must be added a recent ruling of the Privy Council, in compliance with one of the resolutions of the States-General, that all bishops, including the cardinals, were to return to their sees.[3] This regulation eliminated some of the leaders of both parties, the cardinal

[1] La Place, 129; La Popelinière, I, 244; De Thou, IV, 66, 67. The king of Navarre, most of the princes of the blood, cardinals, and nobles being present, chief among whom were the duke of Guise and the cardinal of Lorraine. The prince was declared innocent, all the information brought against him was pronounced false and the letters, forgeries. This rehabilitation was also extended to the vidame of Chartres and Madame de Roye, Coligny's sister and mother of the princess of Condé, and the parlementary arrêt was ordered to be proclaimed in all the courts of parlement of the realm (C. S. P. For., No. 265, § 8, June 23, 1561).

[2] Nég. Tosc., III, 467, and note.

[3] Ordonnance générale . . . . des états assemblés à Orleans, p. 5; Isambert, XIV, 65. In pursuance of this legislation the cardinal of Lorraine resigned a few of his pluralities. He gave the bishopric of Metz to his brother, the cardinal of Guise, and retained for himself the archbishopric of Rheims, with the Abbeys of St. Rémy and St. Denis (Claude Haton, I, 234). On April 1, 1561, the action of the States-General was affirmed in a royal edict which commanded the bishops to return to their dioceses and there reside under pain of seizure of their temporalities, and in every bailiwick in France inventories were to be made of the whole revenues of the priest (Isambert, XIV, 101). It was followed by an edict dealing with the administration of the hospitals and support of the poor (ibid., 105), designed to put an end to corrupt practice on the part of unprincipled and avaricious priests who did not wish to reside at home and so sold their cures to presbyters. Those who had numerous benefices found means to excuse themselves from residence in their cures, in virtue of an article of the edict, which provided that ecclesiastics who had numerous cures, which they held par dispense, or other benefices or charges requiring actual residence in some other church, and who could not by this means reside in their parishes, by residing in one of the parishes or other churches in which they had a benefice or office requiring residence, were exempt from residing in their other cures, provided that they committed them to the care of capable vicars. In

of Lorraine on the one hand and the cardinal de Châtillon on the other, to the discomfiture of both parties. Only the cardinal Tournon, whose great age made him harmless and who really wanted to pass the rest of his life in retirement, and the cardinal of Bourbon whose easy disposition also made him harmless, were permitted to stay with the court.

Philip II of Spain had been an attentive follower of all that had happened in France since the early autumn of 1560 and had been kept thoroughly informed by his indefatigable ambassador. His disquietude over the death of Francis II and the new direction of affairs in France was so great[1] that in January Philip sent Don Juan de Manrique, his grand master of artillery, to Orleans, ostensibly to perform the office of condolence and congratulation,[2] but in reality to win over the constable, to harden the policy of the French government toward the Huguenots, to persuade it against the project of a national council,[3] and to promote Philip's pur-

virtue of this article they were permitted the enjoyment of their revenues after having satisfied the king's officers in each bailiwick. Cf. Claude Haton, I, 221, 222. The revenues of hospitals were assumed control of by the government, and the administration thereof was committed to the care of special administrators. Local judicial officers instead of the clergy, as formerly, were to supervise the distribution of money, wood, wine, and provisions, to priors, monks, nuns, and the poor.

The hospitals of various towns of France and in particular the hôtels-dieu at Paris and Troyes, had already, even before this, been governed by lay commissioners. For a complaint of bad administration of the Hôtel-Dieu at Provins by the lay officers, who enriched themselves at the expense of the poor, and let the house run down, for which reason the King was requested to restore the administration to the clergy, see Claude Haton, I, 223.

[1] The letter which the bishop of Limoges, the French ambassador in Madrid, wrote "après la mort de François II," detailing the Spanish monarch's fear, is almost prophetic (Paris, Négociations relatives au règne de François II, 782–85).

[2] Philip II, to Charles IX, January 4, 1561, K. 1,495, No. 13; to Mary Stuart, January 7, K. 1,495, No. 17; C. S. P. For., No. 870, January 10, 1561. He arrived on the evening of January 23. Cf. Don Juan de Manrique and Chantonnay to Philip II, January 28, 1561, K. 1,494, No. 55, giving an account of his reception at the French court. He left about February 10, 1561 (C. S. P. For., Nos. 933, January 23, 1561, and 984, February 11, 1561).

[3] C. S. P. For., No. 11, March 4, 1561; Despatches of Suriano (Huguenot Society), February 19, 1651. A letter of December 26, 1560, to the King, published in the Revue d'hist. diplomatique, XIII, No. 4 (1899), 604, "Dépêches de Sebastien de l'Aubespine," states the real mission of Don Juan de Manrique.

poses regarding the marriage of Mary Queen of Scots, to Don Carlos, Philip's son.

Catherine de Medici soon divined both the purpose and the danger, and her alarm was correspondingly great, because the increasing confusion in the realm on account of religion every day made Spanish intervention more possible.[1]   One of two results seemed certain to happen: either that things would end with the Huguenots having churches in which they could preach, read, and perform their rites according to their doctrine without hindrance, as they had temporarily obtained churches by the declaration of Fontainebleau, at the end of August, in compliance with the resolution presented by the admiral; or else that obedience to the Pope and to the Catholic rites would be enforced at the point of the sword, and a manifest and certain division in the kingdom would result, with civil war as the consequence.   When Francis II died, a great number who had fled to Geneva and Germany after the conspiracy of Amboise came back to France.   For the government of Charles IX had inaugurated the new reign by a declaration of toleration (January 7, 1561) which, although Calvin disapproved it,[2] may yet with reason be regarded as a liberal edict.   The Protestants were not slow to profit by the change, and flocked back from Switzerland and Germany and resumed their propaganda, one phase of which was a vilification of Rome and the Guises to such an extent that the King protested to the Senate of Geneva regarding their abuse.[3]   Paris soon abounded with Huguenot preachers from Geneva, who relied upon the division in the council or the protection of persons in power for the maintenance of the new edict.[4]

[1] The queen mother to the bishop of Rennes, April 11, 1561, *Correspondance de Catherine de Médicis*, I, 186.   The latter's reply is in Paris, *Négociations*, etc., 871, May 26, 1561.   Cf. Castelnau, I, 555.

[2] Lacombe, *Catherine de Médicis entre Guise et Condé*, 108.   The edict was actually a confirmation of the edict of Romorantin.   See *Mém. de Condé*, II, 266; text of the Edict of Romorantin in Isambert, XIV, 31.

[3] Letter of Charles IX, January 23, 1561, *Opera Calvini*, XVIII, 337.   The reply of the senate under date of January 28 is at 343–45.

[4] *C. S. P. Ven.*, Nos. 250, 272, April, 1561.   Coligny's house was a favorite rendezvous.   He never went to mass, and when his wife gave birth to a child in the spring of 1561 he had it baptized openly in the popular tongue, according to the Calvinist form (*C. S. P. For.*, Nos. 933, 984, 1561).

In some provinces, such as Normandy,[1] Touraine, Poitou, Gascony,[2] and the greater part of Languedoc, Dauphiné, and Provence, congregations and meetings were openly held. Guyenne save Bordeaux, was badly infected with heresy.[3] The new religion penetrated so deeply that it affected every class of persons, even the ecclesiastical body itself, not only priests, friars, and nuns, but even bishops and many of the principal prelates. Among all classes there were Huguenot sympathizers, the nobility perhaps more manifestly than any other class.[4] The congregations of Rouen and Dieppe sent to the King for license to preach the word of God openly. In Dieppe the Calvinists once a day met in a great house, "of men, women and children above 2,000 in company."[5] There were Huguenot outbursts at Angers, Mans, Beauvais, and Pontoise, in April, and at Toulouse in June.[6] At Beauvais when the cardinal of Châtillon, who was bishop there, caused the Calvinist service to be conducted and communion administered in his chapel, "after the manner of Geneva," the canons and many of the people "assembled to good numbers to have wrought their wicked wills upon the cardinal." Some were hurt and killed in the trouble, and one poor wretch was brought before the cardinal's gate and burned.[7] A similar riot took place in Paris, on April 28, in the evening, near the Pré-aux-Clercs.

As a result of these excesses things took a sterner turn. A new measure interdicted Huguenot meetings, even in private houses; and all persons of every condition *in Paris* were required

[1] For the rise of Protestantism in Normandy see Le Hardy, *Histoire du protestantisme en Normandie depuis son origine jusqu' à la publication de l'Edit de Nantes*, Caen, 1869; Lessens, *Naissance et progrès de l'hérésie de Dieppe, 1557–1609: Publication faite pour la I*ère *fois d'après le MS de la biblioth. publ. av. une introd. et des notes*, Rouen, 1877; Hauser, "The French Reformation and the Popular Classes," *American Historical Review*, January, 1899.

[2] *Archives de la Gironde*, XIII, 132; XVII, 256.

[3] "There is not one single province uncontaminated," wrote Suriano, the Venetian ambassador on April 17, 1561 (*C. S. P Ven.*, 272).

[4] See a long letter of Hotman published by Dareste in *Rev. hist.*, XCVII, March–April, 1908, p. 299.

[5] *C. S. P. For.*, 857, January 1, 1561.

[6] *Nég. Tosc.*, III, 456.

[7] *C. S. P. For.*, No. 124, April 20, 1561.

to observe the Catholic religion.[1]　The attitude of Paris was ominous for the future. The populace was wholly Catholic and hostile to religious change,[2] and was strongly supported by the Sorbonne and the Parlement.[3] The Sorbonne freely let it be understood that it would never obey any order issued to the injury of the Catholic religion, asserting that whenever the crown changed faith and religion, the people were absolved from the oath of fealty and were not bound to obey.[4] The words "civil war" were on the lips of all who were attentively observing events. "Between the two parties, justice is so little feared," wrote the duke of Bedford, "and policy has so little place that greater things are to be dreaded."[5]

The responsibility for the government's vacillation at this season is not to be imputed wholly to Catherine de Medici.[6] It is to be remembered that France was under a double regency, and that the weakness of the king of Navarre materially embarrassed affairs. At this moment he seemed to be inclined toward the faith of Rome in the hope of conciliating Philip II of Spain, in order to recover the kingdom of Navarre. The Spanish ambassador and the Guises naturally made the most of his aspiration, the former telling Antoine that although it was impossible to obtain what he claimed from His Catholic Majesty by mere force, he might make a fair agreement with Philip by maintaining France in the true faith.[7]

During these months of tension and tumult, the ambassador

---

[1] C. S. P. For., No. 155, April 30; C. S. P. Ven., No. 255, May 2, and No. 258, May 14, 1561.

[2] Suriano says this hostility of Paris toward Protestantism was greater, perhaps, because it was favored by the nobles, who were naturally hated—"la plebe di questa Città che per professione è nemica delle nove sette, forse perchè sono favorite dalli nobili, li quali sono odiati per natura."—Op. cit., May 2, 1561. Cf. May 16, ab init. (Huguenot Society of London).

[3] "Requête de la Sorbonne au roi," K. 1,495, No. 74, without date but seemingly of this time.

[4] C. S. P. Ven., No. 259, May 16, 1561.

[5] Ibid., For., No. 158, April, 1561; cf. No. 124, April 20, 1561.

[6] Correspondance de Catherine de Médicis, I, 188, and n. 1.

[7] C. S. P. Ven., No. 259, May 16, 1561.

worked out a scheme, which in principle was that of Philip II, but the details were of Chantonnay's own arrangement. The aim was to form a group of influential persons at the court, who should begin by complaints of the government's policy and then proceed to threats and dark hints of the displeasure of Spain, finally presenting a bold front to Catherine, and compelling her to abandon her policy of temporizing and moderation. The constable Montmorency was the objective leader of this cabal, and his persuasion to the enterprise was one of the secret purposes of the mission of Don Juan de Manrique. While this envoy bore letters expressing Philip's esteem to all the most notable Catholics at the French court, there was a distinction between them. The king of Spain wrote in common to the duke of Guise, the constable, the duke of Montpensier, the chancellor, and the marshals St. André and Brissac,[1] and a joint note to the cardinals of Lorraine and Tournon.[2] But Montmorency and St. André each also received a separate letter. The discrimination shows the wonderfully keen penetration of Philip's ambassador, for these two were destined to be two of the three pillars of the famous Triumvirate.[3] In reply the cardinal of Lorraine hastened to inform Philip II of his deep interest in maintaining the welfare of Catholicism[4] But it required time and adroitness to overcome the constable's prejudice against Spain, and his attachment to his nephews.[5]

In the meantime, before the constable was persuaded, the cabal made formidable headway by winning Claude de l'Aubespine to its cause. This paved the way for an action which, if Catherine de Medici could have known it, would have thrown her into consternation indeed. For Claude de l'Aubespine's brother Sebastian, the bishop of Limoges, was Charles IX's ambassador in Spain. On April 4, 1561, the latter addressed a secret letter to Philip II

[1] January 4, 1561; K. 1,495, No. 15.   [2] Ibid., No. 16.

[3] On the whole see De Crue, *Anne de Montmorency*, 294, 295.

[4] January 31, 1561; K. 1,494, No. 21.

[5] For an example of Chantonnay's way of working see De Crue, 296, 297, and the letters in K. 1,494, No. 54, January 15, 1561, and No. 56, February 1, 1561.

of Spain describing the turmoil in France and thanking him, in the queen's name, for the "bons et roiddes offices" of Chantonnay.[1]

Coincident with this event, things in France had come to a head precisely as Philip and his ambassador had planned to have them. At this juncture Montmorency took a decisive stand. When the constable saw that meat was being freely eaten during these Lenten days; that Protestant service was held in the chambers of the admiral and the prince of Condé; that Catherine de Medici invited Jean de Montluc, the heretic bishop of Valence, to preach at court on Easter Sunday, the old warrior's spirit rose in revolt. In vain his eldest son, the marshal Montmorency, pleaded that his father's fears were exaggerated and his prejudices too deep-seated. The old man was firm in his convictions, in which he was sustained by his wife, Madeleine of Savoy, a bitter adversary of Calvinism.[2] Moreover, the political as well as religious demands of the Huguenot party, especially the demands of certain of the local estates, which advocated drastic reform, alarmed him. The whole power of the political Huguenots was directed against the constable, the duke of Guise, the cardinal of Lorraine, and the marshals Brissac and St. André, the leaders of the party being determined to call them to account for their peculations during the reign of Henry II and his successor, and to force them to surrender the excessive grants which had been given them.[3]

On the evening of April 6, 1561, Montmorency, after having expostulated with the queen, invited the duke of Guise, the duke de Montpensier, the prince of Joinville, the marshal St. André, and the cardinal Tournon to dine with him. In his apartments

---

[1] This important document which has not been published by M. Louis Paris, or elsewhere that I can find, is in K. 1,494, No. 70 (printed in Appendix II).

[2] La Place, 122, 123.

[3] This is the judgment of both Catholic and Huguenot historians; e. g., Castelnau, Book III, chap. v, and Benoist, *Historie de l'édit de Nantes*, Book I, 29, who says that the chief motive of St. André and the constable in forming the Triumvirate was fear of being compelled to pay back the immense sums which they had embezzled. Yet the constable in 1561 was a poor man as the result of the heavy sums of ransom he and his house had been obliged to pay during the late war. See De Crue, *Anne de Montmorency*, 236.

that famous association named by the Huguenots the Triumvirate, in which the constable, Guise, and St. André were principals, was formed.[1]

The preparations of the Guises during the former year enabled the Triumvirate rapidly to lay its plans. Spanish, Italian, German, and Swiss forces could be counted upon and procured within a very short time. These forces were to be divided under the command of the duke of Aumale and the three marshals, Brissac, Termes, and St. André. In order to support these troops, the Catholic clergy were to be assessed according to the incomes they enjoyed; cardinals 4,000 to 5,000 livres per annum; bishops 1,000 to 1,200; abbots 300 to 400, priors 100 to 120; and so on down to chaplains, whose annual stipend was but 30 livres, and who were only assessed a few sous. But as some immediate means were necessary, the gold and the silver of some of the churches, and the treasure of certain monasteries was to be appropriated at once, receipts being given for the value of the gold taken, and promise being made that reimbursement would be made shortly out of the confiscations made from the heretics.[2]

Catherine de Medici's plan to govern through the constable Montmorency and the admiral,[3] leaving Antoine of Navarre only nominal authority, received an abrupt shock when the Triumvirate was established. Her policy partook of both doubt and fear, and vacillated more than ever.[4]

But more formidable than the project to organize insurrection at home, thus promoted by the Triumvirate, was the foreign policy it adopted. The Triumvirate formally appealed to Philip II for

---

[1] La Place, 123; Ruble, III, 71; De Crue, 303; Chantonnay to Philip II, April 7, K. 1,494, B. 12, 73; April 9, B. 12, 75. Cf. *Mémoires de Condé*, III, 210 ff.: "Sommaire des choses premièrement accordées entre les ducs de Montmorency, Connestable et De Guyse, ... et le Mareschal Sainct André, pour la Conspiration du Triumvirate, et depuis mises en délibération à l'entrée du Sacré et Sainct Concile de Trente, et arrestée entre les Parties en leur privé Conseil faict contre les Héréticques et contre le Roy de Navarre en tant qu'il gouverne et conduit mal les affaires de Charles IX."

[2] La Planche, 454.

[3] *Nég. Tosc.*, III, 448.

[4] *Rel. vén.*, I, 534.

aid.[1]   The response was not slow in forthcoming, though the
royal word was prudently couched in vague terms.[2]   To make
matters worse, Antoine of Navarre inclined more than ever toward
the faith of Rome in the hope of conciliating Philip II of Spain.[3]

To a man less vain and gullible than Antoine of Bourbon
such a proposition, upon its very face, as the restoration of
Navarre, would have appeared to have been preposterous.
Aside from the blow to its prestige which any loss of territory
entails upon a nation, it is only necessary to look at the
position of Spanish Navarre to perceive that Spain could
better afford to lose a war abroad than to part with this key
to the passes of the western Pyrenees.   There is no need to relate
at length the story of Antoine's alternate hopes and fears, of his
great expectations, and of the empty promises made him.[4]   The
office Antoine held, not the man, made him important to France
and Spain.   For this reason, he was alternately wheedled and
cajoled, mocked and threatened, for more than a year; and all
the time the pitiable weakling shifted and vacillated in his policy.[5]
It is amazing to see how successfully Antoine was led along by the
dexterous suggestions of Chantonnay, and the evasive answers
of Philip II.   It was a delicate game to play, for there was continual fear lest he would discover that he was being made the dupe
of Spain, and prevail upon the queen mother and the prince of
Condé to join him in avenging his wrongs, a not impossible devel-

[1] The original letter is preserved in the Musée des Archives Nationales, No.
665.   See the *Mémoires de Condé*, III, 395.

[2] Philip II to the constable, the cardinal of Lorraine, and Antoine of Navarre,
April 14 and June 12, 1561, Archives nat., K. 1,495, B. 13, 33, 44.   Admission of
this step thus early is made in the *Mémoires du duc de Guise*, ed. Michaud et Poujoulat, sér. I, V, 464.   The Huguenots were early apprised of it by the interception of a messenger of the Triumvirate near Orleans.   Cf. *Bref discours et
véritable des principalles conjurations de la maison de Guyse*, Paris, 1565, 5, 6.

[3] *C. S. P. Ven.*, No. 259, May 16, 1561.

[4] Cf. De Ruble, *Antoine de Bourbon et Jeanne d'Albret*, III, 251 ff.

[5] On Palm Sunday (1561) Antoine went to mass, for which Pius IV hastened
to congratulate him and the church (K. 1,494, No. 74, April 8, 1561), and for some
time after Easter he continued to go to mass, and refrained from eating flesh on the
days prohibited by the church (*C. S. P. For.*, No. 248, May 18, 1561).   But within a
month, he is discovered having public preaching in his house by a Protestant minister, and "daily service in the vulgar tongue" (*ibid.*, No. 265, §13, June 23, 1561).

opment, as Granvella observed, "considering that prudence does not always preside over the actions of men."[1]

The game was the more difficult because Antoine wanted the restoration of his kingly title more than anything else. If he had been willing to become vassal to Spain, as Chantonnay said to St. André, there were a thousand ways to satisfy him. But Spain could not think of alienating any of her provinces, least of all any frontier possession like Navarre or Roussillon.[2] Time and again the prince of Condé told his brother he was a fool to be so wheedled, and Jeanne d'Albret sarcastically said that she would let her son go to mass when his father's inheritance was restored.[3] When the game was likely to be played out, and Antoine, discovering that fine words did not butter parsnips, began to complain or boldly to bluster,[4] a possible substitute for the kingdom of Navarre which Antoine did not want to hold as a Spanish dependency[5] was suggested. At one moment it was Sienna; at another the county of Avignon; at a third the crown of Denmark—to be gotten through the influence of the Guises. The most alluring offer in Antoine's eyes, however, was Sardinia.[6] In return for the crown of Sardinia,

---

[1] "Como todas actiones no se goviernan siempre con la razon."—Granvella to Philip II, May 13, 1561, *Papiers d'état du cardinal de Granvelle*, VI, 541.

[2] Chantonnay's letter of April 18, 1562, is almost entirely given up to a report of a conversation between him and the marshal St. André upon this question. It is very interesting (K. 1,497, No. 24).

[3] K. 1,497, No. 33.

[4] See Vargas to Philip II, from Rome, September 30, 1561, in *Papiers d'état du cardinal de Granvelle*, VI, 357, where he tells the king of one of Antoine's speeches. One of the minor duties of Don Juan de Manrique's mission to France in January, 1561, had been to give Antoine hope in that quarter, in which policy Spain's grand master of artillery, and the papal nuncio worked together. The nuncio was Hippolyte d'Este, the cardinal of Ferrara. His correspondence is published in *Négociations ou lettres d'affaires ecclésiastiques et politiques escrites au Pape Pie IV et au Cardinal Borromée, par Hippolyte d'Est, cardinal de Ferrare, legat en France au commencement des guerres civiles*, Paris, 1658.

[5] K. 1,497, No. 28.

[6] "Sa principal espérance de ce costé-la [Sardinia], se fonde sur les bons et vigoureux offices qu'il se promet de nostre Saint-Père."—Letter II, from St. Germain, January 10, 1561. *Négociations . . . . du cardinal de Ferrare*, Lettre XXXIV, June 26, 1562.

Don Juan de Manrique suggested to Antoine—"Que s'il vouloit repudir la reine sa femme, comme hérétique qu'elle estoit, les Seigneurs de Guise luy feroient espouser leur Nièce, veuve de Francis II."

Antoine was willing to leave all the fortresses of the island in Spain's possession; and to put his children in Philip's hands as hostages.[1]

This digression has somewhat anticipated the progress of events. Charles IX had been crowned at Rheims on May 15 (Ascension Day).[2] The declared majority and the coronation of her son seems to have given Catherine new courage, for in spite of the menace implied in the formation of the Triumvirate, she still labored in the interest of the Huguenot cause. On June 13, as we have seen, the definite exoneration of the prince of Condé was pronounced by the Parlement of Paris,[3] and in the following

[1] Apparently the Sardinians were prepared to say something for themselves in the matter. For St. Sulpice, the French ambassador n Spain, who succeeded L'Aubespine, on October 8, 1562, writes to Antoine to this effect: "On lui a rapporté 'comme les galères d'Espagne, venant d'Italie à Barcelone, et passant près de la Saidaigne, les habitans du pays, s'étaient mis en armes avec contenance de vouloir défendre l'abordée de leurs portes ausd. galères, de quoi s'étant depuis venus justifier par deça; ils avaient remontré qu'ils avaient entendu que ce roi les voulait bailler à un autre prince et qu'ils craignaient que lesd. galères y vinssent pour les contraindre de la recevoir à sgr., ce qu'ils ne voulaient permettre, le suppléant de ne les aliéner de sa courrone,'" etc.—*L'Ambassade de St. Sulpice*, 83. His correspondence abounds with allusions to Sardinia, e. g., 17, 25, 35, 37, 79, 83, 84, 90, etc.

[2] In the presence of the king of Navarre, the constable, the dukes of Guise, Nevers, Montpensier, and Aumale, and of spiritual lords, the cardinal of Lorraine, who was archbishop of Rheims, and the bishops of Laon, Langres, Châlons, Noyon, and Beauvais, the last being the cardinal Châtillon, the only prominent Huguenot, who attended the coronation. The prince of Condé, the admiral, the duke de Longueville, the marshal Montmorency, and his brother Damville, were not present, because they would not assist at mass ("M. Damville is the constable's best-beloved son, a Knight of the Order, one of the paragons of the court and a favourer of the reformed faith."—*C. S. P. For.*, No. 395, §3, August 11, 1561). For a detailed account of the particulars and party issues manifested at the ceremony see De Crue, 309, 310. Catherine de Medici apparently took her time to advise Philip II of the coronation, for her letter (without date) was not received by the King until June 17, K. 1,494, No. 44.

[3] This mightily offended the Triumvirate, and the duke of Guise, the constable, and the marshal St. André forthwith left the court in high dudgeon.

Rochambeau, *Lettres d'Antoine de Bourbon et de Jeanne d'Albret*, Inventaire Sommaire, No. CXLIII, 27 juin 1561—"Attestation de Catherine de Médicis et Antoine de Bourbon, pour affirmer que la retraite du duc du Guyse, de conestable de Montmorency, et du mareschal de St. André n'est due qu'au seul respect et affection qu'ils portent au service du roi et au repos de ses sujets."—Bib. Nat., F. Fr., 3,194, fol. 5.

August an outward reconciliation, at least, was effected between the prince and the duke of Guise.[1]

Encouraged by the positive attitude of the queen mother and the vacillation of the king of Navarre, the Huguenots urged the cause of toleration and presented a request to the King on June 11, 1561, through the deputies of the churches dispersed throughout the realm of France.[2] They declared that the reports of their refusing to pay the taxes and being seditious were false and calumnious; they begged the King to cause all persecutions against them to cease; that he would liberate those of them who were in prison, and that he would permit them to build churches as their numbers were so great that private houses would no longer suffice; finally offering to give pledges that there would be no sedition in their assemblies, and promising all lawful obedience.

The queen mother referred this petition to the Privy Council, but as it involved so important a matter the council was of opinion that it ought to be laid before the Parlement as well as to be considered by the princes of the blood and all the peers and councilors of the Court of Parlement.[3] The Catholic party was quite willing to have this course followed, feeling confident that the Parlement in its official capacity would refuse to register an edict for such purpose. But L'Hôpital[4] and Coligny had hopes that the interest and authority of the princes of the blood and other persons of influence might carry it through the Parlement after all.[5] However, in the end nothing positive was concluded, final resolution being deferred until a colloquy of the bishops and other clergy, who were convoked at Poissy, near St. Germain, for the end

[1] "Procès-verbal de la reconcilation entre le prince de Condé et le duc de Guise en presence du roi Charles IX," in K. 1,494, No. 92; *Nég. Tosc.*, III, 460; *C. S. P. For.*, Nos. 449, August 24, 1561, 461, August 30, 1561; La Place, 139, 140.

[2] "Requeste présenté au roi par les Deputez des Eglises esparses parmi le royaume de France." A printed copy is to be found in K. 1,495, No. 42. It is a really eloquent petition.

[3] Castelnau, Book III, chap. iii; *C. S. P. For.*, No. 304, §3, July 13, 1561.

[4] Suriano definitely says the edict of July was the work of the chancellor. He gives a summary of the edict in a despatch of July 27, 1561 (Huguenot Society).

[5] Cf. *C. S. P. For.*, 1561, No. 237; *Despatches of Suriano* (Huguenot Society), June 25, 1561.

of the month, took place.[1]   Meanwhile a tentative ordinance—
the Edict of July, similar to the Edict of Romorantin—was to
obtain.   This gave the church, as before, entire cognizance of
the crime of heresy and deprived the Parlement, the bailiffs, seneschals, and other judges of any jurisdiction.   In every case local
ecclesiastical courts had to act first; banishment was to be the
severest punishment for heresy; false accusers were to be punished
in the same way that the accused would have been if really guilty;
amnesty was granted for past offenses; and firearms were forbidden
to be carried in towns or elsewhere, with certain exceptions, under
a penalty of 50 gold crowns.[2]   Within a short time, accordingly,
the Protestant assemblies appeared as frequently as before,
although the Calvinist clergy seemed to have become more discreet
in their utterances.[3]

This cleverly designed edict, while seeming to pronounce judgment, really avoided the question at issue.   There was sufficient
leeway still for the holding of Protestant assemblies, and moreover,
even though ecclesiastical affairs were to be referred to the spiritual
courts, the Huguenots were protected by a saving clause (except
for offenses cognizable by the secular power).[4]   Such qualified

[1] Chantonnay to Philip II, July 24, 1561, K. 1,495, No. 52; *C. S. P. For.*,
No. 321, §2, Paris, July 16, 1561.

[2] Isambert, *Anc. lois franç.*, XIV, 109 (Edit sur la religion, sur le moyen de
tenir le peuple en paix, et sur la répression des séditieux).

[3] Suriano, August 25; *Nég. Tosc.*, III, 453–58; Castelnau, Book III; *C. S. P.
For.*, No. 357; Beza, *Hist. ecclés.*, I, 294 (ed. 1841); La Place, 130; D'Aubigné, I, 309.

[4] Castelnau, Book III, chap. iii; he admirably depicts the divided state of mind
of the Parlement which resulted in the edict taking this neutral form.   Suriano
pithily observes: "Con questi dispareri le cose del Regno patiscono assai, et
non si può far niuna deliberatione d'importanza che sia ferma et rissoluta, et di
quà hanno havuto origine tanti editti nel fatto di Religione che sono stati publicati
li mesi passati, li quali non solamente sono ambigui, ma diversi l'uno dall' altro,
et spesse volte contrarii, donde li heretici hanno preso tanto fomento che sono fatti
più indurati et più ostinati che mai" (June 26, 1561).

Charles IX sent the Sieur d'Ozances to Spain to soften Philip's anger as much
as possible.   In a letter of July 18, from St. Germain to his ambassador in Spain,
after stating the motives which have led him to dispatch D'Ozances, he adds:
"Au demeurant, je ne doubte point qu'on sème de beaulx bruictz par delà, touchant le faict de la Religion, et qu'on ne nous face beaucoup plus malades que nous
ne sommes; et, pour ceste occasion il m'a semblé qu'il serait fort à propos que le

toleration, so guardedly given, was probably all that might with safety have been granted to the Huguenots at this early date. But they were far from seeing things in this light. The hotheads among them, in their meetings and in public places, used the most violent language in detraction of the Catholic church and its sacraments.[1] In some places popular feeling against priests was so strong that they were compelled, for the safety of their lives, to disguise their costumes and not to wear the clerical habit abroad, nor long hair, nor have the beard shaved, nor exhibit any other mark which would indicate that they were priests or monks.[2]

Sr. d'Auzances feist entendre au Roy, mon bon frère, les termes en quoy nous en sommes." Then follow details upon the edict of pacification. This letter was sold at auction in 1877. It is catalogued in the *Inventaire des autographes et des documents historiques composant la collection de M. Benjamin Fillon*, Paris, Charavay, 1877 (Series I, 34, No. 132—"Lettre de Charles IX contre-sig. Robertet, à l'évêque de limoges, ambassadeur en espagne; St. Germain, 18 juillet, 1561").

[1] Claude Haton, I, 122.

[2] *Ibid.*, I, 129. In consequence of this state of things we find numerous ordinances passed in the summer of 1561 in restraint of violence; cf. "Edit sur la religion, sur le moyen de tenir le peuple en paix et sur la répression des séditieux, July 1561," Isambert, XIV, 109; "Edit pour remedier aux troubles, et sur la répression des séditieux," October 20, 1561, *ibid.*, XIV, 122; "Edit sur le port d'armes à feu, la vente de ces armes et les formalités à suivre par les fabricants," October 21, 1561, *ibid.*, XIV, 123.

CHAPTER V

THE COLLOQUY OF POISSY. THE ESTATES OF PONTOISE. THE EDICT OF JANUARY, 1562

In the summer of 1561, France saw two separate assemblies convene: the adjourned session of the States-General at Pontoise and the conference of the leaders of the two religions at Poissy. In a sense the cause of the political Huguenots was represented in the former, that of the religious Huguenots in the latter, although the deliberations of the two assemblies were finally combined in an instrument known as the Act of Poissy. The elections in the provinces, each of which sent up two[1] representatives from each bailiwick of the kingdom, had enabled the opposition to go on record,[2] so that the crown had early intimation of the sort of legislation that was likely to be demanded. The business of the estates was

[1] C. S. P. Ven., No. 237, February 17, 1561, says: "one representative with absolute authority to treat and conclude what might be approved by the majority of votes." But La Place, III, 121, says two representatives were chosen from each bailiwick. Cf. De Crue, Anne de Montmorency, 300.

[2] The estates of the Ile-de-France demanded that the council and government of the King should be formed according to the ancient constitution of the realm; that the accounts of the previous administration should be examined; that the queen mother should be removed from the government and be content with being guardian of the King's person; that no stranger be admitted to be of the council; that no cardinal, bishop, or other ecclesiastical person having made suit to the Pope, should have any place in the Privy Council, not even the cardinal Bourbon, though he was a prince of the blood, unless he resigned his hat; that the king of Navarre be regent of the realm with the title of lieutenant-general, and that with him be joined a council of the princes of the blood and others; that the admiral and M. de Rochefoucault should have charge of the education of the King. On these conditions the Estates offered to discharge the King's debts in six years; but in the event of refusal, they declared that the King must live upon the incomes of the royal domain, much of which was mortgaged (C. S. P. For., No. 77, sec. 3, March 31). Cf. Despatches of Michele Suriano (Huguenot Society), June 10, 1561; De Crue, Anne de Montmorency, 300, 301; letter of Hotman to Bullinger, April 2, 1561 in Mém. de l'Acad. des sc. moral. et polit., CIV (1877), 656; Nég. Tosc., III, 455–58. For other information, see "Remonstrances du tiers-état du baillage de Provins," in Claude Haton, II, 1137; "Remonstrance . . . . des villes . . . . de Champagne," ibid., III, 1140, which shows the economic distress.

to find a way out of the financial difficulties which overwhelmed the King.[1]

The spokesman of the third estate, one Jean Bretaigne, mayor of Autun, after a tedious prologue copiously laden with biblical and classic lore, at last came to the pith of things: he summed up in a paragraph of portentous dimensions the burden imposed upon the people by war and the extravagance of the court during the past twenty years, declaring that the people were so penniless that they had nothing to give the King, "save a good and loyal will." Things had come to such a pass that mere economy and retrenchment, nor even an honest and effective administration, although that was demanded and was promised by the King, could save the future.[2] The immense resources of the clergy must be made to restore the dilapidated finances of the monarchy; the church must come to the material rescue of the state, as in the days of Charles Martel. The entire revenue he argued, must be taken of all offices, benefices, and ecclesiastical dignities not actually officiated either in person or in a titular capacity, the Knights of Rhodes and the Hospitalers of St. James included; all the fruits, also, of benefices in litigation which the collators were accustomed to take during the time of litigation should be appropriated by the state, as well as the moneys of deceased bishops and monks. Moreover, one-quarter of the income should be taken of all beneficiaries actually resident in their benefices, in cases where the revenue was from 500 to 1,000 livres; of those having a revenue of 1,000 to 3,000 livres, one-third; of those with incomes running from 3,000 to 6,000 livres, one-half; of those ranging from 6,000 to 12,000 livres, two-thirds. Those of the clergy whose incomes exceeded 12,000 livres and above were to be permitted to retain 4,000 livres, the surplus being applied to liquidate the King's debts,

---

[1] La Place, 158 ff.; La Popelinière, I, 271 ff.; D'Aubigné, Book II, chap. xvi; Beza, *Hist. ecclés.*, ed. 1840, I, 320 ff.; L'Hôpital, *Œuvres complètes*, I, 485 ff. De Thou, Book XXVIII, 74–77; Claude Haton, I, 155. A test vote, however, on religion was taken, resulting in 62 votes for liberty of worship in the case of the Huguenots, and 80 against it (letter of Hotman in *Rev. hist.*, XCVII, March–April, 1908, 300.

[2] *C. S. P. For.*, No. 396, August 11, 1561; La Place, 146, 147, 150.

save in cases where the beneficiaries were bishops, archbishops, primates, and cardinals, to whom 6,000 livres revenue was to be allowed. As to the monastic orders, their whole treasury and revenues were to be appropriated, save enough for their support, for the maintenance of their buildings, and for charity. And this was not all: all houses, gardens, and real property within either cities or faubourgs not actually employed for ecclesiastical uses, were to be confiscated by the government; the clergy were to be made to pay taxes upon the rich furniture and works of art or adornment given them to enjoy either for a length of years or in perpetuity. Finally, all lands providing revenues, either in money or in kind, as oil, wine, and grain, in case of being let to contract or change of control, were to be declared redeemable. If these measures should prove insufficient, then recourse must be had to more drastic means, namely the direct sale of the property of the church. Twenty-six million livres' worth of this could be readily sold, the speaker argued, which would be no more than one-third of the church's possession; the remainder should be administered by a trustworthy commission, which, after paying the stipends of the clergy in the amounts above indicated, should devote the balance to the payment of the debts of the crown.[1]

This formidable programme, which suggests the policy actually followed by France in 1789, in spite of the hot declaration of the constable that the speaker presenting it ought to be hanged,[2] proved so reasonable that the government, without going to the extreme proposed, saw that the moment was a favorable one to secure important aid from the clergy. The clergy, on the other hand, were sharp enough to see that in order to save their property, they would have to make sacrifice of a portion of it. At first they offered the crown a bonus of ten million livres, which it refused as being too small a sum, and demanded a greater subsidy.[3] A temporary settlement at last was made on the basis of 1,600,000

[1] La Place, 150–52; De Thou, IV, 74, 75. The full text, unpublished, of this discourse is in F. Fr., 3970, a volume which contains much unused material for the history of the estates of Pontoise. L'Hôpital's address is one of the documents.

[2] Despatches of Suriano (Huguenot Society), August 24, 1561.

[3] C. S. P. For., No. 538, §5, September 26, 1561.

livres annual revenue to be levied upon the vineyards of the clergy, in order to relieve the King's present needs.[1] But something more fundamental than this had to be done, for these measures only supplied the King with funds for current expenses, and did not admit of redemption of the debt or resumption of the crown lands, which had been mortgaged for about thirty millions of francs. This matter was the subject of investigation and debate through the ensuing November and December. Finally, a scheme was worked out whereby the royal domain was all to be redeemed by the clergy within six years, and the remainder of the debt to be discharged within another six.[2]

The contract of Poissy-Pontoise presents two important stipulations: one, a gift of money to the King; second, the repurchase by the clergy of the domains of the crown and the redemption of the debt. If this contract had been observed, it would have rendered the other assemblies of the clergy useless, but the failure to execute it made necessary the subsequent assemblies of 1563 and 1567, which established a rule of periodicity, as it were, and fixed the next session at 1573. By 1567, the clergy had fulfilled its first obligation and declared itself ready to resume the second by giving to the provost of the merchants and to the *échevins* of Paris the guarantees desired for the redemption of the *rentes*. But the King at the same time insisted upon the continuation of the subsidy of 1,600,000 livres. The clergy protested, demanding his adherence to the contract of Poissy. The crown enforced continuation, but as "an easement" waived claim to the "secular tithe" heretofore exacted, and granted to the clergy, for the first time, the right to collect taxes by its own agents, and the right to judge in a sovereign capacity all cases which might arise from these financial matters. The government observed this convention no better

---

[1] De Crue, 312, 313; De Thou, IV, 74; *Nég. Tosc.*, III, 461; Ruble, *Antoine de Bourbon et Jeanne d'Albret*, III, 160; *Rel. vén.*, II, 21; K. 1,494, fol. 94. Notwithstanding this relief, the King demanded a further subsidy amounting to three million gold crowns from the local Estates to be paid in the following January (*C. S. P. For.*, No. 682, §10, November 26, 1561).

[2] *Ibid.*; cf No. 750, §7, December 28, 1561. Most of this debt was held by Paris. It amounted to 7,560,056 livres.

than the first, and in addition to extraordinary subventions—two million livres in 1572, nearly half of which was squandered by the duke of Anjou in Poland—resorted to compulsory alienations of church property, as in 1563, 1568, 1574, which were made upon order of the King, without recourse to papal affirmation. Purchasers were not wanting for the new credit. The rate of interest fell to 5 per cent. in the autumn of 1561 as a result of these expedients, and, provided civil war could be averted, it seemed probable that the dilapidated finances might be rehabilitated.[1]

Simultaneous with the sitting of the estates at Pontoise to settle the financial issue, the religious issue was being debated by the doctrinal leaders of Catholicism and Calvinism, at Poissy.[2] This solemn assembly had been summoned in June to meet on the second of the following month,[3] in spite of the opposition of the clergy and Spain, who warned Catherine that such a concession would lead to disaster.[4] But delay ensued, and the assembly did not actually convene until September, for the members were slow in coming.[5] The conditions governing the meeting at Poissy were published in council on August 8, namely, that the clergy should not be umpires; that the princes of the blood should preside at the disputation, and that the different proceedings should be faithfully recorded by trustworthy persons.[6] With respect to the other matters the Calvinists were required to make some con-

[1] *Rel. vén.*, I, 409–11. Upon the whole question, see De Crue, *Anne de Montmorency*, chap. xiv; Esmein, *Histoire du droit français*, 632–33.

[2] De Ruble, *Le colloque de Poissy* (1889); Klipfel, *Le colloque de Poissy* (1867).

[3] *C. S. P. For.*, No. 265, §9, June 23, 1561; La Place, 131.

[4] Paris, *Négociations relatives au règne de François II*, 550, 615–22; *Papiers d'état du cardinal de Granvelle*, VI, 137; Klipfel, *Quis fuerit in Gallia factionum status*, Paris 1863, 23.

[5] Theodore Beza, "the Huguenot pope," did not reach the court until August 23, where he was cordially received by the prince of Condé, before whom he preached "in open audience, whereat was a great press" (*C. S. P. For.*, No. 461, August 30, 1561). For the active agency of Beza at court before the assembly at Poissy met, see La Place, 155–57.

[6] The Sorbonne protested against the whole proceeding, but its request was not granted (La Place, 154; cf. *C. S. P. For.*, No. 458, August 28, 1561, No. 485, September 8, 1561).

cessions in order to avoid the reproach of seeming to evade the colloquy. While awaiting the formal opening of the conference at Poissy, Beza was invited by the court to speak before the King, the queen mother, the king of Navarre, and the Council. He was listened to with great attention by all until he began to deny the Real Presence, when the Catholic party tried to stop his address, exclaiming that it was blasphemy, and Beza and his partisans would certainly have been ejected if their opponents had not been restrained by the royal authority and compelled to listen to the end. At its conclusion the cardinal Tournon exhorted the King to continue firm in the faith of his ancestors,[1] and not to permit France to be reduced to the Swiss cantonal system.[2]

Many of the clergy said that it was not pertinent for the colloquy to determine these points, but that it was for the General Council to decide; moreover, it was argued that as the delegates of the Spanish clergy would shortly be coming through France on their way to Trent, why should not they assist as well as the others?[3] Catherine, it is said, had intended that there should be no disputation about dogma. But there is some reason to believe that she confounded dogma with the rites and observances of the church,[4] and it is certain that the Huguenots were determined to push their privilege of free speech to the very limit. Indeed, the conditions predicated by Beza formed the substance of a petition presented by the Reformed leaders to Charles IX.[5]

When the conference met a great attempt to maintain secrecy

---

[1] *C. S. P. For.*, No. 492, September 10, 1561.

[2] "Far diventar questo Regno cantoni di Svizzeri" . . . . (*Despatches of Suriano* [Huguenot Society], Aug. 15, 1561; cf. *English Hist. Review*, VIII, 135). Elsewhere the Venetian ambassador says: "E cosi si va alla via di redurre quella provincia a stato populare, come Svizzeri; e distruggere la monarchia e il regno."— *Rel. vén.*, I, 538. De Thou, Book XXV, observes: "Qui primam, quam Deo debebant, fidem irritam fecissent; qua semel violate, minime dubitaverint regem ipsum petere quo regnum everterent, et confusis ordinibus, in rei publicae formam, Helvetiorum exemplo, redigerent."

[3] *C. S. P. For.*, No. 421, August 19, 1561; *ibid., Ven.*, No. 280, September 8, 1561.

[4] *Despatches of Suriano* (Huguenot Society), September 18, 1561.

[5] "Demandes des ministres protestantes au roi," K. 1,494, No. 95.

was made. No one was permitted to enter except those who had been formally appointed;[1] the duke of Guise carried the keys to the conference hall, and careful search was made at the beginning of each sitting to find any who might be hid.[2]

The principal points in dispute turned upon the use of images; the administration of the sacrament of baptism; the communion;

THE COLLOQUY OF POISSY
(Tortorel and Perissin)

the mass; the laying-on of hands and the vocation of ministers, and finally the consideration of a possible accord in doctrine, in which points the usages of the primitive church and the reasons of separation were involved.[3]

On the second day of the conference (September 16) the cardinal of Lorraine spoke, dwelling upon these principal points: first,

[1] Upon the personnel of the assembly, see the references in D'Aubigné, I, 315, n. 4.

[2] C. S. P. For., No. 516, §7, September 20, 1561.

[3] "Paroles prononcées par Theodore de Beza touchant le sacrement."—K. 1,495, No. 77. 1, "Profession de foi . . . . concerté par les prelats de France;" 2, "Première proposition des Catholiques; première proposition des hérétiques."— Latin, K. 1,495, No. 78; cf. Rel. vén., II, 75.

that the King, being a member of the church and not its head, could not set himself up as a judge in matters of religion and faith, but was subject to the church like every other Christian; second, the definition of the authority of the church was extended even over princes.[1]

Before long, however, it became evident, both that the attempt to reconcile the Catholic and the Calvinist parties was an impossibility, and that the government's policy of accommodation was exciting discontent.[2] The demands of the Huguenots, based on Beza's arguments, were as follows:

1. That bishops, abbots, and other ecclesiastics should not be constituted in any way judges of the Huguenots, in view of the fact that they were their opponents.

2. That all points of difference be judged and decided according to the simple word of God, as contained in the New and Old Testaments, since the Reformed faith was founded on this alone, and that where any difficulties arose concerning the interpretation of words, reference should be made to the original Hebrew and Greek text.[3]

This second article was a rock of contention from the very beginning. The whole Catholic doctrine of tradition having equal weight with Scripture was denied in this article. It was manifest, indeed, from the first that three things would *not* be suffered to be considered: (1) a change of religion; (2) the authority of the Pope; (3) the possible alienation of church property.[4] This state

---

[1] The cardinal's definition of the church was, "the company of Christians in which is comprised both reprobates and heretics, and which has been recognized always, everywhere, and by all, and which alone had the right of interpreting Scripture."—*C. S. P. For.*, No. 507, September 17, 1561; cf. Suriano (Huguenot Society), September 22. His address is given at length in La Place, 179 ff. It was published at the time. Suriano, August 23, 1561, says all the delegates "made very long speeches." Upon the doctrinal tactics of the cardinal of Lorraine at the colloquy of Poissy, see the letters of Languet, *Epist. secr.*, II, 139, September 20, 1561; 159, November 26, 1561.

[2] The first president of the Parlement of Paris was committed to keeping his house because of offensive agitation (*C. S. P. For.*, No. 461, August 30, 1561).

[3] Proposition de Théodore de Bèze, K. 1,494, No. 96.

[4] *C. S. P. Ven.*, No. 280, September 8, 1561.

of things, together with the fact that the prolongation of the session entailed great expense,[1] brought about a change of plan. Five persons, the bishop of Valence, the archbishop of Sens, and MM. Salignac, d'Espence, and Boutellier, were appointed by the queen and agreed to by the clergy, to confer with five representatives of the Calvinists, viz., Peter Martyr,[2] Beza, De Gallars, Marborat, and D'Espine.[3] Within ten days more the prelates and ministers had ceased to confer and were taking their departure.[4] The assembly of Poissy dissolved of itself on October 18, having accomplished nothing,[5] except doctrinally still further to disunite the Protestant world, which otherwise might possibly have had a council of its own, composed of French, Scotch, English, Germans, Danes, Swiss and Swedes, to face the Council of Trent.[6]

Two days later the cardinal and the duke of Guise departed from the court, in spite of the urgency of the queen mother to have them remain, accompanied by the dukes of Nemours and Longueville and other great personages and mustering six or seven hundred horse. Outwardly there was no sign of disaffection. Immediately afterward the constable also left, expressing dissatisfaction with the tolerant policy of the government. It was plain

[1] C. S. P. For., No. 511, September 19, 1561.

[2] Not being a Frenchman, but an Italian—his name was Pietro Martire Vermigli—he received a separate safe-conduct (Suriano [Huguenot Society], August 23; Rev. hist., XCVII, March–April, 1908, p. 302).

[3] La Place, 199.

[4] C. S. P. For., No. 602, October 1,2 1561. For a description of the last days of the Colloquy, see Despatches of Suriano (Huguenot Society), October 16, 1561.

[5] C. S. P. For., No. 624, October 18, 1561. In K. 1,495, No. 66, is a résumé by the Spanish chancellery of Chantonnay's dispatches dealing with the colloquy.

[6] C. S. P. For., No. 753, from Strasburg, December 30, 1561. Writing just a week earlier, on December 23, to his sovereign, Chantonnay strongly condemned the course of Catherine at Poissy because it had militated against the authority of Trent, and had given courage to the heretics to continue their synods.—K. 1,494, No. 104. Other references to the Colloquy of Poissy are De Thou, IV, 84 ff.; De Ruble, Antoine de Bourbon et Jeanne d'Albret, 76 ff.; Corresp. de Catherine de Médicis, I, Introd., ci, 239. Chantonnay's correspondence, covering both the colloquy and the meeting of the estates at Pontoise, is in K. 1,494, No. 89, August 5; No. 90, August 20; No. 101, September 12 (especially valuable for the financial settlement); No. 102, September 15.

throughout the proceedings at Pontoise (and at Poissy) that the chancellor of France, L'Hôpital, and the admiral, had the chief direction of affairs in their hands, although the queen mother and the king of Navarre had the greater show of authority.[1]

The Vatican had been an anxious observer of affairs in France, and early in June, 1561, the Pope had resolved to send the cardinal of Ferrara, Hippolyte d'Este, to France as legate.[2] The principal points of his mission to the French court, where he arrived on September 14, were to entreat the French crown that the annates might still remain as the Pope's revenue; that there might be no change of religion and observance in the church; to solicit the King to recognize the Council of Trent and to break off the colloquy at Poissy.[3] But when the legate presented his credentials, at the instance of the chancellor, who impugned his powers, the estates protested against the entry of any of the Pope's bulls or letters without the King's consent and seal.[4] The Parlement of Paris

---

[1] C. S. P. For., No. 659, §10, November 14, 1561. Of these the chancellor was the more agrressive, opposing the efforts of the clerical party to delay and obstruct action (D'Aubigné, I, 311).

[2] Correspondance de Catherine de Médicis, I, 248; C. S. P. For., Nos. 225 and 245, June 6–13, 1561; No. 273, June 23, 1561. The choice was a tactless one on the part of the Pope and one certain to antagonize Catherine de Medici as well as the political Huguenots, for the cardinal was a relative of the Guises by marriage. Don Luigo d'Este, the duke of Ferrara's brother, was the son of Alphonso d'Este and Lucretia Borgia. He resigned his place in the church and married the duchess of Estouteville, a marriage indicating the Guise policy of aggrandisement (C. S. P. For., No. 904, March 27, 1560). The marriage made bitter feeling between the House of Ferrara and the Guises. "There is a breach between the Dukes of Ferrara and Guise touching the former's mother, who, being very rich, and lately fallen out with her son, had secretly sent to the Duke of Guise, a gentleman with a message that she would come to France and end her life there and be as his mother. Word was sent her that she would be welcome; and if her son would not permit her to come with her substance, he would take into his hands the assignation made by the late king upon certain lands for the payment of 100,000 crowns yearly to the Duke till such time as 600,000 crowns, borrowed from him at the Duke of Guise's last voyage to Rome, were paid off. The Duke keeps his mother with good watch for fear of her escaping to France."—C. S. P. For., No. 446, August 22, 1561. The cardinal traveled with great pomp, having no less than four hundred horses in his train.

[3] C. S. P. For., No. 538, §1, September 26, 1561.

[4] D'Aubigné, I, 311; Rel. vén., II, 87; C. S. P. For., No. 602, October 12, 1561.

went even farther, and refused to confirm the King's letters-patent.
But the King's council overrode this resolution, and recognized
the legate's credentials, although L'Hôpital steadfastly refused to
affix the seal of state to the council's action.

The cardinal began his negotiations by offering on the part of
the Pope to resign the tenths and subsidies exacted by the church,
and promising all the help His Holiness could give with honor,
on condition that the resolution of the estates of Orleans, prohibiting payment of the annates, which the estates of Pontoise had
reasserted, should not be executed. The nuncio argued that this
action was a violation of the concordat of 1516, and that the principle in the case had been decided by the council of Basel, and
accepted by Charles VII in the Pragmatic Sanction. Accordingly,
the nuncio asked for a revocation of the actions taken touching
the property of the church, and that things be restored to the state
in which they originally were.[1] But the cardinal's arguments
were of no effect. The execution of the new law went forward.
The first province where it was applied was Guyenne—within
the government of the king of Navarre, then Touraine, and the
Orleannais.[2]

An even more interested observer, perhaps, of French affairs
than the Pope, was Philip of Spain. The progress of heresy in
France, the seizure of the property of the church there, the attitude
of the French crown toward the Council of Trent, the uncertainty
of Antoine of Bourbon's conduct—these were all disquieting facts
to the Spanish ruler. Philip curtly told Catherine and her son
that her government must abandon its policy of weakness and
dissimulation, that too many souls were being imperiled by her
course, and that coercive measures must be used.[3] The duke of

---

[1] *Despatches of Suriano* (Huguenot Society), September 23, 1561.

[2] *Ibid.*, October 22, 1561. For further details of the negotiations, see *ibid.*,
November 3, 1561; *C. S. P. For.*, No. 682, §9, November 26; Baschet, *Journal
du Concile de Trente*, 89.

[3] Philip II to Catherine, September 29, 1561; to Charles, *ibid.*, K. 1,495, No.
72. To Chantonnay he wrote three days later: "También hazed entender á la
Reyna como por este camino perdera su hijo, esse reyno y la obediencia de sus
vassalos."—K. 1,495, No. 80. The words were not merely urgent advice—they
implied a threat.

Alva had the boldness to declare that unless the government of France revived the rigorous suppressive measures of Henry II, and punished every heretic, His Catholic Majesty was resolved to sacrifice the welfare of Spain and even his own life in order to stamp out a pest which he regarded as menacing to both France and Spain.[1] Singly and together the bishop of the Limoges (who was still at the Spanish court) and D'Ozances, while deploring the malice of the times and "the disasters of which everyone knew," tried to justify their government on the ground that Calvinism had become a necessary evil in France and that it was better to give it qualified toleration than to plunge the country into fire and war. They pointed to the deliberations of the assembly of Fontainebleau, to the States-General of Orleans, to the *arrêts* of the Parlement, and the findings of Pontoise and Poissy in proof; they asserted that the queen mother and the king of Navarre—they were cautious not to style him thus in Philip's presence, however—were "of perfect and sincere intention" not to let heresy increase in France; "the scandal and outrage" of heretical preaching never would be permitted in Paris or at the court, although it was necessary to permit the Protestants to have their own worship outside of some of the towns; that the purpose of the crown was fixed never to change or alter the true religion; that France was not hostile to the Council of Trent, but in her distress was naturally impatient; and finally they importuned the king of Spain not to show his anger, but to give "advice and comfort" for the sake of the friendship which existed between their country and his, and for the repose of Christendom.[2]

---

[1] Weiss, *L'Espagne sous Phillippe II*, I, 114, 115; cf. Forneron, *Histoire de Philippe II*, I, 253, n. 3. See also the remarkable "Rapport sur une conférence entre l'ambassadeur de France et le duc d'Albe, au sujet des affaires du roi de Navarre et des troubles pour cause de la religion (French transcript, apparently of a report of the Spanish chancellery), in K. 1,496, No. 136, December 20, 1561. The Pope indorsed the proposition of Spanish intervention in France (Vargas to Philippe II, November 7, 1561, in *Papiers d'état du cardinal de Granvelle*, VI, 398, 404).

[2] "Aux villes et pays où ils sont là declaires leur bailler quelques lieux prochaine hors des dictes villes"—Résumé des points principaux traités par l'ambassadeur de France auprès du roi Philippe II (Communications du duc d'Alba),

The appeal fell upon deaf ears. Philip coldly replied that it was useless for France to expect the advice or assistance of Spain so long as her government tolerated heresy in any degree whatsoever; that those at the court who were Huguenots, like the admiral and the prince of Condé, should be sent away forthwith, and all others should be coerced; that from the point of view of religion it was blasphemy to permit the Huguenots to have any places of worship, and from the political point of view it was suicide to tolerate them, for "there could never be new things in religion without loss of obedience to the temporal power," in proof of which the King pointed out that in certain of the provinces of France the people were refusing to pay tithes and taxes, at the same time triumphantly asserting that he was better informed of things happening in France than in Spain; that as to the Council of Trent, the Germans would have nothing to do with it and Spain had no need of it, while France was torn by heretical controversy, so that it might well be said that the council sat for the benefit of France alone.[1]

One of the points upon which Philip II dwelt with earnestness in the interviews he granted the two ambassadors of France was the vicious education under which Charles IX's brother Henry,

November 9, 1561, K. 1,495, No. 58; "Propositions faites par M. d'Ozance et l'ambassadeur ordinaire en Espagne, l'évêque de Limoges, dans deux audiences à eux données par le roi Philippe II" (Résumé avec annotations), M'nute, Notes de chancellerie, K. 1,495, No. 69, Madrid, September 17, 1561; "Points principaux d'une négociation spéciale de M. d'Ozance, envoyé de Catherine de Médici avec réponses notées à la marge, point par point: Communications au duc d'Albe après une délibération du Conseil d'état, prise lui absent," November 12, 1561, K. 1,495 No. 89; "Précis des points traités par M. d'Ozance et de l'Aubespine, ambassadeur de France," K. 1,495, No. 94, December 10, 1561; "Réponses à faire par ordre de Philippe II à M. d'Ozance, sur les nouvelles propositions de cet ambassadeur," K. 1,495, No. 98, December 15, 1561; "Memento addressé par l'évêque de Limoges au duc d'Albe" (Note à communiquer au roi Philippe II), K. 1,495 No. 100, December 20, 1561; Philip II to Chantonnay: "Avis de ce qu'on a répondu à M. d'Ozance," December 21, 1561, K. 1,495, No. 102; "Rapport sur une conférence entre l'ambassadeur du France et le duc d'Albe, au sujet des affaires du roi de Navarre et des troubles pour cause de la religion" (copié en Français), K. 1,496, folio 136, Madrid, December 20, 1561.

[1] Summary of Philip II's letter to Chantonnay of January 18, 1562, in K. 1,496, No. 34.

duke of Orleans, was being brought up. He emphatically condemned the Huguenot environment of the young prince. It did
not seem a coincidence therefore, when a plot was discovered in
November to seize the duke of Orleans—afterward Henry III—
who was to have been made *capo di parti* by the Catholics. It was
even said the conspirators aimed also to remove the king and queen
of Navarre, Condé, and the admiral, by poison. The duke of
Nemours was charged with being the principal author of it, and
was to have carried the young duke off to Lorraine or Savoy.[1]
This supposition was given greater probability when the whole
company of the Guises suddenly left the court and departed for
Lorraine. But Catherine was not yet intimidated, though she
prudently dropped the investigation which she had set on foot
when she discovered clues that led to the Escurial and the Vatican.[2]
In spite of the omens, she still adhered to a middle course. The
government resolved to send twenty-five bishops and two archbishops to Trent, although they went "very unwillingly."[3] At
the same time permission was granted to the ministers of the Re-

---

[1] *Despatches of Suriano* (Huguenot Society), November 4, 1561. The *Journal
du Concile de Trente* (ed. Baschet), 89, says the intention was to carry him into
Lorraine, to prevent his becoming tainted with heresy. Lignerolles, an intimate
of the duke of Nemours, later confessed the latter's complicity in the plot to kidnap
the young prince and spirit him away to Savoy, but the affair was hushed up and
Lignerolles was shortly afterward released. The prince de Joinville, Guise's son,
seems to have been more actively interested than his father. The correspondence
between Chantonnay and Philip leaves no room for doubt of the fact that Nemours
was acting as the agent of Spain (K. 1,494, No. 106, October 31, from St. Cloud;
No. 114, November 28, 1561), although Philip repudiated complicity in a letter to
Catherine (K. 1,495, No. 90, November 27, 1561), and Chantonnay declared the
whole story was a trick of the Huguenots.

[2] D'Aubigné, 321. Chantonnay seems to have been apprehensive lest the
circumstances might precipitate the civil war which every one feared (Letter to
Philip II, November 28, 1561, K. 1,494, No. 114), and seized the opportunity
afforded by it to read the queen mother a lecture. The ambassador "used great
threatenings toward the queen mother and the king of Navarre for their proceedings
in religion."—*C. S. P. For.*, No. 659, §§1, 2.

Ruble, *Antoine de Bourbon et Jeanne d'Albret*, III, 245–50; De Crue, *Anne
de Montmorency*, 315, 316. The official inquiry entitled, "Enquête sur l'enlève-
ment du duc d'Orleans," is in F. Fr. 6,608.

[3] *C. S. P. For.*, No. 715, §1, December 12, 1561.

formed churches to preach in private houses or in gardens environed
with houses (the erection of churches being prohibited), if it was
done without tumult.[1]   At court the ministers of the Reformed
churches preached one day, when the queen of Navarre, the prince
of Condé, and the admiral would be present.   The next day either
some Cordelier, Jesuit, Jacobin, Minim, or other of the cloistered
sects, preached, on which occasion, the King, the queen mother,
the king of Navarre, the cardinal of Ferrara, accompanied by
those who leaned toward the see of Rome, would be present.   But
moderation was exacted of both sects.   On one occasion a famous
preacher of the Minims, who had won some credit with the Catholics for his railings, was in the night secretly taken from his
lodgings and carried to the court to answer for his rabid utterances.[2]

But it was increasingly manifest that events, both within and
without France, were passing beyond the grasp of the government.
The Huguenots, sometimes from fear no doubt, but not infrequently
for effrontery, went to their services with pistols and matchlocks,
in spite of the laws against the bearing of arms; and they even
were bold enough to march through the streets singing their psalms,
to the anger and scandal of Catholic Christians.[3]   An outbreak
was imminent at any time.

In Paris, on October 12, the Protestants assembled together
to the number of 7,000 or 8,000 to hear one of their ministers preach,
half a mile from the town.   The Catholics thereupon shut the
gates to prevent their re-entry.   Finding the gates closed, the
Protestants forced them, and many were wounded and some slain
on both sides.[4]   From the provinces word had come in July that
the duke of Montpensier, going to his house in Touraine for the
burial of his mother, and finding numbers in many towns who
made open profession of Calvinism, by virtue of his governorship
of that country, imprisoned about one hundred and forty in Chinon.

[1] *Despatches of Michele Suriano* (Huguenot Society), November 3, 1561;
C. S. P. For., No. 659, §5, November 14, 1561.

[2] C. S. P. For., No. 717, §7, December 13, 1561.   For some of the famous
Catholic preachers of Paris in 1561, see Claude Haton, I, 213, 214, and notes.

[3] Claude Haton, I, 177, 178.

[4] C. S. P. For., No. 617, October 15, 1561.

Whereupon the people, not forgetting his conduct toward them in the previous reign, when he razed the houses of several who were reported to him to be Huguenots, assembled in great numbers— about 12,000 or 15,000, we are told—surely a great exaggeration, and marched so fast upon him that he was besieged in his house and forced to release all the prisoners in order to appease the multitude.[1]

The organized nature of the Huguenot agitations in various localities, especially in southern France, did not escape the keen observation of Philip's ambassador.[2] At Montpellier in Languedoc the Protestant organizations, by September, had taken the form of a definite league, with the sweeping motto: "No mass, no more than at Geneva," whose operations were so thorough that many Catholics were on the point of emigrating to Catalonia.[3]

Quite as formidable as armed and insurrectionary religion at home was the drift of the negotiations of both parties abroad. The formation of the Triumvirate had been taken as a sign by both parties that the issue between them was, as in Germany before the Smalkald war, likely soon to pass from religious difference and political rivalry into military combat; and both sides accordingly prepared against this fatal day. Naturally, the Protestant German princes who had followed the proceedings at Poissy with intense interest[4] were the ones looked to for assistance by the

---

[1] C. S. P. For., No. 304, §4, July 23, 1561.

[2] K. 1,495, No. 47, June 19, 1561. Cf. Despatches of Suriano (Huguenot Society), October 1. Upon these insurrections in the south, see D'Aubigné, I, 322–26; De Thou, II, 235 ff. (ed. 1740); Mém. de Condé, III, 636; Long, La réforme et les guerres de religion en Dauphiné; Pierre Gilles, Hist. ecclés. des églises réformées vaudoises, chap. xxii; Hist. du Languedoc, V, 211.

[3] "Aulx petites villes, elles se sont ralliez les unes avec les autres en ung faict, ung monopole et une ligue ensemble."—Mémoires-journaux du duc de Guise (M. & P., sér. I, VI, 467, col. 2); Letter of Joyeuse to the constable; duplicate to the duke of Guise (September 16, 1561). For the work of this league see pp. 468–71. Guillaume, vicomte de Joyeuse, was lieutenant to the governor of Languedoc and later a marshal of France.

[4] These princes were Wolfgang William, duke of Deuxponts; William, landgrave of Hesse; Frederick the Pious, count palatine of the Rhine (D'Aubigné, I, 333, 334; Le Laboureur, I, 673). The leading Protestant princes of Germany were Augustus, elector of Saxony; Joachim II, margrave of Brandenburg, John

Huguenots. In May, 1561, the prince of Condé had sent Hotman to the chief German princes, begging them not to desert the cause of the true religion in France and saying that Philip II was endeavoring to terrify the queen from making any concessions to the Huguenots.[1] The fact that some of these, as the count palatine of the Rhine, and the landgrave of Thuringia were Calvinists, while others were Lutherans, was not an insuperable barrier to co-operation, although the Lutherans wished that the confession of Augsburg might first be recognized in France. But the prevailing opinion was that the adherents of both of the Protestant faiths should first unite in endeavoring to secure freedom of worship and liberty of conscience in France, and then they might proceed to establish uniformity of religion, if possible.[2] Two propositions were made to the German princes. The first was that if the Guises, or any of their confederates, tried to enlist soldiers in Germany, measures should be taken to stop the effort; secondly, that if the Guises or their accomplices resorted to the use of arms against Condé and Coligny and were supported by Spain, then assistance should be given them. Some of the German princes agreed at once to this latter proposition, provided the expenses of such military support were defrayed by the Huguenots; but others thought that the matter could only be settled in a general assembly of the princes. The circle of Huguenot negotiations at this moment was a wide one and their prospects were bright. For Frederick duke of Saxony; Christopher, duke of Württemberg; Wolfgang William, duke of Deuxponts (Zweibrücken); John Albert, duke of Mecklenberg; John the Elder, duke of Holstein; Joachim Ernest, prince of Anhalt, and Charles, margrave of Baden. These are enumerated in a letter of Hotman, December 31, 1560. See *Mém. de l'Acad. des sc. moral. et polit.*, CIV, 653, and *Bulletin de la soc. prot. franç.*, 1860.

[1] *Mém. de l'Acad. des sc. moral. et polit.*, CIV (1877), 66; *C. S. P. For.*, No. 399, August 12, 1561.

[2] *C. S. P. For.*, No. 319, July 15, 1561, from Strasburg. Hotman visited the elector palatine at Germersheim; the landgrave of Hesse at Cassel; the elector of Saxony at Leipsic, whence he went to Stuttgart. He did not see the duke of Württemberg in person, and was compelled to write to him instead. (See his letter, September 27, 1561, in *Mém. de l'Acad des sc. moral. et polit.*, CIV, 660.) Thence he went to Heidelberg, from which point he wrote a second letter to the duke of Württemberg, and one to the duke of Deuxponts.

at this time Denmark, too, was suing for French favor. Among the ambassadors who came to offer the condolences of their sovereigns for the death of Francis II and to congratulate young Charles, had come an envoy of the Danish king proposing the marriage of his sister to a French prince and himself to marry Mary Stuart. This proposed Franco-Danish alliance could have produced no other effect than to facilitate the Protestant cause in France.[1] On the other hand, the prospect of Swiss support of the Catholic cause in France was not good. Aside from the great expense this alliance had always entailed, the number of the Catholic cantons had been diminished by the secession of Glaris, which had lately gone over to Protestantism, in consequence of which the rest, seeing themselves weakened, had asked aid from the duke of Savoy and the Pope.[2]

The Catholics adroitly emphasized the difference between the two Protestant faiths, with the hope not only of preventing Lutheran support of the Huguenots, but even of securing their aid against the French Calvinists. The duke of Guise went in person to confer with the duke of Württemberg at Saverne (February 15, 1562),[3] while Philip II redoubled his efforts to alienate the king of Navarre.[4] The support of the Spanish monarch was the vital factor in French politics. The French Calvinists had no single *most powerful ally* to support them, such as the Catholic party enjoyed in the assistance of Spain. England was the only Protestant power capable of being a rival to Spain, and England was too cautious or too much occupied with home politics to risk embroilment abroad.

Both Rome and Spain at this moment took a resolute attitude. Shortly after the conference of Poissy came to an end, a consistory

[1] La Place, 121, 122; C. S. P. Ven., No. 249; Arch. nat., K. 1,495, folio 47, Chantonnay to Philip II, June 19, 1561.

[2] C. S .P. For., No. 736, November 26, 1561.

[3] Chantonnay's correspondence shows that agents of the duke of Guise were busy in Germany as early as October, 1561, K. 1,494, No. 105, October 28, 1561. Cf. Hubert Languet, Epist. secr., II, 142, 159, 202; Archives de la maison d'Orange-Nassau, I, 216–18, 226–52; Bulletin de la soc. do l'histoire du prot. français, XXIV.

[4] C. S. P. For., No. 724, §2, December 14, 1561.

of the curia, on October 10, 1561, had resolved to resist the Protestants in France.[1]   The counter-reformation programme deliberated at Trent recognized Philip II as the secular head of the
movement ("à ceste fin d'un commun consentement le tout chef
et conducteur de toute l'enterprise") who was to wheedle or compel the king of Navarre to commit himself in favor of the Catholic
cause in France, of which the duke of Guise was to be formally
recognized as leader.   The Spanish monarch was also to bring
pressure to bear upon the Emperor to compel the Catholic princes
of Germany to prevent the Lutherans and Rhenish Calvinists
from supporting the Protestants of France.   France must be
saved from self-ruin for the sake both of religion and the preservation of other Catholic nations.   Time and circumstances would
show the hour of such intervention, but everything must be prepared in advance.[2]

Aside from his inflexible religious convictions, in Philip's eyes,
policy also pointed toward Spanish intervention in France.   Spain,
Spanish Burgundy, and Flanders were, as Montluc of Valence
declared, "les trois plus belles fleurs de chapeau du roy Philippe;"
each of them bordered France, and France lay between Spain and
them, splitting the Spanish empire like a wedge.   Under these
circumstances the prevention of heresy in France was not merely
an act of religious duty but an act dictated by political expediency.
Moreover, Spain might territorially profit by such a policy.   The
son of Charles V dreamed of acquiring ducal Burgundy, which
his father had failed to secure; the Three Bishoprics might be
wrested away from Charles IX, either violently or as the price of
Spanish aid, and joined to Franche Comté they would materially
strengthen Spain's midcontinental road from Lombardy to the
mouths of the Rhine.[3]

[1] C. S. P. For., No. 602, October 11, 1561, from Rome.

[2] Papiers d'état du cardinal de Granvelle, VI, 432–43:   "Rapport secret du
secretaire Courtville," December, 1561.

[3] Cf. Montluc, bishop of Valence,   "Discours sur le bruit qui court que nous
aurons la guerre à cause de la religion," Mém. de Condé, ed. London, III, 73–82.
A note adds: "Ce discours se trouve aussi au fol. 61 recto du MS R et il est à la
suite d'une lettre de M. de Chantonnay, du 24 mars 1561.   Il dit à la fin de cette

Fear of Spain and of the Guises gave Catherine de Medici more anxiety than the insurrections of the Huguenots.[1] The government was justly apprehensive of Philip II's movements and warned Joyeuse to be on his guard against any effort to throw Spanish troops across the frontier.[2] Reinforcements were sent to Calais.[3] At the same time more captains and companies were sent to Metz, where Vieilleville, the governor, was ordered not to admit anyone known to be a Guisard into the city, as the Guises were suspected of wishing to hand it over to Philip.[4] Precautionary changes were also made in the military posts, in the case of those known to be well-affected to the Guises, the changes

lettre, que l'on disoit communement que ce Discours étoit de l'évêque de Valence (Montluc). Ce Discours a été copié dans ce MS sur l'édition qui en fut faite dans le tems."

[1] On November 23, 1561, Charles IX wrote to the bishop of Limoges in regard to Philip II: "Dites-lui que je le prie si l'on luy a donné quelques doubtes et soupçons de mes déportements, qu'il vous en dye quelcun et ce qu'il la mys en doubte, affin que s'il veult prendre tant de paynes d'envoyer ung homme fidelle ez lieux où il aura oppinion qu'on fera quelques préparatifs, je luy face cognoistre que c'est une pure menterie."—*Catalogue* . . . . *de lettres autographes de feu M. de Lajariette,* Charavay, Paris, 1860, No. 667. Five days later, on November 28, 1561, Catherine de Medici wrote to the same ambassador: "Je me défie tent de seux qui sont mal contens . . . . car je ne veos ni ne suys conselliée de venir aus armes."—*Collection de lettres autographes ayant appartenu à M. Fossé-Darcosse,* Paris, Techener, 1861, No. 193.

[2] *Hist. du Languedoc,* V, 211. Philip II was reputed to have spent 350,000 crowns of his wife's dowry in Germany (*C. S P. For.,* No. 659, §18, November 14, 1561). Catherine sent a special agent, Rambouillet, into Germany to assist Hotman in discovering information about Spain's intrigues there (*C. S. P. For.,* No. 713, December, 1561; *Mém. de l'Acad. des sc. moral. et polit.,* CIV [1877], 661). D'Ozances in Spain received special instructions to decipher Philip II's conduct if possible.

[3] *C. S. P. For.,* No. 265, §11, June 23, 1561. This was in consequence of the apprehension aroused early in May by the appearance of a large body of Spanish infantry and cavalry to survey Abbeville whence they returned toward Guisnes (*ibid.,* No. 248, from Paris, May 18, 1561).

[4] *Ibid.,* No. 712, December 9, 1561, from Strasburg; No. 717, §6, December 13, 1561, from Paris. There had been some anxiety lest the Emperor might avail himself of the distraction in France to seize the Three Bishoprics. But at this moment, on account of the activity of both the Turk and the Muscovite, and because he was angry with the Pope over the Council of Trent, Ferdinand, was friendly to France and cordially received Marillac, the bishop of Vienne (D'Aubigné, I, 332, 333).

all being in favor of the Huguenot party.[1] De Gourdan was removed from Calais and the command given to the sieur de Grammont, who had married a sister of the vidame de Chartres; the prince de la Roche-sur-Yon was made king's lieutenant in Paris; the admiral made governor of Normandy in place of the duke of Bouillon; Condé was sent to Picardy, where the marshal Brissac had lately resigned on account of illness.[2]

"Here is new fire, new green wood reeking, new smoke and much contrary wind blowing," wrote Shakerley to Elizabeth's ambassador, Throckmorton, on December 15, 1561.[3] The words were wisely as well as quaintly used. From the capital to every edge of France unrest, suspicion, conspiracy, insurrection prevailed. The Catholic orders began to fortify the abbeys. Every day Catherine's determination to maintain an even balance of the two religions was producing greater tension and more heat. Violence was ominously on the increase.[4] Robbery was common

[1] "Le conseil du roi, voyant que les mouvements les plus divers agitaient le royaume, décide que chaque gouverneur, lieutenant, sénéchal et autres ministres, se rendissent à leurs gouvernements."—Baschet, *Journal du Concile de Trente*, 89.

[2] *C. S. P. For.*, No. 595, October 9, 1561; No. 602, October 12, 1561; No. 624, October 18, 1561; No. 659, §20, November 14, 1561. The appointments of Coligny and Condé never became operative, owing to the outbreak of civil war early in the next year. They are important only as they reflect Catherine's policy of caution and craft.

[3] *Ibid.*, No. 729. Thomas Shakerley was an Englishman by birth, who had once been a page to Edward VI, while the latter was prince. He had left England nine years before and had spent most of his time in Rome, where, becoming an organist, he "obtained the estimation of a cunning player for the substance and solemnity of music." He came to France in the suite of the cardinal of Ferrara. The Spanish ambassador approached him with an offer to enter the secret service of Spain, which Shakerley patriotically communicated to Throckmorton (*ibid.*, No. 730, §5, December 18; No. 750, §1c, December 28, 1561).

[4] On December 27, the Protestants congregated in the Faubourg St. Marceau, whereupon the priests and Papists assembled at St. Medard and determined to attack them. One of the Protestant soldiers going to remonstrate was run through. The Protestants who were appointed to guard the assembly, seeing this, ran to his succor, but were driven back by the numbers. Other Protestants coming up put their attackers to rout and forced their way into the church, when the prince de la Roche-sur-Yon, the King's lieutenant, arrived with a strong force of horse and foot and carried off several to the Châtelet (*ibid.*, No. 783, January 4, 1561; *Mém. de Condé*, II, 541 ff.; Claude Haton, 179, and note; *Arch. cur.*, IV, 63 ff.; and an article in *Mém. de la soc. de l'hist. de Paris*, 1886).

under pretense of searching for heretics.[1]   In the hope of bettering things, the crown relieved the prince de la Roche-sur-Yon of the lieutenancy and committed it to the marshal Montmorency, from whose religious moderation and popularity much was expected.[2] The capital of France at this season presented a strange and terrible appearance.   Armed bands roamed the streets.   The city more resembled a frontier city in a state of siege than a mercantile or university town.   The students of the Sorbonne paraded the streets and went armed to mass, the authorities being powerless to control them.[3]

The condition in the provinces was as bad; only here the odds seem to have been in favor of the Protestants.   In Guyenne a Huguenot mob sacked a town, committed many outrages, and finally besieged the governor, Burie, in his house.[4]   A worse occurrence was the murder of Fumel, an eminent lawyer in Languedoc, as an "enemy of the religion."[5]   There were riots in Troyes, Orleans, Auxerre, Rouen, Meaux, Vendôme, Bourges, Lyons, Tours, Angers,[6] Bazas.[7]   The Huguenots of Sens erected

[1] C. S. P. For., No. 758, §13, December 31, 1561.

[2] Ibid., No. 789, §2, January 8, 1562.   The prince de la Roche-sur-Yon passed for a Calvinist, while the marshal Montmorency was a liberal Catholic. The queen mother hoped the change would be acceptable to both parties.   Another reason for this change was that the constable and the prince de la Roche-sur-Yon were the principals in a law-suit involving 10,000 ducats income.   It was possible for the lieutenant of Paris to use influence with the Parlement of Paris before which the case was to be tried, and this more obviously favored the constable's side of the suit.   Cf. details in Chantonnay's letter to Philip II, January 5, 1562, K. 1,497, B, 15.

[3] C. S. P. For., No. 925; cf. Castelnau's description of the bandits in the Faubourg St. Marcel, Book III, chap. v.

[4] C. S. P. For., No. 789, §2, January 6, 1562.

[5] Archives de la Gironde, VIII, 207.   The King sent a special officer to put the offenders to death and destroy the village, but it is significant that this commission was not intrusted to Villars, who was sublieutenant in Languedoc and notorious for his treatment of the Huguenots (C. S. P. For., No. 750, §10, December 28, 1561).

[6] Claude Haton, I, 195-98, 236, 237.   His spleen is evidenced, though, in saying that: "à cause de la grande liberté à mal faire et dire qui leur estoit permise sans aulcune punition de justice . . . . si le plus grand larron et voleur du pays eust esté prins prisonnier. il eust eschappé à tout danger voire à la mort, moyennant qu'il se feust déclaré Huguenot et de la nouvelle prétendue religion."—Ibid., I 124.   This is one of the earliest characterizations of the Huguenot faith.   It was afterward currently referred to as the "R. P. R."

[7] Archives de la Gironde, XV, 57.

a church outside the town.   Then finding that they outnumbered
the Catholics they pillaged the treasury of the cathedral and robbed
the monasteries.[1]

Still the queen mother persevered, taking her counsel from the
chancellor L'Hôpital, the admiral Coligny, the prince of Condé,
and his brother, D'Andelot, and adhered to her resolution to permit the Huguenots to enjoy freedom of worship.   On January 3,
1562, the chancellor made an earnest plea for religious toleration
before the Court of Parlement,[2] which was followed by the
most decisive action the government had yet taken, namely the
issuance of the famous edict of toleration of January 17, known
as the Edict of January, which was the first that granted exercise
of the Reformed religion *in public*.[3]

[1] Claude Haton, I, 194, 195, and note.

[2] Chantonnay to Philip II, January 5, 1562, K. 1,497, B. 15.   The Spanish
ambassador violently expostulated with Catherine de Medici, Antoine of Bourbon,
and others after this address was over (K. 1,497, January 11, 1562), for which
Philip II commended him (K. 1,496, No. 34, 3 *verso*).

[3] Isambert, XIV, 124–29; Raynaldus, XXXIV, 292, 293.   The original document is on exhibition in the Musée des Archives at Paris.   It is catalogued
K. 674, No. 4.   Although authorized on January 17, the edict was not printed
until March 13, 1562 (*C. S. P. For.*, No. 930, §11; 934, §1).   The Edict of
July had been only negative in its character, simply forbidding judges and the
magistrates from pursuing the Huguenots, but not in any sense recognizing their
religion.   Castelnau, Book I, chap. ii, makes this very clear.   The Edict encountered strong opposition in the Parlement, which twice rejected it by a plurality
vote (*C. S. P. For.*, No. 849, January 28, 1562; Claude Haton, I, 185, 186).   Benoist,
Histoire de l'Edit de Nantes, I, Appendix, gives the text together with the
first and second mandamus of the King, February 14 and March 11, 1562, expressly enjoining the Parlement "to proceed to the reading, publishing, and regis-
tering of the said ordinance, laying aside all delays and difficulties."   The first
mandamus, "Déclaration et interprétation du roy sur certains mots et articles
contenus dans l'edict du XVII de janvier 1561," declared that magistrates were not
officers within the meaning of the edict (Isambert, XIV, 129, n. 2).   Klipfel,
Le colloque de Poissy, chap. iii, makes the point that the Parlement of Paris was
criminally wrong in arraigning itself upon the side of violence and encouraging the
intolerance of the populace.   The Parlement of Rouen was more complacent, and
seems promptly to have registered it (*C. S. P. For.*, No. 891, §10, February 16, 1562).

The Edict of January is sometimes wrongly dated January 17, *1561*.   The
error arises from the confusion of the calendar in the sixteenth century.   In 1561
the year in France legally began at Easter, which, of course threw January 17, into
the year 1561.   But in 1564 a royal *ordonnance* abolished this usage and estab-

This edict was expressly declared to be *provisional* in its nature, pending the decisions of the Council of Trent, which, by a coincidence, was opened on the day following, January 18, 1562, the first formal session being set for the second Thursday in Lent.[1] The preamble recited that the government's action was taken in consideration of the state of affairs prevailing in the kingdom; that it was not to be construed as approving the new religion; and that it was to remain in force no longer than the King should order; it deprecated the "disobedience, obstinacy, and evil intentions of the people" which made even provisional recognition of Calvinism necessary. Specifically, the edict provided for the restoration by the Huguenots of all property unlawfully possessed by them; it forbade them to *erect* any churches, either within or without the cities and towns (Art. 1) or to assemble for worship within the walls thereof either by day or night, or under arms (Arts. 2, 5). Protestant worship was required to be in the daytime, outside the town gates, in the open, or, if under cover, in buildings occasionally used, and not formally consecrated as churches. For this reason the Reformed ministers preached, some in the fields, others in gardens, old houses, and barns, according to their particular inclinations or convenience. For they were expressly forbidden to build any chapels, or meddle with the churches, upon any account. Access to their meetings was always to be permitted to the King's officers, i. e., bailiffs, seneschals, provosts, or their lieutenants, but *not* to officers of judicature (Arts. 3, 6; and supplementary declaration of interpretation, February 14, 1562). Furthermore, the raising of money among the Huguenots was to be wholly voluntary and not in the form of assessment or imposition. They were to keep the political laws of the Roman church, as to holidays and marriage, in order to

---

lished January 1 as the beginning of the year, which brought forward January 17 into its proper year, 1562. The reform of the calendar by Gregory XIII would alter the *date of the month* also, according to modern reckoning. But it is simpler to let established dates stand. Henry III authorized the use of the Gregorian calendar in France in 1582. For a lucid account of these changes see *Commentaires et lettres de Montluc*, IV, Introd., x–xi by the baron de Ruble.

[1] Baschet, *Journal du Concile de Trente*, 71.

avoid litigation and confusion of property rights; and to refrain from harboring any person who might be accused, prosecuted, or condemned by the government, under penalty of a fine of 1,000 crowns, to be devoted to charity, together with whipping and banishment (Arts. 8, 9, 12). The use of reproachful or vituperative language touching the faith or practice of the Catholic church was made a misdemeanor (Art. 10). Finally, all Protestant synods or consistories were required to be held by permission of or in presence of the lieutenant-general of the province concerned, or his representative, and the statutes of the churches were to be communicated to him (Art. 7, and supplementary declaration and interpretation of February 14, 1562).

In order to prevent seditions, an edict was sent to the judges of the towns, in the name of the King, by which the authorities were ordered to disarm all Catholics in their towns of every species of weapon and to make them deposit their arms in the local city hall or other common point, where they were to be kept under the guard of the *procureur* and the *échevins*.[1]

It is a question worthy of consideration, whether the preachings of the Reformed might not have been peaceably maintained after the Edict of January, the provisional form gradually being modified until complete religious toleration would have been secured, if Spain had not continued to tamper with French politics, and if the persistence of the political Huguenots had not continued to push things to such a point that at last the two causes, originally separate, became the obverse and reverse sides of the same issue and had to stand or fall together. On the other hand, had not these concessions of the crown been too long delayed? Was the edict "dead from birth," as Pasquier wrote?[2]

[1] Claude Haton, I, 177, and n. 1. For other details see Castelnau, Book III, chap. i; *Rel. vén.*, II, 71.

[2] *Lettres de Pasquier*, II, 96. Mignet characterizes the provisions of the Edict of January as "généréuses, simples, et sages." Mignet, "Les lettres de Calvin" (*Journal des savants*, 1859, p. 762), and Haag, *La France protestante*, Introd., xix, as "le plus libéral édit qui ait été obtenu par les réformés jusqu'à celui de Nantes."

CHAPTER VI

THE FIRST CIVIL WAR. THE MASSACRE OF VASSY (MARCH 1, 1562). THE SIEGE OF ROUEN

The progress of events had developed so rapidly as to bely the Edict of January almost as soon as it was passed. The continued absence of the Guises from the court made them open to suspicion, particularly as messengers were passing frequently between Joinville and St. Germain.[1] The nets of conspiracy woven by the Triumvirate were daily being drawn tighter around France. Directed by Chantonnay and the cardinal of Ferrara (who generally spoke in Spanish when together in public, that those near by might not understand),[2] the plans of the Triumvirate were concerted, the Spanish ambassador looking ahead to the day when force would supplant diplomacy.[3]

Ever since its formation, as we have seen, the Triumvirate had sought to win over the king of Navarre. As he was, therefore, sought by both parties, he was much inflated with a sense of his own importance. Antoine still lived in hope of compounding with Philip for the kingdom of Navarre, and to that end still negotiated both with the Vatican and with Spain.[4] But he was getting very tired of the procrastination of the Spanish king, so that there was danger of the thread of his patience being snapped.[5] If war

[1] *C. S. P. For.*, No. 789, §1, January 8, 1562, and cf. No. 750, §3, December 28, 1561. The importation of money from Germany into Lorraine was no secret.

[2] *Ibid.*, No. 729, §3, December 16, 1561. Catherine de Medici, however, could speak the language (*ibid.*, No. 2,155, December 3, 1571).

[3] *Ibid.*, No. 729, §3, December 16, 1561. Chantonnay was morally the leader of the Triumvirate, beyond a doubt, and guided its policy. "The king of Navarre, the duke of Guise, the constable, the cardinal of Ferrara, the marshals St. André, Brissac, and Termes, the cardinal Tournon, have joined together to overthrow the Protestant religion and exterminate the favorers thereof—*which enterprise is pushed forward by the Spanish ambassador here and Spanish threatenings.*"—*C. S. P. For.*, No. 934, §1, March 14, 1562.

[4] *Ibid.*, No. 758, §12, December 1; No. 531, §4, September 23, 1561.

[5] Antoine de Bourbon to Philip II December 7, 1561, K. 1,494, No. 116 (not in Rochambeau).

broke out in France and found him in such a mood, an attempt might possibly be made to overrun Navarre.[1] In consequence, it became necessary to make a more tangible proposition to the Bourbon prince. It took the form of a demand and a promise. The demand was that every Huguenot should be banished from court and the Protestant clergy expelled from the country together with the prince of Condé, the Châtillon brothers, the chancellor, and Montluc, the bishop of Valence. In return Antoine was to receive the "kingdom of Tunis" as a reward. This was the new prize used by Spain to bait the hook, and gradually Antoine was drawn over to the side of Spain and the Triumvirate. The amusing feature of this proffer was not so manifest to the men of that day as to us. Geographical knowledge, even of the Mediterranean coast, was hazy. The constable, for example, thought that Tunis was an island! But Antoine knew more history and geography than Montmorency; he knew that Tunis was a Turkish possession which Charles V had vainly tried to seize, and had to be beguiled with visions of oriental splendor and large plans for its conquest before he became passive. Pending its acquisition, Philip II renewed the offer of Sardinia. Meanwhile Antoine received instruction in the Catholic faith from a teacher recommended to him by the general of the Jesuits,[2] and quarreled with Jeanne d'Al-

[1] *Despatches of Michele Suriano* (Huguenot Society), October 18, 1561. The whole letter is exceedingly interesting.

[2] The Jesuits had long tried to get a legal status in France. Henry II, was favorable to them, but the Parlement of Paris, the secular clergy, and the Sorbonne were bitterly opposed. The Act of Poissy recognized the Jesuits as a college but not as a religious order, to the anger of the Sorbonne. See Douarche, *L'Université de Paris et les Jesuites*, Paris, 1888, chap. iv. At the time of the expulsion of the Jesuits from France in 1761, in reply to the question of the crown as to their legal status, the cardinal de' Choiseul made the following answer: "Lorsqu'ils ont été reçus en France l'an 1561, par le concours des deux puissances, ils se sont soumis et ont été astreints par la loi publique de leur établissement à toute superinten-dance, juridiction et correction de l'évêque diocésain et à se conformer entièrement à la disposition du droit commun, avec la renonciation la plus formelle aux pri-vilèges contraires portés dans les quatre bulles par eux présentées ou autres qu'ils pourraient obtenir à l'avenir." . . . . "*Le véritable état des Jésuites en France paraît donc être, suivant les lois canoniques reçues dans le royaume, l'état des réguliers soumis à la juridiction des ordinaires conformement au droit com-*

bret because she would not let the future Henry IV be taken to mass, or permit him to be present at the christening of the infant son of the Spanish ambassador.[1] By March (1562) it was evident that the king of Navarre was "never so earnest on the Protestant side as he was now furious on the other."[2]

But if the Spanish ambassador used smooth words to the king of Navarre, his language was quite otherwise toward Catherine de Medici. In the name of his sovereign he demanded the banishment of Jeanne d'Albret from court, the compulsory education of Henry of Navarre in the Catholic religion, and so soundly rated her for harboring Coligny and D'Andelot at court that the outraged queen mother demanded his retirement,[3] ordered the marshal St. André back to his government,[4] and the constable to retire to Chantilly, and contemplated doing the same with the old cardinal Tournon. This procedure offended Antoine who imputed her conduct to Coligny and his brother, and in consequence he inclined more than ever toward the Triumvirate.[5] Finally on Palm Sunday (March 22) Antoine cast the die and went to mass, coming from the service with the emblem of the celebration in his hand.[6]

A superficial aspect of peace still prevailed at court, but in the provinces a state of war already prevailed. Sens,[7] Abbeville,[8] Tours, Toulouse, Marseilles, Toul in Lorraine,[9] and most of all

mun." Cf. Eugene Sol, Les rapports de la France avec l'Italie, d'après la série K. des Arch. Nat., Paris, 1905, 119,120. The original document is in the Archives nationales, K. 1,361, N. 1, C.

[1] C. S. P. For., No. 934, §2, March 14, 1562.

[2] Ibid., No. 931, March 9, 1562.

[3] Ibid., No. 924, §8, March 6, 1562; cf. ibid., No. 715, §4, December 12, 1561: "The Spanish ambassador was wondrous hot with the queen."

[4] Lettres du cardinal de Ferrare, No. 14, March 3, 1562.

[5] C. S. P. For., No. 891, February 16, 1562.

[6] Corresp. de Chantonnay, K. 1,497, No. 17, March 25, 1562. This circumstance is noticed by almost all the chroniclers: D'Aubigné, Book V, chap. iii, 1; Mém. de Condé, I, 76, 77; Arch. cur., VI, 59.

[7] Claude Haton, I, 189.

[8] Beza, Histoire ecclés., I, 416.

[9] Collection Godefroy (Bibliothèque de l'Institut), Vol. XCVII, folio 19, March 6, 1562.

Cahors and Agen,[1] where the terrible Montluc figured, were all scenes of riot and bloodshed during the winter months, in which the Huguenots were generally worsted.[2] In Agen it was so bad that the government had to take more than ordinary notice of the situation.   Charles IX called upon the governor of Guyenne to repress "les excès, forces, violences, sacagements d'églises, séditions et escandalles advenus en nôtre pays d'Agenais," and ordered the consuls of the city to send him the names of those who disturbed the peace.

In this condition of things only a spark was needed to throw the whole country into flames.   Force alone could settle the irreconcilable conflict, and it was soon to be invoked.   War was certainly anticipated by both parties.   But contrary to expectation it was not precipitated by Spanish intervention, but by outbreak within France.   It was the massacre of Vassy on March 1, 1562, that threw the country into civil war.

The duke of Guise had spent the winter, as we have seen, working in the interest of the Triumvirate.   On February 15, 1562, he had a conference at Saverne with the duke of Württemberg, whom he adroitly persuaded into the belief that the Calvinists were aiming to involve the German Protestants in their own quarrel, thereby securing his neutrality in event of civil war.   Shortly after his return to France the duke left Joinville with the intention of rejoining the court.   As he was passing through Vassy,[3] his retinue encountered a Huguenot congregation worshiping in a barn outside of the town.   Though the service was strictly in conformity with the Edict of January, the sight angered the duke, whose followers fell upon the company, and the famous massacre ensued.   It was March 1, 1562.   How much provocation was made by the Protestants for this attack is a matter of dispute.   The duke himself and Catholic partisans ever since have asserted

[1] *Inventaire des archives communales d'Agen*, BB., "Inventaire sommaire," XXX, 28 (April 17, 1562).

[2] D'Aubigné, II, 7, gives a long list of cities where disturbances occurred.

[3] Vassy was a little town in the diocese of Châlons-sur-Marne, in a dependency of Joinville belonging to the Guises.

that stones were first thrown at him. Probably the absolute truth will never be known. Ranke, perhaps, sums up the verdict of history best in the statement that "whether the duke intended the massacre or not, it is enough that he did not prevent it."[1]

THE MASSACRE OF VASSY, MARCH 1, 1652
(Bib. Nat., Estampes. *Histoire de France*, Q. b.)

Two weeks later, on March 16, the duke of Guise, accompanied by the chief members of his house, save the cardinal of Lorraine and the duke of Elbœuf, arrived in Paris. The capital, which long since had learned the news of Vassy, received him joyfully.[2] At

---

[1] In the *Mémoires de Condé*, III, 124, there is an elaborate Protestant version of the massacre, preceded by a letter of the duke of Guise. The Guise account is in the *Mémoires du duc de Guise*, 471–88. Cf. D'Aubigné, 131; *Arch. cur.*, IV, 103. The Spanish ambassador's long letter of March 16 is in K. 1,497, No. 14. The quotation from Ranke is in his *Civil Wars and Monarchy in France*, 211.

[2] *Correspondance de Chantonnay*, March 20, 1562, K. 1,497, No. 16. Accounts of this event abound. See La Popelinière, I, 287; Claude Haton, I, 208; D'Aubigné, II, 10; a letter of Santa Croce in *Arch. cur.*, VI, 55; La Noue, *Mém.*

the St. Denis gate he was met by the constable and his four stalwart sons, the eldest of whom was governor of the city, the four marshals of France, and twenty-one knights of the Order. Having arrived at his hotel, the provost of the merchants, who was syndic of Paris, accompanied by many of the chief merchants, visited him, "testifying his joyful welcome," which was further attested by the proffer of two millions of gold in favor of the Catholic cause. The duke made an adroit reply, assuring them that the queen mother and the king of Navarre, with the aid and advice of the King's council, would pacify the realm; that he, as a faithful and loyal subject, must abide where the King commanded, and that he hourly expected a summons to court. On the same day the prince of Condé, returning from the court to Paris with the intention of going to Picardy, finding the duke of Guise in the capital, changed his plans and tarried in Paris, though offering to leave the town by one gate if the duke, the constable, and the marshal St. André would leave by the other.[1] When the Guises perceived that the Huguenots were undismayed by the events, they began to increase their adherents in the city, so that in a short time, it was thronged with nearly ten thousand horsemen. It was impossible, on the other hand, for the Huguenots to concert measures of defense in Paris, and accordingly the prince of Condé soon quitted the capital (March 23) "like another Pompey,"[2] going to Meaux, where Coligny and D'Andelot soon joined him.[3]

Meanwhile Catherine de Medici, fearful lest the person of the King would be forcibly seized by the Guises, and recognizing that

milit., ed. Petitot, 128—very interesting; and a letter of an eye-witness in Bull. de la Soc. de l'hist. du prot. franç., XIII, 5.

On March 16, 1562, an ordinance of the king of Navarre enjoined the captains and lieutenants of each quarter of Paris who were elected by the bourgeoisie to appoint ensigns, corporals, and sergeants, and to enlist all the men capable of bearing arms in their divisions, both masters and servants (Capefigue, 234, 235).

[1] L'Aubespine to his brother, the bishop of Limoges, French ambassador at Madrid (L'Ambassade de St. Sulpice, 22; C. S. P. Eng. For., No. 987, §7; manifesto of the prince of Condé to Elizabeth, April 7, 1562).

[2] This is D'Aubigné's comparison, II, 14, and n. 2.

[3] Delaborde, II, 48; Correspondance de Catherine de Médicis, I, 285, n.; C. S. P. For., No. 987, §12, March 31, 1562.

the king of Navarre had surrendered completely to the Triumvirate, endeavored to remove the King to Blois. But Antoine
hotly protested against so overt a move in favor of the Huguenots
and Spain's ambassador fulminated so strongly against "the evil
reputation" of L'Hôpital,[1] that the court was compelled to go to
Fontainebleau instead.[2] Even this place met with small favor
on the part of the Guises, who would have preferred keeping the
court in Paris. But when they urged the necessity of the queen's
presence in the council in consideration of the grave state of affairs,
Catherine caustically rejoined that she thought "it more meet to
have regard to the health of the King than to inform so many wise
men what was necessary to be done." This speech of the queen
mother, however, was not said altogether in sarcasm. For instead
of following the advice of the constable, who showed signs of
resenting the Guise ascendency, that the crown repudiate and
condemn the massacre of Vassy and announce its determination
to maintain the Edict of January,[3] Catherine in her alarm lest the
rising of the Huguenots sweep the Valois dynasty from the throne
began to incline toward Spain.[4] For the time being the Triumvirate professed itself satisfied, intending after Easter to compel
the court to repair to Bois de Vincennes, in order to have the King
in their midst and thus strengthen with his name the authority
of their actions.[5] Great was the alarm, therefore, when the prince
of Condé, accompanied by the admiral Coligny and D'Andelot,
appeared before the gates of Paris on March 29 with three thousand

---

[1] "La mala reputacion que el chancellerio ne quanto à la fé."—*Correspondance
de Chantonnay*, K. 1,497, No. 16, March 20, 1562.

[2] Tavannes, 271; *C. S. P. For.*, No. 943, March 20, 1652.

[3] Paris, *Négociations relatives au règne de François II*, 880.

[4] "Monsieur le conestable ayst d'opinion que l'on (fasse) une lètre patente par
laquelle le roy mon fils déclère qu'i ne voult poynt ronpre l'édist dernier. . . . . Ne
distes rien deset que je vous dis de l'ambassadeur (Chantonnay) qui ayst yci, mès
au contrère distes qu'i comense à se governer mieulx et plus dousement qu'i ne
solet en mon endroyt."—Catherine de Medici to St. Sulpice, *circa* April 11, 1562,
in *L'Ambassade de St. Sulpice*, 15, 16. This is a characteristic example of the
queen's eccentric spelling.

[5] D'Aubigné, II, 15.

horse.[1]   Immediately all the bridges were drawn up and preparations made to meet an attack.[2]   Already extraordinary arrangements had been made for the defense of Paris.   Strangers were
compelled to leave the city; no persons except gentlemen were
permitted to wear arms and these were limited to sword and
dagger; only six gates were open and these were under double
guard.[3]   Failing to enter the city, the prince quartered his troops
at St. Cloud and took possession of the highroad from Paris to
Orleans at Longjumeau, while in Paris the duke of Guise, the
king of Navarre, and the constable hastened forward the preparations for war.[4]   But the prince of Condé refrained from the use
of force.   He gave out that he had as much right to enter the city
under arms as had Guise, and complained of the fact that Guise
and his following, on March 27, which was Good Friday, had
visited the King and Queen at Fontainebleau, where the latter
"made them strange countenance because the train came in arms
to the court."[5]   The apparent purpose of the prince of Condé
was to cut Fontainebleau off from Paris, for the admiral lay at
Montreuil, but four leagues distant, and thus force a reasonable
settlement, or push matters to an extremity by making himself
master of the Loire, thus cutting France in twain and having all
Guyenne and Poitou and much of Languedoc at his back.   Color
was lent to this belief by the fact that so many men from the northern and eastern provinces were passing southward that a special
body of troops was set to guard the line of the Seine.[6]

[1] *L'Ambassade de St. Sulpice*, 22; C. S. P. For., No. 967, March 31, 1562.
Elizabeth wrote to Condé to "remember that in all affairs second attempts be even
more dangerous than the first."—C. S. P. For., No. 965, March 31, 1562.   On the
political theory of the Huguenots that the King was a captive and that they were
struggling for his relief, see Weill, 66.

[2] C. S. P. For., No. 969, March 31, 1562.

[3] *Correspondance de Chantonnay*, March 25, 1562, K. 1,497, No. 17.   He
reports also that a boat was captured coming down the Seine loaded with 4,000
arquebuses and other ammunition, all of which was taken to the Hôtel-de-Ville.

[4] *Correspondance de Chantonnay*, K. 1,497, No. 17, March 25, 1562.

[5] C. S. P. For., No. 967, §12, March 31, 1562.

[6] *Correspondance de Chantonnay*, April 2-4, K. 1,497, No. 18; April 11, *ibid.*,
No. 22.

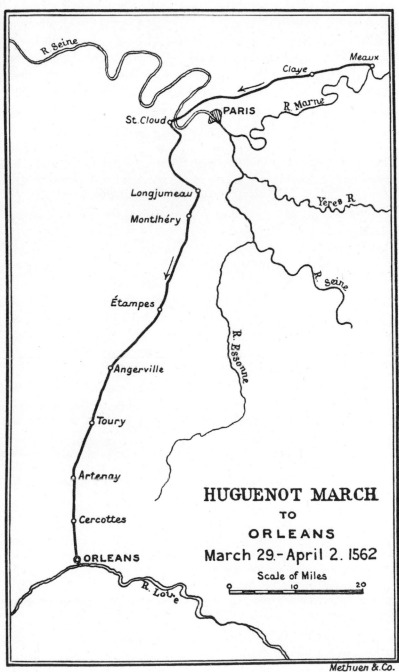

R. Seine

Meaux

Claye

R. Marne

St. Cloud

PARIS

Longjumeau

Yeres R.

Montlhéry

R. Seine

Étampes

R. Essonne

Angerville

Toury

Artenay

HUGUENOT MARCH

TO

Cercottes

ORLEANS

ORLEANS

March 29.-April 2. 1562

R. Loire

Scale of Miles

10   20

Methuen & Co.

But the Catholic leaders guessed Condé's purpose and by a *coup de main* seized the King and his mother and carried them off from Fontainebleau to Melun, a town strong enough to be withheld against any sudden enterprise. Thereupon the prince, perceiving that he had been outreached, marched toward Orleans[1] in spite of an order sent from the King, and undoubtedly inspired by Guise, that he should lay down his arms. An attempt to prevent him from reaching Orleans was blocked by a rapid advance of D'Andelot.

Meanwhile the constable had assumed the direction of affairs in Paris, where on April 5 the Huguenot house of worship near the Port St. Antoine was torn down, the pulpit, forms, and choir burned, and fragments carried away as souvenirs by the mob. Troops patrolled the streets, arresting suspects, and a house to house visitation was made in search of Calvinist preachers. The same day the court came to Bois de Vincennes. During the next few days vain overtures were made to the prince. Coligny and D'Andelot offered to meet the queen mother at such a place as she would appoint, provided the prince of Navarre, the future Henry IV, Damville, the constable's second son, and one of the Guises, were given into Orleans as hostages for them. Catherine was willing to accept the offer, but was overruled by Antoine of Bourbon, the duke of Guise, and Montmorency.[2] Those who were least alarmed still looked for settlement at the hands of the General Council. But there were serious political difficulties, as well as those religious, in the way of this, the three principal ones being: (1) the summons of the council, which many Catholics even wished to be convoked by the Emperor, and not by the Pope; (2) the place of the council; (3) the authority of the council, which many Catholics wished to be above the Pope.[3]

On April 12, 1562, at Orleans, the prince of Condé formally

---

[1] La Noue, *Mémoires*, chap. ii, has described this march.

[2] *Correspondance de Chantonnay*, April 8 and 11, 1562, K. 1,497, Nos. 21, 22.

[3] *C. S. P. Ven.*, No. 283.

assumed command of the Huguenot forces,[1] his chief lieutenants being the admiral Coligny and D'Andelot.[2] The first civil war was a reality. The city on the Loire for some years to come was destined to be the capital of the Protestants, dominating all the surrounding country. Blois and its château, Tours and its castle, Amboise, Saumur, Angers, and many other towns on the Loire and in Maine, were occupied by the Protestants. Orleans was reputed to have bread and wine enough in store to withstand a two years' siege,[3] and the Huguenots seemed to have plenty of money for immediate necessities, thanks to their despoilment of the churches of the region, especially the rich abbey of Marmoutier.[4] Although the purposes of the Huguenots were clandestinely more political than religious, it was expedient to cloak them under a mantle of faith.[5] The political organization of the Huguenots was effected through the medium of an association, a form of organization of which there are many examples, both Protestant and Catholic, during this troubled period. The preamble of the instrument of government disclaimed any private motives or considerations on the part of those who were parties to the association, and asserted that their sole purpose was to liberate the King from "captivity" and punish the insolence and tyranny of the disloyal and the enemies of the church. Idolatry, blasphemy, violence, and robbery, were forbidden within the territory of the

[1] According to Hotman who had left Orleans on May 29, the Huguenot forces consisted of 15,000 foot and 5,000 horse.—Letter to the landgrave, June 7, 1562, in *Rev. hist.*, XCVII March–April, 1908, p. 304.

[2] Condé had entered Orleans on April 2. On the 7th he wrote to the Reformed churches of France, requiring men and money in the interest of the deliverance of the King and the queen mother and the freedom of the Christian religion (*Mémoires de Condé*, II, 212).

[3] *Correspondance de Chantonnay*, April 11, 1562, K. 1,497, No. 22.

[4] *Ibid.*, No. 21, April 8, 1562; De Ruble's edition of D'Aubigné, II, 18–20; C. S. P. For., No. 997, April 10, 1562; No. 1,043, §2, April 24, 1562. Cf. Boulanger, "La réforme dans la province du Maine," *Revue des Soc. savant. des départ.*, 2e sér., VII (1862), 548.

[5] "Leurs desseins cachés ont autre racine que celle de la religion, encores qu'ils le veuillant couvrir de ce manteau."—Catherine de Medici to St. Sulpice, *L'Ambassade de St. Sulpice*, 59, August 9, 1562.

association, in order that all might know that it had "the fear of God before it." The association was to expire after the King had attained his majority.[1]

The essential difficulties in the situation as it obtained at this time are manifest. The Huguenots declared the King to be a captive in the hands of the Guises and themselves claimed to be loyal subjects in rebellion against tyranny.[2] The Guises, on the other hand, branded the Huguenots as rebels and schismatics, although Catherine de Medici still had a lingering hope of restoring peace, and in official utterances carefully refrained from alluding to the prince of Condé as a rebel.[3] Neither side would agree to lay down its arms without the other doing likewise, and neither dared take the initiative in this matter. The situation, therefore, was an irreconcilable one, which nothing but war could settle. The political determinations of the Huguenots were quite as fixed as their religious convictions, for part of their platform was the article agreed upon by the estates at Orleans to the effect that the cardinal of Lorraine, the duke of Guise, the constable, and the marshals Brissac and St. André, should render an account of their stewardship.[4] How far politics governed the situation is evidenced by the fact that late in April the king of Navarre and Montmorency began to weaken in their attitude when it was known that Condé dominated the middle Loire country, Touraine, Maine, Anjou,

---

[1] "Déclaration faicte par monsieur le prince de Condé, pour monstrer les raisons qui l'ont contrainct d'entreprendre la défense de l'authorité du roy, du gouvernement de la royne, et du repos de çe royaume" (Orleans, 1562); cf. *C. S. P. For.*, No. 1,003, Orleans, April 1, 1562.

The prince of Condé is said to have issued a coinage of his own at this time with the superscription, "Louis XIII." Chantonnay, however, says that they were medals (K. 1,497, No. 27, May 2, 1562). See the memoir of Secousse: "Dissertation où l'on examine s'il est vrai qu'il ait été frappé, pendant la vie de Louis Ier, prince de Condé, une monnie sur laquelle on lui ait donné le titre de roi de France," *Mém. de l'Acad. roy. des inscrip. et bell. lettres*, XVII (1751); Poulet, *Correspondance du cardinal de Granvelle*, III, 85. Whitehead, *Gaspard de Coligny*, 303, is convinced the story is a fabrication.

[2] *Correspondance de Chantonnay*, April 11, 1562, K. 1,497, No. 22.

[3] K. 1,497, No. 21, April 8, 1562.

[4] *C. S. P. For.*, No. 1,013, §12, April 17, 1562.

and much of Normandy; when it was learned that the cities of Lyons,[1] Toulouse, Caen, Rouen,[2] Dieppe, Troyes, Bourges,[3] and the provinces of Dauphiné, Provence, and Poitou, had declared for the Huguenot cause; and when troops were pouring into Orleans by thousands.[4]

If the Guises and the marshals Brissac and St. André could have acquitted themselves with so little discredit as Antoine of Bourbon or the constable, it is possible that a compromise might have been made even yet.[5] But such an issue was impossible under the circumstances. The guilt of Vassy still hung over the duke, for he had not yet been absolved either by the Court of Parlement or by the peers of France. Having appealed to force, force re-

[1] *Archives curieuses*, sér. I, IV, 175.

[2] Rouen was taken in the night of April 15. Floquet, *Histoire du parlement de Normandie*, II, 380.

[3] Raynal, *Histoire du Berry*, IV, 35.

[4] The stopping of the couriers in the service of Spain by the Huguenots was a source of great anxiety to Chantonnay. April 8 he wrote to Philip advising that the couriers be sent via Perpignan and Lyons in order to avoid being intercepted, as the Huguenots commanded the whole line of the Loire. Cf. Letters to Philip II, April 24, 1562, K. 1,497, No. 25; K. 1,497, No. 21; K. 1,497, No. 28.

His letter of May 5 (K. 1,497, No. 28) describes the adventure of a courier bearing a dispatch of the bishop of Limoges. He was given twenty blows with a knife, but managed to escape. St. Sulpice reports a similar experience of "le chevaucher de Bayonne" in a letter to Catherine, June 30, 1562. D'Andelot intercepted a letter from the duke of Alva (K. 1,497, No. 26, April 28, 1562) and the prince of Condé one from the bishop of Limoges to Catherine de Medici (K. 1,497, No. 33). The activity of the Huguenots in Gascony gave the French and Spanish governments special disquietude because they continually overhauled the couriers bearing official dispatches between Paris and Madrid. The letters of St. Sulpice contain many complaints because of the rifling of his correspondence (see pp. 30, 35, 37, 38, 41, 59). But the Huguenots were not the only ones who scrutinized letters unduly. Philip II frequently asked to be shown the letters of Charles IX and his mother to his wife, so that St. Sulpice advised Catherine always to send two letters, one of which was to be a "dummy" to be shown to the King (*L'Ambassade de St. Sulpice*, 136). The Spanish ambassador told Philip he would have to come out into the open and declare war to protect his own interests (K. 1,497, No. 26, April 25, 1562). He anticipated as early as this the probable combination of the French Huguenots and the Dutch rebels, and warned Margaret of Parma to be on her guard (*Correspondance de Chantonnay*, K. 1,497, Nos. 30, 33, to Philip II).

[5] *C. S. P. For.*, No. 1,043, §2, April 24, 1562.

mained the only method of settling the great dispute that divided France, and Guise daily assembled horse and foot in Paris in expectation of battle.[1]

The formidable nature of the Huguenot rising by this time had so increased the fear of Catherine de Medici that she completely surrendered to the Triumvirate and resolved to appeal to Spain for help. On April 19 she sent for Antoine of Navarre, the duke of Guise, the constable, and the two marshals, Brissac and St. André, to whom she declared that she had been badly advised hitherto, and that she now trusted to their support. Montmorency at once proposed to ask the nuncio to petition His Holiness to send money and troops to the help of Catholic France. But Spain, not Rome, was the political cornerstone of the Catholic world, and it was now that the momentous resolution was taken to invite Philip II to lend assistance. Catherine de Medici, who shortly before this time had looked upon the prospect of Spanish intervention with apprehension, was now in favor of it. At Catherine's instance the Triumvirate formally invited Spain's support in a joint letter which was accompanied by Antoine of Navarre's written profession of the Catholic faith.[2] Two weeks later, May 8, Charles IX himself formally solicited military assistance of Philip II.[3]

---

[1] On April 24 the cardinal of Lorraine came to Paris with 1,000 horse (C. S. P. For., No. 1,043, §11, April 24, 1562; Corresp. de Chantonnay, April 28, K. 1,497, No. 2).

[2] This famous document, which is dated April 21, 1562, is in K. 1,496, B, 14, No. 61, and is on exhibition in the Musée des Archives. Chantonnay's letter to Philip II on April 24 sheds an interesting light on the situation. In it the ambassador advises the King to write personally to the queen mother, but not to write individually to the others, but rather a single letter, because if Antoine of Navarre were not addressed as King of Navarre he would refuse to receive it, whereas if the letter were written to all in common, this complication might be avoided (K. 1,497, No. 25).

[3] The Spanish King acceded to this request on June 8, 1562 (Philip II to Margaret of Parma; Gachard, Correspondance de Philippe II sur les Pays-Bas, II, 218-23.

He promised to send 10,000 foot and 3,000 cavalry, chiefly Italians and Germans; cf. De Ruble, Antoine de Bourbon et Jeanne d'Albret, IV, 214. At about the same time the constable appealed to Rome through Santa Croce, for a loan of 200,000 écus and a body of soldiers (Arch. cur., VI, 86).

Catholic Switzerland[1] Catholic Germany,[2] Savoy, the Pope,[3] and other princes of Italy were also looked to.[4]   The queen mother

[1] The Swiss Diet, which met at Soleure on May 22, offered 6,000 infantry to be commanded by the captain Froelich (Letter of Hotman in *Revue hist.*, XCVII, March–April, 1908, 305).

[2] *C. S. P. For.*, No. 6, §1, May 2, 1562.   The Spanish ambassador was deeply incensed at Catherine for making this new overture.   The intermediary was the Rhinegrave, but Chantonnay persuaded the leaders not to recognize him (*Corresp. de Chantonnay*, April 28, 1562; K. 1,497, No. 26).   The duke of Savoy offered to furnish 10,000 footmen and 600 horse, 3,000 of the former and 200 of the latter to be at his expense.   This was the fruit of Chantonnay's interview with Moreta, the Savoyard ambassador, early in April, when he discussed with him a possible restoration of the fortresses in Piedmont (K. 1,497, No. 21, April 8, 1562).

[3] The Pope offered to give 50,000 crowns per month.

[4] "Suisses, lansquenetz et reystres, seront en ce pays devant la fin de ce moys, sans vostre secours d'Espagne."—*L'Ambassade de St. Sulpice*, 24, June 12, 1562. It must be understood that in many European states, especially those of Germany, the maintenance of regular troops did not yet obtain as a practice.   Instead, the princes depended upon mercenary forces recruited by some distinguished captain. These troops, which answered to the *condottieri* of Italy were called *Lanzknechts* or *Reiters*.   Languet stigmatizes this practice in *Epist. ad Camerariam*, 28; cf. *Arch. d'Orange-Nassau*, I, 104.   In Protestant Germany there was a feeling that the policy of France threatened to extinguish the gospel in other regions besides France and therefore should be opposed by common consent.   The elector palatine, the landgrave, and Charles, margrave of Baden, planned to send an embassy into France in the name of the Protestant princes to allay the dissensions there, and to ask that the same liberty of religion might be granted as was allowed by the edict of January 17.   Many advocated an open league between all the Protestant states for mutual protection, in the hope that the mere knowledge of such a league would restrain their adversaries (*C. S. P. For.*, No. 11, May 2, 1562).   Opinion was divided in Germany as to whether Condé also should make foreign enrolments, or whether the territories of those who had suffered these levies to be made should be invaded by the Lutherans.   Agents of the Guises circulated a printed apology for the massacre at Vassy (D'Aubigné, II, 16, and n. 2; La Popelinière, I, 327).

Rambouillet and D'Oysel, the agents of France in these countries (St. Sulpice, 77; *Corresp. de Catherine de Médicis*, I, 364) made much of the King of Spain's aid and carried credentials from Chantonnay.   The duke of Guise even sent an agent, the count of Roussy, to England, to discover Elizabeth's intentions, and to ascertain the military state of her kingdom (cf. Beza, *Hist. des églises réformées*, ed. of Toulouse, I, 373; De Ruble, IV, 103 ff.; *L'Ambassade de St. Sulpice*, 13; *C. S. P. For.*, No. 1,037, April 21, 1562).

The argument of the Catholics with the German Protestant princes and imperial cities was that the Huguenots were political dissidents and rebels, and that religion was a pretext with them (*L'Ambassade de St. Sulpice*, 65).   In order to counteract this teaching the Huguenots circulated a pamphlet written by Hot-

did not know that already the Triumvirate had anticipated her request by asking the Spanish King to instruct the regent of Flanders

man throughout the Rhine provinces which attempted to neutralize the differences between Calvinism and Lutheranism. (This curious pamphlet is printed in *Mém. de Condé*, II, 524; La Popelinière, I, 325. In this capacity Hotman was invaluable. Some of his letters at this time are in *Mém. de l'Acad.*, CIV, 662–65.)

The German princes as a whole tried to prevent soldiers from going out of Germany. The landgrave Philip of Hesse arrested an officer of cavalry who was secretly enlisting horsemen in Hesse and who said he was doing so for Roggendorf, tore up the officer's commission before his face, and made him swear to leave his castle without a passport. The duke of Württemberg also took care that no volunteers should march through Montbéliard into France, and Strasburg forbade anyone to enlist under severe penalties. The bishops of the Rhine kept quiet; only in Lorraine and the Three Bishoprics was Catholic enlisting unimpeded. The recruiting-sergeant of the Guises in Germany was the famous Roggendorf, a Frisian by birth who had been driven out of his native land in 1548 and since then had lived the life of an adventurer, part of the time in Turkey. (See an interesting note in Poulet, I, 542, with references.) On April 8 the king of Navarre in the name of Charles IX, signed a convention with him engaging the services of 1,200 German mounted pistoleers and four cornettes of footmen of 300 men each (D'Aubigné, II, 33, n.). These forces entered France late in July and reached the camp at Blois on August 7 (D'Aubigné, II, 76, n. 3).

One reason why the Protestant princes of Germany were unable immediately to make strong protest to the French crown was that the envoys of the elector palatine, the dukes of Deuxponts and Württemberg, the landgrave of Hesse and the margrave of Baden, were unprovided for a month with letters of safe conduct, by the precaution of the Guises, with the result that Roggendorf led 1,200 cavalry in the first week in May across the Rhine and through Trèves into France for the Guises, though the Protestant princes did all they could to hinder the passage and expostulated with the bishops of Trèves and Cologne for allowing them to be levied in their territories. Failing greater things, the Protestant princes of Germany, in July, 1562, put Roggendorf under the ban in their respective states (cf. *C. S. P. For.*, Nos. 244 and 269, June 13 and July, 1562). In the end, despite the enterprise of the Guises, the French Catholics may be said to have been unsuccessful beyond the Rhine, that is in Germany proper, but not in Switzerland or the episcopal states. D'Oysel, who was sent by Charles IX in July to Heidelberg (D'Aubigné, II, 97, and n. 1; Le Laboureur, I, 430) received a short and definite answer "which showed him how groundless were his hopes of aid from that quarter, a document to which so much importance was attributed that it was forthwith printed for wider circulation" (*C. S. P. For.*, No. 414, August 3, 1562, and the Introduction, xi).

The king of Spain's captains had money and were ordered that as soon as soldiers were taken from Germany into France they should enlist men for the defense of his territories (*C. S. P. For.*, No. 11, May 2, 1562). In the bishopric of Trèves soldiers were enrolled easily, as the passage from thence to France was short (*ibid.*, No. 74, May 19, 1562).

In Switzerland the Huguenots endeavored to prevail upon the Protestant

to hold the troops there in readiness "because Madame de Parma would not let a single horse go out of Flanders without orders."[1] By the end of June these troops were ready. They were almost all Spaniards and Italians, then universally regarded as the best soldiers in the world.[2] Philip II, though, was actuated by other motives besides zeal for Catholicism.[3] He feared lest the south of France might attack Navarre, owing to the identification of Jeanne d'Albret with the Huguenot cause, and so sent reinforcements to Fontarabia and Pampeluna; a movement which weakened the prince of Condé by preventing Grammont's Gascon troops from going to Orleans.[4]

The war went forward in spite of lack of funds on both sides. In order to pay the expenses of the war in Brittany Catherine authorized the seizure of the plate in the churches. But the duke of Etampes, who was governor of Brittany, was cautious about carrying out this order. "The people are so religious and scrupu-

---

cantons to prevent the Catholic cantons from lending support to Guise (*C. S. P. Ven.*, No. 285, April 29, 1562). The Guises asked for a levy of foot from the papist cantons of Switzerland in the King's name (*Corresp. de Catherine de Médicis*, I, 289, April 8, 1562). The cantons promised to send 15 ensigns; but the Protestant cantons especially Bern, told the prince of Condé that they would not suffer any soldiers to be levied against him in their territory, on pain of confiscation of goods. Nevertheless the Catholic Swiss managed to make some enrolments, the men quitting home on July 8. On August 7 these mercenaries arrived at Blois, having come by way of Franche Comté (De Thou, Book XXX). They were commanded by Captain Froelich (see D'Aubigné, II, 148; Zurlauben, *Hist. milit. des Suisses*, IV, 287 ff.; Letter of Hotman in *Rev. hist.*, XCVII, March–April, 1908, 307).

[1] *Correspondance de Chantonnay*, K. 1,497, No. 22.

[2] "La fleur du monde."—*L'Ambassade de St. Sulpice*, 41. For details see *ibid.*, 24, 26–29, 36–38, 41, 50–54; *Correspondance du cardinal de Ferrare*, Letter 40, July 3, 1562; D'Aubigné, II, 91, and n. 2; Ruble, *Antoine de Bourbon et Jeanne d'Albret*, 220.

[3] St. Sulpice was dubious of Philip II's purpose and suspected political designs "sous le titre de notre secours" (*L'Ambassade de St. Sulpice*, 39). Nevertheless he believed in Philip's methods of repression—even the Inquisition. See his letter to the French ambassador at Trent on p. 28.

[4] *C. S. P. For.*, No. 46, §3, May 11; No. 86, §1, May 23, 1562. Cf. No. 248— Challoner to Elizabeth from Bilboa, June 24, 1562. Spain established a naval base at La Réole to help Noailles, lieutenant of the King in Guyenne (*L'Ambassade de St. Sulpice*, 61).

lous in these things," he wrote, "that if they found out that we wanted to take it, they would not readily endure it, especially in Lower Brittany." Instead he advised that the plate of the churches be deposited in some principal town in each bishopric, "under color of retaining and guarding it there, and that a tax of from 15 to 20 livres be imposed upon each person for this purpose, figuring that this expedient would produce from 15 to 20,000 livres.[1] The Huguenots let no money pass from the provinces under their control, even going so far as to destroy the government registers in the towns they took.[2]

Every day increased the interest of the populace in the struggle.[3] "If the prince of Condé should come to Paris," wrote an Englishman in Paris, "they could not tarry there, on account of the fury of his soldiers and the populace."[4] In Dauphiné, De la Mothe Gondrin, lieutenant of the duke of Guise, was slain at Valence by the Protestants. It is just to say, however, that he was the aggressor. Accompanied by sixty or eighty gentlemen he went out into the country and came upon a worshiping company of Calvinists "and left not one of them alive." A Huguenot nobleman, Des Adresse who styled himself "lieutenant of the King in Dauphiné," acquired a reputation in the region as sinister as that of Montluc in Gascony. The whole southeast of France seemed up in arms.[5] Grenoble, Macon in Burgundy, Châlons in Cham-

---

[1] *Correspondance de Chantonnay*, K. 1,497, No. 21, April 8, 1562; *C. S. P. Eng. For.*, No. 1,058, April 27, 1562; *ibid.*, No. 6, §2, May 2, 1562.

[2] *Correspondance de Chantonnay*, K. 1,497, No. 33, May 2, 1562. Philip has commented on the margin to the effect that if the Catholics were as active as the Huguenots they would be better off.

[3] Chantonnay particularly notices this in a dispatch of April 18, 1562, K. 1,497. So also does the Tuscan ambassador (*Nég. Tosc.*, III, 481, June, 1562). Traveling in France was dangerous (Windebank to Cecil, *C. S. P. Dom.*, XXII, 53, April 8, 1562).

[4] *C. S. P. Dom.*, XXII, 60, April 17, 1562. Paris wore red and yellow ribbons—the Guise colors. "Ceux de Paris disent publiquement qu'on doit renvoyer la reine en Italie et qu'ils ne veulent plus avoir de roi qui ne soit catholique. Ils en ont d'ailleurs un que Dieu leur a donné, c'est le grand 'roi de Guise.'" Letter of Hotman in *Rev. hist.*, XCVII, March–April, 1908, 305.

[5] D'Aubigné, Book II, chap. iv.

pagne, Moulins in Bourbonnais, where they destroyed the tombs
of Antoine's ancestors,[1] were taken by the Huguenots. Lyons, by
reason of its proximity to Geneva, was radically Huguenot, and
this sentiment was stimulated still more by the great discontent
that prevailed among the lower classes, engaged in silk manufacturing and other industries.[2]   In Normandy it was even worse.
At Rouen the Huguenots routed the Catholics and seized the
government.[3]   On May 14 Maligny took Havre-de-Grace, which
astonished and affrighted the Catholics because it stood at the
mouth of the Seine and made open communication between the
Huguenots and the English easy.   At Caen,[4] Bayeux, and most
places in Lower Normandy, the inhabitants defaced the images
in the monasteries and parish churches, and arrested the King's
revenues coming to Paris.[5]   Caudebec, which revolted on May
15, was besieged by the Guisards, but had placed men in it pre-
viously and so saved itself.   In Dieppe, where the revolt followed
hard upon news of Vassy, a conflict between Protestants and
Catholics resulted in the death of 150 persons.[6]   Terrible cruelties
were committed at Angers[7] by the Protestants.

Amid this almost spontaneous insurrection involving provinces
widely separated from one another, the Ile-de-France and Burgundy adhered to the crown and the Catholic cause, the former
wholly from inclination, the latter in part because of the adroitness

[1] *Correspondance de Chantonnay*, K. 1,497, No. 36, May 28, 1562.

[2] The importance of Lyons so near the cantons of Switzerland and Geneva
is emphasized in *Nég. Tosc.*, III, 488, July 6, 1562.

[3] *Correspondance de Chantonnay*, April 24, 1562, K. 1,497, No. 25.   On the
situation in Rouen, see *Mém. de Condé*, III, 302 ff.; and the diary of a citizen in
Revue retrospective, V, 97.   Montgomery who was in western Normandy about
Vire sent the King's letter back to him after polluting it with filth, at least so says
Chantonnay, K. 1,497, No. 27, May 2, 1562.

[4] See Carel, *Histoire de la ville de Caen sous Charles IX, Henri III et Henri
IV*, Caen, 1886.

[5] The duke of Bouillon, commandant of Caen Castle, made an attempt to
restrain the populace (*C. S. P. For.*, No. 303, §7, July 12, 1562).   He posed as a
neutral, but ultimately became a Huguenot.

[6] *C. S. P. For.*, No. 101, May 27, 1562.

[7] *Ibid.*, No. 68, May 18, 1562; cf. No. 69, §10.

of Tavannes, the brilliant captain, who foiled the Huguenot assault upon Dijon,[1] and saved Châlons-sur-Saône.[2]

In spite of these occurrences, however, abortive negotiations for peace filled the ten days between the 18th and the 28th of May.[3] In Paris it was expected that Condé would attack the city. The government's force was not sufficient to take the field, and twenty-five pieces of artillery were paraded through the streets to make an impression and to induce the clergy and Parisians to contribute money for this religious war-making.[4] Popular opinion in Paris was bitterly hostile to the Huguenots, but the bourgeois were not inclined to go down into their pockets and so, when the cowardly king of Navarre published a proclamation on May 26[5] expelling all Protestants from Paris and leaving their goods at the mercy of their adversaries, it was hailed with delight by the capital. Mobs of Catholics forcibly expelled Huguenots from the city and destroyed their goods. The city was so full of men-at-arms, highwaymen, and robbers at this time that every householder was required to keep a light in his street window until daybreak.[6]

[1] C. S. P. For., No. 69, §16, May 18, 1562.

[2] Forbes, II, 8; cf. Planche, Histoire de Bourgogne, IV, 556.

[3] Upon these negotiations see Mém. de Condé, III, 384, 388, 392, 393, 395.

[4] C. S. P. For., No. 106, §2, May 28, 1562. The King's army had but twenty-two pieces of artillery at the beginning of the first civil war (Rel. vén., II, 101).

[5] C. S. P. For., No. 107, May 28, 1562; No. 174, June 9; Mém. de Condé, III, 462. Another edict of the King put the military government of Paris in the hands of the provost of the merchants and the échevins of the city ("Déclaration portant permission au Prévost des Marchands et aux Echevins de la Ville de Paris, d'établir ès Quartiers d'icelle, des Capitaines, Caporaux, Sergents des Bandes, et autres Officiers Catholiques. A Monceaux, le 17 May 1562;" also in Ordonnances de Charles IX, par Robert Estienne, fol. 187; Mém. de Condé, III, 447]), in compliance with a popular request made a week earlier; "Ordonnance du Roy, donnée en conséquence de la Requête des Habitans de Paris, par laquelle il leur est permis de faire armes ceux qui dans cette Ville sont en état de portes les armes, et d'en former des Compagnies, sous des Capitaines qui seront pas eux choises," May 10, 1562 (Mém. de Condé, III, 422, 423). The Venetian ambassador wisely observed "Perciochè dar liberamente l'armi in mano ad un populo cosi grande e cosi furiosi, benchè fosse cattolico, non era farse cosa molto prudente."—Rel. vén., II, 98; cf. Nég. Tosc., III, 280.

[6] See Chantonnay's letter to Philip II of May 28, inclosing the edict and giving these and other details, K. 1,497, No. 36.

Risings in many parts of the country continued to be heard of;[1] Vendôme, La Charité, Auxerre, Montargis, Poitiers, together with most of the towns of Saintonge and Angoumois,[2] either declared for the prince of Condé or were taken by him. But at Toulouse the Huguenots suffered heavily.[3] In Normandy, there was great fear of English intervention.[4]

Overtures for peace came to nothing because the Huguenots made the withdrawal of the Triumvirate a condition precedent to their laying down of arms.[5] The prince contended that he could not be secure unless the duke of Guise, the constable, and the marshal St. André retired from the court. The queen mother in reply represented that it was not right, during the King's minority, to remove from him such important personages; that the Catholics

[1] "Cependant tout se ruyne et se font tous les jours infiniz meurdres et saccagemens de part et d'autre . . . . vous verrez par les chemyn's une partye de la pitié qui y est, et ce royaume au plus callamiteux estat qu'il est possible."—L'Aubespine à l'Evêque de Limoges, June 10, 1562; *L'Ambassade de St. Sulpice,* 22.

[2] Chaumet, "Procès-verbal des titres et ornements brûlés par les protestants," *Les protestants et le Cathédrale d'Angoulême en 1562,* in *Bull de la Soc. arch., etc.* 4e sér., VI, 1868–69 (Angoulême, 1870), 497.

Gellibert des Seguins, *Aubeterre en 1562;* "Enquête sur le passage des protestants en cette ville, le pillage de l'église Saint-Jacques et la destruction des titres et papiers du chapitre," *Bull. de la Soc. arch., etc.,* 1862, 3e sér., IV (Angoulême, 1864).

[3] The strife in Toulouse was occasioned by an edict of the parlement of Toulouse (May 2) forbidding Calvinist worship and the wearing of arms by the Huguenots (K. 1,495, No. 35; a printed copy of the edict). Both parties fought for three days for possession of the Hôtel-de-Ville where arms were stored. Nearly 5,000 Protestants, it is said, were killed (*Corresp. de Chantonnay,* 1497, No. 36, May 28, 1562; *Commentaires de Montluc,* Book V, 234-37, La Popelinière (who saw it), I, 311 ff.; D'Aubignè, Book II, chap. iv; *Lettres du cardinal de Ferrare,* No. 30, June 23, 1562; cf. *Histoire véritable de la mutinerie, tumulte et sedition faite par les prestres de St. Medard contre les Fideles, le Samedy XXVII juin de 1562;* Bosquet, *Histoire sur les troubles advenus en la ville de Tolose, l'an 1562, le dix-septiesme may,* Nouv. édition, avec notes, Paris, 1862; *Histoire de la délivrance de la ville de Toulouse,* 1862.

[4] Stanclift, *Queen Elizabeth and the French Protestants (1559–60),* Leipzig, 1892.

[5] *Coll. des lettres autographes,* Hotel Drouot, March 18, 1899, No. 19; Cardinal Châtillon to the queen mother, May 28, 1562, protesting that peace is impossible without the banishment of the Guises from court. Cf. *R. Q. H.,* January 1879, 14, 15.

in Paris had taken up arms to oppose the Edict of January, and
that if the Huguenot soldiery would retire to their homes they might
live there as they liked, while a council (of which he should be
a member) considered some better means of settlement.[1] Gradually the hostile armies—the prince of Condé at the head of the
Huguenots and the duke of Guise, the constable, the marshal
St. André and the recreant king of Navarre with the Catholic host
—drew near to each other.[2] An attempt was made to take Jargeau,
eight miles from Orleans; but fearing lest its capture would cut
supplies off from Orleans, Coligny and D'Andelot destroyed the
bridge there. This forced the Catholic captains to change their
intention, and they traversed the Beauce so as to surprise Beaugency, fourteen miles from Orleans, midway between Orleans and
Blois, where there was a bridge across the river. On June 15 the
two forces arrived near the bridge at almost the same time and a
fight seemed imminent. The two armies were about five miles
apart, and about the same distance from Orleans. Both being
south of the Loire, there was no river to hinder an engagement.
There were many vineyards between them, which was an advantage
to the prince, who had more infantry than cavalry, while Guise

[1] "Tous jours sur le point que messieurs de Guise, conestable et mareschal
de St. André se retirent de la cour."—L'Aubespine, sécretaire d'état à son frère M.
de Limoges, ambassadeur en Espagne, June 10, 1562; *L'Ambassade de St. Sulpice*,
22; cf. the same to the same, June 12, p 24. On these unsuccessful negotiations,
see D'Aubigné, II, 33–35; La Popelinière, I, 323; *Mém. de. Condé*, 489; La Noue,
Mém., Book I, chap. ii; Ruble, *Antoine de Bourbon et Jeanne d'Albret*, IV,
chap. xix.

Condé further justified the revolt of the Huguenots on the ground that the
King and his mother were "prisoners" in the hands of the Triumvirate, but the
statement was too transparent to be believed. Catherine herself, in order to dis-
prove it, took the King to Monceaux with her (*Corresp. de Chantonnay*, May 28,
1562, K. 1,497, No. 36), whence she wrote to the Parlement of Paris explaining the
reason of her action. The Parlement promptly approved her course. *Mém.-
journaux du duc de Guise*, 495, col. 2: "Acte par lequel la Reinemère et le Roy
de Navarre declarent que la retraite voluntaire que font de la cour du duc de
Guise, le Connestable et le mareschal de St. André, ne pourra porter préjudice à
leur honneur" (May 28, 1562).

[2] "Nostre camps et à douse lyeu d'Orleans et byentot nous voyront set que
en sera."—Catherine de Medici to Elizabeth of Spain, June 13 or 14, 1562, in
L'Ambassade de St. Sulpice, 31.

had 7,000 horse, D'Aumale having come from Normandy with his force. The Catholic forces were divided: Guise lay north of the river, beyond Beaugency, Paris-ward; D'Aumale's detachment was on the other side of the river at Clerie, midway between Orleans and Beaugency, having the town and the bridge in his hands; while Navarre was established at Vernon, a league from Beaugency.[1]

The condition of the country around Orleans at this time, considering that a state of war existed, was not bad. Condé had plenty of money for the moment, having secured the riches of the churches of Bourges. Food was good and plentiful in Orleans and bread was cheap. Everything the Huguenots took they paid for, as a matter of policy,[2] although large funds were not in sight and they looked anxiously to England for 100,000 crowns, offering the notes of the leaders as security or else the bonds of some of the most notable Reformed churches, as Rouen and Lyons. The Huguenot army made a brave display. Many of the gentlemen were rich and wore long white coats (casaque blanche) of serge, kersey, or stramell, after the old manner, with long sleeves over their armour.[3]   The truce expired on June 21 (Sunday), but only

[1] A parley was held with the usual lack of success on June 21 between the prince of Condé and his brother at Beaugency, which was neutralized for the purpose (D'Aubigné, II, 37, and n. 4). The baron de Ruble discovered the correspondence of the principals in the interview. The king of Navarre exhorted his brother to accept the conditions offered by the King, i. e., to let the Huguenots dwell peaceably in their houses until a council settled the matters in dispute. He promised in any event that the Protestants should have liberty of conscience. But when the prince insisted on having the edict enforced in Paris even, Antoine replied that the crown would never consent to such terms (C. S. P. For., No. 329, §§1, 2, July 17, 1562). Even while the truce existed straggling prisoners were taken daily by either side. (For other military details, see Mém. de La Noue [ed. Panthéon litt.], 284; D'Aubigné, II, 39, 40; Beza, Histoire des églises réformées, I, 540, 541; and the "Discours ou récit des opérations des deux armées catholique et protestante dans les premiers jours de juillet," in De Ruble, Antoine de Bourbon et Jeanne d'Albret, IV, 414).

[2] Not so the royal troops, which were quartered upon the towns of the region and nearly consumed the people by their exactions (Claude Haton, I, 279).

[3] The Catholics, in derision, called the Huguenot gentry "millers." During the interview on June 9 between the prince and the queen mother, the latter said: "Vos gens sont meusniers, mon cousin," a fling which the prince of Condé more than matched by the rejoinder: "C'est pour toucher vous asnes, madame!" This anecdote is related by D'Aubigné, II, 35.

light skirmishing was indulged in while specious negotiations were continued by Montmorency.[1] But the Catholic leaders offered such hard conditions that Condé would not accept them. Among others it was demanded that all preachers should be banished from France, together with the prince himself, the brothers Châtillon, and the other Huguenot leaders, until the King was of age.

During this delay the prince lost the advantage he had possessed. For the duke of Guise, the constable and Marshal St. André returned from Chartres to the camp again, which was between Beaugency and Blois, which lends color to the theory that it was they who overruled Antoine of Navarre and Catherine. After the rupture of the truce, the Catholic army marched to Blois, which they battered for a day and a night, assaulted and entered, although the inhabitants offered to let them in at the gates. When the magistrates of the city offered the keys to the duke of Guise, he pointed to the cannon with him, saying they were the keys he would enter by. At the same time St. André took Poitiers and Angoulême and drove La Rochefoucauld into Saintonge with the aid of Spanish troops.[2] When informed of the duke's proceedings at Blois, Condé marched to Beaugency, which, after bombardment, was entered on July 3, the most part of those who were left to guard it being killed.[3] Then seeing his own fortunes diminishing daily, he retired to Orleans, with scarcely 3,000 horse and 6,000 footmen. The prince was in doubt what next to do; whether to retire to Lyons and join with the baron des Adresse,[4] who had

[1] Cf. Guise's letter to the cardinal of Lorraine, Appendix III; *C. S. P. For.*, No. 238; No. 264, §3, June 29.

[2] *Ibid.*, No. 425, August 5, 1562; *Archives de la Gironde*, XVII, 270. The constable seized Tours and Villars Châtellerault (D'Aubigné, II, 41–44). For the operations of Burie in Périgord, see *Archives de la Gironde*, XVII, 271. At Bazas a local judge, with the aid of Spanish troops actually crucified some Calvinists (*ibid.*, XV, 57).

[3] La Noue admits that the boasted discipline of the Huguenots was disgraced by their atrocities here (*Mém. milit.*, chap. xvi; cf. *C. S. P. Ven.*, No. 288, July 16, 1562).

[4] On the war in Lyonnais, Dauphiné, Provence, and Languedoc, see D'Aubigné, Book III, chap. vii. The notes are valuable. Des Adresse proclaimed all Catholics in Lyonnais, Burgundy, Dauphiné, and Limousin rebels to the King

acquired Grenoble, Valence, and Châlons in Burgundy, despite
Tavannes who kept the field with his forces,[1] and was reputed to
have 8,000 foot and 1,500 horse besides 6,000 Swiss sent from Bern
and Lucerne, or to retire to Gascony where the queen of Navarre
was, or thirdly to go to Rouen and thereby keep Normandy. In
the end, however, he and Coligny stayed in Orleans. The
remainder of his force was either dispersed in the various towns or
dismissed.

The Protestants stood in dire need of outside aid during this
summer.[2] A few days after Condé had retired within Orleans,
D'Aumale took Honfleur (July 21). In París mobs killed almost
hourly men, women, and children, notwithstanding an edict to
the contrary under pain of death. Arms were in the people's
hands, not only in Paris but in the villages. Neither the King nor
the queen mother had the means to rule them, for the king of
Navarre and the duke of Guise were then at Blois, with the result
that Paris did much as it pleased. The leaders contemplated the
recovery of Touraine, Anjou, and Maine, and all the towns upon
the Loire, and then proposed to go into Normandy and recover
Havre-de-Grace, Dieppe, and Rouen. In pursuance of this project the duke of Guise took Loudon and Chinon in Touraine. In
the same month Mondidier was entered by the Catholics upon
assurance that all the Protestants therein should live safely; but
notwithstanding the promises they were all cut to pieces, robbed,
or driven forth. Numbers of men, women, and children were
drowned in the night with stones about their necks, at Blois, Tours,
and Amboise, and those towns which surrendered to the king of
Navarre.

While these events were taking place in the Loire country, the

(C. S. P. For., 340). He was not a Huguenot in the proper sense, but rebelled
against the King, and sided with the Huguenots because he was jealous of La
Mothe Gondrin, who was made *lieutenant du roi* instead of himself in Dauphiné
(see D'Aubigné, II, 49, n. 5).

[1] D'Aubigné, II, 48. He recovered Châlons-sur-Marne in June and Macon
in August (Tavannes, 339, 343).

[2] It was at this moment that D'Andelot was sent to Germany for succor (C. S. P.
For., No. 374, §7, July 27, 1562).

duke of Aumale again approached Rouen on the 29th of June, and planted his batteries before St. Catherine's Mount, but succeeded in doing little in spite of his long battery. He hoped to recover Havre-de-Grace after Guise had seized the towns upon the Loire. The great fear of the French was lest Havre-de-Grace should be given by the Huguenots into the hands of the English, and the atrocious practice of D'Aumale was likely to further such conduct on the part of the Huguenots,[1] for he promised the peasantry not only the privilege of sacking the châteaux of the nobles, but also to relieve them of all taxes. As a result of this vicious policy, trade was dead and whole families of the nobility retired to Dieppe, abandoning their homes.[2]

Violence increased both in the cities and in the provinces. In the southeast Somarive committed great cruelties in Orange, killing men, women, and children wherever he went.[3] But the achievements of Montluc, "the true creator of the French infantry"[4] were the conspicuous feature of the war in the south. By his own confession this famous soldier "rather inclined to violence than to peace, and was more prone to fighting and cutting of throats

[1] At Pont Audemer the duke caused a preacher to be hanged, and afterward some of the best citizens and even boys (C. S. P. Ven., 355, July 23, 1562). There was also fear lest the English would land troops in Guyenne (Archives de la Gironde, XVII, 284).

[2] C. S. P. Ven., No. 354, July 23, 1562; Claude Haton, I, 301; C. S. P. For., 185, June 13, 1562; cf. 246, §24; but see the duke of Aumale's disclaimer to the queen mother, of July 9, asserting that those of Rouen, Dieppe, and Havre were plundering indiscriminately (Appendix IV).

[3] D'Aubigné, II, 52–73. The prince of Orange found himself in a very difficult position. His principality was continually exposed to the attacks of the king of France and those of the Pope from Avignon. Moreover, the conduct of the Huguenots compromised him on account of their violence toward the priests in the sanctuaries (Archives de la maison d'Orange-Nassau, I, 71, 72; Raumer, II, 211 [1561]).

[4] Forneron, Histoire de Philippe II, I, 294. Montluc is unequaled in the keenness of his political penetration. The baron de Ruble says with truth that the old soldier rivals Hotman and Bodin in this respect. Witness the paragraph written in December, 1563, to be found in the memoir he sent to Damville justifying his resignation of the lieutenancy of Guyenne (Commentaires et lettres de Montluc, IV, 297, 298 and note).

than to making of speeches."[1]　The war in the southern provinces, it is plain, was one of both politics and religion. The practices of the Huguenots penetrated the whole administrative machinery. The sieur de Burie, king's lieutenant in Guyenne, was old and overcautious, and not without suspicion of Calvinism,[2] while Duras, the Huguenot leader was so active that the crown had sent the veteran of the siege of Sienna into Guyenne in January, 1560, with a special commission.[3] The Huguenots tried to buy Montluc off through one of their captains formerly with him before Sienna, who came to him saying that the church at Nérac had made him their captain. Montluc's reply nearly took the captain off his feet. "What the devil churches are those that make captains?" was his fierce question.[4] He speedily began to make his name formidable by hanging six Huguenots without process of law "which shook great fear into the whole party."

Montluc's arrival was in the nick of time for the Catholics of the south. He thought that if the Huguenots had been more led by soldiers and not so "guided by ministers, they had not failed of carrying Bordeaux and Toulouse. But God preserved those two forts, the bulwarks of Guyenne, to save all the rest." Montluc was everywhere at once, never resting long in any place, holding his foes in suspense everywhere, and not only was himself in continual motion, but also with letters and messages perpetually solicited and employed all the friends he had.[5] His troops were few in numbers and so ill-paid that he sometimes was reluctantly compelled to ransom his prisoners. "We were so few that we were

---

[1] There are few more interesting annals in the history of war than the racy, egotistical, garrulous, yet sometimes pithy narrative of this veteran leader. The fifth book of Montluc's *Commentaires* is wholly taken up with the war in Guyenne in 1562–63. His correspondence during the same period is in IV, 111–225; add Beza, *Histoire des églises réformées*, which is remarkably accurate and impartial.

[2] Coll. Trémont, No. 51.—Antoine de Bourbon to M. de Jarnac, from the camp at Gien, September 12, 1562, relative to sending forces into the south to join those of Burie and Montluc.

[3] *Commentaires et lettres de Montluc*, II, 345, and note. His title was "conservateur de la Guyenne" (O'Reilly, *Histoire de Bordeaux*, 221).

[4] *Commentaires et lettres de Montluc*, II, 357.

[5] *Ibid.*, 416, 421.

not enough to kill them all," he comments. "Had the King paid his companies I should not have suffered ransom to have been in use in this quarrel. It is not in this case as in a foreign war where men fight for love and honor. In a civil war we must either be master or man, being we live as it were, all under a roof." He was as good as his word and "shook a great terror into the country everywhere." When he appeared before Agen he "wondered that the people should be so damnably timorous and did not better defend their religion." Instead "they no sooner heard my name but they fancied the rope already about their necks." Yet terrible as the old war-dog was, he still waged war according to the rules of the game. He is outspoken in condemnation of the conduct of the Spanish companies sent by Philip.II which joined him before Agen.[1] The importance of Montluc's services in the south was great. He helped save Toulouse and Bordeaux to the government and the subsequent capture of Lectoure, and the notable battle of Vergt in Périgord (October 9, 1562) prevented the Huguenots south of the Loire from joining the forces of the prince of Condé, who thus narrowly lost the battle of Dreux.[2]

As the Catholic cause mended, the situation of the Huguenots darkened. Four thousand Swiss in June had joined Tavannes in Burgundy and thereby Dijon, Macon, and Châlons-sur-Saône were made safe. Late in July 6,000 lansquenets passed through Paris toward the camp at Blois. Pope Pius IV sent his own nephew to the aid of Joyeuse with 2,500 footmen, one thousand

[1] "The French spared the women there, but the Spaniards killed them, saying they were Lutherans disguised. These ruffians slew some 300 prisoners in cold blood—not a man escaped saving two that I saved."—Montluc, II, 457, 458. When these Spaniards later mutinied and deserted in the summer of 1563, not even the Catholics regretted their departure (L'Ambassade de St. Sulpice, 144, 152). For the terms on which they came, see Montluc, IV, 452, 453; D'Aubigné, II, 91, n. 2; 94, n. 4.

[2] See Commentaires et lettres de Montluc, III, 37 ff.; De Thou, Book XXXIII; D'Aubigné, II, 95; Bull. de la Soc. de l'hist., du prot. franç., II (1854), 230; C. S. P. For., 837 and 415, §12 (1562). I have purposely built this account upon Montluc's narration in Book V of his Commentaires. An additional source for Lectoure and the battle of Vergt is his long letter to Philip II, published in L'Ambassade de St. Sulpice, 84–86; add also De Ruble, Antoine de Bourbon et Jeanne d'Albret, 244–56.

of whom were "Hispainolz."[1]   The Huguenots impatiently awaited
the coming of German pistoleers and footmen, to be brought by
Casimir, the second son of the count palatine, accompanied by
D'Andelot who had been sent into Germany for assistance.   But
the German princes were slow in responding, especially to the
demand for money,[2] so that the prince of Condé actually promised
to give them the pillage of Paris![3]   D'Andelot passed the Rhine
on September 22, 1562—three weeks too late to relieve Bourges—
with 2,000 German horse and 2,000 musketeers, who figured in
the battle of Dreux in the next December.[4]   France had seen
nothing like these reiters in days heretofore.   Their coming created
both consternation[5] and curiosity.   Claude Haton in vain sought
the meaning of the word.

The word reiter had never had vogue in France within the life of the
oldest of men, and one had never used the word until the present, although
the kings of France had been served in all their wars by Germans, Swiss,
and lansquenets, who are included under this word and name of Germany or
Allemaigne.   I have taken pains to inquire of numerous persons, who are
deemed to know much what was the signification of this word "reiter," but
I have not found a man who has been wise enough to tell me what I wished
to know.[6]

---

[1] *Mém. de Condé*, III, 756: "Fragment d'une lettre de l'ambassadeur du duc
de Savoye, à la Cour de France.   De Paris du dernier de juillet, 1562;" cf. *Nég.
Tosc.*, III, 492, 493.

[2] See an article by De Crue, "Un emprunt des Huguenots français en Allemagne et en Suisse (1562).   Pleins pouvoirs données à M. d'Andelot par le prince
de Condé—Orleans, 7 juillet, 1562," *Rev. d'hist. dip.*, 1889, 195.

[3] *L'Ambassade de St. Sulpice*, 77; *C. S. P. For.*, 884, October 9, 1562.   His
instructions are in *Mém. de Condé*, III, 630.   See a letter of Hotman, July 27,
1562, to the elector palatine, *Mém. de l'Acad. des inscrip. et belles-lettres*, CIV, 668.
The original is in the archives at Stuttgart.   This letter was communicated to the
duke of Württemberg by the count palatine and was sufficient temptation to lead
the first of the famous hordes of German reiters across the border into France.

[4] Claude Haton, 267.   See in the *Mém. de Condé*, III, some letters relating to
the coming of the reiters in this year.

[5] "Ceux-ci [reiters] sont toujours prêts à se battre, mais en tout le reste, ils
n'obéissent à personne et montrent la plus grande cruauté.   Ils pillent tout, et cela
ne leur suffit pas.   Ils dévastent tout et détruisent les vins et les récoltes."—Letter
of Hotman in *Rev. hist.*, XCVII, March–April, 1908, 311.

[6] Claude Haton, I, 294.

In order to pay the reiters and to find money, a *taille* was imposed upon the Huguenots of all classes, in all towns and villages under their control, upon nobles, priests, merchants, bourgeois, and artisans. But as this means was very tedious, the prince had recourse to the gold and silver vessels, chalices, and crosses of the churches which the Huguenots had pillaged. He also seized upon the government receipts from the *gabelle* and other taxes of the King in all the villages and *élections* controlled by the Huguenots, even the moneys of the royal domain, and the revenues of the churches.[1]

Meanwhile on August 19 the siege of Bourges had begun. The city was defended by about 3,500 soldiers, but the circuit of its walls was very great. It was well provisioned for a time, and had considerable munitions and artillery of an inferior sort, but neither cannon nor culverin. Half the town was protected by a great marsh near by; the other half was fortified. It was the plan of D'Andelot, who had entered Lorraine with 2,000 horse and 4,000 foot, commanded by the duke of Deuxponts, feeling he could do nothing in time for Bourges, to cut off Paris by securing the passages of the river at St. Cloud and Charenton.[2] Accordingly the constable and the duke of Guise, learning of the approach

---

[1] *Ibid.* From an account in the Record Office, indorsed by Cecil, we know what the wages of these hireling troops were: "The pay of every reiter is 15 florins the month. The entertainment of the ritmeisters is a florin for every horse, and each cornet contains 300 men. The lieutenants have, besides the pay of one reiter, 80 florins. The ensign, besides the pay of one reiter, has 60 florins, eight officers having, besides a reiter's pay, 15 florins apiece. The wage and appointment of 4,000 reiters with their officers *per mensem* equals 122,048 livres *tournois*, equals 81,532 florins. The colonel 3,000 florins; 15 officers equals 300 florins. To every ten reiters there must be allowed a carriage with four horses, at 30 florins per month. Total (not counting the money rebated) 127,448 livres *tournois*, or 84,966 florins. Total expense for four months, counting the levy, 569,792 livres *tournois* equals 379,861 florins.

"For levying 6,000 lansknechts: for their levying, a crown per month. The pay of every ensign of 300 men per month, 3,500 *livres tournois*. The whole expense for four months 395,000 livres *tournois* equals 263,337 florins. Sum total with other expenses, 1,759,792 livres *tournois* equals 211,174,175, 2d."

[2] D'Andelot passed the Rhine on September 22, too late to relieve Bourges.

of the reiters, dispatched D'Aumale with a commission to levy all men of war in Champagne, Brie, and Burgundy, both foot and horse, and to sound the tocsin for the purpose of raising new levies for the King if those which he first raised should not suffice, and to make a great camp of all these men for the purpose of combating the reiters.[1]   But D'Aumale dallied so long,[2] to the intense chagrin of his army, which clamored to "frapper dessus les lif-lof de reistres,"[3] that the German troopers were able to cross the river Seine at Chanceaux, whence they took the road above Auxerre, crossed the Yonne, and so joined the prince of Condé at Orleans.

It would have been much better for France, and especially for the provinces of Champagne, Brie, and Burgundy, if D'Aumale had attempted to repulse the reiters, for his soldiers were the ruin of the villages where they lodged, and any action, even defeat, would have been better than license and idleness. When it was known that the reiters had evaded the force sent against them, the King, seeing new villages of France taken every day, sent orders to all those who still adhered to the crown to the effect that they should be on their guard night and day, for fear of being taken by surprise.   For greater security commissions were dispatched

[1] See Claude Haton's vivid description of this recruiting. The new levies did great damage to the country of Brie and Champagne, for they were kept in villages for more than five weeks before going to cámp, and all this time the reiters were approaching closely (I, 295).

[2] Claude Haton, I, 295. He adds that Catherine de Medici sent him secret orders to do so. But there is no evidence of this in her correspondence, and D'Aumale's subsequent blunder in 1569 by which the Huguenots were able to get possession of La Charité justifies the inference that his action was due to incapacity as a general.

[3] The long presence of the reiters in France during the civil wars introduced many German words into the French language, for example bière (Bier); blocus (Blockhaus); boulevard (Bollwerk); bourgmestre (Burgmeister); canapsa (Knapsack); carousser (Garaus machen); castine (Kalkstein); halte (halt); trinquer (trinken and of course reitre (Reiter) and lansquenet (Lanzknecht).   See Nyrop, Grammaire historique de la langue française, I, 51.   Rabelais abounds with such words, e. g., "Je ne suis de cas importuns lifrelofres qui, par force, poultraige et violence, contraignent les lans et compaignons trinquer, voire carous et alluz qui pis est." Rabelais, Book IV, prologue.   So also in Book IV, prol.: "Je n'y ay entendu que le hault allemant."

authorizing the election of a gentleman of honor and credit to be town-captain in every town.[1]

The Catholic and Huguenot position with reference to each other between Paris and the Loire was now somewhat as follows: the former held Chartres, Bonneval, Chateaudun, Blois; the latter St. Marthurin, Montargis, and Gien. On August 31, 1562, the surrender of Bourges took place. The crown guaranteed life, property, and liberty of conscience to the commandant and soldiers and inhabiants of the town, in consideration of an indemnity of 50,000 livres "pour avoir été si gracieusement traités."[2] But the Catholic leaders were in doubt what next to do, for all the Huguenots were within the towns, neither occupying the open country nor having a camp outside the walls. The king of Navarre urged the siege of Orleans, but the council was not in agreement with him for two reasons: first, on account of the plague which was there; secondly because they had hopes that Navarre might prevail upon his brother to desert the Huguenot cause, and so spare them the exercise of force. For these reasons it was resolved not to push the siege of Orleans and to attack Rouen instead, where the duke of Aumale was already.[3]

[1] In Provins, on their own initiative, the townspeople taxed their town, bailiwick, and réssort (sénéschausée) to the amount of 7,000 livres tournois, the sum being imposed upon persons of every class, those who had gone to the war in the King's service alone being exempted. This levy created great discontent, especially among the clergy, who appealed against the bailiff and the gens du roi to the Court of Aids, alleging that the levy was made without royal commission and without the consent of those interested. The bailiff compromised by promising the clergy to restore the money paid by them and not to demand more of them, and so the process was dropped (Claude Haton, I, 296, 297).

[2] On the siege of Bourges see D'Aubigné, II, 77 ff.; Raynal, Hist. du Berry, IV; Mém. des antiq. de France, sér. III (1855), II, 191 ff.; Nég. Tosc., III, 494, 495; Boyer, Doc. relat. au régime de l'artillerie de la ville de Bourges dans le XVIᵉ siècle, 641; in Bull. du Comité de la langue, de l'hist. et des arts de la France, III, 1855-56. The capitulation of Bourges is in Mém. de Condé, III, 634. See also the "Journal of Jean Glaumeau," edited by M. Bourquelot in Mém. de la Soc. des antiq. de France, XXII. Philip II expressed his displeasure at the terms to St. Sulpice, saying, "que aulcunes des conditions semblaient du tout assez convenables des sujetz à leur roi" (L'ambassade de St. Sulpice, 70, 75. Alva's opinion is given at p. 78).

[3] Claude Haton, I, 285. Philip II told St. Sulpice "quant un voyage de Normandie, bien qu'il l'estimait être bien entrepris, qu'il semblait qu'il eut été meilleur de s'adresser à Orleans, où étaient les chefs, afin qu'ils ne se grossissent d'avantage."
—L'Ambassade de St. Sulpice, 75.

The Guises were now fully aware of the formidable nature of the revolt of Normandy, there being danger of their also losing western Normandy, where the duke de Bouillon held Caen castle, but was disposed to be neutral. They planned, therefore, to send the greater portion of their new forces, Germans and Swiss, to the aid of D'Aumale, who had advanced against Rouen after D'Andelot gave him the slip, for they were little needed in the Loire country. Roggendorf, Guise's chief German agent, at this time arrived in Paris with 1,200 German pistoleers, well armed and mounted; the Swiss captain, Froelich had brought fifteen ensigns of Swiss, and the Rhinegrave was in Champagne with two regiments of foot and three hundred pistoleers.[1]

The constable and the duke of Guise in fear of English support, resolved to concentrate the greatest part of their force against Rouen and Havre-de-Grace. Another motive lay in the fact that Paris was in want; for the Huguenots recognized that if Rouen, Havre-de-Grace and Dieppe were well held, coercion of Paris was not impossible. The condition at Dieppe and Havre-de-Grace was the source of more anxiety to the government than any other matter. These towns, owing to their situation, were the chief keys to France, without which neither Paris nor Rouen could be free. Havre-de-Grace was of more use to France than Calais as a port of supply, and daily all those who escaped from Pont Audemer, Honfleur, Harfleur, and the Protestants between Dieppe[2] and Rouen were flocking thither.

The chief hope of the French Protestants was based upon the expected aid of England. Early in April, 1562, the prince of Condé and the admiral had solicited her support.[3] But the anxiety

[1] C. S. P. For., No. 374, §7, July 27, 1562; No. 510, §1, August 10, 1562. For the operations of the reiters around Paris in the summer of 1562 see D'Aubigné, Book III, chap. xii; De Ruble's notes are valuable.

[2] Daval, Histoire de la réformation à Dieppe, 1557-1657. Publ. pour la Ire fois avec introd. et notes par E. Lesens (Société rouennaise de bibliophiles. 2 vols., 1879).

[3] C. S. P. For., Nos. 975, 976, 1,002. This solicitation was in the nature of an acknowledgment of an expression of interest in them made by the English queen. For as far back as March she had sent assurances of her interest to Condé and the admiral (ibid., No. 965, March 3, 1562).

of Elizabeth in the welfare of Protestantism beyond sea was not disinterested, any more than Philip II's catholicism.. The legality of her position as queen required her adherence to everything anti-Catholic, to which may be added the influence of the political aims of Philip II with reference to England, especially his interest in the doings of Mary Stuart and Spanish tyranny in the Low Countries, both of which jeopardized England. Her ambassador in France observed truly when he wrote her: "It standeth Your Majesty, for the conservation of your realm in the good terms it is in, to countenance the Protestants as much as you may."[1] Another practical end to be gained by English support of the Huguenots was the possibility of recovering Calais.[2] Yet in spite of their deep religious animosity and their political hostility to one another, England and Spain were in so peculiarly complicated a relation that neither state wished to go to war. Philip II assured Charles IX that although Elizabeth would squirm at sight of Spanish assistance given to France, she dared not strike back in aid of the Huguenots, and would have to compel herself to view things from afar.[3] The key to this extraordinary situation is to be found in the commerce of the Low Countries. The duke of Alva flatly said that his master could not afford to break with the English because of the commercial injury he would sustain in the Netherlands.[4] The same proposition, reversed, was in like stead true of England; her commercial interests in Holland and Flanders were too great to be risked.

But the good prospect of regaining Calais coupled with the fear lest the reduction of France to Spanish suzerainty would entail greater danger to England in the long run than the loss of

[1] C. S. P. For., No. 973, April 1, 1562.

[2] Ibid., No. 1,013, §13, April 17, 1562. Elizabeth considered the suggestion of her ambassador so favorable that she sent Sir Henry Sidney to France in the spring to aid Throckmorton. See the instructions in C. S. P. For., Nos. 1,063, 1,064, April 28, 1562.

[3] "Et il assure que bien qu'elle prenne à dépit de voir que les catholiques soient secourus de deça, elle est persuadée que son meilleur est de se contenir et regarder de loin ce qui adviendra."—L'Ambassade de St. Sulpice, 55, July, 1562.

[4] "Réponses du duc d'Albe à St. Sulpice, October 8, 1562," L'Ambassade de St. Sulpice, 79; cf. 92, 93, 103.

her commerce beyond sea, at last persuaded Elizabeth to support
the Huguenots, upon certain conditions, the ultimate one being
restoration of Calais to England.[1] Accordingly, in September,
1562, the queen offered to land 6,000 men to guard the towns in
Normandy, to take Havre and Dieppe under her protection, and
receive into them the refugees of the Reformed church, and promised not to abandon Havre without the prince's consent, nor
receive Calais from the opposite party. The vidame of Chartres
agreed to deliver the custody of Havre-de-Grace to the queen's
lieutenant on condition that the latter would recompense him and

---

[1] Throckmorton, English ambassador in France, urgently pressed such a
policy, "even though it cost a million crowns" (C. S. P. For., No. 418, August 4,
1562). It was in the form of alternative offers to the Huguenots. Upon receipt of
Havre-de-Grace, England was to deliver three hostages in guaranty of the compact,
to the count palatine of the Rhine, and to pay in Strasburg 70,000 crowns; also to
deliver at Dieppe 40,000 crowns within twenty days after the receipt of Havre-de-
Grace, and 30,000 crowns within twenty days following, to be employed by Condé
upon the defenses of Rouen and Dieppe and in the rest of Normandy, with the
understanding that Havre-de-Grace was to be delivered to France upon the restoration of Calais, and the repayment of the 140,000 crowns advanced. The
second offer was to this effect: Upon receipt of Havre-de-Grace, England was to
deliver three hostages and deposit 70,000 crowns in Germany, and to send 6,000
men into Normandy to serve at Rouen and Dieppe (C. S. P. For., No. 268, July,
1562; cf. Nos. 662, 663). After prolonged negotiations which were conducted by the
vidame of Chartres, the treaty of Hampton Court was framed on these lines, on
September 10, 1562 (Mém. de Condé, III, 689; Mém. du duc de Nevers, I, 131;
D'Aubigné, II, 79, 80). Elizabeth's proclamation and justification of her action
is at p. 693 of Mém. de Condé.

The alliance between the prince of Condé and the English, with the implied
loss of Calais to France, more than any other fact, reconciled Catherine de Medici
to Spanish assistance. After August she personally urged this aid (L'Ambassade
de St. Sulpice, 58, 59). Still Philip emphatically gave her to understand that
"si l'ambassadeur de Espagne avait fait espérer que son maître déclarerait la guerre
aux Anglais . . . . il avait dépassé ses instructions, car les Espagnols étaient
depuis si longtemps liés avec ces peuples qu'il était impossible de rompre cette
alliance."—St. Sulpice to Charles IX, November 12, 1562 (L'Ambassade de St.
Sulpice, 93).

The constable was at Yvetot in October, 1562, at the time of the descent of the
English upon Havre and wrote to Charles IX that he was unable to take the field.
At a later season he complains to Catherine of the calumnies heaped upon him, and
bluntly says "that he is not in the humor to endure such things."—Coll. de St.
Pétersbourg, CIII, letters pertaining to the house of Montmorency; La Ferrière,
Rapport, 46.

Condé by annual pensions or assigned lands, because of the loss of their estates and goods in France. In pursuance of this compact, on September 24, 1562, the English proclamation for the expedition into Normandy was published. It was time, if success were to crown the enterprise, for in Havre troubles and enemies multiplied and patience with the English was on the point of breaking. "No prey happens to a sleeping fox," wrote the vidame impatiently to the English admiral. On October 1, 1562, the English sailed from Portsmouth for Havre, and on Sunday, October 4, entered the roadstead of Havre at three in the afternoon, and immediately landed as many men as they could with the tide.

The English occupation of Havre-de-Grace startled the government into new activity before Rouen, and the King determined to take it before English assistance could be afforded.[1] The town was well supplied with provisions and had plenty of small arms, but was short of artillery and gunpowder. The garrison numbered about 4,000, under command of Montgomery, the guardsman who had accidentally killed Henry II in tournament, for Morvilliers, the former chief in command in Rouen, had hesitated about the introduction of English soldiers and had been replaced.

In the first week of October the attack of the royal forces upon Rouen was renewed with fury and the fortress on St. Catherine's Mount was taken by them. Desperation soon prevailed in the beleaguered city and there was talk of conditional surrender if that could be effected, until the arrival of a few companies of English revived the courage of the Rouennais and the fight was renewed. But the procrastinating caution of the English by this time over-

---

[1] Archambault to St. Sulpice, *L'Ambassade de St. Sulpice*, 71; Charles IX to St. Sulpice, September 15, *ibid.*, 74. The camps on the Loire were broken up on September 14, only sufficient forces being left to invest Orleans. The soldiers were sent to Normandy via Montargis, Angerville-la-Rivière, and Etampes, leaving posts at Gien, Beaugency, and Pithiviers to keep the lines open between north and south and to prevent D'Andelot from getting to Orleans.

On the siege of Rouen, see Claude Haton, I, 286–89. The city was taken October 26 (Floquet, *Hist. du Parlement de Normandie*, II, 435).

On Huguenot excesses in Rouen, see an arrêt of the Parlement of Rouen, August 26, 1562, in *Mém. de Condé*, III, 613, and another ordering prayers for the capture of Fort St. Catherine, October 7 (*ibid.*, IV, 41).

reached itself.   In spite of the importunities of Throckmorton,[1] the English government was reluctant to venture its arms beyond the seaboard,[2] although Throckmorton's arguments were reinforced by every other English agent in France, Rouen being represented as "such a jewel for them that by no means is it sufferable to become an enemy."[3]   All urgency was in vain.   The instructions to the earl of Warwick, the English commander in Havre-de-Grace, were to the effect that if requested to send aid to Rouen or other places he should make some "reasonable delay," without offending them.[4]   It is easy to see from such instructions and the policy pursued by the English government in France that its interest was purely practical and in no sense sentimental or religious. England wanted to hold Havre-de-Grace in pawn for Calais, under cover of pretending to support the Huguenots.

By mid-October, however, it had become plain that this narrow policy could not be so rigidly adhered to.   The success of the Catholic armies in Normandy was even endangering Havre-de-Grace, and Havre-de-Grace was not nearly so favorable a point of vantage for the English as Calais had been, for there the pale protected the city proper;   in the city at the Seine's mouth the fortifications were weak and, worst of all, the location was a poor one for defense.[5]   With the coming of winter, it would be possible for the French with slight effort to prevent much intercourse by sea between Havre and the English ports, while already the country roundabout was being devastated by the German reiters. D'Aumale was reported to have said—and there was justification of the statement—that the English garrison might make merry as it pleased, the winter and famine would cause them to pack homeward faster than they had come.   Too late the English at

---

[1] See his singular letter to Cecil of July 29, 1562, in C. S. P. For., No. 389.

[2] Cf. articles for the English agent Vaughan, of August 30, in Cecil's handwriting (ibid., No. 550).

[3] Ibid., No. 763, Vaughan to Cecil, October 4, 1562; Forbes, II, 89.

[4] C. S. P. For., No. 790, October 7, 1562; Forbes, II, 93.

[5] Cf. C. S. P. For., No. 803, October 8, 1562; Forbes, II, 101; report of a military expert to Cecil.

last determined to succor Rouen after the fall of St. Catherine's Mount,[1] and relief troops were sent forward to Rouen from Havre-de-Grace and Dieppe. An intrepid English captain named Leighton (he was afterward made governor of Guernsey), with a handful of men, made his way into the city, but substantial assistance did not come until the middle of October. Even then misfortune overtook the English. The approach was made by the river in six small ships, but one of them struck on a sand bar near Caudebec and was intercepted by Damville, so that only 600 English got into the town.[2]

On the morning of the 16th, Montgomery and two of the chief men of the city came out of Rouen, under a flag of truce, and spoke with the queen, returning a second time with fresh proposals, but nothing resulted. The Huguenóts demanded, first of all, liberty of preaching, and of living according to their religion. Besides this, they insisted that the King should not put a garrison in Rouen, and as security for the observance of these conditions they required hostages from the King, to be kept by them at Havre-de-Grace. In the second interview they enlarged the conditions; namely, that the Edict of January might be observed and that they might preach freely *in the cities*, although by the edict preaching was permitted only *outside* of cities.[3] Moreover, they insisted on this agreement being extended to *all* towns of France; and in order to give this convention a general effect, the prince of Condé was to confirm it. For the observance of all these conditions they demanded as hostages the prince de Joinville, eldest son of the duke

---

[1] It was taken by assault by the duke of Guise (*Corresp. de Catherine de Médicis*, I, 414, note; Claude Haton, I, 285; *Mém. de Condé*, IV, 41).

[2] The English aid had been divided into three bodies, that portion which entered Rouen being only the vanguard. It was the middle portion which followed in ships up the river and was captured by Damville. The third body was of the rear guard and returned to Havre-de-Grace (*C. S. P. Ven.*, No. 302, October 14, 1562). In the fight off Caudebec 200 English were killed, and 80 made prisoners, all of whom were hanged by the French—a more rigorous punishment than even sixteenth-century war nominally allowed (*ibid., For.*, Nos. 870, 872, October 17, 18, 1562).

[3] *Ibid.*, No. 901, October 23, 1562.

of Guise, and brother of the marshal Brissac,[1] superintendent of the King's revenues.

Although Montgomery was unaware of it, the government already, alarmed by the English intervention, had made overtures to the prince of Condé in Orleans. But in each case, a condition required would not be yielded. The demand of the Rouennais that the Edict of January be revised so as to permit Protestant worship *in all towns* broke off negotiations with them. In the overtures made to Condé and Coligny, restitution of all in rebellion to their estates and offices was promised, as also the assurance to the Huguenots that they might enjoy their religion peaceably *in their houses*, but *public* worship, even without the towns, was not to be permitted. The Protestant leaders seem to have been inclined to yield to these terms, although they implied a reduction of their religious privileges, but insisted that the crown should assume the payments due to Condé's German auxiliaries. The government balked at this proposal, and the prince and the admiral themselves balked when the king of Navarre declared that D'Andelot's German troopers and the Huguenots should unite to expel the English from France, so that in the end neither set of negotiations was successful.[2]

During the successful assault upon Fort St. Catherine which followed the rupture of these negotiations both Antoine of Navarre and the duke of Guise were wounded, the former by an arquebus-shot in the joint of the shoulder, as it proved, mortally, because mortification of the wound could not be stayed.[3] Montgomery fought furiously in the assault, which lasted seven hours, and threatened to use his sword upon any who might seek to yield. It was a desperate and vain battle, however.[4] The King's forces

[1] *C. S. P. Ven.*, October 27, 1562.

[2] *Ibid., For.*, 932, §4, October 30, 1562.

[3] For details see *Corresp. de Catherine de Méd.*, I, 420, note; Claude Haton, I, 287–91; and a relation in *Arch. cur.*, IV, sér. 1, 67.   Also in *Mém. de Condé*, IV, 116.   The same volume has some letters addressed to the queen of Navarre upon his death.   Cf. Le Laboureur, III, 887.   Claude Haton, I, 292, 293, has an interesting eulogy of him.

[4] Charles IX and his mother were eye-witnesses of this struggle, viewing it from a window of the convent of St. Catherine "from which they could see all that took place within and without the city."—*C. S. P. Ven.*, October 18, 1562.

mined clear to the walls of the town, and the havoc of their explosions could not be remedied. The breach in the walls made by both mine and shot was so wide that some of the royal force rode through on horseback.[1] On Monday, October 26, the besiegers fought their way through and over the walls. In this supreme movement the English and the Catholic Germans came sharply together. No quarter was given the English in the town, the command being given "that they should all pass the sword." Many of them were stripped naked by the victors. The wounded English who were found had their throats cut; the rest were sent to the galleys. The King entered Rouen the day after its capture, making his way over dead bodies which had been spoiled by the soldiers.[2] The royal forces now had unlimited control of the Seine below Rouen; at Caudebec they staked half the river, so that ships and boats were compelled to pass close under their guns.

[1] It had been the queen's hope that Rouen might be saved from sack, and with this object she had offered 70,000 francs to the French troops if they would refrain from pillage. But such a hope was slight, for Rouen was the second city of the realm and one of great wealth (*C. S. P. Ven.*, October 17, 1562). Moreover, "Guise proclaimed before the assault that none should fall to any spoil before execution of man, woman, and child" (*ibid., For.*, No. 920, Vaughan to Cecil, October 28, 1562). Catherine de Médici also throws the responsibility upon the duke of Guise (*Corresp.*, I, 430). For other details of the sack, see Castelnau, Book III, chap. xii. "Le ravage de ceste ville fut à la mesure de sa grandeur et à sa richesse," is D'Aubigné's laconic statement (II, 88). Fortunately, for the sake of humanity, the sack was stayed after the first day. The German troopers committed the worst outrages. The marshal Montmorency is to be given credit for mitigating the horrors. Montgomery, though at first reported captured, escaped to Havre, having disguised himself by shaving off his beard (*C. S. P. For.*, No. 939, October 30, 1562), and abandoned his wife and children, to the indignation of Vaughan, who vented his outraged sentiments to Cecil: "A man of that courage to steal away, leaving his wife and children behind him" (*ibid.*, No. 920, October 28, 1562).

Among those in Rouen who were officially executed were a Huguenot pastor by the name of Marlorat, with two elders of the church, a merchant and burgess of the city, named Jean Bigot, and one Coton; Montreville, chief president of Rouen, De Cros, some time governor of Havre-de-Grace, eight Scotchmen who had passports of Mary Stuart to serve under Guise, and some French priests (D'Aubigné, II, 88; *C. S. P. For.*, No. 950, §14, October 31, 1562; No. 984, §2, November 4, 1562).

[2] *C. S. P. Ven.*, No. 307, October 31, 1562, *L'Ambassade de St. Sulpice*, 91; "Montgoméry qui les faisait tenir s'est sauvé, laissant le peuple livré à la boucherie." —Letter of Catherine de Medici to St. Sulpice.

The Guises now anticipated a swift collapse of the Huguenot cause. All the chief towns in France save Orleans[1] and Lyons were either by inclination or compulsion obedient to the crown, which found powerful support from the property-owning and lawyer class. Politically and financially the government was stronger, although the court was in want of money at this time. The duke of Guise, the most notable captain and soldier in France, the constable and veteran marshals like Brissac and St. André, had made a combination too strong to be overcome. In this strait, the Huguenot leaders grasped at the last straw—the hope that the prince of Condé might succeed the king of Navarre as lieutenant of the realm by winning the support of liberal Catholics and the anti-Guisard element.[2] There was ground for this hope if the Calvinists could be persuaded to be a little less radical, and if the Catholic religion would be suffered without criticism to be and remain the religion of France, and the Huguenots would make no further alteration in their form of worship than the English Reformation had done.[3]

Antoine of Bourbon, since sustaining the wound received at Rouen, had been gradually sinking, and died on board a boat on his way to Paris, October 26, after prolonged suffering.[4]   Condé

---

[1] Orleans had 1,200 horsemen and 5,000 footmen in it, besides the inhabitants, with provisions to last six months. Almost all the weak places had been fortified with platforms, ravelins, and parapets. The counterscarp was roughly finished. There were nine or ten cannon and culverins with a good store of powder. The greatest menace was the plague which daily diminished the number of the Protestants (*C. S. P. Eng.*, 596, §6, September 9, 1562—report of Throckmorton who was on the ground).

[2] *C. S. P. Ven.*, October 17, 1562. The Spanish ambassador had foreseen the possibility of such a contingency and early in April had cautioned Philip II not to play upon Antoine's expectations to the point of exasperation (K. 1,497, No. 17).

[3] *C. S. P. Eng.*, 1,050, November 14, 1562.

[4] "His arm is rotten and they have mangled him in the breast and other parts so pitifully"—in the endeavor to cut out the mortified flesh.—*C. S. P. For.*, 1,040, Smith to Cecil, November 12, 1562. Cf. No. 932, October 30; for other details see *C. S. P. Ven.*, November 8, 9, 10, 13, 1562; *Mém. de Condé*, IV, 116; D'Aubigné, II, 85. The knowledge of his death was kept a secret for two days (*C. S. P. For.*, 1,079, November 20, 1562). The Spanish court wore mourning for four days in honor of his memory (*L'Ambassade de St. Sulpice*, 103). He was a "trimmer"

now, by virtue of the arrangement made at the meeting of the
States-General at Orleans, legally succeeded to his brother's
office as lieutenant of the realm, and proceeded forthwith to send out
commissions to the constable, marshals, and to all the governors
of provinces and places, to repair to him as the King's lieutenant-
general and governor of France.   But in spite of the regulation of
the estates, the court and Catholic party, by the advice of the
cardinals of Ferrara, Lorraine, and Guise, the duke of Guise, the
constable, and marshal St. André, with the special solicitation of
the Spanish ambassador who voiced his master's wishes with "a
lusty swelling tongue," resolved to establish the cardinal of Bourbon in the authority the king of Navarre had held.[1]

to the last, on his deathbed professing the confession of Augsburg, as a doctrine
intermediate between Catholicism and Calvinism (*Despatch of Barbaro* [Huguenot
Society], November 25, 1562).

[1] "Le roi catholique est content que la reine mère ait l'entier gouvernement
des affaires, tout en ayant près d'elle le cardinal de Bourbon."—*L'Ambassade de
St. Sulpice*, 109, January 19, 1562 (1563).

CHAPTER VII

THE FIRST CIVIL WAR (*Continued*). THE BATTLE OF DREUX (DECEMBER 19, 1562). THE PEACE OF AMBOISE (MARCH 19, 1563)

After the fall of Rouen, the chief military design of the Guises seems to have been to protract the war, without giving battle, until the Germans with D'Andelot and Condé either deserted for lack of pay or were corrupted by them. Catherine's wish, on the other hand, was to end the war by composition and not by the sword, fearing to have either party become flushed with success. In pursuance of this policy numbers of the soldiers were permitted to go home, the war being considered to be practically at an end until the spring, except that garrisons of horse and foot were kept in the towns round about Orleans after the manner of a flying siege (*siège volante*). But the rapid advance of the prince toward Paris from Orleans, where he had been waiting for D'Andelot, who mustered his German horse in Lorraine in the middle of September, after he learned of his brother's death, required the duke of Guise to change his plans. Passing by Etampes, which the Guises abandoned at his approach,[1] the prince of Condé marched toward Corbeil in order to win the passage of the Seine, where 4,000 footmen and 2,000 horse of the enemy lay in order to keep the Marne and the Seine open above Paris for provisioning the capital. The Huguenot army numbered about 6,000 footmen; 4,000 of them Germans, and nearly 3,000 horsemen. Most of the Germans were well armed and mounted, and all "very Almain soldiers, who spoil all things where they go."[2]

The duke of Guise, having received word of the approach of the Huguenots upon Paris, abandoned his purpose of going to Havre,

---

[1] "Il y eut toujours dans la ville quatre corps de garde, Charles IX ordonna d'établir à Etampes un magasin de vivre bour fournir son armée."—*Annales du Gâtinais*, XIX, 105.

[2] *C. S. P. Eng.*, No. 1,070, November 20, 1562.

in order to return to the succor of the city. Great difficulty was experienced in accomplishing the return of the army, because it was the depth of winter and the days were short and the roads heavy. "Nevertheless everyone in camp took courage, because he was returning to the good French wines and no more needed to drink the cider of Normandy."[1]

To combat the Protestant force, Guise and the constable had not over 6,000 footmen and 1,000 horsemen at Paris, though this force could be somewhat enlarged by drawing in the troops around Rouen and before Havre-de-Grace. It was fully expected that the prince of Condé would march upon the capital or else take the straight road to Normandy in order to unite with the English and with their help attempt to regain possession of Rouen and Dieppe. Paris was in the greatest alarm. All the people living in the faubourgs were compelled to abandon their houses. The state of the royal army was bad; the soldiers were scattered and disorganized, for the spoil of Rouen had induced every kind of license and debauchery. Moreover, the plague was raging everywhere. In this exigency the duke of Guise abandoned the country roundabout, within two or three leagues of Paris, to the pillage of the Protestants, withdrew his scattered forces within the walls, and feverishly employed every available person in the erection of fortifications, principally upon the side toward Orleans, for which certain unfinished erections of Francis I were utilized. The city was so crowded with people even before the appearance of the troops of the prince that it seemed to be in a state of siege. If Condé at this time could have seized the river above and below the capital by which provisions were received into Paris, the city could have been speedily reduced to famine, as there was even at this time a scarcity of food.[2]

But Louis of Condé was not a man of good judgment and, while

---

[1] Claude Haton, I, 305.

[2] C. S. P. For., 193, December 5, 1562; ibid., Ven., December 3; Forbes II, 27. La Noue gives a motive which led Condé to besiege Paris: "Non en intention de forcer la ville, mais pour faire les Parisiens, qu'il estimoit les soufflets de la guerre et la cuisine dont elle se nourissoit." Mém. milit. do la Noue, chap. ix.

personally brave, he lacked political daring.   To gain time for the
arrival of reinforcements, Catherine and the Guises wheedled him
with empty overtures for peace and sent the marshal Brissac's brother to the Protestant camp near Etampes to propose a plausible
settlement, saying that the Huguenots might have what they desired
if they would aid in expelling the Germans, and especially the English.   The last possibility was what the English agents in France
had most feared, the more because of the undeniable strength of the
Catholic crown party, which had won to itself a great number of the
nobility, and because of the approaching winter, the lack of money
among the Huguenots, the scarcity of food, and the weariness of the
country.   Such abandonment of the English by the prince of Condé
could hardly have been construed as a breach of faith, seeing the
apathy of the English participation after the seizure of Havre-de-
Grace and Elizabeth's slowness in sending him financial assistance.
But the prince refused to treat with an agent and continued his
march toward Paris.   On November 25 his cavalry appeared in
sight of the city and the queen mother and the constable went out to
parley further.   The prince of Condé demanded the post of lieutenant-general of the realm; for the Huguenots the right to have
churches in all towns except Paris and its *banlieue* and frontier
towns; the right of all gentlemen to have private worship in their
own houses, and the retirement of the foreign troops.   To these
demands, the queen replied that no one should have her authority,
adding that the government was already well made up of gentlemen, officers, and ministers, among whom the responsibilities of
state had been divided, so that the government was capable of
being well conducted until the King had attained his majority.
As to toleration, she declared that to grant it would only be to
encourage civil war.[1]

Too late Condé found that he had been trifled with[2] in order

[1] Charles IX to St. Sulpice December 11, 1562; *L'Ambassade de St. Sulpice*,
98; *Despatch of Barbaro* (Huguenot Society), December 7, 1562.

[2] Yet although the negotiations of the prince of Condé at this time were tentative and the statements of the crown not intended by it to obtain, nevertheless
the claims advanced are to be observed, because the lines along which religious
toleration was to develop in France and the outlines of subsequent edicts of tolera-

to give the government time to bring up reinforcements[1] and that the terms he offered had not even been considered. The blame for this unfortunate turn in the war must rest, not upon the queen mother, but upon the Guises. For the duke of Guise and his brother, with the constable, could not but fear, that in the event of peace they would be ruined, and the duke used his own popularity with the masses and the enmity felt by the Parisians toward the queen to gain his ends. When

---

tion, like those of Amboise, Longjumeau, and Bergerac, are foreshadowed in the articles proposed now.

Condé first proposed the following three articles: (1) liberty of conscience with free exercise of religion where demanded; (2) security of life and property unto all; (3) the summons of a free council within six months, or, if that were impossible, then a general assembly of the realm. To these proposals the government replied that Calvinist preaching would not be permitted under any circumstances in Lyons and other frontier towns, which were defined, nor near those with a governor and garrison, nor in those towns which were seats of the parlements. Condé then modified the Huguenot demands, as follows: (1) That Calvinist preaching be permitted in the suburbs of frontier towns, or in certain ones so appointed; (2) that it should obtain only in those other places where it was practiced before the war began; (3) except that it should be lawful for all gentlemen and all nobles to have private service in their own houses; (4) all persons residing in places where preaching was not permitted should be suffered to go to the nearest towns or other places for the exercise of their religion, without molestation. In reply, the government excepted Paris and the *banlieue* from these stipulations. All these conditions the government and Condé accepted on December 3, 1562, Lyons being declared *not* to be a frontier city within the construction of the articles. Certain minor stipulations followed as to amnesty, recovery of property, etc. Cf. *C. S. P. For.*, No. 1,219, December 9, 1562; Beza, *Hist. des églises réformées*, II, 121 ff., ed. 1841.

[1] "M. de Nevers has already here from 800 to 1,000 horse. They look for 600 foot and horsemen, Spaniards and Gascons and Piedmontese, to arrive shortly. All this while they had driven the prince off with talk."—*C. S. P. For.*, 1,168, December 1, 1562—Smith to Throckmorton. These reinforcements reached Paris on the night of December 7, 1562; there were 10 ensigns of Gascons (40 or 50 in an ensign), in all about 500 or 600 men; of the Spaniards, 14 ensigns, "better filled," about 2,500–3,000, all footmen, and few armed. Their weapons were arquebuses and pikes, and some bills and halberds. "With them a marvellous number of rascals, women and baggage" (Smith to Cecil, *C. S. P. For.*, No. 1,205, December 7, 1562; cf. Barbaro [Huguenot Society], December 7, 1562. The Venetian ambassador went out to view them). These reinforcements are much exaggerated in the *Mém. de Condé* (V, 103, 104, ed. London), which rates the Gascons as 3,000 and the Spaniards as 4,000.

duplicity failed, then Catherine's adversaries used intimidation, and the Spanish ambassador at their instigation was sent to her, "either threatening or protesting, or promising and offering aid, and thus upsetting everything."[1] When Paris was full of soldiers negotiations were broken off, the prince of Condé declaring defiantly that the Huguenots would sharpen their swords as they would have need of them.

The only advantage the prince had gained was that he had been able to draw his force close in toward Paris, so that in the last week in November he was camped near the Pont de Charenton. On the 26th he planted his camp on the left bank, a mile from the faubourgs. If the prince of Condé had attacked Paris at once, instead of wasting time at Corbeil in vain *pourparlers*, the whole Huguenot cause might have triumphed, for the government would have been forced to yield almost everything. He might have won the suburbs with little loss, although in want of heavy artillery, and the city could not then have held out long. But now the case was such that he either had to fight—with small hope of winning, let alone of taking Paris—or else come to an accord upon his enemy's terms.[2]

The prevailing opinion was that the prince would not be able to keep his army together for want of provisions and money, especially in mid-winter.[3] This proved to be true. On Decem-

[1] *C. S. P. Ven.*, December 3 and 14, 1562. For an extreme example of Chantonnay's overbearing policy, see Barbaro's account of a conversation with the Spanish ambassador in the letter of January 25, 1563.

[2] *Ibid.*, *For.*, 1,183, December 3, 1562; No. 1,238, §7, December 13, 1562. It is fair to say, though, that Condé was almost without artillery, having but eight guns, so that there was no possibility of breaking the wall. The only way to take the city would have been by an assault with scaling-ladders (letter of Hotman in *Rev. hist.*, XCVII, March–April, 1908, 311).

[3] Claude Haton, I, 307; *C. S. P. Ven.*, No. 314, December 11, 1562. See Throckmorton's earnest plea in *C. S. P. For.*, 1,195, December 6, 1562, for sending financial assistance to him. The English intervention in Normandy was demonstrated to be a safe and profitable venture; besides other advantages which they might draw from Rouen, Havre, and Dieppe (which could safely be recovered) the archbishopric of Rouen was worth 50,000 francs; the two abbeys inside the town 10,000; the abbey of Fécamp 40,000 francs; the benefices within the town valuable; the *gabelle* in salt and other royal rights in Rouen and Dieppe worth 50,000

ber 9 he broke camp and marched off crestfallen, toward Normandy, after burning the camp, to effect a juncture with the English.[1] By this time he had barely 7,000 men, the time of the year telling hard upon the army, for it was compelled to live in the open, while his adversaries had 15,000 or 16,000 men of all nations, one-quarter of whom were mounted. The difficulty of his position was the greater because he was on the left bank of the Seine, with no prospect of passing the river, for the duke of Guise lay at Poissy,[2] while the Rhinegrave and Villebonne were guarding Pont de l'Arche lower down. Warwick was unwilling to venture forth from Havre to the prince's assistance, but hoped, by stopping the shipment of salt and other merchandise up the Seine, to be able to compel the towns of Normandy, as Honfleur, Harfleur, Caudebec, and Rouen, for necessity's sake to come to terms.[3] Being unable to pass the Seine, Condé drew off toward Chartres, followed at the distance of about five leagues by the duke of Guise and the constable, and came to a halt near Montfort not far from Evreux, while Guise lay at a point about ten leagues west of St. Denis, from whence, including Paris, he drew his supplies.[4] All around the two armies the country was destroyed.

crowns, which would double when the English merchants came, so that the military occupation of Normandy would cost less than the profits therefrom. But arguments were in vain to persuade Elizabeth's double policy of caution and parsimony. Sir Nicholas drove Smith's warning of December 7 home by another one to Elizabeth, urging her "to deal substantially" with Condé, "for wanting the queen's force of men it is not likely he will be strong enough to accomplish his intents."

[1] Too late the English government was alive to the danger of its losing all, owing to the narrow policy hitherto pursued, and Cecil hurried Richard Worseley, captain of the Isle of Wight, off to Portsmouth on December 7 to secure 5,000 pounds, as earnest of more money to be sent into France in aid of the Huguenots, whence he was to hasten to Havre, warn the earl of Warwick not to give credit to any reports of peace unless so informed by Throckmorton or Smith, and see that the town was speedily fortified and guarded (C. S. P. For., No. 1,033, December 7, 1562; Forbes, II, 124, 125).

[2] Claude Haton, I, 307; C. S. P. For., No. 1,240, December 13, 1562.

[3] C. S. P. For., No. 1,238, December 13, 1562. On December 14, 1562, Condé wrote anxiously from his camp at St. Arneuil asking for succor, especially that Montgomery, who had gone to England for assistance, might be sent to him. (See Appendix V.) Montgomery was in Portsmouth with Sir Hugh Poulet, who was commissioned to bring over the balance of 15,000 pounds to Havre (C. S. P. For., No. 1,270, December 16, 1562).

[4] Ibid., No. 1,276, December 18, 1562; No. 1,278, December 19, 1562.

The prince's inability to secure provisions, combined with the failure of English support, finally compelled him to give battle to the duke of Guise near Dreux on December 19, the engagement being precipitated by his attempt to force the passage of the Eure, although the odds were against him in every particular, for the duke of Guise was posted at a point so chosen that he could fall back on Dreux if compelled to do so; his flank was protected by a stream and a wood; and his artillery was more numerous than

BATTLE OF DREUX, DECEMBER 19, 1562
(Bib. Nat., Estampes, *Histoire de France*, Q. b)

that of Condé.[1]   The advance guard of the Huguenots was commanded by the admiral; the "battle," in which were the German reiters, by D'Andelot; the rear guard by the prince of Condé himself.   The Huguenot ministers and preachers, armed and mounted, moved about among the men, who sang their psalms in such a loud voice that the camp of the King could easily hear them.   On the Catholic side the marshal St. André was pitted

[1] Guise had 22 cannon; Condé's artillery consisted of 4 field-pieces, 2 cannon, and a culverin, which "never shot a shot" (Throckmorton to the Queen, *C. S. P. For.*, January 3, 1563.   He was an eye-witness of the battle.   Forbes, II, 251).

against D'Andelot; the constable Montmorency commanded the
rear guard, with instructions to hold off until the Huguenot rear
guard entered the fight; while the duke of Guise himself commanded the advance guard against the admiral.[1]

The battle was begun about noon by a victorious charge of the
Huguenot horse, headed by Condé and Coligny, which drove back
the Catholic Swiss and resulted in the capture of six pieces of
cannon and the constable Montmorency who was slightly wounded
in the mouth.   His captors "sent him to Orleans with such speed,
that he drank but once by the way and that on horseback."[2]   The
second charge was less effective owing chiefly to the slowness of
the prince's German reiters who had to have their orders interpreted to them, and partly to the effective artillery fire of the enemy,
and culminated in the capture of Condé, whose horse was shot
under him.   Too late to save the prince of Condé the admiral
made a partial rally of the French and German cavalry, in the
course of whose attack the marshal St. André was killed.[3]   Even
then the issue might have been different if the Huguenot footmen
had not behaved like cowards.[4]   The Protestant loss included
about 800 of the noblesse, and nearly 6,000 footmen and reiters
according to those who buried the dead.[5]   The Catholic loss was
about 2,000, the most conspicuous among the fallen being the
marshal St. André and Montbrun, the youngest son of the constable Montmorency.[6]

[1] Claude Haton, I, 308, 309.   Cf. note for other references.

[2] *C. S. P. Eng.*, No. 228, 229, January 3, 1562; the admiral to Montgomery
(Delaborde, *Gaspard de Coligny*, II, 180), December 28, 1562, from the camp
at Avarot; cf. *C S. P. Eng.*, No. 181, January 2, 1563—the admiral to Queen
Elizabeth; Forbes, II, 247.

[3] De Thou, Book XXXIV, and Le Laboureur's additions to Castelnau, II, 81.

[4] "They did not strike a stroke" and "were defeated in running away."—
C. S. P. For., January 3, 1563; Forbes, II, 251.

[5] Claude Haton, I, 311.

[6] For contemporary accounts of the battle of Dreux, see: "Discours de la
bataille," in *Mém. du duc de Guise*, ed. Michaud, 497 ff.; Beza, *Histoire des églises
réformées*, I, 605 ff.; D'Aubigné, Book III, chaps. xiii, xiv; Tavannes, 392 ff.;
La Noue, *Mém. milit.*, chap. x; De Thou, Book XXXIV; *C. S. P. Eng.*, No. 1,282,
abstract of a printed pamphlet; No. 1,316, December 21; No. 1,323, December

The battle of Dreux was fought on the day of the feast of St. Thomas—almost the shortest day of the year—and the Huguenots had to thank the oncoming of darkness for saving them from pursuit.   Under its cover Coligny drew off toward Auneau where he pitched camp, but some of the Huguenot horse galloped all night toward Orleans.   Fortunate was the Calvinist who could find a cross to put upon his clothing on the morrow.[1]   Twenty-two standards of the prince of Condé were found upon the ground, which were sent to the King and hung in the cathedral of Notre Dame.   Almost all Condé's German footmen were taken prisoners, about 2,000, three-quarters of whom were sent back to Germany on parole, without weapons, and bearing white rods in witness of their abdication; the rest entered the service of the King and were joined with the Rhinegrave's forces under command of Bassompierre, an Alsatian in the service òf Charles IX.[2]

The battle of Dreux, while not a complete rout of the Huguenots, was no less a disaster, because it foiled the efforts of Coligny to effect a junction with the English in Havre and compelled him

22, 1562—letter of the admral to the earl of Warwick; to Queen Elizabeth, Delaborde, II, 178, 179.   For details as to the number of prisoners, etc., see *C. S. P. For.*, Nos. 1,286–88, 1,316, 1,317, 1,335, §§4–6; 1,334, 1,353, §6; 1,563, Nos. 12, 22, 28, narrative of Spanish troops.   Excellent accounts of the battle are to be consulted in De Ruble, *Antoine de Bourbon et Jeanne d'Albret*, II, 366 ff.; Whitehead, *Gaspard de Coligny*, 140–45; and the duke of Aumale's *History of the Princes of Condé* (Eng. trans.), I, 150–68.   The standard treatment of the subject is Coynart, *L'Année 1562 et la bataille de Dreux: étude historique et militaire; extraits divers, correspondance officielles du temps* (1894).

Montaigne has an interesting essay upon some peculiar incidents of the battle. Two curious occurrences happened.   The duke of Guise was the first to alight from his horse and courteously receive the prince of Condé (*C. S. P. For.*, No. 1,326, December.26, 1562); the two slept in the same bed that night (*ibid., Ven.*, December 21, 1,562).   The duke of Aumale was unhorsed and nearly the whole army rode and trampled over him, yet he was unhurt, owing to the heavy suit of armor he wore (*ibid., For.*, No. 375, §3, 1563; cf. No. 400, §2).

[1] The Parlement ordered the bishops of France to declare that in all parishes those who knew who were Huguenots should denounce them within nine days to their priests under pain of excommunication.   This practice led to a large exodus of the Huguenots in many of the towns (Claude Haton, I, 312, 316, 317, and note, 318).

[2] The German form of the name was Bessenstein.

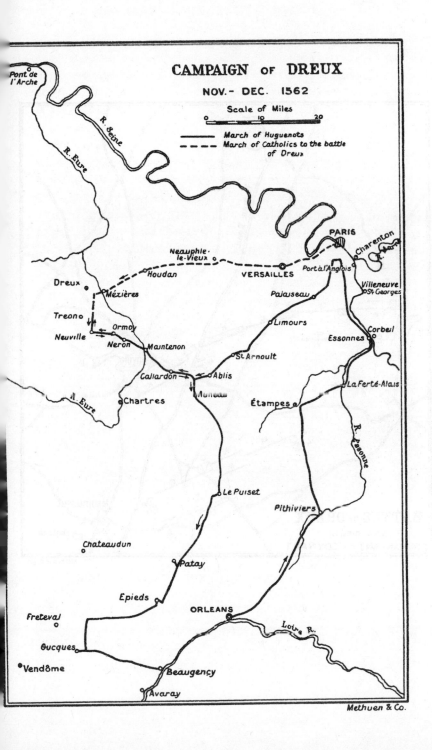

CAMPAIGN of DREUX

NOV.- DEC. 1562

Scale of Miles

0   10   20

——— March of Huguenots
– – – March of Catholics to the battle
of Dreux

Pont de l'Arche

R. Seine

R. Eure

PARIS

Charenton

Neauphle-le-Vieux

Houdan

VERSAILLES

Port à l'Anglois

Dreux

Mézières

Palaiseau

Villeneuve
St Georges

Treono

Ormoy

Limours

Corbeil

Neuville

Neron

Maintenon

Essonnes

St Arnoult

Gallardon

Ablis

La Ferté-Alais

R. Eure

Muneau

Chartres

Étampes

R. Essonne

Le Puiset

Pithiviers

Chateaudun

Patay

Epieds

ORLEANS

Loire R.

Freteval

Oucques

Beaugency

Vendôme

Avaray

Methuen & Co.

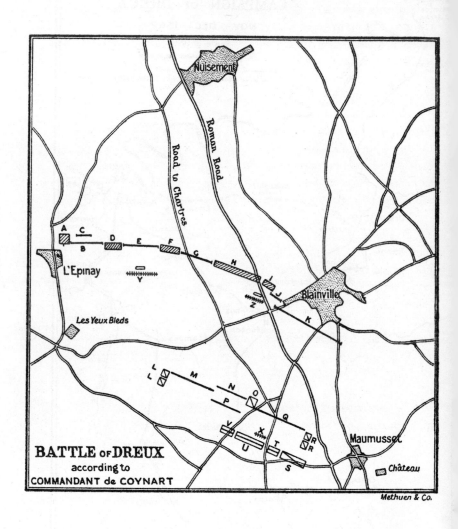

Nuisement

Road to Chartres

Roman Road

A   C
B   D   E   F
        G   H
L'Epinay   I
                            J
                        Blainville
Les Yeux Bleds   K

L   M
L   N   O
        P   Q
        V   X   R
        U   T   R
                S   Maumusset

BATTLE of DREUX
according to
COMMANDANT de COYNART

Château

to fall back on Orleans. Even Spain breathed easier, for anxiety lest the English get Calais was dispelled.[1] Moreover, the French Protestants were in need of money, both Coligny's and D'Andelot's troops being in arrears of pay, the latter's reiters having gone three months without wages.[2] On the other hand the government was in better financial condition through the efforts of the cardinal of Lorraine, who collected some money at the Council of Trent[3] in order to continue the war, and the active efficiency of the Spanish ambassador and the papal legate, who were excellent coworkers.[4] Yet, in spite of defeat, Coligny was resolved to continue the fight, though uncertain what policy to follow. At first he was inclined to go into Dauphiné and join forces with Des Adresse against the duke of Nemours,[5] but the prospect of Catholic relief from Germany in the early spring made it advisable to abandon this plan.

The military situation was much as follows in mid-January, 1563: the Huguenot center was at Orleans, where D'Andelot lay, in control of the middle line of the Loire above Blois and as far northward as Chateaudun and the vicinity of Chartres;[6] Coligny lay at Villefranche (January 12); Montgomery was in Dieppe and the English in Havre. But communication between the Protestant coreligionists was prevented by the way in which the Catholic troops were disposed. Etampes, which the duke of Guise recovered in January, restored the necessary connecting link between Blois and Paris, and the whole line of the Seine was in the hands of the Catholics; Warwick was being besieged in Havre by Vieilleville (he had succeeded the Marshal St. André and was also governor of Normandy), who lay at Caudebec.[7] The marshal

---

[1] C. S. P. For., No. 14, §2, January 3, 1563.

[2] Ibid., No. 16, §2, January 3, 1563, and No. 32—D'Andelot to Elizabeth from Orleans, January 5, 1563; cf. Forbes, II, 263.

[3] Sarpi, Histoire du Concile de Trent, Book VII, chap. xlviii.

[4] C. S. P. For., No. 15, §1, January 3, 1563.

[5] Ibid., Eng. For., No. 35, January 6, 1563; Forbes, II, 270; No. 54, §2, January 7; No. 69, §1, January 11, 1563.

[6] La Mothe Fénélon to St. Sulpice, December 17, 1562; L'Ambassade de St. Sulpice, 163, 164.

[7] C. S. P. Ven., December 27, 1562.

Brissac was at Rouen with seventeen ensigns. The marshal Bourdillon who had been given the bâton of the late marshal Termes was in Piedmont. Paris of course was in the government's hands. In Berry where the upper waters of the Loire and the Seine flow close together the lines of the two hostile parties came in contact. The admiral in the second week in January, 1563, passed the Loire at Beaugency and distributed his men at St. Aignan, Celles, and Montrichard, which lay on the right bank of the stream.[1] At the same time Guise had been minded to cross the river the other way and attack Orleans. This move on the part of each commander brought about a collision of forces near Cléry, in which Guise was repulsed. The condition of the country at the time was terrible, especially for the duke, whose troopers were so pressed that they had to forage twelve leagues from camp.[2] Everywhere the reiters were held in terror, for these raiders frequently made long and rapid marches and fell suddenly upon places, carrying death and destruction with them.

In the meanwhile, the constable had been kept in light captivity at Orleans,[3] a treatment in contrast with that experienced by Condé, who was first kept under strong guard by Damville in the little abbey of St. Pierre at Chartres, both the windows and the street being barred, and later, on January 24, 1563, brought to Paris.[4] Ever since Dreux, the queen mother and the constable had been constantly employed in the endeavor to make a settle-

---

[1] Randolph wrote to Cecil on January 5, 1563: "We thought ourselves happy till we heard of the prince's taking, but despair not as longe as the admiral kepethe the feeldes."—C. S. P. Scot., I, 1,160.

[2] Ibid., For., No. 83, January 13, 1563; No. 84, §3, same date; No. 109, §6, January 17; No 137, §5, January 23, 1563.

[3] Ibid., No. 83, §3, January 13, 1563.

[4] "Coll. d'un ancien amateur," Hôtel Drouot, February 10, 1877, No. 34: Eleanor de Roye to Catherine de Medici from Orleans, December 22, 1562, asking that pity be taken upon the prince of Condé; C. S. P. For., No. 35, January 6, 1563; Forbes, II, 270; No. 146, §3: "This night (January 24) Condé was brought into this town with a strong guard. He came on horseback, and was brought through the town in a coach covered with black velvet, by torch-light, and the windows of the coach open; but the torch was so carried that none could see him." The government had good reason to fear an attempt would be made to rescue him while he was at Chartres.

ment.[1]   In the case of the constable, self-interest was the chief motive: he chafed under confinement and was envious of the duke of Guise.[2]   On the other hand, Catherine's anxiety was of a political nature.   She was fearful lest England permanently acquire Havre-de-Grace.   Her purpose was to make peace with the Huguenots and then unite the parties in a war for the recovery of Havre.[3] But the mistrust of the Huguenots that the overtures of peace were meant to be an accord in appearance only; the ambition of the Guises who saw their power thrive in the struggle; the opposition of Paris, and perhaps above all, the opposition of Spain, were difficulties in the way.[4]   Philip II's joy over Dreux was tempered by his anxiety, and he secretly aimed to thwart any terms of peace at all favorable to the Protestants.[5]   Catherine probably would have preferred to abide by anything rather than have the Guises gain greater profit.[6]   The queen mother urged

[1] "A ce soir bien tard j'ay receu la lettre qu'il vous a pleu m'escripre par la poste et vous puis asseurer Madame qu'il y a deux jours que Madame la Princesse et mon nepveu Dandelot veullent vous envoyer la response et advis de mon nepveu monsieur l'admiral et de toute leur compaigne.   Mais je les en ay engarder sur la tente qu'auyons au retour du Plessis qui devoit estre samedy au matin pour estre rendu certain de vostre volonté, à quoy les voys tous fort affectionnés pour faire une bonne paix," etc., etc.—Montmorency to Catherine de Médicis, Orléans, 12 janvier 1563 (Fillon Collection, No. 2652).

[2] C. S. P. For., No. 35, §2, January 6, 1563; Forbes, II, 270.

[3] Catherine expressed this determination as far back as October 20 in a letter to St. Sulpice (L'Ambassade de St. Sulpice, 87; C. S. P. For., No. 37, January 6, 1563).

[4] C. S. P. Ven., February 2, 1563.

[5] Cf. L'Ambassade St. Sulpice, 93, 108, 114, 116, and Corresp. de Cath. de Méd., I, 508, 548.   This was the real mission of Don Fernando de Toledo, a bastard son of the duke of Alva and grand prior of the order of St. John in Castile, who was sent to France to congratulate Charles IX on the victory of Dreux (cf. C. S. P. For., No. 187, January 29, 1563, from Madrid; No. 190, January 30, from Madrid; No. 234, February 3, from Madrid).   St. Sulpice this early surmised that Alva, at any rate, though he did not yet so suspect the political designs of Philip II, desired the continuation of civil war in France in order that Spain might profit by her distress, and so wrote to Catherine de Medicis.—L'ambassade de St. Sulpice, 93, November 12, 1562.   In consequence of this attitude, religious and political, the arguments of France fell upon deaf ears (see ibid., 122, and note).

[6] Cf. C. S. P. For., No. 35, §2, January 6, 1563; No. 109, § 4, January 17; No. 182, §9, January 28; Forbes, II, 270, 287.

the necessity of peace on account of lack of funds to carry on the war.[1] But her arguments were cast to the winds by the triumphant Guises when money began to pour into France from Spain, Venice, the duke of Tuscany, and from some of the Catholic German princes.[2]

On the other hand, the penury of the Protestants increased from day to day. Coligny was in daily fear lest the reiters would desert him on account of the delay in paying them.[3] In vain he wrote to Elizabeth, urging the speedy remittance of money. The cautious procrastination and niggardly policy of Elizabeth in the end was fatal to his purpose. In vain her ambassador in France, the faithful Throckmorton, urged immediate and liberal action. Warwick also added his plea, informing the home government and the queen that the admiral would be "ruined and unable to hold up his head without her aid in men and money."[4] Elizabeth's notorious parsimony led her to deceive the French Protes-

[1] C. S. P. Ven., February 6, 1563.

[2] Ibid., For., No. 234, February 3, 1563, from Madrid. No. 194, January 30, 1563. The money was used to purchase the services of 3,000 reiters and some new levies of Swiss. Pending their arrival, Charles IX called out the arrière-ban— cavalry of the nobility obliged to serve upon call—to prosecute the war (C. S. P. Ven., February 17, 1563). See the interesting account of the interception of 13,000 écus d'or probably by the Huguenots, though it may have been by robbers, sent from Flanders in February, 1563 (Paillard, "De tournement au profit des Huguenots d'un subsidé envoyé par Philippe II à Catherine de Médicis," Rev. hist., II, 490).

[3] C. S. P. For., No. 145, January 24, 1563; Forbes, II, 300.

[4] Ibid., Eng. For., No. 289, February 12, 1562. "If the admiral," wrote the earl, "should, for want of present aid, be discomfited and driven to make composition, they may reckon not only upon the whole power of France being bent against this place (Harfleur), but that the same will, with the assistance of Spain and Scotland and their confederates, be also undoubtedly extended against England. But if he be now aided with 10,000 men and 200,000 crowns, further inconvenience will be stayed and may serve a better purpose than the employment at another time of a far greater number at larger charges. It would be better for the queen to convert a good part of her plate into coin than slack her aid."—Ibid., Eng., No. 290, February 12, 1563; add Nos. 285, 287. Warwick in seconding Coligny's appeal (ibid., For., No. 294, February 12, 1563) urged haste in the matter of the money, as "if it is not sent in time it will be the ruin of the cause through mutiny of the reiters, who may even kill the admiral;" moreover, as the admiral's forces were all cavalry, English infantry was wanted.

tants with vague promises, a policy so short-sighted that it ultimately lost England the support of the Huguenots and compelled the evacuation of Havre-de-Grace, which otherwise they might have made another Calais. By February the admiral's patience was well-nigh exhausted, and his troops in mutiny, the reiters raiding the country to such an extent that the court and the foreign ambassadors were compelled to retire from Chartres to Blois, not daring to try to go to Paris. As his position became more desperate from want of funds, Coligny determined to strike northward, if possible to effect a juncture with the English on the coast of Normandy, and so while his agents parleyed for peace in order to gain time and deceive the enemy, the admiral, leaving his wagons and baggage behind him in order that his reiters might ride unimpeded, stole away from Jargau on the night of February 1 with 2,000 reiters, 1,000 mounted arquebusiers, and 500 gentry. His purpose was to join Warwick, but when he reached Dreux, where the battle had been fought six weeks earlier, he discovered that it was impossible for him to cross the Seine, and hence, after sending word to the earl that he was in hard straits for money to pay his men and had "much ado to keep them together," he drew off toward Caen.[1]

While Coligny lay at Dives, Throckmorton—it must have been against his own convictions—was sent to confer with him, informing him that if the admiral counted that the payment of his army and the support of the war depended upon Elizabeth alone, he was to understand that the people of England would not willingly contribute to such an expense, since the war was of little profit to them. Therefore Elizabeth advised the Huguenots not to refuse reasonable conditions of peace, the English queen including in the sphere of "reasonable conditions" Huguenot insistence that Calais be restored to England.[2]

In the meantime, while Coligny's position was growing worse

[1] C. S. P. For., Nos. 265, 276, 280, 282, 289, February, 1563.

[2] Ibid., Eng., No. 291. Throckmorton's report of his conference with Admiral Coligny, February 12, 1563. It is astonishing, after this display of selfishness and greed, that Coligny should still have retained patience with, and faith in, Elizabeth.

and worse, the position of D'Andelot in Orleans had also become serious. The duke of Guise invested the city on February 4, and got possession of Portereau (February 6), a faubourg of Orleans across the river, which had been fortified during the previous summer. But the Huguenots still held the town at their end of the bridge and broke several of the arches down. A tiny island lay in the stream and this the duke planned to reach by filling thousands of sacks with sand and gravel and throwing them into the river between the banks at Portereau and the island from whence he would be more able to attack Orleans with cannon.[1] But it being winter time, the river was too deep and the current too strong. Failing this, he planned to cut the river above Orleans in order to let the water into the meadow lands.[2] The spirited siege lasted many days. Every kind of metal was impressed into service by those of Orleans, including shells made of brass, "which was a new device and very terrible," and their ammunition seemed likely to outlast that of their enemy. The Catholic position around Orleans was by no means an enviable one. Food, money, and ammunition were lacking. All Guise's men-at-arms and light horsemen lived at discretion—that is, they quartered themselves on the surrounding villages and forced the poor people of the country to feed them and their horses. The court was doing the same at Blois to the "marvellous destruction" of the country. The lack of powder bade fair to be fatal to the duke's success, for the government's powder factories at Chartres, Chateaudun, and Paris were all blown up, accidentally or otherwise, about this time, that of Paris having occurred on January 28, 1563, with great destruction of property and some lives.[3] In consequence of these

[1] The duke was short of heavy guns and had to send to Paris for them to come to Corbeil by water, from thence to Montargis, and so after by land to the river. The defenders had improvised a mill on the island into a fortress but after the arrival of the heavy guns, so hot a fire was poured upon them that they were compelled to retire across the bridge, "leaving many to the mercy of the fish" (Claude Haton, I, 319).

[2] *C. S. P. For.*, No. 323, February 17, 1653. Both D'Aubigné, Book III, chap. xvi, and La Noue, *Mém. milit.*, chap. x, have vivid accounts of this siege; cf. also De Thou, Book XXXIV.

[3] Barbaro gives details of the havoc wrought by this explosion (*C. S. P. Ven.*, January 28, 1563); cf. *C. S. P. For.*, No. 239, §3, No. 323, § 18, February 17, 1563.

disasters, the Catholic artillery had to send all the way to Flanders for gunpowder. Although some breaches were made in the wall by the Catholics, the duke of Guise delayed final assault, for two reasons: first, because the queen mother hoped to take the city by composition, secondly, because Catholic reinforcements were looked for late in March out of Germany, Switzerland, and Gascony, to the number of ten thousand.

No such silver lining lightened the cloud on the Huguenot horizon. D'Andelot from Orleans, the princess of Condé, Eleanor de Roye, from Strasburg, her imprisoned husband, and Coligny all implored the English queen in vain for speedy relief. The admiral's position by the end of February was desperate. He had been compelled to move into the western part of Normandy, for his 5,000 reiters were "in such rage for their money that he could scarce keep them together," and were being so corrupted by the enemy that he might otherwise have lost them utterly.[1] Powder also was wanting.[2] The condition of Montgomery[3] in Dieppe and of Warwick in Havre was quite as bad. In Havre food was so scarce that rations were reduced to a two-penny loaf to four persons; wood was unprocurable; the water was bad.[4] The spoiling of Normandy from the devastation of Coligny's reiters who were levying upon the country without law or order, and burning and destroying villages without regard to religion, was

---

[1] Throckmorton wrote to Cecil on February 21: "He is to be pitied, for every hour he is in danger of his life and of being betrayed by his reiters."—*C. S. P. For.*, No. 333, §§1, 5, 9, February 20, 1563; No. 339, February 21, 1562.

[2] *Ibid.*, No. 374, March 1, 1563; Forbes, II, 332.

[3] Montgomery to the Rhinegrave, Dieppe, 8 fevrier, 1563: "Les habitans du plat pays m'ont faict entendre qu'ils seroient prestz de se joindre à moy si je me vouloys metre en campagne pour les deffendre des oppressions, pilleries et sacagementz qu'ilz disent estre exercés par ceux qui vous suivent. . . . . Monsieur l'admiral [Coligny] n'est [pas] au pays [l'Orléannais] que me mandez, ou à tout le moings qu'il a faict une extrême diligence et est plus près de nous qu'on ne cuyde, en delliberation de metre bientost une fin à ces troubles, pour nous faire tous jouyr du rang que nous debrons tenir prez la personne du Roi comme ses vrays subjets et loyaulx serviteurs."—Fillon Collection.

[4] *C. S. P. For.*, No. 352, Warwick to the council, February 25, 1563; cf. Forbes, II, 336; *C. S. P. Eng. For.*, No. 327, §3, February 18, 1563; Forbes, II, 334, 380, March 1, 1563; cf. Nos. 333, 344.

terrible. "If the reiters understand that another messenger has arrived here (Caen) from the queen and the money not come," wrote the admiral, "it will be impossibble to save our throats from being cut." Fortunately the very next day the English ambassador arrived in Caen with word for Coligny to the effect that eight thousand pounds in English sovereigns, French crowns, angels, and pistolets were on the way from Portsmouth to Caen.[1] Fire opened on Caen castle on March 1, and the next day the marquis D'Elbœuf surrendered it. Bayeux also capitulated.[2] The fall of these two places and the fearful state of the country,[3] might have broken the resolution of the crown to continue the war.[4] But another fate intervened.

Henry of Guise was mortally wounded on the night of February 18, 1563, by a Huguenot assassin named Poltrot[5] and died on

---

[1] The money reached Havre on February 25 and was brought by Beauvoir, Briquemault, and Throckmorton under guard of eight pieces of artillery to Caen at once (Delaborde, II, 226, 227). The reiters received their pay at once. For some curious information about the avarice of the reiters and the pay given them, see *Papiers d'état du cardinal de Granvelle*, VIII, 129, note; VII, 407.

[2] *C. S. P. For.*, 391; Forbes, II, 346.

[3] Catherine wrote with truth: "Ce royaume est réduit en telle extrémité que la necessité veut que l'on ne perde l'occasion de faire pacifier, principalement pour jeter hors les étrangers, mêmement les Anglais."—*L'Ambassade de St. Sulpice*, 101.

[4] "La guerre," said Catherine with words of simple dignity, which were repeated in the instructions of the special envoys sent to notify the court of Vienna and Madrid, the Vatican and the Council of Trent, "a tellement appauvri le royaume qu'il est réduit à un état digne de commisération. La voie des armes était impossible; le remède propre à un tel mal; l'expérience a démontré, c'est un libre et général concile."—*Corresp. de Cath. de Méd.*, II, Introd., v. Philip II, reproached the regent of Parma for not lending assistance to France. See her letter justifying her conduct in Gachard, *Correspondance de Philippe II sur les Pays-Bas*, I, 266, August 12, 1563.

[5] The marshal Brissac succeeded to the command (*L'Ambassade de St. Sulpice*, 120). For the influence of the death of the duke of Guise in France, see Forneron, *Hist. des ducs de Guise*, II, 80; upon Flanders, *Papiers d'état du cardinal de Granvelle*, VII, 52, 61, 65; Gachard, *Philippe II sur les Pays-Bas*, I, 245. For interesting details see D'Aubigné, Book III, chap. xx; *Mém. de Condé*, IV, 243; *C. S. P. For.*, No. 332, February 20, 1563; No. 354, §§2–5, February 26, 1562, both from Smith to Queen Elizabeth, written from Blois. Cf. Forbes, II, 159; 361, §§1–8, 17, February 26, 424, §10 March 8, 1563; *C. S. P. Ven.*, letters of February

Ash Wednesday following, February 24. The death of the duke of Guise was a heavy blow to the Catholics. His following, because of his personal magnetism, was greater than that of any other Catholic leader, for many noblemen and gentlemen adhered to the Catholic cause more for love of him than for loyalty to the established religion. Moreover, he was an able general uniting quickness of intelligence, determination, experience, popularity, and physical endurance in his talented person. Immediately after

ASSASSINATION OF THE DUKE OF GUISE, FEBRUARY 18, 1563
(Tortorel and Perissin)

Guise was hurt, the queen mother went to the camp with the desire to see the constable. The prince of Condé and the con-

23, 27, and March 2, 23, 1563. It is said the duke received warning from Montluc and Madame de St. André, but that the word arrived too late. The news of his death was kept from Mary Stuart for some time. See *C. S. P. Scotland*, VI, No. 1,173, March 10, 1563; VIII, No. 17, March 18, 1563; No. 30, April 1, 1563; No. 31, April 10, 1563. On the political theory of assassination, see Weill, 69.

Poltrot was put to death on March 18; for the trial, see *Mém.-journ. de François, de Lorraine* (Michaud Coll.), 506, 537 ff.; Paulin Paris, *Cabinet hist.*, Ière part., III, 49 ff. A conspicuous instance of the high-mindedness of Jeanne d'Albret is the letter of consolation she wrote to the duchess of Guise after the assassination of the duke (La Ferrière, *Rapport*, 39).

stable were obviously the men of the hour, and as they could not conduct negotiations while they were prisoners, they were both liberated on March 8, and held a conference together on that day.[1] On March 19 the King, with the assent of his council, formally decreed religious toleration and appointed the prince of Condé lieutenant-general of the realm with exemption for seizure of any of the royal revenues by him during the troubles.[2] It was high time for peace to be made, for the revolt of the provinces was

INTERVIEW ON THE ILE-AUX-BŒUFS
(Bib. Nat., Estampes, *Histoire de France*, Q. b)

increasing. In La Rochelle, Poitou, Guyenne, and Picardy the "Howegenosys" had again rebelled in February, and the lieutenants of these provinces sent to Blois for aid.[3]

[1] *C. S. P. For.*, No. 422, March 8, 1562; Forbes, II, 350, 354, 356; *C. S. P. For.*, No. 437, March 12, 1563; *ibid.*, No. 424, §§25–27; No. 435, March 11, 1562, Condé to Smith.

[2] *Ibid.*, No. 473; 481, March 20, the Rhinegrave to Warwick on the basis of a letter of the queen mother (Beza, II, 17, ed. 1841).

[3] *C. S. P. For.*, Nos. 395, §2, March 3, 1563; 419, §5, March 7; 424, §§3, 4; Forbes, II. "La retarder d'un jour," said De Losses in one of the sessions of the King's council, "c'était exposer la ville de Paris au sac et au pillage, laisser le roi

The terms of Amboise are interesting because they mark the triumph of the aristocratic element in the Huguenot party, whose interests were identified with their political purposes and their feudal position, over the "Geneva party," who were austere Calvinists, and who had an eye single to religion only.[1] D'Andelot, and to a less degree the admiral, were representatives of this latter group.[2] The terms of peace provided that the prince of Condé was to succeed to the place of the late king of Navarre; that the Huguenot army was to be paid by the government; that in all towns where the Reformed religion prevailed, save Paris, it was to be protected; that in every bailiwick the King was to appoint one town where the gospel might be preached; that all gentlemen holding fiefs in low or mean justice might have preaching in their houses for the benefit of their families; that all nobles enjoying high justice might have preaching on their estates; that property confiscated from either church was to be restored.[3] Paris firmly refused at first to tolerate any terms of peace,[4] its Catholic prejudices being aggravated by desire to revenge the murder of the duke of Guise; but the King replied to the demur of the Parlement

et la reine à la merci des protestants encore aux armes." M. Gonnor, later the marshal Matignon, dwelt upon the miserable state of the country and concluded: "Je parle sans passion. Je ne suis pas huguenot et je supplie la cour de ne pas différer l' enrégistrement de l'édit."—*Corresp. de Cath de Méd.*, II, Introd., iii.

[1] "Traité politique par lequel en quelque sorte la gentilhommerie provinciale s'isolait du puritanisme de Génève."—Capefigue, 260.

[2] "C'est trop grand pitié que de limiter ainssy certains lieux pour servir à Dieu, comme s'il ne vouloit estre en tous endroicts."—Fillon Collection, 2,657, the admiral to the landgrave from Caen, March 16, 1563.

[3] "Edict et déclaration faite par le roy Charles IX sur la pacification des troubles de ce Royaume: le 19 mars 1563," Par., *Rob. Estienne*, 1563; Isambert, XIV, 135. The various pieces showing the evolution of the edict are to be found in *Mém. de Condé*, IV, 305, 333, 356, 498, 504. Cf. *C. S. P. For.*, Nos. 428, 430, 431 (March 10, 1563).

Biron was sent into Provence in 1563 with instructions to give an account to the King of the manner in which justice was administered there and how the edict was executed. He was also to find the count of Tendes and Sommerive and express the King's displeasure of their conduct. The royal instructions are evidence of the sincerity with which the government started to execute the edict (La Ferrière, *Rapport*, 46; cf. *Collection Trémont*, sér. 3, p. 124).

[4] *C. S. P. For.*, No. 424, §16; No. 590, April 8, 1563; Forbes, II, 379.

that the city must make up its mind to accept the conditions.[1]
On the other hand, Lyons as obstinately refused to receive the
mass, so that the country round about it remained turbulent well
into the autumn.[2]   Rouen, Dijon, Toulouse, encouraged by the
opposition of the Parlement, refused to recognize the edict.[3]   The
roads were filled with robbers, and the continued presence of the
reiters, to whom an enormous sum in wages was due, was a perpetual menace.

The Germans who had been in the service of the King and
those of the prince of Condé fraternized on the road home.   They
made a great troop to the number of 10,000 or 12,000, taking the
road from Orleans by way of Pluvières and Etampes to Paris, and
arrived there in Easter week, where they staid for five weeks at
least.   When they left they were an entire day crossing the bridge
over the Seine, because of the enormous amount of baggage which
they had.   After having crossed the Seine, the reiters divided into
two bands for better living, one of them skirting the right bank
of the Seine, the other crossing Brie to the Marne, in order to find
better provisions for themselves and their horses.   These latter
traversed Champagne to the River Aube and encamped at Mon-
tier-en-Der near Vassy for six entire weeks, marauding the country

[1] C. S. P. Ven., March 23, 1563. "Response faicte par le Roy (Charles IX)
et son Conseil, aux Presidens et Conseillers de sa Cour de Parlement de Paris:
Sur la remonstrance faicte à sa dicte maiesté, concernant la déclaration de sa
Maiorité, et ordonnance faicte pour le bien, et repos publique de son Royaume"
(Lyons, Rigaud, 1563).

In the first week of May the King summoned the members of the Parlement
of Paris and the authorities of the city to St. Germain, commanding them before
the week was out to obey the Edict of Toleration, to release those imprisoned for
religion, and to lay down their arms (C. S. P. For., No. 703, §3, May 4, 1563).
Paris finally published the edict, but observed it slightly, the Parlement admitting
the "graces" of the edict, but saying it could not in its conscience allow two religions
(ibid., No. 1190, 835, June 2, 1563).   For an example of the violence of the
capital see No. 895, June 15, 1562.   The public criers and the very horses which
they used in the crying of the edict in the city of Paris were in danger of being killed
by the populace, which poured out of the mouths of the streets (Claude Haton, I,
328).

[2] "Le peuple y est fort sedicieux."—Fourquevaux to St. Sulpice, October 13,
1563, L'Ambassade de St. Sulpice, 165.

[3] Correspondance de Catherine de Médicis, II, Introd., iv.

for five or six leagues about.   Their depredations drove the peasantry to such despair that protective associations composed of
the peasantry and nobles were formed to resist their aggressions,
and these fell upon stragglers whenever they found a little group
of them, and cut their throats.   Gradually, however, these despoilers were drawn off out of the land, being accompanied to the frontier by the French infantry under the command of the prince de
Porcien, who was then at Metz, where he had been stationed to
foil any effort the Emperor might make for its recovery.[1]   The
priest-historian of Provins has graphically depicted the depredations of the reiters:

At the beginning of this war [he says] the people of the villages were so
rich and well provided for, so well furnished in their houses with all kinds
of furniture, so well provided with poultry and animals, that it was noble to
see. . . . .   But the soldiers destroyed their beautiful tables, their shining
brass-bound chests, and killed a great quantity of poultry without paying for
it, or else offering a paltry sum in proportion to the number of soldiers who
were lodged in the house.   It was all one whether one man or many were so
lodged, because the soldier who had a house to himself seized everything to his
own profit.   The wives and daughters of the peasantry were compelled to
defend their honor.   Property was seized and every sort of villainy was done
by the soldiers, within the space of the three or four days that they might
remain at a place.[2]

Not since the Hundred Year's War had France beheld a people
more fearful and formidable than were these reiters.   They plundered the wretched people of all their goods, loading their horses
and wagons therewith.   Amid their equipment they carried win-
nowing fans to winnow the grain, flails to beat it in the granges,
and sacks to bind it up in.   They had with them mills to grind
the grain and little ovens to bake bread in.   Wherever they lodged
they tore up floors, broke into closets, and ransacked gardens,

   C. S. P. Ven., March 29, April 10 and 20, 1563.   On the prince de
Porcien, see Le Laboureur, I, 389; also an article by Delaborde in Bulletin de
la Soc. prot. franç., XVIII, 2.   Claude Haton gives some vivid details about this
retirement of the reiters (Vol. I, p. 355).   Cf. Correspondance de Catherine de
Médicis, II, 15, 16, 42.   On the case of the Three Bishoprics see St. Sulpice, ibid.;
C. S. P. Ven., March 29, April 10, 1563; C. S. P. For., Nos. 323, §8, and 419, §5,
420, 455; Nég. Tosc., III, 403.

   2 Claude Haton, I, 279, 280.

courts, and chimneys, in order to find booty.   They even fell upon
the houses and châteaux of the nobles, where they passed, if they
saw they were not strong or well defended.[1]   For this reason those
living in poorly fortified houses vacated them and fled to the towns.
Those who owned strong and well-fortified houses levied soldiers
for their defense.   What happened at Provins happened, doubtless,
in many other places, too.

In the carrefours of Provins, it was proclaimed that no inhabi-
tant of the town, under pain of a fine of one hundred livres *tournois*
and imprisonment, should leave it, and that every man at the
hour of ten in the morning must report with his arms before the
house of his sergeant (*dizainier*) for the purpose of mounting guard
upon the walls, each in his own part of the city.   Everybody in
the surrounding country began to vacate their houses and to drive
their cattle into the town.   On the evening before Easter messengers of Provins reported that the reiters were near.   At this
news watchers were set upon the wall of the town, and a *corps de
garde* posted by the town authorities.   On the morning of the
morrow, which was Easter Sunday, the gates of the town were
not opened until eight o'clock, upon which there poured into the
town an infinite number of wagons and pack-animals laden with
the possessions of the villagers round about.   There was hardly
room to bestow so many people and so many animals.   Divine
service was celebrated in the parish churches, for it was expected
that the reiters would take their course toward the town, and the
people were resolved not to let them enter, but to resist to the very
last drop of blood.

In order to ascertain what was the equipment and the arms of each in-
habitant of the town, a general meeting was called at midday for a view of
arms, but it was not possible to hold the meeting because all the streets and
squares were packed with the refugees and their animals.   In consequence of
this, local meetings were held in each of the quarters of the city.   Thus the
day wore on and consternation abated only when it was learned that the
reiters had gone off toward the Marne, which they crossed above Coulumiers.
On the morrow, Easter Monday, there was no procession in the streets as

[1] See the interesting account of an unsuccessful attempt by the reiters to
storm a château (Claude Haton, I, 347–49).

usual, for fear of a surprise, and it was not until evening that the people who had found refuge within the town, began to depart.[1]

But the undisguised hostility of Spain to the Edict of Amboise was a greater source of danger to France than protests of the Parlement or popular violence. "If the heretics obtain their demands with the aid of the English queen," Chantonnay had threatened on March 6, "the Catholics in their turn will rise, and they will be sustained by the King my master and by all the Catholic princes."[2] But Catherine was in no mood to be intimidated. She openly told him that he treated her as if he governed the country, and charged him with wilful fabrication, sarcastically adding that she could excuse him for so doing in some degree because she knew from whom he derived his opinions, meaning the constable and the two deceased members of the Triumvirate.[3] Philip II's religious convictions were outraged by the toleration of Calvinism allowed in the Edict of Amboise, the more so because the queen mother, in justification of the course of the government, compromised the church at large by declaring that the sole practical solution of the difficulty could be accomplished by a true general council of the church, and *not* by the one sitting at Trent, in defiance of whose conclusions she asserted the legality and inviolability of the edict.[4]

Catherine de Medici was deeply concerned over the conduct of the Council of Trent. For the programme of zealous advo-

[1] Claude Haton, I, 354.

[2] Quoted by Forneron, I, 277, note 1.

[3] *C. S. P. Ven.*, April 21, 1563.

[4] *Correspund. de Cath. de Méd.* Introd., cxlv-vi; cf. *R. Q. H.*, October 1869, 349-51. Charles IX was firmly resolved to enforce the national traditions of the French monarchy with reference to the papacy. The fearless speech of Du Ferrier occasioned a sensation in the council. France was accused of wishing, like England, to secede from Rome and found a national church and it was even proposed to hand the ambassador over to the Inquisition (Frémy, *Un ambassadeur libéral sous Charles IX et Henri III*, 1880, p. 49). So energetic were the remonstrances of Lansac that he was derisively called the "ambassador of the Huguenots" (Frémy, 21).

On April 15, 1563, the King wrote to the cardinal of Lorraine to inform him that, having grown impatient at the slowness of the Council of Trent, he was sending the president Biragues to Trent and then to the Emperor with a mission to have

cates of the counter-Reformation there aimed at church consolidation and the enlargement of papal authority to such an extent that
the immemorial liberties of the Gallican church, confirmed by the
great concordat of 1516, and the rights of the crown over the temporalities of the church in France were seriously threatened. The
complication of the Huguenots with England and the murder of
the duke of Guise had brought this issue to a head. In the month
in which the duke was assassinated there was a significant meeting
of the ambassadors of the ultra-Catholic powers resident at the
French court, in which it was resolved to support the Council in
matters of religion; to prevent future appropriation of church
revenues by the state under pain of excommunication; to stamp
out heresy; and to avenge the murder of the duke of Guise.[1] The
cardinal of Lorraine was the chief representative of France at
Trent and perhaps the most conspicuous prelate there. He was
bitter against the policy of Charles IX, advocating utter suppression
of the Huguenots. His continuance at Trent, therefore, became
a danger to France and Catherine de Medici dexterously found
means to remove him by sending him on special errands to Vienna
and Venice, leaving the case of France at Trent in the hands of
the sieur de Lansac, whose loyalty to the Catholic faith did not
subvert his patriotism.[2]

the council transferred to a freer place if possible. The King declared that if the
reforms demanded by Christianity were not accorded and confirmed by the council, France would not hesitate to convoke a national council. (See the instruction
to D'Oysel in *Corresp. de Catherine de Médicis*, II, 1–3, note.)

[1] "Articles de l'alégation de messieurs les ambassadeurs, estant de present à
la cour; envoyez, l'un par nostre saint père le Pape, l'autre par l'Empereur, Roy des
Romains, l'autre par le Roy d'Espaigne, et le Prince de Piedmont. Au Roy de
France et princes de son sang, au mois de Fevrier, 1563," *Mém. de Condé*, V, 406–8;
cf. *L'Ambassade de St. Sulpice*, 135 and 167.

[2] Lansac and Du Ferrier were the ambassadors of France at Trent. Lansac's
instructions, which outline the policy of France, are in Baschet, *Journal du Concile de Trente*, etc., 251–65; add D'Aubigné, Book III, chap. xxi; St. Sulpice,
28, 64, 102, 114, 130, 141, 160–63. On Lansac, see *Correspondance de Catherine de Médicis*, Index; upon Du Ferrier, consult Frémy, *Un ambassadeur libéral
sous Charles IX et Henri III*, 1880.

The cardinal of Lorraine, while agreeing with Philip II, as to religion and
heresy, looked with resentment upon the King's attempt to appropriate the political

Aside from his religious antagonism, Philip II regarded his own political interests as also jeopardized by the French situation. He was alarmed at the possible recovery of Calais by England,[1] and the progress of heresy and rebellion in the Netherlands, especially at Valenciennes and Tournay, was certain to be encouraged by the example of France, while a common effort of the Huguenots of Picardy and those of the religion across the Flemish border was seriously feared.[2]

destiny of Mary Stuart to his own ends (St. Sulpice to Lansac, December 15, 1562, p. 103). The whole council was filled with disaffection; 150 out of the 230 members present were Italians, most of these pensioners of Rome, so that the others resented their preponderance (Lansac to St. Sulpice, February 10, 1563, *L'Ambassade de St. Sulpice*, 115).

There were conflicts as to precedence; some of the ambassadors like Lansac and Du Ferrier believed in qualified toleration of Protestants (St. Sulpice, 115); many of the members, while believing in the enlargement of the Pope's prerogatives in religious affairs, were opposed to a reduction of governmental rights of control over ecclesiastical temporalities. Philip II's attitude in this respect was identical with that of Charles IX—each wanted to exercise political control over the church within his kingdom (St. Sulpice, 198). Even the cardinal of Lorraine was an advocate of temporal independence (St. Sulpice, 161). See Baschet, *Journal du Concile de Trente;* the Appendix has a valuable bibliography of the history of the Council of Trent. M. Baguenault de la Puchesse' article in *R. Q. H.*, 1869, may be added. The cardinal of Lorraine left Trent on March 23. M. Baschet questions (p. 214): "Que sont devenues toutes les dépêches qu'il a du écrire à la Reine mère, tant sur sa négociation avec l'Empereur, que sur sa visite à la Republique de Venise et son voyage en Cour de Rome, pour l'accomplissement desquels il s'était deplacé de sa résidence au Concile?" He was not aware of the fact, when he wrote in 1870, that Count Hector de la Ferrière had shortly before discovered them in the archives at St. Petersburg (La Ferrière, *Deux années de mission à Saint Petersbourg*, 51). For the cardinal's mission to Venice see *R. Q. H.*, October 1869, 349, 350, and 385, note.

[1] Forbes, II, 271; *C. S. P. For.*, No. 1,193, §5, December 5, 1562. Granvella to the King, March 10, 1563; Gachard, *Correspondance de Philippe II sur les Pays-Bas*, I, 239; cf. Philip to Margaret of Parma, May 16, *ibid.*, I, 249.

[2] The fear was amply justified. Granvella wrote to his sovereign on December 22, 1563: "Le situation actuelle de la France est plus fâcheuse qui j'aie vue depuis la mort du roi François."—*Papiers d'état du cardinal de Granvelle*, VII, 284. Gachard, *Rapport sur les archives de Lille*, 218, cites a remark made in 1562: "Messieurs, acoustez bien ce qui adviendra en France entre les catholicques et les Huguenots; cas, au son flageolet de Franche il vous faudra danser par dechà."

CHAPTER VIII

THE WAR WITH ENGLAND—THE PEACE OF TROYES[1] (1563–64)

The closure of the civil war was a necessary condition precedent to the war France now planned to wage with her "adversary of England" for the recovery of Havre-de-Grace. Catherine de Medici had paid Coligny's reiters in order to close the chasm as soon as possible. The keen-witted representatives of Queen Elizabeth in France—Throckmorton and Smith—had done all in their power to diussade the Protestants from making peace.[2] Too late Elizabeth perceived the result of her procrastination. War between England and France over Havre was inevitable,[3] though in March the French government dissembled its real intention, giving the English to understand that the last portion of the fourth article of the peace, which referred to putting strangers out of the realm, applied to the German reiters.[4]

The English declared that if the French would restore Calais to the queen, Elizabeth would surrender Havre-de-Grace and Dieppe, with all that was held by the English in Normandy.[5] But the French contended that the English, having occupied Havre-de-Grace, were deprived of all right to Calais,[6] and declined to entertain such a proffer, hoping to recover Havre-de-Grace by force[7] and also to remain masters of Calais by virtue of the treaty

---

[1] On this subject see La Ferrière, *La Normandie à l'étranger*, and his article entitled, "La paix de Troyes avec l'Angleterre," *R. Q. H.*, XXXIII, 36 ff. Much of the article is reprinted from the introduction to *Correspondance de Catherine de Médicis*, II.

[2] *C. S. P. For.*, No. 443, March 13, 1563, Smith to D'Andelot; cf. 511, the Privy Council to Warwick, March 23, 1563; Forbes, II, 363.

[3] The prince of Eboli and the duke of Alva proposed that Havre-de-Grace be put temporarily into the hands of Philip II, he to mediate between England and France! (St. Sulpice to Charles IX, July 11, 1563, and to Catherine, August 27; *L'Ambassade de St. Sulpice*, 137, 151.)

[4] *C. S. P. For.*, No. 498, March 22, 1563, Elizabeth to Smith.

[5] *Ibid., Ven.*, No. 319, January 24, 1563.

[6] Charles IX to St. Sulpice, June 20, 1563; *L'Ambassade de St. Sulpice*, 122, 123.

[7] *Ibid.*, 136.

of 1559, which provided that if, during the term of the treaty, which was to endure for the space of eight years, the English acquired other possessions in France, they would immediately lose their right to Calais. To this England replied that France had been the first offender, when French troops were sent into Scotland in aid of Queen Mary; and that thereby the treaty was broken and Calais was due her. Elizabeth refused to see that her own selfish conduct had compelled the Huguenots to make terms, and bitterly upbraided the Huguenot leaders for their "desertion."[1]

The determination to push the war proceeded entirely from the queen, the chief members of the government having opposed it both because of the strength of the fortress, which they thought difficult to take, and also because of the confusion which still prevailed in the kingdom. On April 7 the prince of Condé was established in the lieutenantship. Marshal Brissac, who was chief military commander, a week later quitted Paris for Normandy in company with the Swiss, and the whole artillery lately used before Orleans was sent forward.[2] Artillery and ammunition were sent by the river, and provisions also were forwarded. The campaign was delayed until this time for two reasons: first, to ascertain whether the internal disturbances could be quelled and the reiters gotten out of the kingdom, as otherwise it would have been perilous to make any movement in the direction of the coast; secondly, all the territory of Normandy had been so devasted by the war that

[1] Neither Coligny nor D'Andelot could be prevailed upon to serve in the war against England, although believing they had been shabbily treated by Elizabeth. The admiral openly refused; D'Andelot feigned illness; Condé alone, of the Huguenot leaders, bore arms against his former ally—"l'honneur de la France couvrait son ingratitude."—*Correspondance de Catherine de Médicis*, II, Introd., xii, xiii, xvii; cf. *C. S. P. For.*, Nos. 498, 511, 541, and especially 548, March, 1563. Elizabeth had replied to the envoy sent to her by the prince of Condé to notify her of the peace made by the prince with the King and to treat for the restitution of Havre-de-Grace, that as the envoy had neither power nor commission from the King, she would not negotiate with him, and that nothing must be said about Havre-de-Grace unless the affairs of Calais were first adjusted (*C. S. P. Ven.*, May 18, 1563).

[2] *Ibid.*, *For.*, No. 936, April 17, 1563. Warwick in a letter to Lord Robert Dudley and Cecil of April 23, 1563, estimates the French force around Havre at 10,000 French and 6,000 Swiss (*ibid.*, No. 659; Forbes, II, 398).

the army could not be maintained except at very great cost and inconvenience. Fortunately for the French government anxiety with reference to the Emperor's designs regarding Metz was now removed, the cardinal of Lorraine having persuaded Ferdinand that if the Three Bishoprics were restored they would become a refuge for the heretics from Lower Germany and Luxembourg.[1]

The queen mother appealed to Paris to obtain 200,000 crowns, and a royal edict commanded the clergy to contribute 100,000 écus de rentes annual revenue.[2] At the same time a government octroi upon wines was laid for six years, to the dismay of many towns, which opposed the execution of the edict, claiming that the vine and wine were their sole means of livelihood.[3] The King also went to Parlement to obtain pecuniary supplies there against England, saying that the 200,000 crowns from the city was to be used to pay the reiters of the Rhinegrave, who had mutinied for their pay in Champagne, to quit the kingdom.[4] Paris readily responded, "the Parisians caring not what they gave to recover Newhaven;" it had been "a scourge and loss to them of many millions of francs" during that year.[5]

Meanwhile the position of Warwick in Havre had grown so

---

[1] C. S. P. For., No. 652, Mundt to Cecil, April 20, 1563, from Strasburg; cf. No. 659, Warwick to the Privy Council on the authority of the Rhinegrave, April 23, 1563; Forbes, II, 398. Nevertheless, the French continued to fortify Metz against the future (C. S. P. For., No. 705, May 4, 1563).

[2] The church complied by mortgaging its possessions to this amount (Claude Haton, I, 330). They were redeemed in the March following (Catherine de Medici to St. Sulpice, December 22, 1563; L'Ambassade de St. Sulpice, 203; Journal de Bruslart, 141. The transaction cost the church 3,230,000 livres. Some of the clergy claimed that the King had no right to do this without papal authorization (Claude Haton, loc. cit.).

[3] The rate was fixed at five livres for each measure of wine, and at 6 sous, 8 deniers, for each queue (Claude Haton, I, 330, 331). The farm of this gabelle was sold at Provins for the sum of 600 livres.

[4] ". . . . Led. prince dit avoir moyen de faire sortir . . . . les Allemans qu'il a en grand nombre."—L'Ambassade de St. Sulpice, 101; C. S. P. For., Nos. 688; 748, §§13, 20; 753, §§5, 10; No. 764 (anno 1563); C. S. P. Ven., No. 326, May 18, 1563.

[5] C. S. P. Eng. For., No. 750, §§6, 7, May 16, 1563; No. 753, §5, May 17; No. 770, May 20, 1563.

bad that he had expelled all strangers from the town.[1] Anticipating a siege, a new fosse 30 feet wide, 10 feet broad, and 8 feet deep
had been constructed outside of the old ditch around the town.
The delay of the English government, however, was fatal to the
success of Warwick. All his labors went for naught.[2] On May 22
the French assault upon Havre began in earnest.[3] In the midst
of the tedium and the anxiety Catherine de Medici dominated
all, having no regard for her own convenience, but being in vigorous action at all hours, and under great mental strain most of
the time. Yet her patience, her address, and her assiduous attention during the time of the siege to the councils of the government, and to her continual audiences, were remarkable. "Her
Majesty," wrote the Venetian ambassador, "exceeds all that could
be expected from her sex, and even from an experienced man of
valor, or from a powerful king and military captain." She insisted
on being present at all the assaults, and even in the trenches,
where cannon-balls and arquebus-bullets were flying.[4]

The character of Catherine de Medici from this time forth,
throughout her long and varied career, continued to fill her subjects with astonishment.[5] Not even the most consummate courtier

---

[1] *C. S. P. For.*, 584, April 5, 1563; Forbes, II, 573.

[2] Warwick had barely 5,000 men of all sorts to defend the town (*C. S. P. For.*,
No. 680, Muster of April 29–30, 1563). There was much sickness. Food was scarce.
"The estate of victuals here," wrote the earl to the Privy Council on April 30,
"rests now upon a scarce proportion of one month in bread and corn (of beer we
can make no further account than as long as we are masters of water, to brew),
having neither flesh, fish, butter, nor cheese, nor any meat of the queen's store but
bacon for two days. The clerk of the store here is as bare in money as victuals.
. . . . The enemy's chief hope for taking this town rests upon famine."—*C. S. P.
For.*, No. 676; Forbes, II, 402. Warwick pointed out, however, that if the queen
"would put forth a power upon the sea" and keep the mouth of the Seine open, as
well as prevent relief from being brought from Flanders and Brittany, Havre might
be saved. "Their whole relief must come to them by Picardy side, which
will not suffice long; neither can they be victualled by land any way, if the commodities of the seas be by this means taken away."—*C. S. P. Dom.*, XXVII, 15,
January 12, 1563. Cf. XXVIII, 48, May 8, 1563.

[3] *C. S. P. For.*, No. 786; Forbes, II, 427.

[4] *C. S. P. Ven.*, No. 328, May 28, 1563

[5] *Rel. vén.*, II, 155; cf. II, 45. "Non si può già negare che non sia donna di
gran valore e di gran spirito."—*Ibid.*, I, 548. "Très-sage et très-universelle en
tout."—Brantôme, III, 249.

could have praised her beauty. She had big eyes and thick lips, like Leo X, her great-uncle.[1] She possessed, too, the characteristics of her family. She loved to erect public edifices; to collect books. She made a profession of satisfying everybody, at least in words, of which she was not saving. Her industry in public business was the subject of astonishment. Nothing was too small for her notice. She could neither eat nor drink without talking politics. She followed the army without regard to her health or even her life. Her physical characteristics, if not the admiration, were certainly the wonder of all. She was fond of good-living, eating much and irregularly, and was addicted to physical exercise, especially hunting, which she also followed for the purpose of reducing her weight. With this design, incredible as it may seem, she often rode clad in heavy furs.[2] When fifty years of age she could walk so fast that no one in the court was willing to follow her.

The difficulties of the French in the siege of Havre-de-Grace were very great. The locality was surrounded for the distance of a mile by marsh and by the waters of the sea, which were cut by inaccessible canals. There was a strand of sand on the seaside only about thirty yards distant from the wall at low tide. The besiegers passed along the shore, somewhat concealed by the sand and gravel cast up by the sea, and wedged themselves and their artillery between this strand and the sea, and opened fire. By the end of July the French had approached so near the walls of Havre-de-Grace that they were almost able to batter them point-blank, and the besieged went out to parley and demanded four days' time to communicate with England.[3]

The garrison was reduced to a sorry plight, for the French were about to storm the place, as they had already battered effectually and dismantled a bulwark and several towers of the fort and filled up the whole moat, so that with but a little more work they would have opened a road for themselves securely with a spade. They had, moreover, a battery of forty cannon, so that while only twenty

---

[1] *Rel. vén.*, I, 375.

[2] *Ibid.*, I, 429.

[3] *C. S. P. Ven.*, No. 338, July 27, 1563; *L'Ambassade de St. Sulpice*, 141, 142.

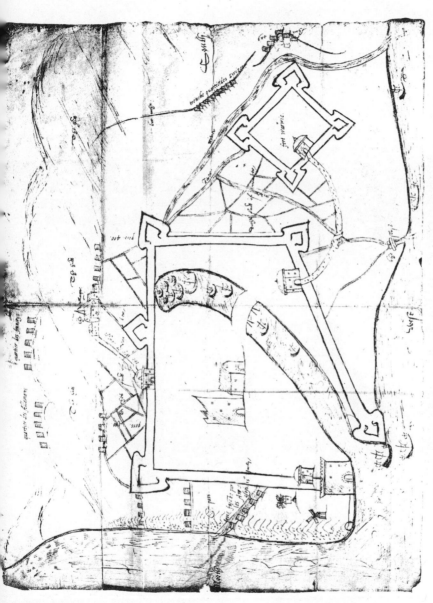

SKETCH MAP OF THE FORTIFICATIONS OF HAVRE-DE-GRACE

Dated July 15, 1563. Original in Public Record Office, State Papers, Foreign, Elizabeth, Vol. XI, No. 919.

or thirty shots each day formed the usual feature of a siege at this time, the French now fired more than a hundred and twenty shots.[1] At last on July 28 Warwick agreed to surrender Havre-de-Grace, and to embark in four days. Two days later the English admiral Clinton appeared in sight, with thirty ships and five galliots. The French artillery was then directed toward the sea, so the admiral set sail the next evening with the fleet, and the French army entered on Sunday, August 1, 1563.[2]

The capture of Havre was of immense immediate advantage to France, especially to Normandy, Havre being the door through which all the traffic and commerce entered, not only to Rouen, but also to Normandy, and to a great part of France. Without this commerce Normandy-of-the-Seine suffered greatly.[3]

But Elizabeth was reluctant to believe that she had been beaten, and the autumn of the year witnessed tedious negotiations.[4] The chief difficulty between the two crowns turned on the restitution of Calais. The French insisted that they were absolved from the terms of Cateau-Cambrésis through the action taken by England in the matter of Havre-de-Grace; that thereby forfeiture of the

---

[1] I have come upon an interesting item in the history of the art of war in connection with this siege of Havre. In January, 1563, a Corsican, resident in Spain, by the name of Pietro Paolo del Delfino offered his services to St. Sulpice. "Il va dans l'eau," wrote the ambassador to Catherine, "et m'a assuré qu'avec certains engins il empéchera que nul navire venant d'Angleterre puisse aborder aud. Havre sans grand danger." In June Delfino arrived at Bois de Vincennes, where he was well received, according to his own statement (*L'Ambassade de St. Sulpice*, 112, and n. 4). But I do not find any further mention of him. Was this invention a sort of torpedo? We know that shells were first used in the siege of Orleans in this year.

[2] *C. S. P. Ven.*, No. 341, August 6, 1563; on the progress of the siege and the condition of Havre cf. *ibid.*, *For.*, 1563, Nos. 754, §6; 762, 806, §§ 4, 5; 828, 835, 852, §4; 853, §4; 857, §8; 871, 881, 894, 907, §2; 941, 967, 973, §2; 977, §4; 982, §9; 998, 1007, 1021, 1024, 1026, §7; 1044, §4; 1049, 1081, 1086, 1100, 1208, 1296. In Appendix VI is a letter of Admiral Clinton to Lord Burghley, July 31, 1563, in which he says that the plague, not the arms of France, has conquered them.

[3] *C. S. P. Ven.*, No. 343, August 14, 1563.

[4] *Correspondance de Catherine de Médicis*, II, Introd., xxvi–xxviii; *L'Ambassade de St. Sulpice*, 177, 194, 195.

English right to Calais was made.[1]   Elizabeth, on the other hand, would not make peace unless her pretensions were recognized.[2]

In the meanwhile, in the seas of Flanders, France, and England thousands of acts of piracy were committed, and trade in the Channel was quite interrupted.[3]   A partial agreement at last was patched up.   On April 11, 1564, the treaty of peace was signed at Troyes,[4] the articles yielding Havre-de-Grace to France, in return for 120,000 gold crowns, a sum which the English grudgingly took, though they had demanded a half million, the terms also providing for property indemnifications and freedom of commerce between the two nations.

Nothing was specified as to Calais.   After three years of negotiations the question still remained unsettled.   In June, 1567, Sir Thomas Smith, Elizabeth's ambassador, demanded the restitution of Calais.   Charles was evasive, saying that the messenger must be content to wait till the King had obtained the consent of his council, before whom the King told Smith openly that he would not restore Calais, but would hold it as the possession of his ancestors, to which the queen of England had no just right. When the ambassador replied, citing the word of the treaty, the chancellor answered that the promise had been given under the express conditions that the English queen should not in any way molest the subjects or territory of France or Scotland, but from what had taken place at Havre-de-Grace it appeared manifest that she had forfeited all claims which she might have had to Calais. The King's rejoinder was notable in that it is so excellent an example of the French doctrine of "natural frontiers," Charles IX

[1] "Adieu le droit de Calais," wrote Robertet, Charles IX's secretary, on July 4, 1561, to St. Sulpice (L'Ambassade de St. Sulpice, 142).

[2] C. S. P. Ven., 347, November 11, 1563; ibid., For., No. 6, January 4, 1564; No. 47, January 15.

[3] Ibid., Ven., No. 348, November 18, 1563; Archives de la Gironde, XVII, 293.

[4] The text of the treaty is in Rymer's Foedera, XV, 640.   La Ferrière has an extended account of the negotiations in Correspondance de Catherine de Médicis, II, Introd., xxxiv–xliv.   For other details see C. S. P. For., 1564, Nos. 6, 47, 250–53, 297, 307–10, 314, 347, 363, 364.   On the great commercial importance of the treaty of Troyes, see De Ruble, Le traité de Cateau-Cambrésis, 193, 194.

replying to the effect that the queen ought not to regret the loss of Calais, knowing that of old it was the possession of the crown of France, and that God had willed it to return to its first master, and that the two realms ought to remain content with the frontiers created for them by nature and with a boundary so clearly defined as the sea.[1]

[1] *C. S. P. Ven.*, 1564, No. 388.

CHAPTER IX

EARLY LOCAL AND PROVINCIAL CATHOLIC LEAGUES

Thanks to her own enterprise in pushing the war which had culminated with so much honor to France, and partly also to her skilful handling of the factions at court, Catherine de Medici was now in enjoyment of supreme power. The entire weight of the government rested on her shoulders, there being no longer any other person who controlled public affairs. The Guises and Châtillon factions were full of animosity toward one another, for Madame de Guise refused to recognize the admiral's acquittal for the murder of her husband;[1] Montmorency was deeply offended because the young duke of Guise received the grand-mastership and the gift of the duchy of Châtellerault, and so feigned to have the gout in order to avoid service before Havre; Condé was doubly angry at the queen, both because she withheld the promised lieutenant's commission and because the daughter of Marshal St. André, who left a great fortune, was not permitted to marry his son. The parties were, therefore, in a triangular relation toward one another and Catherine's art was bent upon maintaining the balance in order to hold her own.[2]

The population of the wittiest city in Europe was quick to perceive the animosities and paradoxes that existed. "The Parisians have three things to wonder at," the saying went, "the constable's beads, the chancellor's mass, and the cardinal Châtillon's red cap. One is ever mumbling over his beads and his head

---

[1] "A Paris arriva toute la maison de Lorraine vestue de deuil, pour faire une solemnelle demande de justice exemplaire sur la mort du duc de Guise."—D'Aubigné, II, 204; the request bearing date September 26, 1563, is in *Mém. de Condé*, IV, 667.

Coligny was so fearful of suffering violence in Paris from the bigotry of the populace or at the instigation of the Guises, that he would not enter the city.

[2] On these feuds see *C. S. P. For.*, anno 1563, No. 748, §§1–6, 15; No. 753, §1; No. 770; No. 896, §3; No. 912, §4; No. 1,003, §3; No. 1,212; No. 1,233, §4; No. 1,249; No. 1,287; No. 1,337, §3; No. 1,431; No. 1,445, §8; *Proceedings of the Huguenot Society*, letters of April 20, 30, May 1, 21, 27, 31.

is ever occupied with other affairs; the other hears mass daily and is the chief Huguenot in France; the third wears a cardinal's cap and defies the Pope."[1]   The queen mother had hoped that religious animosities would be forgotten in the course of the war with England. But she was disappointed. The peace of Amboise could not be enforced. Even in Paris armed troops and armed guards had to patrol the streets to prevent outbreaks of violence.[2]   It was impossible to disarm the Catholics, who made house-to-house searches to ferret out Huguenots.[3]   Under the terms of pacification the Protestants were permitted to return to Paris, but who dared avail himself of so precarious a liberty? Instead, they were compelled to sacrifice their property.[4]   In the provinces the same condition of things prevailed—in Languedoc, in the Orléannais, in the Lyonnais.[5]   In Languedoc the association of the Huguenots maintained its organization, raised money, levied troops.[6]   Yet in spite of its failure to enforce pacification, the government required the demolition of the walls of towns known to be Huguenot strongholds, as Orleans, Montauban, and St. Lô, a procedure which the Protestants strongly resisted; so that a condition of petty civil war existed throughout much of France, the Edict of Amboise notwithstanding.[7]   Summarized, the troubles of France at this time may be said to have been the feud between the house of Guise and that of Châtillon—a feud which compro-

---

[1] C. S. P. For., No. 1,558, December 29, 1563. "Le connétable lui même, tout en étant homme de bien catholique, était cependant carnale, et voulait avoir appui des deux cotés."—Baschet, Journal du Concile de Trente, 240.

[2] For examples see C. S. P. For., No. 982, §§1, 2, an episode of the last week of June, 1563; ibid., Ven., No. 333; Correspondance de Catherine de Médicis, II, Introd., xxix.

[3] A law was made in August forbidding the wearing of any weapon but sword and dagger; concealment of firearms was an offense punishable by confiscation of lands and goods (Edict of Caen, August 24, L'Ambassade de St. Sulpice, 147; C. S. P. For., No. 1,394, October 1563; ibid., No. 912).

[4] C. S. P. For., No. 1,003, July 14, 1563; ibid., Ven., No. 330, June 10.

[5] Correspondance de Catherine de Médicis, II. Introd., xxxii, xxxiii (many examples).

[6] C. S. P. For., Nos. 896, §§3, 17; 912, §4.

[7] Ibid., Nos. 1,155, 1,387, 1,394, 1,431, 1,445, anno 1563.

mised the crown and most of the other great families of the kingdom; the queen's ambition to govern, which led her to nourish
the quarrel; religious intolerance; the poverty of the crown; the
uncertainty of its foreign relations; and finally the detriment to
its commerce on account of the war with England, which deprived
France of four or five millions of gold.[1]

Even before peace was made between France and England
it had been decided that the King should make a tour of the provinces for the better pacification of the country.[2]   A programme
of administrative and financial reform was developed at the same
time.   The army was to be reduced; in place of the royal garrisons
there was to be a "belle milice" of forty ensigns of footmen, ten
each in Picardy, Normandy, Languedoc, and Dauphiné.   These
troops were to be supported partly by the crown, partly by the
provinces.   The Scotch Guard was to be cut down.   Through
the church's aid twelve millions of the public debt, including the
unpaid balance of the dowries of Elizabeth of Spain and the duchess of Savoy, were to be paid off within six years and the alienated
domains of the crown redeemed.[3]   Already Charles IX's majority
had been declared at Rouen, during the course of the siege of
Havre[4]—a dexterous stroke of the queen mother to thwart the
ambitions of the factions.[5]

---

[1] The fisheries of France, however, were profitable. "They quietly make
their herring fishery . . . . without impeachment. . . . . Their fish-markets were
never better furnished."—C. S. P. For., No. 1,356, Throckmorton to the queen
November 1, 1563.

[2] Castelnau, Book V, chaps. vii–ix.

[3] "Instructions pour le Sieur de Lansac, envoyé en Espagne, janvier 1564,"
L'Ambassade de St. Sulpice, 223.

[4] August 18, 1563.   The official promulgation is in Mém. de Condé, IV, 574.
Déclaration faicte par le Roy en sa majorité tenant son lict de justice en sa cour de
Parlement de Rouen, Robert Estienne, Paris, 1563.

[5] L'Ambassade de St. Sulpice, 101, 102; R. Q. H., XXIV, 459; Claude Haton,
I, 363, and n. 2; Correspondance de Catherine de Médicis, II, Introd., xxiii; C. S. P.
For., No. 1,190, September, 1563.
The declaration, by a technicality, contravened the testament of Charles V
(1374), which for centuries had been the law regulating the King's majority.   Charles
IX was born on June 17, 1550, so that he was in his fourteenth year, though not yet
fourteen years old.   The Parlement of Paris for more than a month refused to

In the early spring of 1564 the court set out from Fontainebleau, and thence went to Sens and Troyes, where the peace was signed; from Troyes the way led to Bar-le-Duc and Nancy. But the journey of the King, instead of allaying the disquietude of the Huguenots, alarmed them still more. For the strongest overtures were made to the King to break the peace of Amboise, not only by provincial authorities[1] but also through the ambassadors of certain of the Catholic powers.

The Council of Trent had finished its labors with somewhat unseemly haste on December 4, 1563, on account of the anticipated decease of Pius IV,[2] and strong pressure was brought upon the French and Spanish governments to accept its findings.[3]   The Pope, in consistory, accepted them in their integrity, on January 26, 1564.[4]   But various European governments, especially France, strongly objected to the findings as prejudicial to the interests of monarchy.[5]   On the first Monday in Lent the cardinal of Lorraine

register the edict, not on political, but on religious grounds. It objected to "la mention de l'édit de pacification d'Amboise, introduite sans motif dans la déclaration de l'édit de la majorité, ce *que semblait reconnaître deux religions*."—*Correspondance de Catherine de Médicis*, II, Introd., xxiv. The Venetian ambassador gives an interesting character-sketch of Charles IX at this time (*Rel. vén.*, I, 419).

[1] The estates of Burgundy declared in a memorial that it was impossible to maintain double worship in France and petitioned that Protestant worship might be abolished in that province, May 18, 1563 (D'Aubigné, II, 205; *Mém. de Condé*, IV, 413; Castelnau, Book V, chap. vi.

[2] "S'étaeint tous départis avec une hâte extrême causée sur la disposition du pape."—Testu to Catherine de Medici, *L'Ambassade de St. Sulpice*, 207. "Les évêques français se déclarent obligés de partir, se voyant privés de ressources."—Baschet, *Journal du Concile de Trente*, 239.

[3] The Pope sent the bishop of Vintimilla to Spain to persuade Philip II to enforce the Tridentine decrees in favor of the counter-Reformation (*L'Ambassade de St. Sulpice*, 174, 200, 217, 218). See also a letter of Luna, Philip II's ambassador at Trent, of November 17, 1563, in *Correspondencia de los principes de Alemania con Felipe II, y de los Embajadores de Este en la Corti di Vienna (1556–98)* in "Documentos inéditos," CI, 24.

[4] *Annales Raynaldi*, 1564, No. 1; Labbé, XIV, 939; cf. *R. Q. H.*, October, (1869), 402.

[5] For the grounds of objection see *R. Q. H.* (October, 1869), 365, 366, and 401–8; Frémy, *Diplomates du temps de la Ligue*, 45. In Vol. LXXXVI, *Coll. de St. Pétersbourg*, is a collection of letters, many of them from Lansac and the cardinal of Lorraine while at the Council of Trent. These are the letters whose disappearance Baschet wondered at and deplored (La Ferrière, *Rapport*, 58).

presented the decrees of Trent to the King in council and others of the Parlement, urging that their adoption was necessary for the repose of the kingdom. The debate which followed, in a certain sense was a test of strength between the moderate Catholic party, led by the chancellor L'Hôpital and the Guises. Much objection was made to the findings, especially by the chancellor, who asserted that they were contrary to the privileges of the Gallican church, and that the cardinal's party was now trying to compass by craft what they had failed to do by force of arms. The cardinal rejoined with words to the effect that L'Hôpital was unmindful of the benefits he had received of them (the Guises), using the word "ingrate" (*ingrat*). To this the chancellor haughtily returned that he had never received any benefits from the cardinal or his family, that he had only filled the post of *maître de requêtes*, which was not a high office, and that he did not desire to pay his debts at the expense of the King's sovereignty by voting in favor of the decrees. In the end, France refused to accept all of the findings.[1]

With the closing of the Council of Trent, the representatives of the ultra-Catholic powers, notably Spain and Savoy, intimated to Charles IX that their sovereigns would assist him in the extirpation of heresy in France. The offer was both a promise and a menace, the implication being that the Catholic world at large would not tolerate the recognition of Protestantism accorded by France and that a joint action of the powers most concerned might compel the king of France to live up to his title of Most Christian King. The cardinal of Lorraine had carried the idea of the Triumvirate to Trent with him,[2] and on the floor of the Council had proposed the formation of an association to be called "The Broth-

---

[1] Charles IX to St. Sulpice, February 26, 1564, *L'Ambassade de St. Sulpice*, 229; D'Aubigné, II, 223; L'Estoile, I, 19; *Bulletin de la Soc prot. franç.*, XXIV, 412. Catherine makes no allusion to this scene in her letter to Elizabeth of Spain at this season (*L'Ambassade de St. Sulpice*, 237). But on a subsequent occasion, when the cardinal of Lorraine dropped the remark that the Council of Trent ought to be called *Spanish*, the queen mother replied "qu'il avait raison, et que aussi lui même s'était montré tel et plus de ce parti que de tout autre."—*Ibid.*, 383.

[2] *R. Q. H.*, XXXIV, 462; Frémy, *Diplomates de la ligue*, chap. i.

erhood of Catholics in France." He offered to secure the co-operation of his nephews, relatives, and friends, and returned to France with the consent of the Pope for that purpose.[1] The Triumvirate, as we have seen, had already made overtures to Spain, to which Philip II had responded with cordial, if no very definite sentiments, and from the time of the promulgation of the Edict of January and the formation of the Triumvirate, the idea of a Catholic league in which the Pope and the king of Spain were to be the chief pillars, begins to take shape.[2] The mission of Louis de St. Gelais, sieur de Lansac, to Trent and Rome in this month, was partly to prevent the formation of such a league, and partly to persuade the Pope to approve the French government's appropriation of the property of the church. Granvella was not unfavorable to the idea, though in his eyes such a league should be formed, not for the purpose of intervening in France, but as a defensive measure, lest Catherine endeavor to profit by the critical situation prevailing in the Spanish Netherlands and interfere there in order to divert the discontent of the French from home affairs, and to prevent the Protestants of the Netherlands from assisting their coreligionists in France.[3]

The outbreak of civil war after the massacre of Vassy and the seizure of Havre-de-Grace by the English had convinced Philip II that the time to act had come in France, and Spanish troops and Spanish money were put at the disposal of the Guises, although Philip denied to England that he was giving succor to Catholic France.[4] In May, and again in August of 1562, the Triumvirate appealed to Philip II,[5] and on June 6 the Spanish King wrote to the regent in the Netherlands to send the Triumvirate assistance. But

[1] Tavannes, 291.

[2] Vargas, Spanish ambassador in Rome, to the cardinal Granvella, February 22, 1561 (*Papiers d'état du card. de Granvelle*, VI, 512, 513; *R. Q. H.*, XXXIV, 460).

[3] On January 16, 1562, Granvella wrote to Perez from Brussels that it was already impossible to prevent this (Gachard, *Correspondance de Philippe II sur les Pays-Bas*, I, 198).

[4] Philip II to Quadra, Spanish ambassador in England, August 4, 1562 (*Papiers d'état du cardinal de Granvelle*, VI, 606).

[5] La Popelinière, Book VIII, 591, 634, gives the text of these appeals.

the order was easier to give than to execute, and exactly a month later (July 6) both Margaret and Granvella replied, asserting the impractibility of carrying out Philip's wishes on the ground that no money could be procured from the estates for such a purpose.[1] In the meantime, the cardinal-legate in France, convinced that "in order to lay the ax at the root of the evil, there was no shorter way and no better expedient than recourse to arms,"[2] and impatient of Spain's slow reply to the petition of the Triumvirate,[3] stirred up both the Vatican and the court of Madrid to livelier action.[4] As a result, although it was against their better judgment, Margaret and Granvella prevailed upon the Council of State in August to appropriate 50,000 écus for the war in France, and in September 3,000 Italians were sent from Franche Comté to the aid of Tavannes in Burgundy.[5]

The elements of the future Holy League are here manifest as early as 1561–62. But apart from the course being followed out in high political circles, at the same time, popular associations for the maintenance of the Catholic religion were being formed within France. The years 1562–63 witnessed the formation of

[1] "Les états ne payeraient un maravédis aux bandes d'ordonnance si on voulait envoyer celles-ci en France."—Gachard, *Correspondance de Philippe II sur les Pays-Bas*, I, 206.

[2] "Pour coupper la racine du mal, il ny puisse avoir de plus courte voye, ny de meilleur expédient que alluy d'armes."—*Lettres du cardinal de Ferrare*, Letter xxx, 1563.

[3] "Après la déclaration que seigneurs ont envoyée en Espagne des deniers qu'ils y ont demandez, ils ne voyant pas qu'on se haste beaucoup de leur respondre."—*Ibid.*

[4] *Nég. Tosc.*, III, 492.

[5] *Papiers d'état du cardinal de Granvelle*, VI, 620, September 13, 1563. It is interesting to observe the objections of Margaret of Parma and Granvella. According to the former, "l'impossibilité de donner secours au roi de France était notoire, à moins qu'on ne voulût la perte et la ruine totale des Pays-Bas."—Gachard, *Philippe II et les Pays-Bas*, I, 211; Margaret to Philip, August 6, from Brussels. The latter deplores the reduction of the forces of the country because "les ligues et confédérations (c'est ainsi qu'on les appelle) formées contre lui, continuent."—*Ibid.*, August 6, 1562. Three future patriots of the Netherlands were in this session of the Council of State—William of Orange, Egmont and Hoorne. Cf. Gachard's note.

several provincial leagues and town associations, which were the real roots of the Holy League.

The people of the capital had begun to manifest their prejudices in an organized military form as early as 1562, and the government, instead of suppressing this tendency, encouraged it. On May 2, 1562, the Parlement of Paris passed an ordinance ordering the *échevins* and all loyal Catholics in each quarter of the city to organize under arms, with captains, corporals, and sergeants.[1] But the preponderance of Paris in the formation of the Holy League has been exaggerated. When it became a national affair, Paris, as the capital and most Catholic city of France, seized hold of it and made it her own. But it is inverting things to say that Paris gave the League to the provinces. Rather Paris identified herself with their interests, and reflected their passions and their character, "fierce in Languedoc, sullenly obstinate in Brittany, everywhere modified in its nature and its devotion by the politics of the towns."[2]

The south of France was far more aggressive than the north in this particular, and anti-Protestant associations were formed in many provinces to the disquietude of the government, which knew not how to control them.[3] The earliest of such local associations formed by the Catholics seems to have been one of Bordeaux, where the people were organized after the Protestant attempt to gain possession of the Château Trompette in Francis II's reign.[4]

---

[1] La Popelinière, Book viii, 499); *Rel. vén.* II, 99.

[2] "Cependant la ligue ne s'est pas renfermée dans l'enceinte de Paris. Paris, qui l'avait incertaine et hesitante encore, la renvoya aux provinces, toute brûlante et toute armée. Elle s'associa à leur intérêts, réfléta leur passions et leur caractère, feroce en Languedoc, durement obstinée en Bretagne, partout modifiée dans sa nature et sa durée par la politique locale des municipalités."—Ouvré, *Essai sur l'histoire de la ligue à Poitiers* (1855), 6.

[3] Ranke, *Civil Wars and Monarchy in France*, 226, notices this contrast between the north and the south.

[4] This local organization did not seem strong enough for Montluc, whose activity against the Protestants in 1562 was already notable and who was suspicious lest some Huguenots might creep into the body and betray it; so the power was taken out of the hands of the *jurats* of the city at his suggestion and vested in the hands of Tilladet, governor of Bordeaux, who also had possession of the keys

This association formed in Bordeaux is the germ of the Catholic League which later expanded over the Bordelais and Gascony. Other portions of France followed suit. In November, 1562, the Association of Provence was formed at Aix and terrorized the Huguenots.[1] Toulouse was notoriously Catholic, and street wars between Catholics and Protestants were of common occurrence. A more than usually violent outburst of popular fury here culminated on March 2, 1563, in the formation of a Catholic League, of which the cardinals Armagnac and Strozzi, lieutenants of the King in the sénéschaussées of Toulouse and Albi, the president of the Parlement, Du Faur, who was advocate-general of the crown, certain eminent knights of the Order, and the famous Montluc, were sponsors. The immediate occasion of this outbreak at Toulouse seems to have been the combination of fury and fear of a plot which the Catholics felt when they learned of the duke of Guise's assassination. When the outbreak began, the president of the Parlement of Toulouse hastily dispatched a messenger to Montluc entreating him to come to their assistance. Upon Montluc's arrival at Toulouse the leaders prayed him to put himself at the head of the troops in the province against the Huguenots.

Montluc at first made some difficulty about consenting to this request, because he had no permission from Damville, the governor of Languedoc, in which province Toulouse was located, and who, moreover, was not one of his friends.[2] Finally, however, he

of the city. This proceeding was destined to be revolutionary in the development of the municipality. The *jurats* pleaded their ancient privileges, which were as old as the English domination, which Louis XI had confirmed after the wars of the English in France were over. But the parlement of Bordeaux approved the change and thus the form of government of the greatest city of the Gironde was altered by stress of circumstances (O'Reilly, *Hist. de Bordeaux*, II, 241–44; Montluc, *Lettres et commentaires*, IV, 214, note). Cf. Gaullieur, *Histoire de la réformation à Bordeaux et dans le ressort du parlement de Guyenne*. Tome I, "Les origines et la première guerre de religion jusqu'à la paix d'Amboise" (1523–63), Paris, 1848.

[1] "Tellement que les pauvres fidèles trembloyent dans Aix et plusieurs firent constraints de s'enfuyr."—*Mém. de. Condé*, IV, 240. At p. 278 is an account of the formation of this league. Cf. *Discours véritable des guerre et troubles advenus au Pays de Provence en l'an 1562.*

[2] This was Henri Damville, the second son of the constable Montmorency.

yielded to their request, and measures were taken to put an army on foot in thirty days.   Those who composed this assembly drew up the compact of a league or association on March 2, 1563, which was to be observed by the clergy, the nobility, and the third estate in the towns and dioceses within the jurisdiction of the parlement of Toulouse, both in Languedoc and Guyenne.   According to the articles of this association the members engaged to bear arms, and to make oath between the hands of those commissioned by the Parlement, or by the King's lieutenant in the country, to march whenever required for the defense of the Catholic religion.   The parlement of Toulouse approved and authorized this association on March 20, provisionally and without charges, "subject to the good pleasure of the King."   In the name of this league taxes were laid, men were levied, and an inventory of arms made in every *généralité* and diocese.[1]

Montluc had come to Toulouse, fresh from the formation of another and earlier league for the preservation of the Catholic faith, in Agen, which had been organized on February 4, 1563.   This league was a direct consequence of the siege of Lectoure and the battle of Vergt.   Montluc had received orders to report, with the marshal Termes, to the King in the camp before Orleans.   But the Agenois was not quite pacified and the gentry of the country were so filled with alarm, that they concluded, so Montluc naïvely says, "that in case I should resolve to go away to the King, as his Majesty commanded, and offer to leave them without a head, they must be fain to detain me in the nature of a prisoner."[2]   The upshot of things was that the "Confederation and Association of the town and city of Agen and other towns and jurisdictions of

---

[1] This association, in the words of D'Aubigné, was the "prototype et premier example de toutes les ligues qui ont depuis paru en France."—Vol. II, 137.   Extended accounts of its origin may be found in the *Annales de Toulouse*, II, 62 ff.; De Thou, IV, Book XXXIV, 496, 497; La Popelinière, Book VIII, 602, gives the text of the compact, which shows the financial measures adopted in the support of the league; *Lettres et commentaires de Montluc*, ed. De Ruble, II, 398; *Hist. du Languedoc*, V, 249 ff.   Protestant accounts are in Beza, Book X; D'Aubigné, III, chap. xviii.

[2] *Commentaires* (Eng. trans.), Book V, 232.

Agen" was formed and organized on February 4, 1563, with a captain, lieutenant, sergeants, corporals, and other necessary officers, in order to extirpate the Huguenots from the region. It was an oath-bound covenant.[1]

The examples of Agen and Toulouse were contagious, and the popular hatred of the Huguenots, on account of the assassination of the duke of Guise, induced the spread of these local leagues. On March 13, 1563, the Catholic lords of Guyenne also entered into a league at Cadillac on the same plan and for the same object as that of the Catholics of Agen and Languedoc.[2] Like the earlier ones, the league of Guyenne was organized by parishes, districts, sénéschaussées and provinces, under the direction of one supreme chief assisted by a council chosen from the third estate. In the north of France, as has been observed, the tendency of the Catholics to associate was not so strong as in the south. There is evidence of a weak association of the Catholics in the towns of the Rouennais and the lower part of the Ile-de-France in 1563,[3] and of a town league in Anjou and Maine.[4] But no formidable Catholic association was formed north of the Loire, until the appearance of the Confrérie du St. Esprit in 1568, under the marshal Tavannes.

The nucleus of many of these Catholic associations, before they expanded into provincial leagues, in most cases seems to have been a local guild or confraternity[5] of some nature. These were

[1] "Ordonnance de Blaise de Montluc, chevalier de l'ordre et lieutenant du roi en Guyenne, sur l'opinion qui devoit estres les sujets fidèles à sa Majesté en la sénéchaussée d'Agenois, et sur l'ordre qu'ils devoient tenir pour résister aux entreprises des sujets rebelles."—Ruble, *Comment. et Lettres de Montluc*, IV, 190; La Faille, *Annales de Toulouse*, II, 62. The preamble is a recital of Catholic grievances and Huguenot violence.

[2] D'Aubigné, II, 213, and n. 6; *Commentaires et lettres de Montluc*, IV, 214.

[3] *C. S. P. For.*, No. 1,000, anno 1563.

[4] Mourin, *La réforme et la ligue en Anjou*, 21, 22.

[5] It is interesting to observe how history is repeating itself in the formation of these local associations or confraternities against the Huguenots. In 1212 in the course of the war against the Albigenses the "Confraternitas ad ecclesiae defensionem Massiliae instituta" was formed at Marseilles by Arnaud, the papal legate. See Martène, *Thesaurus anecdotorum*, sub anno.

closely connected with the body of tradesmen, each trade having its patron saint, its sacred banner, and devoted bands; but some of the more aristocratic people were joined with the artisans.   The members had fixed places of meeting and certain days on which to assemble, common exercises, and often a common meal.   They swore to use their wealth and their life, if need be, for the defense of their faith.[1]

The new rôle now begun to be played by these ancient guilds is an interesting phase of the religious wars.   If France in the sixteenth century was laboring in the throes of a religious revolution, she was also in a state of industrial transformation.   In origin the economic revolution was independent of the Reformation, yet so influential were its social and economic effects upon the Reformation that in a very true sense the religious movement may be said to have been the subordinate one.[2]   The identity and fulness of this change in the old order of things coincides with the Reformation, which in large part became the vehicle of its expression.   The crisis coincides with the reign of Charles IX and Henry III, although the beginnings of it are very manifest in the time of Louis XI (cf. the ordinances of 1467, 1474-76, 1479).   The change particularly involved the guilds, whose traditional practices had now reached the point of an industrial tyranny.   More and more, from the middle of the fifteenth century, control of the guilds had tended to fall into the hands of a few.   This growth of a social hierarchy within the guilds had serious political and economic results.   For inasmuch as city government was so largely an out-growth of guild life, this exclusiveness threw political control of the cities into the hands of a "ring" composed of the upper bourgeoisie, who formed an

---

[1] Martin, *Histoire de France*, IX, 201; Anquetil, I, 213.

[2] "Si la Réforme acquit une si grande importance, au point que les esprits superficiels y virent l'origine des libertés actuelles, c'est qu'auparavant avait éclaté une révolution sociale et économique, dont les luttes religeuses ne furent que les arrière-maux.   Tant que les historiens, dans leurs études sur la Réforme, ne tiendront pas compte de ce dernier point de vue, ils n'écriront à son sujet que les romans ou des pamphlets."—Funck-Brentano, Introd. to new ed. of Montchrétien's *L'Œconomie politique*, LXXI.

oligarchy and gradually squeezed the lower classes out of all participation in the government. The general body of the commonalty everywhere, in France, in Germany, in England, tended to disappear or to be replaced by a select group from the inner circle of the guild. The lower bourgeoisie was shut out of the council at Nevers in 1512, at Sens in 1530, at Rheims in 1595.

But the economic revolution implied in this change was of far greater importance than the political. The *gens de métier* became a monopolist, a capitalist class, controlling the "hoards" of the guilds as well at being the ruling class in local politics. The old guild was transformed into a mercantile association, operated in favor of a few rich families who were possessed of capital and regulated wages and fixed the term of apprenticeship to their own advantage. In order to secure cheap labor the masters increased the number of apprentices, lengthened the time of service, raised the requirements of the *chef-d'œuvre*, made membership in the guild increasingly difficult, and reduced wages by employing raw, underpaid workmen in competition with skilled labor. The result was that the distance widened continually between the upper and lower working classes.[1] The social democracy and honorable estate of guild life, as it had been in the thirteenth and fourteenth centuries, passed away and was replaced by a strife between labor and capital, between organized labor and free labor, which brings the sixteenth century, remote as it is in time, very near to us in certain of its economic conditions.

To be sure there were some things which partially neutralized this antagonism, such as better facility in communication, the increase of production, the activity of exchange, the invention of new industrial processes, and the opening of new industries, notably printing and silk manufacture.[2] But nothing compensated the workman for the rise in the price of necessities of life due to the influx of gold and silver from America, for his wages

[1] Hauser, "The Reformation and the Popular Classes in France in the Sixteenth Century," *American Historical Review*, January, 1899, 220.

[2] See Hauser, *Ouvriers du temps passé;* Pariset, *Histoire de la fabrique lyonnaise,* 1901; Roussel, "Un livre de main au XVIe siècle," *Revue internationale de sociologie,* XIII (1905), 102, 521, 825.

did not rise in proportion. In consequence the cleavage grew
more and more sharp. The result of this tendency was that poor
workmen, despairing of getting economic justice from the guilds,
took to working in their own quarters. So common was this practice in the sixteenth century that a new word was coined to define
this unapprenticed class—*chambrelons*. These plied their trades
in their own houses and sold the product of their handicraft anywhere. As early as 1457, and again in 1467, the masters complain
of this practice.[1] It is easy to understand the disastrous influence
of this new form of industry upon guild labor, since the new class
of workmen was not subject either to the same money charges or
to the same restrictive regulations. It was "unfair" competition
for the old order of things which reposed upon the maintenance
of an economic equilibrium between demand and supply, between
labor and capital, was upset by the new tendencies.

To the toiling masses trodden down by the masters and econom
ically tyrannized over, the Reformation came as the first *organized*
movement of discontent, and hosts of dissatisfied workmen throughout Germany and France hastened to identify themselves with
Protestantism, not for religious reasons, but because the Reformation constituted exactly that for which they were seeking—a protest. The situation was further aggravated by the influx of
foreign workmen, chiefly from Germany, where this economic
revolution was earlier and more fully developed than elsewhere
in Europe, in great industrial centers like Nürnberg, and where
small German workmen were more completely shut out than
was the case in France or England. These men—such as cobblers, shoemakers, carpenters, wool-carders, and other simple
artisans—wandered over the country from one province to another,

[1] Eberstadt, "Der französische Gewerberecht und die Schaffung staatlicher
Gesetzgebung und Verwaltung in Frankreich vom dreizehnten Jahrhundert bis
1581," *Schmoller's Forschungen*, XVII, Pt. II, 270. This is a pioneer work in the
economic subject here briefly outlined. The reader will find Unwin's *Industrial
Development in the Sixteenth and Seventeenth Centuries*, London, 1905, an admirable
survey of the same subject, dealing chiefly with England, but with frequent reference
to the continent, where the conditions were much the same. There is a copious
bibliography prefixed to the work. The article by M. Hauser referred to in the
American Historical Review, January, 1899, should also be examined.

carrying the economic gospel of free labor and the religion of
Lutheranism with them. Naturally they imbued their French
fellow-workmen with their sentiments—and to such an extent
that for years, during the early course of the civil wars, the
Huguenots were commonly called "Lutherans." Before 1560, the
greater portion of the Protestant party was made up of wool-
combers, fullers, drapers, weavers, shoemakers, hosiers, dyers,
tailors, hatters, joiners, glaziers, bookbinders, locksmiths, cutlers,
pewterers, coopers, etc.[1] Even as late as 1572, when the Huguenot movement had for twelve years been led by noblemen like
the Châtillons and the Rohans, the Venetian ambassador still
characterized the Huguenots as "a sect which consists for the most
part of craftsmen, as cobblers, tailors, and such ignorant people."[2]

Coupled with this religious and economic revolution, went also
a change in the manners of society, which pervaded all classes—
a change which began in the reign of Francis I and was continued
under Henry II. The new internationalism of France, due to the
Italian wars, was probably the initial cause of this. Returned
soldiers, laden with the pay of booty of warfare, brought back into

---

[1] Weiss, *La chambre ardente*, cxlv. The early identification of the French
nobility with Calvinism has been exaggerated. One must be cautious in the use
of the term "nobility," for it is to be remembered that the eldest son received the
largest share of the inheritance and that younger sons and small nobles, in many
instances, had much in common with the small farmers in the provinces. As
Mr. Armstrong aptly says: "All that separated them from their neighbors was
'privilege,' and to this they clung all the more desperately."—Armstrong, *The
French Wars of Religion*, 4. In the decade between 1550 and 1560 there is an
increase in the number of aristocratic names identified with French Protestantism,
but it was not till 1557 that the first great noble espoused its cause and that
covertly. This was Antoine of Bourbon. In the same year Coligny and D'Andelot also inclined to it (Whitehead, *Gaspard de Coligny, Admiral of France*, 63–66).
On the whole matter, see Lavisse, *Histoire de France*, V, Pt. II, 238–42.

[2] Relazione IV, 242. The great store-house of information on this head is
M. Noel Weiss, *La chambre ardente*, 1889—the trials for heresy during the years
1547–49 of the reign of Henry II—a book which has revolutionized the point of
view of the history of the French Reformation (see a review of this work in *English
Hist. Review*, VI, 770).

In the town of Provins there were but a few Huguenots. Among them were
1 doctor; 2 lawyers; a notary; 1 barber and surgeon; 1 dyer; 3 apothecaries; 1
draper; 1 fuller; 1 salt dealer.—Claude Haton, I, 124, 125.

France the manners and customs of Italy, which commingled with the manners and customs introduced by wandering workmen from Germany and Switzerland.[1]

The revision of the statutes of the guilds was one of the minor features of the reform programme of the political Huguenots in the States-General of Orleans and the *Cahier-général* of the third estate which was compiled from the local *cahiers* presented by the deputies shows traces of the interest of France at large in the issue.   Unfortunately these fuller local records are lost.[2]   But this revision only looked to a modernizing of the mediaeval language of the *ordonnances*, which chiefly dated from the fourteenth century, and did not contemplate an entire recasting of them, so as to make them harmonize with the new industrial conditions.   Only one man in the assembly seems to have appreciated the real condition of things.   This was the chancellor L'Hôpital.   Not content with the mild reorganization of the guilds recommended by the third estate, on the last day of the session, January 31, 1561, the chancellor drew up the famous ordinance of Orleans.[3]   The intent of this statute was indirectly to restrain the enlarged economic tyranny of the guilds, to lessen the burden of apprenticeship, and to establish freer laboring conditions.   This purpose the gov-

---

[1] It would be a narrow view of the history of France at this time to infer that religious and economic changes were the only sort.   The truth is, the reigns of Francis I and of Henry II, were an age of transition in religion, in institutions, even in manners.

"La corruption des bonnes mœurs a continué en tous estatz, tant ecclesiastique que aultres, depuis les cardinaux jusques aux simples prebstres, et depuis le roy jusques aux simples villagloix.   Chascun a voulu suyvre son plaisir; on a délaissé mesne l'ancienne coustume de s'habiller. De temps immémorial, nul homme de France n'avoit esté tondu ni porté longue barbe avant le régne dudit feu roy; ains tous les hommes, garcons et campagnons portoient longs cheveux et la barbe rasée au menton. . . . . Les prebstres et évesques se sont faict tondre des derniers; et ont porté longue barbe, ce qui a esté trouve fort estranger depuis le commencement du règne dudit feu roy, ont commencé les nouvelles façons aux habillemens toutes contraires à l'antiquité, et a semblé la France estre ung nouveau peuple ou ung monde renouvelé."—Claude Haton, I, 112.

[2] The *cahier* of the estates of Orleans was published at the eve of the French Revolution (*Recueil des cahiers généraux des trois ordres*, chap. i).

[3] Isambert, XIV, 63 ff.

ernment aimed to attain by dissolving the confraternities, for by striking at these it really struck the guilds, since many of these associations were one and the same. No distinction was made between associations whose character was religious or charitable, and those composed of patrons and workingmen; all the confraternities were grouped together and governmental supervision was provided for. They were not legislated out of existence by the new action, but reduced to a partial dissolution. Their accumulated hoards of capital were ordered to be expended for the support of schools and hospitals and similar institutions in the towns and villages where these various guilds were, and only a limited amount of money was left in their hands. The municipal officers, in co-operation with those of the crown were made personally responsible for the execution of this measure in every bailiwick. It is important to notice the significance of this course. The government, in fact, was pursuing a policy of partial secularization of the property of these confraternities for the benefit of the people at large, and compelling distribution of the great sums locked up in the hands of the guilds in much the same way that the church had come to possess enormous sums in mortmain. This legislation, if it had really been effective, would have destroyed the guilds.

The guilds thus put upon the defensive, owing to the reforming policy of the crown and the political Huguenots, sought to save themselves by pleading that they were religious associations. By this adroit movement they gained the support of the Catholic party. But the crown refused to yield, and we find the *Confréries de métiers* directly supervised in letters-patent of February 5, 1562, and December 14, 1565. Coupled with these measures, we find others forbidding banquets, festivals, and like celebrations (edicts of December 11, 1566, and of February 4, 1567) which by this time had become centers of religious agitation among the Catholics. But the government could not maintain its course. The identification of the guilds and confraternities with the Catholic party gave them great and unexpected support. Under the new order of things they became the nuclei of local and provincial Catholic leagues.[1]   In other words, the labor party became identified with the Huguenots, while the upper bourgeoisie, controlling the guilds, adhered to the Catholic cause—at Rouen in 1560 the merchants actually declared a lock-out against workmen who attended preachings[2]—and became the nuclei of the provincial leagues, exactly as in France in 1793 every Jacobin club became an arm of the Terror government.

It was said at the time, and has often been asserted since, that these local Catholic leagues were but protective associations in the beginning and formed to repel Huguenot violence.[3]   The Huguenots practiced as violent methods as their religious opponents and their offenses were as numerous; but with the exception of the Huguenot association in Dauphiné, there is no early example of a Protestant association similar to the leagues of the Catholics

[1] I am indebted for much of this information to M. Henri Hauser, "Les questions industrielles et commercielles aux Etats de 1560," *Revue des cours*, XIII, No. 6, December 15, 1904.   Cf. Funck-Brentano, Introd. to Montchrétien, *Traicté de l'œconomie politique*, LXXIV–VI.

[2] Hauser, "The Reformation and the Popular Classes in France in the Sixteenth Century," *American Historical Review*, January 1899, p. 223.   "The trade-unions fell under the sway of the religious brotherhoods, which excluded the non-Catholics and were soon to lead the revolutionary movement of the League."—*Ibid.*, 227.

[3] "L'origine des ligues en ce royaume vient des Huguenots."—Tavannes, 222; Martin, *Histoire de France*, IX, 125.

"En face des Protestants, qui s'associaient et s'organisaient contre les catholiques, ceux-ci avaient de bonne heure formé des unions locales pour résister aux entreprises des hérétiques.   Ces premières ligues ont seulement un but religieux. Elles sont généralement composés de bourgeois dévoué à la royauté et sincèrement émus des dangers auxquels est exposé la catholicisme."—*La grande encyc.*, XXII, 234, *s. v.* "Ligue," article by M. de Vaissière.

"La jalousie entre les deux Religions ne se borna pas l'émulation d'une plus grande régularité; elles cherchèrent s'appuyer l'une contre l'autre de la force des confédérations et des serments.   Depuis long-temps la Romaine entretenoit dans son sein des associations connues sous le nom de confréries.   Elles avoient des lieux et des jours d'assemblée fixés, une police, des repas, des exercices, des deniers communs.   Il ne fut question que d'ajouter à ce la un serment d'employer ses biens et sa vie pour la défense de la Foi attaquée.   Avec cette formule, les confréries devinrent comme d'elles-mêmes, dans chaque ville, des corps de troupes prêtes à agir au gré des chefs, et leur bannières, des étendarts militaires."—Anquetil, I, 213.

in the provinces. The Protestant local organizations were not so highly developed, in a military sense, as early as this, nor were they of the same form as those of the Catholics. Montluc himself, than whom there is no better judge, testifies that in the war in Guyenne in 1562 "they showed themselves to be novices, and indeed they were guided by their ministers." The Protestants had a sort of triumvirate, it is true, in the two Châtillon brothers, and the prince of Condé, but their work only remotely partakes of the policy of the real Triumvirate; even their appeal to Elizabeth did not contemplate such radical conduct as the Triumvirate displayed.[1]

No Huguenot leader ever thought of subordinating the government of France to a foreign ruler for the maintenance of the faith he believed in,[2] as the Guises, Montmorency, and St. André did. Condé's declaration that the civil war was caused by the Triumvirate's action had much truth in it. The rules of the association which the Huguenots formed at Orleans, on April 11, 1562, were as much a body of military regulations for the discipline of the army as they were a political compact, as a reading of the articles will prove.[3] There was little of the politico-military character of

[1] Coligny expressly denied having made any promise to return Calais to England, and as to the occupation of Havre, he said: "J'en ignorais les termes jusqu'à la venue de Throckmorton en Normandie, et lorsque j'en ai signé la confirmation, je n'ai jamais pu croire qu'il y eut autre clause que l'assurance donnée à la reine du remboursement des sommes qu'elle nous avançait."—*Correspondance de Catherine de Médicis*, II, Introd., xiii. See the extended discussion of this controverted subject in Whitehead, *Gaspard de Coligny*, Appendix I, where he shows that the admiral is to be exonerated from the odium of having sought to betray Havre-de-Grace into the hands of the English and puts the blame for this article of the treaty of Hampton Court upon the vidame de Chartres.

[2] The conduct of La Rochelle in the fourth civil war is the most pronounced instance of Huguenot willingness to subordinate French territory to a foreign domination and this action was of the municipality, not of a single Huguenot leader, nor did it, of course, imply the subjection of the government of France to English rule as the Triumvirate contemplated in the case of Spain.

[3] *Mém. de Condé*, IV, 93: "Traicté d'Association faicte par Monseigneur le Prince de Condé avec les Princes, Chevaliers de l'Ordre, Seigneurs, Capitaines, Gentilhommes et autres de tous estats, qui sont entrez, ou entreront cy-apres, en la dicte association, pour maintenir l'honneur de Dieu, le repos de ce royaume, et l'estat et liberté du Roy sous le gouvernement de la Roy sa mere."

The third article provides for implicit obedience to the prince of Condé, "chef

the Catholic leagues about it.   It is not until after the Bayonne episode that we find a solid federation of the Reformed churches beginning to form, and the first test of the Protestant organization was made at the beginning of the second civil war.[1]   This is not the place, however, to dwell upon its development.   In due time the subject will be taken up.

The edict confirming the act of pacification (March 19, 1563) in its sixth article forbade the formation of any leagues in the future, and ordered the dissolution of those already in existence.[2] This prohibition was a dead letter from the beginning.   The government not only was unable to prevent the formation of new leagues; it was even unable to suppress those already in existence.[3] When the first civil war ended, there were three well-organized Catholic leagues in southern France, namely those of Provence, of Toulouse, and of Agen.   Catherine de Medici, who, for some months to come, continued to give substantial manifestation of her desire for peace,[4] in announcing the act of Amboise to Montluc,

et conducteur de toute la Compagnie," i. e., the army; *there was no league*.   Minute regulations follow for the government of the camp, for services of prayer both morning and evening, etc.   The fourth article, which has to do with the ways and means of raising revenue, is the nearest approach to *political* organization: ". . . . nous jurons and promettons devant Dieu et ses Anges nous tenir prests de tout ce qui fait en nostre pouvoir, comme d'argent; d'armes, chevaux de service, et toutes les autres choses requises, pour nous trouver au premier Mandement du dict Seigneur Prince."—*Mém. de Condé*, III, 210–15.   Cf. La Popelinière, Book VIII, 582 ff., upon the same subject.

[1] In 1567 when the Huguenot chiefs tried to seize Charles IX by surprise at Meaux, thus precipitating the second civil war, the Venetian ambassador, Correro, expressed astonishment at the perfection of the Huguenot organization (*Rel. vén.*, II, 115).

[2] Edit de confirmation de l'édit de pacification du 19 Mars 1562, sec. 6: "Nous . . . . prohibons et défendons, sur peine de crime de leze-majesté à tous nos dits sujets, quels qu'ils soient, qu'ils n'ayent à faire practique, avoir intelligence, envoyer ne recevoir lettres ne messages, escrire en chiffre n'autre escriture feincte, ne desguisée, à princes estrangers, ne aucuns de leur subjects et serviteurs, pour chose concernant nostre estat sans nostre sceu et exprès congé et permission."— Isambert, *Recueil des lois*, XIV, 145; the "Ordonnance explicative" of April 7 is on p. 333; cf. *Mém. de Condé*, IV, 311; La Popelinière, Book X, 724.

[3] We find repeated orders for their dissolution, e. g., F. Fr. 15,876, fol. 201.

[4] Lettres-patentes of Charles IX extended the right of Protestant worship to Condom, St. Sevère, and Dax, towns which did not figure in the edict of March 19

demanded the dissolution of these associations. Instead of so doing, however, Candalle, Montluc's chief agent in Guyenne, continued his activities. On March 13, 1563, as has been noticed, in defiance of the impending edict of pacification (which was completed and only awaited promulgation) the Catholic seigneurs of Guyenne, at Cadillac (near Bordeaux) entered into a league identical in purpose and in form with those of Agen and Languedoc.[1] This league, which is the germ of that which spread over Gascony, seems to have been denounced to the government by Lagebaston, the president of the parlement of Bordeaux, between whom and Montluc there was friction, partly because of Montluc's preference for Agen as a working capital for the region, partly because of his notorious dislike of the lawyer class, whose disposition to regard forms of law and vested right interfered with Montluc's high-handed and arbitrary management of affairs.[2] This new league in such glaring violation of the edict, called forth a sharp letter of rebuke from the queen mother to Montluc on March 31. After alluding in a general way to "les maulx" due to the existence of "les partialitez et les associations, qui se sont faictes" she says:

J'ay esté advertye qu'il s'en est faicte une autre en la Guyenne dont est chef Monsieur de Candalle, laquelle encores qu'elle ayt esté faicte à bonne intention durant la guerre, si n'est-ce que, cessant la dicte guerre et se faisant la paix, elle n'est plus nécessaire et ne la peult ung roy trouver bonne, ny que ceulx qui veullent estre estimez obéyssans ne peuvent soustenir sans encourir le mesme cryme de rebellion dont ilz ont accusé leurs adversaires. Et pour ceste cause, et que le Roy monsieur mon filz n'est pas délibéré d'en souffrir plus aucun, de quelque costé qu'elle procedde ny permectre plus à ses subjectz, de quelque religion qu'ilz soient, d'avoir autre association qu'avec luy

(Ruble, *Commentaires et lettres de Montluc*, IV, 257, 272, and notes). A royal ordinance was later issued giving a list of those towns where Calvinist worship was permitted, specifying that it must be conducted in the faubourgs, however (*Mém. de Condé*, IV, 338).

[1] Within a month the government received anonymous information of Candalle's activity (*Archives de la Gironde*, XXI, 14 [April 16, 1563]). Cf. "Lettre de Candalle à la reine, du mai 20, 1563 (F. Fr. 15,875, fol. 495). In the same volume, fol. 491, is a joint declaration of the gentlemen of Guyenne upon the purposes of this association.

[2] *Commentaires et lettres de Montluc*, IV, 214.

et selon son obéyssance, il fault, Monsieur de Monluc, que, pour le bien de son service, comme il le vous commande expressément par ses lettres, que vous, qui estes son lieutenant-général par delà, faciez rompre celle qui s'est faicte sans permectre qu'ilz ayent aucune force, puissance ou authorité que celle que vous leur baillerez, ny aucune volunté que d'obéyr à ce que par vous, pour le bien du service du Roy monsieur mon filz, leur sera commandé; pour lequel effect j'en scriptz, comme faict le Roy monsieur mon filz, une lectre audit s^r de Candalle et à tous ceulx qui y sont comprins, comme nous en avons esté bien amplement advertiz.[1]

Until the ambition of the Guises created an opposition to them among the old-line nobility, and so identified the Huguenot movement with the interests of the aristocracy,[2] the French Reformation found its chief support among the lower bourgeois class in the towns. The proportion naturally varied from place to place. Lyons, partly from its proximity to Geneva, but more because of its strong commercial position and its great manufacturing interests, among which the silk industry was of most importance, was the greatest Huguenot city in France.[3] Where we find Protestantism prevailing in feudal districts, it is largely to be ascribed to

[1] *Correspondance de Catherine de Médicis*, I, 552, col. 2. At the same time Catherine wrote to certain members of the Parlement of Bordeaux. Montluc's reply, both the personal letter he wrote to the queen mother (April 11), and the more official remonstrance he forwarded to the King, is a palpable lie. He wrote to the queen "Je vous puis asseurer . . . . que despuis la nouvelle de la paix, il n'y a eu traicté d'association aucune; que, au moindre mot que j'en ay dict, tout ne soit cessé comme s'il n'en avoit jamais esté parle."—*Commentaires et lettres*, IV, 206. Cf. his similar declaration to Charles IX, on p. 214. The clergy of Bordeaux sustained Montluc in this deception, and when the queen's suspicion continued, justified the association on the ground of religion. *Corresp. de Catherine de Méd.*, I, 552, note. Candalle in a letter of May 20, 1563, still evaded the truth in writing to the queen (F. Fr., 15,876, fol. 495), and Catherine, upon more suspicious information from d'Escars, determined to satisfy herself of certain facts, and sent two commissioners to Guyenne to secure better information (*Commentaires et lettres de Montluc*, IV, 270, note). Unfortunately for the government, the Parlement of Bordeaux resented their coming as an invasion of their jurisdiction, and the inquiry degenerated into a quarrel between the Parlement and the commissioners (*ibid.*, IV, 292, n. 1; *Corresp. de Catherine de Médicis*, II, 114, 115).

[2] Claude Haton, I, 266.

[3] "A Lyon, les catholiques y sont pour le jour d'huy en plus grand nombre des troiz partz pour une que les huguenotz; mais les dits huguenotz sont les principaulx et ceulx qui ont les forces en mains."—Granvella to the emperor Ferdinand I, April 12, 1564, *Papiers d'état du cardinal de Granvelle*, VII, 467.

the influence of Protestant gentleman-farmers, often retired bourgeois, who purchased the county estates of the older nobility who had
been bankrupted by the wars in Italy and Flanders, or else preferred
to live at court. The strongholds of French Protestantism were
the river towns, on the highways of trade, or sea-ports like Rouen
and La Rochelle. Dauphiné, which fattened on the commerce out
of Italy through the Alpine passes, and Provence which bordered
the Mediterranean, both of which "cleared" through Lyons;
Lower Poitou, where La Rochelle was, and Normandy on the Channel
were the chief Protestant provinces of France. Normandy was
probably the most Protestant province of all, for here Calvinism
not only obtained in the ports and "good" towns, but in the country areas as well.[1]

But there are evidences of the penetration of Protestantism
into the country districts elsewhere as well—in Orléannais, Nivernais, Blésois, the diocese of Nîmes and even in isolated parts of
Champagne and Gascony.[2] In general, however, the French
peasantry were strongly Catholic.

The reason for this is, first, a social one: while the revolution of the fifteenth and sixteenth centuries was ruinous for the artisan, it was profitable to
the peasant. The rent paid to the landlord, immutably fixed in the twelfth
or thirteenth century, represented under the new values of money a very light
burden, while the fall in the price of silver considerably raised the nominal
worth of the products of the soil, when the villein sold them. The price of
land was falling rapidly at the very time when the French gentry, ceasing to be

[1] The coast trade with England and Holland probably explains the prevalence
of Protestantism in Lower Normandy, at least in part. But the reasons of the
prevalence of rural Huguenotism on an extensive scale in Normandy are quite
obscure. On this subject see La Ferrière, *Normandie à l'étranger*, 2–5, 82; Hauser,
"The French Reformation and the French People in the Sixteenth Century,"
American Historical Review, January 1899, 225, 226.

[2] Hauser, *op. cit.*, 226, 227. I find in Montluc an interesting allusion to the
prevalence of the Reformed belief among the peasantry of Guyenne, which M.
Hauser has not noticed. It occurs in a letter of "Instruction au cappitaine Monluc
[Pierre-Bertrand, called captain Peyrot] de ce qu'il dira à la royne et au roy de
Navarre, de la part du sieur de Monluc, touchant l'état de Guyenne," March 25,
1561, and is as follows: "Et ce, à cause des insollences, scandalles et contemne-
ments que *les paisans* dudit païs leur ont faict depuis ung an en cà," etc.—*Commentaires et lettres de Montluc*, IV, 115.

an aristocracy of gentlemen-farmers and becoming a court-nobility, were compelled to sell their estates to meet their expenses and, as was said, to put their mills and meadows on their shoulders. When a lord wished to sell at any price a part of his estates, there was always, in the parish, a countryman who had been, as one may say, saving money for centuries, and who, realizing at last the dream of bygone generations, bought land. Thus did the French villein become a landowner. The reign of Louis XII and the beginning of that of Francis I was for the French peasants an epoch of real prosperity; his situation presented a striking contrast with that of the German peasant who, at the same date, was in danger of relapsing into bondage. We may easily understand why there was not in France, as in Germany, a peasants' revolution both social and religious.[1]

But there are other reasons for the religious growth of the Huguenot cause among the people not so hard to find. Their ministers preached in the French language and avoided the use of Latin, which tended to mystery and obscurity; after sermons the service was continued with prayer and the singing of psalms in French rhyme, with vocal and instrumental music in which the congregation joined. In their church polity, the Huguenots had carried changes farther than had the Reformation elsewhere in Europe. In Germany and England the Reformation still adhered to many of the institutions of the mediaeval church, retaining the episcopate and inferior clergy, as deacons, archdeacons, canons, curates, together with vestures, canonical habits, and the use of ornaments.[2]

No reliable estimate can be made of the proportion between Catholics and Huguenots in the sixteenth century. A remonstrance of 1562 to the Pope declared that one-fourth of France was separate from the communion of Rome.[3] The Venetian

---

[1] Hauser, "The French Reformation and the French People in the Sixteenth Century," *American Hist. Review*, January 1899, 224. For further information upon this change in the condition of the lower and middle classes in France in the sixteenth century see Avenel, "La fortune mobilière dans l'histoire," *Revue des deux mondes*, August 1, 1892, pp. 605, 606; *idem*, "La propriété foncière de Philippe-Auguste à Napoléon," *Revue des deux mondes*, February 1, 1893, pp. 128, 129; April 15, 1893, pp. 796, 797, 801–3, 812, 813; August 15, 1893, pp. 853–55; Lavisse, *Histoire de France*, V, Pt. I, 262–65.

[2] Remonstrance sent to the Pope out of France, C. S. P, For., No. 1453 (1562).

[3] *Ibid.*

ambassador thought "hardly a third part of the people heretical" in 1567.[1] The *échevins* of Amiens declared three-quarters of the inhabitants of Amiens were Protestant in the same year.[2] Charles IX in a remonstrance to Pius IV asserted that a fourth part of France was Protestant.[3] Montluc, no mean observer, estimated that one-tenth of the population of Guyenne was Protestant.[4] If this proportion be applied to France at large, the Huguenots would have numbered something like 1,600,000. Beza, who presided over the synod of La Rochelle in 1571, claimed that the Huguenots had 2,150 congregations, some of them very large, as in the case of the church of Orleans, which was said to have 7,000 members. At the time of the Colloquy of Poissy, Normandy was said to have 305 pastors, Provence 60.[5] But the number of Huguenots in Normandy, Provence, or the Orléannais was exceptionally large. The average congregation must have been small. If we assume that the population of France was sixteen millions[6] and that one-tenth of the people were Calvinist, we would have a total of 1,600,000 Protestants for all France, which would give an average of about 750 members to each congregation on the basis of Beza's statement as to the number of the Huguenot churches. This is certainly much too high a figure. Personally I believe the average was less than half of this. If the congregation averaged 400 members each, on Beza's calculation there would have been

[1] *Rel. vén.*, II, 121.

[2] Du Bois, *La ligue: documents relatifs à la Picardie d'après les registres de l'échevinage d'Amiens* (1859), 5.

[3] *Mém. de Condé*, II, 812.

[4] Montluc, Letter 48, March 25, 1561, *Comment. et lettres*, IV, 115. "Cette appréciation de Montluc est digne d'être signalée à cause de sa conformité absolue avec les conclusions de l'érudition actuelle. On admit généralement que le parti protestant, à l'époque même de sa plus grande force, n'a jamais compté plus de dixième de la population en France."—Note appended by M. de Ruble.

[5] *Synodicon in Gallia*, I, lix.

[6] A Venetian syndicate interested in France in 1566 estimated the population to be between fifteen and sixteen millions (*Rel. vén.*, III, 149). I assume this estimate to be more reliable than most. According to Levasseur, economically France could support a population of 20,000,000 in the sixteenth century (Foville, "La population française," *Revue des deux mondes*, November 15, 1891, 306).

860,000 Huguenots in France. A Venetian source of the year 1562 sets the number at 600,000.[1] This may be too low, but all things considered, I believe it not far from the truth. The total Protestant population of France I do not believe to have exceeded three-quarters of a million before 1572, and after that date it is often difficult to distinguish between Huguenots and Politiques.

Such was the state of things when the first civil war came to an end.

[1] *C. S. P. For.*, No. 935, §4, March 14, 1562.

CHAPTER X

THE TOUR OF THE PROVINCES.[1] THE BAYONNE EPISODE

"I am always *en voyage*," wrote the Venetian ambassador to the senate. "Since the beginning of my embassy the King has not staid more than fifteen days in any one place. He goes from Lorraine to Poitou, and then to Normandy and the edge of Belgium, back again to Normandy, then to Paris, Picardy, Champagne, Burgundy."[2] Dr. Dale wrote in the same strain to Lord Burghley: "The Spanish ambassador has a saying that ambassadors in France are eaten up by their horses, since they are constrained to keep so many because of the habit of the court of moving from place to place continually."[3]

But there was point to Charles IX's famous tour of the provinces in 1564–66. The unsettled condition of the country, if no other reason, accounts for Catherine's great design of completing the pacification of the kingdom by having the King tour the realm. The route lay through Sens[4] (March 15) to Troyes (March 23)[5] where the peace with England was signed on April 13; thence to Châlons-sur-Marne, Bar-le-Duc, Dijon (May 15), Macon (June 8), and thence to Lyons, where the court arrived on June 13. The King traveled with his ordinary train, that is, with his mother, his brother, the duke of Anjou, the constable, and the archers of the guard, in order to spare the people the burden of

[1] Upon the details of this famous tour see *Correspondance de Catherine de Médicis*, II, Introd., xlv ff.; D'Aubigné, Book IV, chap iv; Jouan, *Voyage du roi Charles IX*, new ed.; *L'Ambassade de St. Sulpice*, 243, 254, 255, 270, 272, 274–76, 287, 300, 319.

[2] *Rel. vén.*, I, 108.

[3] *C. S. P. For.*, No. 43, March 7, 1574.

[4] "Entrée du roy Charles IX et de la reyne-mère Catherine de Médicis en la ville de Sens, le 15 mars 1563," Relation extraite du MSS d'Eracle Cartault, chanoine, et des déliberations de l'Hôtel-de-Ville. Préface de M. H. Monceaux, 1882.

[5] Coutant, "Dépenses du roi Charles IX à Troyes le mercredi 5 avril 1564 après Pâques," Annuaire admin., etc., pour 1860 (Troyes); "Depenses du roi Charles IX à Troyes le samedi 8 avril 1564," Annuaire admin., etc., pour 1859 (Troyes).

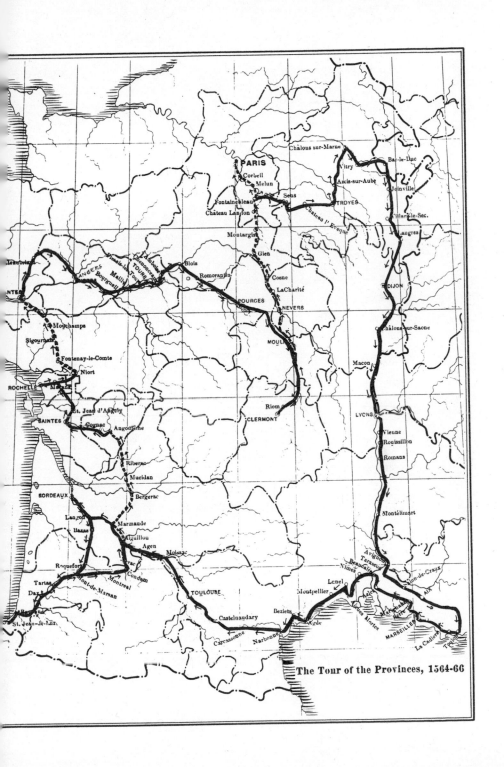

The Tour of the Provinces, 1564-66

great entertainment, and those princes and nobles who wished to follow were accompanied only by their ordinary servants.[1] If the Huguenots viewed the King's sojourn at Bar-le-Duc with apprehension,[2] it was not without anxiety that his Catholic subjects saw Charles IX visit the great city located at the junction of the Rhone and the Saône rivers.[3] Lyons seems to have imbibed something of Calvinism from the very waters of the arrowy river whose source was the lake of the citadel of Calvinism.[4] The rumor was current that a greater conspiracy than that of Amboise was on foot; that the King and queen were to be deposed and slain, and that Lyons would unite with Geneva to form a greater Calvinistic republic.[5]

But Lyons welcomed the King graciously, and gave him sumptuous accommodation.[6] Charles was charmed with the reception given him and amazed at the wealth and commercial prosperity of the city.[7] Situated at the confluence of the Rhone and the

[1] Claude Haton, I, 364.

[2] The visit of the King to Bar-le-Duc (to attend the baptism of the child-prince Henry of Lorraine) profoundly stirred the Calvinists of France and Switzerland. Charles IX in person, Ernest of Mansfeldt, governor of Luxembourg, representing Philip II, and the dowager-duchess of Lorraine, Christine of Denmark, acted as god-parents.

[3] Fourquevaux to St. Sulpice, May 19, 1564, L'Ambassade de St. Sulpice, 266.

[4] Armstrong, French Wars of Religion, 22, admirably observes: "Geneva was practically a French republic, constantly recruited by raw refugee material, and circulating in return trained ministers and money, giving unity to measures which local separation was likely to dissolve. Hence came the propagandism, the organization for victory, the reorganization after defeat, the esprit de corps, the religious zeal which whipped up flagging political or military energies."

[5] See a letter of Alva in K. 1,502. Montluc later informed Philip II of it (Commentaires et lettres, V, 25, letter of June, 1565). The rumor seems not to have passed unheeded, for the marshal Vieilleville cautioned the King and his mother to be moderate in their course, saying that the Huguenots were many and the soldiers few (Papiers d'état du cardinal de Granvelle, VIII, 632). On the state of Geneva at this time see Roget, L'église et l'état à Genève du vivant de Calvin; étude d'histoire politico-ecclésiastique, 1867.

[6] The constable to St. Sulpice, June 21, 1564, in L'Ambassade de St. Sulpice, 273.

[7] L'Ambassade de St. Sulpice, 275, 276; Nég. Tosc., III, 515, 516; Nyd (l'abbé) "Notes écrites en 1566, à la fin d'un missel de l'abbaye de Malgrivier (événements

Saône rivers, the wines and grain of Burgundy came to Lyons for market, while it was the natural entrepôt of the commerce out of Italy, besides much that came from Spain and Flanders. There were four fairs there each year. The great industry of the city was silk manufacturing. In 1450 Charles VII had granted it the monopoly in this. Francis I in 1536 relieved the silk operatives of all taxes and military service. The bulk of the commerce was in the hands of Italians, of whom there were said to be above twelve thousand in the city—chiefly Florentines, Genoese, and Milanese.[1] There were also many Germans and Swiss, whose presence gave the governor, the duke of Nemours,[2] great anxiety, because large quantities of arms were smuggled into the city in the guise of merchandise.[3]

The court had not been long upon its tour through the provinces before Catherine de Medici discovered that the petition of the estates of Burgundy for the abolition of Protestant worship was not merely a local prejudice, but the sense of the provinces.[4] The elements of this public opinion were various: The clergy—not all, however—wanted the findings of the Council of Trent accepted *in toto;* all of them were dissatisfied with the recognition of the rights of the Protestants; the alienation of their lands was a grievance to the clergy, the more so because speculators had bought them at a low price because of the doubt as to the validity

rel. à Lyon, 1562–66)," *Bull. du Com. de la langue, de l'hist. et des arts de la France,* IV, 300 (1857). The copper and lead mines of the Lyonnais had been profitable in the Middle Ages, but the wars of the English in France and the Black Death ruined the industry. See Jars, "Notice historique des mines du Lyonnais, Forez et Beaujolais," MS, Bibliothéque de Lyons, No. 1,470.

[1] *Rel. vén.,* I, 35–37.

[2] A letter of his published by La Ferrière, *Deux années de mission à St. Pétersbourg,* Paris (1867), 56, 57, casts an interesting light upon the state of the city at this time.

[3] *L'Ambassade de St. Sulpice,* 266.

[4] La Cuisine, *Histoire du parlement de Bourgogne,* I, 60; Castelnau, Book V, chap. vi, says the petition was printed. The bishop of Orleans, Jean de Morvilliers, in a letter dated August 21, 1563, called the queen mother's attention to this growing prejudice (Frémy, *Les diplomates de la Ligue,* 30–32).

of the title.[1] The Guises were angry that the prosecution
of Coligny for the murder of the duke had been abandoned.[2]
Among high and low alike there were unprincipled folk who had
hopes of profiting by confiscations and forfeitures imposed upon
the Huguenots.[3]

The queen mother was too good a politician not to pay heed
to these signs of popular feeling, more especially as the voice of
the provinces chimed with those in high authority, who not
only urged that the war be renewed against the Protestants but
also hinted broadly of foreign support in aid of the crown. At
first Catherine answered graciously, yet guardedly, to the effect
that a peace which had been so solemnly made, by the advice of
the princes of the blood and the council, could not be too lightly
cast aside.

The miserable effects of the war were everywhere evident.
Agriculture had almost ceased in a country famous for its fertility,
and the whole country had been so plundered and harassed by
both parties that the poor people, being stripped of all their substance, often preferred to fly to the forests rather than to remain
continually exposed to the mercy of their enemies. Wandering
soldiers and dissolute women, with stolen goods in their possession,
infested the roads.[4] As to trade and manufacturing, the mechanic
arts still were plied only in the largest and strongest towns; even
here merchants and tradesmen had shut up shop and gone off
to war, not always out of religious zeal, but in the hope of enriching
themselves by spoliation. The nobility were divided; the clergy
incensed. The civil war had been accompanied by the attendant
aids of violence, robbery, murder, rape, and justice had not been

---

[1] *L'Ambassade de St. Sulpice*, 129–31. Philip II, as has been observed, expressed his disapproval of this practice (*ibid.*, 152), and when the French government
endeavored to make it apply to the property of the French church in the Low
Countries, he set his foot down hard (*ibid.*, 188). An endeavor was made to restrain
speculation in church property by law.

[2] For details see *ibid.*, 152, 156, 165, 185, 186, 226.

[3] *Castelnau*, Book V, chaps. vi and x is very clear in the statement of various
motives.

[4] Claude Haton, I, 368.

administered in the courts for months. The very methods resorted to for the preservation of religion rendered it hateful in the eyes of many men of both parties. Both parties were bigoted in belief and in practice. The iconoclasm of the Protestants, who tore down church edifices hoary with age and sanctified by tradition, expelling the inmates, both male and female, if doing them no worse injury, familiarized society with changes wrought by violence and made the people callous to one of the most precious possessions of a nation—a reverence for tradition.[1]

To all these difficulties the prevalence of the plague must be added. Since the century of the Black Death Europe had not so suffered from this scourge as in the sixteenth. It recurred intermittently, being especially violent in the years 1531, 1533, 1544, 1546, 1548, 1553, 1562-64, 1568, 1577-80.[2] No part of Europe was spared. France, England, Spain, the Low Countries, Germany, and Italy, all suffered. But certain portions of France suffered more than others, as Bas-Languedoc, Provence, the Lyonnais, Burgundy, Champagne, the Ile-de-France, and Normandy. The west and especially the southwest were relatively exempt. Apparently the disease followed the trades-routes along the river valleys, for Toulouse, Lyons, Châlons-sur-Saône, Macon, Châlons-sur-Marne, Langres, Bourges, La Charité, Orleans, Tours, Moulins, Sens, Melun, Dijon, Troyes, Château-Thierry, Soissons, Beauvais, Pontoise, Paris, Rouen, and the Norman ports suffered most.[3] As always, Italy was the immediate source of the epidemic, which was communicated from place to place by the movements

---

[1] See the wonderful word-picture drawn by Castelnau at the beginning of Book V, and Montluc, Books V, VI, *passim*. For the brigandage that prevailed see Montluc, IV, 343 (letter to the King from Agen, March 26, 1564).

[2] Frankiin, "La vie d'autrefois," *Hygiene*, chap. ii, especially pp. 67–75. For the plague of 1563–64 in Languedoc see *Hist. de Languedoc*, XI, 447 (Toulouse), 464 (Montpellier, Nîmes, Castres, etc.). It was at its height in July, 1564. It seems to have come into Languedoc from Spain. See also *Papiers d'état du card. de Granvelle* (March 11, 1564), VII, 387, 401; VIII, 36, 382, 470; C. S. P. *For.* (1564), Introd., xi–xii, and Nos. 544–53, §2; No. 592; Claude Haton I, 332. Those exposed to the infection were required to carry white wands as a sign (*C. S. P. Ven.*, No. 824, November 20, 1580).

[3] Claude Haton, I, 332.

of trade. Lyons paid dearly for its commercial pre-eminence, for the ravages of the plague were terrible there.[1] It was at its height when the court was there in July, 1564. The English ambassador, Smith, gives a fearful picture of the state of the city. Men died in the street before his lodgings. His servant who went daily for his provisions sometimes saw ten and twelve corpses, some naked, lying in the streets where they lay till "men clothed in yellow" removed them. A great many bodies were cast into the river, "because they will not be at the cost to make graves. This day," he writes on July 12, "from break of day till ten o'clock there laid a man naked in the street, groaning and drawing his last breath, not yet dead. Round the town there are tents of the pestiferous, besides those which are shut up in their houses."[2] Almost every third house was closed because of the plague. The city authorities vainly tried to combat the disease by providing that visits were to be made twice a day by those appointed; but as there were but five "master surgeons" in the whole city, medical attention must have been slight. Persons affected with the plague were to be removed to the hospital—the oldest and one of the best in Europe at that time. Corpses were to be buried at night and the clothes of the dead burned.[3] "About the Rhone men dare eat no fish nor fishers lay their engines and nets, because instead of fish they take up the pestiferous carcasses which are thrown in." New sanitary regulations were made. All filth was to be cast into the river and not allowed to pollute the streets or the river banks. Fires of scented wood were kept burning between every ten houses in the street. Pigs and other animals were not allowed at large. Meat, fish, and vegetable stalls were to be inspected and all decayed provisions destroyed.[4]

It is interesting to observe the efforts made by local authorities to prevent the spread of the disease and the relief measures that

[1] Vingtrinier, *La peste à Lyon*, 1901.

[2] *C. S. P. For.*, No. 553 (1564).

[3] On the state of medical science at this time see Franklin, "La vie d'autrefois," *Hygiene*, chap. ii; cf. *C. S. P. For.*, No. 544, July 1, 1564 (summary of a pamphlet printed by the city authorities).

[4] Claude Haton, I, 224–28.

were taken. As soon as the plague was discovered, the town authorities usually set guards to watch the houses of those stricken and appointed barbers and gravediggers to treat ill and to inter the dead. These attendants were supported and paid by a tax laid upon the town. Those who were ill were sent to a house of isolation appointed to be a hospital, which was often upon the walls of the town, remote from the people. In Provins the church and cemetery were immediately adjacent to the hospital! The mortality was great. In Provins in 1562 there were eighty persons stricken, of whom sixty died, among them four of the attendants. Two of the barber-surgeons refused to serve and were proceeded against by the town bailiff and were hanged in effigy because the principals in the case had made their escape. Diseased houses were sprinkled with perfumes and aromatic herbs were burned in them in order to purify them.[1] As always, the dislocation of society and the depravation of morals worked havoc in the community. Crimes of violence were common.[2]

Little by little, however, this picture of misery faded into the background of the queen's mind and the question of political expediency, which was always the lodestar of her policy, became her primary consideration.[3] The Catholics plucked up courage as the court progressed[4] and Huguenot suspicion of the queen's course was early aroused. Shortly after the tour of the provinces had begun, and while the court was till at Troyes pending the signature of the treaty of peace, there was a jar between D'Andelot and the queen mother, who would not permit him to choose his own captains and other officers as was customarily permitted to colonels.

[1] Claude Haton, I, 332.

[2] "Non-seulement la France fut agitée en ceste année de guerres, diminution des biens de la terre et de peste, mais aussi fut remplie et fort tormentée des voleurs, larrons et sacrilèges, qui de nuict et de jour tenoient les champs et forcoient les églises et maisons, pour voller et piller les biens d'icelles pour vivre et s'entretenir." —*Mémoires de Claude Haton*, I, 332 (1562).

Smith declared that Lyons was the "most fearful and inhuman town he had ever seen. Men show themselves more fearful and inhuman than pagans."— C. S. P. For., No. 553, July 12, 1564.

[3] Castelnau, Book V, chap. x.

[4] Claude Haton, I, 378.

Partially in consequence of this affront, and partially to avoid being compromised more with Qeen Elizabeth, D'Andelot, the prince of Condé, and the cardinal Châtillon all remained away from the sessions of the council while the terms of peace were under consideration, and when the court resumed its migration, no one of these attended it.[1] Indeed, after the court left Châlons-sur-Marne, so wide was the breach between the prince of Condé, the admiral and all of that faction, and the court, that the chancellor L'Hôpital was the only official who continued to treat them with deference.[2] The consideration shown Jeanne d'Albret only partially relieved the suspicions of the Protestants.[3]

We find the anxiety of the Protestants over the situation reflected in the proceedings of the provincial synod of the Reformed churches of the region through which the court had been traveling during this season, namely the churches of Champagne, Brie, Picardy, the Ile-de-France, and the French Vexin.[4] This synod assembled on April 27, 1564, at La Ferté-sous-Jouarre, and was composed of forty-five ministers. Letters were read from many parts of France and abroad, among which was one from Beza bidding the Huguenots to be on their guard as the priests were contributing money for the purpose of rooting out the truth. It was agreed by the body to reply that the Protestants were suspicious of the intentions of the queen mother.[5] In its resolutions the synod condemned the policy of the magistrates who cloaked their religious animosity under the guise of the law,[6] and complained that the Catholics were

[1] C. S. P. For., No. 327, §11, April 14, 1564; No. 389, §12, May 12, 1564.

[2] Ibid., No. 755, October 21, 1565.

[3] Jeanne d'Albret had an interview with Catherine after the court left Macon; she demanded possession of Henry of Béarn, and leave to return to her estates. But the queen mother, feeling that to grant either of these requests might injure her cause with Philip II, sought to satisfy her with the gift of 150,000 livres and the assignment of Vendôme as the place of her residence (Corresp. de Catherine de Médicis, Introd., II, l).

[4] C. S. P. For., No. 384, § 7; Papiers d'état du cardinal de Granvelle, VII, 529. His opinion of the synod is expressed in Vol. VIII, 17; Correspondance de Catherine de Médicis, II, 179, note; Claude Haton, I, 384.

[5] C. S. P. For., No. 358.

[6] Castelnau, Book V, chap. x, p. 284, attests this miscarriage of justice.

carrying the King about the country in order to show him the ruin of their churches.[1] The moderate La Roche even went so far as to declare that the Reformed church never could have peace while the queen mother governed.

Justice and historical accuracy, however, require that it be said that the Huguenots' own conduct was sometimes in violation of the privileges granted them by the Edict of Amboise. Their iconoclasm toward the images and the pictures which the Catholics considered sacred was outrageous; they failed to confine their worship to authorized places, so that the magistrates were acting within their rights in so far repressing Protestant worship; their provincial synods not infrequently were inflammatory political assemblies.[2] On the other hand, the Catholics wilfully molested the Huguenots, interfering in their congregations, and compelling them to pay tithes and other dues for the support of the Catholic poor and even—Castelnau says—to support their provincial leagues.[3]

But the Huguenots went too far in their suspicion of the government. Beza, at the synod of La Ferté-sous-Jouarre had been apprehensive of a joint attack of France and Savoy upon Geneva, not knowing that the French aim was to renew the alliance with the Catholic cantons in order to prevent Spanish ascendency there.[4] Bern and Zurich were the pillars of French ascendency in the Alpine country. France counted upon them more than upon all else to prevent Spanish recruiting, and to close the Alpine passes to Spain's army. To this end Bellièvre, the marshal Vieille-

---

[1] C. S. P. For., 755, October 21, 1564.

[2] No one can read the Huguenot historian, La Popelinière, Vol. II, Book XI, without prejudice, and not be convinced of the fact that the French Protestants infringed both the letter and the spirit of the Edict of Amboise. The fact that Damville, who had succeeded his father the constable as governor of Languedoc in 1562, and who was a moderate Catholic, was required to be so drastic in his measures of repression that the Protestants complained of him to Charles IX, supports this view. Cf. Corresp. de Catherine de Médicis, II, Introd., l and li.

[3] Castelnau, Book V, chap. x; La Popelinière, loc cit.

[4] L'Ambassade de St. Sulpice, 328; Papiers d'état du cardinal de Granvelle, VIII, 398.

ville, and the bishop of Limoges, who had returned from Madrid, where he was succeeded by St. Sulpice, were sent into Switzerland in the early spring of 1564 to penetrate the designs of Spain, and to promise an early payment of the French debts due to the cantons in return for their military support in the wars of Henry II.[1] Bellièvre's particular mission was to the Grisons. The position of the Grisons was a precarious one, for Spain could attack them from the Valteline, or starve them by prohibiting the exportation of grain into the country from Lombardy. By using such threats the Spanish governor of Milan hoped to compel the adherence of the Grisons to a treaty which would open to Spanish and imperial arms the great Alpine routes of the Splügen, the Bernina, and the Stelvio, thus connecting the territories of the two branches of the Hapsburg house and shutting France out from eastern Switzerland. Bellièvre fraternized with the popular element, and by May, 1564, had almost completely neutralized the success of his Spanish rival in spite of Spanish gold. Fortunately for France the Ten Jurisdictions declared in her favor and the Grisons, though very Spaniardized, luckily had a French pensioner as its chief magistrate, the Swiss captain Florin.

Meanwhile the negotiations of the bishop of Limoges and the marshal Vieilleville had progressed so far that the treaty of alliance was all but signed. Late in October Bellièvre received from Freiburg the text of the articles of alliance which the bishop of Limoges and the marshal Vieilleville proposed to submit to the Swiss diet. Encouraged by this success, he went to Glarus in order to overcome the influence of the Zurich preachers who were outspoken enemies of the French alliance, and if possible to settle the difference between that state and Schwytz. By great dexterity he prevailed upon the two cantons to accept a uniform treaty. But he could not push negotiations to a conclusion until hearing from his colleagues.

Spain made a supreme effort to secure the opening of the

---

[1] It was rumored also that the queen mother was ready to sacrifice the Italian protégés of France to curry favor with Spain (*Papiers d'état du cardinal de Granvelle*, VIII, 395–400, note; *L'Ambassade de St. Sulpice*, 300, 335).

passages between the Tyrol and the Milanais, but failed because the Grisons promised France that they would accept the principle of a renewed alliance, leaving the settlement of details pending, so that although the supremacy of France in Switzerland was not absolutely assured, at least the adherence of the three leagues to her seemed assured.

But the Escurial and the Vatican were leagued to destroy French influence in Switzerland. Spain gave up hope of compelling the cantons to make a direct alliance with her, but by means of commercial threats and commercial inducements counted on still keeping the Alpine passes open to her arms. Her maxim was, where the grain of Lombardy goes, there Spain's armies may go, too. To neutralize this danger the French energetically opposed any renewal of an alliance between the Vatican and the Swiss cantons. The Grey League, later won by the commercial promises of Spain, separated from the other two in the end, but its defection was not so serious as it might have been, since according to the joint constitution the vote of two leagues in matters of foreign policy compelled the adherence of the third. But in order further to strengthen the hold of France, the French ambassadors had recourse to a sort of referendum in order to secure an approval of the majority of all the Swiss towns in favor of the French alliance, in addition to the official action of the three leagues. The success of this stroke was complete and the general diet of the three leagues gave its adherence to the treaty of Freiburg concluded by the bishop of Limoges and the marshal Vieilleville on December 7, 1564.[1] The poverty of France, however, seriously endangered the continuance of this alliance. When it was concluded, France tried to stave off payment of her debts, which amounted to more than 600,000 livres, yet demanded the execution of the articles of Freiburg. Glarus, Lucerne, Schwytz, Appenzell, Valais, the Grisons, Schaffhausen, and Basel bitterly complained, the last also because of the burdens laid upon the importations of her commerce into France through Lyons.

[1] "Traité et renouvellement d'alliance entre Charles IX, roi de France, et Messieurs les Ligues de Suisse, faite et conclué en la ville de Fribourg, le 7 jour de Déc., 1564" (Dumont, Corps dip., V, Pt. I, 129).

In this conflict which France carried on against Spain and the Holy See in Switzerland, Charles IX was supported by the German Protestants, who of course were hostile to both houses of Hapsburg, and France may be credited with considerable address in smoothing the ruffled feelings of Basel and Schaffhausen, and softening the Protestant prejudices of Zurich. This is simply another way of saying that the foreign policy of France in Switzerland was a Protestant policy. Even Bern yielded and joined the general treaty of alliance instead of insisting upon a particular treaty, as she had at first done.[1]

The Huguenots, however, suspicious of the impending reaction at home and misreading the diplomacy of France in Switzerland, grew more and more fearful and began to turn their eyes again toward the prince of Condé as a leader. But fortune and the craft of Catherine had lured the prince away from his own; he had become a broken reed, dangerous to lean upon. In July, 1564, Eleanor de Roye, the brave princess of Condé, died.[2] The Guises and the queen mother, who were now in co-operation,[3] at once began to practice to lure Condé away forever from his party, and the former at the same time, in order to make the alliance between France and Scotland more firm, conceived the idea of marrying the prince of Condé to Mary Queen of Scots.[4] As another possibility

---

[1] Abridged from Rott, "Les missions diplomatiques de Pomponne de Bellièvre en Suisse et aux Grisons (1560–74)," *Rev. d'histoire diplomatique*, XIV, 26–41 (1900); cf. *Papiers d'état du cardinal de Granvelle*, VIII, 630, 631; D'Aubigné, II, 210. M. Rott admirably observes (p. 42): "Ainsi donc, cinquante ans et plus avant Richelieu, la politique confessionnelle de la France s'inspirait déjà dans les rapports avec l'étranger, de principes fort différents de ceux qui dirigeaient son action à l'interieur du royaume."

[2] *Papiers d'état du cardinal de Granvelle*, VIII, 72. The prince of Condé had secured leave to leave the court in order to visit her at Vitry in May, where she then lay ill. Her mother was Madeleine de Mailly, sister of the admiral and granddaughter of Louise de Montmorency, sister of the old constable (*ibid.*, VII, 630, and note; cf. *C. S. P. For.*, 592, August 4, 1564).

[3] "All go and come by the cardinal of Lorraine, for without him nothing is done."—Smith to Cecil, November 13, 1564, *C. S. P. For.*, 793, §2.

[4] Granvella to Mary Stuart, November, 1564, *Papiers d'état du cardinal de Granvelle*, VIII, 570; cf. 550, 591, 599.

Randolph to the earl of Leicester: "The prince of Condé is become a suitor

the Guises cherished the hope of marrying their niece to Charles IX and thus recovering the ascendency they had enjoyed under Francis II.[1] The corollary of such a plan was the reduction of the Protestants of France. To these ideas Philip II, was stoutly opposed, though he concealed his opposition thereto; Mary was too valuable for his projects to be suffered to become a tool of the Guises. Their purposes were limited to France; his purposes embraced Christendom.[2]

In 1575 the Venetian ambassador wrote, à propos of one of the courtships of Queen Elizabeth: "Princes are wont to avail themselves of matrimonial negotiations in many ways."[3] These words sagely summarize the efforts of much of the diplomacy of the sixteenth century. By a singular combination of events and lineages, Mary Stuart was necessarily almost the cornerstone of the universal monarchy Philip II dreamed of forming in Europe; her possession of the Scottish crown, her claims to England, her

here, supported by the cardinal."—*C. S. P. Scotland*, IX, 67, November 7, 1564. Mary Stuart expressed her repugnance at such a prospect by saying: "Trewlye I am beholding to my uncle: so that yt be well with hym, he careth not what becommethe of me."—Randolph to Cecil, *C. S. P. Scot.*, II, 117, November 9, 1564. Another match, proposed simply for the purpose of leading Condé along, was between the young duke of Guise and the prince's daughter, Margaret, who was a little child.—*C. S. P. For.*, No. 642, §3; Smith to Cecil from Valence, September 1, 1564; No. 650, *ibid.*, September 3, 1564; No. 784, November 7, 1564. Smith to Cecil: "News is that the prince of Condé and the cardinal of Lorraine have intervisited each other." Cf. *Papiers d'état du cardinal de Granvelle*, VIII, 127. Bolwiller who disapproved of these plans in the interest of Philip II (*ibid.*, VIII, 381, note) evidently believed the prince won over to Catholicism (*ibid.*, VIII, 156). A propos of Condé's relapse he sarcastically wrote to Granvella on July 8, 1564: "Ce que l'on est en oppinion que L'Admiral ét D'Andelot se doibvent renger et hanger leur robbe, si le font, lors me semblera—il veoir une vraye farce, et pourront les femmes dire lors estre dadvantaige constante que les hommes, mesme madame de Vandosme et duchesse de Ferrare demeurans en l'oppinion où l'on les void."—*Ibid.*, VIII, 129.

[1] *Corresp. de Catherine de Médicis*, II, 106, note; *L'Ambassade de St. Sulpice*, 164; *C. S. P. Scot.*, II, 153, Randolph to Cecil, March 1–3, 1565. Mary Stuart in 1564 was twenty-two years of age, Charles IX barely fourteen (*Papiers d'état du card. de Granvelle*, VIII, 347, note).

[2] Cf. the luminous letter of Philip to Granvella, August 6, 1564, in *Papiers d'état du card. de Granvelle*, VIII, 215, 216.

[3] *C. S. P. Ven.*, November 6, 1575.

relationship with the Guises, united with the religion she professed, made the furtherance of her power the most practicable means to that end. Whether Mary's future husband were Don Carlos or the Austrian archduke was a matter of detail in Philip's plan—the end remained constant. Mary Stuart was of too much value to Philip II's political designs to risk such a marriage as the Guises contemplated.[1] Her hand might be disposed elsewhere with greater advantage.

Those intense religious convictions of the Spanish King which made him believe he was the divinely ordained instrument of the counter-Reformation, united with his political purposes and ambitions, required him to keep a watchful eye upon France.[2] The Netherlands, France, Italy, England, Scotland were like so many squares of a vast political chessboard upon which he aimed so to move the pieces he was in command of as ultimately to seize possession of those countries, and redeem them from heresy. Mary Stuart was an important personage in Philip's purposes. He wanted to put her on the throne of Elizabeth and thus unite

[1] Fortunately for Philip, a whim of passion helped the Spanish King's purposes, and Catherine and the Guises failing to carry the match between Mary Stuart and the prince were content to keep the prince alienated from his party. The prince of Condé had become enamored of one of the queen mother's maids-of-honor, Isabel Limeuil, while the court was a Roussillon, and had seduced her.

On this liaison see *Corresp. de Cath. de Méd.*, II, 189, note; Louis Paris, *Négociations*, Introd. XXVI, XXVII; *Nég. Tosc.*, III, 572, and especially La Ferrière, "Isabel de Limeuil," *Revue des deux mondes*, December 1, 1883, 636 and the duc d'Aumale, *Histoire des princes de Condé*, I, Appendix, xix. A suggestion of the manners prevailing at court is found in the following information: "Orders are taken in the court that no gentleman shall talk with the queen's maids, except it is in the queen's presence, or in that of Madame la Princesse de la Roche-sur-Yon, *except he be married;* and if they sit upon a form or stool, he may sit by her, and if she sits in the form, he may kneel by her, *but not lie long,* as the fashion was in this court."—*C. S. P. For.*, 1091, April 11, 1565.

[2] Unknown to Charles IX, the Spanish ambassador Chantonnay, whose recall Catherine had insisted upon for months past and who was finally replaced late in 1564 by Alava traversed the provinces of France in disguise, in the interest of his master, journeying through Auvergne, Rouergue, Toulouse, Agen and Bordeaux, before he reported at Madrid for new duty.

St. Sulpice to Catherine de Medici, June 12, 1564; *L'Ambassade de St. Sulpice,* 711, *Papiers d'état du cardinal de Granvelle*, VII, 592. For some correspondence between Philip II and Granvella, and Granvella and Antonio Perez regarding

Scotland and England under a common Catholic rule. For a time he dreamed of marrying her to his own son, Don Carlos, until Catherine interfered and offered her daughter Marguerite as a less dangerous alternative to France. The death of Don Carlos,[1] the eternal irresolution of the Spanish King, the development of new events, continually altered the details of Philip's purposes, but his essential aim never varied an iota.[2]

The subjugation of France, not in the exact terms of loss of sovereignty, perhaps, but no less in loss of true national independence was a necessary condition of Philip's purposes. The kingdom of France was situated in the very center of those dominions whose consolidation was to be the Spanish King's realization of universal rule. Spain bordered her on the south; the Netherlands on the north; in the east lay Franche Comté. Besides these territories which were directly Spanish, the Catholic cantons of Switzerland and Savoy were morally in vassalage to Spain. Beyond Franche Comté lay the Catholic Rhinelands,

Chantonnay's recall see Gachard, *Correspondance de Philippe II sur les Pays-Bas*, I, 251–53. Upon Chantonnay's successor, Alava, see *L'Ambassade de St. Sulpice*, 227, 228, 236; *Papiers d'état du cardinal de Granvelle*, VIII, 393; *Correspondance de Catherine de Médicis*, II, 359, 534; Poulet, I, 570, n. 1; Forneron, *Histoire de Philippe II*, II, 256.

On the secret service of Philip II, see Forneron, I, 218, 290, 334; II, 304, 305; *Papiers d'état du cardinal de Granvelle*, VII, 498, 499; VIII, 128, 182.

Alava exceeded his instructions in threatening France with war. Philip II, far from wishing war with France, repudiated his ambassador's statements (*R. Q. H.*, January 1879, p. 23).

[1] Upon one of the fits of madness of Don Carlos see letter of the Bishop of Limoges to Catherine de Medici in La Ferrière, *Rapport*, 48, 49. The Raumer Letters from Paris, Vol. I, chap. xv, contain an interesting account of Don Carlos, with long extracts from the sources. The editor rightly says that Ranke in his treatise on the affair of Don Carlos, as acute as it is circumstantial, has adopted the only right conclusion for the solution of this mysterious episode of history. See also *Wiener Jahrbücher*, XLVI; Forneron, *Hist. de Philippe II*, II, 103 ff.; Louis Paris, *Négociations*, etc., 888; *Papiers d'état du cardinal de Granvelle*, VIII, 317, note; *L'Ambassade de St. Sulpice*, 17, 29, 101, 597; Lea, in *Amer. Hist. Rev.*, January, 1905; *English Hist. Rev.*, XIV, 335.

[2] Cf. *Papiers d'état du card. de Granvelle*, VIII, 334 and note; cf. 215, 343, 344, 595, 596. Philip found a new prospective husband for Mary Stuart in the person of the archduke Charles. He had abandoned the idea of marrying Mary Stuart to his son even before the death of Don Carlos.

bound to the other branch of the house of Hapsburg. Beyond Switzerland and Savoy lay Italy, save Venice entirely, and Rome in part, a group of Spanish dominions.

Catherine de Medici combated Philip II both at Madrid and Vienna. But by the side of the negative purpose to thwart Philip's proposed alliances, Catherine de Medici had purposes of her own of the same sort. The daughter of a house made rich by banking and which never lived down the bourgeois tradition of its ancestry in spite of all its wealth and power, even though popes had come from its house, Catherine was fascinated by the thought of marrying Charles IX to the eldest daughter of the Hapsburgs, and her favorite son, the future Henry III, then known as the duke of Orleans-Anjou, to the Spanish princess Juana, sister of Philip, hoping to see some of Spain's numerous dominions pass to France as part of Juana's dowry.

In the pursuance of this double marriage project, the queen early began to beset Philip II for a personal interview, and urged her daughter to persuade the king to the same end, using Pius IV's cherished idea of a concert of the great Catholic powers to consider the condition and needs of Christendom with some adroitness as a screen to her own personal purposes.[1]

Much of her correspondence with St. Sulpice relates to an interview with Philip II for the purpose of arranging these matters, upon which she had set her heart, and the time of both the ambassador and the Spanish King was consumed with repeated interviews none of which was ever satisfactory, and all of which were tedious.[2] The natural reluctance of Philip II to commit himself to any positive course, united with the great aversion he felt toward the queen mother because of her wavering religious policy—for rigid adherence to Catholicism was Philip's one inflexible feature—led the King to follow a course of procrastination and duplicity for months, during which, however, he never evinced any outward sign of

[1] See R. Q. H., XXXIV, 461.

[2] Catherine turned to her own advantage an almost forgotten wish of Philip II that he might see her, expressed in July, 1560, when his anxiety was great because of her lenient policy toward the French Protestants (R. Q. H., XXXIV, 458).

impatience; his countenance remained as imperturbable as that of a Hindu idol, and never by any expression reflected his thought.[1]

Foolish pride and undue affection led Catherine even to use the Turk as a means of pressure upon Spain in order to accomplish this double marriage project. In the year 1562 an ambassador of the Sultan passed through France, having come by way of Venice to Lyons, and going thence via Dijon and Troyes to Paris.[2] Turkey, after crushing the revolt of Bajazet,[3] was seeking to avenge the accumulated grievances which she had suffered from Austria and Spain, especially the latter, for Philip II's expedition to Oran and his capture of its fortress, which was regarded as impregnable, had been a bitter blow to the Porte.[4] Exasperated by Spain, Turkey whose war policy was guided by the able grand vizier, Mohammed Sokolli, prepared a vast expedition to expel her from all points which she occupied in Africa. But such a campaign was not possible until Malta, lying midway in the straits of the Mediterranean, was overcome.[5] Europe, which still preserved an acute memory of the protracted siege of Rhodes, looked forward with dismay to the prospective attack upon Malta, so that Catherine de Medici's cordial reception at Dax of another Turkish ambassador—he was a Christian Pole in the employ of the Sultan—in the course of the tour of the provinces was a political act that was daring to rashness.[6] In order to force Philip II's hand Catherine even intimated that

---

[1] Challoner, English ambassador to Spain, to the queen: "Hardly shall a stranger by his countenance or words gather at any great alteration of mind, either to anger, or rejoicement, but after the fashion of a certain still flood;" quoted by Forneron, I, 319, n. 2, from Record Office MSS No. 466.

[2] See the extremely interesting account of the passing of the Turkish embassy through Provins, in Claude Haton, I, 342–44.

[3] On the conspiracy of Bajazet and his flight to Persia see D'Aubigné, Book III, chap. xxviii.

[4] *Négociations dans le Levant*, II, 729.

[5] *Ibid.*, 730.

[6] Spain suspected the Sultan was desirous of securing a French roadstead for his fleet during the siege of Malta. See *Commentaires et lettres de Montluc*, V, 38, note; D'Aubigné, 221, and n. 1; *Papiers d'état du cardinal de Granvelle*, VIII, 162; *L'Ambassade de St. Sulpice*, 398; *R. Q. H.*, XXXIV, 473–78.

Charles IX might marry Queen Elizabeth, although this proposition was too great a strain upon the credulity of Europe to be given any consideration.[1] Soon after St. Sulpice reached Spain, we find Toulouse suggested as the place for the desired interview,[2] and thereafter for thirty-eight months this conference was one of the dominant thoughts in Catherine's mind.[3]

The queen mother's original plan had been to avoid the heat of the south by passing the winter at Moulins, and visiting Languedoc and Guyenne in the next spring.[4] But the influence of impending change impelled her forward in the maze of tournaments, balls, and masques.[5] Although she was in "a country full of mountains and brigands,"[6] so that she feared "que cette canaille sacageassent quelques uns de sa cour," and strengthened Strozzi's band as a precaution, nevertheless Catherine's resolution seems to have increased in degree as she moved southward. Probably the fact that the prince of Condé was in the toils encouraged her; certainly the necessity of exhibiting something positive that would please Spain, in view of the approaching interview, actuated her. But apart from her own motives, outside pressure had been brought to bear upon her to this end, when at Bar-le-Duc, where the King went to attend the baptism of the infant child of Charles III, duke of Lorraine, who had married Charles IX's sister, Claudine, in

[1] *Corresp. de Cath. de Méd.*, II, Introd., lxxxvi, lxxxvii; *R. Q. H.*, XXXIV, 470.

[2] *L'Ambassade de St. Sulpice*, 14, Letter of March 27, 1562.

[3] Perez writes to Granvella on November 15, 1563: "La reine mère de France tourmente sa majesté catholique pour la déterminer à une entrevue."—*Papiers d'état du card. de Granvelle*, VII, 256; and two weeks later (December 4, 1563) we find Philip II writing to Alva, saying that "L'ambassadeur de St. Sulpice lui a proposé une entrevue avec la reine de France," and desiring the duke's opinion in the matter (Gachard, *Correspondance de Philippe II sur les Pays-Bas*, I, 277). The actual text is in Philip's correspondence, No. XXVI.

[4] *L'Ambassade de St. Sulpice*, 226.

[5] "Ne se passoit jour sans nouvelle sorte de combatz, passe-temps et plaizirs. . . . . L'on dréçoit joustes, tournoy, commédies et tragoedies."—Fourquevaux to St. Sulpice, *L'Ambassade de St. Sulpice*, 266; cf. *Papiers d'état du cardinal de Granvelle*, VIII, 466. For an account of one of these entertainments, see Castelnau, Book V, chap. vi.

[6] "Le pays est tel que vous avez entendu, pleins de montagnes et bandoliers."—Catherine to St. Sulpice, January 9, 1564, *L'Ambassade de St. Sulpice*, 331.

March.[1] Later "when the court came to Lyons information was brought to it that if the King and his advisers should continue to resist the general rising against the Huguenots, it would be turned against itself."[2] In this instance, however, the pressure came, not from Spain, but from Pope Pius IV whose agent, the Florentine Ludovico Antinori, was sent to France to urge the extirpation of Calvinism and to plead the cause of the findings of the Council of Trent.[3] Catherine obeyed the signs. But as a sudden rupture of the peace of Amboise would have been attended with dangerous consequences she proceeded cautiously.[4]

The first[5] definite intimation of the reaction was an edict issued on July 24, prohibiting Calvinist worship within ten leagues of the court, notwithstanding the fact that authorized places of Protestant worship were affected by it. A fortnight later, on August 4, came a more sweeping edict—the so-called Edict of Roussillon[6] which forbade all persons of whatever religion, quality, or condition to molest one another, or to violate or maltreat images,

---

[1] Charles III had been educated in France and was a French pensioner to the amount of 250,000 francs annually (*Rel. vén.*, I, 451). On this Spanish pressure to revoke the Edict of Amboise see *Papiers d'état du cardinal de Granvelle*, VII, 461, 468; Poulet, I, 576, note; Castelnau, Book V, chap. ix; *R. Q. H.*, XXXIV, 462, 463. The Huguenots quickly divined it (Languet, *Epist. secr.*, II, 268, November 18, 1563; *Arch. d'Orange-Nassau*, I, 136).

The anxiety of the French Protestants over the King's visit of Lorraine is well expressed in the letter of Lazarus Schwendi to the Prince of Orange. August 22, 1564, in *Arch. d'Orange-Nassau*, I, 191.

[2] Ranke, *Civil Wars and Monarchy in France*, 226.

[3] Davila, *Guerre civile di Francia*, III, 144. On September 27, 1564, the prévôt Morillon wrote to the cardinal Granvella: "L'édit de France contre les apostatz me faict espérer que la royne mère passera plus avant, puisque la saison est à propos; et si elle ne le faict, je crains qu'elle et les siens le paieront."—*Papiers d'état du card. de Granvelle*, VIII, 361.

[4] Castelnau Book V, chap. x. Granvella expressed impatience at Catherine's slowness in repressing the Huguenots. See his letters to vice-chancellor Seld and Philip II at this time in *Papiers d'état du cardinal de Granvelle*, VIII, 598, 599, 632, 633.

[5] Unless the order forbidding Renée of Ferrara to hold Protestant service even in private while at the court, be taken as the first; see *R. Q. H.*, XXXIV, 467.

[6] Near Lyons, where on account of the plague the court was stopping July 17 to August 15; it belonged to the cardinal Tournon, who held it in apanage.

or to lay hands upon any sacred objects upon pain of death; magistrates were likewise enjoined to prevent the Huguenots from performing their devotions in any suspected places, but to confine them to such places as had been specified; finally, the Huguenots were forbidden to hold any synods or other assemblies except in the presence of certain of the King's officers, who were appointed to be present at them.[1] The pretext of both of these edicts was the trespass upon the terms of Amboise by the Protestants, and fear of a Protestant conspiracy. But in reality the action of the government constituted a partial yielding to that Catholic pressure which already had made itself manifest at Nancy.

The Edict of Roussillon completely ignored a petition of the Huguenots presented to the King while at Roussillon, which shows the pernicious activity of the local Catholic leagues already. The complaint specified that infractions of the Edict of Amboise had been committed by the Catholics, especially in Burgundy; that Catholic associations everywhere were being formed against them; that the priests openly lauded the King of Spain from their pulpits; that their synods were broken up by the enemies of their religion.[2]

After a sojourn of a month at Roussillon, the pilgrimage of the court was again resumed. At Valence (August 22) Catherine received word that Elizabeth of Spain had given birth to still-born twin babes. On September 24 Avignon was reached, where a stay of two weeks was made during which Catherine consulted the famous astrologer Nostradamus. Hyères and Aix were stages on the road to Marseilles[3] (November 3–10), whence

---

[1] Isambert, XIV, 166; Castelnau, Book V, chap. x; La Popelinière, II, Book XI, 5, 6; Chéruel, *Histoire de l'administration monarchique de la France*, I, 196.

[2] D'Aubigné, II, 211. On the last complaint see *Correspondance de Catherine de Médicis*, II, 195, 203, and notes. These Catholic associations generally at this time went by the name of "Confréries du St. Esprit," as D'Aubigné's allusion shows.

[3] For an episode showing at once the manners of some in the court, and the Catholic intensity of the people of Marseilles, see *Papiers d'état du cardinal de Granvelle*, VIII, 475.

it led to Nîmes[1] (December 12), and Montpellier[2] (December 17), and thence to Agde and Beziers,[3] where progress for some time was blocked by heavy snow-falls. The snows irritated Catherine and to placate her impatience she was shown historical evidence that both Blanche of Castile and the queen of Charles VII had once been snowed-in in these parts for three months.[4] 'Unlike his mother, Charles IX enjoyed it, building a snow fort in which he and his pages withstood a siege by some of the gentlemen of the household.[5]

During this enforced sojourn Catherine de Medici received word of the famous conflict between the marshal Montmorency, who had been made governor of Paris,[6] when the court started *en tour*, and the cardinal of Lorraine. On January 8, 1565, the cardinal of Lorraine sought to enter Paris with a great rout of armed retainers. The marshal demanded the disarming of the company, in compliance with a royal *ordonnance* of 1564 forbidding the carrying of arquebuses, pistols, or other firearms,[7] not knowing that the cardinal had a warrant from the queen mother

[1] Lamathe, "Délibération des consuls de Nismes au sujet de l'entrée de Charles IX dans ladite ville (1564)," *Rev. des Soc. savant des départ.*, 5ᵉ série, III (1872), 781.

[2] While here, Catherine dispatched the marshal Bourdillon into Guyenne for the purpose of dissolving the league formed at Cadillac on March 13, 1563 (D'Aubigné, II, 213). As we shall see, the mission was fruitless.

[3] *Correspondance de Catherine de Médicis*, II, Introd., lviii. The editor adds: "De toutes les villes du Midi, c'était [Beziers] celle qui comptait le plus de Protestants." On account of the alarm evinced by the Huguenots of the south—300 gentlemen of Beziers visited the King in a body—Charles IX, when at Marseilles on November 4, "confirmed" the Edict of Amboise. Yet so apprehensive was the court that whenever it stopped an effort was made to disarm the local populace (*C. S. P. For.*, No. 788 [1564]).

[4] On the incident of Catherine reading a MS chronicle about Blanche of Castile, see the extract of the Venetian ambassador in Baschet (*La diplomatie vénetienne*, 521, 522).

[5] *Correspondance de Catherine de Médicis*, II, Introd., lix.

[6] Claude Haton, I, 378.

[7] The order of the King of December 13, 1564, prohibiting any nobles whoever they might be, unless princes of the house of France, from entering the government of the Ile-de-France is still unpublished. It is preserved in a report of the Spanish ambassador, Arch. nat., K. 1,505, No. 31. It is to be distinguished from the

authorizing his men to wear arms if so desired. The cardinal haughtily refused to obey, and a fight took place in the street near the corner of St. Innocents, in which one man was killed.[1]

The reactionary policy of the government stimulated the local Catholic leagues in Languedoc during this winter of 1564–65.[2] The religious prejudice which these associations manifested was influenced by the bitter jealousy existing between the Guises and the Montmorencys. From the hour of the clash between the cardinal and the marshal, the Guises plotted to compass the ruin of the house of Montmorency, and sought to find support in the Catholic leagues of the southern provinces. The tolerant policy of the

---

general *ordonnance* of the year before—"Lettres du roy contenans defenses à toutes personnes de ne porter harquebuzes, pistoles, ni pistolets, ni autres bastons à feu, sur peine de confiscation de leurs armes et chevaulx," Paris, 1564. Cf. Isambert, XIV, 142.

[1] All the historians notice this episode. See D'Aubigné, Book IV, chap. v; *Corresp. de Catherine de Médicis*, II, Introd., lix, lx, and 253–56 where the letters of the marshal and the queen mother on the subject are given. The editor, in a long note, sifts the evidence. Other accounts are in Claude Haton, I, 381–83 (other references in note); *C.S.P.For.*, No. 942, January 24, 1564; *Mém. du duc de Nevers*, V, 12, 13; Castelnau, Book VI, chap. ii.

In *Papiers d'état du cardinal de Granvelle*, VIII, 600–2, is an account from the pen of Don Louis del Rio, an attaché of the Spanish embassy at Paris; and on pp. 655, 656 is the "Harangue de l'admiral de France à MM. de la court du parlement de Paris du 27 janvier 1565 avec la réponse." The baron de Ruble has written the history of this incident in *Mém. de la Soc. de l'hist. de Paris de l'Ile-de-France*, Vol. VI.

According to a letter of Mary Stuart to Queen Elizabeth, February 12, 1565, the resentment due to the old lawsuit over Dammartin flashed out at this time. But it must have been a conjecture on her part, for she adds: "I have heard no word of the duke of Guise or monsieur d'Aumale."—*C. S. P. Scot.*, II, 146. The prince of Condé's Catholic leanings at this critical moment are manifested in a letter to his sister, the abbess of Chelles, in which he states that he is annoyed at the outrage committed on the cardinal of Lorraine by the marshal Montmorency; that the union of these two houses is more than necessary; that if he had been with the cardinal, he would have given proof of his good-will by deeds. See Appendix VII.

[2] "Les confraires du Sainct-Esprit et autres reprenoient plus de viguer, et les provinces ne pouvoient plus souffrir les ministres ny les presches publics et parti-culièrs, et se sé paroient entièrement des huguenots; qui estoient argumens certains qu'en peu de temps il se verroit quelque grand changement."—Castelnau, Book VI, chap. ii.

marshal Montmorency and his brother Damville was seized upon by the Guises to make them odious.[1] The secular clergy and still more the Jesuits and Capuchins were very active in this work, going from town to town and village to village, urging Catholics vigorously to defend their faith, and their fiery preaching materially advanced the tendency to union among the provincial leagues.[2]

Under the effective leadership of the sieur de Candalle, the league of Agen had had an astonishing spread over Guyenne, exhibiting a strength of organization and an audacity which foreshadows that of the Holy League of 1576, in whose genesis, indeed, it represents an evolutionary stage. What made the league of Guyenne so peculiarly formidable, however, was not so much its perfection of organization and its wide expansion, as the fact that it was organized and had existence without the knowledge or consent of the crown, and in transgression of the royal authority, which forbade such associations. This highly developed stage of existence was arrived at by the league of Agen in August, 1564, from which date it may properly be called the league of Guyenne.[3]

Naturally the Guises approached Montluc with their plan. While the court was sojourning at Mont-de-Marsan (March 9–24, 1565), waiting the arrival of the Spanish queen and the duke of Alva at Bayonne, an intimation was given to Montluc that a league was in process of formation in France "wherein were several great persons, princes and others," and an agent of the Guises at this

---

[1] Ardent Catholics, like Cardinal Granvella, believed both the marshal Montmorency and Damville to be Protestants at heart (*Papiers d'état du cardinal de Granvelle*, VIII, 278).

[2] "Des catholiques formèrent des 'unions' pour défendre l'honneur de Dieu et de la Sainte Eglise, et ces unions, en se rapprochant constituènent la Ligue."— Beulier, "Pourquoi la France este-elle restée catholique au XVIe siècle," *Revue anglo-romaine*, January 11, 1896, 257. The Jesuits worked hard in France for Philip II. Forneron, II, 304, quotes an interesting letter to this effect from a Jesuit working in France.

[3] The procès-verbal of this league is in *Mémoires de Condé*, ed. London, VI, 290–306. For the court's sojourn at Agen see Barrère (l'abbé), "Entrée et séjour de Charles IX à Agen (1565)," *Bull. du Com. de la langue, de l'hist. et des arts de la France* I (1854), 472.

For the King's sojourn at Condom (1565) see Barrère (l'abbé), *ibid.*, 476.

time endeavored to persuade Montluc to join the association.[1] But Montluc was cautious; he had no great affection for the Guises and, moreover, leagues and such associations were against the law, which he, as a crown officer, was pledged to support. Grammont who was opposed to Montluc had already complained of his conduct to the queen mother.[2] Besides, there were private reasons, whose nature will be soon developed, which made him hesitate. Montluc carried his information to Catherine de Medici, who, not yet perceiving that the ambition of the Guises was the chief motive, was not at once seriously alarmed, since the anti-Protestant policy of the government made it indifferent now to such associations. Accordingly, when the court reached Bordeaux (it arrived there on April 9) and the Huguenots renewed their complaints against Candalle and his associates, the King ignored the petition, recognizing that many of the nobles were members of the league of Guyenne. Instead, he gave the league a quasi-legal status by proclaiming that the crown would not listen to any more complaints against Candalle and his associates.[3]

But the queen mother was genuinely alarmed a few weeks later when the real purpose and scope of the proposed league were revealed to her through an intercepted letter which the duke of Aumale had written on February 27, 1565, to the marquis d'Elbœuf. The duke of Montpensier, the vicomte de Martigues, Chavigny, who was a Guise protégé, D'Angennes, and the bishop of Mans, were named in this letter as the chiefs of an association, which had for its avowed end the abasement of the house of Montmorency.[4]

[1] *Commentaires et lettres de Montluc*, III, 80, 81; De Thou, V, Book XXXVII, 32; Anquetil, I, 213.

[2] Collection Godefroy, CCLVII, No. 7, July 18, 1564.

[3] De Thou, IV, Book XXXVII, 32.

[4] A printed copy of this important dispatch, entitled "Coppie d'une lettre du sieur d'Aumale au sieur marquis d'Elbœuf son frère, sur l'association qu'ils delibèrent faire contre la maison de Montmorency" (February 27, 1565), is to be found in the Bib. Nat., L *b*. 33: 172. It evidently was circulated as a political pamphlet by the Huguenots. But where is the original? Portions of it are as follows: "Mon frere . . . . j'ay receu de vostre homme la lettre que m'avez escripte. . . . . J'en ay par plusieurs fois cy devant escript à Messieurs de Montpensier, d'Estampes, Cehavigny: par où ils auroyent bien

Catherine, apprehending the consequences certain to result from such an extension of the feud of the two houses, implored the King, at a large meeting of the council held on May 18, 1565, to divulge what had been ascertained—that a secret association had been discovered in defiance of the law, having political aims detrimental to the monarchy, and a system of government for the levying of men and money without the King's authority. The counselors, with one accord, denied their knowledge or implication, and protested their devotion to the cause and the law. Catherine was thoroughly alarmed, and appealed to Montluc for advice. What followed may be told in his own words:

I heard then some whisper of a league that was forming in France, wherein were several very great persons, both Princes and others, whom nevertheless I have nothing to do to name, being engaged by promise to the contrary. I cannot certainly say to what end this League was contrived; but a certain gentleman named them to me every one, endeavoring at the same time to persuade me to make one in the Association, assuring me it was to a good end; but he perceived by my countenance that it was not a dish for my palate. I presently gave the Queen private intimation of it; for I could not endure such kind of doings, who seemed to be very much astonished at it, telling me it was the first syllable she had ever heard of any such thing; and commanding me to enquire further into the business, which I did, but could get nothing more out of my gentleman; for he now lay upon his guard.

Her Majesty then was pleased to ask my advice, how she should behave herself in this business, whereupon I gave her counsel to order it so that the

peu juger la volonté que j'ay tousjours lue de nous venger, et combien je desirerois l'association que vous dites (*verso*) prevoyant assez combien elle estoit necessaire non seulement pour nous, mais aussi pour tous les gens de bien à qui l'on en veult plus que jamais.

"Et pour ceste cause, mon frere, je trouverois merveilleusement bon que les dicts Sieurs y voulsissent entendre, laissant les villes, d'autant qu'il n'y a nulle asseurance en peuple, comme je l'ay dernièrement encore cogneut. Mais avec la Noblesse, de ma part je suis tout resolu et prest, et n'y veux espargner aucune chose, et le plustost sera le meilleur. Qui me fait vous prier, de regarder et en bien adviser tous parensemble, et mesmes avec le seigneur de Montpensier, et de m'en mander ce que vous aurez deliberé, à fin que par là je resolue avec les Seigneurs et Noblesse qui sont de deça et mes Gouverneurs, qui feront tout ce que je vouldray.

"Au demeurant, vous avez bien entendu le nombre de Chevaliers de l'Ordre qui ont esté faicts, qui sont bien pres de trente ou plus, dont monsieur de Brion en est des premiers. Aussi des preparatifs que lon fuit à la Court pour aller à Bayonne recevoir festoyer la Roine d'Espaigne."

King himself should say in public that he had heard of a League that was forming in his Kingdom, which no one could do without giving him some jealousy and offence; and that therefore he must require everyone without exception to break off this League, and that he would make an Association in his Kingdom, of which he himself would be the Head; for so for some time it was called, though they afterwards changed the name, and called it the Confederation of the King. The Queen at the time that I gave her this advice did by no means approve of it, objecting, that should the King make one, it was to be feared that others would make another; but I made answer and said that the King must engage in his own all such as were in any capacity of doing the contrary, which, however, was a thing that could not be concealed, and might well enough be provided against. Two days after, her Majesty being at supper, called me to her and told me that she had considered better of the affair I had spoke to her about, and found my counsel to be very good, and that the next day, without further delay, she would make the King propound the business to his Council; which she accordingly did, and sent to enquire for me at my lodging, but I was not within. In the evening she asked me why I did not come to her, and commanded me not to fail to come the next day, because there were several great difficulties in the Council, of which they had not been able to determine. I came according to her command, and there were several disputes. Monsieur de Nemours made a very elegant speech, remonstrating "That it would be very convenient to make a League and Association for the good of the King and his Kingdom, to the end, that if affairs should so require, every one with the one and the same will might repair to his Majesty's person, to stake their lives and fortunes for his service, and also in case any one of what religion soever, should offer to invade or assault them, or raise any commotion in the state, that they might with one accord unite, and expose their lives in their common defence." The Duke of Montpensier was of the same opinion, and several others saying that they could not choose but so much the more secure the peace of the Kingdom, when it should be known that all the Nobility were thus united for the defence of the Crown.

The Queen then did me the honor to command me to speak; whereupon I began, and said, "That the League proposed could be no ways prejudicial to the King, being that it tended to a good end for his Majesty's service, the good of his Kingdom, and the peace and security of his People; but that one which should be formed in private could produce nothing but disorder and mischief; for the good could not answer for the evil disposed; and should the cards once be shuffled betwixt League and League, it would be a hard matter to make of it a good game; that being the most infallible way to open a door to let strangers into the kingdom, and to expose all things to spoil and ruin; but that all of us in general, both Princes and others, ought to make an

Association, which should bear the title of the League, or the Confederation of the King, and to take a great and solemn oath, not to decline or swerve from it upon penalty of being declared such as the oath should import; and that his Majesty having so concluded, ought to dispatch messengers to all parts of the kingdom, with commission to take the oaths of such as were not there present, by which means it would be known, who were willing to live and die in the service of the king and state.   And should anyone be so foolish or impudent as to offer to take arms, let us all swear to fall upon them; I warrant your Majesty I will take such order in these parts, that nothing shall stir to the prejudice of your royal authority.   And in like manner let us engage by the faith we owe to God, that if any Counter-League shall disclose itself, we will give your Majesty immediate notice of it; and let your Majesty's be sub-scribed by all the great men of your kingdom.   The feast will not be right without them, and they also are easy to be persuaded to it, and the fittest to provide against any inconvenience that may happen."

This was my proposition, upon which several disputes ensued; but in the end the King's Association was concluded on, and it was agreed, that all the Princes, great Lords, Governors of Provinces, and Captains of Gens d'armes should renounce all Leagues and Confederacies whatsoever, as well without as within the Kingdom, excepting that of the King, and should take the oath upon pain of being declared rebels to the crown; to which there were also other obligations added, which I do not remember. . . . . In the end all was past and concluded, and the Princes began to take the oath, and to sign the articles.[1]

The weakness of the crown's position in these circumstances is evident.   Recognizing its inability to crush these local associations and fearing lest control of them would pass over wholly to the

---

[1] *Commentaires et lettres de Montluc*, III, 80–86.   I have used the seventeenth-century translation of Cotton, 274, 275, which preserves something of the spirit of the original.   De Thou, never having seen the document in question, expresses his doubt of Montluc's veracity in the matter, and argues the improbability of the King's having followed Montluc's advice on the ground that the crown had con-demned all secret associations as destructive of domestic tranquillity.   "Why should the King make a league with his subjects?" asks De Thou.   "Far from deriving any advantage from it, would it not diminish his authority?   Would the King not incite his subjects to do exactly what he wanted to avoid, and by his own example accustom them to town factions; to foment and support parties in the kingdom?"—De Thou, IV, Book XXXVII, 33.   Unfortunately for the truth of De Thou's hypothesis, the facts are the other way, for there is documentary proof that Charles IX followed out Montluc's suggestion, and sent the declaration to all his officers requesting their adherence to it.   The baron de Ruble discovered the proof in F. Fr. 20,461, fol. 58.   See his edition of Montluc, III, 86, note; cf. D'Aubigné, II, 218, and n. 6.

Guises, the crown tried to save its power and its dignity by fusing them into a single confederation under the King and forbidding the formation of future associations without royal consent. But the power of the crown was not commensurate with its show of authority. The leagues continued to multiply and to remain independent of the crown's coercion. In the year 1565 the situation is different in degree but not in kind from that which existed in 1576 when the Holy League was formed.

Even the Spanish affiliations of the Holy League existed potentially at this time through the treason of Montluc.[1] For the wily Gascon, whose character was a combination of daring determination, religious bigotry and envy, in recommending the measures he did was really taking steps to cover up his own tracks. Montluc, despite his professions of allegiance, was angry at the queen mother, and quite ready to knife her in the dark. His heart was filled with rebellious envy of Vieilleville, because the latter had been given a marshal's bâton. Disappointed in this expectation he asked for the post of colonel-general which D'Andelot filled.[2] Instead Montluc had to be satisfied with the office of governor of Guyenne, which he regarded as ill compensation of his services.[3] In consequence of these grievances, even before the recovery of Havre, Montluc had entered into correspondence with Philip II, to whom he represented the necessity of Spanish intervention in France, on account of the double danger by which France was threatened through the purposes of the Protestants and Catherine de Medici's toleration of them. The Spanish King at first hesitated, but soon availed himself of the opportunity thus afforded, for two strings were better

[1] The credit of having made this important discovery is due to the baron de Ruble, *Commentaires et lettres de Montluc*, IV, 317–26, 329, 330, 346, 347, 362, 363. But it was Forneron who showed the world the magnitude of Montluc's treason (*Hist. de Philippe II*, I, 293–330). Suspicion of Montluc's course, however, prevailed in his own day. He was charged with having agreed to deliver over the province of Guyenne to Philip II in 1570 and issued a cartel against his adversaries denying that he had any intelligence with Spain. See Appendix VIII.

[2] D'Andelot's appointment to this post created intense feeling among the Catholic officers. Strozzi, Brissac, and Charry openly refused to obey him (D'Aubigné, II, 207; Brantôme, V, 341).

[3] Forneron, I, 294, n. 3.

than one to his bow. Profound secrecy covered the negotiations.
Philip's love of mystery and the delicacy of the matter led him to
conceal the plan even from his ambassador in France, and operate
through Bardaxi, a cousin of a Spanish captain of that name, who
had been pursued by the Inquisition and had fled to France, where
he sought service under Montluc in recompense of which he finally
was rehabilitated.[1] Montluc proposed the formation of a league
between the Pope, the Emperor, the Spanish King, and the leading
Catholic princes of Germany and Italy to avert a union of the
Huguenots with outside Protestant princes for the overthrow of
the Catholic religion in France.[2] He enlarged upon the moral
"benefit" of such a league to France, now ridden by the Huguenots
to the imminent ruin of the monarchy, and pointed out to Philip II
the peculiar interest he had in crushing Calvinism.[3] The plan
was for Philip II to kidnap Jeanne d'Albret who was to be given
over to the Inquisition, and to seize possession of Béarn, and thus
accomplish two purposes at once—destroy the hearth of Calvinism
in France, and establish Spanish power north of the Pyrenees.[4]
Fortunately for France, the French ambassador at Madrid, St.
Sulpice, was informed of the plan, though he did not know of Montluc's treason, by a servant of the Spanish queen, and Catherine
de Medici's energetic steps in the protection of Béarn nipped the
scheme in the bud.[5]

This joint plan of Montluc and Philip II for the seizure of Béarn

[1] Montluc, ed. De Ruble, IV, Introd., ix.

[2] It will be observed that Montluc independently had come to the same conclusion as Granvella.

[3] Montluc, ed. De Ruble, IV, 317–26, February 8, 1564.

[4] Forneron, I, 330. D'Aubigné, II, 294, wrongly ascribes this plot to the
Jesuits. The traditional Protestant account, attributed to Calignon, chancellor of
Navarre, is printed in *Mém. du duc de Nevers*, II, 579; also in *Mém. de Villeroy*.
The account in *Arch. cur.*, VI, 281, is much colored. Catholic historians have
denied the existence of such a plot, e. g., the abbé Garnier in *Mém. de l'Acad.
des inscrip.* (1787), Vol. L, 722. But since the publication of Montluc's *Correspondance* there is no doubt of it.

[5] Forneron, I, 303–6. Cabie, *L'Ambassade de St. Sulpice*, 483, gives the text
of the ambassador's letter to Catherine, and his note of thanks to the queen's
embroiderer who divulged the plot.

and the capture of its queen telescoped with another plot against her to which Philip and Pope Pius IV were parties. On September 28, 1563, a papal bull excommunicated the queen for heresy, and she was cited before the Holy Office for trial.[1] To Catherine's credit she at once took a firm stand in favor of the queen of Navarre.[2]

It was not in the nature of Philip II to be daring in daylight. Precaution was second nature to him. Lansac's mission to Madrid to protest against the action of Pius IV coincided with Montluc's overtures to the Spanish King. The discovery of part of the plan made Philip timid about pushing it at all until a more favorable time at least. Accordingly he gave Montluc little encouragement, save offering him an asylum in Spain if events should compel him to quit France on account of his treasonable correspondence,[3] while to Lansac he said that "what the Pope had done against 'Madame de Vendôme' was very inopportune and would be remedied."[4] In a word, Philip II dissembled his participation in the Pope's conduct, asserting that the procedure had been taken without his knowledge, and that while he deplored the queen of Navarre's apostasy he could not be unmindful of the fact that she was kith and kin of the queen of Spain, his wife![5]

There probably was a certain amount of spite work in Philip's repudiation of the Pope at this time. One of the important political issues raised at the Council of Trent was the question of precedence between the ambassadors of France and Spain. Lansac, Charles IX's ambassador to the Council, claimed the honor of

[1] D'Aubigné, II, 204, 205; *Mém. de Condé*, IV, 669. Charles IX's letter of November 30, 1563, to St. Sulpice gives some details of the process (*L'Ambassade de St. Sulpice*, 186, 187).

[2] *Correspondance de Catherine de Médicis*, II, 119, 120. Her letter to her daughter in Spain, not in the correspondence, which M. Cabie cites in *L'Ambassade de St. Sulpice*, 208, displays real courage. Charles IX said he could not abandon Jeanne d'Albret "sans être vu déserter de ses plus proches parents" (*ibid.*, 247). The instructions to Lansac, who was sent to Spain to protest in the name of France against the papal action, show fine scorn (*ibid.*, 224).

[3] *Commentaires et lettres de Montluc*, IV, 327, note.

[4] *L'Ambassade de St. Sulpice*, 228: "Réponse de Philippe II au sr. de Lansac en sa première audience, 18 fev. 1565."

[5] *Ibid.*, 247.

going before the count of Lara, Spain's representative, at which Philip was "picqué oultre mesure."[1] The papal party in vain implored Lansac to yield. Lansac replied that "la France ne pouvait renoncer aux droits qui lui avaient été reconnus dans tous les précédents conciles, et que, plutôt que de laisser rien innover sur ce point, ' j'étais résolu, selon le commandement de mon maître, après avoir protesté de nullité de ce concile, de m'en aller incontinent avec tous les prélats de ntre nation, sans entrer dans aucune dispute ne composition.' "[2]   Philip II refrained from making any observation to France upon the disputed point[3] pending the decision of the Pope.[4]   But such a course was impossible.   The contest over the question became the absorbing topic of conversation at Rome.[5]   The Pope was between Scylla and Charybdis.[6]   Spain claimed precedence for Philip II through the crown of Castile— "chose peu véritable"—and argued that the services of Philip II to the church justified her pretension; to which France rejoined that her king was historically first son of the church, the Most Christian King, who "had bled and suffered for the preservation of the Catholic religion in his kingdom, for which he had combated to the hazarding of his entire state."[7]   Finally being compelled to decide, Pius IV made a choice in favor of France, to the immense chagrin of Philip II who actually fell sick of the humiliation and recalled his ambassador Vargas from Rome as a sign of his displeasure.[8]

[1] *L'Ambassade de St. Sulpice*, 5.

[2] Letter to St. Sulpice, February 10, 1563, *ibid.*, 115.

[3] *Ibid.*, 135.

[4] Pius IV was so perplexed that he tried to avoid pronouncing in the matter. "On avait décidé, à la dernière fête de St. Pierre, de supprimer cette cérémonie, afin de n'offenser personne."—Charles IX to St. Sulpice, July 24, 1563, *ibid.*, 141.

[5] Du Ferrier, French ambassador at Venice to St. Sulpice, April 12, 1564, *ibid.*, 252.

[6] Cf. the report of the conversation between Archbishop Cispontin, the papal secretary, and D'Oysel (*ibid.*, 273, July, 1564).

[7] "Instructions données par Charles IX à L'Aubespine le jeune, envoyé en Espagne," *ibid.*, 277, June 24, 1564.

[8] *Ibid.*, 279, 281, 282, 299. "It is an error to regard, as most historians do, the course of the relations of Philip II to the see of Rome as a single consistent development, for the earlier part of his reign was dominated by

The catalogue of Spain's grievances against France, besides the question of religion, the dispute over precedence, and France's refusal to accept the findings of Trent which Philip II had recognized[1] included still another complaint. This was the border difficulty between the Spanish provinces of Artois and Luxembourg, and France. It was a complex question, partly religious, partly political, partly commercial. Like the Huguenot rebellion, the growing insurrection in the Low Countries was of a double nature —religious and political. Each side looked to the other for sympathy and support and neither was disappointed. The Huguenots retaliated for the assistance afforded the government of France by Spain during the first civil war by aiding the revolt of the Netherlands. This intimate connection of events on each side of the line is an important fact to be observed.

It was in 1563, as Granvella had divined,[2] that the intrigues of a principle utterly different from that which inspired the latter. In the sixties and early seventies the Spanish king devoted himself primarily to the maintenance of the principles of the counter-Reformation; he abandoned political advantage in the interest of the faith, united with the ancient foes of his house for the suppression of heresy, dedicated himself and his people to the cause of Catholicism. . . . . But in the later seventies there came a change. The spirit of the counter-Reformation was waning in France: the old political lines of cleavage had begun to reappear; Philip began to discover that he was draining his land to the dregs in the interests of a foreign power who offered him no reciprocal advantages, and reluctantly exchanged his earlier attitude of abject devotion to the interests of the church for the more patriotic one of solicitude for the welfare of Spain. . . . . Viewed from the Spanish standpoint, the story of this long development is a tragic but familiar one—reckless national sacrifice for the sake of an antiquated ideal, exhaustion in the interests of a foreign power, which uses and casts aside but never reciprocates. But it adds one more to the already long list of favorable revisions of the older and more hostile verdicts on the Spanish monarch. Philip's attitude toward the papacy, though not always wise or statesmanlike, was at least far more honorable and loyal to the church than it is usually represented (as, for instance, by Philippson): the first part of his reign is marked by his single-hearted devotion to the cause of Rome, and even at the last that devotion does not falter, though the interests of his conntry forced him in to adopt a more national policy toward the papacy than that with which he had begun."—R. B. Merriman, Review of Herre, *Papsttum und Papstwahl im Zeitalter Philipps II* (Leipzig, 1907), in *American Historical Review*, October, 1908, pp. 117, 118.

[1] *Papiers d'état du cardinal de Granvelle*, VIII, 177, July 30, 1564; R. Q. H., 1869, p. 403.

[2] *Papiers d'état du cardinal de Granvelle*, VII, 669.

the French Protestants in Flanders became a matter of serious apprehension. Valenciennes was the most aggressive city of the religion in Flanders, and Margaret of Parma actually was afraid of Montigny doing as Maligny had done at Havre. Already the prince of Orange was the recognized leader of those who sympathized with the Huguenots. To this class England's support of the prince of Condé, and above all, the assassination of the duke of Guise, came as a real stimulus. Valenciennes, Tournay, Antwerp, even Brussels were stirred. In May, 1563, the demonstrations of the Calvinists at Valenciennes and Tournay became so bold that it required six companies of infantry to keep them overawed. But this measure, instead of accomplishing the result expected, aggravated the situation, for the marquis de Berghes, the commander, was so ostracized by the nobles, that he lost courage. Philip II grew alarmed and wrote to his sister on June 13, 1563, that the example of France counseled most drastic suppression. In reply the regent and the cardinal Granvella implored Philip to come to the Netherlands, but he pleaded ignorance of the language and poverty as excuse. Meanwhile the Orange party practiced so successfully with the duchess of Parma that she inclined toward conciliation instead of coercion. This threw the regent and De Berghes into alignment, who proposed to convoke the States-General to remedy the evils—a programme which the nobles enthusiastically advocated.

The similarity between the Flemish movement and the programme of the political Huguenots in France is very close.[1] With the design of suppressing heresy in its two most active centers, Granvella proposed to imitate the method used at Paris, of exacting a profession of faith together with a pledge to observe the laws, of all citizens who wished to stay in the city. Recalcitrants were to be disarmed, compelled to sell their property, one-third of the proceeds of which was to be confiscated for the support of the soldiers and municipal expenses, and the culprits were then to be banished

---

[1] Granvella said as much to Philip II, July 14, 1563. See *Papiers d'état du card. de Granvelle*, VII, 124; cf. Gachard, *Correspondance de Philippe II sur les Pays-Bas*, I, 277 (Philip II to Alva, December 14, 1563).

from the country. This drastic policy called forth a mingled protest and threat from the prince of Orange, whose wealth and German connections, aside from other qualities he possessed, gave him great influence. The government begged for money and troops, "como la liga va cresciendo."[1] Orange's tactics were to persuade the provincial estates to refuse to vote subsidies or to throw the weight of the finances upon the church much after the manner of things done at Pontoise. This he began to do in Brabant where the indefinite postponement of a grant of money provoked mutiny among the soldiers. In September De Berghes went out from office, having distinguished himself by not putting a single heretic to death. The change was immediately followed by the burning alive of a Protestant preacher and the protestations of the quartet, Orange, Hoorne, Egmont, and Montigny, became bolder.[2] Finally the nobles of Flanders resolved to protest to the King of Spain. Philip II, always hesitating and undecided, did not respond. To a petition which was sent him demanding the recall of the cardinal, he replied by a flat refusal. The nobles showed their offense by absenting themselves from the Council of State and used their influence to detach the regent from Granvella. At last, after months of negotiation, Philip II yielded. Granvella retired to his splendid palace at Besançon in Franche Comté and the nobles resumed their seats in the council. But the four were irritated at Philip II's delay in responding to their demands for reform. It was evident, moreover, by November, 1563, that something like a common purpose actuated the chief provinces—Flanders, Artois, Holland, Zealand, and Utrecht.[3]

The Calvinists were especially numerous in the Walloon provinces, and preachers from Geneva and England were active among them. The government undertook to restrain their assemblies, and the conflict broke out. This conflict, it is important to remark, did not turn upon the question of religion in and of itself, but upon the manner of treating the heretics. Philip wanted to

[1] Granvella to Perez, August 6, 1563, *Papiers d'état du cardinal de Granvelle*, VII, 177.
[2] *Ibid.*, 231.　　　　　[3] *Ibid.*, 262.

apply the edicts of his father, which required the death penalty for heresy; but the government and Spanish officials in the Low Countries, Catholics though they were, were opposed to so severe a penalty and would rather have treated those offending as criminals than as heretics. But with Philip the extirpation of heresy was a question of conscience.

Valenciennes still remained the most prominent place of dis-affection,[1] but Brussels was much infected.[2] But more formidable than local spirit was the marked tendency toward a union of the provinces[3] and the growing interest of the Huguenots in the Dutch and Flemish cause,[4] so much so that Cardinal Granvella strongly hinted at Spanish pressure being forcibly exerted upon France for the reduction of the Huguenots.[5] The cardinal hoped to see Charles IX and his mother more docile in receiving the advice of Spain since the withdrawal of Chantonnay, who was made Philip II's ambassador at Vienna. But the theft of Alava's cipher by the Huguenots threw him into despair.[6] The reciprocal con-nection between politics and religion in France and the Low Countries made the Spanish government watch the movement of events in France with vigilance.[7] So acute was the situation owing to Huguenot sympathy with the cause of insurrection across the border,[8] that although Granvella ridiculed the wild rumor that Montgomery was coming to Flanders, he nevertheless apprehended the possibility of a rupture with France and was relieved to know

---

[1] See Paillàrd, *Histoire des troubles de Valenciennes, 1560–67.*

[2] *Papiers d'état du cardinal de Granvelle*, VIII, 270.

[3] For proof see *ibid.*, 55, 56, and note.

[4] "Les Huguenots de France sollicitent continuellement ceulx des Pays-Bas pour se révolter," writes Granvella to the Emperor on June 3, 1564 (*ibid.*, 18).

[5] *Ibid.*, 99; cf. 104, note.

[6] *Ibid.*, 23, 393; *L'Ambassade de St. Sulpice*, 5, 275, 280, 284, 300, 305; *Cor-respondance de Catherine de Médicis*, II, 197s.

[7] "Si cela de la religion succède bien en France, les affaires vauldront de mieulx."—*Papiers d'état du cardinal de Granvelle*, VIII, 152, July 15, 1564.

[8] The presence of many Belgian students at the French universities undoubtedly contributed to this sympathy. See Gachard, *Correspondance de Philippe II sur les Pays-Bas*, I, 372.

that precautions had been taken against any chance enterprise of the Huguenots along the edge of Artois and Hainault.[1]

Margaret of Parma and the nobles sent ambassadors to Spain to ask concession on two points: (1) that the provinces be governed by native officials; (2) that the punishment of heresy be moderated. The King hesitated long. It was not until October 17, 1565, that he gave decisive pronouncement in dispatches issued from Segovia. In them he ordered the maintenance of the Inquisition, the enforcement of the edicts, and the impoverishment of those who resisted. In a word, Philip II would not yield. The discontent against the administration of the King of Spain now turned against the King himself. William of Orange used the notable words, "We are witnessing the beginning of a great tragedy."

In the face of the growing resistance the duke of Alva strongly advised Philip II to convert the towns into fortresses.[2] For the Flemish cities were, as yet, commercial groups, not fortified burgs. With the possible exception of Gravelines, no one of them was capable of making a sustained defense.

This suggestion happened to coincide with the English occupation of Havre-de-Grace and the possible return of Calais to England in return therefor. Such a contingency could but be viewed with anxiety by Spain,[3] and this fact, coupled with the uncertainty of developments in France induced Philip to follow out Alva's suggestion by strengthening Gravelines. France at once became alarmed over Calais and protested in the same breath against the building of fortifications at Gravelines and the duty upon her wines.[4] In retaliation the French government also strengthened the garrisons on the

[1] *Papiers d'état du cardinal de Granvelle*, VIII, 390, 527, 550, 556, 593.

[2] *Ibid.*, VII, 281.

[3] The counselor d'Assonleville wrote to Cardinal Granvella after the peace of Troyes, "Adieu, Callais! conbien qu'elle nous duiroit bien hors de mains des François!"—Poulet, I, 570.

[4] *L'Ambassade de St. Sulpice*, 191, 194, 209, 221. Each state appointed a commission in 1563 to adjust this difficulty and other border complications on the edge of Artois and Luxembourg (for instances, see *L'Ambassade de St. Sulpice*,

edge of Picardy, under the direction of the prince of Condé (who was governor of the province), to the immense indignation of Spain.[1] The Spanish erections around Gravelines reacted also upon the state of things in Flanders. For new and heavier taxation was the indispensable point of departure for carrying out such measures, "unless one were willing to see everything said upon the subject vanish in smoke." The sole effective remedy for the state of things prevailing in the Flemish provinces was, of course, to reorganize the finances and the administration of justice in accordance with the demands made by the nobles. But instead of attempting to do this, the government aimed to weaken the opposition by dividing the leaders, and the long silence of Philip II covered an attempt to draw away Egmont, who was regarded as the ringleader of the Flemish nobles at this time.[2] The Spanish government dreaded to summon the estates, as Orange insisted should be done, for fear of things in Brabant and the other provinces going the road of things in France under like conditions.[3]

In order, therefore, to provide for funds without asking the estates to vote subsidies, over which there was sure to be a conflict, the Spanish government in the Netherlands undertook to raise the needed money by tariffs. The cloth trade of England and the wine trade of France were the two commodities so taxed. In 1563 a duty was laid on French wine.[4] In the case of England, the

224, 227, 228, 240, 254), whose conferences were prolonged through the years 1564–65. See the long note in Gachard, *Philippe II sur les Pays-Bas*, I, 270.

In Collection Godefroy, XCIV, No. 16, will be found a "sommaire de la négociation de Calais, entre le président Séguier et le conseiller du Faur, députés de Charles IX, et les ambassadeurs de Philippe II;" original, signed by Séguier and Du Faur. In the same collection, XCVI, No. 6, is a delimitation treaty pertaining to the Picard frontier, signed by Harlay and Du Drac, at Gravelines, December 29, 1565. Charles IX refused to ratify it.

[1] *Papiers d'état du cardinal de Granvelle*, VIII, 18.

[2] "Un eslavon tan importante desta cadena."—*Ibid.*, VII, 215.

[3] For Granvella's opinion of the demand for the Estates-General, see his letter to Philip II, April 18, 1564 (*ibid.*, 492–94).

[4] *Ibid.*, 294, note, and especially 495–97; cf. *L'Ambassade de St. Sulpice*, 188, 193.

excuse given for the high duty placed on imported cloth was precaution against the plague.[1] France at once protested against
the tariff and threatened to retaliate by taxing the herring and cod
trade, though the Spanish ambassador at Paris, represented that
such action would entirely destroy the wine trade and would compel reprisal.[2]

Flemish merchants were doubly alarmed at the state of things,
for England, too, threatened reprisal by removing the cloth market
from Antwerp to Embden and imposing tonnage duties on merchant
ships of Flanders driven by stress of weather into English ports for
safety during storm.[3] But the government in Flanders was obdurate. Granvella declared England's threat to remove the staple
to Embden to be "puerile rhodomontade." He believed that
not only would the prohibition against the import of English cloth
compel Elizabeth to redress the grievances of Spanish subjects
against England, but that it might even make the English government more lenient toward the Catholic religion. Furthermore,
he argued, the tax would operate like a protective tariff to stimu-
late the manufacture of cloth in the Low Countries. "If not a
single bolt of English cloth ever comes into Flanders again," he
wrote "it will be to the permanent profit of the Pays-Bas. We saw
this clearly last year during the plague when the prohibition having
temporarily suspended the importation of this kind of goods, there
was manufactured in the single county of Flanders 60,000 pieces
of cloth, or more than the sum total of the three preceding years."[4]
In the case of French wines the Flemish government even estab-

---

[1] "Non admettre à couleur de la peste."—Granvella to the duchess of Parma,
Papiers d'état du cardinal de Granvelle, VII, 411.

[2] This was a mere threat, however, as such a course would have injured France
as much as the Netherlands.

[3] See the letter of the president Viglius to Granvella, April 17, 1564, in *Papiers
d'état du cardinal de Granvelle*, VII, 476; cf. 481. On this whole question, so far
as England is concerned see Brugmans, *England en de Nederland in de eerste
Jaren von Elizabeth's regeering* (1558–67), Groningen, 1892; cf. *English Historical
Review*, VIII, 358–60.

[4] *Papiers d'état du cardinal de Granvelle*, VII, 496, 497. Cf. the observation
of Assonleville in a letter to Granvella, Poulet, I, 570. The cardinal's prophecy
was partially fulfilled (*Papiers d'état du cardinal de Granvelle*, VIII, 40, 41).

lished a maximum law for their sale which cut the throat of French merchants worse than ever.[1] The French government carried the action of the Flemish government up to Madrid, where for months the duty on wine and the buttresses of Gravelines were matters of repeated interviews between St. Sulpice and the King, and were still unsettled questions at the time of the conference at Bayonne.[2] Meanwhile the conflict of the Flemish reform party became more acute because it became complicated with the question of religion.

In the light of all these circumstances, it is no wonder that Philip II hesitated long before giving his consent to an interview with Catherine de Medici.[3] Even then he imposed a number of conditions and regulations. He would not go in person to Bayonne—the place appointed; his wife was to be accompanied by the duke of Alva; display was to be avoided by either side both for motives of economy and to prevent having undue political significance attached to an interview which was to be understood to be purely personal. Philip II's most striking regulations, however, were those which had to do with the French *entourage*. No one in the least tainted with heresy was to accompany the court. The queen of Navarre, whom the Spanish King carefully alluded to as "Madame de Vendôme," the prince of Condé, the admiral,

[1] "Qui est autant que couper la gorge aux marchands."—"Mémoire envoyé pour le roi de France à St. Sulpice," January, 1564, in *L'Ambassade de St. Sulpice*, 210.

[2] See "Note du Ministère de France en réponse aux griefs presentés par l'ambassadeur d'Espagne" in *Papiers d'état du cardinal de Granvelle*, VIII, 584–86. Other references to this commercial matter are in VII, 62, 164, 375, 411, 476, 481, 495–97, 584, 668; *L'Ambassade de St. Sulpice*, 175, 181, 188, 191, 193, 194, 200, 206, 209, 210, 213, 217, 221, 224, 304, 350, 351; *Papiers d'état du cardinal de Granvelle*, VIII, 6–15; 514, 515; Gachard, *Correspondance de Philippe II sur les Pays-Bas*, I, 244, 246, 247; Poulet, I, 567, and n. 2. There is a memoir on the mission of Assonleville to England, April–June 6, 1563, in the *Bulletin de la commission royale d'histoire*, sér. III, I, 456 ff.

Undoubtedly Spain's harsh commercial policy toward France was also influenced in part by jealousy of the commercial relations of France and England, for the treaty of Troyes established freedom of trade between the two nations. For the great importance of this treaty in the history of commerce see De Ruble, *Le traité de Cateau-Cambrésis*, 193–95.

[3] St. Sulpice sent this important information in a letter of January 22, 1565 *L'Ambassade de St. Sulpice*, 338).

and the cardinal Châtillon were specifically named with abhorrence. The queen mother acquiesced in this prohibition, save in the case of the prince of Condé, protesting that, on account of his rank, it would give great offense to forbid his presence, as well as create belief among the Huguenots that the meeting contemplated something disadvantageous to them. History has shown that Catherine's instincts were perfectly right in this particular; since after the massacre of St. Bartholomew the Huguenots—indeed almost the whole Protestant world—jumped to the conclusion that that disaster was preconcerted at Bayonne. In vain St. Sulpice argued political expediency, saying France and Spain must not be judged alike, and that "experience had proved that the way of arms had resulted in more dangers than profit to France." Philip II's answer was metallically hard; he would not consent to the presence either of Jeanne d'Albret or the prince of Condé at Bayonne, because it would be a reproach to him and to Spain for his wife to have had converse with a heretic.[1]

The last stage of Charles IX's long tour of the provinces was from Bordeaux[2] to Bayonne[3] where the French court arrived on May 22, 1565. But that indolence of spirit which is so much associated with Spanish character seems as early as the sixteenth century to have become habitual,[4] so that the Spanish queen was forced to travel in the heat (six soldiers of Strozzi's band died with their armor on from heat prostration[5]), which aggravated the plague prevailing in certain parts.[6]

[1] *Ibid.*, 366. Catherine de Medici pushed her insistence perilously far, asserting that Alava, the Spanish ambassador in France, had intimated that objection would not be made to the presence of the prince of Condé, since his exclusion might endanger the peace. Philip II promptly declared that if Alava had made Catherine believe so, he had acted in violation of instructions. "Mémoire envoyé à Catherine sur les réponses du roi catholique," May 7, 1564, in *L'Ambassade de St. Sulpice*, 375.

[2] Egmont passed through Bordeaux on his way to Spain while the court was there (*R. Q. H.*, XXIV, 479).

[3] The reasons for the selection of Bayonne are set forth in *R. Q. H.*, XXXIV, 472.

[4] "Les lenteurs . . . . qui sont habituelles en Esgapne."—*L'Ambassade de St. Sulpice*, 363.

[5] F. Fr. 20,647, fol. 11. For other details of the preliminaries of Bayonne, see *L'Ambassade de St. Sulpice*, 335–38, 347, 350, 351, 353, 354, 357–60, 362, 363, 366, 374–78, 382.

In conferences of state, especially international conferences, things of importance are confined within four walls. The sixteenth century was *par excellence* the age of closet politics. The world upon the outside saw only the fêtes[1] that marked the interview at Bayonne. But these festivities were no more than the flecks or wreaths of glittering foam that float upon the bosom of the water for an instant and then are gone. The real business at Bayonne was politics. But the great importance for three hundred years[2] attributed to this famous interview is today proved to have had slight foundation in fact. The light of recent research has dissipated the traditional belief that Philip II and Catherine de Medici planned the massacre of the French Protestants at Bayonne, and finally consummated it on St. Bartholomew's Day.[3] The truth is that not what was contemplated but *what was imagined was contemplated* at Bayonne became the important historical influence of the future. An assumed fact came to have all the force of reality. The principals in this unfortunate conference, in point of truth, were far apart from one another. Philip II's interests were wholly political, and personalities were merely incidental to his main purpose. On the other hand, the queen mother's interests were chiefly personal, being centered in plans to achieve brilliant marriage

[1] Cf. *Recueil des choses notables qui ont esté faites à Bayonne-Paris*, 1566; and the *Mémoires de Marguerite de Navarre*, Book I.

[2] See De Thou, Book XXVII; Mathieu, *Histoire de France*, I, 283; La Popelinière, Book XI, 8. The prince of Orange and William of Hesse both believed that the massacre of St. Bartholomew was concerted at Bayonne (*Archives de la maison d'Orange-Nassau*, III, 507; IV, 108).

[3] Some of the literature upon this famous interview is as follows: E. Marcks, *Die Zusammenkunft von Bayonne: Das französ. Staatsleben u. Spanien in d. J. 1563–67*, Strassburg, 1889; Combes, *L'entrevue de Bayonne de 1565*, Paris, 1882; Maury, in *Journal des savants*, 1871; Loiseleur *La St. Barthelémy*, Paris, 1883; Lettenhove, *La conférence de Bayonne*, 1883; La Ferrière, *R. Q. H.*, XXXIV, 457, and the same in *Correspondance de Catherine de Médicis*, II, Introd.; Philippson, *L'Athénæum belge*, July 1, 1882; De Croze, *Les Guises, les Valois et Philippe II;* Boutaric, *La Saint Barthélemy, d'après les archives du Vatican* (*Bib. de l'Ecole des Chartes*, sér. V, III, 1); Raumer, *Frankreich und die Bartholomäusnacht*, Leipzig, 1854; Wuttke, *Zur Vorgeschichte der Bartholomäusnacht;* Soldan, *La Saint Barthélemy* (French trans.), 1854.

alliances for her children, for whose sake she ruinously compromised herself and France.

If Catherine had been less vain and less foolishly affectionate, she would have striven harder for the solution of things more vital to France.   It is true she was far from ignoring these issues entirely, but she weakened the cause of France in respect to them by subordinating these to her main purpose, so that she awakened the greater suspicion of Spain by her attempts to avoid answering in those matters of most concern to Philip II and by her continual harping upon the things that were nearest to her heart, but not of most moment either to France or to Spain.   When the duke of Alva drove her into a corner and compelled her to answer the questions he put to her concerning greater politics, Catherine's replies were fatal to her aspirations. What were these matters?

Alva's instructions were strict.   He was to demand the expulsion of the Huguenot ministers from France within thirty days; the interdiction of Protestant worship; acceptance of the decrees of the Council of Trent; profession of the Catholic religion by all office holders.[1]   This policy of suppression and compulsion outlined by his sovereign was wholly in keeping with his, the duke's, own judgment.   But with greater penetration and less hesitation than Philip II, Alva recognized clearly the intimate connection between the politics of Flanders and the politics of France, and favored the adoption of a parallel line of conduct at once in the Low Countries.   He was convinced that France was incapable of managing her own affairs and was a menace to other states, politically and religiously.[2]   The means of repression which Spain had often urged had not produced the results desired: they had only delayed the total ruin of the nation.   Suggestion and insinuation must be replaced by a more drastic policy.   Assassination was a recognized, perhaps a quasi-legitimate political recourse in the eyes of the men of the sixteenth century.   The old generation of French Catholics upon whom Spain could rely, the cardinal de Tournon, the duke of

[1] R. Q. H., XXXIV, 483, and n. 2.

[2] For Alva's judgment on the government of France see *Papiers d'état du cardinal de Granvelle*, VII, 276; cf. *L'Ambassade de St. Sulpice*, 341–43.

Guise, the marshal St. André, had passed away—one of them assassinated at the hands of a Huguenot. Tavannes and Vieilleville were reluctant to sacrifice country to religion, especially when a rival nation would profit thereby. The constable was the only old-time figure of prominence remaining, and he could not be relied on since the conflict between the marshal Montmorency and the cardinal of Lorraine, for he favored the side of his nephews and so was believed to be not far distant from the party of the admiral.[1] Power had fallen into the hands of the Huguenots, whose leaders now excelled in personal force. "The shortest, the most expeditious way, is to behead Condé, the admiral, D'Andelot, La Rochefoucauld, and Grammont," Alva told the duke of Montpensier[2] and Montluc, the two most earnest French converts to this policy.[3]

But it was yet a far cry from this cool advocacy of assassination of the Protestant leaders to the wholesale slaughter of August 24, 1572. There is really no positive connection between the conference of Bayonne and the massacre of St. Bartholomew.[4]

---

[1] Nég. Tosc., III, 523; R. Q. H., XXXIV, 492–512, n. 4. Alva frankly said that he wished the constable were gone with the rest—"el condestable que valierá mas que faltára como los otros."—Papiers d'état du cardinal de Granvelle, VII, 277.

[2] The duke of Montpensier was a notoriously bigoted Catholic. The Venetian ambassador said of him: "Il quale è tenuto più atto a governare un monasterio di frati che a comandare ad eserciti."—Rel. vén., II, 155.

[3] R. Q. H., XXXIV, 485. Montluc put a memoir in Alva's hands which proposed an alliance between the crowns of France and Spain for the purpose of crushing the Protestants in France. In event of the French king's refusal to become a party to this alliance, Montluc outlined the means of defense which Philip II would have to resort to. This memoir is published by the baron de Ruble in Commentaires et lettres de Montluc, V, 23 ff. In this striking document the veteran soldier, after setting forth his favorite thesis that French Calvinism was antimonarchical in its nature, makes a survey of the religious state of the provinces. He concludes that while Protestantism was rampant everywhere in France, in five-sixths of the country the Catholics were superior. The place of great danger is Guyenne. The mutual safety of France and Spain requires the subjugation of this province. France cannot or will not do this alone (cf. Correspondance de Catherine de Médicis, I, 342, n. 3; 343, n. 4). It remains, therefore, for the king of Spain to do so. This is the historical argument for all of Montluc's subsequent course of treason with Philip II.

[4] This has been triumphantly proved by Count Hector de la Ferrière, who has shown that M. Combes, L'Entrevue de Bayonne de 1565 et la question de St. Barthelémy d'après les archives de Simancas, Paris, 1881, has mistranslated the very documents upon which he relied (R. Q. H., XXXIV, 511 ff.).

The slaughter of the French Protestants *as a sect* was never advocated by any prince in Europe, not even Philip II. There is no evidence at the Vatican of any Catholic or papal league for the extirpation of the Protestants. Such a solution of the religious problem was not contemplated, save by one person in Europe at this time—Pope Pius V. It is this pontiff who has the sinister distinction of having advocated general destruction of the Protestants, rather than a discriminating assassination of the Huguenot leaders.[1] The most radical action touching the Huguenots

[1] Pius V was elected pope January 17, 1566 (see Hilliger, *Die Wahl Pius V zum Päpste*, 1907). He had been grand inquisitor before his elevation, and imparted a ferocious zeal to the holy office (see Bertelotti, *Martiri di Libero Pensero e Vittime della Sta. Inquisizione nei Secoli, XVI, XVII, e XVIII*, Rome, 1892). The violence of his character and his bigotry led to his committing several acts injurious to the Catholic cause, but it was due to him that the Spanish, Venetian, and papal fleets defeated the Turks at Lepanto. He wrote on March 28, 1569 to Catherine de Medici: "Si Votre Majesté continue, comme elle a fait constamment, dans la rectitude de son ame et dans la simplicité de son cœur, à ne chercher que l'honneur de Dieu toutpuissant, et à combattre ouvertement et ardemment les ennemis de la religion catholique, *jusqu' à ce qu'ils soient tous massacrés* (ad internecionem usque), qu'elle soit assurée que le secours divin ne lui manquera jamais, et que Dieu lui préparera, ainsi qu'au roi, son fils, de plus grandes victoires: ce n'est que par *l'extermination entière* des hérétiques (deletis omnibus haeritics) que le roi pourra rendre à ce noble royaume l'ancien culte de la religion catholique."—Potter, *Pie V*, 35; letter of the Pope to Catherine de Medici, March 28, 1569. The original Latin version of this letter, the salient words of which are in parentheses above, is in *Epistola SS. Pii V*, ed. Gouban, III, 154, Antwerp, 1640. The editor was secretary to the marquis de Castel-Rodrigo, ambassador of Philip IV to the Holy See. An abridged edition was published by Potter, *Lettres de St. Pie V sur les affaires religieuses de son temps en France*, Paris, 1826. The letter is one of congratulation written to Catherine de Medici upon the Catholic victory of Jarnac and the death of the prince of Condé. (Cf. the letter of April 13, 1569, on p. 156 to the same effect.) Nevertheless, even the Pope regarded the total destruction of the French Protestants as a result more devoutly to be wished for than practicable. Pope Pius V, however, was not the first advocate of destruction, for as early as 1556 François Lepicart gave the same advice to Henry II: "Le roy devroit pour un temps contrefaire le luthérien parmi eux [the Protestants], afin que, prenant de là occasion de s'assembler hautement partout, on pût faire main-basse sur eux tous, et en purger une bonne fois le royaume."—*Bayle's Dictionary*, art. "Rose."

The doctrine of assassination for heresy originally proceeded from the mediaeval church, in which it can be traced back as far as the beginning of the Crusades. Urban II asserted that it was not murder to kill an excommunicated person, provided it was done from religious zeal. ("Non enim eos homicidas arbitramur quod adversus excommunicatos zelo catholicae matris ardentes, eorum quoslibet trucidasse

at large, it may safely be said, that was regarded practicable in 1564–65 was to forbid and prevent future conversion,[1] or else the

contigerit."—Migne, *Epistolae Urbani*, CLI, No. 122; Mansi, XX, 713; the same words are used by Ivo of Chartres, X, 331, and by Gratian in the *Decretum* [causa 32, quaestio 2, canon: *De neptis*].) The passage stands in the revised edition, to which Gregory XIII prefixed the injunction that nothing should be omitted, and the gloss gives the following paraphrase: "Non putamus eos esse homicidas qui zelo justitiae eos occiderunt."

In 1208 Innocent III proscribed the count of Toulouse (Teulet, *Trésor des Chartes*, I, 316), and in the same pontificate the Fourth Lateran Council declared that the Pope might depose anyone who neglected the duty of exterminating heresy and might bestow his state on others (Harduin, *Concilia*, VII, 19). The same canon reappears in the *Decreta* of Gregory IX (Lib. iv, tit. 7. cap. 13). St. Thomas Aquinas declared that the loss of political rights was incurred by excommunication (*Summa* [ed. 1853], III, 51). The teaching that faith need not be kept with a heretic was well established by the church in the thirteenth century. It was pleaded by the Emperor in the case of Huss—"quoniam non est frangere fidem ei qui Deo fidem frangit."—Palacky, *Documenta Joannis Hussi*, I, 540.

The spirit of this teaching survived in the sixteenth century. In 1561 some citizens of Lucca, having embraced the Protestant belief, were obliged to flee from the city. The government of the republic, under suggestion from Rome, passed a law on January 9, 1562, that whoever killed one of these refugees, though he had been outlawed, yet would his outlawry be reversed; and that if he himself needed not this privilege, it could be transferred to another (*Archivio storico italiano*, X, app. 176, 177). On January 20, Pope Pius IV wrote to congratulate the city on this pious legislation: "Legimus pia laudabiliaque decretaque civitatis istius Generale Consilium nuper fecit ad civitatem ipsam ab omni heresum labe integram conservandam. . . . . Nec vero quicquam fieri potuisse judicamus, vel ad tuendum Dei honorem sanctius, vel ad conservandam vestre patrie salutem prudentius."—*Ibid.*, 178, 179.

When Henry of Valois made oath to respect liberty of conscience in Poland he was informed that it would be sin to observe the oath, but that if he broke it, the sin of making it would be regarded as a venial offense: "Minor fuit offensio, ubi mens ea praestandi quae pelebatur, defuit."—Hosii, *Opera*, II, 367.

The Ridolfi plot, it may be added, casts a very clear light upon the teaching and conduct of Pius V.

[I owe some of the information given above to a curious accident. In 1899, among a number of books which I purchased in London, I found a number of fragmentary notes dealing with this question. There is nothing to indicate their authorship, but in recognition of the assistance of some scholar to me unknown this acknowledgment is made. It may be added that the books purchased dealt with France in the fourteenth century].

[1] This was Montluc's idea, which he broached both to the cardinal of Lorraine and Philip II, in the form of an edict which he himself improvised, and which we know that the king of Spain actually read (*Commentaires et lettres de Montluc*, IV,

wholesale exile of the Huguenots from the realm.[1]   The alternative of total destruction was not contemplated anywhere in Europe or at any time, except in the single case mentioned.

No such crime as the massacre of the Huguenots was planned at Bayonne, nor perpetrated as the result of that conference.   The principals in the case were too far apart in intention and conviction for so gigantic a programme.   The paramount purpose of the queen mother was to marry Charles IX to the elder daughter of the Emperor, Margaret of Valois to Don Carlos, and the duke of Orleans (the future Henry III) to Donna Juana, Philip II's sister.   But Alva was crafty.   By a series of adroit questions which tantalized her hopes and preyed upon her fears, he compelled Catherine de Medici to commit herself upon the very political issues which she wished to avoid discussing, until she was hopelessly compromised.   In vain she doubled like a fox pursued by the hounds   and   tried   to   throw   the   duke   off   upon   a   false scent.

"France must be cleared of this vicious sect," said Alva.   In order to avoid replying, Catherine attempted, by a question, to turn the conversation to the subject of a universal league, whether it should be against the Turk or against the heretic.   Alva was not thrown off.   The queen resorted to sarcasm.

"Since you understand the evil from which France is suffering so well," she said, "tell me the remedy."

Alva sidestepped the direct shot, by suavely rejoining:

"Madame, who knows better than yourself?"

"The King, your master," said Catherine ironically, "knows better than I everything that passes in France. What means would he employ to overcome the rebellious Protestants?"

Alva resorted to the Socratic method, hoping to involve the queen in the toils of argument.

359–62.   There are two Spanish translations of the first document in the Archives nationales.   Philip indorsed the letter to Bardaxi in his own handwriting: "la carta para el cardinal de Lorena."—*Ibid.*, IV, 362, note.

[1] *Papiers d'état du cardinal de Granvelle*, IX, 306; Gachard, *Correspondance de Philippe II sur les Pays-Bas*, I, 368; letter of Margaret of Parma to Antonio Perez, September 27, 1565.

"Has the religion gained or lost since the peace of Amboise ?" he inquired insidiously.

"It has gained," replied she.

The answer, in Spain's eyes, was a condemnation of the policy of France; it was a thorn in the road of the queen's ambitious hopes of marriage alliance. In her exasperation, Catherine upbraided her daughter for out-Spaniarding the Spaniard.

"I am a Spaniard, I admit," said Elizabeth. "It is my duty."[1]

Catherine broached anew the possibility of Philip II consenting to have his sister marry her Benjamin—Henry duke of Orleans—and conferring Artois as dowry upon the pair.

"The king would never consent to sacrifice one of his provinces," said Alva brusquely.

"But to give a Spanish province to the duke of Orleans," argued the queen mother, blinded by maternal affection, "would be the same then as giving it to his own brother."

Alva taxed the queen with maintaining a heretic, L'Hôpital, in the chancellorship, and of opposing the Tridentine decrees. Catherine emphatically denied the first charge, although her daughter again supported Alva's indictment by declaring that even during the life of her father, L'Hôpital had passed for a Huguenot; as to the second, she said the crown of France objected to the political application of certain findings of the Council of Trent, which she hoped to have adjusted. Alva saw the vulnerable point in her reply and inquired if she aimed to call another assembly like the Colloquy of Poissy.

"I recognize the danger of such assemblies," said Catherine, "but the king, my son, is strong enough to compel discussion only of those subjects which he may designate."

"Was it so at Poissy ?" sneered Alva.

[1] The monotony of life and the tyranny of Spanish etiquette must have borne hard upon the little queen of Spain. But in the midst of the miseries of this "royal slavery," as M. le comte de la Ferrière calls it, it was a crowning humiliation to be condemned to be the instrument of Philip's political intrigues. That her young spirit rebelled, though hopelessly, against the stiuation is evident, from a pitiful letter written by her to her brother's ambassador in Spain (La Ferrière, *Rapport*, 28).

The queen's reply was a tirade against the cardinal of Lorraine, whom she blamed for the failure of the colloquy.

In the end there *was* a promise given by the queen mother at Bayonne. But it was verbal, not written, and so governed by circumstances that the edge of Spain's intentions was dulled. Compromising the agreement certainly was; convicting it is not, for, aside from the fact that its fulfilment was dependent upon an impossible condition of things, Catherine never permitted herself to express in writing what the terms of this promise were. Our knowledge of it is dependent upon Alva's letters of June 15 and July 4; upon Philip II's construction of it in a letter addressed by him to the cardinal Pacheco[1] on August 24, 1565, and the dispatch of the Venetian ambassador Suriano, who was with the French queen, to the senate on July 22, supplemented by what information St. Sulpice picked up during the last days of his mission in Spain.

It is evident from the careful reading of these documents that the real triumph at Bayonne was scored by the papacy; that Spain won a sterile victory, and France met an indecisive defeat. Spain and France, being unable to carry their own purpose through as each desired, compromised on a course which was an intermediate plane of agreement to them, but which, *according to the letter*, was a supreme triumph for Rome, and would have been a complete victory for Rome *if the terms had ever been executed*. The man of the hour was the cardinal Santa Croce, nuncio in France. His services are thus reported by the Venetian ambassador in France on July 2:

> On the eve of departure, the queen, perceiving the discontent of the duke of Alva, summoned the nuncio, who was not far away, to Bayonne, in order to have him at hand. It is he who has found a solution; he has satisfied both parties. I shall be able to inform you shortly as to the nature of his solution.[2]

Three weeks later (July 22) the promised word was sent to Venice in the form of a cipher dispatch,[3] the information in which

[1] On Cardinal Pacheco see Poulet, I, 7, note and Index.

[2] *Correspondance de Catherine de Médicis*, II, Introd., lxxxiii, lxxxiv.

[3] The key to it was discovered in 1885. Suriano had been Venetian envoy at Trent. He was not the regular ambassador of the senate in France and his dispatches seem to have been in another key from that of Marc Antonio Barbaro the accredited ambassador.

had been communicated to him in strictest secrecy.[1]   This intensely important document reads as follows:

Now that I have received positive information, I shall tell everything to your Signory that has happened. Since his arrival, the duke of Alva has not ceased to urge the queen to give his master a manifestation of her good will toward the cause of religion by some manifest act, and he had urged her to cause the decisions of the Council of Trent to be observed throughout the whole realm of France, for which his Catholic majesty would show his satisfaction. The queen had yielded readily to this proposition and had told him that she was very inclined to convene an assembly of prelates, of theologians, and savants, to examine the decisions made at Trent, *without occupying themselves with doctrine*, but confining themselves to the reform of abuses. The duke had found this offer strange and had not concealed his discontent over it. According to him, this was to oppose a council to a council, which would be the worst of results and mightily displease the king his master. Since he urged the necessity of this measure, before passing to any other consideration, and was so obdurate, the queen, being very pained to see him depart so unsatisfied, and things being so desperate, notified the nuncio, who was not lodged at Bayonne like all the ambassadors, and ordered the *mareschal de logis* of the palace to prepare accommodation for him and to have him come immediately. He came at once and being informed by the queen, went to find the duke, but was very badly received by him. The duke blamed and reproached him for not remaining firm in his opinion. The queen holding to the idea of this assembly of prelates and theologians, and the duke opposing it, the nuncio found another expedient which seemed to give satisfaction to all. He broached it to the queen, and with her consent communicated it to the duke. This remedy, at the twelfth hour, was very opportune. It is this: This assembly shall be held: but under certain conditions. The first is that the persons chosen to participate in it shall be of such influence as to be able to demand that no Huguenot shall sit in it; secondly, the assembly must conform to that which the queen had at first proposed; that is to say, all disputes over dogma and doctrine shall be forbidden. The queen, having accepted this, authorized the nuncio to communicate her consent to the duke, who showed himself satisfied. Both of them then came together to find the queen again, and on the next day, in the presence of the queen of Spain, the cardinal Bourbon, the marshal Bourdillon, and the leading nobles, the whole was confirmed.

Great benefit can come from this: by eliminating everything that pertains to dogma, and avoiding doctrinal difficulties, all the other resolutions which are of less importance will be strengthened, especially as the

[1] *Correspondance de Catherine de Médicis*, II, Introd., lxxxv.

Huguenots, the only ones who can give trouble will be excluded. There is no doubt about both the king and the queen being disposed to the Catholic religion, since they have given proofs of it. I am, moreover, assured by what the queen has said, that there is no intention to touch any of the privileges of the Holy See, nor, per contra, any of the concessions made by the popes to the kings who were predecessors of the king now reigning. The execution of this convention thus arranged is not to take place until the return of the king to Paris.

The King of Spain, in the letter cited to Cardinal Pacheco, expressed his contentment with this agreement,[1] not perceiving that the application of it was capable of a great amount of flexibility. In his blindness he thought that the nuncio had broken the loaf so as to give the greater portion to Spain; while in reality the greater part was in the hands of the Pope, Philip II having actually but the difference between a fragment and no bread. In fine, no plot was entered into at Bayonne; no crime was ever committed in pursuance of an agreement arranged there. The "plot" agreed upon at Bayonne between Catherine de Medici and Philip II of Spain consisted of an ambiguous promise, the fulfilment of which was dependent upon an impossible condition of things.[2]

The affair of Bayonne was not a crime; it was a colossal blunder. The destruction of the ambitious marriage expecta-

[1] Combes, 47.

[2] "For a whole fortnight Catherine resisted the pressure of her daughter and the Spanish envoys, who found support in the drastic proposals of the leaders of the French Catholics. Within the last three days of the interview, however, concessions were made which satisfied Alva and his master, though Granvella and Alva exhibited some skepticism. The queen was prompted, ... not by Alva's alleged threat that the King must lose his crown, or his brother Henry his head, but merely by her fear that the total failure of the interview would hinder the attainment of her ends. These concessions consisted in the engagement to accept the decrees of the Council of Trent and in an enigmatical promise of punishment or remedial measures. The latter, however, probably did not refer to the judicial murder or assassination of the Huguenot leaders—a scheme suggested by Montpensier's confessor and welcomed by Alva—but to the expulsion of the ministers and subsequent enforcement of orthodoxy. The execution of these measures was postponed until the conclusion of the journey, but it seems probable that Catherine never seriously intended an act which would have been the inevitable sign of civil war."—Armstrong in *English Historical Review*, VI, 578, 579 (review of Marcks, *Die Zusammenkunft von Bayonne*, Strasburg, 1889).

tions of the Valois was the least loss.   The irreparable thing
was that France forfeited the confidence of her Protestant
subjects.   The secrecy that enveloped the conference made the
Huguenots apprehensive of the worst.   They believed that a
Franco-Spanish alliance was made at Bayonne for their over-
whelming; and the second civil war was the outcome of their
misgivings.[1]   And when finally, *for other reasons*, the massacre
of St. Bartholomew befell them, not merely Protestant France but
Protestant Europe was convinced that the false hypothesis had
been demonstrated.   The count Hector la Ferrière admirably
summarizes the situation:

> To maintain and loyally to adhere to the edict of pacification; to open to
> the daring sailors of France the Indies and America, which Spain and Portugal
> were endeavoring to close to them; and finally to rally Catholics and Protestants
> under the same banner against the foreigner—this was the only true French
> policy.   The Spaniard at this time was the enemy of France.   She encount-
> ered him everywhere in her path; at Rome, at Vienna, at the Council of Trent
> he disputed her precedence; in Switzerland by gold and by the menaces of his
> agents he interfered with the renewals of the French treaties with the Catholic
> cantons; at the very time when Catherine and Elizabeth of Valois were ex-
> changing false promises of alliance and friendship, Menendez was sailing for
> Florida, bearing orders for the massacre of all the French found there.[2]

[1] For example La Noue, chap. xii (1567).

[2] *Correspondance de Catherine de Médicis*, II, 509, 510; *R. Q. H.*, XXXIV.

CHAPTER XI

THE TOUR OF THE PROVINCES (*Continued*). THE INFLUENCE
OF THE REVOLT OF THE NETHERLANDS UPON
FRANCE. THE AFFAIR OF MEAUX

From the field of Philip II's empty victory the court resumed
its pilgrimage, crossing the Loire and traversing Guyenne which
was "in good repose," visiting Angoulême, Cognac, Saintes,
La Rochelle, and Niort *en route* to Nantes. The country was the
veritable dominion of Calvinism in France, but as yet the Huguenots let their hopes belie their fears.[1] The progress through the
western provinces was purposely slow, for Catherine still hoped
against hope that Fourquevaux, who had succeeded St. Sulpice
at the Spanish court, might persuade Philip II to think more favorably of her matrimonial schemes,[2] until finally, late in December,
the bitter truth came out; only the younger daughter of the Hapsburgs might marry a Valois, even though he was king of France.
The queen mother had been weighed in the balance by Catholic-
Hapsburg Europe and had been found wanting. Then it was
that Catherine turned her eyes toward eastern Europe in the hope
of finding in Poland a recompense for the fondled and despicable
Henry of Valois. Strange are the vicissitudes of history! The
effect of Philip II's resolution was to put a mountebank on the
throne of Poland and cast Marguerite of Valois into the arms of
the son of Jeanne d'Albret.[3]

Long before this time, however, Spain had begun to be impatient
for the fulfilment of the compact of Bayonne. But procrastination was Catherine's trump suit. She averred that the plague

[1] "Tous les bruis que l'on fayst courer ne sont pas vray . . . . Et y a tent de
noblèse au demourant que tou les souir à la sale du bal je panserès aystre à Baionne
si j'y voyais reine ma fille," writes Catherine to the duke of Guise (*Correspondance de Catherine de Médicis*, II, 315).

[2] Fourquevaux, I, 6, November 3, 1565. Cf. *Correspondance de Catherine
de Médicis*, II, 326—Catherine to Fourquevaux, November 28, 1565.

[3] For the beginnings of Catherine's negotiations in Poland see *Correspondance
de Catherine de Médicis*, II, Introd., cv, 404; Capefigue, 412 ff.

was too prevalent to make it safe for the court to return to Paris until winter,[1] and when the cold weather diminished the danger from that source, pleaded the poverty and famine of the realm as an excuse.[2]   It was an excuse the validity of which was everywhere manifest.   France truly had been in the dire pangs of hunger and intense cold during the celebrated winter of 1564–65.[3]   Claude Haton, the priest-historian of Provins, who was a close observer of meteorological phenomena has given a graphic description of this season.

The winter at its commencement in November [he says] was very mild and was so until December 20, the vigil of St. Thomas the apostle, without either cold or frost in the mornings.   The rain was so warm that it was thought that the winter would be mild and open, but on the vigil of St. Thomas there came a great cold, accompanied in the morning by a cold rain, which by mid-day turned into snow, and which fell all the rest of the day in so great abundance that the earth, which was very wet, was covered on the morrow to the depth of a foot, king's measure, and more, with snow.   With this snow came a northeast wind, which froze everything under a coating of thick ice.   This cold continued down to the last day of December.   The ice was so thick that a man could cross the river without breaking through.   The snow lay so heavy upon the fields that in the open places the drifts were as high as a man.   After the snow-storm had passed the cold redoubled, so that even the best clad suffered whenever they went out doors.   There was not a house in the village where the water did not freeze, if it was not set close by the fire; and I do not exaggerate when I say that in many good and well-built houses wine froze before the great chimney, though the latter was heaped up with wood.   I saw in many houses iron pots suspended above the fire with icicles hanging over the edge.   Every night and morning when the people got up there was frost upon the coverlet, from the evaporation of the bodies of the sleepers.   There was not a wine-cellar where the wine did not freeze in the casks, unless care was taken to keep charcoal fires burning there.   In some wine-cellars it was necessary to close every aperture in order to prevent the wine from freezing. It frequently froze so hard that it was necessary to pierce the bung-hole with a red hot poker in order to draw it out.   On the night of the 23–24 December, as also on Christmas night, the ice was so heavy upon the trees that the boughs

[1] *Correspondance de Catherine de Médicis*, II, 320.

[2] "C'est la rareté et la cherté des vivres qui nous chasse," said Catherine to the Venetian ambassador (cited by La Ferrière, *Correspondance de Catherine de Médicis*, II, Introd., cii).

[3] See the rhyme upon it in L'Estoile, ed. Michaud, series 2. Vol. I, p. 17.

were broken.   These things had not been seen in France since the year 1480.[1]
The greatest cold was on the day of the feast of the Innocents (December
28).   Many men who were exposed died in the roads.   The crests of cocks
and poultry were frozen and fell off some days afterwards, and many were
found dead under their roosts.   The sheep also died.

Early in January the ice began to melt.   It grew uncommonly warm for
the season, so that fire became unnecessary.   On the day following the edict
of the king, about noon, a soft warm rain began to fall, which caused the snow
to vanish rapidly.   This lasted for five days, so that the earth was covered
with water.   And then came a second cold for three entire weeks, until the
28th of the month, and snow with a high wind came, which drove the snow
everywhere and piled it in great drifts.   The winter grain was frozen in the
furrows.   God knows how much the poor people who had no wood suffered.
Most of them stayed in bed night and day without getting up except to eat once
in twenty-four hours.   The poor of Paris and others who had no means, were
compelled to burn their furniture.   Those who had made no provision for the
winter, chiefly of wood, were compelled to purchase at high prices, for it was
not possible to do carting because of the condition of the roads; in many cases,
moreover, the bridges were destroyed.   When the thaw came, the high waters
penetrated houses and churches in Provins to the depth of three, four, and
even five feet, washing out the very dead in the cemetery.[2]   At Paris the flood
damaged the Pont-au-Change and caused many houses to topple.   Vine-
growers found themselves in great difficulty.   Those who were wise cut their
vines back to the root, in order that they might sprout better again, and were
repaid for so doing, for they were the only ones that bore.

The spring was fair and mild, so that barley and oats were sown.   Yet
much ground lay bare because in the fields sown with winter wheat the roots
were all killed, so that no grain grew.   The walnut trees seemed to be dead
through all the month of April and half of May, for they did not put forth
their buds.   Pear and apple trees bore a few blossoms.   In some places there
were plums and cherries, but not everywhere.[3]

[1] Cf. Babinet de Rencogne, "Sur un débordement de la Charente et la cherté des
vivres en 1481," *Bull. de la Soc. art.*, etc., 1860, 3e sér., II, 3 (Angoulême, 1862).

[2] Cf. Boutiot. "Notes sur les inondations de la rivière de Seine à Troyes
depuis les temps les plus reculés jusqu' à nos jours," *Annuaire admin. pour 1864*
(Troyes), p. 17.

[3] Claude Haton, I, 395–98.   This statement, even if there were no other
evidence, is confirmed for the south of France by the court's experience in the
foothills of the Pyrenees in January, 1565 (cf. *Hist. du Languedoc*, V, 465).   For
the west of France see *Chroniques Fontenaisiennes* (Paris, 1841), 84, 85, and the
"Journal de Louvet," published in the *Revue d'Anjou* in 1854.   One quotation
may suffice: "Au mois de febvrier, il tomba sy grande quantité de neige au païs

The winter was just as bad in Gascony, Provence, and Langue-doc. On the day of the Feast of St. John the Baptist (June 24) it snowed![1] Even the poor people were compelled to build fires, though they could not afford the fuel. The vines throughout central France were so badly injured that not a third part of the crop remained. The grain likewise was destroyed. Water courses were swollen and overflowed their banks, and in the meadows of the Seine people had to take care lest they be drowned. As a result of the cold spring, the harvest of 1565 failed over almost all the realm to such an extent that it was necessary to abolish the tolls between provinces and to permit free trade in grain. Paris imported wheat from Champagne, Picardy, Anjou, Lower Brittany, Burgundy, and Auvergne, the least stricken of the provinces.[2] The Parlement of Paris passed an ordinance forbidding speculation in foodstuffs and compelled those possessed of a surplus of grain to throw what was not needed for their own necessity upon the market.[3] A measure (*boisseau*) of wheat, from January to April cost from 12–15 sous (= 1½ pecks at from 36 to 45 cents), and after April the price rose every week until harvest time, to the sum of 25 sous *tournois* (approximately 75 cents). Wheat was very dear in Paris and throughout all Brie, the Ile-de-France, Valois, Soissonais, and Picardy; less so in Champagne, Burgundy, and Lorraine, where there was rye and barley enough for the people. The stock starved because the grain was consumed by the people. Many people went over into Champagne in order to purchase rye and barley to make bread with until the harvest came. Fortunately grain was plentiful in Champagne, and wheat fell to 7 and 6 sous

d'Anjou et fust l'hyver si froid, que les rivières furent glacées et qu'on marchoit et passont par-dessus, et que tous les lauriers et romarins gelèrent, et qu'au dégel les eaux crurent et furent si grandes qu'elles rompirent des arches, ponts et chaussées, et fust ceste année appelée l'année du grand hyver." I know of no article upon this subject as a whole. M. Joubert, *Etude sur les misères de l'Anjou aux XVᵉ et XVIᵉ siècles*, 1886, pp. 35 and 161, has a little to say. The subject deserves treatment. The sources of course are almost wholly local.

[1] Claude Haton, I, 331.

[2] *Idem*, I, 409.

[3] Catherine's order to the marshal Montmorency, as governor of Paris, dated November 19, 1565, is in *Correspondance de Catherine de Médicis*, II, 325.

per measure (from 19 to 22 cents), and corn in like proportion after the harvest. Because of the hard times which they had experienced, many accumulated great stores in the expectation that in a short time there would again be a dearth.

Wine was very dear until the vintage. In the months of August and September before the grapes were gathered, it was not possible to purchase wine by the cup at taverns, even for silver; it was with great difficulty that sufficient wine was procurable for church service. But after the vintage the price dropped to 14 *livres tournois* ($8.70) *la queue du creu*, whereas it had been as high as 80 before ($49.60).[1]

As so often appears elsewhere in history, the economic distress and strain of poverty was followed by psychological manifestations of a religio-sociological sort, among the lower and poor classes. In 1565, in the villages of Champagne and Brie and especially in the bailiwicks of Sens, Melun, Montereau, Nogent, Troyes, Châlons, Rheims, Epernay, Château-Thierry, Meaux, and Provins, the belief spread among the peasantry that in honor of the Virgin they ought to refrain from working in the fields on Saturday after midday, and that this Saturday rest had been formally ordered by the Virgin in revelations and apparitions. A young girl of Charly-sur-Marne, near Epernay, boasted of having received

---

[1] The authorities of Provins made requisition of the grain possessed by private persons and appropriated all save that which was necessary for the owners, which was sold to the townspeople at the maximum price of 20 sous per *boisseau*. The abbot of St. Jacques and the prior of St. Ayoul baked bread to be distributed to the poor. One of the wealthy citizens from Easter till harvest made daily distribution of bread to more than three hundred poor, besides furnishing them with work (Claude Haton, I, 409).

The *boisseau* (Med. Latin, *boissellus* [Du Cange, *s. v.*]) was an ancient measure of capacity equivalent to 13.01 litres, approximately 12 quarts. In remote parts of France the term is still sometimes used to indicate a décalitre. The *boisseau* was used for both dry and liquid measure. On the other hand the *bichet* (Med. Latin, *bisselus* and *busellus*, whence the English bushel) was a dry measure, representing from one-fifth to two-fifths of a hectolitre (from 4.4 to 8.8 gallons) according to the province. The *setier*, was a larger dry measure of 6 pecks (Paris measure). The *muid* (Latin *modius*) also was of variable capacity. That of Paris equaled 36 gallons. The *queue du creu* was a large wooden cask, about equivalent to a hogshead and a half, and was used only for wine. The calculations of terms of American money are on the theory that the *livre tournois* in 1565 was equivalent to 3.11 francs, according to the estimate of the vicomte d'Avenel in *Revue des deux mondes*, June 15, 1892, p. 795.

these confidences, and showed miraculous signs of her mission. But the cardinal of Lorraine caused her to be arrested and questioned, and she was burned alive as a witch.[1]

Instead of going to Paris, the court passed the winter at Moulins in Bourbonnais,[2] where the famine was most slightly felt. By this time the expectations of the Catholics and the fears of the Huguenots were beginning to bear their bitter fruit, and in the state of public tension every incident was magnified. At Angers, in November, the Rohans, having forbidden Catholic worship upon their domains, the King had had to compel them to reinstate it by threatening to dispossess them of their châteaux; at Blois the cardinal Bourbon reproached the queen mother for suffering the edict to be violated by permitting the queen of Navarre and the prince of Condé to maintain court-preachers in their entourage. The Catholics of Dijon demanded that in future Calvinist ministers be forbidden to attend the last hours of the dying, a petition which the cardinal of Lorraine supported in order to make the chancellor L'Hôpital commit himself. The answer of the latter sustained the edict's grant of the right of selection in the matter of religion. Of greater anxiety still was the influx of Huguenots into the town of Moulins, Montgomery among the rest, who for the first time since the fatal tournament of June 30, 1559, looked upon the court.[3]

The memory of the conspiracy of Amboise haunted the queen like a specter, and was the more vivid because of the *rapproche-*

[1] Claude Haton, I, 418. For information on this subject see Reuss, *La sorcellerie au 16e et au 17 siècle, particulièrement en Alsace d'après des documents en partie inédits;* Jarrin, *La sorcellerie en Bresse et en Bugey* (Bourges, 1877); Pfister, "Nicolas Rémy et la sorcellerie en Lorraine à la fin du XVIe siècle," *Revue hist.*, XCVII, 225.

[2] "Molins è città, ed à posta vicina all' Alier, sopra il quale ha un ponte; è la principale del ducato di Borbon. Vi è un bellissimo palazzo, fabbricato già dai duchi di Borbon, posto in fortezza, con bellissimi giardini e boschi e fontane, e ogni delicatezze conveniente a principe. Tra le altre cose vi è una parte dove vi si teniano de infinite sorte animali e ucelli, delli quali buona parte è andata de male; pur vi restano ancora molti francollini, molte galline d'India, molte starne, è altre simil cose; è vi son molti papagalli vi diverse sorte."—*Rel. vén.*, I, 32, 34.

[3] When the court was a Blois so great was the number of strangers that the Knights of the Order made a house-to-house canvass.

ment between the leaders of the Huguenots and the Montmorencys, who had met together at Paris in November at the marriage of the amorous prince of Condé to Mlle. de Longueville. The incident was sharp enough to strike fire between the Catholic-Guisard and the Huguenot-Montmorency party. For when the papal nuncio indignantly demanded the cardinal of Beauvais' renunciation of the purple, the constable bluffly said: "I am a papist. But if the Pope and his agents still seek to trouble the kingdom, my sword will be Huguenot. My nephew will never renounce his dignity. The edict gives him the right to it." It is no wonder Catherine de Medici was anxious to hear of the report of these words at Madrid and what Philip II would say.[1] The interdiction of the Protestant worship at Moulins on January 9, 1566, on the very day that Coligny returned from the wedding festivities, was her own reply.

The very next day she guarded against new fire being struck between the factions by compelling at least outward reconciliation between the admiral and the cardinal of Lorraine. On January 10, 1566, in the presence of the court, she addressed the cardinal, saying that the repose of the kingdom was destroyed by private quarrels and especially by two of his, the one with the marshal Montmorency, the other with the admiral for the murder of the duke of Guise.[2] At the same time the queen mother, in order to preserve peace between the rivals, hit upon the novel scheme of lodging the cardinal and the admiral in the same house, so that each had to use the same stairway in order to reach his apartments, telling both that each was keeper of the other, and that if either of them experienced any injury it would be imputed to the other.[3]

---

[1] *C. S. P. For.*, *anno* 1565, p. 524; cf. *Nég. Tosc.*, III, 523. For details upon the history of the six months between July and January, see *Correspondance de Catherine de Médicis*, II, lxxxvii–cv.

[2] *C. S. P. For.*, *anno* 1566, No. 17. Before the end of the month the old scores were officially "shelved" by decrees of the King in council (January 29 and 31, 1566). Many of the sources allude to this hypocritical reconciliation: De Thou, V, Book XXIX, 184; Poulet I, 125—letter of Granvella from Rome; D'Aubigné, II, 223–25; *C. S. P. For.*, No. 57, January 29, 1566; Castelnau, Book VI, chap. ii.

[3] *C. S. P. For.*, No. 41, January 23, 1566.

The cardinal of Lorraine, for fear of losing all his influence, accepted the situation (he did not stir from the side of the queen),[1] and was compelled to abide by the situation *telle quelle*, as Sir Thomas Smith wrote to Cecil.[2] But nothing could mollify the anger of the constable against the Guises, and when the duke of Guise at length came to court in February, Montmorency left it forthwith.[3]

While the factional feeling thus grew more embittered, serious and noble effort was yet made to carry out the demands of the States-General of Orleans and Pontoise—demands which were principles of the political Huguenots. This programme was supported by the queen mother, who seems in this way to have sought to placate the fears of the Huguenots for their faith. The year 1566 is notable for the fact that greater recognition was then accorded the political demands of the Huguenots than at any time hitherto, so that large progress was made in the betterment of the administrative system of France.

The King in his address to the council said that at his accession he had wanted to travel through all the provinces desolated by the late civil wars, in order to hear the complaints of his subjects and to remedy conditions in the best manner possible; that it was for this cause that he had convoked the assembly and so enjoined them, in virtue of the royal authority, to apply themselves diligently to affairs.

Then the chancellor spoke: after dwelling upon the general evils of the state, he asserted that the root of all the evils was the bad administration of justice; that the King had become convinced of this in the course of the tour of the provinces; that for himself he could not refrain from calling things by their right name and from speaking as he thought; that those who were appointed to administer justice were guilty of great excesses; that these evils had increased owing to the impunity and the license which obtained.

[1] *C. S. P. For.*, No. 120, February 22, 1566.

[2] *Ibid.*, No. 150, March 6, 1566.

[3] *Ibid.*, No. 136, February 25, 1566. "The constable lies at Chantilly ill at ease."—*Ibid.*, No. 406, May 21, 1566. Poulet, I, 190, Morillon to Granvella, March 5.

I do not deny [he added] that there are too many laws and ordinances in France and that the multitude of the laws and the number of the judges is the cause of much unnecessary and tyrannical litigation. But it is no less true that when new evils arise there is a necessity of new remedies, and that when the ancient laws have been abrogated either by inobservance or by license, it is necessary to make new ones in order to cure current evils and to arrest the course of public calamity. The public welfare requires new legislation. If the new laws are not observed, on account of the venality and avarice of the ministers of justice, they must be punished severely and these public pests who fatten upon the blood of a miserable people must be driven from office. Superfluous offices, moreover, must be abolished and the ruinous multiplication of legal causes stopped.

The justice of the last charge was particularly manifest. Since the time of Francis I it had been the practice of the crown to sell offices and even to create them for purposes of revenue only.

The chancellor further asserted that the King could not suffer those who had not the right to make laws to attribute to themselves the power to interpret them; he proposed to diminish the excessive number of the courts, and raised the question whether the demands of justice would not be better met if the Parlement ceased to be so sedentary and became ambulatory instead—a suggestion which, it is interesting to observe, found a partial realization in the seventeenth century in the establishment of the Grands Jours d'Auvergne. He insinuated that it was advisable to subject the judges to censure and to compel them to render account of the manner in which they exercised their office, and that it might be better to establish judges for two or three years than to permit the holding of office in perpetuity.

After longer deliberation, in February, 1566, the famous ordinance of Moulins was framed. It contained eighty-six articles, and dealt radically with the evils of the time and imposed drastic reform, especially in the administration of justice.

This act declared the royal domain inalienable, limited and regulated the right of remonstrances of parlement, organized circuits of inspection by magistrates especially appointed to go throughout the realm, instituted certain changes in the judicial administration, and pledged the word of the crown to appoint capable and honest magistrates.[1]

It profoundly modified both the public and private law of France. In the former sphere the ordinance strengthened the legislative power of the crown by laying down the principle that the King's ordinances must be observed in spite of remonstrances on the part of the parlements, and even if the latter refused to register them; the *maîtres des requêtes* were enjoined to punish severely any infraction or failure to observe the ordinances. The powers of the governors in the provinces were much reduced; they were forbidden to exercise the right of pardon, to levy taxes, or to institute fairs and markets. The judicial power of the great *villes* was almost entirely suppressed. The communal judges were deprived of all civil jurisdiction and retained cognizance only of petty offenses; at the same time, the attempt was made to restrain seigneurial jurisdiction. The right of written proof was recognized in cases involving 100 livres or more.[2] No less than 1,500 superfluous offices, treasurerships, secretaryships, etc., were abolished. In the matter of religion some of the articles were a confirmation of the edict of 1563. Another article abolished entirely all confraternities, and prohibited the formation of all leagues.[3]

The financial administration came in for a most searching investigation. The flaunting arrogance of some of the King's treasurers is remarkable. Numbers of them had had houses, and even châteaux which rivaled the King's own in elegance, the means to purchase and furnish which they had secured by plundering the people and robbing the government. One treasurer—among

[1] *C. S. P. For., anno* 1566, Introd. The text of the *ordonnance* is in Isambert, XIV, 189; De Thou, Book XXXIX, 178–84, has much upon it. It is he who records the speeches of the King and the chancellor. It is interesting to observe that very similar conditions prevailed in Germany at this time. See the account of the Diet of Spires (1570) in Janssen, *History of the German People*, VIII, 75 ff.

[2] Cf. Cheruel, *Histoire de l'administration monarchique de la France*, I, 196–203; Glasson, *Histoire du droit et des institutions de la France*, VIII, 170 ff.

[3] The clergy of Guyenne were so incensed at this prohibition that they threatened to leave the country (*Archives de la Gironde*, XIII, 183).

four who were hanged at Montfaucon—was found to owe the crown over three million livres.[1]

The young duke of Guise, who had refused to be a party to the farcical reconciliation between his house and the Chatillons soon found means to leave the court. In May the duke of Nemours and the duchess of Guise were married at St. Maur-des-Fosses. It was a match which sowed dragon's teeth once more. For Nemours forsook his wife, who was a Rohan, having induced the Pope to nullify the marriage. The Huguenots murmured indignantly against the insult done the Rohan clan whose powerful family influence was now joined with the Châtillons and Montmorencys.[2]

Catherine de Medici was not the ruler to govern France with a firm yet facile hand under the circumstances that existed in 1566. Irrespective of foreign influences, which we shall presently come to, the economic distress[3] of the country, the rivalry of the great houses, and the religious acrimony prevailing made a combination of forces that needed another sort of ruler to reconcile them—a ruler such as Henry of Navarre was to be. The queen mother, while a woman of force, was so deficient in sincerity that no one could have confidence in her; so jealous of power that she would brook no other control of the King, whose sovereignty she confounded with her maternal oversight of him, making no distinction

[1] See the case of the magnificence of the house of a Parisian shoemaker, who had purchased the estate of a king's treasurer and enormously enriched himself with gold and silver. Under a pretext the queen mother secured entrance to the house. Claude Haton, I, 412, gives a detailed description of its magnificence.

According to an estimate of January 15, 1572, the income from the "Parties Casuelles," that is to say, from offices vacated by the death of particular possessors thereof, and from the "Paulette," was two million francs and yet the corruption in the administration was so great that the King received but a quarter of this amount (Cheruel, I, 208).

[2] De Thou, V, Book XXXVII, 185; D'Aubigné, II, 224; C. S. P. For., Nos. 343, 344, 347, 387, April 28; May 3–4, 16, 1566; Forneron, Hist. des ducs de Guise, II, 59.

[3] "On ne sait encore quant on délogera d'icy, combien que les laboureurs des champs ayent ja faict présenter deux requestes au Roy pour se retirer et sa suite à Paris jusques à ce que la récolte soit faict."—Tronchon to M. de Gordes, July 4, 1567; quoted by the duc d'Aumale, Histoire des princes de Condé, I, Appendix XVI.

between Charles IX the ruler and Charles IX the son. Catherine time and again marred or ruined the progress she had made with the aid of one party's support by her own envious fear of that party's predominance. Her "bridge policy,"[1] instead of uniting France, kept it divided. To maintain the balance of power—an immemorial Italian policy—her Italian nature resorted to duplicity and deception continually. Accordingly, suspicion prevailed at court and suspicion prevailed in the provinces, the more so in the latter because of the Huguenots' uncertainty about what was done at Bayonne, and doubt as to Philip II's course. Men were doubtful of their neighbors; towns were fearful of other nearby towns. "All the way of my coming hither," reported Sir Thomas Hoby, the new English ambassador to France, "I found the strong towns marvelously jealous of strangers, insomuch that only by the sound of a bell they discovered a number of horsemen or footmen before they come; but also, after they are entered they have an eye to them."[2]

When the court finally moved to Paris, the great nobles came thither with such numerous trains[3] that the queen sent four companies of the King's guard ahead of his coming, and ordered the marshal Montmorency to require the retirement from the city of all those who were not of the ordinary household of each nobleman and gentleman. In vain the marshal, anxious to protect his party against the Guisards, resisted the order and complained that the queen was interfering with his authority. The King ordered Lansac and De la Garde to accomplish what Montmorency was unwilling to do.

If choice must be made as to who were the worst offenders in this respect, the greater blame lies with the Protestants. It was not only impolitic, it was insolent on their part to permit Montgomery to swagger around Paris as he did, "booted and spurred

[1] "Politiquè de bascule," R. Q. H., XXVII, 274.

[2] C. S. P. For., No. 275, April 12, 1566.

[3] It was estimated that, beside footmen, captains, men-at-arms, there were 20,000 horsemen attached to the various factions (C. S. P. For., No. 470, May–June, 1566).

with all his men."[1] Apparently the queen had not the daring
to compel his withdrawal, as she did that of the Guises' recruiting
sergeant, Roggendorf.[2] Her policy for the time being was to
favor the Châtillon-Montmorency faction.[3] Backed by the joint
support of the admiral and the constable, the queen accordingly
undertook to bring certain unsettled or indefinite matters of
religion and the church to a conclusion. On May 31, 1566,
Charles IX sent a series of articles to the cardinal Bourbon for
consideration by the clergy of Paris, then sitting at St. Germain des
Près. Two of these had to do with the baptism of infants where
one of the parents was a Catholic, and the maintenance of Protestants schools. Three concerned church temporalities, namely,
the redemption of the fourth part of the temporals of the church,
given to the King during the late civil war; the subsidy which was
to expire in eighteen months; and the preparation of an edict
defining the privileges and jurisdiction of the church. The residue
of the articles dealt with infractions of the Edict of Amboise, such
as restraint of preaching according to the edict, and the molestation of former Protestants who had returned to the church of Rome
by the Huguenots. By an awkward coincidence, the sending of
these articles exactly coincided with the arrival of the papal legate
in Paris, who came to request the promulgation of the decrees of
Trent in conformity with the agreement made with the cardinal
de Santa Croce at Bayonne.[4]

Catherine de Medici's policy at this time was that of the political
Huguenots. She hoped that the question of religion would settle
itself with time, and to divert attention from that issue, and also

---

[1] C. S. P. For., No. 667, August 21, 1566.

[2] Ibid., No. 715, September 14, 1566.

[3] Hugh Fitzwilliam to Cecil: "The constable is of great authority with the
king and the queen mother; and being mortal enemy to the house of Guise is with
his nephews and the Protestants for his life."—C. S. P. For., No. 741, October
3, 1566.

[4] Nég. Tosc., III, 515. "A man might easily perceive by the sour countenance
the queen made that she liked not all that he had said. After he had saluted
divers persons the king made him somewhat too short an answer for so long a
demand."—C. S. P. For., No. 444, June 1, 1566.

because there was great need of it, she energetically continued the administrative and economic reforms begun at Moulins. L'Hôpital began so searching an investigation of the conduct of the King's treasurers that some of them were hanged and others banished. The constable was of service here, although his notorious avarice tarnished the honesty of his work.[1] Yet there was peril even in a policy so just and so much needed by France. Sooner or later such a course would unearth the dishonesty of bigger thieves than the small collectors of the revenue who, in many cases undoubtedly suffered for the peculation of their superiors. The administration was full of "grafters" such as St. André had been, who would not scruple to conceal their thievery behind the smoke of another civil war. The queen mother knew this only too well from former experience, not being unaware of the fact that one of the causes of "the late unpleasantness" was the demand of the estates that the Guises should make an accounting and be forced to disgorge their ill-gotten gains. The government resorted to various devices to raise money and an imposition was laid upon inn-keepers. The most singular expedient, though, was the offer of a Genoese syndicate to pay the King a lump sum for the privilege of taxing dowry gifts and for a license to endure eight years to levy a crown on every first-born infant, and after, for every boy born into a family five sous, and for every girl babe, three sous.[2] This preposterous measure actually passed the council, and was only prevented from becoming law by the good sense of the Parlement.[3]

But the events happening in the Netherlands were of greater importance to France at this time than anything within her borders. From the beginning of the insurrection there the Huguenots had recognized the important bearing of that struggle upon their own movement, and as the shadow of Philip II fell in greater length

---

[1] "The king has made peace with his treasurers for a certain sum by the constable's means, whereof something cleaves to his fingers."—*C. S. P. For.*, No. 733, §2, September 28, 1566.

[2] According to the estimate of this syndicate France had a population of from fifteen to sixteen millions (*Rel. vén.*, III, 149).

[3] *C. S. P. For.*, Nos. 1,111–15, April 18–19, 1567.

each year across France, the interest of the French Protestants in the rebellion of the Low Countries increased.[1] As Huguenot preachers in Flanders sowed the double seed of Calvinism and revolt, so Protestant preachers exiled from the Low Countries sought refuge in France.[2] This intercourse became a formidable historical issue by 1566. The issue was understood from the beginning by all parties concerned, and Philip II and his ministers were determined to profit by the lessòn of France and to prevent similar trouble by crushing all opposition in the bud. The Turkish attack upon Malta[3] had been very favorable to the Protestant cause, and the raising of the siege in September, 1565, probably influenced the King of Spain in his resolution to extirpate heresy in the Low Countries.[4] The Flemish government suspected William of Orange who by July was openly allied with the Gueux[5] and his brother, Louis of Nassau, of direct intercourse with Condé

[1] *Papiers d'état du cardinal de Granvelle*, IX, 594, 595; Poulet, I, Introd., l–lii, n. 2; Gachard, *Don Carlos et Philippe II*, I, 303; C. S. P. For., No. 641, August 13, 1566. Coussemaker, *Les troubles religieux du XVIe siècle dans la Flandre maritime 1560–70*; Van Velthoven, *Documents pour servir à l'hist. des troubles religieux du XVIe siècle dans le Brabant;* Verly, *La Jurie espagnole, 1565–95;* Kervyn de Lettenhove, *Les Huguenots et les Gueux: Etude hist. sur vingt-cinq annels du XVIe siècle (1560–1585)*, Bruges, 1883–85, 6 vols.; Poulet, *Correspondance du cardinal de Granvelle*, I, Introd., lvll–lxxvi; II, Introd., iv–vii; De Thou, V, 204–37; D'Aubigné, Book IV, chap. xxi.

[2] The most notable of these was Francis Junius, who was driven out of Antwerp. The Spanish ambassador demanded his arrest but the prévôt de l'hôtel refused, alleging with right that Junius was the ambassador of the count palatine and entitled to immunity (*Correspondance de Catherine de Médicis*, II, Introd., cviii).

[3] On this famous siege of Malta see D'Aubigné, Book IV, chap. xix; De Thou, Book XXXVIII. It was begun on May 17, 1565.

Mingled with this fear was apprehension lest even the Turk might become an ally of the Flemings and the Protestant French (Poulet, I, 357, Morillon to Granvelle). That it was not an utterly fantastic notion of him alone, see the letter of Margaret of Parma to Philip II, in *Corresp. de Philippe II*, I, No. 411, and Gachard. *Corresp. de Guillaume le Taciturne*, VI, 408.

[4] *Archives de la maison d'Orange-Nassau*, I, 259–89; Poulet, I, 207; Gachard, *La Bibliothèque Nationale à Paris*, I, 88. "Avec la liberté des consciences, que aulcungs prétendent, nous ne nous trouverions pas mal si, suyvant l'exemple des François, nous tumbions aux mesmes inconvenientz."—Letter of Granvella, April 9, 1566, in Poulet, I, 209.

[5] Sir Francis Berty to Cecil: "The Prince of Orange since Wednesday shows himself openly to take the Gueux part, and divers of his men wear their badge. This town is marvellously desolated; great riches are conveyed out, chiefly by strangers."—C. S. P. For., No. 582, July 20, 1566, from Antwerp.

and Coligny,[1] and sent Montigny—the faithless member of the patriotic quartette composed of Orange, Egmont, Hoorne, and himself—to Paris in the spring to pick up information.[2] The fear lest Montgomery might come to Flanders, which Granvella had once laughed at, by the summer of 1566 had some basis of reality, although the braggadocio character of this adventurer discounted alarm.[3]

Knowledge of the solidarity existing between his revolted subjects in Flanders and the Huguenots[4] which Montluc had warned Philip of even two years before,[5] coupled with information concerning the dealings of Louis of Nassau with Protes-

[1] Poulet, I, 307.

[2] We know of Montigny's treason from a dispatch of Granvella to Philip II, July 18, 1565, in which the cardinal tells the King that Montigny is still successfully pretending to be a Calvinist and is in correspondence with the Châtillons and Montmorency. He had already been at least nine months in the pay of Spain. He got 20 écus per diem for one job (*Papiers d'état du cardinal de Granvelle*, IX, 404, 595). Montigny came to Paris ostensibly to attend the wedding of the duke of Nemours' son to the admiral's niece at Easter time. We get a line on Philip II's methods at this point, for the Guises themselves were having secret and treasonable dealings with Spain, yet did not know of Montigny's relation to Philip II and treated him with scorn and contempt (*ibid;* Poulet, I, 329; cf. Finot, *L'espionnage militaire dans les Pays-Bas entre la France et l'Espagne aux XVIe et XVIIe siècles*).

[3] Poulet, I, 304; Edward Cook to Cecil: "Montgomery has told him that the French Protestants are resolved to succour those of Flanders."—*C. S. P. For.*, No. 661, August 18, 1566. This letter is analyzed in the *Bull. de la comm. roy. d'histoire*, 3e sér., I, 129. Granvella's confidant in Brussels, the prevost Morillon, wrote with truth on July 7: "Je croy que si avons mal cest année ce ne sera du costel de France."—Poulet, I, 350. Cf. Reiffenberg, *Corresp. de Marguerite de Parme*, 88; Gachard, *Corresp. de Philippe II*, I, 429, 431, 436; at p. 473 is a letter dated October 15 in Italian from the duchess of Parma to Philip expressing fear of Huguenot projects.

[4] Louis of Nassau without doubt was in close connection with the leading French Protestants. See *Archives de la maison d'Orange-Nassau*, I, 229; II, 196, 403. It was extremely difficult to repress the ardor of the Protestants at Valenciennes, owing to its nearness of the French border and the number of Calvinist preachers whom the Huguenots sent into the country in June, 1566 (*ibid.*, II, 135). For the influx of Calvinist preachers into the country as early as 1561 see Languet, *Epist. secr.*, II, 155. The prince of Condé was reputed to have sold a tapestry for 9,000 florins, which he gave to the cause there (Poulet, I, 439).

[5] Montluc to Bardaxi, October 27, 1564: *Commentaires et lettres de Montluc*, IV, 368.

tant Germany[1] and France, stirred the Spanish King's habitual indecision into action. He sounded Charles IX as to the possibility of sending Spanish troops directly across France to the Low Countries and asked him to restrain his subjects from coming thither with arms,[2] crowds of whom went to Flanders disguised as merchants.[3] Simultaneously Margaret of Parma begged the Emperor to take the same course.[4] But the government of France could not have honored Philip II's request, even if it had been so minded, without risking an immediate rising of the Huguenots. As a matter of fact, it had no desire to do so. The resentment felt by France toward Spain on account of past scores at Trent, Rome, and in Switzerland, was now all eclipsed in her rancor because of the massacre by the Spaniards of her ill-fated colony in Florida in September, 1565.[5]

[1] Poulet, I, 64; Reiffenberg, 91; *Archives de la maison d'Orange-Nassau,* II, 175, 178.

[2] *Corresp. de Philippe II,* I, 433.

[3] The government of Charles IX even winked at the secret levies made by the prince of Condé for the benefit of Louis of Nassau, from behind the mask of an official repudiation of the complicity of any French in Flanders, denying that the prince of Condé was ever in Antwerp in disguise (Poulet, I, 521, 3; Gachard, *La Bibliothèque Nationale à Paris,* II, 206. The last assertion, of course, was true. On July 24 a royal proclamation was issued at Alva's instance, forbidding French subjects to go into the Low Countries "pour négotiation ou autrement."—Poulet, I, 364; Gachard, *op. cit.,* II, 27.

[4] "Hinc illae lachrymae et ille metus," wrote the provost to Granvella (Poulet, I, 405). It was the wish of the Emperor that the King of Spain would go in person and without an army to the Low Countries in order to pacify it by kindness and not by force (*Archives de la maison d'Orange-Nassau,* II, 505; Raumer, I, 173, December, 1566). But Philip II could not make up his mind to come in person to the Netherlands, although advised to do so by all. For years he continued to entertain the thought and continually put it off. See a letter of the Duchess of Parma to Duke Henry of Brunswick upon the coming of the duke of Alva, January 1567, .in *Archives de la maison d'Orange-Nassau,* III, 21 ff.

[5] On April 3, 1565, St Sulpice sent word to Charles IX that Philip II had sent Menendez to Florida "avec une bonne flotte et 600 hommes pour combattre *les Français et les passer au fil de l'épée.*"—*L'Ambassade de St. Sulpice,* 364. When Fourquevaux succeeded him the French government had not yet learned of the massacre. St. Sulpice's fragmentary information is to be found at pp. 400, 401, 404, 414. The abortive efforts of France to secure redress are spread at length in *Corresp. de Catherine de Médicis,* II, 209, 330, 337, 338, 341, 342, 360; and in Fourquevaux, I, Nos. 4-7, 9, 15, 21, 28, 43, 47, 55, 66. The editor's account in the

Alexander VI's bull had divided the western hemisphere between the Spanish and the Portuguese. Florida belonged to Spain. France had built Fort Caroline on Spanish territory. As peace existed in 1565, France argued that the massacre by Menendez was a violation of international law. To this Spain replied that Florida belonged to her by discovery and as all treaties between Spain and France were silent as to any change of ownership, there really had been no such change in law. Consequently the French settlers were intruders and heretics to boot. The answer was crushing, Fourquevaux was heavily handicapped, for he could not openly espouse the cause of Frenchmen who were heretics. Before news of the massacre reached France, Philip II, knowing the facts, inquired if the French expedition had been commanded or sanctioned by the French King. The only answer possible was a negative. An affirmative answer would have been tantamount to a declaration of war. "Then the incident is closed," was the Spanish reply. This was followed by a demand that Coligny, under whose sanction the expedition had sailed, should be punished.

France was likewise at odds with the Emperor. The reason for this is to be found in the strong attitude the empire had lately taken on the question of Metz.[1] Understanding of this question entails a glance backward. In 1564 the baron Bolwiller, a native

Introd., xv–xxi is admirable. In the *Correspondencia española*, II, 126–28, is to be found Philip II's letter to Chantonnay, February 28, 1566, in reply to the ambassador's letter of advice about Coligny's enterprise. The blood of French colonists who had been massacred in Florida cried out for vengeance, and from the hour of its knowledge the subject of reprisal was a matter of common talk in the Norman ports (*C. S. P. Dom.*, Add., XIII, 227). On September 24, 1566, Sir Amyas Paulet, the English ambassador informed his government that he had information that a squadron was about to sail for this purpose, although it was "late for so long a voyage" (*ibid.*, 31). On the whole history of this ill-fated colony see Gaillard, "La reprise de la Floride faite par le capit. Gourgues (1568)," *Notices et extr. des manuscr. de la Biblioth. Nat.*, IV, and VII (1799); Gourgues, *La reprise de la Floride*, publiée avec les variantes, sur les MSS de la Bibl. Nat. par Ph. Tamizey de Larroque, 1867; Gafferel, *Histoire de la Floride française*, 1875; Parkman, *The French in North America*. The newest literature upon the subject is Woodbury Lowery, "Jean Ribaut and Queen Elizabeth," *American Historical Review*, April, 1904, and the same author's *The Spanish Settlements within the Present Limits of the United States: Florida, 1562–74* (New York, 1905).

[1] De Thou, V, 37–40.

of upper Alsace, but at that time bailiff of the Emperor in the grand
bailiwick of Haguenau, revived the plan he had conceived in 1558,
of recovering Metz by a surprise.[1] Bolwiller represented that no
time was to be lost if France was to be prevented from fixing her
hold upon the Three Bishoprics forever. Philip II favored the
enterprise and offered 20,000 sous cash, and the assignment of
8,000 écus annual revenue of the territory, "pour celluy ou ceulx
qui'lz luy rendroyent la ville du dict Metz."[2] For with Metz in
the hands of the Hapsburgs once more, the chain of provinces
connecting the Netherlands with Spain through mid-Europe would
have been practically complete, lying as Metz, Toul, and Verdun
did, between Franche-Comté and Luxembourg.[3] This was at
the time when Condé was recreant to his people and was dallying
with the widow of the marshal St. André, and the idea was conceived and abandoned of buying the prince over and bribing him
to betray Metz to Spain.[4] Spain, however, in order to avoid a
rupture with France wished to conceal her own participation in
the plot to recover Metz, and urged the Emperor Maximilian to
undertake the venture.[5] The plot was to tempt Metz to revolt

[1] Papiers d'état du cardinal de Granvelle, VII, 381, note. In 1558 Bolwiller
made an inroad into France (Bulletin des comités historiques, 1850, p. 774; a summary
of a letter concerning this episode to be found in the archives of Basel). On
Bolwiller see Papiers d'état du cardinal de Granvelle, IX, 36, note. The new plan
was occasioned by the issue of letters-patent of Charles IX on October 9, 1564, forbidding sale or alienation of any regalian rights of the Three Bishoprics without his
consent (text in Papiers d'état du cardinal de Granvelle, VIII, 394).

[2] Bolwiller to Granvella, October 16, 1564, on the written authority of Philip
II (ibid., VIII, 429).

[3] "Je tiens que les François, par voye de faict, y (Toul) mectront la main,
comme ilz ont jà commencé, et le mesmes à Metz et Verdung."—Papiers d'état
du cardinal de Granvelle, VII, 465; Granvella to the Emperor, April 12, 1564.

[4] Ibid., VIII, 504-6.

[5] Ibid., IX, 44. Granvella to Perez, February 26, 1565; p. 111, Philip II to
Chantonnay, then stationed at Vienna, April 2, 1565. Bolwiller intrusted the
action to Egelolf, seigneur de Ribeauspierre (the German form is Rapolstein),
a noble of Upper Alsace. His mother was a Fürstenburg. (See ibid., IX, 24,
note.) Strange vicissitude, that a descendant of that house in the next century
should have been Louis XIV's right-hand agent in his seizures on the Rhine through
the Chambers of Réunion, playing an identically opposite part from that of his
ancestors.

against France by offering to convert it into a free imperial city, it being expected that the Lutherans in the city would support the movement.[1] The alertness of the French government, however, foiled the project's being undertaken in April. In August Bolwiller renewed his plan, alleging to Chantonnay that the people of Metz were ready to provide 20,000 écus, and that there were arms in plenty stored in secret. He urged prompt action now for the French government had begun the erection of a citadel in the city.[2]

By this time Philip II was so anxious to see France despoiled of Metz and so impatient at Maximilian's delay, that it was even considered advisable by some to take advantage of the check given the Turks at Malta and have the Emperor make peace with them in order to have his hands free in the Three Bishoprics.[3] As for himself, Philip II dared not make an overt move against France, lest in the event of war with Spain, Charles IX appeal to the Huguenots, with the result that Protestantism would profit by the diversion.[4]

But meanwhile things in Metz had got beyond control of either

[1] *Papiers d'état du cardinal de Granvelle*, IX, 71—Bolwiller to the cardinal March 20, 1565.

Metz was early famous for its interest in the Reformation. The laxness of the episcopal discipline in the first part of the sixteenth century contributed to the growth of this spirit, and finally led to a Catholic reaction. The city was more inclined, however, to Calvinism than to Lutheranism. Charles V prohibited the exercise of the Lutheran faith, but nevertheless, the Protestants of Metz made an alliance with the Smalkald League. Under the French domination the city passed definitely from Lutheranism to Calvinism. The French governor, Vieilleville, was a moderate in policy and granted the Huguenots a church in the interior of the town. During the first civil war the Protestants in Metz remained tranquil, but soon afterward Farel visited the city for the third time, and thereafter the city's religious activity was considerable. The cardinal of Lorraine suppressed Protestant preaching in the diocese and closed the church. When Charles IX visited Metz in 1564 the edifice was destroyed and Protestant worship was forbidden. After the death of the Marshal Vieilleville, the count de Retz was made governor. One of the motives of the support of the Huguenot cause by John Casimir, the prince palatine, was a promise made by the Huguenots that he would be given the governorship of Metz. On the subject as a whole see Thirion, *Etude sur l'histoire du protestantisme à Metz et dans le pays Messin*, Nancy, 1885; Le Coullon, *Journal (1537–87) d'après le manuscrit original*, publié pour la première fois et annoté par E. de Bouteiller, Paris, Dumoulin, 1881.

[2] *Papiers d'état du cardinal de Granvelle*, IX, 462, 463.

[3] Granvella to Perez, October 15, 1565; *ibid.*, IX, 594, 595.

[4] See Philip II's letter to Chantonnay, October 22, 1565; *ibid.*, IX 609 ff.

Spain or the empire. The Calvinists in both France and the Netherlands had been quick to see the advantage afforded, for the former by gaining possession of the territory could connect France and the Palatinate, thus aiding themselves and their coreligionists at one and the same time, since by so doing the land route of Spain through Central Europe, via Milan, Besançon, and Luxembourg, would be cut in half. Matters came to a head in May and June, 1565, in what is known as the "Cardinal's War." On May 5 the Emperor Maximilian had issued a decree affirming his suzerainty over Metz, Toul, and Verdun. The cardinal of Lorraine at once recognized the validity of this decree, which was equivalent to treason to France. Thereupon, in the name of Charles IX Salzedo an ex-Spaniard[1] and leader of the French party in Metz assumed the title of governor of Metz and appealed to the French King for support against the cardinal. The issue was really one between France and Spain. The Guises naturally supported the cardinal. The "war" which followed was not formidable, although the issue as stake was of great importance. But the cardinal soon discovered that discretion was the better part of valor and yielded to the King, more especially as neither Philip II nor Maximilian raised a hand for fear of betraying themselves, for the cardinal feared that if he resisted longer Charles IX would refuse to pardon his treasonable conduct. He was not unaware of the fact—he did not even deny it—that it was known that he had been in treasonable communication with Bolwiller and the archbishop of Trèves.[2]

If Charles IX and the queen mother had known the full extent of the cardinal of Lorraine's treasonable conduct at this time they

---

[1] He had served in Italy in 1555 and became the cardinal's bailiff and revenue-collector in the bishopric of Metz after the treaty of Cateau-Cambrésis (*Commentaire et lettres de Montluc*, I, 228).

[2] For an account of the "Cardinal's War" see De Thou, V, Book XXXVII, 37–40. There is another account in the *Mém. de Condé*, V, 27, supposed to have been written by Salzedo himself. In F. Fr. 3, 197, folio 92, there is an unpublished letter of Salzedo's (see Appendix IX), and another of the duke of Aumale upon this incident. Chantonnay comforted Philip for the disappointment over Metz by telling him, that while the restoration of the Three Bishoprics was indeed important, because of their bearing upon the situation in Flanders, the trouble had averted a

might not have been so lenient toward him. For he was guilty
not only of treasonable intercourse with the empire, but directly
with Spain also. The one supremely important result of this
petty war over Metz is that at this time the cardinal—and with
him the whole Guise house—began those secret negotiations with
Philip of Spain which culminated in the establishment of the Holy
League. Shortly after the end of his ignominious war around
Metz, burning with anger and shame, the cardinal sent a secret
agent to Franche Comté, who found Granvella at Beaudencourt
in July, 1565, to whom he recited the cardinal's grievances, saying
that owing to the death of his brother the duke of Guise and the
insolence of the marshal Montmorency, he had no hope in the
justice of Charles IX. The agent then went on to point out the
great danger threatening Catholic Europe by reason of what had
recently happened at Metz, and, speaking for the cardinal of Lorraine, expressed the wish that Philip II would enter into a league
with the house of Guise, the duke of Montpensier—Alva's convert
at Bayonne—and certain others for the protection of the Catholic
faith in France and the overthrow of the Châtillons, the prince of
Condé, "Madame de Vendôme," and other Huguenots. This
formidable overture was made under the seal of secrecy. The
cautious Granvella listened but refrained from committing his
master to the proposition.[1] Again, Philip II hesitated to implicate
himself so directly in French affairs, as the cardinal of Lorraine
urged, just as he had hesitated the year before with Montluc, and

marriage alliance between France and Austria which would have been more
calamitous (Letter to Philip II, October 30, 1565, in *Papiers d'état du cardinal
de Granvelle*, IX, 625).

Two years later we find the tricky cardinal of Lorraine still protesting his
innocence to Catherine and praying her not to be suspicious of him (Letter of
December 6, 1567, Fillon Collection, No. 316).

[1] Forneron, I, 346, on the basis of Alva's letter to Philip on May 19, 1566, and
the cardinal's own letter, written at the same time (both preserved in K. 1,505,
No. 99, and K. 1,509), assumes that the secret intercourse between Philip II and
the Guises began in the year 1566 and ascribes the immediate occasion of it to the
troubles in the Low Countries. He missed the inception of it by a year. Granvella's letter conclusively shows that it began in July, 1565. Every word of this
letter is of weight. It is to be found in *Papiers d'état du cardinal de Granvelle*, IX,
399–402.

while he waited events in the Low Countries went from bad to worse.

In August, 1566, a furious outburst of iconoclasm swept through the churches of Flanders.

Commencing at St. Omer, the contagion rapidly spread, and in a fortnight 400 churches were sacked in Flanders alone, while in Antwerp the cathedral was stripped of all its treasures. Images, relics, shrines, paintings, manuscripts, and books shared a common fate.[1]

The event stirred Philip to action. He determined to send the duke of Alva to Flanders to repress things with an iron hand.[2]

On November 18, 1566, the duke of Alva formally requested the French ambassador at Madrid to secure Charles IX's permission for a Spanish army to cross France.

The remedy has become little by little so difficult [said the duke] that deeds not words and remonstrances, are now necessary. Having exhausted all good and gracious means to reduce things in the Low Countries, the King is constrained, to his great regret, to have recourse to force. Public assemblies, preaching, the bearing of arms, and violence prevail in the land and the King's ministers amount to nothing.

The duke then outlined the plan. Ten thousand new Spanish recruits under three ensigns were to be sent to Luxembourg, Naples, Sardinia, and Sicily to take the places of as many veteran troops there, for the King was unwilling to use Italian infantry. A thousand heavy-armed footmen and three or four hundred mounted arquebusiers, all Spanish, were to be drawn from Milan, the most loyal of Spain's Italian dependencies. An indefinite number of reiters and other mercenaries could be had for the asking. These

---

[1] Johnson, *Europe in the Sixteenth Century*, 328. For interesting details by an eye-witness, see Bourgon, *Life and Times of Sir Thomas Gresham*, II, 121 ff.

[2] Poulet, I, 509; Gachard, *Don Carlos et Philippe II*, 354; *La Bibliothèque Nationale à Paris*, II, 213. The disastrous news reached the King on September 5. For ten days he was ill with a high fever in consequence. Fourquevaux, writing from Segovia on September 11, to Charles IX, gives some details of Philip's illness and how he was treated by the physicians and then adds: "Les Espagnols sont bien marriez d'entendre que les Lutheriens dud. pais (Flanders) ont commencé s'empoigner aux eglises et reliques, et à fere marier les prebtres et nonnains, avec infiniz autres maulx qu'ilz font, qui est le semblable commencement des doleurs qui advindrent en votre Royaume du temps des troubles."—*Dépêches de M. Fourquevaux*, I, 124, 125.

troops would proceed to the Netherlands through Savoy by way of Val d'Aoste or Mt. Cenis, Montmélian, Chambéry, and La Bresse, into Franche Comté and Lorraine, unless—and this was the crux of Alva's interview with Fourquevaux—the winter season made it impossible to traverse the mountain passes, in which case His Catholic Majesty desired leave of France to take them by sea to Marseilles or Toulon and thence to march them northward up the Rhône to La Bresse and so reach Franche Comté.

No one knew better than Alva the formidable nature of this proposition to France and he used all his artifice to conceal its danger, dwelling on the mutual connection between the Huguenot and the Flemish movement and the benefit that France would derive from the crushing of the rebellion in the Low Countries. Fourquevaux in reply declared that the Huguenots would fly to arms again, if a Spanish army should enter France, to which the duke rejoined that the presence of a Spanish army would so overawe them that they would not dare to do so. The ambassador then inquired whether the Emperor could support Philip, seeing that he was engaged in a war with the Turks[1] and was incapable of raising funds in his behalf. Alva told him that the German princes would perceive that the Flemings were merely rebels and that "no prince or soldier in Germany, even were he a Lutheran, would refuse to take the pay of Spain."[2] But Fourquevaux refused to be convinced by Alva's smooth words. He had information that Spain was borrowing ships from Malta, Genoa, and the papacy and Savoy and warned Charles IX to strengthen the garrisons in Languedoc and Provence.[3]

[1] The Austrian lands were invaded by the Turks in the autumn of 1566 (*Négociations dans le Levant*, II, 721; Languet, *Epist. secr.*, I, 15).

[2] It was a pose of Philip's that the expedition was purely political; cf. Gachard, *Les bibliothèques de Madrid et de l'Escurial*, 94 ff., based on the correspondence of the archbishop of Rossano.

[3] Dispatch to Charles IX, December 9, 1566 (Fourquevaux, I, 147–52). He waited in great anxiety for instructions from Paris, daily growing more suspicious because the Spanish King said not a word to him on the subject, although he sent for him in audience on January 14, 1567 (*ibid.*, 167–72; dispatches of Jan. 5 and 18, 1567). The tremendous financial operations of the Spanish government (consult Gachard, *Don Carlos et Philippe II*, II, 369, 370) filled him with

This information threw the court of France into great excitement. Catherine de Medici declared that the heretics would take up arms immediately, under such circumstances.[1] The King wrote to Fourquevaux on December 24 not to spare any efforts to penetrate the designs of Spain.[2] Sixteen thousand troops were sent into the Lyonnais at once.[3] The marshal Vieilleville returned to Metz.[4] The government began the erection of a great citadel in Verdun and to fortify the frontier against Luxembourg.[5] D'Andelot was sent to Switzerland to make new enrolments.[6] An agent was sent into Normandy with instructions to pass along the coast and take the names of master mariners and sailors.[7] The queen of Navarre began to mobilize forces in Béarn.[8] All this time the duke of Alva kept endeavoring to quiet French alarm by reiterating that he would use all means in his power to avoid troubling France and that the army destined for Flanders, now increased by 1,500 light horse composed of Spaniards, Italians, and Albanians, would go by the valley of the Rhône only as a last recourse.[9]

Finally, in the middle of February, the duke of Alva's preparations were made. Don Juan de Acuna, who had been sent to

alarm, and he made an unsuccessful effort to bribe the secretary of one of Philip II's ministers. He gathered that the Spanish forces would likely sail for Barcelona and disembark at Nice or Genoa (*ibid.*, 176, 177, February 13, 1567).

[1] Forneron, I, 347, on authority of Alva's dispatch in K. 1,507, No. 2; cf. *Nég. Tosc.*, III, 527.

[2] Gachard, *La Bibliothèque Nationale à Paris*, II, 228. The dispatch was delayed on account of the illness of the courier and the heavy snows he encountered in the Pyrenees, and did not reach the ambassador until January 15, 1567 (Fourquevaux, I, 168). The correspondence of Bernardo d'Aspremont, viscount of Orthez, governor of Bayonne—unfortunately much scattered in the volumes of the Bibliothèque Nationale—shows the standing danger the southern provinces of France were in from Spanish invasion (*Commentaires et lettres de Montluc*, III, 400, note).

[3] Poulet, II, 183.   [4] D'Aubigné, II, 229, note.   [5] Poulet, II, 495.

[6] D'Aubigné, II, 228; Zurlauben, *Hist. milit. des Suisses*, IV, 335.

[7] We learn this from a letter of George Paulet. See Appendix X.

[8] Poulet, II, 183; *Dépêches de M. Fourquevaux*, I, 173.

[9] *Dépêches de M. Fourquevaux*, I, 174, February 4, 1567. Philip II took these military preparations of the French with remarkable equanimity—even Charles

Savoy to make arrangements with the duke for the transit of the
Spanish army, returned, after having made a satisfactory settlement. The army was to go through Savoy, via the Mt. Cenis
and Chambéry, cross the Rhône at Yenne, and so proceed to Besançon in Franche Comté, where it was to be joined by German con-
tingents. This averted the danger threatening Languedoc and
Dauphiné, but threw it upon French Burgundy and Champagne.[1]
It was a roundabout route for the Spanish troops in the Milanais,
but it was impossible to send them directly through Switzerland
by way of the Grisons, Constance, Basel, and Strasburg without
inflaming these localities; above all, Geneva would thereby have
been menaced, and any movement imperiling that city would have
fired the entire Calvinist world.[2]

In the face of common peril Bern, Freiburg, and Valais concluded a defensive league on February 20, while Basel and Zurich
took up arms with French approval. Fear of a joint attack of
Spain and Savoy upon Geneva prevailed throughout Switzerland,
which was divided into two camps, the five cantons of the center
favoring designs upon Geneva and the Vaud. Spain aimed

IX's positive refusal to allow the Spanish army to traverse France (March 24,
1567). He seemed to be sincerely anxious to avoid friction with France (see his
letter to Granvella, February 17, 1567, in Poulet, II, 255, 256). The danger in the
Low Countries was too great to allow any outside controversy. The clandestine
operation of Protestant preachers in Spain itself and the smuggling of heretical
books into the land, concealed in casks of wine, disquieted him more than France did
at this season. (For information on this head see Poulet, II, 126, 142, 199; Nég.
Tosc., III, 506; Weiss, Spanish Protestants in the Sixteenth Century.)

[1] Fourquevaux (February 15, 1567), I, 180, 181. Granvella apparently,
immediately after learning of the image breaking, and anticipating that either the
King himself or the duke of Alva, would have to go to Brussels, sent a remarkable
memoir to Philip II, in which he discusses all the various routes by which he might
go, and the advantages and disadvantages of each of them. The physical difficulties
of governing the Low Countries from Madrid are very evident (see Poulet, I,
469–80).

[2] The Pope's nuncio had pointed out to Philip II what a splendid achievement
the overcoming of Geneva would be for Christendom. The scheme was an old
one. See a letter of Pius IV to Francis II, June 14, 1560, in Raynaldus, XXXIV,
64, col. 2. The King, after some weeks of consideration, declared that he could
not think of it; that even the duke of Savoy was against the project. (See Gachard,
Corresp. de Philippe II, II, 552, and his Les bibliothèques de Madrid et de l'Escurial,

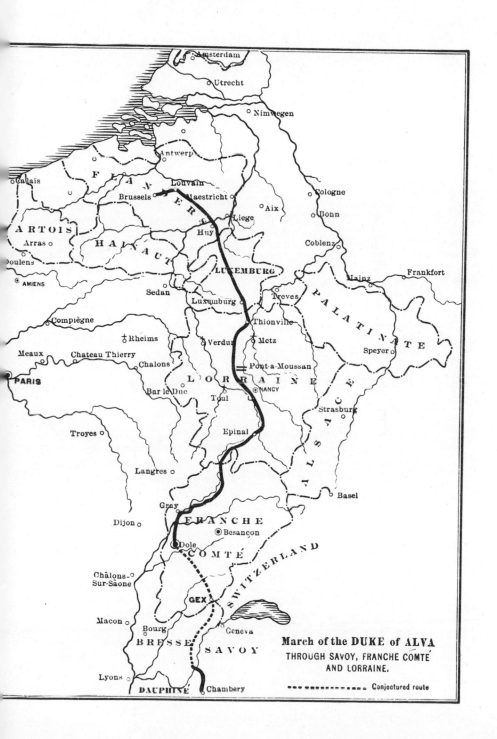

March of the DUKE of ALVA
THROUGH SAVOY, FRANCHE COMTÉ
AND LORRAINE.

---·-·-·-·---- Conjectured route

to profit by the impression produced by the passage of her troops close to the Swiss frontier to force certain military advantages and dispossess France from the exceptional situation she had lately secured in the Alps. The western cantons were offered cheap salt from Franche Comté, and those of the center grain from the Milanais. The duke of Lorraine also offered salt at a low price from his duchy. As a result Bern found herself deserted by western Switzerland and apparently single-handed about to be called upon to protect Geneva from Spanish attack. Perhaps if Spain had been certain of the support of Savoy at this juncture, this might have happened, but the duke of Savoy was content to profit by the fear of the Bernois to compel them to restore the three bailiwicks which they had formerly agreed to do in the treaty of Lausanne, October 30, 1564, but had delayed to fulfil. Charles IX himself advised Bern to yield in this par-ticular and in August the settlement with the duke of Savoy was made.[1]

All that Philip now requested of France was leave for French subjects to provide the army with supplies in its course. Again Fourquevaux urged his sovereign to be cautious; the fact that France was just recovering from a year of famine and could ill spare sustenance for others was not so important as the necessity of avoiding every occasion of civil war.[2]

On May 10, 1567, the duke of Alva sailed from Cartagena and arrived at Genoa on May 27. St. Ambroise at the foot of the Alps was the point where his munitions and provisions were concentrated. Here on June 2 the duke had a grand review of his troops. There

100.) On the political ambition of the duke of Savoy see *Rel. vén.*, I, 453. He had made a treaty with Bern in 1565 (Collection Godefroy, XCIV, fol. 21). There are three excellent German monographs on Switzerland in the sixteenth and seven-teenth centuries: Planta, *Die Geschichte von Graubunden in ihren Hauptzügen*, Bern, 1892; *idem, Chronik der Familie von Planta*, Zurich, 1892; Salis-Soglio, *Die Familie von Salis*, Lincau-im-B., 1891. For a review of the last two see *English Historical Review*, VIII, 588.

[1] See *Revue d'histoire diplomatique*, XIV (1900), 45–47.

[2] "Mais le faisant, c'estoit remectre le feu et le glaive dans la France plus et plus cruel qui'lz n'y ont esté."—*Dépêches de M. Fourquevaux* (March 15, 1567), I, 189.

were 19 ensigns (3,230 men), from Naples, under the command
of Alonzo de Uloa; 10 ensigns from Sicily (1,620 men) under
command of Julian Romero; 10 ensigns of Lombard troops (2,200
men) under command of Don Sancho de Londono; 10 Sardinian
ensigns with four companies of recruits in addition (1,728 men)
under command of Don Gonzalo de Bracamonte, making a total
of 49 ensigns of Spanish infantry (8,778 men).   The duke's cavalry
was composed of five companies of Spanish light horse and three
Italian and two Albanian companies and two companies of Spanish
arquebusiers on horseback, in all 1,200 horses.[1]   On the march
a company of 15 musketeers was placed between each ensign.
This was the first instance in modern warfare when muskets were
used in the field.   Hitherto this weapon had been so enormously
heavy that it was used in siege work only, balanced upon a triangle
of wood or iron.[2]

[1] I have given the figures of Mendoza, which probably is the strength of the
forces when they arrived.   The official roster is in the *Correspondencia*, No. CXXII.

[2] "The front of every company by a new invention was flanked with fifteen
supernumeraries, armed with musketoones, and rests wherein they laid the barrow
that could not be managed by the hands.   For before his time, such huge muskets
as unmanageable were drawn upon carriages and only used at sieges, from whence
being transmitted into the field, and those that carry them mixed with the lesser
musketeers, they have been found extraordinarily serviceable in battle."—Stapyl-
ton's transl. of Strada, Book VI, 31.

Brantôme's statement is more graphic: "Il fut luy le premier qui leur donna
en main les gros mousquetz, et que l'on veid les premiers en guerre et parmy les
compagnies; et n'en avions point veu encores parmy leurs bandes, lors que nous
allasmes pour le secours de Malte; dont despuis nous en avons pris l'usage parmy
nos bandes, mais avec de grandes difficultéz à y accoustumer nos soldats comme
j'en parle au livre des couronnelz.   Et ces mousquetz estonnzarent fort les Flamans,
quand ilz les sentirent sonner à leurs oreilles; car ilz n'en avoient veu non plus que
nous: et ceux qui les portoient les nommoit-on Mousquetaires; très bien appoinctéz
et respectéz, jusques à avoir de grands et forts gojatz qui les leur portoient, et
avoient quatre ducats de paye; et ne leur portoient qu'en cheminant par pays:
mais quand ce venoit en une faction, ou marchans en bataille, ou entrans en garde
ou en quelque ville, les prenoient.   Et eussiez dict que c'estoient des princes, tant ils
estoient rogues et marchoient arrogamment et de belle grace: et lors de quelque
combat ou escarmouche, vous eussiez ouy crier ces mots par grand respect: *Salgan,
salgan los mosqueteros! Ajuera, ajuera, adelante los mosqueteros!*   Soudain on leur
faisoit place; et estoient respectéz, voire plus que capitaines pour lors, à cause de
la nouveauté, ainsy que toute nouveauté plaist."—Brantôme, *Vies des Grands
Capitaines:*   "Le Grand Duc d'Albe."

The route lay via Alessandria de la Paille, St. Ambroise, Aosta, Turin, the Mont Cenis, St. Jean de Maurienne, and the valley of the Arve through Savoy. In spite of his small array it was necessary to divide the army into three parts, the advance guard, the "battle," and the rear guard. The "battle" each day occupied the place abandoned by the advance guard and was itself in turn replaced by the rear guard, the three divisions of the army marching one day apart. The duke of Alva commanded the advance guard, his son Don Ferdinand Alvarez de Toledo the "battle;" while the rear guard was under the command of the Italian, Ciappin-Vitelli, Marquis of Cetona formally in the service of the Grand Duke of Tuscany. The army thus divided occupied fourteen days in traversing Savoy. It was a long and toilsome journey through a wild and mountainous country, where the difficulties of the march were increased by constant dread of famine. In many places the country was completely sterile. In Burgundy the march was easier and twelve days brought the army via Dôle and Gray to Fonteney near Toul, whence twelve days more brought Alva by Thionville to Luxembourg (July 29), where he was joined by new forces.[1]

In spite of the length of the march and the hardships of it, the duke retained his traditional iron discipline and the soldiers were not allowed to forage upon the country or to break ranks.[2]

[1] Mendoza, *Comentarios*, II, chaps. i–iii. There is a French translation of this work by Loumier (Soc. de l'histoire de Belge), 2 vols., 1860.

[2] "The duke arrived in the Low Countries offending none in his passage nor being himself offended by any one, though the French appeared in arms upon the marches of Burgundy and Colonel Tavannes by command from the French king with 4,000 foot and some troops were defence of course of the borders, 'costed' the Spanish army. Indeed I do not think that ever army marched so far and kept stricter rules of discipline, so that from Italy even to the Low Countires, not only no towns but not any cottage was forced or injured."—Strada, VI, 31.

The only instance of plundering seems to have been in the case of the property of the prince of Orange in Burgundy (*C. S P. For.*, 1562, August 7, 1567). This discipline is all the more remarkable, considering the fact that there were fifteen hundred women with the army. "Lon a sceu le passaige du duc d'Albe et de sa trouppe; quon dict estre de six mille espaignolz et quinze cens femmes."—Guyon to M. de Gordes, July 11, 1567. Cited by the duc d'Aumale, *Histoire des princes de Condé*, I, Appendix XVI.

On August 12, 1567, the duke of Alva entered Brussels. General terror prevailed in the Low Countries upon his arrival. The Prince of Orange left the land. Count Egmont, naïvely declaring that he had done nothing wrong, remained; his friend Hoorne imitated his example. Alva at once sent away all the Flemish soldiers and quartered the city with the new troops. In order to facilitate his policy the duke created a special tribunal, *not* composed of lawyers "because they would not condemn without proofs." This was the famous Council of Troubles which the people called the "Council of Blood." The members of it held no commissions from the King, but were the simple agents of the duke of Alva. The most celebrated of them was a certain Vargas, a criminal himself, against whom action had been suspended in return for his infamous services.

If the policy of the Spanish government in Flanders took a new and different form with the coming of Alva, the revolution there was no less changed. The cardinal Granvella some months before this time had written to Philip II: "It is a general rule, in matters of state, that popular enterprises, if they do not terminate in the first outburst, generally vanish in smoke if the remedy for them be applied before they have time to follow up the movement."[1] He added that contemporary history afforded some striking examples of the truth of this observation. But the provinces he had lately governed were not of this category. For it is clear that a change had taken place in the nature of the Flemish revolt in the years 1565-67. The revolution by this time had passed through the earlier stages of defiance and rebellion and developed an organization with a definite, set purpose before it. The formation of the Gueux was the clearest manifestation of this change. In its inception this famous group was an aristocratic body, composed solely of nobles, and the Spanish government had little fear then of its becoming a popular association.[2] Granvella saw the simi-

[1] Poulet, II, 183, December 25, 1566.

[2] Morillon to Granvella, April 7, 1566: "Pas ce boult veult l'on gaigner le magistrat des villes et le peuple: que ne sera si facille comme l'on pense."—Poulet, I, 203. The following is explicit: "Et dict encores plus que, s'il se fust joinct à la première lighe des seigneurs, la religion fust bien avant venue, car de là, dict-il,

larity of the Gueux to the Huguenot association formed at Orleans in 1562, but he did not anticipate the popular nature it was soon to develop.[1]

He was soon disillusioned. What was believed by the Spanish government to be a somewhat close political and aristocratic combination of nobles before long became a popular confederation of congregations having a religious propaganda, as well as a political purpose.[2] Despite this change, however, Philip's minister did not yet believe the Gueux to be formidable. As Alva had declared at Bayonne that all that was necessary to destroy the Huguenot party in France was to kill the "big fish," so he now believed that if the leaders of the Gueux were cut off, their movement would die

'tanquam ex fonte emanasse has undas,' et que le Roy le doibt entendri ainse et y pourveoir avant toutte euvre, puisque de celle là est née la seconde de la religion."— Poulet, II, 75. Cf. 118: "la première lighe et la secunde engendrée d'icelle."— Granvella to Viglius, November 23, 1566. As late as May 9, 1567, it is called "la gentille ligue" (Poulet, II, 434). Granvella, in a letter to Philip in 1563, attributed the formation of the association to Count Hoorne (*Papiers d'état du cardinal de Granvelle*, VIII, 12). Noircarmes, who was better informed, makes Brederode the moving spirit of it (Poulet, II, 613, 614).

The Gueux even had a branch organization, though one historically different in origin, in Franche Comté, in the Confrérie de Ste. Barbe. The seigneurs of the house of Rye enjoyed high civil and ecclesiastical station in both Burgundies in the fifteenth and sixteenth centuries. Marc and Claude François of Rye, father and son, were rivals and political enemies of the Perrenots—the family of Granvella and Chantonnay—and regarded them as upstarts. The Confrérie de Ste. Barbe was organized by them in Franche Comté on lines similar to the Gueux and had dealings with the latter—the members even wearing their emblem. Cardinal Granvella accused the seigneurs of Rye of aiming to establish Protestantism, in Franche Comté from Flanders. This probably was true but in a less degree. Protestant agitation was a means to an end, not an end in itself, it seems to me. If otherwise, such a *catholic* title for the association is very singular. On the Confrérie de Ste. Barbe consult Poulet, I, 29; II, 44, 141. I am somewhat inclined to think that Tavanne's Confraternity of the Holy Spirit in ducal Burgundy may not impossibly have been influenced by the Confrérie de Ste. Barbe in the adjoining county of Burgundy, for Tavannes had a long political conflict with the Parlement of Dôle in Franche-Comté (see Collection Godefroy, CCLVII, Nos. 22, 23), and was familiar with things there.

[1] Poulet, I, 223.

[2] *Ibid.*, II, 269. This revised form of the Gueux in which Calvinism is interjected is often alluded to as the "second league" in the letters which pass between Granvella and the provost Morillon, e. g., *ibid.*, 280, 437, 600.

too.[1] But Alva soon discovered that the Gueux were hardly ever weakened by the detachment of certain of the nobles either by bribery or intimidation.[2] By the time of his arrival, under Brederode's able leadership, the Calvinists of the Flemish provinces had worked out a scheme of union in which every congregation was at once a parish, a rating precinct, a military hundred, and a political unit. Antwerp, whose population was so large and so cosmopolitan that police scrutiny could be easily evaded, and from which it was easy to make one's escape, was the capital of the association, as Orleans first, and later La Rochelle, was for the Huguenots.[3]

The Flemish government was soon alive to the necessity of breaking the power of this confederation.[4] Membership in the confederation, if proved, was heavily punished. The retirement of the prince of Orange from the land was believed by the government to be due to a prudent effort to avoid being so compromised. It was certainly true of Brederode. But Egmont and Hoorne remained, declaring they had done nothing, and renewed their oath of allegiance to the King.[5] Nevertheless Granvella sarcastically quoted Lycurgus that neutrals were more odious than enemies. "After the towns have been cleared out," wrote the provost Morillon, "it will be time to attack the garden in order to destroy the weeds and roots there," and Spain's agent at Amsterdam at the same time wrote: "God may pardon those who are the cause of *one* and the *other* league; but I assure you, unless I am much mistaken, that those who have made others to dance, have some other purpose than we know. Time will discover it."[6]

This somewhat long dissertation upon the nature and development of the confederation formed by Philip's II revolted subjects

[1] Poulet, II, 42.   [2] For some examples see *ibid.*, 183.

[3] This organization seems to have been perfected by February, 1567. Poulet, II, 244, has a brief note on this matter. For an extended article see *Bulletin historique et littéraire de la société de l'hist. du protestantisme Français*, March, 1879. Cf. Gachard, *Corresp. de Guill. le Taciturne*, II, cx, cxi, and notes. Marnix was treasurer-general of the confederation (Poulet, II, 262, n. 1).

[4] Poulet, II, 335, 336, 396. "Sine qua factum nihil," wrote the provost, whose conception of government was Draconian in simplicity, to his confidential friend (*ibid.*, 353).

[5] *Ibid.*, 469 and 508.   [6] *Ibid.*, 396, 438.

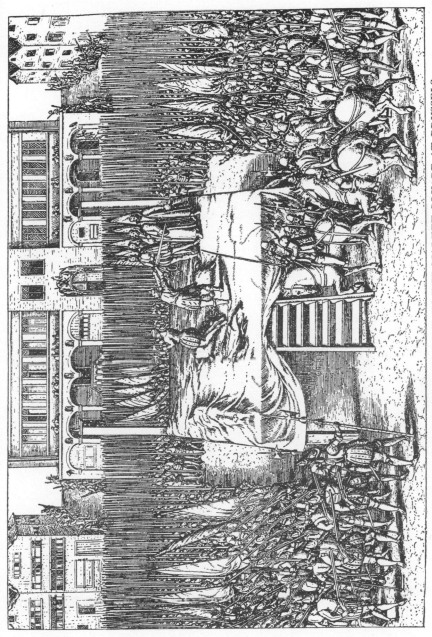

EXECUTION OF EGMONT AND HOORNE IN THE MARKET SQUARE AT BRUSSELS

Original copper plate by Franz Hogenberg.

in Flanders is not a digression beside the mark. The number of Huguenots to be found in the Low Countries in 1566–67, intriguing with their coreligionists against Spain was very great. The duke of Bouillon and the prince of Porcien were the most prominent of these.[1] In the aggregate the number was so great and their participation so serious a matter for the government, that the maintenance of the frontier against the French was urged upon Alva as the first necessity, immediately after his arrival at Brussels.[2] France for her own part began to erect a citadel at Verdun and to strengthen the Picard frontier, whose towns received new troops in June, and when word came that there were German troops in Luxembourg awaiting Alva's arrival, D'Andelot was sent to the frontier of Champagne with 6,000 Swiss which the government had levied.[3] This action ruffled Philip II's temper, for to him it was flaunting his failure to break the alliance of the Swiss with France in his very face. His ambassador in France protested energetically and charged the queen with duplicity.[4] At Madrid the nuncio inquired with curiosity of Fourquevaux, in what spirit Philip II—who had had an audience with the ambassador the day before—received the news of France's activities in Switzerland. "I told him," wrote the ambassador to Charles IX, "that it was the usage and custom of great kings and princes whenever they saw their neighbors arming, to assure themselves also of their realms

[1] See Gachard, *Corresp. de Philippe II*, 461, 471, 473; Poulet, I, 461, 521; II, 102, 106, 139, 143, 187, 394, 440, 451, 659, 675.

[2] Morillon to Granvella, August 31, 1567, in Poulet, II, 605: "La première chose que l'on doibt faire sera de munir et asseurer les frontières et renvoier chascun à son gouvernement, d'aultant que les François semblent voulloir esmouvoir, du moingz les Hugonaux." The cardinal had advised the duke of Alva to do this in the May preceding, when he was at Genoa on his way northward (Poulet, II, 448, 454).

Montluc's repeated warnings to Philip II, in the course of their secret correspondence, of the succor French Calvinists were giving to his Flemish rebels (K. 1,506, Nos. 46–48) led the King to enlarge the system of espionage which he maintained in France. The movements of the admiral, the prince of Condé, and other leaders, were carefully reported (*Commentaires et lettres de Montluc*, V, 75, note). On the whole practice see Forneron, I, chap. xi.

[3] Mundt to Cecil from Strasburg, July 8, 1567 (*C. S. P. For.*, No. 1, 418).

[4] *Correspondance de Catherine de Médicis*, III, Introd., v.

and states."[1]   Calais was a double source of anxiety, first because
Spain, in pursuance of Alva's recommendation, had not been content with fortifying Gravelines, but had actually built a fort of
earth only five paces from the turnpike which marked the French
limit; secondly, because at this embarrassing time Elizabeth of
England had conceived the thought of reviving the English claim
to Calais.[2]   With the purpose of fathoming her son-in-law's designs
Catherine sent the younger L'Aubespine to Madrid.[3]   War with
Spain was already on the lips of some in France.[4]

In spite of the wisdom of these military precautions on the part
of the French crown, the Huguenots grew alarmed lest there was
a movement on foot to repress the edict.[5]   There was designed
intention in the unadmirable conduct of the prince of Condé, and
perhaps some in that of Coligny too.   The prince craved chief
command of the army, and a war with Spain was in a direct line
with his aspirations.   He had been well treated since the peace
of Amboise, having been given the government of Picardy and the

---

[1] Fourquevaux (July 17, 1567), I, 237. St. Sulpice had held similar language
in 1564: "Le meilleur moyen pour le prince d'avoir la paix est d'être toujours en
état de repousser ses voisins."—L'Ambassade de. St. Sulpice, 269.

[2] C. S. P. For., No. 1,402, July 6, 1567. Sir Henry Norris writes to Cecil on
March 25, 1567: "A better time than this could not be found to demand Calais,
they being in such distrust of their own force, wherefore it might be understood that
some preparation of arms was making in England."—Ibid., No. 1,048. A year
earlier than this Cecil had been advised to make common cause with the Emperor,
the one to recover the Three Bishoprics, the other Calais (ibid., No. 326, April 29,
1566; cf. ibid., Ven., 394, July 3, 1567). There is a brief account of the negotiations
in Bulletins de la Comm. royale d'histoire, séries IV, Vol. V, 386 ff. Cf. C. S. P.
For. (1587), Nos. 1039, 1044, 1046, 1083.

[3] Correspondance de Catherine de Médicis, III, Introd., iii; C. S. P. Ven., Nos.
389, May 16, 1567.

[4] Correspondance de Catherine de Médicis, III, Introd., iv.

[5] "The prince of Condé wrote to the queen mother against the king's revoking
the edict of pacification, who assured him on the faith of a princess that as long as
she might prevail, she should never break it, and if he came to court, he would be
as welcome as his heart could devise, and as for the Swiss they were to defend the
frontiers in case the Spanish forces should attempt to surprise any peace."—Norris
to Queen Elizabeth, August 29, 1567, C. S. P. For., No. 1,644. Catherine de
Medici ordered the dispersal of the Huguenot bands on the Picard border in
1567 (R. Q. H., January, 1899, p. 21).

county of Rotrou, which was erected into a duchy under the name of Enghien-le-François. But his appetite for power was insatiable. In July, after angry speech with the King, Condé had retired from court, and was followed by the admiral, who gave out that that he had discovered "some practice that wholly tended to his confusion."[1]

It was small politics. In this time of external danger from the furtive designs of Philip II and the blustering enmity of England, the honorable course of every subject of France was to stand by the King and the nation. The Huguenot leaders compromised the cause at large by indulging their personal vanity, their petty spite, their pique at such an hour. Friction there was, disagreement there was over the interpretation and the working of certain parts of the edict of Amboise. The Catholics, for example, complained that the intention of the edict was evaded by the Huguenots, asserting that in cases where the right of preaching was permitted to all barons and high justiciars only for themselves and their tenants, and for others of lower degree for their household only, congregational worship was held under cover thereof.[2]

The bigotry of Paris and its vicinity, though, was the worst source of disaffection. In the city district captains were chosen

---

[1] The words are from a letter of Sir Henry Norris to the earl of Leicester in *C. S. P. For.*, No. 1,537, July 21, 1567, and sound like a paraphrase of the admiral's language. The implication is that Coligny's withdrawal had some connection with the purported stealing of Alava's cipher in the May before. See *C. S. P. For.*, No. 1,230, May 24, 1567. But according to Fourquevaux, I, 227, the Spanish ambassador accused Catherine de Medici of the stealing, *not* Coligny. If this be true, then Coligny must have wanted to find a pretext for leaving the court without arousing the suspicion or animosity of the King, as might have been the case if he had done so openly out of sympathy for the prince of Condé. Claude Haton, I, 406, says that Coligny was piqued because Strozzi was given the command of the new forces instead of himself. The prince of Condé retired to Valéry, Coligny to Châtillon. D'Andelot soon afterward followed suit, resigning his post as colonel-general of infantry on the ground that the marshal Cossé refused to obey his orders, and retired to Tanlay near Tonnerre. The fine château is still standing.

Thenceforward it was of interest to the prince to stir up doubt and distrust among the Huguenots by misrepresenting the true reasons for the crown's military preparation (*Correspondance de Catherine de Médicis*, III, Introd., vi; *C. S. P. For.*, anno 1567, p. 305).

[2] *C. S. P. For.*, No. 1,629, August 23, 1567.

by the populace to watch against Protestant activity—the nucleus of the famous Sixteen (*Seize*) of Paris in 1589-94. It would have been the height of political inexpediency, under such circumstances, to have tried to enforce the letter of the edict in the Ile-de-France. The July amendment of the edict of Amboise prohibiting exercise of Protestant worship throughout the Ile-de-France except in such places as should be licensed by the King, and the further one prohibiting Protestants from filling public offices in the cities,[1] I believe was framed for the purpose of avoiding conflict and not with any reactionary purpose. It is certainly of significance that the liberal chancellor L'Hôpital favored them.[2] Patience and experience would have worked out the solution of such difficulties as these. It was criminal in the prince of Condé to fan the ashes of the late civil war into flame once more. For in this tense state the prince deliberately exaggerated and misrepresented things for his own purpose and a spark from Flanders—Alva's arrest of the counts Egmont and Hoorne on September 9—kindled France into flame again.

The arrival of the news in France unfortunately coincided with the session of two synods of the Huguenots, one at Châtillon-sur-Loing, the other at Valéry.[3] Dismay prevailed in them. The preachers cried out that the arrest of Egmont and Hoorne[4] was the proof of a secret alliance between Spain and France for the overthrow of Calvinism. The truth of Bayonne was out at last! Coligny's iron will might still have kept them in order, however, if in the midst of this excitement word had not also come that 6,000 Swiss whom Charles IX had enrolled to cover the French frontier against the duke of Alva had entered France. The double news was too much for the excited minds of the Huguenots. The admiral and the prince who had failed to perceive the true policy of France in Switzerland, in desperation turned to the constable for

[1] Claude Haton, I, 405.

[2] *C. S. P. Ven.*, July 12, 1567.

[3] La Popelinière, XI, 36, 37.

[4] See Rosseeuw-Saint-Hilaire, "Le duc d'Albe en Flandre. Procès des comtes d'Egmont et de Hornes (1567-1568)," *Séances et travaux de l'Acad. des sc. moral et polit.*, 4e sér., XVI (LXVIe de la collect.), 1863, p. 480.

a word of truth and comfort. But the old Montmorency, who
desired to have his son, the marshal Montmorency, succeed him
in the office of constable[1] (which the prince of Condé coveted
for himself), roughly rejoined: "The Swiss have their pay; don't
you expect them to be used?"[2] The words were brutally and
thoughtlessly said. They merely imported anger. The Huguenots interpreted them to mean that they were to be overcome by
military force, and Protestantism coerced, if not extinguished.
The synod of the Huguenots at Valéry[3] resolved upon war. The
conference was held in the admiral's château at Châtillon under
the outward guise of a banquet. There were present the prince
of Condé, La Rochefoucault, the cardinal of Châtillon. D'Andelot,
Bricquemault, Teligny, Mouy, Montgomery, and other nobles of
mark, besides some Huguenot ministers. The conference lasted
the entire week, at the end of which it was resolved that all the
Huguenots in France should be notified in every *bailliage* and
sénéschaussée, by the deacons and other officers of their congregation; that they should be called upon to furnish money according
to the means which they had, for the payment of reiters from
Germany, which the count palatine of the Rhine was to levy;
and that all the young men of the religion capable of bearing
arms were to be enrolled for military service.[4]

The plan was as bold as it was simple. It was to gain possession
of the King's person by a sudden *coup de main,* for which purpose
a force of 1,500 horse was to be brought secretly to Valéry. The
court at this time was residing at the Château de Monceaux near
Meaux, and was without more than nominal military protection.[5]

[1] *C. S. P. For.,* No. 1,155, May 1, 1567.

[2] D'Aubigné, I, Book IV, chap. vii.

[3] This château was a gift to the prince of Condé by the widow of marshal
St. André, who was infatuated with him. After the prince's second marriage she
wedded Geoffrey de Caumont (Claude Haton, I, 363). See also Clément-Simon,
La Maréchale de Saint-André et ses filles, Paris, 1896.

[4] The rendezvous was a Rosay-en-Brie (La Popelinière, Book XII, 37;
D'Aubigné, IV, chap. vii; Claude Haton, I, 424, 425).

[5] The Venetian ambassador Correro, in his relation of the conspiracy, expresses astonishment that the secret of the Huguenot leaders did not leak out, and

On the evening of September 24, the queen learned of the rendez-vous at Rosay-en-Brie. A midnight council was called. The Swiss, who had reached Château Thierry, were hastily summoned. The Lorraine party and the duke of Nemours advised immediate return to Paris. The chancellor and Montmorency endeavored to persuade the King against so doing.[1] The former pointed out that to go to Paris would be for the King to commit himself to the most bigoted of his subjects and destroy the possibility of an amicable settlement, while the constable argued that Meaux was a fortified city capable of withstanding a siege, and that to leave it might be to court defeat in the open country. In the dilemma the Swiss colonel Pfiffer cast the die.

"May it please your Majesty," cried he, "to entrust your person and that of the queen mother to the valor and fidelity of the Swiss. We are 6,000 men, and with the points of our pikes we will open a path wide enough for you to pass through the army of your enemies."[2]

---

attributes the fact to the perfection of the Protestant organization (quoted by La Ferrière in *Correspondance de Catherine de Médicis*, III, ix). It seems to me that this feature was less due to perfect organization than to the promptitude with which Condé and Coligny endeavored to carry out the project. The lesson of the conspiracy of Amboise seven years before could not have been lost upon them. Moreover, the queen mother did have some intimation, notwithstanding her surprise when the shock came. For on September 10, while the court was staying at Monceaux, some armed bands of horsemen were seen hovering around, which which caused the King's hasty removal to Meaux (*C. S. P. For.*, No. 1,683, September 13, 1567, Norris to Leicester). From that hour Catherine was on the alert, though she refused to attach alarmist importance to the signs she had seen until her eyes were opened.

[1] Claude Haton, I, 434.

[2] Zurlauben, *Hist. milit. des Suisses*, IV, 351; Laugel, "Les régimens suisses au service de France pendant les guerres, de religion," *Revue des deux mondes*, November 15, 1880, pp. 332 ff. Pfiffer had served in France during the first civil war and was made a colonel after the battle of Dreux. There is a life of him in German by Segesser, *Ludwig Pfyffer und seine Zeit*, Bern, 1880. Other versions of this incident are in D'Aubigné, II, 230–32; Claude Haton, I, 428, 429; Castelnau, VI, chap. iv; De Thou, Book XLII; *Nég. Tosc.*, III, 530. La Popelinière, XII, 38, 39, gives a good account of the behavior of the Swiss. The duke of Bouillon, an eye-witness of these incidents, has left a striking account in his *Mémoires*, ed. Petitot, 75.

"Enough," Charles rejoined. "I would rather die free with you than live a captive among rebels."[1]

The return to Paris began at four o'clock in the morning. "When the Swiss arrived at Meaux," wrote Correro, "I vow they were the most villainous looking gang I have ever seen. Yet in battle array they were admirable. Three times they turned upon the enemy and lowering their pikes charged upon them like savage dogs in serried ranks and in good order, without one being a pace in advance of another. Thus the King was able with his suite to get to Paris."[2] He reached the Louvre that night, travel-worn, hot, famished, and so angry that his fierce disposition never lost the memory of that humiliation.[3]

The affair of Meaux came like a thunder-clap to most of France. The suddenness of the Huguenot action and the all but complete success of it astonished men. "This movement," wrote the Vene-tian ambassador, "of which several thousand men had knowledge, was conducted with such precaution that nothing leaked out until it was all but an accomplished fact. This could not possibly have been done without the perfect intelligence that exists among the Huguenots, and is a striking manifestation of their organization throughout the realm."[4]

In the light of this judgment, it remains to describe the Hugue-not form of government.

The ecclesiastical—and political unit—of French Calvinism was the congregation. Congregations were grouped "according to number and convenience" into colloquies or classes which met from two to four times each year, the division being made by the

---

[1] For Charles IX's own version of the affair of Meaux see a letter of the King to the baron de Gordes, begun at Meaux and finished at Paris, September 28, 1567, in Duc d'Aumale, *Histoire des princes de Condé*, I, Appendix XXII. His letter to Montluc of the same date is in *Archives de la Gironde*, X, 437.

[2] *Rel. vén.*, II, 187.

[3] The Guises made capital out of the event of Meaux and sedulously exploited the King's animosity. Martin, *Histoire de France*, IX, 216, suggests that Charles IX's conduct on St. Bartholomew's Day may have been influenced by this episode.

[4] *Rel. vén.*, II, 112, 113.

authority of the provincial synod.[1] In church matters, no church had any primacy or jurisdiction over another, nor one province over another.[2] Ministers brought with them to local classes or provincial synods one or two elders chosen out of their consistories.[3] Elders who were deputies of churches had an equal power of voting with the pastors.[4] The authority of a provincial synod was subordinate to that of the national synod,[5] and whatever had been decreed by provincial synods for the government of the churches in their province had to be brought before the national synod.[6] The grand lines of division followed the historic provincial divisions of France, but smaller provinces and parts of the larger ones, as Guyenne and Languedoc, were associated together. The national synod of 1559 divided France into sixteen Protestant provinces, as follows: (1) The Ile-de-France, Chartrain, Picardy, Champagne and Brie; (2) Normandy; (3) Brittany; (4) Orleans, Blesois, Dunois, Nivernais, Berry, Bourbonnais, and La Marche; (5) Touraine, Anjou, Loudunois, Maine, Vendôme, and Perche; (6) Upper and Lower Poitou; (7) Saintonge, Aunis, La Rochelle, and Angoumois; (8) Lower Guyenne, Périgord, Gascony, and Limousin; (9) Upper and Lower Vivarais, together with Velay, and Le Forêt; (10) Lower Languedoc, including Nîmes, Mont-

---

[1] "Discipline of the Reformed Churches in France Received and Enacted by Their First National Synod at Paris in 1559," chap. vii, canon 1, published in Quick, *Synodicon in Gallia*, 2 vols., London, 1692.

The first consistorial regulation which we possess has been published by the Protestant pastor, Eugene Arnaud, from a manuscript at Grenoble. It bears the title "Articles Polytiques par l'Eglise Réformée selon le S. Evangile, fait à Poitiers 1557." See *Synode général de Poitiers 1557, Synodes provinciaux de Lyon, Die, Peyraud, Montelimar et Nîmes en 1561 et 1562, assemblée des Etats du Dauphiné en 1563, etc.*, par E. Arnaud. Grenoble, ed. Allier, 1872, 91 pages.

At the synod of Lyons (1563) the canons of the three preceding national synods held at Paris, Poitiers, and Orleans, were reduced to a single series of articles. The deliberations of most of the provincial synods still remain in manuscript or are lost (Frossard, *Etude historique et bibliographique sur la discipline ecclésiastique des églises réformées de France*, 18).

[2] Chap. vi, canon 1.

[3] Chap. viii, canon 2. Chap. v, canon 1, provides that "a consistory shall be made up of those who govern it (the individual churches), to-wit, of its pastors and elders." In some cases deacons discharged the elder's office (chap. v, canon 2).

[4] Chap. viii, canon 8. Elders were elected by the joint suffrage of pastor and people, upon oral nomination (chap. iii, canon 1).

[5] Chap. viii, canon 9. [6] Chap. viii, canon 14.

pellier, and Beziers; (11) Upper Languedoc, Upper Guyenne, Toulouse, Carcassonne, Quercy, Rouergue, Armagnac, and Upper Auvergne; (12) Burgundy, Lyonnais, Beaujolais, Bresse, Lower Auvergne, and Gex; (13) Provence; (14) Dauphiné and Orange; (15) Béarn; (16) the Cevennes and Gévaudan.[1]

This administrative partition, however, did not remain fixed. Some provinces, like Brittany, had so few Protestants in them, that the Huguenots therein could not stand alone, and the first civil war brought out the weakness of this system. Accordingly, in 1563, the map of France was partitioned anew, and the former sixteen "provinces" were reduced to nine. Some of the changes made are interesting. For example, the Chartrain was cut off from the Ile-de-France and attached to the "province" of Orleans, manifestly in the endeavor to keep a connecting link between Normandy and the Loire country. Brittany was strengthened by the annexation of Anjou, Maine, and Touraine which formerly constituted an independent "province," which obviously drew it into closer connection with the stronger Calvinistic provinces. The "province" of Upper and Lower Poitou was combined with Saintonge, Aunis, and Angoumois, thus knitting together all the country watered by the Charente, the Clain, and lesser streams. Burgundy, Lyonnais, Beaujolais, Bresse, Lower Auvergne, and Gex absorbed the small Huguenot province composed of Vivarais, Velay, and Le Forêt. But the most interesting consolidation was in the south of France. Formerly Upper Languedoc, in which were Nîmes, Montpellier, and Beziers; Lower Languedoc, comprising Upper Guyenne, Toulouse, Carcassonne, Quercy, Rouergue, Armagnac, and Upper Auvergne; Provence; Dauphiné, and Cevennes-Gévaudan had each formed separate "provinces." But in 1563 this immense territory was all united to form the great Huguenot province of Languedoc. The only ancient provinces which remained unchanged in 1563 were Normandy,[2] Béarn, and Lower Guyenne, with Périgord and Limousin.

[1] Chap. viii, canon 15.

[2] The synod of Nîmes in 1572 also divided Normandy into two provinces (*Synodicon in Gallia*, I, 111, 112). At the same time Metz was annexed to Champagne.

The Huguenot ecclesiastical organization and its political organization were one and the same. The congregations, the "colloquia," the synods, constituted both taxation units and military cadres.[1] The strength of the Huguenot organization, however, before the massacre of St. Bartholomew, I believe has been exaggerated, except in Guyenne where, in the vicinity of Nérac especially, Montluc early came in contact with a powerful combination of the Huguenots.[2] The strong elements in the Protestant organization were its simplicity and the vigilance of all, from provincial chiefs to simple pastors, who made up for scarcity of numbers by the most zealous activity.[3] "If our priests," wrote the Venetian Correro in 1569, "were half so energetic, of a certainty Christianity would not be in danger in this country."[4] It was not until after 1572 that the Huguenot organization reached a high point of military and political development, when a solid federation of the Reformed churches was formed at Milhaud in 1574, with rating precincts, military hundreds and civil jurisdictions.[5]

Exactly as the early organization of the Huguenots has been overemphasized, so has the republican nature of the early Huguenot movement been exaggerated. Apart from whatever religious motives may have actuated them, the Protestant nobles were influenced by political ambition; the bourgeoisie by the hope of adminis-

[1] *Rel. vén.*, II, 115, and n. B; *Commentaires et lettres de Montluc*, II, Book V, 338; L'Ambassade de St. Sulpice, 107; *Mémoires de Philippi*, 360, col. 1 (ed. Buchon); Collection Godefroy, CCLVII, No. 46; Claude Haton, I, 425.

[2] The democratic revolutionary character of the Huguenot movement in Guyenne probably owes some of its intensity to the memory of the revolt of 1548 and the merciless suppression thereof (observation of M. Henri Hauser, *Rev. hist.*, XCVII (March–April, 1908), 341, n. 6, a review of Courteault *Blaise de Montluc*).

[3] "Temevano prima i cattolici, non perchè fossero inferiori di numero (che . . . . del popolo minuto non vi è la trigesima parte ugonotta; la nobilita è più infetta; e s' io dicessi di un terzo, forse non fallirei); ma perchè questi; sebben pochi, erano però uniti, concordi, e vigilantissimi nelle loro cose."—*Rel. vén.*, II, 120.

The Huguenots fired guns instead of ringing bells as a signal of alarm (*ibid.*, 107). The *tocsin*, even before St. Bartholomew, was the Catholic signal.

[4] *Rel. vén.*, II, 115.

[5] *Correspondance de Catherine de Médicis*, I, 552; Ranke, *Civil Wars and Monarchy in France*, 287; Forneron, *Les ducs de Guise*, II, 221; Anquetil, *Histoire des assemblées politiques des réformes de France*, I, 18.

trative and economic reform; the masses by the general spirit of discontent. The Huguenots did not present a united front until after St. Bartholomew, when the fusion of the political Huguenots with the Politiques reduced the "religious" Huguenots to a left-wing minority. Before 1572 the political ideas of the Reformed, if not still inchoate, were not harmonized into one homogeneous cause, backed up by a compact and highly organized political system. Individual political theorists or fanatic devotees, of course, were to be found in the Huguenot ranks, but there was no systematic political philosophy to guide their conduct before the massacre of St. Bartholomew. It was this catastrophe that crystallized Huguenot opinion and organized combination on a large scale.[1] In Guyenne, alone, where, as has been said, the Huguenot organization was most completely developed at an early date, does any clear republican idea seem to have early obtained.[2]

[1] Forneron, II, 164 ff.; *Hist. de Languedoc*, V, 543, 544; Armstrong, "The Political Theories of the Huguenots," *English Historical Review*, IV, 13; Merriam, *History of the Theory of Sovereignty since Rousseau*, 13–15; Beaudrillart, *Jean Bodin et son temps*.

[2] "Si le roy tenoit sa loy, le royaulme en seroit mieulx régy et gouverné, les antiens, qui ont tenu les concilles, ont bien regardé à cella quant ilz ont uny nostre foy avec la continuation de la monarchie des princes, car ilz ont bien poysé que le peuple, qui est gouverné sous ung monarque, est beaucoup plus assuré et tenu en la craincté de Dieu et à l'obéyssance qu'il doibt porter à son roy, que non celluy qui est soubz une républicque, en laquelle sa loy admene tout le monde et destruict les monarchies. Qui me voldra nyer que le roy prent ceste loy qu'il ne faille que sa personne mesmes et son royaulme soit régy et gouverné par les gens qui auront esté esleuz par les estatz, qui sera son conseil sans lequel le roy ne pourra faire chose aucune. Et s'il veult une chose et le conseil une aultre, le pays ne fera sinon ce que le conseil ordonnera, parce qu'il aura esté (esleu) par les estatz; et si le roy mesmes veult quelque chose pour luy ou pour aultre, fauldra que, le bonnet à la main, il le viegne demander à son conseil et les prier, là où en nostre loy il commende au conseil et à tous, tant que nous sommes. Que l'on regarde dès ceste genre ce que se faict en Angleterre et en Escosse, et si ce n'est plustost manière d'aristocracie ou de démocracie que non de monarchie. Et quand le roy sera grand, il voldra demander sa liberté, laquelle ne luy sera concédée et s'il faict semblant de la voloir avoir par force, son conseil mesmes luy couppera la guorge et feront un aultre roy à leur plaisir."—*Commentaires et lettres de Montluc*, IV, 297, 298 (December 1563). The baron de Ruble, in a note remarks: "Nulle part peut-être, pas même dans les écrits de François Hotman et de Bodin, les réformes politiques que promettait le calvinisme ne sont exposées avec autant de clarté que dans ce mémoire de Montluc."

CHAPTER XII

THE SECOND CIVIL WAR (1567–68)

In this wise, after a respite of four years, the second civil war was precipitated. There was an exodus of Huguenots at once from Paris, some repairing to the prince of Condé, some to the duke de Rohan, others to Montgomery in Lower Normandy where a war of the partisans began at once.[1] The capital was in a furious mood and the King's presence alone prevented the Parisians from massacring the Protestants there and the Montmorencys.[2]

The chief effort of the Huguenots was to seize the towns on the Seine above and below Paris, in order to stay provisions, and so to compel the government to submit.[3] The capture of the Pont de Charenton[4] by Condé's forces was a heavy blow to the government, as Charenton chiefly supplied Paris with wheat and flour. The Parisians fully expected to be attacked and made preparations therefor by breaking up the stones in the streets and piling them in heaps for ready service or taking them into their houses; at the same time they destroyed pent-houses and other similar insignificant structures in order that they might the better hurl their missiles.[5] So suddenly had the war been begun that the blockade of Paris for the time being was almost complete.

[1] Paulet to Cecil, October 13, 1567; *C. S. P. Dom.*, Add.

[2] *Nég. Tosc.*, III, 549. On September 29, 1567, permission was given the populace of Paris to arm themselves.—Lettres patentes du Roy Charles IX pour l'establissement des capitaines de la ville de Paris et permission aux citizens d'icelle de prendre les armes. Felibien, *Histoire de Paris*, III, 703, 704.

[3] La Popelinière, XII, 39; Claude Haton, I, 439; La Noue, chap. xiv; *C. S. P. For.*, No. 1,427, September 30, 1567. Norris gives the names of the towns taken by the prince of Condé's forces.—*State Papers, Foreign*, Elizabeth, Vol. XCIV No. 1,338. See Appendix XI. According to Baschet, *La diplomatie vénitienne*, 543 and note, the prince of Condé planned to burn Paris.

[4] La Popelinière, Book XII, 51, 51 *bis*. The slaughter at the bridge was terrible. The King's captain and the color-bearer, who managed to escape to Paris, were hanged by Charles IX.—*C. S. P. For.*, No. 1,804, November 2, 1567.

[5] *Ibid.*, No. 1,763, October 14, 1567.

Lagny on the Marne,[1] Charcnton, Porchefontaine, Busanval, Argenteuil, St. Ouen, Ambervilliers, and St. Denis constituted the inner
zone of Huguenot control while farther out Montereau on the highroad to Sens, Etampes on the road to Orleans and in the heart
of the wheat district that supplied the capital,[2] Dourdan at the
junction of the Blois-Chartres roads, and Dreux on the road

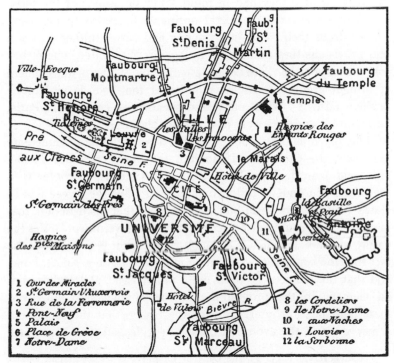

PARIS AND ITS FAUBOURGS IN THE SIXTEENTH CENTURY

toward Normandy, formed an outer circle. So closely was Paris
invested that the windmills 'in the faubourgs of St. Denis, St.
Honoré, and Port St. Martin were burned by the Huguenots. The
churches for leagues around were plundered of copes, chasubles,
tunics, and other rich silk and satin garments. The Huguenot
gentry made shirts and handkerchiefs out of the lace and linen of

[1] Claude Haton, I, 444–46.
[2] C. S. P. Ven., No. 407, October 18, 1567.

the clergy.   But all gold and silver taken, as altar-vessels, crosses, chalices, were turned into the general spoil for the sake of the cause.[1]   Forced loans were imposed upon small merchants and even the peasantry were constrained to forced labor,[2] so that the latter fled by hundreds to Paris.

The ravages of the Huguenots were so great that they defeated the very purpose they had in mind.   For thousands of the peasantry, under cover of a liberal ordinance intended to provision Paris,[3] drove their cattle into the city and carted thither the grain and provisions they had stored up against the winter, where they sold it cheap, rather than see it destroyed by "volleurs quilz pillent et brulent granges, maisons, moulins et font tout le mal qu'ilz peullent faire."[4]   Wine, meat, and bread were not dear in Paris; beechnut oil and oats were at a reasonable price.

The queen mother, who looked to Alva for the most immediate aid,[5] sent the chancellor L'Hôpital, the liberal marshal Vieille-ville, and Jean de Morvilliers, bishop of Orleans, to confer with the prince of Condé in order to gain time.   But the prince was so elated with his successful blockade of Paris that his demands rose in degree, and could not be accepted by the government.   Yet the nature of these demands is to be observed, for it is evidence of the fact that the conflict was becoming more and more a *political* one, and that the religious issue, if not a minor issue, at least was but an element in the programme of the Huguenots.   Moreover, these demands are interesting for the reason that they represent a new stage in the evolution of the struggle and that henceforth

[1] Claude Haton, I, 439–45, and La Noue, chap. xvi, give some graphic details.

[2] Claude Haton, I, 444, 445.

[3] "Ordonnance du Roy, portant permission à toutes personnes, d'apporter, et faire apporter, conduire et amener à Paris, tant par eau que par terre, toutes espèces de vivres, bleds, vins et autres; sans payer pour iceux aucunes daces, subsides, ou imposition quelconques."—Paris, R. Estienne, 1567.

[4] "Lettre addressée aux échevins de Rouen par un de leurs délégués," *Bulletin de la Société de l'histoire de Normandie*, 1875–80, p. 279. The whole letter is of interest.

[5] Alva's reply October 24, 1567, is in *Correspondance de Philippe II*, II, 594. Cf. Gachard, *La Bibliothèque Nationale à Paris*, I, 395; II, 459; and *Histoire des troubles des Pays-Bas*, ed. Piot, I, 293 (chap. xlvi).

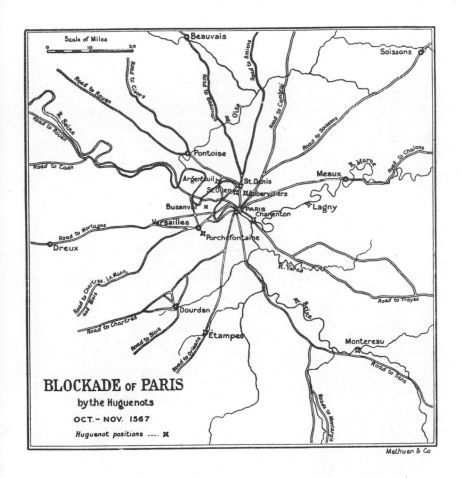

Scale of Miles

Beauvais

Soissons

Road to Amiens

Road to Gisors

Road to Rouen

Road to Pontoise via Pois

R. Seine

R. Oise

Road to Caen

Pontoise

Road to Camiloi

Road to Soissons

R. Marne

Road to Chalons

Meaux

Argenteuil
St.Denis
St.Ouen
Aubervilliers

Lagny

Busanval
PARIS
Charenton

Road to Mortagne
Versailles

Dreux
Porchefontaine

R. Yères

Road to Chartres, Le Mans, and Blois

R. Seine

Road to Troyes

Dourdan

Montereau

Road to Chartres

Road to Blois

Étampes

Road to Sens

Road to Orleans

Road to Montargis

BLOCKADE OF PARIS

by the Huguenots

OCT.- NOV. 1567

Huguenot positions .... ✕

Methuen & Co

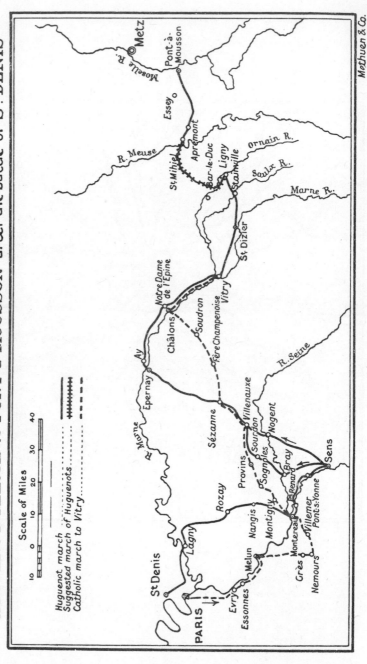

HUGUENOT MARCH TO PONT-à-MOUSSON after the battle of ST DENIS

Scale of Miles

Huguenot march ....
Suggested march of Huguenots ....
Catholic march to Vitry ....

Methuen & Co.

they are a permanent contention of the Huguenots and ultimately are embodied in the Edict of Toleration. The prince, whose chief object was to overthrow the Guises and get the government of the King and the management of affairs into his own hands[1] insisted on the free exercise of religion throughout the realm without limitation or distinction of places or persons; that all taxes lately authorized should be remitted and all new forms of taxation imposed since the reign of Louis XII abolished; that an accounting be made of the money granted for defraying the King's debts; that all those who had been deposed from their offices on account of religion should be reinstated; and that four fortified towns be placed in his hands as security for the good intentions of the crown. Furthermore, the prince demanded the dismissal of the Swiss and Spanish regiments.[2]

In due time the prince of Condé discovered that delay was disastrous. Although his force had daily increased by new accessions from the south,[3] nevertheless the Huguenot position was not so strong as it appeared. Paris rallied to the cause of the King and gave him 400,000 écus, while the clergy advanced 250,000.[4] The duke of Guise was in Champagne with troops of Champagne and Burgundy, besides eight companies of men-at-arms.[5] Moreover, recruits were pouring in to help the King, some from the duke of Savoy,[6] some from Piedmont under command of Strozzi, whose approach the admiral and De Mouy tried to prevent, and some from Pope Pius V, who bestirred himself in behalf of France as

[1] C. S. P. For., No. 1,789, October 27, 1567.

[2] These demands were presented in writing to the queen's emissaries. De Thou, Book XLII; Claude Haton, I, 447; D'Aubigné, II, 232–34, have summarized them. La Popelinière, Book XII, 41–43 gives the text. There is a monograph by Baguenault de Puchesse: Jean de Morvillier, évêque d'Orléans: Etude sur la politique française au XVIᵉ siècle, d'après des documents inédits, Didier, Paris, 1870.

[3] La Popelinière, Book XII, 50 bis; C. S. P. For., No. 1,856, October 10, 1567.

[4] Davila, I, 195.

[5] C. S. P. For., No. 1,777, October 22, 1567.

[6] A list of officers and the number of horsemen commanded by each who were sent to the king of France by the duke of Savoy.—C. S. P. For., No. 1,735, September, 1567.

soon as he was informed of the renewal of hostilities once more.[1]
The Huguenots made strenuous efforts to break the Swiss alliance
and to persuade the Protestant Swiss cantons to withdraw. But
fortunately for the French crown, the cantons remained firm,
for without the assistance of Swiss troops, Charles IX would have
been hard put to it for an army, for he dared not accept the all too
interested offers of Philip II.[2]   As in the first civil war, both parties looked to Germany for assistance[3] and the queen mother
sent Lignerolles "to practice the stay of the reiters, and on
his return, to the count palatine to desire him not to succor the
prince and his associates, affirming that their rising was not
of any zeal of religion, but only to rebel against their prince."[4]

[1] He wrote to Philip II, to Emanuel Philibert of Savoy, and the Venetian
government urging them to succor Charles IX "against the rebels and heretics"
within his kingdom, and to the duke of Lorraine to stop the reiters.—Potter,
Lettres de St. Pie V sur les affaires religieuses de son temps en France, Paris, 1828.
To Philip II, October 13, 1567—Potter, p. 1 (ed. Gouban, Book I, No. 22, p. 50);
to the duke of Savoy, October 18, 1567—Potter, p. 8 (ed. Gouban, Book I,
No. 25, p. 54); to Priuli, Venetian ambassador in France, October 18—Potter, p. 6
(ed. Gouban, Book I, No. 24, p. 53).   At the same time the Pope wrote to the
duke of Nevers in terms of rejoicing that Charles IX had escaped at Meaux.—
Potter, p. 3 (ed. Gouban, Book I, No. 23, p. 51), October 16, 1567.   Within
a month the Pope's word began to be made good, for 10,000 pieces of gold were
en route to France in the middle of November.—Potter, p. 10 (ed. Gouban,
Book I, No. 26, p. 56), letter to the duke of Savoy of November 16, 1567.   In it the
Pope says he has written the duke of Lorraine to stop the reiters about to enter
France.

[2] The question of payment of the Swiss still remained to be settled and
Charles IX was at his wits' end and actually offered a mortgage of his frontier
towns, save Lyons and the frontier of Burgundy, paying 5 per cent. interest in
order to quiet the importunate demands of the cantons.—*Revue d'histoire diplomatique*, XIV (1900), 49, 50.

[3] Request of Charles IX to the bishop of Mainz to permit the reiters to pass,
December 9, 1567.—Coll. Godefroy, CCLVI, No. 4.   John Casimir, second son
of the elector palatine, Frederick III, levied troops for the Protestants.   When
protest was made against this action, he gave an evasive reply.   See Languet,
Epist. secr., I, 27; *Archives de la maison d'Orange-Nassau*, II, 163, 164; La Noue,
ed. 1596, p. 897.

On the other hand the landgrave was hostile to the prince of Condé and was
fearful also of compromising himself with the Emperor and Spain.—*Archives de
la maison d'Orange-Nassau*, III, 128, 164; Languet, *Epist. secr.*, I, 35.

[4] *C. S. P. For.*, No. 1,864, December 15, 1567.

The Huguenots also made overtures to Philip II's revolted subjects.[1]

By the middle of October the prince of Condé discovered that he was lying between two enemies, Paris and the new troops coming up, and every day added to his peril. There can be little doubt but that the queen mother purposely protracted the negotiations, knowing that by so doing Condé's security would be diminished. Signs were not wanting to indicate that matters were coming to a head. On October 7 the King sent a herald to the prince to proclaim that all who were with him should unarm and repair to Paris, whereby they might save their lives and goods, which, if they refused to do so, should be confiscated.

The same day the constable declared how the King, trusting to bring certain of his subjects to good conformity by his clemency, had sent his chancellor to assure them that his edicts made for religion and pacification should be inviolably kept, and that no man should be molested for the same; and that touching other small articles he was in full mind to have satisfied them. Notwithstanding, they would not submit themselves to any reason; wherefore the King was fully resolved to declare them rebels and prosecute them accordingly, for the maintenance whereof he would venture both body and goods. On October 8 proclamation was made that if the prince with his associates would submit themselves to the King within three days he would freely pardon all that was past; but if they refused, they were to be accounted as rebels and it was to be lawful to all the King's subjects to kill all such as they should find armed. In expectation of battle, the constable was made lieutenant-general of the King's army.[2]

Yet despite the precariousness of his situation the prince was still confident. His pride was hardened by the capture of Orleans by La Noue on September 28,[3] and of Soissons.[4] He enlarged the

---

[1] This is shown by a passage in which the elector of Saxony makes mention of an alliance which the French nobles had offered (*Archives de la maison d'Orange-Nassau*, III, 131, 134). Although the prince of Condé in December declared that he had not entered into a treaty with the Flemish Calvinists (*ibid.*, 143), it is probable that these proposals were accepted some months later. There is in existence the minute of a treaty with Condé and Coligny dated August, 1568 (*ibid.*, III, No. 321, p. 285).

[2] *C. S. P. For.*, No. 1,756, October 10, 1567.

[3] La Popelinière, XII, 52 *bis*; D'Aubigné II, 236. La Noue himself, with characteristic modesty, scarcely mentions this feat.

[4] "Journal de Lépaulart relig. du monastère de Saint-Crepin-le-Grand de Soissons, sur la prise de cette ville par les Huguenots en 1567," *Bull. d. Soc. arch.*, XIV (Soissons, 1860).

Protestants' demands, requiring that Calais, Boulogne, and Metz[1] be delivered to them as surety, that the King disarm first and that one church of every "good town" in France be permitted to those of the religion; and that 300,000 francs be granted the prince to pay his troops, "whereby they may return hence without pillage."[2] The crown scornfully rejected the terms and assumed a rapid offensive. On the night of November 6 Strozzi's band destroyed a bridge of boats planked together which the prince had made in order more effectually to cut off Paris; on the following day another point on the river which threatened Paris was captured by the duke of Nemours, and on the 9th Condé was compelled to withdraw from Charenton after breaking the bridge and firing the town. On November 8 the prince had made the blunder of weakening his main force by sending D'Andelot to seize Poissy and Montgomery to get possession of Pontoise, the two open places in the inner zone of steel drawn around Paris.[3] The crisis of real battle came in their absence, on November 10, the battle of St. Denis. It was a fierce and bloody fray beginning about 3 o'clock and lasting till dark, in which both sides suffered severely. Montmorency, "more famous than fortunate in arms," was twice slashed in the face by a cutlass and then shot in the neck and the small of his back by pistol bullets fired by the Scotch captain named Robert Stuart[4] serving with the Huguenots. The old veteran, thinking his assailant did not recognize him, cried out: "You do not know me. I am the constable." But the Scot, as he fired, replied: "Because I know you, I give.you this!"[5] Though the white-liveried horsemen of Condé passed through and through the King's soldiery and though the constable was mortally wounded the battle was not won by the prince.[6] On November 14 the Hugue-

[1] C. S. P. For., No. 1,804, November 2, 1567. Metz was captured late in October by the Huguenots, but not the citadel.

[2] Ibid., No. 1,822, November 16, 1567.   [3] La Popelinière, XII, 52.

[4] On the identity and career of Robert Stuart, see Claude Haton, I, 458, n. 2.

[5] C. S. P. Ven., No. 410, November 11, 1567. Montmorency lingered two days and died on November 12.

[6] There are accounts of the battle of St. Denis in La Noue, Mémoires, chap. xiv; Mém. du duc de Bouillon, 379; D'Aubigné, Book IV, chap. ix; Claude Haton, I, 457; Nég. Tosc., III, 551 ff. The editor has subjoined a note (2) giving the literature of the subject.

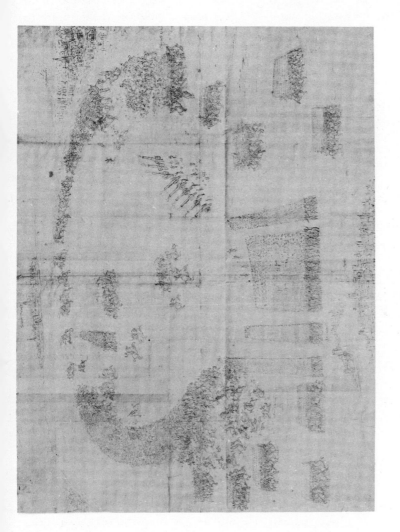

THE BATTLE OF ST. DENIS

From photograph of the original sketch, probably made by the son of Sir Henry Norris, English Ambassador in France. Original in Public Record Office, State Papers, Foreign, Elizabeth, Vol. XCV, No. 1813. It is dated November 10, 1567, and measures 31½ x 23⅜ inches.

not army filed out of St. Denis "without sound of trumpet or stroke of drum."   The prince established temporary headquarters at Montereau toward Sens, but later moved up the Marne to the vicinity of Troyes with the duke of Guise following slowly after him, in order to effect a junction with the reiters of duke Casimir of the Palatinate, which the government was unable to prevent.[1]

The presence of the Huguenot forces seemed like the return of the reiters to the folk in Champagne, who hid their treasures in stables, gardens, chimneys, and the like.   Some concealed their money and jewels in crannies in the walls; others hid them in the swaddling clothes of babes.   But even this was to no purpose, for the soldiers plucked the children from the very breasts of their mothers and stripped them in order to find what was hidden upon them.[2]

After the battle of St. Denis two opinions divided the King's council.   Some urged the queen, who was at Fontainebleau, to make new overtures; others, who reflected the opinion of Paris, were for pursuing the war.   The queen mother acted upon the first suggestion, but nothing came of the overtures because the King insisted upon disarmament of the Huguenots before considering their terms.[3]   Active preparations were therefore made to

[1] Claude Haton, I, 495; *Correspondance de Catherine de Médicis*, III, Introd., xv.
The duke of Guise was criticized for not having pursued the Huguenots more hotly and cut the road by Charenton, or Corbeil, or at the ford of Lagny, which might have been done, for their army was in great disorder and depressed on account of the losses which it had suffered.   The reason of the delay is probably to be found in the fact that the breach between the Guises and the Montmorencys was wider than ever at this moment.   For the duke of Montpensier and the duke of Montmorency each claimed command of the vanguard.   The King finally decided in favor of the former, whereupon Montmorency laid down his command.   See Claude Haton, I, 461, 462 and note; *Bulletin de la Société d'histoire de Normandie*, 1875–80, p. 279; C. S. P. For., No. 1,833, November 24; No. 1,837, November 29, 1567; *Nég. Tosc.*, III, 557.

[2] Claude Haton, I, 495 and note.

[3] The admiral sent Teligny to the King on November 13 for this purpose.—C. S. P. For., No. 1,822, November 16, 1567; cf. No. 1,836.   We know, from a letter of Charles IX to his brother, what the King's terms would have been: (1) in the case of nobles, authorization of Protestant worship to those possessed of high justice or possessors of "pleins fiefs de haubert" i. e., fiefs that were noble, yet did not confer title, provided it were conducted within their own dwellings in the pres-

push the war in the provinces, somewhat to the surprise of the
Catholic gentry who had thought it was finished on the field of
St. Denis.[1] Camps of artillery, the infantry, and the Swiss were
established at Voulton, St. Martin-des-Champs, Gymbrois, and
other points in Champagne and Brie, while the cavalry was lodged
in other parishes. Garrisons were also posted in the châteaux
and *maisons fortes* of the Huguenots in the region. Without
counting the territory covered by the advance guard of the King's
army, a strip of territory was occupied over ten miles long and six
wide, and containing more than fifty thousand persons.[2] For
the feeding of this host, an ordinance of the master of the camp
ordered the seizure of all the local bakeries, the necessary grain being
commandeered from the merchants and farmers of the locality.
Besides these provisions the soldiery, since they were quartered

ence of their families and not more than fifty outside persons, and without arms;
(2) absolute limitation of other worship to the places specifically granted in the
edict of Amboise; (3) surrender of places and property seized by the Huguenots;
(4) suppression of the Protestant cult within the walls, of Lyons, but permission
to worship at two leagues' distance from the city; (5) interdiction of levies of money
or men in the future and the discontinuance of Protestant associations and synods.
—*Correspondance de Catherine de Médicis*, II, Introd., xiv. It is a very remarkable
fact that these precise terms had been recommended to Charles IX as a basis of
settlement by Montluc in a memoir sent to the King in February 1565. See *Commentaires et lettres de Montluc*, V, 3–9. Montluc made the further recommendation
that the governments be divided by *sénéchaussées* instead of by rivers, on the ground
that rivers sometimes divided towns into two jurisdictions. His friction with
Damville (cf. *ibid.*, 103–6) probably accounts for the proposed change. Montluc
also advised abolition of the *vice-sénéchaux* (*ibid.*, 8).

[1] See the proclamation of Charles IX commanding the provost Paris to
search out all gentlemen who have retired to their homes since the battle of St. Denis;
and ordering them to return to the army under pain of forfeiture of their fiefs and
property. Printed in Appendix XII. In the second part of *Coll. de St. Pétersbourg*,
Vol. XXI, is a group of letters from Charles IX to the duke of Anjou running from
December 2, 1567. In every page the question of the military operations of the
second civil war comes up. It is evident that the gentlemen of the *maison du roi*
complained loudly of the service required of them, especially because they were so
ill lodged.—La Ferrière, *Deux ans de mission à St. Pétersbourg*, 24.

[2] During the occupation of the army all Protestant children who had been
baptized in the Reformed religion by preachers were rebaptized according to the
rites of the Roman religion, and godfathers and godmothers were given them and
new names which were approved by the church.—Claude Haton, I, 512 and note.

on households, freely consumed bread, meat, wine, and other food where they were, without payment.

The presence of the King's troops was a heavy drain upon the resources of the region, more especially since the summer had been so dry that the crops were thin. Indeed so great was the drought that even swamps grew dry and there were public prayers and processions for rain in all the parishes of France. Fortunately rain fell in time to save the vines so that the wine did not fail, else the condition of France would have been one of great distress.[1]

On November 20 two thousand horsemen arrived in Paris from Flanders. The hope of the French Protestants was chiefly pinned upon John Casimir of the Palatinate, son of the elector Frederick, and a force of German reiters, the expectation of whose coming had induced Condé to move eastward toward Troyes. The count palatine drew a sharp line in his own mind between religion and politics. He would have been quick to resent any invasion of his rights as a ruler. But he did not understand French politics, and looked upon the Huguenot movement as a purely religious one to which he felt bound to give support because he was a zealous Protestant.[2] The French government sent the bishop of Rennes and Lignerolles to endeavor to dissuade the count palatine; they affirmed that the rebellion of Condé was not for any zeal of religion but for political advantage. But the prince's emissary outmatched the bishop and his colleague, assuring the count palatine that the sole cause of the Huguenot insurrection was the preservation of the free exercise of religion, together with their honor, lives, and goods.[3] The argument of Charles IX that the estate of himself and realm was so intermingled with that of religion that the count palatine could not touch one without offense to the other, was not convincing to Casimir.[4]

[1] Claude Haton, I, 504–12.

[2] On December 6 he published a declaration in favor of the Huguenots.— *Bulletin de la Société du prot. franç.* XVI, 118. See also *C. S. P. For.*, No. 1,920, the elector to Charles IX, January 4, 1568.

[3] *C. S. P. For*, No. 1,911, from the camp at Dessay, January 3, 1568.

[4] *Ibid.*, No. 1,806, November 3, 1567; No. 1,864 § 2, December 15, 1567. His resolution to assist the Huguenots led to the dismissal of his ambassador at the

336   THE WARS OF RELIGION IN FRANCE

To add to Catherine's anxiety the Emperor revived the old
project to seize the Three Bishoprics,[1] a project made doubly
dangerous by the new machinations of the cardinal of Lorraine.
For, in order to safeguard the Catholic cause in France and to save
Metz from being lost entirely after the Huguenots had captured
the citadel in October, the cardinal of Lorraine, had resumed his
secret negotiations with Spain.   Instead, however, of writing direct
to Philip II he wrote to Alva, for time was pressing and the danger
great.   On November 1, 1567, a chaplain of the cardinal appeared
before the duke in Antwerp bearing a letter imploring Alva to
come to the assistance of the French crown and offered to put him
in possession of certain places in France.   At first Alva was so
incredulous that he imprisoned the bearer[2] until he was satisfied
of the verity of his mission.   Nevertheless he immediately sent
3,000 horsemen into the country of Seyn (between Wied and Bas-
Isenberg) whose ruler was a pensioner of Spain, ordered count
Mansfeldt to go to Luxembourg, and dispatched a message to the
margrave of Baden for 1,000 horsemen with the object of preventing Germans going to France or the war there from spreading to
the Spanish provinces.   Finally, when persuaded of the truth of

French court on December 17th.—*Ibid.*, No. 1,889.   In *ibid.*, No. 1,956 there is an
abstract of a long letter of the elector palatine written to Charles IX in remonstrance of the action of the King, and in justification of his own course.

[1] A meeting of the electors was called for January 6, 1568, at Fulda, ostensibly
for the purpose of preventing German enrolments for the war in France, but in
reality that the Emperor might broach the possibility of recovering the Three
Bishoprics.—Mundt to Cecil, January 6, 1568 in *C. S. P. For.*, No. 1,927.   I
cannot understand how Hubert Languet could have fallen into the error of thinking
that the queen mother made no opposition to the enlistment of troops in Germany
for the Huguenot cause, as he says in *Epp. Arc.*, I, 43.   The statement puzzled
Ranke (p. 233) who left it unsolved.   The dispatch of Norris in *C. S. P. For.*,
No. 1,864, December 15, 1567, to the effect that Lignerolles was sent to Germanyy
by the queen for this purpose clears up the matter.   Catherine's correspondence
fails us on this head.   But it is well known that many of her letters are scattered
in private collections and were not procurable by La Ferrière.

[2] Alva had no flattering opinion of the cardinal of Lorraine.   In 1572 he
wrote to Philip II: "Quand en faveur il est insolent et ne se souvient de personne,
tandis que, quand il est en disgrace, il n'est bon à rien."—Gachard, *Correspondance
de Philippe II sur les Pays-Bas*, II, 267.

the cardinal's overtures, Alva said that if circumstances so developed as to make such action on his part an imperative duty before the King of France could be apprised, he would do so; and that if the King were overwhelmed by the Huguenots, he would believe it his duty for the sake of protecting the Catholic faith to occupy the places offered by the cardinal, which might be held in pawn by Spain as collateral for French repayment of her services.[1] But the treasonable designs of the cardinal of Lorraine went even farther than an offer to surrender some of the border fortresses of France into Spanish hands. As early as this time the possible deposition of the house of Valois was contemplated by the Guises in favor of the Spanish-Hapsburg dynasty. For the cardinal went on to say that in event of the early death of Charles IX and his brothers Philip II of Spain would be heir to the throne of France through his wife, Elizabeth of Valois. "The Salic law is a pleasantry," he added, "and force of arms could overcome any opposition"![2] "This last," wrote Alva to Philip, "is a different matter and I cannot risk taking a hand in it without express instructions from your Majesty."

The habitual self-control of the Spanish monarch must have been heavily taxed to subdue his emotion when he learned of this astonishing negotiation. But he was true to his second-nature. Without apparent excitement he endorsed the document thus: "This point is one upon which more time is needed to reflect, because it would be difficult to do what the cardinal asks without compromise. On the other hand, it is hard to decline for such a cause what is thrown into my arms. However, I think that a

---

[1] Gachard, *ibid.*, I, 593, 594, Alva to Philip, November 1, 1567. On the margin of this dispatch Philip wrote this piece of casuistry with his own hand: "Me parece muy bien que hiziese lo que aqui dice, y tanto mas que aquello no hera romper la paz, pues yo no la hizé, ni la tengo, sino con el rey de Francia, y no con sus vasallos ereges, como seria, si esto se hiziese no estando él libre, como aqui se dice."

[2] "En caso de muerte del rey y de sus hermanos, tomarse ya la voz que el cardinal dize de rey de Francia para V. M., por el derecho de la reyna nuestra señora; que la ley salica, que dizen, es baya, y las armas la allanarian" (*ibid.*, 594).

decision in this matter is not urgent.   Let the duke inform me
what he thinks about it, according to the state of things there."[1]
Was it caution, or hesitation, or procrastination ?

As an intermediate course, one less compromising and perhaps
quite as effective in the long run, Alva suggested, although with
some misgiving, to the cardinal of Lorraine that he come in person
to the relief of the French crown.[2]   While he was debating this
question with himself, news came of the battle of St. Denis and
of the approach of the reiters; and hard upon this, word from
Catherine de Medici asking for the aid of 2,000 Spanish arquebusiers against the reiters.[3]   The duke of Alva, in reply, after
chiding Catherine for not accepting the offers of assistance he had
made immediately after Meaux,[4] offered to send 2,000 arquebusiers
and 2,000 cavalry,—he could not now spare the great force he had
proffered earlier—to the assistance of the duke of Aumale against
the reiters,[5] although admitting, with grim pleasantry, that there
was a certain humor in casting firebrands into a neighbor's house
when one's own was burning.[6]   But the offer came too late to be
of service, thus fortunately sparing Catherine from the humiliation

[1] "Esto es el punto en que me parece que ay mas que mirar, porqué esto se
podria mal hazer sin romper; y por otra parte, parece que seria duro dexar de
abrazar á quien por tal causa se pone en mys manos; y pues creo que por este caso
avra tiempo, qu'él me avise de su parecer sobre ello, segun allá estubienen las
cosas."—Gachard, loc. cit.

[2] Philip II approved this.—Gachard, Correspondance de Philippe II, I, 598:
to Alva, November 12, 1567.

[3] Gachard, I, 606–7, from Paris, December 4, 1567; Correspondance de Catherine de Médicis, Letter CLII; Correspondance de Philippe II, I, 605–7.   The
queen mother seems to have been frightened after the battle of St. Denis for she
disclaims blame in advance, "before God and all the Christian princes," if, in
default of help, she be forced to make peace with the prince of Condé.   At about
the same time, she also wrote to Philip II in the same strain (quoted in part by
Forneron, I, 348 from K. 1,507, No. 29).   I do not find that this letter has been
printed.

[4] Correspondance de Catherine de Médicis, II, 62.

[5] Gachard, Correspondance de Philippe II sur les Pays-Bas, I, 608.

[6] "Porqué seria mala burla yr á meter fuego en casa agena, començandose á
arder la propria."—Ibid., 597: Alva to Philip II, November 6, 1567.

of having introduced in France a power whose purpose was the overthrow of France.[1]

In the meantime, while Condé was encamped between Sens[2] and Troyes, the reiters had entered Lorraine to the number of about six thousand.[3] Their coming thwarted the plans of the duke of Guise, who was on the frontier with the marshal Tavannes, for it prevented the French commanders from joining with Count Mansfeldt and the duke of Lorraine and compelled them to fall back.[4] The junction of Condé and the reiters was effected on December 28, and a camp established at Dessay. The King's army of all sorts comprised 30,000 footmen and half as many horse.[5] Nevertheless, despite the adverse prospect, the government did not waver. The capital was intensely loyal. In response

---

[1] It was à propos of Catherine de Medici's weakness at this time that the marshal Vieilleville bluntly said to Charles IX.: "Ce n'est point Votre Majesté qui a gagné la bataille [of St. Denis]; encore moins le prince de Condé. C'est le roi d'Espagne."—Weiss, L'Espagne sous Philippe II, I, 119.

[2] On the military state of Sens at this time see Charles IX's postscript to his mother's letter to Fourquevaux of December 7 in Correspondance de Catherine de Médicis, III, 89, note.

[3] Norris, writing to Queen Elizabeth on December 15, in one place says, "the reiters are 4,000 with 4,000 lansquenets" (§2); later in the course of the same letter, which is a long one and probably the information of several days running, he says, "6,800 with 6,000 lansquenets" (C. S. P. For., No. 1,864, December 15, 1567). This seems to be confirmed by another report from France, December 26, which says "the reiters who have arrived amount to 6,500 men" (ibid., No. 1,882).

[4] Ibid., No. 1,864 §2, No. 1,882, December 15–26, 1567. The reiters came "with certain pieces of artillery and 700 or 800 empty wagons, trusting to be no greater losers by this dissension than by the last" (ibid., No. 1,864, §3, Norris to Elizabeth).

[5] Ibid., No. 1,889, December 28, 1567; No. 1,911, January 3, 1568. In ibid., Nos. 1,976 and 2,011, the following is given as the strength of the two armies: "Army of the King, 20,600 horsemen and 10,000 Swiss footmen; the numbers of the other footmen are not set down. Condé's army, footmen 13,000; horsemen 11,900 where of reiters 6,200"—January, 1568. List of the troops of the prince of Condé with their commanders, amounting in all to 15,000 or 16,000 foot, and 14,000 horse, exclusive of those in garrison or serving in other parts of France—February 15, 1568. Norris wrote in February, 1568: "The prince has crossed the Seine, and is at present nothing inferior in number to the King's army in infantry, but they are not esteemed so good for battle by reason of the Switzers. He has 3,000 more cavalry than the king has."—Ibid., No. 1,981.

to a call of the King, the Parisians made a general muster of 30,000 and offered 1,200,000 francs for the maintenance of the war.[1]

Tentative efforts, however, were even yet made to make peace, to the indignation of the Parisians.[2]   The insistence of Charles IX, though, upon an immediate laying-down of arms was an effective obstacle to any cartel that might have been arranged.   In reply to the articles sent by the King to the prince of Condé, the latter responded that the Protestants had no intention to prescribe the law to the King, but only humbly to require such things as were necessary for the liberty of their consciences and the preservation of their lives and goods, namely, that the edict of Orleans should be observed without any alterations; that bailiwicks should be appointed for the free exercise of religion; that they should be preserved in the enjoyment of their estates and offices; that those of Lyons should have the same liberty as the rest of the subjects of the realm; that synods should be permitted, and that the Edict of Pacification should be declared irrevocable.[3]

---

[1] C. S. P. For., No. 1,864, §4, December 15, 1567.   Names of the different noblemen commanding in the army of the King of France (ibid., No. 1,918, January 4, 1568).   Letters-patent of Charles IX, dated December 16, 1567, ordered the exodus of all of the "pretended Reformed religion" from Paris and enjoined the seizure of all their benefices and lands, which were to be annexed to the crown property, and the sale of all the goods of such subjects (ibid., Nos. 1,877, 1,878, December 21–24, 1567).   In January a supplementary order commanded the sale of all goods and movables of those with the prince of Condé, and the annexation of all their lands and hereditaments to the crown (ibid., 1,914, January 3, 1568)—decrees which "were not left unexecuted in any point to the utmost" (Norris to Cecil, ibid., No. 1,889, December 28, 1567, §1).   Cf. Charles IX's letters-patent of February 21, 1568, bidding that the houses and real property held by base tenure belonging to rebels shall be sold in the same manner as personal property (ibid., No. 2,200, February 21, 1568).   The same sort of measures were practiced elsewhere.   For instance, in Agen, Protestant merchants suffered confiscation of grain and wine to the amount of 1,014 livres, 7 sous (Arch. Commun., Agen, Reg. CC, 302).

[2] The original letter of Charles IX, written from Paris, December 17, 1567 to the duke of Anjou, reciting the terms of peace to be presented to the prince of Condé was sold in Paris in 1845.   The duke's instructions were to renew hostilities if the terms were not accepted.   In Coll. Godefroy, XCVI, No. 8, is the safe-conduct given to the cardinal Châtillon by the duke of Anjou.   It is dated December 25, 1567.

[3] C. S. P. For., No. 1,890, January 4, 1568.

In his answer Charles IX declared that he would never agree to treat with the prince of Condé or any other subject as with an equal; he promised to pardon what had passed if the Protestants would lay down their arms within three days and retire to their houses and give up the places taken by them; that where certain gentlemen complained of having been prosecuted for exercising their religion in their houses, he was content that this should cease, provided that there were not more than fifty persons present exclusive of their families; that he intended to keep his forces in his hands and to dispose of and govern towns as he pleased; that the town of Lyons, being full of strangers, should not be allowed the exercise of religion; that all enrolment of men, associations, and synods, must cease; and finally, that the King would immediately dispatch his letters-patent to assure the prince and his company of their lives, goods, and the liberty of their consciences, if these conditions were complied with.[1]

The truth is, the French government prepared for war with great reluctance. Philip II's anxiety lest the queen would come to terms with her adversaries was a just one.[2] The King's expenses amounted to nearly a million livres per month,[3] and he had "to quiet such storms as daily arose in his camp amongst his nobility, partly for religion and partly for ambition."[4] Unless Spain came strongly to the relief of the Catholic cause in France, it was apparent that Condé could go almost wherever he pleased in the country, his force was so great.[5] Many of the King's soldiers were ill-minded to fight against their countrymen and many

[1] Ibid., No. 1,919, January 4, 1568.

[2] Gachard, Correspondance de Philippe II sur les Pays-Bas, II, 7, to Alva, January 22, 1568.

[3] C. S. P. Ven., No. 430, September 11, 1568; "A Florentine merchant greatly esteemed by these majesties and very useful to them in money matters called upon me today and gave me information concerning the king's inability from want of money to continue the war." Account of the sums of money paid to the troops, native and foreign, in the French king's service during the month of January 1568, amounting to 987,052 livres, or 116, 646£ 9s. sterling. The amounts reduced from French to English money by Cecil (C. S. P. For., No. 1,978, January 1568).

[4] Ibid., No. 1,914, January 3, 1568. For an amusing instance see No. 1,670

[5] Ibid., No. 2,024, February 12, 1568.

deserted. The Swiss were wearied by travel and the inclemency of the season and there was much disease among them.[1] The leaders wrangled for the command.[2] There was mutiny and desertion in the ranks of the Scotch Guard, thirty of whom deserted to the prince, or rather to their old commander Montgomery.[3] All along the line of the King's forces there was opposition to the war. The chevalier Battres told Charles IX that many of the nobles were determined to hazard the King's displeasure rather than to stain their hands in their kinsmen's blood.[4] The marshal Cossé showed unwonted courage in his advocacy of moderation[5] —a policy which he openly admitted and approved in the Council meeting (February 10). The germ of the Politique party is thus early discoverable.[6]

The duke of Anjou, who had been made commander-in-chief of the Catholic forces,[7] seeing the Protestant army considerably augmented and that they had crossed the Seine and controlled the passages over the Yonne and the Loire, sent most of his troops back to Paris, and scattered the rest along the banks of the Seine,

[1] C. S. P. For., No. 2,024, §1, February 24, 1568.

[2] "The King's army, finding what disorder the want of a good head has bred hitherto, are now content to accept any, be it not a marshal of France. It is now said that Mons. de Tavannes shall be M. d'Anjou's lieutenant" (ibid., No. 2,024, February 24, 1568).

[3] Some of them were captured by the King's forces in a skirmish near Châtillon between the duke of Nevers and Montgomery, and broken upon the wheel. The poor wretches under the torture compromised twenty-five others of the Guard, who on March 6 were also horribly put to death (ibid., No. 2,062, March 12, 1568). After the peace of Longjumeau the Scotch captains who had joined the prince of Condé were deprived of their commissions, although the action was contrary to the edict. In fact a reorganization of the whole maison du roi was made (ibid., No. 2,135, April 18, No. 2,178, May 12, 1568. The vacancies were filled by Swiss instead (ibid., Nos. 1,981, 1,987, February 1 and 6, 1568), so that the famous Scotch Guard in the end became the King's Swiss Guard, which lasted down to the Revolution.

[4] Ibid., No. 1,981, February 1, 1568.

[5] He was accused of having "pretermitted many fair occasions to have fought with the prince."

[6] Ibid., No. 2,024, §2, February 24, 1568.

[7] Claude Haton, I, 498 and note; C. S. P. For., No. 1,833, November 24, 1567.

to guard the road between Troyes and Paris. The Catholic camp in Paris was established in the faubourg St. Marceau, where were lodged all the gendarmerie, both foot and horse, the artillery and the Swiss. But most of the cavalry was quartered in the villages, where the horses could get better grazing, to the detriment of the country round about, for the soldiers amused themselves by pillage, so that the better towns and châteaux were compelled to fortify themselves as though against the enemy.[1] Strenuous efforts were made to provision Paris against a future siege, and to establish magazines of provisions and ammunition in the towns of the Ile-de-France and Champagne. To this end the government bought up grain in the early spring of 1568, paying 50 livres per muid, or 10 sous, 5 deniers, per bichet.[2]

As the prince drew nearer to the city, the conduct of Paris became a matter of anxiety. Although bigotedly Catholic, the populace of the capital had no mind to experience another siege in the cause of religion, and the popular rage against the government, especially toward Catherine de Medici, became so intense that she dared not go abroad without being heavily guarded. The popular voice claimed that the queen mother nourished the quarrel and consumed the revenues of the King,[3] a belief which the Guises cleverly fostered, if they were not the immediate authors of it.[4]

[1] Claude Haton, I, 524.

[2] These high prices were partly owing to the fact that speculators had bought up much of the grain, which rose in April to between 60 and 70 livres per muid. But in May, with the promise of a good harvest, the price dropped over one-half, from 15 sous tournois per bichet to 7 sous 6 deniers, to the great regret of the merchants who had counted upon a scarcity. On the other hand, the price of oats went higher, being sold at from 10 to 12 sous per bichet, or boisseau, for there was very little to be had after the passage of the troops; and because it ripened earlier, almost all of it was taken (Claude Haton, II, 523).

[3] C. S. P. For., No. 2,024, February 24, 1568.

[4] So ominous was the temper of the Parisians that even the minor gates of the Louvre were equipped with drawbridges (ibid., No. 2,040, §4, March 1, 1568). Part of the indignation of Paris was due to the outrages of some reiters in the King's army from Luxembourg and Lorraine, who robbed priests and despoiled churches, notwithstanding that they were in Catholic service, so much so that "the Parisians had rather had the prince of Condé's people should approach Paris as they" (ibid., Nos. 2,040, 2,041, March 1, 1568).

"The money of the kingdom today is in the hands of a single class," wrote the Venetian ambassador. "The clergy is ruined. Without counting the property of the church which has been mortgaged or sold with the authorization of the Pope, the church since 1561 has paid out 12,000,000 écus for the King. This would be immaterial, for it is but a seventh of its annual revenue, if the church had not suffered so much from the civil war. The nobles are at their wits' ends and have not a sou on account of the war. The country folk have been so pillaged by the soldiery, whose license is frightful, that they are reduced to beggary. Only the bourgeoisie and the *gens de robe longue* still have money. It is difficult for the King to obtain money without force. In addition to these troubles with his subjects the King has lost all his credit with foreign merchants and cannot raise an écu outside the kingdom without giving collateral. But good may come out of this calamitous state, for the King and his subjects have come to such a dead stop that peace may result."[1]

Under these circumstances the crown earnestly renewed negotiations for peace. Even astrology was invoked by the superstitious Catherine and the signs of the zodiac were sagely said to point toward peace. For the queen, walking one day in her garden, discoursing of the peace, called unto her Messire Nonio, an Italian famed for his knowledge of astrology, of whom she asked what he found by the stars touching peace; to which he presently answered that the heavens did not promise it, nor was the earth yet ready to receive it; since the effect of the eclipse of the sun was then in its greatest force, and likewise the virtue of the conjunction of Saturn and Mars which was in Aries last year; but the wise man concluded with the oracular statement that the heavens did not *constrain* the inferior powers but only *disposed* them.[2]

On February 28 the King sent the marshal Montmorency, Morvilliers, the bishop of Limoges, and D'Allny, one of his secretaries, to confer with representatives appointed by the prince of Condé, the cardinal Châtillon, the bishop of Valence, and Teligny

[1] *Rel. vén.*, II, 145.

[2] *C. S. P. For.*, No. 2,040, §3, March 1, 1568.

at Longjumeau. The prince made two notable conditions to the demands already outlined—that all the articles, agreements, and capitulations should be confirmed by *all* the Parlements of the realm, and that certain cautionary towns—he named Boulogne or La Rochelle[1]—be given to the Protestants as guarantees of the just purposes of the government. These two demands are of interest because they became invariable demands of the Huguenots in the future and foreshadowed important terms in the edict of Bergerac (1576) and that of Nantes of 1598. Those of the King replied that to make such demands impugned the King's honor, that the prince of Condé ought to trust the crown without requiring guaranties of assurance. As to the particular demands, Charles IX declared he did not think it meet to make the edict of 1563 perpetual[2] and protested against the political and military organization of the Protestants, "insomuch as this liberty remaining, the King shall never be assured in his realm." On March 4 the commissioners of the prince, tired of the parleying and vexed at the diversion the King tried to introduce by proposing a double alliance between the warring houses in the marriage of the duke of Guise with the prince's eldest daughter, and of D'Andelot's eldest son to the duke's sister, demanded express answer regarding church edifices; better observance of the edict by the King's officers; Huguenot schools, etc. To these Charles IX assented and the Huguenots waived the matter of confirmation by provincial Parlements and the surrender of certain cautionary places for the time being. It remained to settle the question of the reiters' pay.

---

[1] *Correspondance de Catherine de Médicis*, III, 136. La Rochelle was already the Huguenots' most important point and already large supplies of gunpowder and ammunition, chiefly from England, were being brought in there (cf. the captain of La Rochelle to Queen Elizabeth, *C. S. P. For.*, No. 2,057, March 10, 1568). La Popelinière, XII, 68–70, has a dissertation upon the history and institutions of La Rochelle.

The peace of Longjumeau put an end to Montluc's plan for the seizure of La Rochelle, for which he had received the King's sanction in February. See the documents in F. Fr. 15,544, fol. 187; 15,548, foll. 163 ff.

[2] In the controversy between the count palatine and the King the former had asked that the word "perpetual" be inserted in the edict, so that the edict might not be revoked at will (*C. S. P. For.*, No. 1,968, 1567–68).

Five hundred thousand livres in the royal chest at Amboise were appropriated by the crown and the balance of the obligation was provided for by the cardinal of Bourbon and the dukes of Montmorency and Longueville, who went security for it.[1]

As finally concluded on March 26 the terms of Longjumeau were in reality a confirmation of the edict of March, 1563, which was not enlarged as the prince of Condé had at first demanded, except that the edict in its new form also applied to Provence.[2] The terms of Longjumeau were suppressed for a short time and the army not dismissed, however, because it was thought perilous to disarm until the reiters had taken their leave.   These maraud-

[1] The balance was to be paid in two instalments at Frankfurt (*C. S. P. For.*, No. 2,135, April 18, 1568).   All gifts and pensions were revoked until the debt was paid (*ibid.*, No. 2,248, June 4, 1568).   In Coll. Godefroy, CCLVII, Nos. 35, 41–43 are a number of documents dealing with the pay of the reiters at this time.   The whole sum required for the reiters was 1,440,000 livres, and the government at once set to work to collect it.   The first collection seems to have been a sort of *don patriotique* made by a house-to-house visitation, showing how pressing was the necessity.   The government tried to borrow the money which John Casimir had raised for the Protestants, but which was not used on account of the peace, and offered to pay 16 per cent. interest for it (*C. S. P. For.*, March 28, 1568).   On March 23 the King issued letters patent forbidding all notaries and others receiving any contract for annuities or mortgages before the sum of 1,400,000 livres *tournois* had been raised (*ibid.*, No. 2,085).   The duke of Alva was in a state of great anxiety for fear lest the reiters would come into the Netherlands and thought he discovered a plot to throw St. Omer into their hands (*ibid.*, No. 2,230, April 25, 1568).

All the records abound with allusions to the rapacity of the reiters: "La nazione tedesca, nazione avara" (*Rel. vén.*, II, 125 and notes).

"Les reîtres trouvaient beaucoup meilleur l'argent qu'on leur promettait d'Angleterre que les cidres de Normandie."—La Noue.

"L'importunità dei Tedeschi che mai cessavano de domandare donazioni o paghe."—Davila, I, 137.

"Ils consommeraient un gouffre d'argent—Facheux, avares, importuns."— Brantôme, III, 196, 310.

[2] But restricted as they were, the terms yet mightily offended the Guises, especially the cardinal of Lorraine who "did marvellously storm that the king would condescend to any peace with his subjects, whereat the king said he would agree thereto,, 'maugre luy.'"   On the entire negotiations see *C. S. P. For.*, No. 2,025, Feb. 24; Nos. 2,040–41, March 1–4; No. 2,054, March 9; Nos. 2,057, 2,058, March 10–11; No. 2,092, March 27, 1568).   The final draft was completed on March 23; the edict was signed by Charles IX on March 26.   It was published at Paris on the next day (*ibid.*, Nos. 2,092–93).

ers, who followed war as a trade and with whom faith and piety were not virtues, had not ceased their depredations during the course of the negotiations. The people "being everywhere environed both with their own or foreign enemies, dared not approach town or village, all being replenished with reiters or those who entreated them as ill, whereby they miserably died in the fields."[1]

The publication of the edict encountered bitter opposition throughout the country.[2] At Toulouse the King's messenger who brought the royal order for its registration by the Parlement was actually tried, condemned, and executed for the "offense," so inflamed was the public mind.[3] At Rouen a furious multitude assailed the magistrates and mobbed the dwellings of those of Huguenot inclination. The same thing happened at Bourges. At Orleans the soldiers murdered several at the gates of the city, with impunity. In Languedoc there were commotions and slaughters.[4]

The strife in the south of France, in Provence, Languedoc, and Guyenne, had never entirely ceased since the inception of the first civil war. The King's tour of the provinces had overawed the combatants to a certain extent and in Languedoc Damville, who had succeeded his father on April 28, 1563,[5] managed to keep things with a pretty even hand, enforcing the edict of Amboise throughout his jurisdiction.[6] But the hostility of Montluc, whose government of Guyenne adjoined Languedoc, toward Damville, was a serious bar to pacification, for Montluc not only sought to diminish Damville's authority by complaining to the

[1] *Ibid.*, No. 2,058, March 11, 1568. Granvella expressed fear of universal famine in France, followed by the plague (Gachard, *Correspondance de Philippe II*, II, 17).

[2] The preachers and the doctors in Paris in their sermons decried the King and his Council (Claude Haton, II, 527 and note; cf. *ibid.*, 531; *Rel. vén.*, II, 121).

[3] *C. S. P. For.*, No. 2,273, June 17, 1568; *Hist. du Languedoc*, V, 482 ff.; *Commentaires et lettres de Montluc*, V, 18, 88, 142, 156; D'Aubigné, Book IV, chaps. xii–xiv.

[4] *C. S. P. For.*, Nos. 2,115, 2,135, April 8–10, 1568.

[5] *Hist. du Languedoc*, V, 441.

[6] For details see *ibid.*, 443–64.

King of him, but also secretly connived with the doings of ultra-Catholic partisans in Toulouse and elsewhere.[1]

So intense was the hatred in the south of France between the Catholics and the Huguenots that there was scarce any intermission of hostilities at all after the peace of Longjumeau, especially in Provence. The duke of Joyeuse, who commanded the royal forces here, was a man after Montluc's own heart. Early in 1568 he had passed up the Rhone for the purpose of aiding the counts of Tende and Suze. He had with him 2,000 foot and from five to six hundred horse, and easily overcame the little fortresses until he reached Pont St. Esprit in February. Failing to take this, the army was divided. Joyeuse crossed the Rhone at Avignon on March 7, took Loudun, Orsenne, and Tresques, then, retracing his steps, he again joined the count of Tende and renewed the siege of Pont St. Esprit. The Protestants under the command of Montbrun gave battle in the plains of Montfran near Aramon, and were badly defeated May 24, 1568. When peace was made Joyeuse returned to Avignon. Most of the towns of lower Languedoc were carefully garrisoned by him, but Montauban, Castres, and Montpellier resisted. Everywhere he exacted disarmament and the oath of fidelity.[2]

[1] Montluc even ascribed the ravages of the plague to Damville in order to create popular prejudice against him! (*Hist. du Languedoc*, V, 449). His own words are: "Pour se montrer au peuple, qui avoit une marvelleuse envie de le voir, n'y pouvant arrêter à cause de la grande peste qui y est." (Cf. his letters to Damville, December 31, 1567, and August 26, 1569, in *Commentaires et lettres de Montluc*, V, 103 and 159.) Montluc was doubly incensed at this moment because the peace of Longjumeau canceled orders which he had received in February to attempt to take La Rochelle by sea (*ibid.*, VII, 148 ff.; V, 107 note, 109 note, 184 note).

[2] *Bulletin de la Soc. acad. du Var.*, 1876.

CHAPTER XIII

THE THIRD CIVIL WAR (1568). NEW CATHOLIC LEAGUE.
THE BATTLE OF JARNAC

The peace of Longjumeau, more than any treaty of the civil wars, was a tentative settlement, an armistice merely. It was chiefly compelled by the lack of funds of both parties and from its signature was more openly opposed and protested against than any other of the treaties. Suspense over the probability of a third and worse war prevailed from the beginning. For while many on each side returned to their homes, there were many others who had no place to which to retire, for whom vagabond life had attractions and who preferred war to peace and plundering to honest labor.[1] Both sides were too suspicious and too fearful to lay down their arms. So many of the Huguenot captains kept their troops in the fields that the King wrote to no less than 212 places charging the governors thereof to scatter these bands. Many known to have been in arms hid them in secret places and were, in consequence, not permitted to return to their native places until such arms were given up. The Catholic resentment seems to have been strongest in Paris[2] and Burgundy, though in the former the provost of the merchants made the singularly sane plea to the King to have an especial regard for justice lest its denial might stir the Protestants to new strife. In general, though, wherever the King's garrisons were stationed there was trouble.

It was not long before the Guise opposition organized. Failing of their hold upon Charles IX, the Guises directed their efforts upon his brother, Henry, duke of Anjou, whose Catholic senti-

---

[1] Claude Haton, II, 525. He repeats at different times the current play upon words which designated these free-booting nobles as "gens-pille-hommes" (gentil-hommes). In general, in his estimation, the nobility had much degenerated. See Vol. I, Introd., p. lxii.

[2] Volunteer bands of searchers visited Huguenot houses, to inquire into their faith (C. S. P. For., No. 2,191, May 17, 1568). At the court, certain of the nobles promised Charles to assure for all members of their retinue to be good Catholics (ibid., Nos. 2,191, 2,235, 2,236, 2,243, 2,248, May 17 to June 4, 1568).

ments[1] were less impeachable than those of Charles and who
began to "show some tokens of an ambitious heart," was a sworn
Catholic, and showed great offense at his royal brother's action
in "very courteously" entertaining the cardinal Châtillon, the
count Rochefoucauld, and Brocarde, the Protestant governor of
Orleans.[2]   On the night of March 29 a secret conference was
held at the Louvre of the leaders among the Guise party, in which
it was proposed that a pacific attitude be pretended until the disarming of the prince of Condé's forces and the withdrawal of the
reiters had taken place, and then suddenly to seize Orleans, Soissons, Auxerre, and La Rochelle—the Huguenot strongholds—for
which duty Lansac, Martigues, Chavigny, and Brissac were to
be appointed, reinforce the garrison of Paris, and send the ferocious
Montluc into Gascony to subjugate the strongest Protestant provinces, seize the sea-ports, and drive a Catholic wedge in between
Poitou and the territories of the queen of Navarre, who already
had taken the precaution to strengthen her defenses.   By some
means, perhaps through the marshal Cossé, who was a Politique
at heart, the cardinal Châtillon learned of the plot the very next
day, and straightway informed the marshal Montmorency, another
moderate, of it.   At the same time the plan was discovered from
another source to the prince of Condé.   When Charles IX was
taxed with information of it, he swore that the whole thing was
done without his knowledge, accused the cardinal of Lorraine of
treasonable practice, and calling for pen and ink wrote to Condé
promising "good and sincere" observation of all that had been
agreed upon at Longjumeau.[3]

It will be observed how completely this plan of the Guises for
the subjugation of Guyenne and Gascony is in alignment with
the views of Montluc which he had expressed to Philip II.[4] Hitherto

[1] "D'Anjou has marvellously stomached these dealings, and has kept his
chamber, having uttered most despiteful words against them of the religion, saying
that he hoped to march upon their bellies" (C. S. P. For., No. 2,177, May 12, 1568).

[2] Ibid., No. 2,115, §1, April 8, 1568.

[3] See the revelations of Norris to Cecil in ibid., No. 2,100, March 30, 1568.
As earnest of the royal purpose the marshal Montmorency set at once about
disarming the people of Paris.

[4] Commentaires et lettres de Montluc, V, 22, 23.

the King of Spain had been sustaining two separate lines of secret correspondence, one with Montluc direct; the other with the cardinal of Lorraine through the duke of Alva. These two lines now are fused into a larger whole, at least so far as the Spanish king is concerned.[1] Montluc is the military, the cardinal of Lorraine the diplomatic, agent of Philip's purposes.

The development of the Holy League has now advanced another stage in its evolution. The old warrior had not discontinued his secret relations with Spain, in spite of his warm denial of the fact to the queen mother, who taxed him with it,[2] but through Bardaxi still kept in communication with Philip II. We find him writing twice to the King in February 1567 and Philip responding in terms of encouragement in the following month.[3] Guyenne was peculiarly vulnerable to such an attack as was now contemplated, and Montluc was certainly the best captain to execute it. The army of the Huguenots there was in a bad state.[4]

The instrument was already forged to Philip II's hand in the local Catholic leagues in France. His interest in these was one of the silent activities at Bayonne. The instructions to the duke of Alva and to Bardaxi were almost identical. "As the queen mother lacks either fixity of ideas or honesty of purpose"—the words are those of the procès-verbal framed in the Spanish council-chamber, it is necessary to encourage the practices of Montluc and the Catholics."[5] It must have been a source of delight to the Spanish king to observe the rapid increase of these associations. There are two changes to be noticed in these provincial leagues: their increasingly popular character, and their tendency to fuse together. Hitherto they had been local in their operations. Now a process of federation is to be observed by which the provincial leagues are gradually welded into one whole—in a word the mighty Sainte

[1] Probably neither the cardinal nor Montluc knew that the other had been in secret correspondence with Philip II. Knowing Philip's methods, it is likely that he kept them in ignorance of it. This was his way (cf. Forneron, I, 327).

[2] Ruble, *Commentaires et lettres de Montluc*, IV, 328, 329, letter of March 5, 1564.

[3] *Ibid.*, V, 76, 77 and notes.   [4] *Ibid.*, V, 145.

[5] Cited by Forneron, *Histoire de Philippe II*, I, 327.

Ligue of 1576 potentially exists now.[1] The federative tendency of these associations was a natural result of their increase in number and membership. It was not a haphazard development at all. Design is evident throughout.[2]

The renewal of civil war in 1567 had given a great impulse to this spirit of association.[3] Nowhere was it more pronounced than in Burgundy. Tavannes, who was governor of Burgundy, in the year 1567 (July 18), formed a league under the name of the Confrérie du St. Esprit. Churchmen, the nobility of Burgundy, and wealthy bourgeois who wished to preserve the Catholic religion were united together in the service of the King. The version of its origin in the *Mémoires de Tavannes* is so interesting that I venture to quote it:

Seeing so much discontent and so many threatening enterprises among the Huguenots, the queen, for safety's sake, in the beginning of the year 1567 caused a levy of 9,000 Swiss [the actual number was 6,000 to be made under pretext that they were to be for the service of the duke of Alva in the Flemish War. The prevailing unrest and the rumors of insurrection gave the sieur de Tavannes, who penetrated the designs of the queen and the purpose of the Huguenots, the thought that a prudent man might also take precautions of his own. He reasoned that the Huguenots did not have more zeal for their cause than the Catholics for the old religion, and that those who would preserve it would give their lives and employ their last sou to succor the King; in a word, oppose league to league. He therefore organized the Confrérie du St. Esprit, which in reality was a league of the ecclesiastics and the nobility of Burgundy, with rich men from the towns, who voluntarily swore to serve in the

---

[1] The ordinance of Moulins specifically alluded to the growing popular nature of these confraternities: "Qu'on abolisse entièrement les confréries établies sous prétexte de religion parmi le *petit* peuple, les festins, les répas, les bâtons (bâtons de Confrérie, qui servent à porter aux confréries l'Image de quelque saint, ou la représentation de quelque mystère) et autres choses semblables, qui donnent lieu à la superstition, aux troubles, à la débauche, aux querelles, et aux monopoles" (De Thou, V, Book XXXIX, p. 183, in the article prohibiting them). But it was as impossible then as now to enforce a law in the face of a public opinion which did not sympathize with the provision. Public opinion not merely favored their formation; the very officers of the crown promoted their organization. La Popelinière, XI, 12, makes this point.

[2] "Discorso sopra gli umori di Francia di M^r. Nazaret, 1570," Barberini Library 3,269, fol. 63. See Appendix XIII.

[3] D'Aubigné, III, 2.

interest of the Catholic religion against the Huguenots, sacrificing both person and property for the sake of the King.   Without using coercion he gave orders for the enrolment of men-at-arms and the collection of money, created warders, spies, and messengers, in imitation of the Huguenots, in order to discover their machinations.   The oath subscribed to justified this design.   Each parish of Dijon paid its men for three months, and each town contributed 200 horse and 250 footmen.   Burgundy could furnish 1,500 horse and 400 men on foot, paid for three months of the year.   The sieur de Tavannes summoned an assembly in the Maison du Roi, ... and there caused the oath to be read.

The oath began:

We swear by the most holy and incomprehensible name of God, the Father, Son, and Holy Spirit, in whose name we have been baptized, and we promise on our honor and the peril of our lives that, henceforth, at all times, through the chiefs and those who shall be named by the King under these articles, we will make known any enterprise that may work contrary to our said law and faith of which we have made profession in our baptism, and which we have maintained by the grace of God to the present, and also to make known every enterprise, which may clothe itself in hatred of the maintenance of the said faith, against the said royal Majesty, madame his mother, and messieurs his brothers, who rule over us by divine permission.

And further on in the oath:

We swear and promise in the present writing to render all friendship and fraternity the one to the other, to aid each other reciprocally against all phases of the opposite party, if they shall undertake any enterprise against any one of the signatories to the cause of this party; and for the sake of said aid we promise respectively, the one and the other, to employ all our persons, our credit, and our favors without sparing anything.   And we promise to observe all the articles above sworn to without regard to friends, parents, or any relationship which we may have with those who undertake the contrary.[1]

In the following year, on April 2, 1568, "La Fraternité des Catholiques de Châlons-sur-Saône" emerged.

A l'imitation de la majesté du Roy nostre sire [so runs the instrument], et soubs sa protection et bon plaisir . . . . nous avons faict entre nous et pour tous autres Catholiques qui adjoindre se vouldront une fraternité qui s'appellera Confrairie et Société des Catholiques.

[1] *Mémoires de Tavannes*, ed. Michaud and Poujoulat, séries I, VIII, 288, 289; Pasquier, Book IV, letter 23; Collection Trémont, Nos. 1,367, 1,382; cf. La Popelinière, XI, 7-12; Pingaud, *Les Saulx-Tavannes*, p. 61.

And it is added—sign of omen—

Et au cas qu'il advint que Dieu ne veuille que les persones de sa majesté et de messieurs ses frères . . . . fussent oppressés de sorte que ne sceussions avoir advertissement de leurs volontez, promettons rendre toute obeissance au général chef qui sera esleu.[1]

Six weeks later, on May 18, 1568, through the activity of Tavannes, a similar association was formed in Berry and was confirmed at Bourges by the archbishop, Jacques le Roy.[2] A month later La Ligue Chrétienne et Royale, "for the defense of the Catholic church in France and for maintaining the royal authority in the House of Valois," to which was appended the significant proviso, "so long as it shall govern in the Catholic and Apostolic religion" appeared in Champagne under the auspices of Henry of Guise, then eighteen years of age and governor of the province. The nobility, the bishop, and the clergy, in a meeting at Troyes, concluded, signed, and took an oath to this league on June 25.[3] Exactly a month later, on July 25, the Beauvaisis followed the lead of Burgundy, Berry, and Champagne, and formed an "Association Catholique" for the same purpose.[4] The movement also spread west of the Seine, into Maine and Anjou, where the clergy, the nobility, and the third estate, on July 11, 1568, established an association whose members swore "de vivre et mourir en la religion catholique et de nous secourir les uns et les autres contre les rebelles et hérétiques sectaires de la nouvelle religion." Forty persons signed the oath.[5]

In Toulouse, the former league was revived in September, 1568, with new energy under the patronage of the cardinal of Armagnac and actual leadership of a secular priest who preached

[1] State Papers, Foreign, Elizabeth, XCVII, No. 1 711. A printed pamphlet. See Appendix XIV.

[2] Raynal, Histoire du Berry, IV, 79–83. The text of the act is found in Thauvessière's Histoire du Berry, 189.

[3] The text is given in Claude Haton, II, 1152. Cf. Vicomte de Meaux, Luttes religieuses en France, 177, 178; Capefigue, La réforme et la ligue, 360.

[4] Feret, Clermont-en-Beauvaisis pendant les troubles de la ligue, Clermont, 1853.

[5] State Papers, Foreign, Elizabeth, C, No. 1,863. See Appendix XV.

war upon the Protestants with a crusader's zeal. On September
12 the latter gathered those desirous of reviving the association
in the cathedral of St. Etienne where a solemn oath was taken by
all, who promised to devote life and property to the support of the
catholic religion. The league thus formed was officially entitled
La Croisade, with the motto: "Eamus nos, moriamur cum Christo."
All its members wore a white cross.[1] Even some of the smaller
towns followed the example of the provinces and large cities. At
Anduze in Lower Languedoc at this same time the churches formed
a Catholic union.[2] The movement actually spread into Lower
Navarre where in the same month, September, the sieur de Luxe
and some others, at the instigation of the cardinal of Lorraine,
perhaps, formed a league at St. Palais for the purpose of driving
out the Calvinist preachers in St. Palais. They seized La Rive,
the pastor at St. Palais, Tarde, pastor at Ostabanès, both of whom
were imprisoned in the house of De Luxe. But the prompt conduct of Jeanne d'Albret and the prince of Navarre, who won his
spurs in the siege of Garris, speedily crushed this association.[3]

In view of this spontaneous organization of the Catholics everywhere, it was inevitable that the peace of Longjumeau would be
of short duration, even if there had been no special circumstances
to bring it to an end.[4] The Guises, after the discovery of their

[1] *Hist. du Languedoc*, XI, 509–10 and XII; *Preuves*, No. 300, p. cxiii; *Cabinet historique*, II, 217. This league was much more formal in its organization than any of the others. In addition to securing the authorization of the Parlement, the leaders had secured the sanction of Pius V in the March *preceding*. The bull was granted March 15.

[2] *Cabinet historique*, II, 219.

[3] Bordenave, *Hist. de Béarn et de Navarre*, 139–45. I venture to suggest the cardinal of Lorraine as a possible instigator, from Bordenave's words: "quelques autres . . . . sollicitez par quelques uns des *principaux du conseil* de France." Philip II threw new troops into Spanish Navarre at this time, either in consequence of Jeanne d'Albret's energetic action or to co-operate with the league, if it were successful. Fourquevaux ascertained the fact, but was in the dark as to the reason for it (*Dépêches de Fourquevaux*, II, 25, November, 1568).

[4] A letter of Coligny, July 29, 1568, shows that the Huguenot leader was aware of the formation of these provincial leagues. After complaining of the assassination of one of D'Andelot's lieutenants, he protests against the general violence: "Ce que faict croire que ce sont des fruictz et offices des confraires du Saint-Esprit et

secret conference of March 29, for the time being sought to dissemble their feelings and purposes, and not to offend the King's anger. When it was observed in the royal presence that great inconvenience was likely to arise in France for want of obedience to the edict, the cardinal of Lorraine, hearing the remark, replied "Sur ma conscience, il n'y a rien plus necessaire."

The feud between the Guises and Montmorencys seemed likely to involve the state in war before very long.[1] The quarrel between the two houses was the more intense at this time owing to the fact that the duke of Anjou's retention of the lieutenantship, in which office the Guises supported and maintained him for their own purposes, gave offense to the marshals, Montmorency, Damville, and Vieilleville; the more so because they were all moderate Catholics and were dissatisfied with the duke's bigoted Catholic leanings and affiliation with the Guises; they argued that "it had not been seen heretofore, that the King should have a lieutenant," that the continuance of such a title, especially in time of peace, was a prejudice to their station,[2] adding signifi-

sainctes ligues qu'ils appellent; mais si on voit que infiniz meurtres et massacres qui se sont faictz avec une effrénée licence en tous les endroictz de ce royaume depuys la paciffication il n'en ayt esté faict aucune justice ou chastiment, quelque déclaration que Vostre Majesté ayt faicte de sa volonté et intention, je n'en espère pas davantage de cestuy-cy, estant bien facile à cognoistre que ce sont choses projectées et délibérées avec les gouverneurs des provinces, et que cela ne se faict poinct sans adveu ou pour le moins sans un tacite consentement."—*Correspondance de Catherine de Médicis*, III, 163, note.

[1] Montmorency continually threw his influence in favor of peace and moderation, slapping the Guises, however, in his utterances. "The Duke Montmorency said there was nothing more necessary for the maintenance of the king's estate than the sincere observance of the edict of pacification, and such as labour to the contrary are neither friends to the king nor his crown; and for his own part if the king did not foresee in time with due execution of justice this growing mischief, he was resolved with his leave to depart the court with his friends and allies, and so to withdraw himself from such as under the pretext of maintenance of their religion, continually nourished this division, and in the end put out the glory and renown of the French empire."—*C. S. P. For.*, No. 2,177, §1, May 12, 1568.

On June 17 Norris wrote to Cecil: "Montmorency has come to the court. The process between him and the duke of Guise for the county of Dammartin will in the end break into open enmity."—*Ibid.*, No. 2,273.

[2] "The four marshals agree all in one against the Cardinal."—*Ibid.*, No. 2,235, May 31, 1568.

cantly that they "being marshals knew what appertained to their charges." The strife between the factions soon became so severe as to dismay some, especially the cardinal of Bourbon, who threatened "that in case the King would take no better order than he had done, he would depart the court and give the world to understand how he had at heart the honour of his house and the welfare of his friends." The chancellor L'Hôpital, having vainly endeavored to soften the strife, asked leave to be discharged of his office —an event which the cardinal of Lorraine would have hailed with delight. As it was, the Guises used Anjou to abuse the position of the chancellor.[1]

The continued presence of the reiters and the Swiss also added to the anxiety of those who were peaceably inclined, for "there was not a town or a village in the Ile-de-France that was not furnished with soldiers," the country indeed teeming so much with them that traveling now was more perilous even than during the wars.[2] The 6,000 Swiss still remained within four leagues of Paris at the last of May. The reiters of the prince stopped in Burgundy and plundered the country; while the prince of Condé vainly demanded that they be paid at once.[3] At Dijon five of them were slain by the desperate populace and a massacre of thirteen of the inhabitants followed.[4] Many thought that the war would be renewed the moment the harvest was gathered.[5]

Late in May the duke of Montmorency left Paris for Chantilly, while his brother Damville stayed in the capital. The action of

[1] "All things are ruled now by M. d'Anjou, who though young is a most earnest and cruel enemy against the favourers of religion, and has his privy counsellors, the cardinal of Lorraine being the chiefest, and further has his chancellor, who seals all such things as the good old chancellor of the King refuses to seal; who neither for love nor dread would seal anything against the statutes of the realm."—*Ibid.*, No. 2,178, May 12, 1568. On the whole affair, see *ibid.*, No. 2,177, §2, May 12, 1568.

[2] *Ibid.*, No. 2,115, §2, April 8; No. 2,177, §3, May 12, 1568.

[3] Duc d'Aumale, *Histoire des princes de Condé*, II, App. I.

[4] *C. S. P. For.*, No. 2,235, May 31, 1568.

[5] "The garrisons in the Ile de France are thought to attend no other thing but till the corn be off the ground to begin where they left off."—*Ibid.*, No. 2,178, May 12, 1568.

each was significant. At Chantilly the cardinal Châtillon and other Protestant nobles deliberated, while in Paris Damville's house was frequented by those hostile to the cardinal of Lorraine's authority, notably the four marshals, all of whom inveighed against him and were popularly believed to be forming a new opposition to him.[1]   The Huguenot leaders, Condé, Coligny, D'Andelot, all lay in various castles throughout the Ile-de-France, with captains, soldiers, and gentlemen around them, and so distributed that no river separated them one from the other, while one ford between Paris and Rouen was kept open to enable those of the religion in Picardy to keep in touch with the prince.[2]   So skilfully was the distribution made that the leaders could have been able to unite within a day and a half if necessary.[3]

The strain upon Charles IX soon began to tell. He was heard to say that he would rather lose his crown outright than live in continual fear, and as the feud became intenser, the King yielded and finally showed his hand by displacing the marshal Montmorency as governor of Paris, though he dared not go quite so far as to put Henri d'Anjou in his room, but chose his youngest brother, the duke of Alençon.[4]

We discover at this time the germ of the Politique party.[5]   If the Guises had been aware of the astonishing diplomatic stroke Montmorency had conceived in his retreat at Chantilly and

[1] C. S. P. For., Nos. 2,235, 2,243, 2,248, May 31, June 2–4, 1568.

[2] As to localities see Duc d'Aumale, Histoire des princes de Condé, II, 284.

[3] C. S. P. For., No. 2,296, June 22, 1568.   They feared a plot to capture them by trickery, as Egmont and Hoorne had been trapped in Flanders.   According to report, Lavallette was to have seized the prince, Chavigny the admiral, and Tavannes D'Andelot.   The warning was probably given by some secretary whom Coligny had corrupted, for shortly after this time several secretaries to the Catholic leaders were dismissed (ibid., No. 2,256, June 7, 1568; cf. D'Aumale, Histoire des princes de Condé, II, 12, n. 2, and p. 287).   Coligny also bribed the secretary of Don Francesco de Alava, Spanish ambassador in France (see C. S. P. For., No. 1,230, May 24, 1568 and Introd., p. xxvi).

[4] Ibid., Nos. 2,256, 2,304, 2,323, June 7, 28, July 5, 1568.   For an instance of the feeling between the prince and the cardinal see Sir Henry Norris to the queen, ibid., No. 2,248, June 1, 1568 and Duc d'Aumale, Histoire des princes de Condé, II, 12 and n. 1.

[5] This was the time the word first appeared (D'Aumale, II, 12, note 3).

which he had communicated to the Huguenot leaders, they might not have pressed the case of Anjou so insistently. This scheme was to separate the King's brother from his attachment to the Guises and at the same time enlist English aid in support of religious toleration in France—the aim of the Politique party—by nothing less than bringing about the marriage of the Valois prince with Queen Elizabeth. At the same time Montmorency, by gaining the favor of the duke, would work the cardinal out of power. To this end the duke approached the English envoy in France.[1]

Day by day the animosity of the parties grew. In a certain sense the peril of the times was greater than during a state of war. Daily murder by dagger and by drowning, and violation of property took place throughout France, to such an extent that it was said more had been murdered since the publication of the peace than were in the war which it was supposed to have concluded.[2] But although the animosity of the parties was strong enough to incite them to war, the renewal of hostilities was yet very dependent upon the fluctuation of events in the Netherlands,[3]

[1] C. S. P. For., No. 2,295, Norris to Cecil, June 23, 1568. On the whole negotiation see Robinson, "Queen Elizabeth and the Valois Princes," Eng. Hist. Rev., II, 40; Hume, Courtships of Queen Elizabeth, 114–49. Hume, however, is in error, p. 115, in believing that the negotiation arose after the peace of St. Germain in 1570. The intercourse must have been kept very much in the dark, judging from the obscure allusions in the following: Sir Henry Norris to the earl of Leicester, C. S. P. For., No. 2,241, August 20, 1568—Marshal Montmorency is very desirous to have answer to the letter which he wrote to Leicester; the queen to the duchess of Montmorency, ibid., No. 2,472, August 27, 1568—Thanks her f or her courteous and honorable entertainment in her house, and near her person of the daughter of her chamberlain, Lord Edward Howard. Walsingham warned his government at this time against spies of the cardinal of Lorraine in London. See Appendix XVI.

[2] "More have been murdered since the publishing of the peace than were all these last troubles. Daily murders are committed without any punishment to the offenders, others violently taken out of their houses in the night and led to the river being without remorse drowned."—C. S. P. For., Nos. 2,383, 2,339, 2,407, July 31–August 7, 1568.

[3] The proceedings here on both sides are measured by the success in Flanders (ibid., No. 2,273, June 17, 1568; Archives de la maison d'Orange-Nassau, II, 47; Dépêches de Fourquevaux, II, 24).

and at this moment the balance there was inclined in Spain's favor.[1]

William of Orange, while not in alliance with the French, nevertheless sought to avail himself of the services of the 4,000 reiters which John Casimir had raised for the French Protestants, whose use was no longer required by the Huguenots after the peace of Longjumeau. A horror of Spanish cruelty was beginning to pervade Germany and brought him sympathy and support.[2] Calvinist Europe built high hopes upon this assistance for the Dutch.[3] But Orange was straitened for money[4] and it was not until the middle of August that he was ready to return to give Alva battle with an army of 6,000 horsemen and four regiments of foot, besides the Lorrainers and Gascons who were all gunners. According to the plan of the prince, three armies were to enter the Netherlands at once, the French under a Huguenot leader named Cocqueville, through Artois; the Count of Hoogstraeten between the Rhine and the Meuse, and Louis of Nassau through Groningen..

But the whole plan failed. Cocqueville raised seven or eight hundred men with the intention of provoking Artois to revolt.[5] Failing to take Doulens by surprise, Cocqueville pillaged the abbey-town of Dammartin. The duke of Alva energetically protested to Charles IX against this violation of the Spanish provinces by French subjects, and the marshal Cossé was sent into Picardy. The foreigners in Cocqueville's band were summarily beheaded at St. Valéry, the leader himself was sent to Abbeville for trial for treason and executed, and the whole expedition came to naught.[6] The enforced delay of the prince of Orange, united

[1] In February, 1568 the wholesale condemnation of the people of the Low Countries had been pronounced by the inquisition and confirmed by the Philip II, (*Archives de la maison d'Orange-Nassau*, III, 171).

[2] *C. S. P. For.*, No. 2,432, August 17, 1568, Mundt to Cecil from Strasburg.

[3] Languet, *Epist. secr.*, I, 60; *Epist. ad Camer.*, 79 and 84.

[4] Languet *Epist. secr.*, I, 64; *Archives de la maison d'Orange-Nassau*, III, 208.

[5] *Archives de la maison d'Orange-Nassau* III, 207; Coll. Godefroy, CCLVI, No. 7, Marshal Cossé to the King, June 20, 1568.

[6] See Haag, *La France protestante*, art., "Cocqueville." The admiral Coligny disavowed any complicity in the enterprise. For the fate of the other columns see *Archives de la maison d'Orange-Nassau*, III, 212, 220, 227.

with this repulse, was fatal to the Netherland project. On July 21, 1568, Louis of Nassau was defeated at Jemmingen by Alva, Spanish tyranny was fixed more firmly in the Low Countries, and Egmont and Hoorne were shortly afterward sent to the scaffold.[1]

Everything was now out of joint. The success of the Dutch would have emboldened their French coreligionists to renew the struggle with some hope of success.[2] But the Catholic victory in the Low Countries hardened the resolution of the French government. Hitherto chiefly the lesser nobility of France had been successfully coerced by the French crown. Now the cardinal of Lorraine intended to do the like with the higher nobles, compelling them either to abandon their religious and political contentions or to take up arms.[3] At the same time military preparations began to be made which could not but be viewed with alarm by the Huguenots. The crown was stronger in cavalry, in infantry, in artillery, and in munitions. The country as a whole was with the King, and the chief cities were in his hands. "The great cities," said Coligny mournfully, "are the tombs of our armies."[4]

So carefully were the preparations made that the King remained armed while the Huguenots were scattered and unarmed,[5] saving

[1] *Ibid.*, 239, 255. The prince of Orange anticipated the disaster of Jemmingen, for he disapproved of the rash policy of his brother. See a letter on this head written by him to Louis of Nassau in July, 1568 (*Archives de la maison d'Orange-Nassau*, III, 257, and the latter's reply, July 17, *ibid.*, III, 264, 265). Alva had been so certain of Spanish victory that in advance of it he offered Charles IX the use of Spanish troops (*C. S. P. For.*, No. 2,379 §2, July 29, 1568).

[2] "They (Huguenots) attend the success of the war in Flanders."—*Ibid.*

[3] In September, 1568, a royal edict was promulgated forbidding the *public* profession of any but the Catholic religion, and revoking all former edicts. Text in *Recueil de Fontanon*, IV, 294. Montluc claims that he was the author of the idea and that he sent a rough draft of such an edict to Charles IX (De Ruble, *Commentaires et lettres de Montluc*, V, 153, 154). In intimation of this policy, in August an oath of allegiance and obedience had been exacted by Charles IX of all the Huguenot leaders (*C. S. P. For.*, No. 2,419, August 9, 1568; cf. No. 2,407, August 7 and Duc d'Aumale, *Hist. des princes de Condé*, II, 9).

[4] *Rel. vén.*, II, 123.

[5] Claude Haton, II, 532; *Coll. des autographes de M. de L—— de Nancy* (Paris, 1855), No. 477; Henry, duke of Anjou to Matignon, King's lieutenant in Normandy, October 8, 1568, recommending him to distribute the gendarmerie in places most suitable to protect the country.

large numbers of individual nobles who yet stood upon their guard. In northern and central France, La Rochelle excepted, the government controlled all the towns. In Provence and Languedoc, however, many of the towns were governed by the Protestants.[1] In order to prevent the communication of intelligence between the various parts of France under Protestant control, Charles IX even had refused to permit Condé to levy money upon the Huguenots for payment of the reiters, notwithstanding the governments' own poverty, although the prince cunningly suggested such an action.[2] The outlook was dark indeed. The Huguenots nowhere save in the south seemed strong enough to take the field, and it seemed hopeless for them to expect to join with their coreligionists of the north owing to the vigilance of Montluc in Languedoc and Tavannes in Burgundy and to the fact that the whole course of the Loire was patrolled by forces of the government. Moreover, the general contribution being stopped, both resources and communication were at an end; the gentry too were impoverished by the late war to a very great extent, having "consumed as much in eight months as they had gathered in four years before,"[3] so that the wisest of the Huguenot leaders were of the opinion that the religion was not in a state to attempt anything by open arms.

While he tried to augment his forces Condé sought to remedy matters by appeal to the King,[4] complaining of the outrages inflicted on the Huguenots[5] (Montluc had even hanged seven gentlemen of the entourage of the queen of Navarre, in Languedoc), being careful not to impute these wrongs, however, to the King, but reprobating the malignancy of the cardinal of Lorraine and accusing him of secret intelligence with Spain.[6] The cardinal,

---

[1] *C. S. P. For.*, Nos. 2,352, 2,379, July 14 and 29, 1569.

[2] *Ibid.*, No. 2,379, July 29, 1568; on the calculative policy of the French crown see Languet, *Epist. secr.*, I, 92 and La Noue's comments in *Mémoires militaires*, chap. xii.

[3] *C. S. P. For.*, No. 2,379, July 29, 1568.

[4] Letter of August 23, 1568 analyzed in De Thou, Book XLIV.

[5] See the complaints of the prince of Condé to the King, under date of June 29 and July 22, 1568 in Duc d'Aumale, *Histoire des princes de Condé*, II, App. I.

[6] See the gist of the prince of Condé's petition, summarized in *C. S. P. For.*, No. 2,451, August 23, 1568. As an instance of the care of the government to be

thus assailed, parried through the King, who two days later issued a proclamation, which after reciting the complaints of murder, robberies and other wrongs alleged by those of "the pretended Reformed religion," declared that the King, having sent his *maîtres des requêtes* into the provinces where these acts of violence had been perpetrated, was satisfied of the substantial justice of the administration, and asserted that the complaints had either been manufactured by the Huguenot leaders, or else grossly exaggerated. The proclamation closed by commanding all judges and other officers, on pain of deprivation, to search out and punish wrongdoers, so that those of the religion might not have ground for complaining that justice was not done them.[1]

Such a proclamation was mere verbiage, however, and was intended to lull the anxiety of the Huguenots while the government's preparations went forward. It deceived none of the Protestant leaders. The signs of the times were too plain to be concealed. Arms were secretly levied and stored in La Rochelle, Saintes, Châtellerault, St. Jean-d'Angély.[2] To these signs was now added another unmistakable indication. In August, 1568 the concentration of fourteen companies of gendarmes and several bands of infantry in Burgundy, where the two most conspicuous of the leaders of the Huguenots then were—the prince of Condé and Coligny[3]—ostensibly to prevent the prince from delivering his German reiters to the prince of Orange, precipitated civil war anew.

Protestant historians have contended that the government of Charles IX was wholly to blame for the renewal of war. But

forehanded, agents of the crown secretly measured even the height of the wall in the case of towns of doubtful allegiance. Coligny complained of the attacks which his gentlemen and those of his brother D'Andelot suffered. At Dijon the prince of Condé prosecuted a person whom he accused of secretly having measured the walls of Noyers (Claude Haton, II, 537, note).

[1] *C. S. P. For.*, No. 2,464, August 25, 1568; cf. No. 2,484.

[2] Claude Haton, II, 539; Le Laboureur, II, 593.

[3] *C. S. P. For.*, No. 2,441, August 20, 1568; Condé was at Noyers, Coligny at Tanlay (Yonne): D'Aubigné, Book III, 5, note; Duc d'Aumale, *Hist. des princes de Condé*, II, 367.

it may be fairly said that Charles IX acted not only according to his right, but according to policy in seeking to prevent the union of the Huguenot and Dutch interests. France was not yet prepared to espouse an open anti-Spanish policy, though she was already secretly so inclining,[1] and the projected alliance of the prince of Condé and the prince of Orange[2] would have been certain seriously to compromise her with Spain. Finally, it may be added, that there was not a little of self-ambition in Condé's action.[3]

This attempted co-operation of the prince of Condé and the prince of Orange drew the French government into close association with the duke of Alva. But the diplomatic relations now established between the courts of Paris and Madrid were of much greater importance and the negotiations were energetically forwarded by the cardinal of Lorraine, who on November 21, sent the cardinal of Guise into Spain charged to treat of marriage between Philip II and Marguerite of Valois,[4] or if that proved unacceptable, to suggest Philip's marriage with one of the daughters of the Emperor, while Charles IX was to marry the other. At the same time Alva proposed that the duke of Anjou—the future Henry III —should marry the queen of Portugal.[5] The far-reaching effect of such a series of alliances is manifest. The two houses of Hapsburg would become dynastically united again in a common family and politico-religious purpose, into which association France would be woven.

The government had secretly prepared for the sudden invest-

[1] Languet, *Epist. secr.*, I, 64, 69.

[2] *Ibid.*, I, 75; *Archives de la maison d'Orange-Nassau*, III, 284–86. The prince of Orange at this time was near Cleves having an army but no money. See a letter of the prince of Orange to the duke of Württemberg and the margrave of Baden asking for pecuniary assistance. September 17, 1568 (*ibid.*, III, 291). His plans again failed. He tried to enter Picardy for the purpose of uniting with the Huguenots. But the alertness of the marshal Cossé again prevented Genlis as it had foiled Cocqueville, and the prince was compelled to abandon his purpose. At Strasburg his army was dissolved (*ibid.*, III, 295, 303, 313–16; Languet, *Epist. ad Camer.*, 89; *Epist. secr.*, I, 75).

[3] Even La Noue, 804 and Beza II, 277, assert this.

[4] Elizabeth of Valois, queen of Spain, had died October 3, 1568.

[5] *C. S. P. For.*, Nos. 2,640, 2,666, November 22, December 8, 1568.

ment of La Rochelle, intending to "spring" the war suddenly at that point, but had been compelled to alter the plan. This change of plan induced the resolution to attempt to capture the prince and Coligny,[1] the purpose of the Guises (with whom the King and his mother were not acting) probably being to send them to the scaffold, as Alva had done with Egmont and Hoorne.

But the deception and duplicity which they used to allay the suspicions of the prince and the admiral offended the bluff, soldierly honor of Tavannes, who, though a bigoted Catholic, would not stoop to such a dishonorable course of action.[2] While feigning to obey the orders to capture the two leaders, he contrived to apprise them of their danger by managing so as to have his letters intercepted by them.[3] Thanks to this timely warning, escape was made possible. On August 23, 1568 Condé and Coligny, accompanied by the members of their families and D'Andelot's—the princess of Condé being pregnant—crossed the Loire in sudden flight, guarded on the road by a hundred horsemen. The fugitives were bound for La Rochelle, which was safely reached without mishap, though not without peril.

From the safe retreat of this famous port and stronghold the prince of Condé issued a manifesto protesting that he and his followers intended nothing prejudicial to the King, but only to protect those of the religion from the tyranny and oppression of their enemies. A form of oath was adopted, to be taken by the nobility, officers, and others of the prince's army, regulations were issued for the maintenance of discipline in the army, for the preventon of desertion, private plundering, and avoidance of excess of baggage, camp-followers, disorders, and quarrels.[4]

---

[1] *C. S. P. For.*, No. 2,441, August 20, 1568.

[2] Tavannes, chap. xxi.

[3] *C. S. P. For.*, No. 2,477, August 29, 1568. Norris states the fact that Condé and the admiral were warned by the letters they intercepted. The duc d'Aumale (*Hist. des princes de Condé*, II, 13) has shown the deliberate intention of Tavannes so to do.

[4] D'Aubigné, III, 24: "Le prince . . . . ht publier les loix militaires." Issued from La Rochelle, September 9, 1568. Summary in *C. S. P. For.*, No. 2,514. De Serres gives the text at p. 158. Delaborde gives the admiral Coligny the credit

The government at once took up the gage of battle and prepared to push the war. On September 25, 1568, an edict proscribed the Reformed faith, exiled the pastors thereof, and excluded Protestants from public offices and from the universities.[1] As far back as July the government had begun negotiations with the Pope to secure license to alienate from the lands of the church 200,000 crowns per annum. This had failed when first petitioned,[2] but the cardinal of Lorraine by the end of August had managed to raise 1,200,000 francs, although half of it had to go to pay old debts to the Parisians.[3] The holy father, having at last been persuaded of the good of the cause, consented to the alienation of 100,000 crowns annual rent of the clerical lands, upon condition that the money be strictly employed for the compulsion of those who denied the authority of Rome and the revocation of the Edict of Toleration.[4] The debate upon the measure pertaining to the church lands brought about a clash in the King's Privy Council between the cardinal of Lorraine and the chancellor L'Hôpital, on September 19. The latter protested against the withdrawal of the Edict of Toleration, on the ground that it would induce the war at once

for these regulations (III, 522). Cf. *C. S. P. For.*, No. 2,486, discourse of the cardinal Châtillon, who attributes the evils of France to the cardinal of Lorraine and refutes the charge of ambition brought against the Huguenot leaders. The cardinal fled to England at this time (see La Ferrière, *Le XVIᵉ siècle et les Valois*, 217; D'Aubigné, III, 12, note 31). He died in 1571. There was a rumor that Coligny, too, had gone to England (Languet, *Epist. secr.*, I, 109).

[1] Fontanon, IV, 292, 294; Claude Haton, II, 540; (September 25) *C. S. P. For.*, No. 2,561, §1, September 30, 1568; *ibid.*, *Ven.*, No. 433, September 28, 1568. A supplementary edict suppressed all offices of judicature and finance held by the Huguenots (*C. S. P. For.*, No. 2,674, December 16, 1568).

[2] *Ibid.*, No. 2,363, July 20, 1568.

[3] *Ibid.*, No. 2,467, August 27, 1568.

[4] *C. S. P. Ven.*, No. 430, September 11, 1568. Other sources of revenue were a loan upon the security of the wine duties for several years—a heavy burden upon the people (Claude Haton, II, 547)—which yielded about 300,000 crowns per annum. In addition, the King raised a benevolence of 50,000 crowns from Paris, and Venice loaned 100,000 crowns (*C. S. P. For.*, No. 2,640, November 22, 1568) later increased to 200,000. The Pope later authorized the sale of 50,000 crowns' worth of the temporalities of the church, but the sales were so managed by certain of the clergy that the government got little from them (*ibid.*, No. 233 April, 1569, summary of an ordinance of Charles IX).

and lead to the overrunning of the country again by the reiters, and refused to affix the royal seal to the proposed ordinance, without which the papal writing was of no force in France. The cardinal retaliated by taunting the chancellor with being a hypocrite and asserted that his wife and daughter were Calvinists. L'Hôpital retorted by sarcastically alluding to the notorious administrative practices of the Guises, at which the cardinal became so angry that he would have seized the venerable chancellor by his great white beard if the marshal Montmorency had not stepped between them. In his rage the cardinal, turning to the queen mother, declared the chancellor's vicious policy of toleration was at the bottom of the evils of France and that if he were in the hands of the Parlement of Paris his head would not tarry on his shoulders twenty-four hours longer.[1] The issue of this episode was not long in forthcoming. On September 28 Michel de l'Hôpital was dismissed from office[2] and the seal given to the archbishop of Sens, Biragues, a pupil of the Guises and a henchman of Philip of Spain.[3] It was he who rescinded the Edict of January and the other two edicts of pacification and exiled all Huguenot preachers from France within twenty days, forbade all exercise of the Reformed religion on pain of death, and dismissed from office and the universities all those who were Protestants.

The new civil war was represented as a war of religion; indeed as a crusade, the King going to evensong at La Sainte-Chapelle, on Michaelmas Eve, where the heart of St. Louis was interred, and on the morrow marching in procession with the relics of St. Denis, as did the former kings of France before they took the road of the cross. The duke of Anjou, the King's brother, was appointed lieutenant-general of the realm on September 1, and proclamation made to the companies of gendarmerie and the bands of archers, to assemble at Orleans, now become the Catholic headquarters.[4]

---

[1] For details see Norris to Cecil, *C. S. P. For.*, No. 2,550, September 25, 1568.

[2] Taillander, *Vie de L'Hôpital*, 200.

[3] Even Biragues, now the chancellor, was in the secret pay of Spain (*Papiers d'état du cardinal de Granvelle*, VIII, 387).

[4] *C. S. P. For.*, No. 2,490, September 1; No. 2,529, September 15, 1568. The two Protestant places of worship in Orleans were burned (*ibid.*, No. 2,561, § 2,

Charles IX, in October, went in person to Orleans, in order by his presence, to enlarge the enlistments, and also to overcome the suspicion that the whole movement was made at the instigation of the Guises. The government of Paris was left to the King's youngest brother, the duke of Alençon, assisted by the duke of Montmorency. In the meantime the prince of Condé had remained in the vicinity of La Rochelle during September, while his army was gathering.[1] When the army was massed, he moved up the Loire with his forces.

The emulation that had characterized the Huguenot nobility in the last war now served Condé well. The provinces were alive with activity during this autumn. The young prince of Navarre, the future Henry IV, was to win eminence in the coming struggle, and at this time was at Bergerac where forces were assembled to assist Condé.[2] The Catholic and governmental forces were no less alert. The King's captains were employed in all parts of the realm to levy men. Montluc, discovering a plot in Bordeaux to deliver the town to those of the Reformed religion, executed the greater part of those so accused. At Toulouse, Auxerre, and Lyons all men were constrained to go to mass. In Provence and Languedoc the peasantry even rose against the Protestants. To crown all both sides levied reiters in Germany.[3]

September 30, 1568). Things would have gone worse with the Protestants of Orleans had it not been for the Politique marshal Vieilleville, whose government it was, and who did all in his power to protect the Huguenots (*ibid.*, No. 190, March 24, 1569).

[1] Jeanne d'Alb who had been at Nérac, reached La Rochelle on September 28, having crosse the Garonne "under the nose of Montluc" (Olhagaray, 575), who, it is said had orders to intercept her (Palma Cayet, Part I, 166). Montluc glosses over his negligence in this particular (*Commentaires*, III, 175).

[2] *C. S. P. For.*, No. 2,561, September 30, 1568. D'Andelot was in Brittany, *ibid.*, No. 2,527, September 15, 1568), but on September 16 he crossed the Loire (La Noue, chap. xix) with 1,500 horse and 20 ensigns of foot (D'Aubigné, III, 13, note 7) in spite of the strict injunctions of the King to prevent him (D'Aubigné, III, 14, note).

[3] *C. S. P. For.*, No. 2,610 §2, October 29, 1568. Duke William of Saxony earnestly begged Charles IX to employ his soldiery (*ibid.*, No. 2,640, §5, November 22, 1568) and the margrave of Baden accepted a command of reiters in the King's army (Le Laboureur, II, 724). The duke of Deuxponts offered 8,000 reiters and

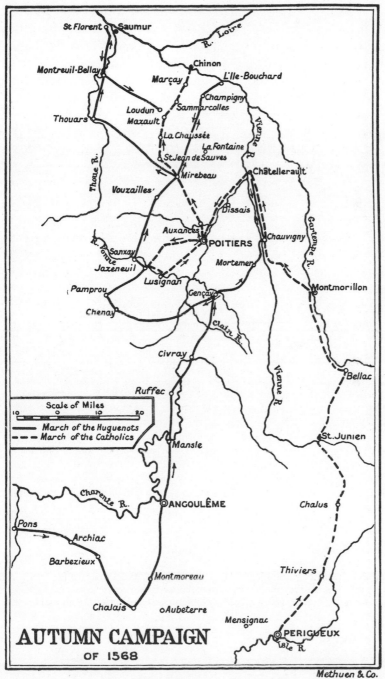

St Florent ○ ● Saumur

R. Loire

Montreuil-Bellay ●
Chinon ●
Marçay
L'Ile-Bouchard

Loudun ○ Champigny
Sammarcolles
Mazault

Thouars ●

Thoue R.

La Chaussée
La Fontaine
St Jean de Sauves

Mirebeau

Vouzailles

Vienne R.

Châtellerault

Dissais

Auxances
POITIERS
Chauvigny

R. Vonne
Sanxay
Jazeneuil
Mortemer

Pamprou ●
Lusignan
Gençay

Chenay
Gartempe R.

Montmorillon

Clain R.

Civray

Vienne R.

Ruffec ●
Bellac ●

Scale of Miles
10   0   10   20

—— March of the Huguenots
--- March of the Catholics

St. Junien ●

Mansle ●

Charente R.

Chalus ●

Pons ●
◎ ANGOULÊME

Archiac
Barbezieux
Thiviers ●

Montmoreau
Mensignac
Chalais ●
○ Aubeterre
◎ PERIGUEUX
Isle R.

AUTUMN CAMPAIGN
OF 1568

Methuen & Co.

The lower course of the Loire was the fighting-line, for command of which both sides aimed.[1]   The tactics of Anjou were to avoid an engagement, if possible, and to prevent Condé's forces from crossing, which he succeeded in doing through a stratagem.[2]   The passage of the Loire being stopped, and the river towns being all garrisoned, especially Saumur, the prince of Condé, after taking the castle of Champigny which belonged to the duke de Montpensier, fell back on Loudun.   The country was so wet that neither horse nor foot could do much.   The prince excelled in cavalry, the Catholic army in infantry.[3]   In the provinces the Catholic preponderance was marked.   The duke of Aumale in Champagne had 18 companies of men-at-arms and 25 ensigns of footmen, awaiting the coming of the reiters; Marshal Cossé was in Picardy with 15 companies of men-at-arms and 2,000 footmen. The reason for the presence of so many troops so far from the actual seat of the war is to be found in the fact that the movements of the prince of Orange, who had entered France in December,[4] gave great anxiety to the government.   The prince was now on

40 ensigns of lansquenets to Condé (*C. S. P. For.*, No. 2,666, §1, December 8, 1568). They were to have no pay for two months, expecting to pay themselves by seizing the towns and castles belonging to the house of Guise in Lorraine and Champagne. In the end England paid for their services (see the record of the receipts in *C. S. P. For.*, No. 2,011, September 10, 1571; No. 2,123, November 13, 1571). The Catholic reiters were to be paid by a forced loan exacted of the Parisians (*ibid.*, No. 2,666, December 8, 1568).

[1] North to Cecil, *C. S. P. For.*, December 30, 1568, January 11, 1569.

[2] For description of it see *C. S. P. For.*, No. 2,640, §15, November 22, 1568. The engagement of Jazeneuil that followed, November 17, was a blow to them (see La Noue, chap. xxi; D'Aubigné, III, 37; *C. S. P. For.*, No. 2,640, §1).   The minute account of the duc d'Aumale may be found in *Hist. des princes de Condé*, II, 26–34.   Whitehead, *Gaspard de Coligny, Admiral of France*, 204–9, has an admirable account.

[3] Condé's army before the defeat at Jazeneuil was estimated at 12,000 foot and 4,000 horse, all well mounted and armed, besides a very large number of irregular troops.

[4] Fourquevaux to Catherine de Medici, January 13, 1569, on the authority of a letter of the Spanish ambassador in France, dated January 7, 1568 (*Dépêches de Fourquevaux*, II, 47).   Alava must have regarded the news as highly important, for the courier was only six days in making the journey to Madrid.

the borders of Picardy, but his horsemen rode as far as Compiègne
and Rheims, to the amazement of the court and the consternation
of the Guises, who dispatched the cardinal of Guise to Madrid
for the help of Philip II.[1]   If the two princes could have effected
a junction in the meantime, Paris would have been between ham-
mer and anvil.   As it was, the danger was so great that the King
hastily began to raise an additional army in December, calling
out ban and arrière-ban, and in order that the capital might be able
to withstand a siege, if worst came to worst, drew all the provisions
of the country roundabout Paris for a space of ten miles into the
city.

The position of the various armies was an interesting one.   In
east France the reiters of the duke of Deuxponts were endeavoring
to join Orange who delayed his movement to await their coming,[2]
while Alva dogged his steps.[3]   In the west Condé was vainly
striving to cross the Loire in order to join Orange and the Protestant reiters, while the duke of Anjou was straining every nerve to
keep him back.   In the midst of all, Paris lay calm but tense[4]—
the undisturbed center of the cyclone of war.   Both armies suf-

[1] Fourquevaux, II, 31, 54.

[2] Coll. Godefroy, XCVI, William of Orange to Charles IX, December 21,
1568.

[3] Alva sent word to Charles IX at all hazards to hold the prince of Condé back,
himself promising to take care of Orange.   The King sent the Spanish duke a very
large commission, not only to levy upon the country for necessities but even to enter
the French walled towns—so far were the two crowns now in accord (*C. S. P.
For.*, No. 2,666, December 8, 1568).

[4] The alarm of the government at this hour over Paris may be measured by
two police regulations of the time.   One ordered search to be made throughout the
town twice a week, in all hostelries and other places, and forbade mechanics to
leave their houses on certain days.   The other allowed those of the religion who
had been forbidden to leave their houses on certain days to appoint one of their
servants to go about the town on their affairs.   He was to have a certificate signed
by the captain and *commissaires* of the quarter, and to be unarmed.   The *commissaires* were to make a weekly search in the houses of those of the religion, to make
procès-verbal of the names of all the domestics, signed by the master of the house, and
to remove all arms found therein (*ibid.*, No. 2,671, December 11; No. 2,684, December 23, 1568).   Both ordinances were registered by the Parlement.   During the
Christmas season no Calvinist was permitted to stir out of doors (*ibid.*, No. 2,688,
§3, December 26, 1568).

fered from the terrible weather of December. The soldiers of each side were dying of famine and privation.[1]

The hope long deferred that Condé had cherished of Orange joining him made him heartsick at last; the latter could not come, for Alva, the duke of Aumale, and the Catholic reiters under a German colonel named Schomberg—a name destined to become illustrious—were too closely watching his movements.[2] Even had these impediments been removed, the Seine and the Loire would have had to be crossed—an impossible feat.

The winter of 1568–69 was occupied with Huguenot and Catholic negotiations for foreign support and with preparations for a renewal of the war when the spring came. Meanwhile the delay of France to pay its debts in Switzerland had gradually provoked a change of public sentiment in the forest cantons, which pushed them a few years later into espousal of Spain. The loss of its ascendency in Switzerland was a particularly hard blow to France. For the policy of Spain had been to rouse a religious war in the Alpine lands, so that her intervention would find easy entrance. The five cantons of the center were the fulcrum of Spain's diplomatic efforts. Day by day the tension became greater, the five cantons inclining more to Spain, their neighbors leaning to France, while between the two groups Bern and Zurich continued neutral, refusing to aid the prince of Condé with either men or money.[3]

Military events were insignificant. Anjou remained with

---

[1] "The good disposition and order that is kept in the prince's army is much to be commended, nothing like oppressing the country where they pass, as that of M. d'Anjou, which was waxed hateful by their insolent behavior, both to Protestants and Catholics. M. d'Anjou has bestowed the greatest part of his army in the towns upon the river of Loire."—*C. S. P. For.*, No. 12, January 4, 1569.

The presence of the royal army in Anjou, under the command of the duke of Anjou, was a heavy burden upon the people of the province, which already had suffered heavily from the depredations of the Huguenots in the preceding year. The municipal council of Angers, on November 4, was called upon to furnish 800 pairs of stockings, 1,500 pairs of shoes, powder, bread, hay, straw, oats, pikes, shovels, mattocks, and other implements. The town was filled with sick and wounded soldiers (Joubert, *Les misères de l'Aniou, etc.*, 36).

[2] Orange was also in want of pay for his troops (Languet, *Epist. secr.*, I, 82).

[3] *Revue d'histoire diplomatique*, XIV (1900), 51–52, 64.

his army in Limousin, and the prince of Condé in Périgord. On December 23, 1568, there was a skirmish near Loudun. In January Condé marched to the relief of Sancerre. The town was of very strong situation and Brocbart, the Huguenot commandant, filled a great number of wine-vats with sand and earth and used them for gabions, and so managed to hold out against five assaults,[1] although the place was so invested by the Catholic army that the prince could do nothing to relieve it. Failing this, he marched upon Saumur in the vain hope of forcing a crossing of the Loire at some point, on the way putting the garrison of 150 men in the abbey of St. Florens at Pont-de-Cé to the sword. Both armies suffered terribly from the weather and the condition of the country.[2]

In the King's council the Politique party still labored for peace, and in the interim made an unsuccessful effort to restore the Edict of Toleration.[3] The cessation of hostilities, however, was complete enough to alarm the Pope, who feared another truce would be made and used exhortation and promise in order to prevent any compromise with heresy.[4]

The Dutch and English were attentive observers of the movement in France, the former especially, for they felt that they and the French Protestants were engaged in a common cause. From England came numbers of English gentlemen to La Rochelle, in order to follow Condé in the war, and the Channel and the Bay of

---

[1] C. S. P. For., No. 22, January 10, 1569; No. 151, March 5, 1569; La Popelinière, Book XV; De Thou and D'Aubigné add nothing new.

[2] On the hardness of the winter of 1568–69 see La Noue, chap. xxiv; Hist. du Lang., V, 514; Commentaires et lettres de Montluc, V, 156; Whitehead, Coligny, 202.

[3] Coll. Godferoy, CCLVII, No. 57. Remonstrance of Jean de Montluc against the continuance of the war, December 2, 1568. In the council of the King a motion was made that the Protestants should be permitted to enjoy the benefit of the edicts granted before; that Condé should be given the government of Saintonge, and be given leave to aid Orange against Spain. But neither Catherine de Medici nor the King would listen to the proposal, and the cardinal of Lorraine argued that it would be dangerous to further Condé in any way (C. S. P. For., No. 23, January 10, 1569).

[4] Potter, Pie V, 19; ed. Gouban, Book III, No. 4, p. 135, letter to the cardinal Bourbon, January, 1569; ibid., p. 23; ed. Gouban, Book III, No. 5, p. 138, letter to the cardinal of Lorraine, same date.

Biscay were thronged with English and Dutch privateers.[1]
Elizabeth, as the saying went, wanted "to throw the stone and hide
the arm." Although the English ambassador, Sir Henry Norris,
protested the innocence of his government and the queen wrote
with her own hand that she would not interfere in France, Englishmen were landed at La Rochelle and in Brittany and English vessels
brought over gunpowder, shoes, and arms.[2]

While Anjou held the line of the Loire, the French government
established its military base at Château-Thierry on the Marne
in order to prevent communication between the Protestant German
princes, especially the elector palatine and the duke of Deuxponts;
or between the Dutch and its own revolted subjects. To this end it
was planned that the duke of Aumale, with a force of reiters sent
by the margrave of Baden and the count of Westelburg, and some
troops proferred by Count Mansfeldt[3] should be sent against the
prince of Orange, while the duke of Anjou was to go against the
prince of Condé.[4] But William of Orange effected a junction

[1] C. S. P. Ven., No. 439, November 9, 1568 and No. 448, January 6, 1569.
The distress of commerce and the legal complications arising from the semi-piratical
acts were very great (see C. S. P. Dom., 1547–80, pp. 378, 386, May 29, 1570,
July 29, 1570).

[2] Ibid., Ven., No. 448, January 6, 1569. The cardinal Châtillon was the
Huguenot agent in England (see ibid., For., No. 71, January 22, 1569; No. 82,
January 30, 1569). On his financial negociations see the detailed note of the baron
de Ruble in D'Aubigné, III, 61.

[3] Count Mansfeldt to the duke of Aumale, January 22, 1569, Coll. Godefroy,
CCLVII, No. 58; C. S. P. For., No. 172, March 15, 1569. They came, not merely
with weapons and bringing horses, but with great vans, flails, and harvest tools,
with which to plunder the fields.

[4] The forces of D'Aumale were 5,500 reiters, 26 companies of French horsemen,
and 30 ensigns of foot, besides others. The troops that the King had were 26
companies of gendarmes, 15 companies of the regular French army, 4,500 Swiss,
2,500 reiters, and his household troops. Montmorency retired to Chantilly owing
to the combination against him (C. S. P. For., No. 75, January 25, 1569. For
the details see Archives de la maison d'Orange-Nassau, III, 315). There had
been a fierce strife between the factions of Guise and Montmorency for D'Aumale's
place, the three marshals, Montmorency, Vieilleville, and Cossé resisting his appointment. The hostility of the Parisians to Montmorency, though certainly not
the accusation of the cardinal of Lorraine that the constable's son had secret intelligence with the prince of Orange, militated against him. The English ambassador even believed that Montmorency and the duke of Bouillon might appear in

with the duke of Deuxponts[1] in spite of D'Aumale's effort to prevent him.[2]

The attitude of the Lutheran princes had now become more definite in favor of the Huguenots.[3]

The international Protestant plan was to drive its blows in on either side of Lorraine and thus sever the chain through central Europe by which Philip II held his dominions together, and to separate the two houses of Hapsburg.[4] The conduct of the Emperor furthered this project, for when Charles IX sent La Forrest to the Emperor to protest against the action of the Lutheran princes of Germany and to continue the talk of his marriage with the Emperor's daughter, Ferdinand, while expressing his regret at the troubled state of France, received the marriage proposition coldly

arms for Condé. Sir Henry Norris to the queen: "On the 23d ult. the duke of Montmorency required the captains and *échevins* of Paris to come to the Louvre to speak with him, and declared that their disorders and unaptness to be ruled was not unknown to the King. Lignerolles, of the court of Parlement, and captain-general of twenty-two ensigns, answered that Paris was like to a ship, whereof the master, neglecting his charge, it is requisite that the pilots do put hand to the helm; whereunto Montmorency coldly replied, 'qu'il parloyt en curtault de butique' " (*C. S. P. For.*, No. 50, January 15, 1569).

[1] *Archives de la maison d'Orange-Nassau*, III, 516.

[2] Claude Haton, II, 516 and note; *C. S. P. For.*, Nos. 42, 50, January 11, 15, 1569.

[3] It appears that the German princes thought of sending a deputation into France to remonstrate with Catherine de Medici. At least the minute of a letter to the queen has been preserved which intimates as much. In it they deplore the sad effects of the persecutions in France (see *Archives de la maison d'Orange-Nassau*, II, 99–100, June, 1567). On January 24, 1569, a decree of the elector of Saxony commanded all captains and soldiers who were his subjects and who might be serving under the duke of Alva or the King of France, to return home within two months after the date of the publication of the decree; and further ordered his officers to arrest any persons whom they might find setting forth for these services. —Dresden, January 24, 1569 (*C. S. P. For.*, No. 74). In March, Augustus of Saxony, the count palatine, and other German princes sent 50,000 silver crowns to Condé (*ibid.*, *Ven.*, No. 452, March 15, 1569).

[4] William of Orange with his two brothers went into Germany in order to push the plan in conjunction with the duke of Deuxponts—D'Aubigné, III, 45, 60 (*C. S. P. For.*, No. 131, February 24, 1569). For the detail of this movement see Gachard, *La Bibliothèque Nationale à Paris*, II, 275, 278, 280. The duke of Aumale has published some of his letters at this time (*Hist. des princes de Condé*, II, 406 ff.).

and complained of the damage done by the French army under the duke of Aumale within the limits of the empire,[1] and recommended that Charles try peaceful methods instead of force for the pacification of his kingdom.[2] Parallel with the project to co-operate with the prince of Orange and the duke of Deuxponts, Coligny planned a revival of Huguenot activity in the south of France so that this diversion would weaken resistance to the other. The aim was, with the aid of the "viscounts" to break a way across the upper Loire, and so open the road to German assistance.[3]

The combined array against D'Aumale was too great for him to make head.[4] Nor was the adverse double military situation the sole anxiety of the French government. Montmorency and the duke of Bouillon were so disaffected that there was even expectation of their openly joining the Huguenots. The cost of the two armies amounted to 900,000 livres a month, besides the gendarmerie and artillery, which was about two million each quarter.[5] There was owing to the gendarmerie 12,000,000 of livres for six quarters; to the 6,000 Swiss with the duke of Anjou 300,000 livres; to those with the duke of Aumale 100,000 livres besides what was owing to the French infantry. Both of the King's commanders were so short of funds that they were forced to seize church-plate and even reliquaries.[6]

In these extremities Charles IX viewed the renewal of war on the opening of spring with alarm and began to think of making peace for a term, with no intention of keeping it, but merely in order to avoid a catastrophe and with the hope that some of the Huguenots might be disarmed in the interim. But suddenly the

---

[1] D'Aumale at this time lay at Phalsburg and Saverne, with 4,000 reiters, 2,000 French horse, and 10,000 footmen. His penetration within the imperial frontier offended and alarmed Strasburg where a French faction had unsuccessfully plotted to betray the town.

[2] See News-Letter from La Rochelle, January, 1569, in Appendix XVII.

[3] C. S. P. For., No. 105, February 10, 1569.

[4] Ibid., No. 151, March 5, 1569; Claude Haton, II, 517.

[5] Ibid., For., No. 155, March 5, 1569; on the desertions from D'Aumale's army see No. 172.

[6] Ibid., No. 105, February 10, 1569.

cloud was lifted. The royal army under the nominal command of the duke of Anjou, but really commanded by the veteran Tavannes, who had orders to give battle at all cost before the duke of Deuxponts could arrive, won the decisive victory of Jarnac on March 13, 1569. It was a fierce and bloody battle.

The prince of Condé, after having been dangerously wounded and taken prisoner, suffered a foul death at the hands of some unknown assassin in the royal army, who shot him with a pistolball.[1] In the engagement the Scotchman, Stuart, who had killed the constable at St. Denis, was taken and brought to the duke, who said to him: "So here you are, you traitor, you who have frequently boasted that you wished to kill the queen, my mother. Now you shall receive your deserts." At that moment the marquis de Villars, the old constable's brother-in-law, appeared, and with his own hands executed vengeance.[2]

In Paris when news of the battle of Jarnac was brought a grand procession was authorized by the clergy and the Parlement. All the stores and shops were closed as though it were a holiday. The clergy, bearing the relics of the saints, marched first to the convent of the Cordeliers, and then to that of the Jacobins, where a fiery sermon was preached by a Jacobin of Auxerre named Mammerot. After the sermon the *Te Deum* was celebrated, and then the militia of the city assembled under the command of the four captains, and a grand review was held in the streets. The celebration ended

[1] For comtemporary accounts of the battle of Jarnac see La Popelinière, Book XV; Jean de Serres, 315 ff; D'Aubigné, Book V, chap. viii; Claude Haton, II, 548 and notes. The best modern accounts are Gigon, *La bataille de Jarnac et la campagne de 1569 en Angoumois*, Angoulême, impr. Chasseignac (Extrait du *Bulletin de la Société archéologique et historique de la Charente*), 1896; Patry, in *Bull. Soc. protest. franç.*, LIII, March 1902; Duc d'Aumale, *Histoire des princes de Condé*, II, Book I, chap. i; Whitehead, *Gaspard de Coligny, Admiral of France*, 204–9, an extremely lucid account. The evidence upon the assassination of the prince is sifted by Denys d'Aussy, "L'assassin du prince de Condé à Jarnac (1569)," *R. Q. H.*, XLIX, 573, and summarized (with some new additions) in Whitehead, 206, note 2. The text of the famous dispatches, which were found in the gauntlet of the prince of Condé are printed in full in Duc d'Aumale, *Histoire des princes de Condé*, II, App. iii.

[2] *C. S. P. Ven.*, No. 454, March 15, 1569; cf. Brantôme, III, 329.

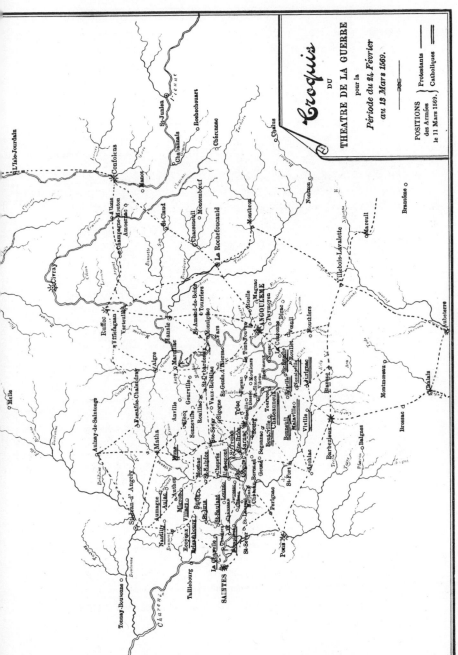

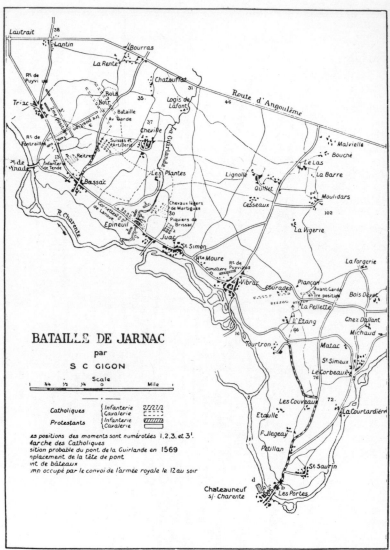

BATAILLE DE JARNAC

par

S C GIGON

Scale

Catholiques { Infanterie / Cavalerie
Protestants { Infanterie / Cavalerie

es positions des moments sont numérotées 1,2,3, et 3¹.
Marche des Catholiques
sition probable du pont de la Guirlande en 1569
nplacement de la tête de pont
nt de bâteaux
mn occupé par le convoi de l'armée royale le 12 au soir

by a great bonfire in front of the Hotel-de-Ville, and the firing of cannon.[1]

The Pope took the victory of Jarnac as a direct answer to prayer.[2]

[1] Claude Haton, II, 549, 550.

[2] Compare the Pope's letter of March 6, informing Charles IX that he has sent troops to him under Sforza and has prayed to God for victory (Potter, *Pie V*, 28; ed. Gouban, Book III, letter 9, p. 148) with the letter of congratulation of March 28, after he had learned of the battle (*ibid.*, p. 31; ed. Gouban, Book III, letter 10, p. 151). The duke of Anjou sent the flags and standards captured at Jarnac to Rome (Potter, *Pie V*, p. 54; ed. Gouban, Book III, 167, letter 17, April 26, 1569).

CHAPTER XIV

THE THIRD CIVIL WAR (*Continued*). THE PEACE OF ST. GERMAIN

By the death of Condé the Admiral Coligny became the actual leader of the Protestant cause in France[1] the more so when his brother d'Andelot died on May 7,[2] although the young prince of Condé and his cousin, Henry of Navarre, were theoretically so regarded.[3] In the nature of things, the leadership of two boys— the former was seventeen, the other sixteen years of age—could only be a nominal one.

After the first shock of dismay at the prince's death had passed, the Huguenots were not dispirited. It is true that numbers of the Protestant gentry returned home.[4] But the Huguenot position was strong in upper and lower Poitou, for the line of the Charente from Angoulême to Saintes was theirs, besides St. Jean-d'Angély, La Rochelle, and the islands of Marins and Oléron.[5] The admiral rallied his forces at Tonnay-Charente,[6] which he could do with impunity since the duke of Anjou raised the siege of Angoulême on April 12.[7]

The hope of the court was to prolong the war, since the King controlled most of the towns and the river passages, "while the religion, their conquered country excepted, had but the fields,"[8] until the resources of the Huguenots would at last become exhausted—money, men, munitions. But the queen of England loaned 20,000 livres to the Protestants, the jewels of Condé and

---

[1] "L'amiral demeurant toujours le principal gouverneur et conseiller en toutes les affaires des huguenots."—Castelnau, Book VII, chap. vi.

[2] Jean de Serres, 333.

[3] D'Aubigné, III, 58.

[4] Claude Haton, II, 557.   [5] *Ibid.*

[6] D'Aubigné, III, 57; Jean de Serres, 326, gives details.

[7] Jean de Serres, 331.

[8] *C. S. P. For.*, No. 294, June 6, 1569.

Jeanne d'Albret being taken as security.[1] Jeanne d'Albret in person directed the foreign negotiations of the Huguenots.[2] The anxiety of the Huguenots was greatest over the effect which Condé's death might have upon the foreign assistance which they were looking for, and letters from the prince of Navarre and the other leaders of the Huguenot army in Saintonge earnestly urged the reiters' advance to the Loire.[3] Coligny's hope was by making a detour by way of Cognac and Chalais to reach the Loire and effect a junction with Deuxponts. To his great relief, the prince of Orange and the duke of Deuxponts wrote assuring the admiral of their continued adherence.[4] As good as his word, Deuxponts, who was at Pont-à-Mousson on January 11, 1569, entered France near Langres, having passed by Joinville, the seat of the Guises in Lorraine, where the old duchess of Guise was then staying,[5] and advanced upon Dijon where he arrived on April 26.[6]

The real center of the government's activity was Metz, which became the basis of operations against Deuxponts and Orange.[7]

[1] Queen Elizabeth was perfectly safe in making the loan, as the jewels were worth three times the sum advanced (Bourgon, *Life and Times of Sir Thomas Gresham*, II, 334-36). *C. S. P. For.*, No. 258 May 12, 1569; Duc d'Aumale, I, 70, note 2; John Casimir and the duke of Deuxponts both promised reiters.

[2] *C. S. P. Ven.*, No. 460, September 15, 1569.

[3] *Ibid., For.*, No. 252, May 9, 1569; the prince of Navarre and other leaders of the Huguenot army in Saintonge to the duke of Deuxponts and certain noblemen in his camp, and to the prince of Orange, earnestly urging them to advance on the Loire, and declaring that notwithstanding the death of the prince of Condé their other losses have been small and that their forces are not diminished or disheartened thereby. Not published in *Lettres missives de Henri IV*.

[4] *Archives de la maison d'Orange-Nassau*, III, 316; Languet, *Epist. ad Camer.*, 105; *Epist. secr.*, I, 81. Copies of five letters written by De Francourt, the agent for the Huguenot party with the duke of Deuxponts' and the prince of Orange, to the Huguenot leaders, expressing regret for the death of the prince of Condé, and assuring them of the continued adherence of the duke of Deuxponts and his reiters to their cause are cited in *C. S. P. For.*, No. 207, April, 1569. The duke of Lorraine is said to have offered Deuxponts 100,000 crowns if he would withdraw his reiters (*ibid.*, No. 234, April 18, 1569).

[5] Claude Haton, II, 517.   [6] D'Aubigné, III, 66.

[7] Preparations looking forward to this movement had begun as far back as March, when the expulsion of all who would not conform to Catholicism was ordered by the cardinal of Lorraine as bishop of Metz and a prince of the empire

Active efforts were made to repair the duke of Anjou's losses and to strengthen his position.[1] The offer of Spanish support which Alva had made was now formally accepted, for after the mission of Castelnau to the margrave of Baden to get relief, he was sent into Flanders to solicit the assistance of Alva, since it now had become the common interest of both crowns to crush the Protestants.[2] The French commanders, the dukes of Nemours and Aumale, had received orders to prevent the approach of Deuxponts at all cost,[3] but Aumale, partially on account of carelessness, partly because of misinformation, failed in his task, and by clever management Deuxponts at last succeeded in crossing the Saône above Bar into Auxerre and Berry, scaled the walls of Nevers, thereby shortening the road between him and the Huguenot army, and finally captured La Charité upon the Loire on May 20, after ten days of siege, and thus controlled the link which united Huguenots and reiters.[4]

(C. S. P. For., No. 194, March 26, 1569; cf. Charles IX's proclamation to the same effect on April 6; see also Nos. 179, 197, the opposing petitions of the clergy of Metz and of the Protestants, dated March 19 and 30 respectively).

The correspondence of the duke of Alençon pertaining to the second civil war is in two volumes listed Nos. 36, 36 bis, in the St. Petersburg collection. The duke remained in Paris, and attended to the forwarding of powder, provisions, and money. In a letter of November 17, 1569, he writes to Charles IX that it is impossible for him to send the sums demanded unless he sells the plate and jewels of the King. In another he sends information of the duke of Tuscany, who was ready to loan 100,000 écus upon the jewels of the crown. He advises that this be done. According to his estimate they were worth 500,000 livres (La Ferrière, Rapport sur les recherches faites à la Bibliothèque imperiale de St. Pétersbourg, 27).

[1] Proclamation by Charles IX: Commands all gentlemen and soldiers to repair to the camp of the duke of Anjou by the 20th of June, properly armed and equipped for service. Requires his officers to search out the names of such as disobey this order and send them to him, in order that they may be punished in such manner as he may think fit (C. S. P. For., No. 281, May, 1569). The King is levying a new army and is disfurnishing his garrisons in Picardy and Normandy (ibid., No. 287, June 3, 1569). Alva promised 4,000 Spanish troops (Nég. Tosc., III, 591).

[2] Castelnau, Book VII, chap. v. Alva advised him to treat Coligny et al. as he had treated Egmont and Hoorne.

[3] Ibid., loc. cit.; C. S. P. For., No. 236, April 23, 1569.

[4] Duke of Anjou to Catherine de Medici, May 23, 1569, Coll. Godefroy, CCLVI, No. 12; La Popelinière, Book XVI; Castelnau, Book VII, chaps. v, vi; D'Aubigné, III, 67 and note 2; Archives de la maison d'Orange-Nassau, III, 317; La Noue,

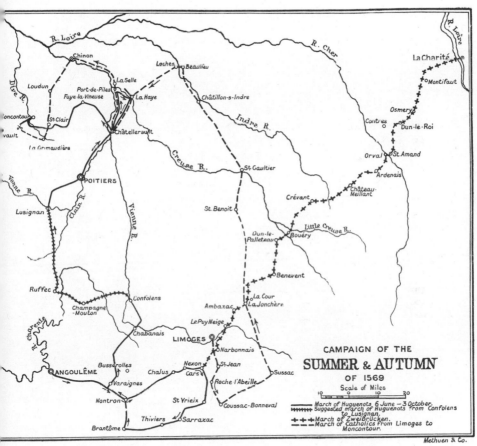

R. Loire
Chinon
Loches
Beaullieu
La Charité
Montifaut
Dive R.
Loudun
La Selle
Port-de-Piles
Fuye-la-Vineuse
La Haye
Châtillon-s-Indre
R. Cher
R. Loire
Osmery
Contres
Dun-le-Roi
Oncontour
St Clair
Châtellerault
Indre R.
vault
La Grimaudière
Creuse R.
St Gaultier
Orval St Amand
Ardenais
Vienne R.
POITIERS
Château
Meillant
St Benoit
Crévant
Lusignan
Clain R.
Vienne R.
Little Creuse R.
Dun-le-
Palleteau
Bouéry
Charente R.
Ruffec
Benevent
Confolens
La Cour
La Jonchère
Ambazac
Champagne-
Mouton
Le Puy Neige
Chabanais
LIMOGES
ANGOULÊME
Busserolles
Narbonnais
Chalus
Nexon
Cars
St Jean
Sussac
Varaignes
Roche l'Abeille
Nontron
St Yrieix
Coussac-Bonneval
Thiviers
Sarrazac
Brantôme

CAMPAIGN OF THE
SUMMER & AUTUMN
OF 1569
Scale of Miles
10   0   30

March of Huguenots 6 June – 3 October.
Suggested march of Huguenots from Confolens
to Lusignan.
March of Zweibrücken.
March of Catholics from Limoges to
Moncontour.

Methuen & Co.

If the Huguenots had been dispirited after Jarnac, they had reason to feel elated after the capture of La Charité. Although the duke of Anjou kept the field in Saintonge, Angoumois, and Limousin, the army was so mutinous for want of pay, so depleted by desertion and disease, that it was far from formidable.[1] Paris was in consternation after the capture of La Charité and anticipated seeing the high hats and great feathers of the reiters before long.[2] The *échevins* of the city were ordered with all speed to make sale of the property of the Protestants to provide means for a new army, which had to be made up of peasant levies, "all their soldiers

chap. xxiv; *C. S. P. For.*, No. 286, June 3, 1569, Sir Henry Norris to the Queen: "The duke of Deuxponts' army being before La Charité, he caused 600 French harquebusiers and certain companies of reiters to pass over the river, besieging the town on both sides, and having made a breach which was scant scalable, they made a proud assault, not without loss of some of their soldiers, and entered the town by force, and put to the sword as many as they found within the same. The Cardinal, to save his brother from the stigma of the loss of La Charité, made Count Montmeyo the scapegoat" (*C. S. P. For.*, No. 293, June 7, 1569). For other details see Hippeau, "Passage de l'armée du duc des Deux-Ponts dans la Marche et le Limousin en 1569," *Rev. des Soc. savant des départ.*, 5e série, V (1873), p. 571; Le Bœuf (Jean), *Histoire de la prise d'Auxerre par les Huguenots, et de la délivrance de la mesme ville, les années 1567 et 1568*, avec un recit de ce qui a précédé et de ce qui a suivi ces deux fameux événemens et des ravages commis à la Charité, Gien, Cosne, etc. et autres lieux du diocèse d'Auxerre, le tout précédé d'une ample préface sur les antiquités d'Auxerre et enrichi de notes historiques sur les villes, bourgs et villages et sur les personnes principales qui sont nommées dans cette histoire, par un chanoine de la cathédrale d'Auxerre, Auxerre, 1723.

[1] Castelnau, Book VI, chap. vi; *C. S. P. For.*, No. 286, June 3. The reiters and the Swiss in the royal service were paid, to the disadvantage of the King's subjects, so that many captains resigned (*ibid.*, No. 351, July 27, 1569). "L'esquelz n'estoient si sanguinaires ni saccageurs d'églises et de prebstres que ceux des huguenots, toutesfois estoient aussi larrons les ungs que les aultres pour serrer sur leurs harnois ce qu'ilz trouvoient à leur commodité; et par ainsi fut la France pleine d'estrangers pour la désoler et quasi rendre déserte" (Claude Haton, II, 547).

The temper of the Catholic army is shown in a dispatch of the duke of Montpensier to Catherine, May 1, 1569, from the camp at Villebois, reciting the death of young Brissac, the marshal's son before Mussidan. The town was taken by storm. "J'en trouve meilleu est qu'ils n'ont laissé reschapper ung tout seul de tous ceuls qui estoyent dedans que tout n'ayt esté passé par le fil de l'épée, ce qui semble être le vray droict de ceste guerre."—Collection Fillon, No. 2,656.

[2] "The admiral minds . . . . to refresh his reiters, and after the harvest to march towards Paris."—*C. S. P. For.*, No. 311, June 30, 1569.

and men of the greatest value being already abroad."[1]   The queen
mother, having received letters complaining of lack of funds and
mutiny in his army, bitterly reproached Aumale for negligence
and cowardice in letting the duke of Deuxponts capture La Charité, and hastily started for the army in Saintonge, in company with
the cardinals of Lorraine and Bourbon, where she went right among
the soldiers with words of encouragement.[2]

BATTLE OF LA ROCHE-L'ABEILLE, JUNE 25, 1569
(Tortorel and Perissin)

But mutiny of the army, and the capture of La Charité, with
the prospective union of Coligny and the duke of Deuxponts, was
not all that worried the queen and the cardinal.   Casimir of the
County Palatine was reported to be coming with 6,000 horse and
as many foot; moreover, the Emperor was hostile.[3]   The extremity
of the government was so great that compromise was necessary,
and Catherine had in mind to patch matters up by offering her

[1] C. S. P. For., No. 272, May 27, 1569.

[2] Ibid., No. 300, Norris to Cecil, June 14, 1569.

[3] Ibid., No. 286, June 3, 1569.   He required Charles IX, in the name of the
empire, to withdraw his troops from Metz (ibid., No. 286, Norris to Cecil, June 3,
1569; ibid., No. 305, Mundt to Cecil, from Frankfourt [?], June 23, 1569).

daughter Marguerite of France in marriage to the young Henry of Navarre—a plan whose consummation three years later precipitated the massacre of St. Bartholomew.[1] Marshal Damville, the second son of the old constable, whose Politique leanings already had made him conspicuous, was significantly appointed the King's lieutenant in Languedoc. Toleration was in the air once more.

But all of a sudden the Catholic cause revived for an instant.[2] Coligny fell ill, and the progress of the Huguenot army was thereby impeded. Worse still, the duke of Deuxponts was stricken with a burning fever, so that he died the very day of his arrival in La Marche.[3] Strozzi with some Italian forces attacked Coligny at La Roche-L'Abeille on June 25, when the rain was pouring in such torrents that the matchlocks of the Italians were useless, so that the soldiers on both sides clubbed their weapons—in the expressive words of D'Aubigné, "rompre croce sur cap"—that is, broke the crosses of their arquebuses over the heads of their antagonists.[4] In the conflict Strozzi was taken prisoner. From this time forth

[1] *C. S. P. For.*, No. 286, June 3, 1569; Claude Haton, II, 692. Marguerite herself is evidence for this: "La maison de Montmorency aient ceux qui en avaient porté les premières paroles."—*Mém. de Marguerite de Navarre* (ed. Guisson, 23), 24.

[2] "Depuis que je y suis, jé fayst marcher vostre armaye en tele diligense, que cet les reystres eusent vole u marcher jeudi, le jour de la feste Dyeu, je me pouvès dyre le plus heureuse femme du monde, et vostre frère le plus glorieux, car vous eusiés heu la fin de cete guere, aystent réduis le duc de Dus Pons."—Catherine de Médicis à Charles IX de Limoges, 12 juin 1569, Fillon Collection, No. 127.

[3] The duke of Deuxponts died on June 11, 1569, of excessive drinking. See Janssen, VIII, 50; D'Aubigné, III, 69, note 1; Jean de Serres, 364; *Commentaires et lettres de Montluc*, III, 208. Fortunately for the Huguenots his death made little difference in the disposition of his army, for Wolrad of Mansfeldt, his able lieutenant, succeeded to the command. His prudence saved the reiters after the battle of Moncontour (see Niemarn, *Geschichte der Grafen v. Mansfeldt*, 1834).

[4] D'Aubigné, III, 73, 74: a graphic account; cf. *Bulletin de la Soc. archéol. et hist. du Limousin*, IV.

"On l'appela *arquebuse à croc* quand on l'eut munie d'un axe de rotation reposant sur une fourchette ou *croc* et facilitant le pointage. L'arquebuse à croc était souvent d'un poids considérable. Elle lançait parfois des balles de plomb de 8, 12 et 13 livres. Jusqu'au commencement du XVIe siècle, on mettait le feu à la charge au moyen d'une mèche allumée que le coulevrinier portait enroulée autour du bras droit. A Pavie, les Espagnols se servirent d'une arquebuse perfectionnée

the army of the King was simply a disorderly mass of men. Famine and fever so reduced it that the duke of Anjou was not able to defend himself, let alone invading the enemy's territory. To increase his forces, he put arms in the hands of the peasantry of Limousin, with the result that a local *jacquerie* prevailed in the province. Lansac was repulsed in assaulting La Charité; Châtellerault (July 12) and Lusignan (July 20) were taken by the Huguenots.[1] The Catholics failed before Niort, to whose relief the brilliant La Noue came after his own seizure of Lucon.[2]

Under these circumstances the government was compelled to content itself with maintaining the line of the Loire save at La Charité, while it sought foreign succor.[3] But the Swiss could not be expected until the middle of September, and Coligny sought

par eux, dans laquelle la mèche était mise en contact avec l'amorce pour faire partir le coup, au moyen d'un *serpentin*, sorte de pince qu'une détente faisait agir, sans que le pointage en fût derangé. Disposer la mèche à la longueur voulue, en aviver le feu avant de tirer constituait l'opération de maniement d'arme designée sous ce nom compasser la mèche."—*La grande encyclopédie*, III, art. "Arquebuse."

[1] La Popelinière, Book XVII; D'Aubigné, III, 80, 81.

[2] D'Aubigné, Book V, chap. xii; Jean de Serres, 355, 356.

[3] Schomberg offered to make a levy of 4,000 Poles; 8,000 Swiss were asked of the Catholic cantons (*C. S. P. For.*, No. 351, July 27, 1569). To support them Paris was mulcted for 700,000 francs and confiscation of Protestant lands to the crown eked out the balance (*ibid.*, No. 355, July 29, 1569).

The following summary from Sir Henry Norris' letter to Queen Elizabeth sets forth the government's fiscal policy at this time: "On the 1st instant the king went to the Palais, where in the end, the Parlement made a general arrest of all the goods, lands, and offices of those who bore arms against the king, and that all their lands held in fee—or knight-service—should revert to the crown; and that for the other lands, first there should be alienated for the sum of 50,000 crowns by the year, and given to the clergy, in recompense of their demesne, which the king had license to sell, and the remainder bestowed on such as had suffered loss by the religion and done service in these wars. It is accounted that this attainture will amount to 2,000,000 francs a year. The same day they made sale, by sound of trumpet, of the admiral's goods in Paris. Some moved to have him executed in effigy, which was thought unmeet, as serving only to irritate him to proceed the more extremely. The king borrows 300,000 £ and offers to perpetuate the Councillors of Parlement's offices to their children, on their giving a certain sum of money; besides this they tax all citizens throughout the realm to make great contributions. The cardinals of Bourbon and Lorraine, to show an example to the clergy, have offered to sell 4,000 £ rent of the monasteries of St. Germain and St. Denis" (*C. S. P. For.*, No. 375, August 5, 1569).

to profit by the situation to take Saumur and thus secure a crossing
on the lower Loire also, and Poitiers, for which purpose he divided
the Protestant army,[1] to the intense alarm of the government,
which tried, through the queen mother, to delay action by drawing
the admiral into an empty parley.   This is the moment when the
marriage of Henry of Navarre with Marguerite of France was
first broached.   But the admiral and Jeanne d'Albret were not

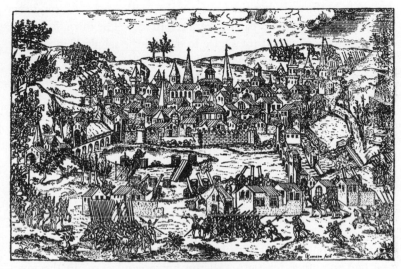

SIEGE OF POITIERS, 1569
Tortorel and Perissin)

to be deceived, and the siege of Poitiers was resolutely continued.
(It lasted from July 25 to September 7, 1569.)   The Catholic
party fully appreciated that the importance of the war depended
upon the success or failure of the Huguenots before this city, into
which the young duke of Guise, then but nineteen years of age,
had thrown himself on July 12 with all the ardor of his father before
Metz.   If Coligny took the town, some notable prisoners of war
would have fallen into his hands, the dukes of Guise and Mayenne
and the abbess of La Trinité, a sister of the cardinal of Bourbon[2]

[1] D'Aubigné, II, 38, 39.

[2] Louise de Bourbon, abbess de Fontevrault, daughter of François, comte de
Vendôme, and of Marie de Luxembourg, died in 1575.

and the ill-starred prince of Condé, the ransom of whom would have abundantly provided for the reiters in the service of the Protestants.

Poitiers was one of the most mediaeval towns in France. The remains of its towers and fortifications, its narrow bridges, the ruined palace of the ancient dukes of Aquitaine, everything recalled the life of a vanished past.[1] The admiral's guns soon made two breaches in the wall, but the fire from the castle and platform drove his men back and the breaches were repaired. The town, however, was too large in circuit for Guise to defend the whole,[2] since many vineyards and fields were within its walls, in consequence of which the French had made a line of double trenches within the town. On August 19 the Huguenots made a furious assault, broke through the wall, and drove the Guisard forces back of the inside trenches. The enemy was "so straitly pent" that for sixteen days the soldiers had to live upon horse-flesh. The most remarkable incident of the siege was the driving-out of a great number of people, old men and women and children, who were unable to fight and could not be fed on account of the lack of provisions. So reluctant were they to go that they had to be whipped through the gates. Fortunately the duke of Guise took pity upon them at last, although in the city bread was so scarce that the food of one had to suffice for ten. All the horses and asses in the town were slain, the gentry out of honor to their position sating their hunger on the former. Of wheat, barley, and other grain there was none, nor was there a green thing left growing in the city. Even rats and mice were consumed.[3]

[1] For a graphic description of Poitiers in the sixteenth century see Ouvré, *Histoire de Poitiers*, 24, 25.

[2] *Rel. vén.*, II, 271.

[3] All the historians narrate the history of the siege of Poitiers (see Claude Haton, II, 375 ff.; La Popelinière, Book XVII; D'Aubigné, Book V, chap. v; Claude Haton, II, 534; De Thou, Book XLV; Liberge, *Ample discourse de ce qui s'est fait au siège de Poitiers*, 1569, new ed., 1846, by Beauchet-Felleau; *Mém. de Jean d'Antras*, ed. Cansalade and Tamizey de Larroque, 1880; see also Whitehead, *Gaspard de Coligny, Admiral of France*, 215, 216; Babinet, *Mém. de la Soc. des antiq. de l'ouest*, séries II, Vol. XI). The story of the siege is also related in an unpublished letter of Charles IX to the duke of Nevers, September 10, 1569, F. Fr., 3,159, No. 195.

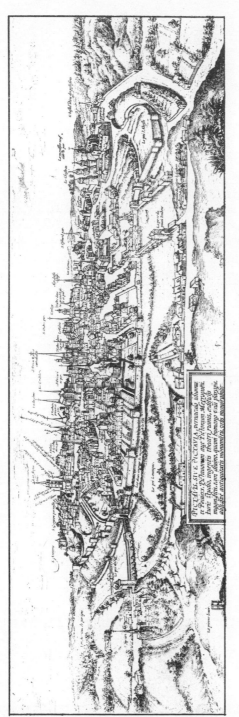

POITIERS IN THE SIXTEENTH CENTURY

The strength of Coligny (he had about 10,000 footmen and 8,000 to 9,000 horse) made it impossible for Anjou to dislodge him by direct attack. His own strength, as appeared by a general muster on September 3, consisted of 1,500 French gendarmes, 700 Italian horse, 1,000 Walloons, and 4,000 reiters, besides La Vallette's regiment of 400 horse—it was much reduced during the siege—and the duke of Longueville's and some other companies. Of footmen he had 6,000 French, 4,000 Swiss, 2,500 Italians, and 2,000 Walloons. Although this army in actual numbers excelled that of Coligny, in reality it was considerably inferior. The troops were many of them without officers, the 6,000 French were drafted peasantry unused to the use of arms; all of them were suffering from hunger and many from fever. The duke of Anjou, therefore, with the approval of his mother, determined to try to draw off Coligny from before Poitiers by a feigned attack upon Châtellerault.[1] For this purpose he crossed the river Creuse on September 4 and planted his artillery before the town. The honor of the first assault was given to the Italians, which offended the French, who refused to support them.[2] Nevertheless a breach 40 feet wide was made in the wall, so that the admiral, judging the place to be in great danger, sent 7,000 horse and 8,000 foot to the city's relief, September 7. It was fatal impatience on Coligny's part, for the action relieved Poitiers from the danger of being taken.

There was now no other recourse for the Huguenots except to give battle. But Coligny was unwilling to do this at once, desiring to wait until the devastation of the country round about still further reduced Anjou's forces. In the interval he withdrew across the Vienne. But the mercenaries in both armies clamored for battle, for there was great want of money on both sides, the King's Swiss being unpaid for three months, the reiters five, the admiral's also being behindhand for three months' wages.[3]

[1] Catherine de Medici to the duke of Anjou: approving of his false attack upon Châtellerault (see Appendix XVIII), not published in the *Correspondance*.

[2] *Nég. Tosc.*, III, 595.

[3] Both La Noue, chap. xxvi, and D'Aubigné, III, 119, emphasize the condition of the army.

On September 30, at Moncontour, the two armies clashed in a preliminary engagement. But three days later on Monday, October 3, 1569, the real battle was joined. It must have been an impressive and thrilling sight before the conflict began. In the Huguenot army the preachers moved about encouraging the men, who sang the solemn psalms of the Calvinist worship with fervor. Across the plain, the Swiss and Germans in the royal host, after the German fashion, knelt and kissed the ground.[1]

BATTLE OF MONCONTOUR, OCTOBER 3, 1569
(Tortorel and Perissin)

At the first shock it seemed as if the Huguenots would win, and they cried in exaltation, "Victory, victory! The Evangel has won the victory and has vanquished the mass of the popes. Down with the Papists!"[2] The admiral began the fray by charging Anjou's center with 2,000 reiters and such French gendarmes as he had, but was himself attacked on the flank by the duke of Aumale and Villars so furiously that he was compelled to fall back.

[1] The custom of kissing the ground at the moment of charging the enemy seems to have been peculiar to the Swiss and the Germans (D'Aubigné, Book V, chap. xvii, 120; Brantôme, VI, 221 and 522).

[2] Claude Haton, II, 581.

The Protestant infantry which had followed the horse into the battle, was thus left unsustained, and when the duke of Guise's light horse charged, the lansquenets broke in flight, abandoning the artillery. In the midst of the melée various companies of reiters, seeing the battle lost, ran to their baggage, seized their most valuable effects, and decamped in haste. Mansfeldt's reiters alone fought well; the others were of slight service. Matters were little better with the hirelings of the King. Many of the leaders on both sides were injured in the course of the battle; Guise in the hand and foot, Bassompierre, a German captain destined to become a very prominent man at court, in both arms; Anjou was borne to the ground off his horse but escaped injury; Coligny was hurt in the face by a pistol-ball. Among the Catholic dead was Montbrun, captain of the Swiss guard. He was haughty and cruel, and a despot with his men, but it is to his credit that he sought to prevent the soldiery from abusing the peasantry.[1] The most of the Huguenot dead were the German reiters and lansquenets, many of whom were killed by their Catholic compatriots or the Swiss, who distinguished themselves by their ferocity.[2] The fight endured for four hours, from 11 until 3 o'clock, at the end of which time the forces of Anjou overthrew the admiral, routed both his horse and foot, and captured his artillery and baggage. But for the good fortune that some of Coligny's horse intercepted a treasurer of the King coming out of Limousin with 30,000 francs, the distribution of which among his reiters quieted their murmurs, Coligny might have been all but deserted by the German horse.[3] As it was, he was able to fall back on Niort and thence make his retreat to the far south.[4]

Fortunately for the Huguenots, the enemy did not attempt pursuit of them, but instead undertook the siege of St. Jean-d'Angély, which lay directly in the way southward, to the disgust of the

---

[1] Claude Haton, II, 585.   [2] Ibid., 582.

[3] La Noue, chap. xxvi. Both Henry and Louis of Nassau were in this engagement, the latter having quitted his university studies for war.—Languet, Epist. secr., I, 117; Archives de la maison d'Orange-Nassau, III, 323.

[4] Jean de Serres, 526, 527. See the letter of Norris, December 19, 1569, Appendix XIX.

liberal marshal Cossé and even Tavannes, who urged that the King, in the light of this great victory, might now make peace with good grace.[1]   Others, considering the strength of St. Jean-d'Angély thought that the war would be protracted into the depth of winter and that the capture of St. Jean-d'Angély would be of small importance while La Rochelle still remained.   Instead of accepting the advice, the government hardened its policy.   A reward of 50,000 crowns was offered for the head of Coligny,[2] 600,000 francs were distributed among the soldiers and 300,000 sent into Germany to make a new levy against the spring.[3]

On October 16 Charles IX arrived before St. Jean-d'Angély and beheld the greatest part of the royal troops ranged in order of battle.   Anticipating a desperate resistance upon the part of those in the city, the King's infantry requested to be equipped with the gendarmes' cuirasses.   One incident will illustrate the desperate valor of the besieged.   On the night of October 21 they made a sortie, entered the enemy's trenches, slew twenty men, took two ensigns prisoner, and all the arms they found in the *corps de garde*, and returned into the town.   The Protestant garrison was not over 1,500 men, but in spite of the odds against him (he had no artillery except falconets and muskets, while Anjou had eleven guns, great and small), the Huguenot commander, Pilles, refused to surrender.   Instead, when the governor of the town urged him to surrender rather than make resistance, the desperate captain had him hanged and his body cast into the river. The attack upon St. Jean-d'Angély opened on October 25, but

---

[1] Delaborde, III, 162.

[2] *Mém. de Condé*, I, 207; D'Aubigné, III, 113, 114; *Arch. cur.*, séries I, VI, 875.   Pius V's letter of felicitation to the queen mother, October 17, 1569, characterizes Coligny as "hominem unum omnium fallacissimum, execrandaeque memoriae, Gasparem de Coligny, qui se pro istius regni admirante gerit."— Potter, *Pie V*, 67, ed. Gouban, Book III, letter 43, p. 236.   The admiral's office had been declared vacant on July 15, 1569 (Coll. Godefroy, CCLVII, No. 69).

[3] *C. S. P. For.*, Nos. 456, 459, 464, 486, October 5, 6, 10, 27, 1569.   This was far from paying the reiters what the government owed them.   They had been serving for thirteen months and received pay but for three; 2,000,000 crowns were still owing (*ibid.*, No. 543, December 19, 1569).

although the wall was badly battered, no sufficient breach was made for days. The town resisted every attack until December 2, when it at last surrendered.[1]

Yet in spite of the double victory of Moncontour and at St. Jean-d'Angély, hard experience was proving the wisdom of the course advised by Tavannes and Cossé. The King was without money to pay the Swiss and the reiters who threatened to mutiny at any minute. The country round about the army was so denuded that there was great misery for want of food and multitudes of the soldiers fell sick.[2] Finally, on November 24, in a sitting of the King's council, Charles IX was formally petitioned by certain of its members to make peace overtures to his revolted subjects,[3] and expressed his willingness to comply with the request.

The hand of the government was forced by events; the courageous resistance of St. Jean-d'Angély, Montluc's action in resigning his commission, and the growing strength of the Reformed among the southern "viscounts," made the crown think eagerly of peace. As an earnest of this purpose, the King sent the liberal marshal Cossé in company with De Losses, the new captain of the Scotch Guard, to La Rochelle to confer with the queen of Navarre and La Rochefoucault. But Jeanne d'Albret was not minded to use haste, to which the marshal meaningly rejoined that "there were many of rank in the Protestant army who would not give her that advice."[4] Yet even if she had wanted to, the queen of Navarre could not have hastened a settlement. For at this time there was a real division of opinion existing between the Huguenot nobles and the people of the Huguenot towns like St. Jean-d'Angély and La Rochelle. The former class were weary of war and wanted to return to their homes and were in favor of peace and inclined to make their own terms, even to the extent of ignoring the claims of their coreligionists

---

[1] On the resistance of St. Jean-d'Angély see D'Aubigné, Book V, chap. xix; La Noue, chap. xxvii; La Popelinière, Book XX.

[2] *Ibid.*, No. 511, November 21, 1569. Both the duke of Alençon and the princess Marguerite, Henry IV's future wife, were among the number. The disease was smallpox (*ibid.*, No. 502, November 3, No. 543, December 19, 1569).

[3] Delaborde, III, 72; *Nég. Tosc.*, III, 608.

[4] *C. S. P. For.*, Nos. 514, 515, 576, November 24, 25, 1569.

of the towns. The latter felt aggrieved at seeing themselves thus
deserted, when they had done so much to maintain the general
cause of the Huguenots, not merely in contributing money but
by making such heroic resistance as that of the people of St. Jean-
d'Angély, and Jeanne D'Albret sympathized with them. She
would not listen to talk of peace, being firmly convinced that it
was but another ruse, like that at Longjumeau, and resolutely
declared that there would be time enough to consider terms of
peace when their forces were more equal; that nothing short of
the free exercise of the religion as granted by former edicts would
avail; that even if all the Huguenot nobles consented to the terms,
her own signature and that of Henry of Navarre would never be
affixed to any half-way terms of pacification.[1] But at last, after
long debate, the queen of Navarre yielded, and sent the admiral's
future son-in-law, Teligny, who had conferred with Coligny, to
the King to request "a good assured and inviolable peace,"[2] probably being in part influenced by the treatment of St. Jean-d'Angély, whose garrison was suffered to march out, bag and baggage,
with colors flying. The Huguenots demanded liberty of conscience, the restitution of their goods, estates, and offices to those
of the religion, and the reversal of all sentences against them,
together with guaranties for the observance of the articles.[3]

[1] C. S. P., For., November 24, 1569, Jeanne d'Albret to the princes of Navarre
and Condé. Not in Rochambeau, Lettres d'Antoine de Bourbon et de Jehanne
d'Albret.

[2] An awkward delay occurred at this time owing to the fact that Teligny's
safe-conduct provided for his coming to the King, but made no statement as to his
departure. On December 14 the queen of Navarre and her son demanded "un
passe-port plus ample" from the King. When it came with a revised form, negotiations were resumed (Commentaires et lettres de Montluc, III, 263, note; C. S.
P. For., No. 643, January, 1570). For details of these protracted negotiations see
La Popelinière, Book XXII; Delaborde, III, 176 ff.). In Appendix XX will be
found a long document consisting of a great number of articles proposed by the
queen of Navarre, the princes of Navarre and Condé, and the other chiefs of the
Huguenot party, for the pacification of France, and divided under the heads of
religion, restitution of goods and estates, council and justice, arms, and finances,
together with measures to be taken to insure the performance of the edict
(February 4, 1570).

[3] C. S. P. For., No. 644, January 1570, articles sent by the queen of Navarre
to the King.

The essential issue, and that which protracted the debate so long was the demand for *chambres mi-parties*,[1] and that the crown give over certain cities into the hands of the Huguenots to be garrisoned and governed by them alone. On February 3, 1570, the King replied, promising to grant amnesty for the past, the restoration of their estates and offices to the Huguenots, the expulsion of the reiters, with liberty of the religion within private dwellings and in two towns which he would appoint.[2] But Jeanne d'Albret, who conducted the negotiations for the Huguenots, refused to be satisfied. In a long letter to the queen mother a week later she recapitulated the former negotiations at great length and complained of the government's want of good faith, especially alluding to the cardinal of Lorraine and the duke of Alva.[3] As a matter of fact the government was not yet willing to give in. The cardinal of Lorraine still hoped to hasten forward a new levy of reiters in Germany when spring should open, and held out the vain hope of the restoration of the Three Bishoprics if the Emperor would lend France this assistance and stay the Protestant levies.[4] But the Emperor himself had something to say about the matter and asserted that he would not consider the proposed marriage of his daughter with the French King until peace was concluded in France.[5] Aware of the Emperor's attitude, the queen of Navarre resolutely demanded terms of peace in conformity with the demands of the Huguenots.[6]

[1] *Hist. du Lang.*, V, 508, note. The parlement of Toulouse was a special object of criticism by the Huguenots. In the act of peace they were exempted from its jurisdiction.

[2] *C. S. P. For.*, No. 672, February 3, 1570; cf. *R. Q. H.*, XLII, 112–15, copied from Record Office; Delaborde, *Coligny*, III, 180.

[3] *C. S. P. For.*, No. 682, February 10, 1570. Not in Rochambeau.

[4] *Ibid.*, No. 674, February 5, 1570. This information had been conveyed to Jeanne d'Albret by a packet which had been intercepted (*ibid.*, No. 689, February 17, 1570).

[5] Waddington, "La France et les Protestants allemands sous Charles IX et Henri III," *Revue Hist.*, XLII, 256 ff.

[6] The queen of Navarre to Charles IX. Has received his letter and communicated his reply to her son and nephew, and the noblemen who are with them. Assures him that it is impossible for them to live without the free exercise of their

The arguments of peace urged by the marshal Cossé and others who shared his thought had less influence upon the King and his counselors as the storm of war drove off toward the south,[1] to the elation of Pius V, who overwhelmed Charles IX with protests against pacification.[2] South of the Loire the principal interest of the third civil war is attached to the doings of that famous group of Huguenot warriors known as the "viscounts," with whom Coligny had failed to connect before the battle of Jarnac. A brief account of the earlier achievements of this group, who sometimes fought together, sometimes separately, and had three or four thousand footmen and three or four hundred horsemen in their command,[3] is necessary at this point. There were ten of these captains: Bernard Roger de Cominges, vicomte de Bruniquel; Bertrand de Rabastenis, vicomte de Paulin; Antoine de Rabastenis, vicomte de Montclaire; the vicomte de Montaigu; the vicomte de Caumont; the vicomte de Parat; Geraud de Lomagne, vicomte de Sevignac (near Beaucaire), a brother of Terride, who was a Catholic and implicated with Montluc in the project to deliver Guyenne to the King of Spain;[4] the vicomte d'Arpajon; the vicomte de Rapin; and the vicomte de Gourdon.[5] Three of these, and the most conspicuous, save Rapin,

religion, which in the end he will be constrained to grant, and declares that all those who advise him otherwise are no true subjects to him (*C. S. P. Spain*, No. 683, February 11, 1570).   Not in Rochambeau.

[1] De Thou definitely says Paris and the court were indifferent as to the fate of the remoter provinces so long as the war did not touch them too (Vol. VI, Book XLVII, p. 37).

[2] "Compertum nobis est nullam esse Satanae cum filiis lucis communionem; ita inter catholicos quidem et haereticos nullam compositionem, nisi fictam fallaciisque plenissimam, fieri posse pro certo habemus."—Potter, *Pie V*, 86 (ed. Gouban), Book 4, letter I, p. 269; Pius V to Charles IX, January 29, 1570.   At p. 272 is a letter in a similar vein to the duke of Anjou, written on the same day.

[3] De Ruble, *Commentaires et lettres de Montluc*, VII, 184, note; V, 135; letter of Montluc, October 31, 1568.

[4] *Ibid.*, IV, 335.

[5] It is to be regretted that there is no monograph upon the history of these viscounts.   It would be quite worth doing.   Communay, *Les Huguenots dans le Béarn et la Navarre*, and Durier, *Les Huguenots en Bigorre*, 1884, are valuable collections of documents.   The sources are largely in the local archives of Upper

the viscounts of Paulin, Bruniquel, and Arpajon were natives of the diocese of Albi, a stronghold of heresy from mediaeval times; the first had seen service in Piedmont in the reign of Henry II, and the ancestors of all three of them had fought against Ferdinand of Aragon in 1495.[1] The viscount of Rapin was a leader of the great Huguenot rising in Toulouse in 1562, and was made Protestant governor of Montauban in 1564 by the prince of Condé.[2] He was so bitterly hated by the people of Toulouse that he was accused of wanting to destroy the city utterly and remove the very stones to Montauban. He had fought in the second civil war, but was betrayed into the hands of the magistrates of Toulouse and condemned and executed there on April 13, 1569, in defiance of the King's orders to the contrary. The Huguenots took terrible reprisal for this outrage, devastating the environs of Toulouse for leagues around, even inscribing on the ruins "Vengeance de Rapin."[3]

These four viscounts were the nucleus of the group and began their career in the first civil war. But save Rapin, none became conspicuous then. During the second war the others were drawn to the standard. They operated in Languedoc and Quercy at first, aided by the peasantry who seem to have turned toward them as natural enemies of the higher nobles.[4] In the summer and autumn of 1568 their united hosts made a mighty raid up the valley of the Rhone from Montauban through Rouergue and the Cévennes, where part of the troops crossed the Rhone under the viscount of Rapin and joined the Protestant army of Dauphiné and Provence under a former lieutenant of Des Adresse. The rest remained in Languedoc. Later Rapin recrossed the river

Languedoc, Guyenne, Quercy, the Agenois, and Rouergue. My information is gathered entirely from the two works name above and Montluc; D'Aubigné; *Hist. du Languedoc*, V; Courteault, *Blaise de Montluc*, Paris, 1908; and Marlet, *Le comte de Montgomery*, Paris, 1890.

[1] *Hist. du Lang.*, V, 155, 156.

[2] De Ruble, *Commentaires et lettres de Montluc*, IV, 354, 399, note.

[3] *Hist. du Lang.*, V, 501; *Commentaires et lettres de Montluc*, II, 399, note; V, 268 note.

[4] *Hist. du Lang.*, V, 495.

into Vivarais with the hope of joining the prince of Condé. But the governor of Provence, the count of Tende, aided by the viscount of Joyeuse, the Catholic general in these parts, blocked his passage. In the midst of this plight relief came to the viscount of Rapin in the person of his former comrade in arms. But at least Joyeuse had prevented the union of the viscounts with the prince of Condé.

The people of Vivarais resented the occupation of the country by these guerilla chieftains, much as their ancestors two hundred years before had risen against the Free Companies during the reign of Charles V. The towns organized an army of their own and distinguished themselves by routing the viscounts upon one occasion. In January, 1568, the viscounts succeeded in their early purpose, penetrated the Catholic army and crossed the Loire at Blois. The relief of Orleans and their union with the prince of Condé before Chartres hastened the peace of Longjumeau.[1]

During the interim between the armistice of Longjumeau and the outbreak of the third war, the viscounts, in common with most of the Protestant forces of the south, seem not to have disarmed, but stayed in the vicinity of Montauban, the Huguenot capital of the far south. When war was renewed, Joyeuse and Gordes, governor of Dauphiné, unsuccessfully tried to keep the Huguenots east of the Rhone from joining them in Languedoc. At Milhaud in Rouergue a great council of war was held at which practically all the Protestant fighting forces of the south save Guyenne and Gascony were represented.[2] In conformity with the plan there arranged, the viscounts remained in Quercy and Languedoc while the main army crossed the Dordogne with the purpose of joining the prince of Condé. But in Périgord it was met and scattered, on October 25, 1568, by the duke of Montpensier and Marshal Brissac. The viscounts continued to operate in Languedoc against Joyeuse and others. The success of their activities, especially the destruction of Gaillac (September 8, 1568) was what led to the

[1] *Hist. du Lang.*, V, 495, 496; La Popelinière, Book XIII.

[2] *Commentaires et lettres de Montluc*, III, 208.

In *State Papers, Foreign*, Elizabeth, Vol. CXV, No. 990 is a document showing the provinces held by the Protestants. It is undated but the mention of the viscounts in it shows that it is of this time (printed in Appendix XXI).

revival of the league at Toulouse under the cardinal of Armagnac on September 12, in the cathedral of St. Etienne. The recall of Joyeuse with the Catholic troops of Languedoc to the north to assist the duke of Anjou, left a clear field in Provence and Langue-doc. The loss of Jarnac, March 13, 1569, where the prince of Condé was killed, may in part be ascribed to the fact that the vis-counts refused to respond to his orders for them to come to him, so that the united forces of Anjou and Joyeuse overwhelmed the Huguenots. A similar reverse befell the Protestants on June 8 following, in the Ariège near Toulouse, where Bellegarde, the seneschal of Toulouse, routed the viscounts and captured the vis-count of Paulin, who would have suffered the fate of the viscount of Rapin, had not Charles IX, less for magnanimity's sake than to rebuke the parlement of Toulouse for violating the royal orders before, refused to have him delivered up to it.[1] The shattered bands of the viscounts joined Montgomery, a leader of their own kind, who had been detached by Coligny from his own army, in the same month.

The reason for Montgomery's appearance in the south is to be found in the peril threatening Béarn and Navarre at this time. Montluc had conceived the idea that Béarn might be conquered while its ruler was absent. The parlement of Toulouse energeti-cally favored the project and on November 15, 1568, had issued an *arrêt* placing Béarn under its jurisdiction.[2] In the early months of 1569 efforts were made with some success to corrupt the captains in the Béarnais army.[3] When the plan was broached to the duke of Anjou he enthusiastically approved it. The time was auspicious, for it so happened that the suggestion coincided with his victory at Jarnac. Exactly a week after the battle[4] he detached the seigneur de Terride with instructions to report to Montluc, for the duke thought Montluc could not be spared from

---

[1] *Hist. du Lang.*, V, 576, note.

[2] Bordenave, 166; *Hist. du Lang.*, V, 575.

[3] Bordenave, *Hist. de Béarn et de Navarre*, 268–77.

[4] Olhagaray, *Histoire de Foix, de Navarre et de Béarn* (1609), 578, however, gives the date March 4.

Guyenne.[1]   This order was a bitter disappointment to Montluc, who wanted to conquer Béarn himself, and he ever thereafter cherished a hatred against Marshal Damville[2] who was away from his government at the time with the duke of Anjou, believing that Damville's jealousy of him was responsible for it.   This may very probably have been so, for, as will be seen later, the enmity between the two was extreme.

Terride's campaign began well.   One by one, in rapid order, the fortified towns of Béarn collapsed before him—Pontacq, Morlaas, Orthez, Sauveterre, and Pau—the birthplace of Henry of Navarre, while the country round about was wasted with fire and sword.   The queen of Navarre's lieutenant was driven to find refuge in Navarrens, whose château, reputed to be impregnable, had been built by Henri d'Albret during his enterprises against Spain.   On April 27, 1569, Terride began the siege of the castle of Navarrens.[3]

Montgomery, who arrived at Castres on June 21[4] bearing the double commission of the two Protestant princes,[5] in the course of four weeks found himself in the neighborhood of Toulouse and at the head of the united forces of the viscounts and some levies made in Albigeois.   Montgomery's energy amazed Montluc who was soldier enough to give his enemy credit for really wonderful achievement.   He had never been in the country before and all the forces he had brought with him were three score and ten horses, and he had no other forces but those of the viscounts in the beginning. He had to cross the Garonne river, too, the entire length of which

---

[1] Bordenave, *Histoire de Béarn et de Navarre*, 216.

[2] *Commentaires et lettres de Montluc*, III, 245.

[3] In F. Fr., 15,558, fol. 293, is a memoir of Jean de Montluc to the King, of July, 1569, enumerating the munitions and provisions of the army before Navarrens.

[4] *Mém. de Gaches*, 90.

[5] I do not know that the actual text of this joint commission is known.   Montgomery, in his letter at this time styled himself as follows: Lieutenant-général du roy en Guyenne, despuis la cousté de la Dordoigne jusques aux Pyrénées, en l'absence et sous l'autorité de messeigneurs les princes de Navarre et de Condé, lieutenant et protecteur de Sa Majesté, conservateur de ses édits et aussi lieutenant-général de la reine de Navarre en son comté de Bigorre!—De Ruble, *Commentaires et lettres de Montluc*, III, 266, note.

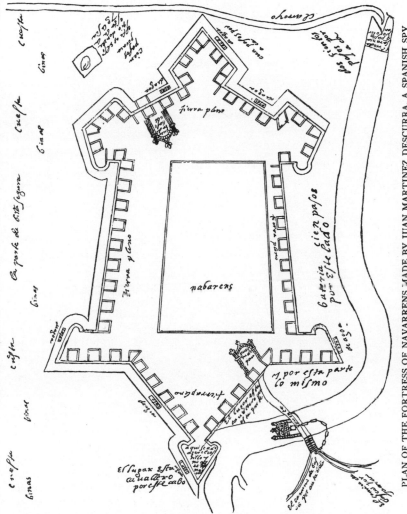

PLAN OF THE FORTRESS OF NAVARRENS ᴍADE BY JUAN MARTINEZ DESCURRA, A SPANISH SPY
In Archives nationales, K. 1499, No. 84.

was watched by spies.   The belief of the Catholic captains in Languedoc was that Montgomery intended to organize the defense of the places the Protestants were possessed of, and this erroneous opinion seems to have been given currency by the Huguenots themselves, "who had ever that quality to conceal their designs better than we," testifies Montluc.   "They are a people that rarely discover their counsels, and that is the reason why their enterprises seldom fail of taking effect."

By rapid marching Montgomery reached Navarrens incredibly soon.   Terride, his soldiers wearied out by a siege which had endured for three months and a half in midsummer, loaded with spoil, licentious and mutinous to an extent that shamed even the reiters, abandoned the siege and fell back on Orthez.   But the city was not proof against the attacks of the viscounts.   In broad daylight the walls were carried *par escalade*.   On August 13, Terride, who had taken refuge in the castle with so much haste that he was without provisions or munitions, surrendered.   He himself was spared by Montgomery for the purpose of being exchanged for the latter's brother, but died before the transfer was made.   His captains, almost to a man, were put to death.   Some of these were former officers in the Béarnais army and were legally guilty of treason, but the real motive of Montgomery was reprisal for the ravages done by Terride's army.   At the beginning of the war the queen's lieutenant, the heroic baron de Larboust, either in the hope of sparing Béarn, or anticipating what would be meted out again, had proposed to neutralize Béarn, putting it into the custody of the count de Grammont, even offering to oppose Montgomery if it were done.   Terride refused and paid the price of his wilfulness and bigotry.   Béarn was saved by Montgomery, in the most brilliant and most honorable campaign of his checkered career.[1]

[1] Montgomery's itinerary is printed in Appendix XXII.

The two parts of Montgomery's expedition south of the Dordogne, first the union with the viscounts, and second, the campaign against Terride are to be distinguished, although they have been much confounded.

The sources and authorities for the history of this brief war are: Communay, *Les Huguenots dans le Béarn et la Navarre;* Durier, *Les Huguenots en Bigorre;*

The Catholic failure to conquer Béarn goaded Montluc's slumbering hatred of Damville to fury, for he believed the utter collapse of the Protestant cause would have followed the conquest.[1] He blamed Damville for it, asserting that Terride's overthrow was due to his slowness. But the marshal had had great difficulty in returning to his government. The Huguenots were in full possession of Quercy and the Albigeois, and the region around Toulouse was so much overrun by them that Damville was unable to reach Toulouse until the end of June.[2] It took Montgomery even with the viscounts immediately at hand, nearly five weeks (June 21–July 27) to prepare for the relief of Navarrens, though the desperate condition of things there required haste, and with the entire civil as well as military burden of Languedoc upon him, a burden that necessarily had accumulated, too, during his absence, Damville could hardly be expected, with justice, to have got ready to go against Montgomery before the middle of August, by which time the siege of Navarrens was over. The truth is, Montluc and Damville radically disagreed as to the policy to be pursued in the south. Montluc's patent covered the territory of Guyenne only. But Montluc, with a mere soldier's disregard for forms of law, believed that it was a soldier's duty to go where the need was greatest. He made the proposal that when Damville should have won a town in Languedoc he would come to attack another in Guyenne. To this the marshal demurred, asserting

Bordenave, *Hist. de Béarn et de Navarre*, Book VII; Montluc. *Comment. et Lettres*, III, Book VII, pp. 254–89, and his letters for September, 1569 in Vol. V, pp. 164 ff.; D'Aubigné, Book V, chap. xiv; La Popelinière, Book XVIII; *Hist. du Lang.*, V, 578–87; Dupleix, *Histoire de France*—his father was one of Montluc's captains and for some time marshal of the camp to Biron in Guyenne; Marlet, *Le comte de Montgomery*; Courteault, *Blaise de Montluc*, chap. xi. The baron de Ruble, ed. Montluc, V, 211, note, says: "Les documents inédits sont presque innombrables. Outre les lettres conservées à la Bibliothèque Nationale, principalement dans la collection Harlay, St. Germain, vol. 323 et suivants, nous citerons, aux archives de Pau la série B 952 à 958: les registres consulaires d'Auch, les registres de Larcher aux archives de Tarbes, les registres consulaires de Bagnères-de-Bigorre." The local archives of Bigorre contain many of Montgomery's letters. Some of them have been published in *Arch. de la Gascogne*, VI.

[1] *Commentaires et lettres de Montluc*, III, 286.

[2] *Hist. du Languedoc*, V, 164.

that it was his duty to attempt to recover what had been lost in his government and pointed to his commission. Montluc derided the plea and accused Damville of being so proud "a grand lord, son to a constable and a marshal of France," that he would not work with a poor gentlemen.[1]

In the late summer (1569) Montgomery victoriously returned from Béarn, having reached the highest point of his reputation. Within six weeks he had gathered an army, marched leagues through a strange and hostile country, crossed the Garonne and raised a siege against equal forces, and turned the Catholic conquest of Béarn into defeat. It seemed a dream both to friend and foe.

[1] Damville ignored the railings of Montluc until November, when he wrote to the King in vindication of himself, giving a full account of their campaign against Montgomery (De Ruble, *Commentaires et lettres de Montluc*, V, 243–57, notes; Coll. Godefroy, CCLVII, Nos. 75 and 84. The first is printed in *Archives de la Gironde*, II, 148; *Hist. du Lang.*, V, 521, note 2; the latter is given in tome XII, preuves, note 304). Damville seems to have anticipated an inquiry, for he carefully laid aside all of Montluc's letters from May 26 to October 22, 1569. On February 27, 1570, Damville sent the King a stinging indictment of Montluc's course. In it he declared Montluc was a rash impostor and accused him of forcing the people of Guyenne to pay unjust ransoms; of violating women; of misusing public moneys; and asserted that he courted investigation of his own conduct (De Ruble, *Montluc*, III, 394; V, 269, and notes; *Hist. du Lang.*, V, 520, note 3; the letter was first published by Le Laboureur in the *Additions to Castelnau*, II, 130, from a copy in the Dupuy Coll., Vol. 755. M. Tamizey de Larroque discovered the original in the Coll. Godefroy in the Bib. de l'Institut). Most men of the time, however, deplored the contest between these two Catholic chiefs of the south, without taking sides (see *Archives de la Gironde*, II, 148). Montluc's Spanish spy, Bardaxi, naturally reproaches Damville (K. 1,574, No. 154). Probably no judgment may fairly be pronounced until all the sources have been carefully examined. A life of Damville is a work sorely needed; it is a rich subject for some historical student. The recent work of M. Courteault, *Blaise de Montluc*, 538–40, 551–53, 557–59, goes at length into this feud between Montluc and Damville. In the main the author sides with the marshal—"Damville acceptait les faits accomplis et ne jugeait pas utile de combattre Mongonmery" (p. 551). He declares that "prudemmement, il [Montluc] a passé dans son livre ce grave incident sous silence" (p. 551). He admits, however, that if the King had ordered an investigation Damville would have had something to answer for (p. 559).

There are numerous letters of Charles IX to Montluc in the St. Petersburg archives. In them Charles harps upon the disagreeable conduct of Montluc toward Jeanne d'Albret, and tries at one and the same time to repress the queen's indefatigable propaganda lest it anger Spain, and to restrain Montluc because of his outrageous conduct and the illustrious blood of the queen of Navarre (La

Nobly did his enemy say: "In all the wars there never was performed a more notable exploit." If Montgomery had failed, Coligny would have had no place to retire to after the loss of Moncontour. For he came from that field of Protestant overthrow with the relics of an army only, mostly gentry and reiters, for the infantry was almost all cut to pieces or captured, without baggage, without money, even the horses needing to be reshod. It was well that the admiral could throw himself into the arms of Montgomery and the viscounts who enriched him with the spirit of their success and drew thousands, literally, to the Huguenot standard by the magic of their achievements. His following increased so rapidly that by the time he reached Montpellier he again had between ten and twelve thousand men.[1] On January 3, 1570, Coligny and Montgomery united their forces. The dissension between Montluc[2] and Damville gave them and the viscounts almost unrestrained

Ferrière, *Rapport*, 22.) Letters of the marshal Montmorency and of marshal Damville are also in this volume. Those of the latter cover the history of all the campaigns of Montgomery in Béarn. He condemns Montluc for the death of Terride. The marshal's laconic language is strikingly in contrast with Montluc's rhetorical complaint (La Ferrière, *Rapport*, 44). If we may believe Brantôme, "dans toutes les guerres Montluc gagna la pièce d'argent; auparavant il n'avoit pas grandes finances, et se trouva avoir dans ses coffres cent mille escus." Charles IX once sharply reminded Montluc in a letter of November, 1562, that he was getting 500 livres per month for his table. (La Ferrière, *Blaise de Montluc d'après sa correspondance inédite*, Mém. lus à la Sorbonne, 1864.)

[1] Coligny was quick to seize the opportunity afforded in the south to continue the war there until the crown came to terms with the Huguenots. After the King's capture of St. Jean-d'Angély, Coligny crossed the Loire to join Montgomery (cf. Delaborde, III, 157, 161, 169, 170; *Montluc*, III, 347, October; *C. S. P. For.*, No. 577, December, 1569; Letters from La Rochelle to the cardinal of Châtillon). The cardinal has received letters from his brother the admiral, dated from Montauban November 22, informing him that the princes are well, that their army is increasing, that the reiters are content and have received pay, and that there is no difficulty in joining with Montgomery and the viscounts. Their army will consist of 6,500 horse and 12,000 arquebusiers. For the proclamation issued from Montauban see Appéndix XXIII. In *C. S. P. For.*, No. 667, January, 1570, is an extract of a letter from La Rochelle, describing the position of the armies of the admiral and the count of Montgomery, who are on either bank of the Garonne, and in good spirits and health.

[2] De Ruble, *Commentaires et lettres de Montluc*, V, 263, 264. Letter of Montluc to Charles IX, January 9, 1570. He writes almost broken hearted.

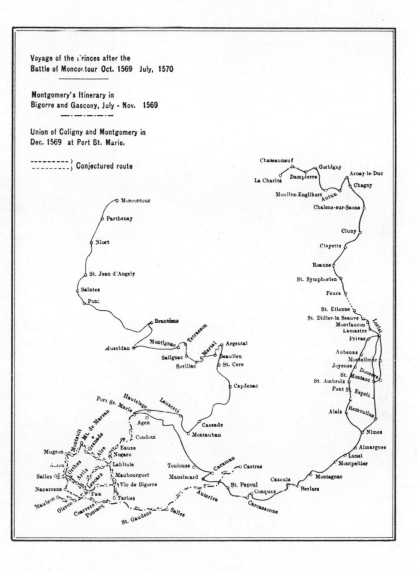

Voyage of the Princes after the
Battle of Moncontour Oct. 1569   July, 1570

Montgomery's Itinerary in
Bigorre and Gascony, July - Nov.   1569

Union of Coligny and Montgomery in
Dec. 1569 at Port St. Marie.

------- } Conjectured route
------- }

Chateauneuf   Oarbiguy
                  Dampierre   Arnay-le-Duc
La Charité   Chagny
      Moulins-Engilbert   Autun
                          Chalons-sur-Saone

Moncontour

Parthenay   Cluny

Niort   Clayette

                                   Roanne
St. Jean d'Angely   St. Symphorien

Saintes   Feurs

Pons   St. Etienne   Loriol
                       St. Didier-la-Seauve
         Brantôme   Montfaucon
                              Lamastre
   Montignac Tetrasson   Privas
Museidan   Aubenas
         Salignac   Mastel   Montellmar
             Sovillac Beaulieu   Joyeuse   Donzere
                      St. Cere   St. Ambroix St. Montant
                                              Pont St   Esprit
                   Capdenac
                                   Alais   Remoulins
         Hautelage   Nimes
Port St. Marie   Lauzerte
          Agen   Almargues
       Condom   Lunel
    Eauze   Montpellier
Mugron Nogaro
      Lahitole   Toulouse   Caraman   Castres   Montagnac
Salles Maubourguet   Mansiscard   Cazouls Beziers
Navarrens Vic de Bigorre St. Papoul Conques
Mauleon   Pau   Tarbes   Auterive   Carcassonne
  Oleron Coarreze Pontacq   Salles
       St. Gaudens

freedom in Upper Gascony and Languedoc, where they grew enormously rich on the spoils of war, and carried their depredations to the very walls of Toulouse which was actually invested from January 22 to February 20, 1570.[1]

When the news of Terride's downfall was known to Montluc he made overtures to Damville in spite of his resentment. A council of war was held at Auch, but instead of coming himself the marshal sent Joyeuse to say that he thought it his duty to pass his time in his own government, considering the charge the country was under to sustain the war. It is interesting to observe the ancient ideas of provincial separation and autonomy asserting themselves at this time. In vain Montluc argued that the real enemy was in Guyenne and that the local hostility of the Huguenots in Languedoc was a little matter in comparison; that all Catholics were equally the King's subjects and that the country was the King's.[2] Joyeuse answered that the estates of Languedoc would not pay for Montluc's army unless he employed their money in recovering the places in their province. The decision abandoned Guyenne, leaving it alone and single handed, for the King's forces were engaged in the protracted siege of St. Jean-d'Angély and could not come to its relief. "J'ay tousjours ouy dire que plus près est la chemise que la robbe," said Montluc satirically.[3]

The old man was on the point of discharging his army and retiring to Libourne or Agen, but the duty of a soldier forbade him. If he now abandoned the open country in so critical a condition, it would ever have been a reproach to him. He thought better of himself and attacked Mont-de-Marsan instead, where he placated

[1] So great was the desolation inflicted that the King was obliged to remit the taille in Agenois (Arch. municip. d'Agen reg. consul., fol. 262). The Protestants were so encouraged that even those living in Agen, Montluc's own town, dared to revolt (Bull. du Com. de la langue et de l'hist. de France, I, 478; Reg. munic. d'Agen, fol. 254). An interesting comparison might be made between the rules for the government of the camp issued by Coligny at this time—they are in K. 1,575, No. 7—and those issued by the prince of Condé at Orleans, in April, 1562. For an example of the severe discipline in the Protestant army see Claude Haton II 568; cf. De Thou, Book XXX.

[2] De Ruble, Commentaires et lettres de Montluc, III, 74.

[3] Ibid., 314.

his outraged feelings by refusing the petition of the garrison to
capitulate and secretly gave orders for the massacre of the entire
number save the captain, Favas.[1]   This feat of arms insured the
future of Gascony and the Landes, for the city served as a granary
for all the surrounding country from whence, however, to the
detriment of France, much grain was exported to Spain.[2]   After
this exploit, feeling the impossibility of maintaining his forces in
the field, Montluc disbanded his army, sending his son to Lectoure
and himself retiring to Agen.   It goaded him to the quick that the
crown approved throughout of Damville's conduct and either
ignored his own complaints, or criticized him for what he had done.
"I was born under a planet to be ever subject to calumny," he
growled.   "Age deprives a man of his heat: for in my younger
days the greatest. prince upon earth could not have made me
swallow such a pill."

It may have been that Damville had friends at court and Montluc none; it may have been that the marshal's pride of long descent
made him indifferent or even contemptuous of Montluc in some
degree.   But if we look closely at things it is evident that the
spirit of provincial separation was the fundamental source of the
difficulty between them.   This spirit penetrated to the very bottom.
Both Montluc and Damville were making war with men levied
from the country in which they were—with militia instead of regular troops.   The consequence of this was that every man in the
host had an eye to the welfare of his family or his friends instead of
to the King's business; moreover, many had relatives or friends
with the enemy, which made them fight reluctantly; finally, they
were ill-paid and had to subsist on plunder, which debauched
discipline.   The true remedy would have been for Charles IX to
have raised the useless siege of St.-Jean-d'Angély and to have come

---

[1] De Ruble, *op. cit.*, III, 315–29; Montluc's sangfroid is amazing as he writes.

[2] Delaborde, III, 157, 161, 169, 170.   Early in 1569 Montluc sent a complaint
to Charles IX protesting against this export of grain.   This trade redounded to the
advantage of the commander of the Gascon coast, who was a brother of the bishop
of Agen, and Montluc's complaint gave rise to an acrimonious correspondence
preserved in Coll. Harley St. Germain, No. 323, which throws some light on the
interesting question of trade in the sixteenth century (see *Commentaires et lettres de
Montluc*, III, 395, note).

in person into the southland, where the authority of the King might have overcome the local forces of separation; and where the regulars would have plied war as a trade, as the circumstances demanded.

The Catholics of the south had an example before their eyes in the reiters with the admiral, of the efficiency of regular troops over local forces. Coligny owed his future to them and Montgomery. The way the reiters made war excited the admiration of trained soldiers like Montluc. They so barricaded the villages in which they quartered themselves that nothing was to be got by assault and in the open country they were always mounted at the least alarm. It was very hard to surprise them. They were careful of their horses and arms and so terrible in action "that a man could see nothing but fire and steel." The very grooms fought.[1]

The reverses experienced at Poitiers, Moncontour, and St. Jeand'Angély had not been fatal to the Protestants. In the middle of December Coligny wrote to the captain of La Charité that he felt ready to resume the offensive in the spring, having in La Rochelle, Cognac, Angoulême, Montauban, Castres, La Charité, and Montpellier a chain of impregnable fortresses extending from the seaboard clear to the heart of France, and controlling the Loire.[2] A survey of the map will show the strength of the Huguenots in this part of France. All of Provence and Lower Languedoc was in full control of the Protestants, Montauban, Albi, and Castres, constituting a line of defense on the west. In Upper Languedoc they were not so strong and the condition of the Catholics was less precarious, since Toulouse, Auch, Agen, and Cahors, formed a quadrilateral in the very center. The Huguenots controlled many of the lesser towns, so that Montluc complained that time and again he had to pass through their hands "and for the least affair trot up and down with great trouble from city to city. Would to God that, as they do in Spain, we had made our constant

[1] See Montluc's observations in III, 368, 369. He gives a spirited account on p. 367 of an attack of the reiters on Monbrun, describing the way they fought in the close quarters of a town.

[2] C. S. P. For., No. 543, December 19, 1569.

abode in the good towns; we had then both more riches and more authority."[1]

Guyenne was safely Catholic if it could continue to hold its own; for this important fact Montluc richly deserves credit.[2] But Guyenne, Gascony, and Upper Languedoc were isolated from the Catholic north by a broad Protestant strip running south-eastward from La Rochelle to Montpellier through Saintes, Cognac, Angoulême, Chalais, Bergerac, Montauban, Albi, Castres, Béziers, and Montpellier, which united Saintonge on the seaboard with Provence and Dauphiné. But, on the other hand, Béarn was separated from the main trunk of Calvinism and was not yet safe, in spite of Montgomery's success, unless it were bound to the main trunk. The Huguenot leaders realized this, and one of Coligny's adroitest strokes, after Moncontour, was the seizure of Port-Ste. Marie, below Agen on the Garonne, with the aid of the German reiters.[3] The capture of this place (November 29, 1569) insured the passage of the Garonne to the Huguenots[4] and accomplished for those of the far south what the possession of La Charité insured to those of central France, for it bridged the Garonne. Later, when Bernard d'Astarac, baron de Martamot, early in the following January (1570) recovered Tarbes[5] on the Adour, the Huguenots had a chain of fortresses running straight north from Béarn through Condom and Nérac to Bergerac and Angoulême, and Catholic Gascony and Guyenne were cut in twain.

Montluc, having fortified Agen, the capture of which would have been another disaster to the Catholics, then set to work to contrive how to break the bridge of boats which Coligny had constructed. A mason who had once built a floating mill for the marquis de Villars above Port-Ste. Marie came to him and suggested loading the mill with stone, cutting it loose, and letting it float down stream with the hope of breaking the bridge. The Garonne at this

[1] Ruble, *Commentaires et lettres de Montluc*, III, 262.

[2] He took it long before historians attributed the honor to him (*ibid.*, 382).

[3] *Ibid.*, 366.

[4] "Il devoit considérer l'importance de la place qui estoit sur deux rivières."— *Ibid.*

[5] *Ibid.*, V, 266.

time was swollen with winter rains. The leaders were skeptical of the scheme, as the bridge was known to be protected by heavy cables above stream. But the captain Thodeas, an engineer with Montluc, supported the mason, after secretly surveying the structure. The novel battering-ram accomplished the work intended. Shortly before midnight the mill was loosed from its moorings, one of the soldiers being drowned in unchaining it. Coligny's artillery, when it loomed through the darkness, made a desperate attempt to sink it by fire from the batteries at either end of the bridge, but in vain. The mill struck the bridge with such a shock that cables, chains, and boats all went to pieces with a crash. Two of the boats went down as far as St. Macaire and some, it was said, were picked up as far down as Bordeaux.[1]

The destruction of the bridge was a heavy blow to the Protestants for it cut their forces into two parts. Besides Montgomery, very many of the reiters were caught on that side of the river toward Gascony. But Coligny's enterprise robbed adversity of its sting. He improvised a bridge of two boats, upon which five or six horses could be carried at once, the boats being hauled by cable, after the Italian manner. It required an hour and a half to go and return, yet at last, with great pains and difficulty the whole company of reiters was got across stream. Montluc had proposed to Candale and La Valette that an attack be made upon Montgomery who was quartered at Condom, south of Nérac. But they were so slow in responding that Montgomery, too, was able to pass over, first his horse and then his foot, one after the other, it requiring five or six days for all his forces to make the transit.[2]

But the admiral and Montgomery followed up this clever deed by a blunder so bad that the Reformed suffered for it for years afterward, and were saved from losing Béarn, perhaps, as they had almost lost it before, by the intervention of the Peace of St.

---

[1] All this happened on the night of December 15 and 16 (*Commentaires et lettres de Montluc*, III, 384, 385). De Thou, V, Book XLV, 666–68, and Popelinière, Book XXII, both tell the tale. A learned dissertation in *Hist. du Lang.*, XII, note 5, clears up a number of obscure points in these accounts.

[2] The last of them got across by January 3, 1570 (*Montluc*, III, 384–91, and his letter of January 9, in V, 261–64).

Germain. Coligny's original plan was to pass the rest of the winter and until harvest in Gascony and Guyenne, with Port-Ste. Marie as his base and to have heavy artillery brought from the fortresses of Béarn with which to take all the towns upon the Garonne as far as Bordeaux. The bridge assured them control of two of the richest provinces of France, for they were absolute masters of the field. By this means Bordeaux would have been at their mercy, for the sea power of the Huguenots at Blaye[1] was sufficient to close the city upon the sea side. It could not have held out for more than three months, for already corn was selling there at ten livres per sack. Bordeaux itself was rich and strong but situated in a barren country, so that, deprived of the Garonne and Dordogne, it could presently be reduced to famine. As for the Protestant army it would have fared well. The lesser towns like Libourne and Lectoure must inevitably have succumbed with their stores, and the viscounts were in full possession of Comenge and Loumaigne, the most fertile counties of all Guyenne. There were numerous stores of grain here, for it was a practice of the dealers and even gentlemen, to accumulate three or four years' store in anticipation of a dear year. Had the Huguenots once got Bordeaux in their clutches, they might have boasted that they had the best and strongest angle of the kingdom, both by land and sea, commanding five navigable rivers. The bridges over the Charente at Saintes and Cognac, being in their hands, no one could pass from Saintonge to Bordeaux where La Noue lay, "as valiant a man as any that ever was in France." The river system of the southwest —the Charente, Ile, Dordogne, Lot, and Garonne—could have been made to bind the whole region into a compact whole if this plan had been carred out, and from behind these natural barriers the Protestants might have defied all the King's armies.

Yet although Coligny's army tasted of Bordeaux wine and his reiters watered their horses in the Garonne, he did not go on. He failed to see that the most vital need of the Huguenots was to gain complete mastery of the sea. This is what La Noue perceived and Coligny did not. After the loss of Rouen they had but one

[1] For a description of Blaye see *Rel. vén.*, I, 22, 23.

important port town at their command, La Rochelle, which the blunders of the government in the second civil war had permitted the Protestants to make their own, on which depended Brouage, reputed the fairest and most commodious haven in all the kingdom, and the chief staple for salt in all the southwest.[1]

The sequel to such a course, it is true, must probably have been the erection of the southwest of France into an independent state. Such a result, looking at the France of today, is repugnant to our feelings. But we must look at things as they were then and judge accordingly and without prejudice. In the first place, it is to be remembered that in Béarn there was already the nucleus of such a state to build upon; and secondly that Guyenne and Gascony for centuries had been possessions of another sovereignty, and that their attachment to France was barely over a century old. In the sixteenth century it was impossible to divorce religion from politics and the only solution was the separation of those which disagreed on matters of religion, as the division between the Protestant Dutch and the Catholic Flemish provinces in 1578–79 proves. The Peace of Augsburg had laid down the principle *cujus regio, ejus religio*, and no other policy could have prevailed in Germany at that time. But France was trying to make a monarchy, institutionally and necessarily Catholic, adapt itself to two religions, which could not be done as long as politics and religion, church and state, were united. Even after twenty-eight years more of struggle, neither the trial and experience of all those years nor the genius of Henry IV ever made the Edict of Nantes anything more than a *modus vivendi* which first proved intolerable to the Huguenots because of their own political ambitions, and finally to the monarchy of Louis XIV, whose motto was as truly: "Un roi, une loi, une foi" as it was "l'état, c'est moi." The French monarchy in the nature of things, in the sixteenth century, could not be one-half Catholic and one-half Protestant, any more than the United States, as Lincoln said, could exist one-half slave and one-half free. What France would have lost by the creation of an independent state in the southwest would have been compensated for

[1] For a description of Brouage see *Rel. vén.*, I, 27.

by other gains in other ways.   Such a state in southwest Europe would have been an effective agency for peace, in the sixteenth and seventeenth centuries.   It not only would have relieved its Catholic neighbors of the religious dissidents within their borders; it would have been a checkmate upon the undue aggrandizement of either France or Spain, operating like Holland and Switzerland as a buffer state and for the maintenance of the balance of power.   The Spanish marriages of France in the next century probably never would have been, with their attendant train of dynastic and territorial complications during the reign of Louis XIV.   The Grand Monarque perhaps never would have conceived the thought of browbeating the rest of Europe, and certainly never would have been able to carry the idea out to the extent he did.

In abandoning his original plan in January, 1570, Coligny not merely altered the immediate future of France; perhaps he changed its destiny for centuries to come.   Instead of securing peace and security for the Huguenots by cutting the Gordian knot and establishing an independent Huguenot state, with Béarn as its cornerstone, he threw the solution of the question back upon France. He had dreamed of a Huguenot France beyond sea.   Why not one at home?   Instead Coligny had become possessed with the idea that neither the King nor his ministers would seriously think of peace as long as the war could be kept confined to provinces remote from Paris and therefore, in order to force the hand of the King, it was necessary to force war upon him in the very heart of the kingdom.   In other words, he conceived a new design, namely, to throw the war into the center of France once more, to march upon Paris, and, before its gates, dictate the terms he desired.

In pursuance of this new policy, the army of the admiral and the viscounts, with Montgomery, moved up the Garonne.   Toulouse was invested for a month (January 22–February 20, 1570), as we have seen, without success and the country fearfully wasted.[1]

---

[1] The sources are unanimous on this point, both Protestant and Catholic (La Noue, *Disc. polit. et milit.*, chap. xxix; La Popelinière, Book XXII; Montluc, *Comment.*, III, 395; Brantôme, ed. Lalanne, IV, 322; *Hist. du Lang.*, V, 527–29, note; Delaborde, III, 189).   The outrages of the reiters were so great that a special order of the day was required to govern their conduct (see K. 1,575, No. 17).

Want of provisions for men and horses at the end of this time compelled the host to move toward Carcassonne and Montréal.[1] As the country between Montpellier and Avignon was almost totally in control of the Huguenots, Coligny soon moved thither, whence he followed up the right bank of the Rhone to Vivarais and Forez. Illness overtook him here and he was in great danger.[2]

HUGUENOT ATTACK UPON A CATHOLIC CHURCH
(Bib. Nat., Estampes, *Histoire de France*, Q. b)

For a time it seemed certain that fate would call Louis of Nassau who had joined him from Orange, to the leadership of the army.[3] By the time of the admiral's recovery, it was time for action if his design was to be executed, for things were in a greater state of doubt and uncertainty regarding the peace than ever.

The prospect of peace darkened as the winter began to break and preparations in both camps grew more active. In February

[1] During the nine months which elapsed between the battle of Moncontour and the peace of St. Germain, the Huguenot army marched over 300 leagues.

[2] La Popelinière, Book XXII; La Noue, chap. xxix; *Revue hist.*, II, 542, 543.

[3] La Noue's observation on this point is curious; cf. Delaborde, III, 205.

the marshal Cossé prepared to expel the Huguenots from La Charité in order to deprive them of their only means of communication
across the Loire River, by which assistance could be brought from
Germany. This place had been one of the cities demanded from
the government as pledge of good behavior, but the crown was
determined not to yield in this particular. Queen Elizabeth had
strongly assured the King that she had not directed nor licensed
any of her subjects to carry arms or munitions to La Rochelle, but
guarded herself against possible compromising evidence being
discovered in future by adding that she "generally must permit
merchants to resort indifferently to France."[1]

While the negotiations thus dragged on through March and
April,[2] a new element of excitement was introduced by the conduct of the reiters in the Catholic army. These adventurers,
many of whom were Protestant in faith, tired of idleness and determined either to renew the war or secure their wages, on April 17
sent the King an address in which, in the same breath, they asserted their loyalty to Charles IX and their belief that those of
the Reformed religion were only fighting for liberty of conscience
and the preservation of their lives. Though guardedly put,
reading between the lines, this memorial implied peace at once or
immediate renewal of the war. Coincident with this manifesto
the princes of Navarre and Condé joined in a note to the King
declaring their resolution never to yield. To these causes of disaffection must be added the further one that many in the rank and
file of the Huguenot party believed that the Protestant leaders were
seeking to serve their own ends more than the common good; and
accused them of being more anxious for the preservation of their
privileges than for the free exercise of religion.

[1] Cf. Elizabeth's declarations of neutrality to Norris, *C. S. P., For.*, No. 704,
February 23, 1570). Across the Channel the cardinal of Châtillon did all he could
to secure the support of the English queen for the Huguenots (*ibid.*, No. 742, the
cardinal to Cecil, March 9, 1570; cf. Delaborde, *Coligny*, III, 185; La Ferrière,
Le XVIe siècle et les Valois, 254–56; and a letter of the cardinal to the prince
of Orange, April 23, 1570, *Arch. de la maison d'Orange-Nassau*, III, 373–77). But
it was not from England direct, but from Germany, under the stimulus of English
gold, that France looked for assistance to come to the Huguenots (*C. S. P. Ven.*,
No. 476, February 26, 1570.

[2] See Appendix XXIV.

Matters continued thus to hang fire for several weeks. The King went to Mont St. Michel in the middle of May to keep the feast of Corpus Christi there, where, while professing his desire to conclude the peace, Charles IX nevertheless imposed a tax of 60,000 francs monthly upon those who had failed to bear arms in the late conflict. At the same time there was a large exodus of nobles from the court, many gentlemen, weary of long service in arms, soliciting and securing leave to retire. The talk of peace, too, continued to be current in the court,[1] although Charles IX's secret dealings with Montluc, the alienation of 50,000 *écus de rente* of the property of the church,[2] and the fact that the marshal Cossé at this same time advanced out of Orleans with 2,000 horse and 4,000 French footmen and was soon joined by 8,000 Swiss and 30 companies of men-at-arms belied this.

Montluc had been on the point of resigning his commission for months past on account of the friction with Damville, but repented when there was prospect of the liberal marshal Cossé succeeding him, fearing lest, with another such as Damville, the Catholic cause throughout the south would be ruined.[3] He still clung to the hope of seeing Béarn conquered notwithstanding Terride's failure, and in June, 1570, the opportunity seemed to have come. With the aim of diverting the war from the Ile-de-France, and throwing it into the provinces once more—the farther the better—Charles IX grasped at a new expedition against Béarn. Montluc was given the commission.[4] Notwithstanding his years and his infirmity and the penury of the government, which had neither munitions nor money to spare, Montluc managed to raise a considerable force.[5]

[1] *State Papers, Foreign*, Elizabeth, Vol. CXII, No. 693 J, the cardinal of Lorraine to ———, May 4, 1570, see Appendix XXV.

[2] *Coll. des autographes de M. Picton*, No. 67. Order signed by the cardinals of Lorraine, Bourbon, and Pellevé, June 24, 1570, for the alienation of 50,000 *écus de rente* of the property of the church.

[3] *Commentaires et lettres de Montluc*, III, 332.

[4] The actual document is still preserved in the Archives nationales, K. 1,725, No. 41. It is dated June 16, 1570, and countersigned by L'Aubespine.

[5] He borrowed 4,000 livres, chiefly in Bordeaux; the munitions came from Toulouse and Bayonne. The provinces were required to furnish the supplies

He had resolved to besiege the little fortified town of Rabastens, near Tarbes, which he had chosen as the point of attack because he could draw upon Gascony for supplies from this place more easily than by beginning at St. Severs, which bordered on the Landes, "a country only fruitful in sands."[1] But the expedition came to an untimely end. In an unguarded moment Montluc exposed himself and "a harquebus-shot clapt into his face" with such force as to break his whole visage in, so that the cheek-bones were taken out in splinters. The town was taken, nevertheless. How it suffered may be read in the words of him who meted out its punishment.

My Lieutenant, who had marcht on the one hand of me when I went on to the Assault . . . . came to see if I was dead, and said to me: "Sir, cheer up your spirits, and rejoyce, we have entred the Castle, and the Soldiers are laying about them, who put all to the sword; and assure your self we will revenge your wound." I then said to him, "Praised be God that I see the Victory ours before I dye. I now care not for death. I beseech you return back, and as you have ever been my friend, so now do me that act of friendship not to suffer so much as one man to escape with life." Whereupon he immediately returned and all my servants went along with him, so that I had no body left with me but two Pages, Monsieur de Las, and the Chirurgeon. They would fain have sav'd the Minister, and the Governor, whose name was Captain Ladon, to have hang'd them before my Lodging, but the Soldiers took them from those who had them in their custody, whom they had also like to have kill'd for offring to save them, and cut them in a thousand pieces. They made also fifty or threescore to leap from the high Tower into the Moat, which were there all drown'd. There were two only saved who were hid, and such there were who offer'd four thousand Crowns to save their lives, but not a man of ours would hearken to any Ransom; and most of the women were kill'd who also did us a great deal of mischief with throwing stones. There was found within a Spanish Merchant whom the Enemy had kept prisoner there, and another Catholick Merchant also, who were both saved; and these were all that were left alive of the men that we found in the place, namely the two that some one help't away, and the two Catholick Merchants. Do not think, you

(*Commentaires et lettres de Montluc*, III, 400). The consular registers of Agen and Auch still preserve the records of his requisitions. According to the report of a Spanish spy, in K. 1,576, No. 5, the forces consisted of 10,000 footmen, 1,500 horse, and 18 pieces of artillery. This is surely exaggerated. His *Commentaires* imply that his men were few in number and he expressly says that he was short of munitions and artillery.

[1] *Commentaires et lettres de Montluc*, III, 401.

who shall read this Book, that I caused this slaughter to be made so much out of revenge for the wound I had received, as to strike terror into the Country, that they might not dare to make head against our Army. And in my opinion all Souldiers in the beginning of a Conquest ought to proceed after that manner, with such as are so impudent as to abide Canon; he must bar his ears to all Capitulation and Composition, if he do not see great difficulties in his Enterprize, and that his Enemy have put him to great trouble in making a Breach. And as severity (call it cruelty if you please) is requisite in case of a resolute opposition, so on the other side mercy is very commendable, and fit, if you see that they in good time surrender to your discretion.[1]

Since his assumption of the command at La Rochelle La Noue had displayed an energy that drove the enemy to despair. On land and on sea he became a terror to them. Sometimes it was by arresting the King's galleys and bringing them as prizes to La Rochelle or Brouage;[2] sometimes it was by driving them out, as at Rochefort, by digging a trench which poured waters waist deep down upon them; sometimes it was by battle in the open field. La Noue outmatched Puygaillard at every point, notwithstanding that his antagonist had the King's picked troops. In the plain of Ste. Gemme, near Luçon, their armies clashed in a fierce, stubbornly fought engagement. Nearly all the captains of his enemy's two regiments and 500 arquebusiers were killed and as many more taken prisoner. The brilliant captain at last won, although he was so badly injured by an arquebus shot in the left arm that amputation was necessary. Yet in the hour of his own intense suffering he magnanimously lamented "the death of so many brave gentlemen."[3]

[1] *Commentaries of Blaise de Montluc*, translated by Cotton, 368, 369. This occurred on July 23, 1570. To consummate Montluc's humiliation, Charles IX filled his place, without giving him opportunity to resign, by appointing the marquis de Villars to be his successor. He did not reach Guyenne until October 22. In the meantime his brother, Jean de Montluc, bishop of Valence, and *commissaire des finances* in Guyenne, and as much a Politique as the other was a bigot, exercised authority for him. Gascony was governed by the seigneur de Vigues (*Commentaires et lettres de Montluc*, III, 434).

[2] *C. S. P. Spain*, No. 687, February 15, 1570.

[3] *Ibid., For.*, No. 1,023, June 20, 1570, La Noue to the cardinal of Châtillon; *ibid.*, No. 1,107, July 22, 1570; Hauser, *La Noue*, 20–22. He received the name "Iron Arm" (Bras-de-fer) from the circumstance that he afterward wore a mechanism made of iron, with which, at least, he was able to guide his horse.

Much more decisive than this engagement, however, was Coligny's action. The admiral had been lingering at Montbrison in
Auvergne during May for the purpose of guarding the upper Loire.[1]
Alarmed by the formidable army under the marshal Cossé, Coligny
now determined to strike suddenly and hard in order to preserve
La Charité. This resolution precipitated the battle of Arnay-le-Duc
on June 15, 1570.[2] The result of this victory was startling. The
government capitulated almost at once. All the essential terms
of peace had been thrashed over during the spring and in less than
a week after the battle Charles IX held in his hands the articles
of pacification demanded by the Huguenots, chiefly stipulating
for the free exercise of religion within three towns in every province
and at Charenton, amnesty for the past and restitution of offices
and estates. But the crown flatly refused the right within ten
miles of Paris, or even for Protestant noblemen attending court
in their own chambers and offered two towns in each province instead
of three. When this was refused it was finally settled to adopt
August 1, 1570, as an *annus normalis*, and permit Calvinist worship
to be held in all towns in the possession of the Huguenots on that
date. The two points of contention still unsettled were the payment of the reiters and determination of the surety-towns. The
government at first proposed that the payment of the reiters be
equally apportioned between the subjects of both religions, but
finally shouldered the burden. As to the surety-towns—the most
important point of all as far as practical politics was concerned—
great difficulty was experienced before agreement was made.
The King at first offered to yield La Rochelle, Angoulême, and
Montauban, and to trade Perpignan or Lansac for La Charité.[3]
Later, Angoulême was withdrawn and Cognac substituted, to the
displeasure of the Huguenots, and La Charité definitely yielded.
As to other matters, namely, restitution of honors, offices, estates,
privileges, equality of justice, amnesty, release of prisoners, and

---

[1] On Coligny's campaign in Rouergue and the Cévennes in the spring of 1570,
see *Revue hist.*, II, 537–39, letters of the cardinal of Armagnac of April 1, April 11,
and May 10.

[2] Delaborde, III, 209–15.   [3] *Nég. Tosc.*, III, 618.

the like, these of course were provided for, and Protestant nobles enjoying "high justice" were to be permitted to enjoy free exercise of the Calvinist faith, including baptism in their houses, for their families, and all others in their dependence,[1] an evidence that the feudal element in the Huguenot party was more considered than the bourgeoisie.[2]

The papal nuncio, understanding that the Huguenots had demanded the exercise of their religion in the counties of Verre and Avignon, which belonged to the Pope, declared that no peace could be made with those who were outside of the church.[3] At the same time the Spanish ambassador, being informed that it was part of the Huguenot programme to secure the restitution of William of Orange and his brother Louis of Nassau to their French possessions, also protested warmly against the peace. Spain offered direct assistance to France of men and money, and the city of Paris and the clergy offered to maintain the war at their own expense for eight months longer. But these protests were ineffectual. The Spanish ambassador's mouth was stopped by the rejoinder that the French King had as much right to make a treaty of peace with his subjects as Philip of Spain had to make terms with the Moriscos,[4] and so, though apprehensive of French

---

[1] The parlement of Toulouse strongly protested against the edict (*Hist. du Lang.*, V, 538, note 5). The Peace of St. Germain was registered by the Parlement on August 11, 1570 (*C. S. P. For.*, August 11, 1570; cf. Delaborde, III, 230, 231). The Pope wrote with mingled alarm and regret over the Peace of St. Germain to the cardinals of Bourbon and Lorraine, on September 23, 1570 (Potter, *Pie V*, 103, 107, ed. Gouban, Book IV, letter 7, pp. 282, 285.

[2] For an excellent discussion of the feudal interests and policy of the Huguenots in the civil wars, see Weill, *Les théories sur le pouvoir royal en France pendant les guerres de religion*, 73–80.

[3] See the letter of the papal nuncio to Philip II, June 26, 1570, in Appendix XXVI. The Pope had protested even earlier than this (brief of Pius V to the cardinal of Lorraine, March 2, 1570, disapproving of the conditions of peace). The King, even if vanquished, ought not to have consented to such detestable terms. The Pope's sorrow is the greater because of the cardinal's assent to them (La Ferrière *Rapport*, 55).

[4] In 1562 on account of fear lest the Moriscos might enter into relation with the Moors of Africa, the government of Spain forbade the use of arms among them. In 1567 an attempt was made to suppress their language and abolish their national

and German Protestant assistance being given to Orange and fearful of an attack upon Franche Comté, the Spanish ambassador was forced to be content with the promise of France that no hostility was intended or would be permitted in France toward Spain.

The Peace of St. Germain was the broadest and most substantial body of privileges yet secured by the French Protestants. Antedating the Edict of Nantes by twenty-eight years, it might have been as great and as permanent an instrument as the latter, if the ambition of the Guises and the intervention of Spain in French affairs had not overthrown it. France itself, government and people, was tired of ten years of strife and disposed to peace. The economic interests of the country were anxious for peace. Only zealots for the religion and those who sought to fish in troubled waters reprobated the terms of St. Germain and sought to continue the struggle. It is true that mutual suspicion still prevailed. Some of the Huguenots anticipated new encroachments again, destructive of the peace, and that the King only aimed to disarm the Protestants in order to overwhelm them later. But time, in all probability, would have qualified this feeling. Religion, unless artificially exaggerated, had ceased to be the primary issue of France by 1570. The real issue was Spain. For all parties alike in France had begun to chafe because of the power acquired by foreign military influences, especially that of Philip—a feeling which ultimately was destined to unite the country on the basis of a national patriotism and embolden Henry of Navarre to expel the Spaniard and establish the Bourbon throne on a truly national basis.

An incident which took place at the court in mid-July, when the terms of peace were under consideration, illustrates this all but universal hatred of Spain. One day the Spanish ambassador entered the King's chamber for audience. Soon afterward the marshal Tavannes came in, who was somewhat deaf and accus-

customs. A terrible war ensued. Don John of Austria finally suppressed the revolt after it had lasted for ten years. But in 1570, in anticipation of a Turkish attack from the west the Moors again rebelled and Spain had to compromise (*Archives de la maison d'Orange-Nassau*, III, 361; cf. Lea, *The Moriscos of Spain*).

tomed to speak in a loud voice. Perceiving the ambassador he gruffly remarked in a voice so audible as to be heard by Alava:

These Spaniards would do better to govern their own members and not interfere by trying to govern other people's countries. For I well know that the Spaniards have no wish but to foment civil wars, so that both one party and the other may be weakened and they themselves become stronger than both. For my own part, I would rather see a hundred white capes [the Huguenot costume] than one red cross [the device the Spaniards wore]; because, after all, the first are our brethren and our kindred, while the latter are the natural enemies of our country.[1]

It was an opportune time for France to undertake an anti-Spanish policy, and it was soon predicted that she would follow such a course.[2] Aside from the discomfiture of the Guises owing to the peace, a condition which peculiarly discountenanced the cardinal of Lorraine, the duke of Guise was in disgrace also. For he was discovered to have made overtures of marriage to Madame Marguerite, the King's sister, and the lady herself for whom a Portuguese match was being considered as a blow to Spain, was reputed to have expressed a preference rather to stay in France than "to eat figs in Portugal." Guise, when the discovery was made that he had raised his eyes to the princess, hastily attempted to divert suspicion by marrying the princess of Porcien. But the episode injured the influence of the Guises, and brought Montmorency forward as the man of the hour.[3]

Under the new régime, the government set about carrying out the terms of pacification, enforcement of which chiefly depended upon the upright and just conduct of the four marshals.[4] By the

[1] C. S. P. Ven., No. 485, July 20, 1570.   [2] Nég. Tosc., III, 439.

[3] "Montmorency bears the vogue in court."—C. S. P. For., No. 1,216, Norris to the Queen, August 31, 1570. To enhance his prestige at this time, Montmorency's claim of right of precedence at court which the duke of Mayenne contested was decided by the Privy Council in his favor (C. S. P. For., No. 1,083, July 9, 1570).

[4] Christopher de Thou to the King, December 2, 1570 defending the Parlement against the accusation that it is unjust to the Calvinists: "Mais un tel crime et si execrable ne se scauroit asses punir, et seroit plus tost à craindre que nous fussions reprehensibles de trop grande rémission que de grand severité, qu'ils appelent cruauté." He and his colleagues wish that the duke of Anjou might enter into possession of his appanage in order that the duchy of Alençon may be in the jurisdiction of the Parlement of Paris and not in that of Normandy (Collection la Jarriette, No. 2,796).

end of September the camps were wholly broken up and the reiters either over or on their way across the frontier.[1] To be sure, radical Protestants continued to complain of infractions of the edict.[2] But the one serious infraction of the edict was in the fifteenth article, providing that all scholars, the sick and the poor, should be received in the universities, schools, and hospitals without difference or distinction on account of religion. The Catholic party, in the hope of abridging the development of the competing religion soon persuaded the King to nullify this provision. In compliance with a petition praying that the crown would forbid any of the Reformed religion from holding any post of authority in the University of Paris, and also that the university authorities might have power to search for and seize all heretical books, Charles IX on October 8, 1570, issued a proclamation forbidding any Calvinist from holding any office or teaching in the University of Paris and giving the authorities thereof the right of search for heretical books.[3] On November 20, this was followed by a more sweeping decree forbidding any persons from keeping schools or holding office in any college, or lecturing on any art or science in public or in private unless recognized and approved by the Roman church.[4] Nevertheless, these petitions, complaining of infractions of the edict, were more smoke than fire. The only internal issue of great importance was an economic one.

Apart from the destructiveness of the war, nature again dealt

[1] Sir Henry Norris under date of September 23, testifies that "the state here is very quiet, where all strife and old grudges seem utterly buried, and men live in good hope of the continuance thereof, since the occasioner of all the troubles [the cardinal of Lorraine] in this realm is out of credit" (*C. S. P. For.*, No. 1,285, Norris to Cecil). The reiters in the course of their return home, pillaged the fair of Champagne (Claude Haton, II, 592 and note).

[2] Thirty articles complaining of infractions of the Edict of Pacification, and desiring that they may be redressed, with the King's answers in the margin (*C. S. P. For.*, No. 1,323, October, 1570).

[3] *Ibid.*, No. 1,359. Pierre Ramus was excluded from the College of Presles by this decree.

[4] Ordonnance du Roy sur les defences de tenir Escolles, Principaultez, Colleges; ny lire en quelque art; ou science que ce soit, en public, privé ou en chambre, s'ilz ne sont congenuz et approuvez esté de la Religion catholique et romaine. Avec l'Arrest de la court du Parlement. Poictiers, B. Noscereau, 1570.

hardly with France in this year. There were heavy rains over all Europe which either rotted the grain in the fields or washed it out. A great inundation of the Seine occurred on June 2, 1570, and the plague began to grow more virulent once more.[1] There was a certain amount of reason in the demand for a new session of the Estates to consider the economic distress of France, but the King was wise in refusing the request, for in event of its meeting, the enemies of Spain would have been sure to endeavor to fan the ashes of the late civil war into flames again. As a solace to those demanding economic relief Charles IX promised to abolish sundry superfluous offices and to tax the nobles instead of the commons for the relief of his debts which amounted to 37,000,000 francs. An earnest of this intention is manifest in an ordinance requiring parish wardens to keep accounts and to make a declaration of the revenue of their churches and to send this information to the royal bailiffs. Every parish was forced to obey this edict, which was a novelty indeed. But the parish authorities took advantage of the situation and not merely rendered an account of their incomes, but also gave the King a minute account of the ruin they had suffered at the hands of the Huguenots. The bailiffs received these declarations and sent them to the Privy Council of the King, where the evidence was reviewed and every church taxed accordingly. The churches which had been burned by the Protestants were lightly taxed, and those which were found to be incapable of payment were authorized to sell their possessions, their vessels, jewels, or lands, or else impose a tax on the parish.[2]

But the thrifty bourgeoisie of France were too lucrative a source of income for the King to keep his promise not to tax them more. In March, 1571, an edict was issued providing that bolts of woolen cloth should be sealed with a leaden seal before sale, and that each bolt should be taxed 3 francs, 4 deniers. The new impost, which was very unpopular, was ascribed to the Italian influence at court.[3]

[1] Claude Haton, II, 610 and 617.

[2] Ibid., 629.   [3] Ibid., 740.

CHAPTER XV

THE MASSACRE OF ST. BARTHOLOMEW

The dominant politics of France in the years 1570-72 were foreign, not domestic, and had to do with Spain. The clouds hung heavy over Spain's dominions in spite of the suppression of the Moriscos, and dark was the prospect ahead for Philip II. In the east only was light. The great victory at Lepanto over the Turks, fought on October 7, 1571, though of general benefit to Christendom, was of greatest advantage to Spain.

It is at this juncture that the duke of Anjou, the King's brother, becomes a conspicuous political figure, one, indeed, of international importance. In order to confirm the confidence of the Huguenots, but especially to strengthen France against Spanish preponderance, the idea was again put forward of marrying Anjou to Queen Elizabeth.[1] At the same time the plan was broached of marrying young Henry of Navarre to the sister of the duke of Württemberg. But again Montmorency came to the forefront and revived the plan suggested in 1569 of marrying the princess Marguerite, Charles IX's youngest sister, to Henry of Navarre. Coligny for the Huguenots, and Walsingham and Norris for England, urged the double plan.[2] The Ridolfi plot proved to Elizabeth that England, like France, had her greatest enemy in Spain.

The consternation of the Guises and Spain at the discovery of this double marriage project was great. The Guises sought to break the proposed marriage of Anjou and Queen Elizabeth

---

[1] The vidame of Chartres to the Marshal Montmorency, October 3, 1570. See Appendix XXVII. The scheme originated with the vidame de Chartres and the cardinal Châtillon (see La Ferrière, "Les projets de marriage d'une reine d'Angleterre," *Revue des deux mondes*, September 15, 1881, p. 310; cf. Hume, *Courtships of Queen Elizabeth*, 115. In 1563 the prince of Condé had actually proposed the marriage of Charles IX and Elizabeth (*Revue des deux mondes*). August 15, 1881, p. 861.

[2] *C. S. P. For.*, No. 1,521, January 27, 1571. Walsingham to Cecil.

THE MASSACRE OF ST. BARTHOLOMEW

From a picture by François Du Bois of Amiens (†1584 at Geneva). The original, in the Museum Uriaud at Lausanne, is 3½ × 5 feet

In the middle of the picture Coligny is being thrown out of the window, below which stand the dukes of Guise and Aumale and the bastard of Angoulême. Teligny, the admiral's son-in-law is trying to escape over the roof. In the background is the Louvre, with Pilles being beset in the doorway. The bodies of Bricquemault and Cavagnies are hanging from the gibbet in the street. On the hill-top in the right of the picture the gibbet of Montfaucon is seen. On the left bank of the Seine some Huguenots are escaping by the Porte de Nesles—Montgomery is the man on horseback outside the gate. The windmill stands on Mont Sainte Geneviève.

by offering him Mary Stuart, and that of Henry of Navarre with the King's sister by offering the cardinal d'Este as a prospective husband, since he was universally expected to succeed his brother, the duke of Ferrara who was without issue.   Tuscan influence was used to this end.   Spain and the papacy, for their part, dangled before the eyes of the duke of Anjou the post of command over the fleet preparing against the Turks.[1]   The gulf between France and Spain, however, was too wide to be bridged by such an offer. Disappointed at Bayonne, Catherine was dreaming of the elder

[1] Such an offer, in the nature of things, could not have been accepted.   Aside from the fact that France at this juncture was unwilling to further any cause advocated by Spain, there was too much practical advantage to France in maintaining the *entente cordiale* with the Turks.   Turkish influence might be brought to bear upon the Emperor to neutralize his opposition to French enterprise in Poland; moreover, France had but recently concluded an advantageous commercial treaty with the Sultan.   For accounts of the relations of France and Turkey at this time see Du Ferrier, *Un ambassadeur liberal sous Charles IX et Henri III*, 44–102;   Flament, "La France et la Ligue contre le Turc (1571–73)," *Rev. d'hist. dip.*, XVI, 1902, p. 619;   Janssen, *History of the German People*, VIII, chap. v, "Turkish wars up to 1572."   The league of the Christian powers, whose efforts culminated in the famous engagement of Lepanto was formed in May, 1571.   The king of Spain, the Pope and Venice were the principals thereof.   Spain was to provide one-half of the forces, the Venetians one-third, and the Pope the remainder.   The capture of Cyprus by the Turks in the spring of 1570 was the immediate cause of its formation (cf. *La vraye et très fidelle narration des succès, des assaults, defences et prinse du royaume de Cypre*, faicte par F. Ange de Lusignan, Paris 1580; *Commentari della guerra di Cipro e della lega dei principi cristiani contro il Turco*, di Bartolomeo Sereno, 1845; Herre, *Europäische Politik in cyprischen Krieg, 1570–73*, Leipzig, 1902—there is a review of this in *English Hist. Review*, XIX, 357; Miller, "Greece under the Turks 1571–1684," *English Hist. Review*, XIX, 646).   Europe expected a double attack on the part of Mohammedanism, both in the Mediterranean and by land against Hungary and Transylvania, as in 1530.   Venice trembled for Zara in Dalmatia.   These fears were not misplaced.   The warlike preparations of the Sultan went so far as to offer pardon to all malefactors, except rebels and counterfeiters, who would serve in the galleys.   The allied fleet lay at Candia during the winter of 1570–71 awaiting reinforcements.   But there was a vast amount of anxiety and discontent among the allies, for nothing but the sense of a common peril could have united Venice and Spain, or Venice and the Pope.   In the politics of Europe Venice was a neutral power, and neutrality in the religious politics of the time, in Philip II's eyes, was almost tantamount to heresy.   Moreover, as was inevitable, the tediousness of the preparations and the corruption of officials of the fleet was so great that men even died of hunger inflicted through fraud.   Only Venice's administration seems to have been efficient.

daughter of the Hapsburgs as the future wife of Charles IX. Such a marriage appealed to her as a practical way of playing one house of Hapsburg against the other, although she plausibly represented it as a new tie that would bind France and the Hapsburgs in greater amity.[1]

The counter-claims of France and Austria to the Three Bishoprics, and the renewal by France of her former relations with Turkey, retarded this negotiation.[2] The greatest hindrance, though, was the opposition of Philip II. It was with the object of frustrating the designs of France that Philip II had transferred his ambassador in France, Chantonnay, from Paris to Vienna.[3] At Bayonne, the queen mother had exerted all her influence in vain to prevail upon the court of Spain to commit itself. When Fourquevaux succeeded St. Sulpice at Madrid, he, in turn, continued to urge that Charles IX should marry the princess Anne; that Marguerite of Valois should marry Don Carlos, and Henry of Anjou the infanta Juana, Philip's sister. But Philip II still hesitated between Mary Stuart and Anne of Austria, and suggested the younger daughter of Maximilian as prospective spouse for Charles IX.[4] Matters remained thus undetermined for years. The marriage of Mary Stuart to Darnley in 1565 and the death of Don Carlos in July, 1568 raised Catherine's hopes. But they were dashed to pieces after the death of Elizabeth of Valois, on October 3, 1568, when Philip II himself became the suitor for the hand of Anne of Austria. French and Spanish diplomacy thereafter plotted and counterplotted, until in 1570 the French King had to endure the chagrin of seeing his expected queen become the fourth bride of Philip of Spain and himself be satisfied with the younger sister, whose physical charms[5] did not compensate for the injury to his pride.[6]

---

[1] *L'Ambassade de St. Sulpice*, 150.

[2] *Négociations dans le Levant*, III, 13.   [3] *L'Ambassade de St. Sulpice*, 261, 267.

[4] *Dépêches de M. Fourquevaux*, II, 28; III, 41.

[5] Sir Thomas Smith, the English ambassador in France, described her in January, 1571 as "a pretty little lady, but fair and well-favored."—*C. S. P. For.*, No. 8.

[6] Even at the official ceremony (Godefroi, *Ceremonial français*, II, 20) of betrothal in the cathedral at Speyer the latent hostility of France and Spain was

But Philip gained another point of advantage over the French King, a point which the latter never discovered. The duchy of Lorraine, was a fief of the empire and had been so ever since the Middle Ages. Situated in the penumbra between France and Germany, the duke of Lorraine's position had become a complex one and he was a vassal of France for the border duchy of Bar. As a sign of his amity toward the Emperor, Charles IX at the time of his marriage agreed to release the duke of Lorraine from his fealty to France. This waiver stirred the patriotic indignation of the keeper of the seal, Morvilliers, who resigned his office, declaring that he would not be an agent for separating from the crown of France any principality owing allegiance to it. Unfortunately for the future, the King appointed a secret partisan of Spain to the post. This was Biragues, a Milanese by birth, whose sinister influence was to play no mean part in the future.[1]

As might be expected, the winter and spring of 1571-72 were filled with cross-negotiations of great importance. The greatest Catholic-Spanish fear was lest a positive alliance be made between France, England, and Holland, and perhaps the Protestant German states for the liberation of the Netherlands, that league to have greater binding force through the double marriage of the duke of Anjou and Queen Elizabeth and Henry of Bourbon to Marguerite of France.[2] Spain, to prove France, made final demand

manifested. The Spanish ambassador refused to give precedence to the ambassador of Charles IX, and so absented himself, the Venetian envoy being compelled to do the same, because of the alliance between these two powers (C. S. P. For., No. 1,355, Cobham to Cecil, October 22, 1570). For other details cf. Nos. 1,267, 1,275, 1,377, 1430. On the negotiations see Mém. de Castelnau (ed. Le Laboureur), II, Book VI, 467.

[1] Rel. vén., II, 255. Killigrew in a letter to Lord Burghley, December 29, 1571, shrewdly observed, à propos of the change, that "divers of the followers of Guise have not letted to say that the duke of Alva knew the way to Paris' gates." —C. S. P. For., No. 2,196. For an example of Biragues' intriguing, and this of the most shameful sort, in connection with the proposed marriage of Henry of Navarre and Marguerite of Valois see La Ferrière, Rapport, 43. The Huguenots had hoped for L'Hôpital's recall.—Nég. Tosc., III, 641.

[2] Janssen, History of the German People, VIII, 117 ff.

of Charles IX: namely, that he forcibly suppress the activity of the prince of Orange in France; that Spain be permitted to levy Catholics in France to serve in the Low Countries; that France restrain the preparations of the Huguenots, especially those of La Rochelle, from aiding the Dutch cause on the sea; that France renounce her alliance with Turkey and join the Holy League against the Ottoman; and finally, that Charles IX abandon the project of marrying his sister to the prince of Navarre.   Charles IX's replies were very vague.   To the first of these demands he replied that his country was too much exhausted by the late wars to take up arms for any cause; to the second he said that if he permitted Catholic levies to be made in France, the Huguenots would not believe them to be for service abroad but would again take up arms; as to the preparations at La Rochelle, it remained to be seen if their purpose was not mercantile instead of military.[1]

The attitude of the various parties in France toward the crown's Spanish policy was a peculiar one.   The Huguenots and moderate Catholics of course urged the marriage of the King's brother to Queen Elizabeth with the greatest zeal.   But even intense Catholics, like Tavannes, singular as it seems, urged the match, with Machiavellian ingenuity estimating that the King, by incurring the deeper enmity of Spain, would be compelled to avail himself of their services, and thus, in the end, the cause of Catholicism in France would be promoted.[2]   The queen mother, with characteristic caution, professed much inclination for the match, but urged that it could not be attempted without hazarding the King's honor.   Meanwhile Montmorency, pushed it with all his ability, alternately urging Catherine de Medici and Lord Burghley by an assiduous correspondence.[3]

[1] C. S. P. For., No. 1,590, March 5, 1571.

[2] This is the keen observation of the Venetian ambassador (cf. C. S. P. Ven., 515, August 1, 1571).

[3] The duke of Montmorency to Lord Burghley, May 20, 1571, see Appendix XXVIII.   On the whole negotiation see La Ferrière, "Elisabeth et le duc d'Anjou," Revue des deux mondes, August 15, 1881, p. 857; September 15, 1881, p. 307.

How purely political as an issue religion had become by this time in Europe is made almost cynically manifest in the conferences between the advocates of the French-English match for the purpose of overcoming the religious disparities represented by the principals in the proposed match. From the beginning of the negotiations it was evident that every compromise made in religion would have to be made by France. The incongruities of age and religion and the complications of politics were great. The hardest thing, perhaps, to estimate, is the influence of Elizabeth's vacillation. Catherine de Medici, on the whole, seems to have been anxious for the match. So protracted and so intricate were the negotiations that the duke of Anjou, with mingled prejudice and despair, declared that "all was but dalliance."[1] It was speciously urged upon the duke that no attempt was being made to effect his sudden conversion to the Anglican religion, but that he should forego the use of private mass, and "examine whether he might not with good devotion use the forms of prayers appointed throughout her realm, the same being in effect nothing but that which the Church of Rome uses, saving that it is in the English tongue, which, if he pleased, might be translated into French; and further, that the usage of the divine service in England did not properly compel any man to alter his opinion in the great matters being now in controversy in the church."[2] To this it was rejoined that "religion was a constant persuasion confirmed by time" and that "relenting in religion, being a matter of conscience, was an inconvenience of more weight than any that might happen to the queen."[3] For a while Anjou,

[1] The words were used to De Foix (*C. S. P. For.*, No. 1,632, April 1, 1571, Walsingham to Burghley).

[2] *Ibid.*, No. 1,739, May 25, 1571; No. 1,813, Francis Walsingham to Lord Burghley: He told her that he had delivered a form of the English prayers to Monsieur de Foix, which form the Pope would have by council confirmed as Catholic if the Queen would have acknowledged the same as received from him (Note in margin, "an offer made by the Cardinal of Lorraine as Sir N. Throgmorton showed me"). That the Queen was bound to prefer the tranquillity of her realm before all other respects. There was never before offered to France like occasion of benefit and reputation.

[3] Report of conference between Walsingham and De Foix, *C. S. P. For.*, No. 1,732, May 25, 1571.

although after the Edict of St. Germain he had staunchly protested that no preaching be allowed anywhere in his territories—
which the King granted—wavered between policy and conscience.
One day while visiting Madame Carnevalet, the wife of his tutor,
he said with affected gaiety: "Carnevalet, thou and I were once
Huguenots, and now again are become good Catholics." "Aye,"
she said, "we were so, and if you proceed in the matter you wot of,
you will then return to be a Huguenot."[1]

Spain did everything possible to thwart the negotiation. Her
ambassador in the presence of the King's council inveighed
against the plan, asserting that the kingdom of France was going
to ruin, but he was cautious not to allege any ground but that of
religion.[2] Finally the counter-practices of the Guises and the
Spanish ambassador, partly by appeals to religious scruples and
partly by the means of lavish promises, overcame Anjou's hesitation and he flatly refused to consider the marriage.[3] The King
was furious. "Brother," he said, "you should have used some
plainness with me in this matter and not leave me to wade so far
to abuse a prince I so much esteem and honour. You allege
conscience to be the cause but I know it is a late pension offered
unto you by the clergy, who would have you still remain here for
a champion of the Catholic faith. I tell you plainly, I will have
no other champion here but myself, and seeing you have such a
desire to remain here on such respects, it behooves me the more
narrowly to look to you; and as for the clergy, seeing they have so
great superfluity, and I so great necessity, the benefices being at
my disposition, I will take a new order; and as for those who make
the offer, I will make some of them shorter by the head."[4]

[1] Anecdote reported by Walsingham to Burghley, C. S. P., For., No. 1,813,
June 21, 1571.

[2] Ibid., Ven., No. 576, August 16, 1571; ibid., For., No. 1,928, August 17, 1571.

[3] Ibid., No. 1,883, July 27, 1571. De Foix and Montgomery were deeply
discouraged, the former protesting to Walsingham that he had "never travailled
more earnestly in any matter in his life" (ibid., No. 1,732). "The queen mother
never wept so much since the death of her husband" (ibid., No. 1,886, July 30,
1571). "The queen mother was in tears. . . . . M. de Limoges said that . . . .
he never saw the King in greater chafe, and the Queen Mother wept hot tears"
(ibid., January 8, 1572).

[4] Ibid., No. 1,886, July 30, 1571.

Nevertheless, despite the fact that the cause was a lost one, the matter was protracted so long that the negotiators of the affair themselves perceived the humor in it. Elizabeth protested that "of herself she had no mind thereto, yet the continual crying unto her of her Privy Council, the necessity of the time, and the love of her subjects, had turned her mind to marriage," while the duke of Anjou reasserted his belief in his future damnation if he yielded anything in the matter of religion. Smith, the English envoy, solemnly averred that "the matter of religion would be the most honourable to break off with," both for his mistress and the duke, and in the same breath asked whether it would suffice if the duke were suffered for a time to have his mass private in some little oratory or chapel—this so that there should be no scandal to any of the Queen's subjects. The queen mother replied that the duke must have the exercise of his religion open, lest he should seem to be ashamed of it, and that he was now of late so devout that he heard two or three masses every day, and fasted the Lent and vigils so precisely "that he began to be lean and evil-coloured," so that she was angry with him and told him that she "had rather he were an Huguenot than be so foolishly precise to hurt his health." She told the English ambassador that he would not be content to have his mass in a corner, but insisted upon "high mass and all the ceremonies thereof according to the time, and in song after all solemn fashion of the Roman church, and a church or chapel appointed where he might openly have his priests and singers and use all their ceremonies."

"Why, Madame," ejaculated Smith, "then he may require also the four orders of friars, monks, canons, pilgrimages, pardons, oil and cream, relics, and all such trumperies. The queen of England will never agree to any mass, let alone great high mass, with all the ceremonies of Rome according to the season, priest, deacon, subdeacon, chalice, altar, bells, candlesticks, paten, singing men, 'les quatre mendiants et tous les mille diables' "— at which tirade all but Anjou laughed.[1]

It is at this moment that the duke of Alençon comes forward

[1] C. S. P. For., No. 20, January 7, 1572.

into the light around the throne. Since the duke of Anjou was "so extraordinarily, papistically superstitious"[1] both sides turned toward him, nothwithstanding the absurd disparity between his age and that of Queen Elizabeth. Even Elizabeth's hardy modesty blushed at the thought of such a match,[2] and the objection of inequality in their ages was backed up by guarded expressions of repugnance on account of the disfigurement the young duke had suffered from small-pox.[3]

The Huguenot pressure eagerly supported the proposed marriage between Queen Elizabeth and the duke of Alençon, for the duke was as easy in religion as his brother was straight.[4] The admiral Coligny urged it upon Lord Burghley, pointing out that it would strengthen the treaty of Blois,[5] while others urged that England would have a practical advantage from the fact that Alençon was as rich in lands as his brother, and that the duchy of Alençon adjoined Normandy, where the whole of the nobility was devoted to the duke, and hoped by his means to be restored

[1] C. S. P. For., No. 23, January 9, 1572, Smith to Burghley.

[2] The Queen to Walsingham: Directs him to express her great regret to the French king and the queen mother that she cannot assent to their proposal brought by M. de Montmorency for her marriage with the duke of Alençon, and to assure them that the only impediments arise from the great disparity in their age, and from the bad opinion that the world might conceive of her thereby (C. S. P. For., No. 496, July 20, 1572; cf. No. 375, May 25, instructions to the earl of Lincoln).

[3] This objection was one so difficult to make without giving offense that it required all the delicacy of the English envoys to say anything at all. In C. S. P. For., No. 494 under date of July 20, 1572, will be found a draft of instructions to Walsingham in Burghley's handwriting on this matter, and by him endorsed: "Not sent." Burghley evidently preferred to leave this delicate subject to his sovereign. See the queen to Walsingham, ibid., No. 502, July 23, 1572, printed in full by Digges, p. 226.

[4] Smith's comments to Burghley are candor itself. "These two brethren be almost become 'Capi de Guelphi et Gibellini.' The one has his suite all Papists, the other is the refuge and succour of all the Huguenots, a good fellow and lusty prince."—Ibid., No. 23, January 9, 1572. He glosses over Alençon's imperfections by the remark that "he is not so tall or fair as his brother, but that is as is fantasied," and adds: "Then he is not so obstinate, papistical, and restive like a mule as his brother is."—Ibid., No. 28, January 10, 1572.

[5] See below for details of this treaty. Coligny's letter is analyzed in C. S. P. For., No. 500, July 22, 1572 (not in Delaborde).

to their ancient privileges and liberties, and that then England could make "a bulwark and defense" out of Normandy for her own protection.[1]

It is a difficult story to take seriously, for each one of the actors felt its hollowness and unreality. One feels that it was a gigantic bubble produced by English and French councilors of state to amuse and occupy each other by its brilliancy and wavering instability. Yet the greatest statesmen in England were driven nearly to distraction by their endeavors to keep it in the air. At first this diplomatic affair assumes an almost farcical comedy aspect: then it darkens into tragedy. It is a game of chess in which the players are grave and reverend statesmen and the pieces queens and princes, with this distinction, that the pieces are always likely to move of themselves and create unexpected combinations. Yet, for all its hollowness, the story deserves attention, for as long as it lasted it absorbed the attention of the persons concerned, and it illustrates most admirably Elizabeth's and Catherine's tortuous methods of diplomacy.

When the negotiations began, Elizabeth was already thirty-eight years old and of vast experience in promoting and then avoiding marriages. As a coy and bashful damsel, she could always plead her repugnance to the marriage state, and as the head of a Protestant nation, religion was another rock of refuge when anxious or angry suitors pressed her too closely. She had fooled Philip and she had kept the poor Austrian archduke gamboling before her. What could the pockmarked François d'Alençon expect but disaster? Yet it was he who came the nearest to pinning her down to a state of matrimonial stability.

The two things in Catherine's character which seem to be especially prominent in this tale of love and lying are her thirst for power for herself and a mother's natural ambition for her children.

Alençon's appearance is the one thing about him which is seriously discussed. He was born 1555 and was therefore twenty-

[1] La Ferté to ———; draft, endd. by Burghley: Windsor, 6th September, 1572.—C. S. P. For., No. 555.

two years younger than Elizabeth. This was, of course, an enormous objection, or, at least, one which could always be urged. His age is the official and public objection, but his face and stature affected Elizabeth far more.[1] As to his character we have the testimony of the English and Venetian ambassadors. Smith, in January, 1572, calls him "a good fellow and a lusty prince" and says "he is not so obstinate, papistical, and restive like a mule as his brother is." Dale, in the quaint letter in a Hatfield MS says of him: "As touching his behavior he ys the most moderate yn all the court; never present at any of the licentious acts of his brethren, nor here nor at Rochelle; of much credit, and namely with them of the religion; thus he ys and hath ben hetherto; what may be hereafter God knoweth." On the whole, the English ambassadors favored him, Walsingham the least. Evidently he was not an unpleasant person, but a young and inexperienced lad, ambitious to do great things, resenting his treatment at the court, and so plunged into the current of things, only to be deceived and ruined by the superior cunning of his supposed friends. His shortcomings may be excused on the ground of his environment and bringing up; may even be praised as being more manly and significant than the effeminate Henry.

Alençon's motives in attempting to win Elizabeth are obvious. His position in France was most unpleasant to him: suspected by his brothers, made fun of and pestered by the Guises and the "mignons" of the court; condemned to a life of subordination and idleness by the accident of his birth, the prospect of the hand of the Queen of England seemed most glowing, even though she was a heretic and more than twenty years older than he. But why should Catherine and Elizabeth ever consider such an intrinsically absurd proposition?

Elizabeth was face to face with several problems, foreign and domestic, upon the solution of which depended her throne and her very existence. It is hard to remember as one looks back upon her long and splendid reign that there was hardly a moment in it when she was free from the danger of overthrow and execution.

[1] *C. S. P. For.*, No. 502, July 23, 1572, the Queen to Walsingham.

This danger, at this time, had just manifested itself in the Ridolfi plot in which the duke of Norfolk, the greatest noblemen of England, Spain, Mary Stuart, and the Pope had all combined. Naturally the Catholic nobles rallied around Mary, the probable successor to the throne, while the Protestants were at a loss to know what to do in view of the unsettled succession. So great was the excitement that Elizabeth always hesitated to call a Parliament for fear it would attempt to urge her on to marriage. Negotiations, not to speak of marriage, with France would immensely relieve the situation. They could be used before Parliament to show that Elizabeth was doing her best; hopes of a settled succession would at once reassure the country and diminish Mary's importance, both as a center of conspiracy and as a source of danger in other ways. To be sure, this possible marriage might excite the Catholics to renewed efforts to save their faith, but the fact that France was Catholic and that from it might come much of their help would militate against disturbance. Negotiations might bring about most of these results and would in any case gain time and postpone the solution of the difficulties.

A second problem before Elizabeth was the maintenance of the Protestant faith. So far as this enters the negotiations it is mostly a pretext, but there was, nevertheless, an actual problem. Negotiations for marriage with a Catholic prince might stir up the Catholics to renewed activities and raise hopes which it might be difficult to allay, but, on the other hand, Elizabeth could hope for relief from the Huguenot movement in France, and the rebellious Dutch, while the alliance with a Catholic prince would immensely strengthen her in her own middle ground. To allow him to bring the mass with him might cause trouble, but still one prince could not do much when queen and council were carefully watching him.

Scotland was another source of continual anxiety to the English ministry. The government was unsettled and the power likely to fall at any time into the hands of those who would turn it over to France. Of course this danger would be entirely removed by a French marriage, though as events proved, negotiations did not stop the intrigues. A similar point of attack existed in Ireland where the least encouragement was sure to raise rebellion. A French marriage would make danger in that quarter also less likely.

But perhaps the greatest source of danger was from Spain. There were countless reasons why Philip should declare war—religion, the seizure of his treasure by Elizabethan seamen, the treatment of Mary (though this did not at first much concern him), and Spanish repression in the Netherlands. English negotiation with France would be of value to England, if for nothing else, in keeping France and Spain apart. It was hoped, moreover, that once England and France were united, the combination might check Philip in his dealing with the Netherlands and the English Catholics and in the cruelties visited on Englishmen in Spain.

But there were grave objections to a marriage. It would introduce a new and unknown element into English councils. Suppose, as a Catholic, the King should join that party; or worse, ally himself with Mary herself, plot the death of Elizabeth and a Catholic restoration. Or suppose he should become king of France? or that his child should be heir to both thrones? The thought of becoming a French dependency was intolerable to England. In any case it would mean a break with Spain and how could England be sure that France was not merely tempting her to that, finally to leave her to face Spain alone? Plainly, marriage was too close and dangerous a union—as for negotiations, that was another matter, and it was simply for the negotiations themselves that Elizabeth entered upon them. This is proved, I think, by her entire policy. Whenever France seems most willing she draws away; but when France seems likely to abandon such fruitless endeavors, she at once becomes affable and yielding. Sometimes her ministers urged her to definite and decided action, but she always managed to find a loop-hole, if either they or circumstance had forced her into too dangerous agreement.

France, on the other hand, could not be content with mere negotiations. She, too, had several definite problems. Rent by civil war, with enormously powerful barons on the one side and a clamorous people on the other, while outside the realm stood Spain and England, only too glad to promote and foster her difficulties, the crown was in a struggle for existence as real as that of Elizabeth. To join Spain would be for France to lose her integral existence and to be swallowed up in the maw of the Hapsburgs. Therefore the English alliance was the only refuge. Besides there were many other advantages. It would stop England's meddling in French affairs and would calm and reassure the Huguenots. But there was the rub: did the Huguenots need to be reassured? Could France safely commit herself to a liberal policy? To Catherine it was not so much that, as the question of her own authority and personal ambition for her family; she had no intention of giving place to the Huguenots any more than she had to the Guises. And so she wavered when the Guises were becoming too powerful, and helped along the marriage; when the Huguenots began to be too authoritative, she frowned on it.

To the Huguenots the marriage was a question of enormous advantage—if it were accomplished, the Calvinists might hope, not only for success in France, but in the Low Counrties as well; while to the Guises, on the contrary, the alliance meant the ruin of their hopes for Mary and for absolute dominion in France.

But to all the risk was great. Elizabeth was by no means firmly seated upon her throne and seemed to be manifesting a reckless carelessness in the leniency of her treatment of the late conspirators. The English ambassadors noted that any "roundness" of treatment at home at once caused a quickening of the negotiations. The real objection, both with France and with England, was fear of duplicity. Neither could trust the other. Each insisted that the other should commit itself first; neither would consent, with the result that all came to naught. This was just what Philip expected. Naturally a French-English league would have seriously hampered him, but he had found by long and trying experience that when Elizabeth talked of marriage, she was only amusing herself with a polite fiction. Not once does he take the matter seriously. So the Spanish attitude was one of unconcern, which in itself added to the fear of both Elizabeth and Catherine, for each supposed some secret understanding with Spain on the part of the other.

With such motives and in such troubled waters the negotiations went on. In the end Elizabeth could not "digest the inconvenience" of the proposed marriage, and failing to cement the new friendship of France and England by this form of alliance, it was then suggested that a political compact, not a marriage alliance, be made between the two powers.[1] But there were great difficulties in the way of this project. For, although the English desired a closer union with France, they were nevertheless not unprepared to treat with Spain, and to use the prospective alliance with France for the purpose of bringing Philip II to terms. England was unwilling yet to be considered as an open enemy of Spain, in spite of the fact she was well aware of Alva's plot with Lord Seton and other Scotch and English refugees in Flanders.[2]

Trade considerations were of great influence in governing this attitude. England could not afford to forfeit her commercial intercourse with Spain and Flanders for the none-too-sure friendship of France, since the staple in Flanders was worth between two and three millions.[3] France could not offer any staple or

[1] Walsingham to Lord Burghley: " . . . . and if he sees no hope then to further what he may the league."—*C. S. P. For.*, January 17, 1572; *Hatfield Papers*, II, 46.

[2] Charles IX to M. de la Mothe-Fenelon: Directs him to inform the queen of England that the duke of Alva does all he can to encourage the 500 or 600 English refugees in Flanders in their enterprise against England, in which they will be assisted by Lord Seton with 2,000 Scots, who have determined to seize on the prince of Scotland, and send him into Spain. Directs him and M. de Croc to watch and do all in their power to frustrate this design (*C. S. P. For.*, No. 330, May 2, 1572; cf. Introd., xii, xiii and No. 257).

[3] On the efforts of Alva to revive the commerce of Flanders see D'Aubigné, Book V, chap. xxxii, p. 265; *C. S. P. For.*, Nos. 94, 95, January 28 and 31, 1572; Motley, *Rise of the Dutch Republic*, chap. v; Altmeyer, *Histoire des relations commerciales des Pays-Bas avec le Nord pendant le XVI siècle;* Bruxelles, 1840; Reiffenberg, *De l'etat de la population, des fabriques et des manufactures des Pays-Bas pendant le XVe et le XVIe siècle*, Bruxelles, 1822.

port advantages to England comparable with those England enjoyed elsewhere.[1] England accordingly proposed that the league be extended to include the Protestant princes of Germany and that they should join together "in defense against any who for matters of religion should use force against any of them;" secondly, that France would bind herself not to support the cause of Mary Stuart in Scotland; and thirdly, that France would not seek any greater trade advantages in the Low Countries than she had in former times. France balked at the proposed extension of the alliance to Germany and it was dropped; as to Scotland, she was willing to make a partial sacrifice of honor for the sake of political advantage.[2]

But England's fear of contributing to the aggrandizement of France was too keen to permit her to have free rein in the Netherlands,[3] though Walsingham proposed a way to prevent the possibility of French ascendency there, and declared that the grandeur of France abroad was less to be feared by England than the continuance of civil war in France or the destructive policy of Alva in the Netherlands.[4] Burghley was as cautious as his mistress. "If the seaports fall into the hands of the French," he wrote, "they will regulate not only the commerce of our merchants abroad but the sovereignty of the Channel, which belongs to us."[5] The

[1] "The answer of the Merchant Adventurers to the French king's offer to establish a staple in France" in *C. S. P. For.*, No. 515, July, 1572: It would be no commodity for them to have a privilege in France, as those things in which they are principally occupied, viz., white cloths, are chiefly uttered in Upper and Lower Germany. Besides, if they alter their old settled trade, they would also have to seek for dressers and dyers in a place unacquainted with the trade. It is dangerous to have the vent of all the commodity of the realm in one country, especially seeing the French have small trade to England. There is besides such evil observance of treaties and so evil justice in France. The drapers of France so much mislike the bringing of cloth into France that they will not endure it, insomuch as January last, by proclamation, all foreign cloth was banished. The converting of the whole trade of England into France would be hurtful to the navy, for that the ports there are so small that no great ship may enter.

For the Merchant Adventurers in the sixteenth century see Burgon, *Life and Times of Sir Thomas Gresham*, I, 185–89.

[2] *C. S. P. For.*, No. 278, April 20, 1572, Queen Elizabeth to Charles IX.

[3] Walsingham, *ibid.*, No. 135.

[4] *Ibid.*, No 143, September 26, 1571.   [5] *Ibid.*, No. 247.

jealous determination of England to monopolize the commerce of the Low Countries was, the greatest obstacle to the formation of the alliance. For England most of all feared lest France would not content herself with Flanders and Artois.[1]

In the delicate business of state which burdened him at this season, Charles IX showed more acumen than either his new-found friends of Protestant faith or the Catholics had expected to find, because while exerting himself to keep the peace with Spain on the one hand, on the other he endeavored to conciliate his Protestant subjects. Unlike his elder brother, Francis II, Charles IX was of strong physical frame, being big boned and vigorous, until the fatal taint of his heritage and his excesses undermined his constitution[2] and brought on the disease of consumption of which he died. He was gross, even brutish in inclination, rejoicing in base physical sport and disinclined to books.[3] But in the present

---

[1] Walsingham to Lord Burghley: Has been asked whether that enterprise having good success, and the French king lending all his forces to the conquest of Flanders, the queen of England would be content to enter foot in Zealand, Middleburgh being delivered into her hands. They fear that the French king will not be content with Flanders, whatsoever is promised (*C. S. P. For.*, No. 2,202, December 31, 1571).

[2] *Rel. vén.,* I, 543; *C. S. P. For.*, No. 687, February 15, 1570. Sir Henry Norris to Cecil. The King keeps his chamber, which they marvel not at who know his diet.

[3] For a character-sketch of Charles IX see Baschet, *La diplomatie vénitienne,* 539–41; cf. *Rel. vén.*, II, 43 and 161. Lord Buckhurst, in a letter to Queen Elizabeth of March 4, 1571, gives an account of one of Charles' hunting parties in the Bois de Vincennes, which illustrates his temperament. "After dinner,'' he relates, "the King rode to a warren of hares thereby, and after he had coursed with much pastime, he flew to the partridge with a cast of very good falcons; and that done, entered the park of Bois de Vincennes, replenished with some store of fallow deer. Understanding that Lord Buckhurst had a leash of greyhounds, he sent to him that he might put on his dogs to the deer, which he did, but found that the deer ran better for their lives than the dogs did for his pastime. After this the King and all the gentlemen with him fell to a new manner of hunting, chasing the whole herd with their drawn swords, on horseback, so far forth as they being embosked were easily stricken and slain; they spared no male deer, but killed of all sorts without respect, like hunters who sought not to requite any part of their travail with delight to eat of the slain venison."—*C. S. P. For.*, No. 1,589, March 4, 1571. In the spring of 1573 the French consul in Alexandria sent Charles three trained leopards for deer-hunting (Coll. Godefroy, CCLVI, No. 51). In June, 1571, the King was somewhat seriously injured while hunting, by striking

politics Charles IX showed little of the rashness of his physical nature.[1] Nevertheless the King went 'farther than caution approved in dealing with his new-found friends. He would have disarmed the suspicion of Spain, and the Guises[2] to some degree, at least, if he had drawn close to the duke of Montmorency, whose moderate Catholicism, however impeachable, was not the detested heresy of the French Protestants. But instead of so doing, the King, unable to dissemble as much as his mother, openly manifested a great admiration for the admiral Coligny, than whom neither the Guises nor Spain had a more resolute foe. The admiral was received in Paris upon his arrival there early in September, 1571, with distinguished honors.[3] His popularity

his head against the branch of a tree (*C. S. P. For.*, No. 1,777, June 8, 1571). In March, 1572, he again was injured (letter of the King to the duke of Anjou, March 21, 1572, in Coll. Pichon, No. 28). His passion for the chase often led him to neglect the business of state, conduct which Coligny once sharply reproved (*C. S. P. For.*, No. 2,156, November 29, 1571), and he was frequently ill from fatigue or exposure (*L'Ambassade de St. Sulpice*, 301). The King himself inspired the French translation of a Latin treatise of the sixteenth century on hunting, by Louis Leroy de Coutances, *Libre du roy Charles*. His patronage also inspired another work on the same subject: "Du Fouilloux, La Vénerie de Iacques du Fouilloux, Gentil-homme, Seigneur dudit lieu, pays de Gastine, en Poitou. Dédise au Roy Très-Chrestien Charles, neufiesme de ce nom. Avec plusieurs Receptes et Remèdes pour guérir les Chiens de diverses maladies. Avec Privilege du Roy. A Poitiers, Par les de Marnefz, et Bouchetz, frères. circa 1565." Charles IX was also given to low practical jokes. For example this is reported of him from Paris, September 18, 1573: The King, in an old cloak and evil-favoured hat, withdrew himself "to a little house upon the bridge from all the ladies, and there cast out money upon the people to get them together, and made pastime to cast out buckets of water upon them while they were scrambling for the money."—*C. S. P. For.*, Paris, September 18, 1573.

[1] Walsingham reported to Burghley in August 12, 1571: "This prince is of far greater judgment than outwardly appears. There is none of any account within his realm whose imperfections and virtues he knows not," although, he adds, "those who love him lament he is so overmuch given to pleasure."—*Ibid.*, No. 1,921.

[2] In May 1571 the Guises were in discredit. The duke went to Joinville, the cardinal of Lorraine to Rheims, the duke of Mayenne started for Turkey. Guise did not come back to Paris till January 1572 (Bouillé, *Histoire des ducs de Guises*, II, Book IV, chap. iv).

[3] "He appeared at all hours near his majesty's chair upon the same terms as the lords who had never left the court" (*C. S. P. Ven.*, No. 576, September 15, 1570). Coligny first became a member of the *conseil du roi* at this time (Soldan, *Vor d. St. Barthomäusnacht*, 39). Blois was practically the capital of France at

with the King was at once a menace and a challenge to Philip II and the Guises.[1]   An added difficulty, as the result of this policy, was that Catherine de Medici, seeing her son so well affected toward the admiral, grew jealous of the latter's influence, lest it supplant her own, and intrigued against him.

Despite the failure of the marriage alliance, France still had two strings to the Ulysses bow she was drawing against Spain— support of the Dutch, and the union of France by means of the marriage of Henry of Navarre and the princess Marguerite. Spain's suspicions that the Huguenot naval preparations at La Rochelle were in favor of the Dutch[2] had not been based on groundless suspicion. William of Orange's own brother, Louis of Nassau, had remained in France after the Peace of St. Germain, urging an alliance between France and England against Spain,[3] or else French intervention in the Netherlands.[4]   The count of Nassau enlarged upon

this time. Paris was avoided both to save creating suspicion among the Huguenots and because of its Guisard sympathies. "He would change from white to black the moment he was in Paris" said Walsingham of the King. Capefigue, *Hist. de la réforme*, III, 92, points out Blois was "le siège naturel d'un gouvernement qui voulait s'éloigner du catholocisme fervent. Placé à quelques lieues d'Orleans, donnant la main à la Rochelle, et par la Rochelle, se liant au Poitou, à la Saintonge, au Béarn."

[1] The King conceives of no other subject better than of the admiral, and there is great hope that he will use him in matters of the greatest trust, for he begins to see the insufficiency of others, some being more addicted to others than to him, others more Spanish than French, or given more to private pleasures than public affairs (*C. S. P. For.*, No. 1,921, August 12, 1571).

[2] Alva to Philip II, April 5, May 22, 1572, in Gachard, *Correspondance de Philippe II*, II, 239.   In December, 1570, the marshal Cossé was sent to La Rochelle.   In March, 1571, Cossé and Biron were sent a second time.

[3] See Walsingham, Letter of August 12, 1571, to Leicester. He gained a great ascendency over Charles IX (Languet, *Epist. ad Camer.*, 132–36, 140. "Count Ludovic is the King's avowed pensioner."—*C. S. P. For.*, No. 2,156, November 29, 1571.   Some of his correspondence is in *Archives de la maison d'Orange-Nassau*, III.

[4] On the secret interview of Charles IX, Louis of Nassau, and La Noue at Blois, see D'Aubigné, Book VI, chap. i, 282; *Mémoires de la Huguerye*, I, 25. The Dutch cause suffered fearfully in this autumn. On November 1 and 2 a frightful storm made terrible inundations on the coast; hundreds of vessels were wrecked; in West Frisia alone nearly 20,000 persons were drowned (*Archives de a maison d'Orange-Nassau*, III, 385).

the vast designs of the Spanish monarch and showed how sinister they were to France as well as Holland, artfully alluding to the peace of Cateau-Cambrésis, "a peace dishonorable to France;" he dwelt upon the tyranny of Alva and the horrors of the inquisition; he demonstrated that all the inhabitants of the Low Countries, both Catholics and Protestants, hated the Spanish domination; that all the maritime towns were ready to receive French and Dutch garrisons, if but those of Spain could be driven out; that with the sea-power of France thrown into the scale, the Dutch could conquer Spain; and finally proposed the formation of an international league to overthrow Spain, and asserted that France might acquire Flanders and Artois and the empire Brabant, Guelders, and Luxembourg as reward of their services. So alluring was the prospect portrayed to Charles IX that he almost cast off the mask he wore of pretended friendship for Spain.[1] He told Philip's minister, Alava, than whom "there was no prouder man or one more disdainful in countenance"[2] when the ambassador complained to the French King that certain ships of the prince of Orange were being harbored at La Rochelle,[3] that "his master should not look to give laws to France."[4]

[1] For details, see Capefigue, III, 44.   Charles IX gave evasive replies to all the remonstrances of the Spanish ambassador (Languet, *Epist. secr.*, I, 177, August 15, 1571).

[2] *C. S. P. For.*, No. 1,578, Walsingham to Cecil; *Nég. Tosc.*, III, 694.

[3] Gachard, *Correspondance de Philippe II sur les Pays-Bas*, II, 239—Alva to Philip II, April 5, 1572; cf. p. 250; *Archives de la maison d'Orange-Nassau*, III, 441.   The Prince of Orange in 1569 began the practice of issuing letters of marque and reprisal in virtue of his position as sovereign prince of Orange.   As a result in the next year the English Channel and the Bay of Biscay were crowded with vessels hostile to Spain.   The most famous of these marauders soon destined to become known as the "Beggars of the Sea" was Adrian de Bergues.   On one occasion within the space of two days, he overhauled and captured two merchant fleets, the one of 40, the other of 60 sail (*Arch. de la maison d'Orange-Nassau*, III, 351). Upon the importance of La Rochelle as a seaport, see La Noue, chap. xxviii. Some of Strozzi's correspondence when in command of the fleet before La Rochelle in 1572 is in F. Fr., XV, 555; cf. *Nég. Tosc.*, III, 760-63.

[4] *C. S. P. For.*, No. 1,921, August 12, 1571.   Languet makes Charles IX's reply less emphatic than this. Languet, *Epist. secr.*, I, 177, August 15, 1571.   I am inclined to believe that Walsingham colored the anecdote. Languet shows the hesitations and vacillations of Charles IX, pp. 132, 136, 140.   The Spanish

Meantime the proposed marriage of Henry of Navarre to Marguerite, the King's sister, progressed. A full year before the nuptials were concluded, the jewels and apparel for the ceremony were already provided. The difficulty of arranging a religious form for the ceremony acceptable to both Catholics and Protestants was the great hindrance.[1]

Again Spain made unavailing protest. Henry of Bourbon still bore the title of king of Navarre, though the kingdom had been lost to the house long before his birth and was, in fact, entirely in the possession of Spain. Her fear was lest the new bond of marriage

ambassador's grounds of fear for Flanders were the more substantial because the garrisons that had occupied St. Jean-d'Angély, Niort, Saintes, and Angoulême during the late war were newly stationed in the border fortresses of Picardy. To Alava's alarmed inquiry Charles IX blandly replied that "the reason why these troops were sent to the frontiers was to give them employment, because if the King had disbanded them all at once the soldiery might have mutinied for lack of pay" (C. S. P. Ven., No. 499, February 19, 1571; No. 575, August 1, 1571).

[1] "The only impediment to the marriage between the prince of Navarre and the lady Margaret is religion."—C. S. P. For., No. 2,038, Walsingham to Cecil, September 16, 1571. The whole matter was referred to eight counselors to settle: those of the Huguenots were Jeanne d'Albret, La Noue, Louis of Nassau, and Francourt (C. S. P. For., March 29, 1572; Archives de la maison d'Orange-Nassau, III, 417). The Pope made objection that, aside from the difference of religion, the parents of Henry of Navarre and Marguerite of Valois were relatives within the third degree, and refused to grant the dispensation for the marriage (Nég. Tosc., III, 712–14). To this demur the Huguenots triumphantly argued that it was not necessary for the Pope or any other priest to give dispensation, since it was a *royal* marriage and it was not fitting for the King's authority to be demeaned by that of the church (Claude Haton, II, 661). There was violent opposition by radical Huguenots, especially the pastors, to the marriage, and fear lest the Pope's refusal to grant a dispensation might lead to a rupture between France and Rome like that of England under Henry VIII (Nég. Tosc., III, 733 and 740). Finally it was arranged that the marriage should be celebrated by a priest of the church of Rome, and that Henry would accompany his wife to mass in the church where the ceremony was to be held, but that he was to retire before the service so that he was neither to be present at the mass nor hear it said (ibid., 662 and note, 663, note). The cardinal of Lorraine, with his usual "trimming" wrote to the queen mother: "Madame, je vous baise très humblement les mains de ce qu'il vous plaît me mander la conclusion du marriage de madame vostre fille, puisqu'il est au contentement de vos majestés et selon les désirs des catholiques."—Collection des autographes, No. 278, April 17, 1572.

For the preliminaries of the marriage of Marguerite of Valois and Henry of Navarre see Revue des deux mondes, October 1, 1884, pp. 560–64.

might unite the parties of France in war for the acquisition of Navarre. It was in vain, however, that Spain sought to prey upon the fears of Charles IX, endeavoring to excite the King's jealousy against the growing power of the house of Bourbon and pointing out that of the twelve provinces of the kingdom ten were in the hands of governors who were bound by blood or interest to the Bourbons.[1] So eager were many of the gentry of France for war with Spain, either in Navarre or Flanders, that one of Coligny's officers, when asked whether France meant to lose the favorable opportunity of attacking Spain, scornfully rejoined, "What can we do? We are good for nothing, for we have to deal with a scared King and a timid queen, who will not come to any decision." By December, 1571, war with Spain was on every lip and the government began to collect money.[2]

---

[1] *C. S. P. Ven.*, No. 516; August 15, 1571. Spain and France clashed in Switzerland, too, at this time. For Switzerland refused to permit forces to fight the Turk on the ground that the Swiss were unused to maritime warfare, yet the Grisons and the Tyrol raised two regiments for the French King (*ibid., For.*, No. 189, March 25, 1572, from Heidelberg or Strasburg).

[2] "There have been no other speeches but war with Spain"—Killegrew to Lord Burghley, December 8, 1571; *C. S. P. For.*, No. 2,163; cf. *Nég. Tosc.*, III, dispatches of April 17 and 20, 1572 and *C. S. P. For.*, Nos. 2,156, 2,162, November 29, December 7, 1571. Alva fully expected war (Gachard, *Correspondance de Philippe II sur les Pays-Bas*, II, 259, Alva to Philip II, May 24, 1572).

In the spring of 1572 Schomberg was dispatched to Germany to contract alliances with the Lutheran princes (*Arch. de la maison d'Orange-Nassau* III, 403; *C S. P. For.*, No. 189, March 25, 1572). The German princes anticipated that if the Low Countries were united to the crown of France that power would become too formidable. They wanted France to content herself with Flanders and Artois. As for Brabant and the other provinces that were once dependent upon the empire, their purpose was to put them upon their old footing and to give the government of them to some prince of Germany, who could not be other than the prince of Orange. Holland and Zealand were to be united to the crown of England (Walsingham, 143, French ed., letter of August 12, 1572 to Leicester). Yet momentous as the French project in the Low Countries was, it was but part of a grander scheme, for France aimed also to acquire a decisive influence in Germany, with the ultimate purpose of acquiring so great ascendency over the German states as to be able to transfer the crown of the empire, for centuries hereditary in the house of Hapsburg, to the head of the French prince (*Rel. vén.*, I, 445). This project was part of the mission of Schomberg in Germany (*Arch. de la maison d'Orange-Nassau*, IV, Introd., 23, 268–73). In Germany the elector

At this juncture, when all Europe was keyed to concert pitch of political tension, when anything seemed likely to happen and no one of the great powers dared make an overt move, the Gordian knot was cut.   On April 1, 1572, the most notable event in the Low Countries since the iconoclastic outburst occurred.   For on that day the count van der Marck, commander of the Beggars of the Sea, captured the port of Brille.   From that time onward the Dutch and Flemings had a maritime point of their own on the mainland and were no longer dependent on the precarious shelter of English and Norman ports.   The effect of this blow to Spain was great. Within the week—on Easter Day—Flushing, and soon afterward Middelburg, rebelled against the billeting of Spanish troops sent by Alva to replace the Walloon garrison there.[1]

The Gueux were masters of the sea and when Dordrecht also rebelled, the inland water routes were endangered too.   No vessel could come from Holland, Guelders, or Frisia and no communication could be made from the north with Brabant.   Even Amsterdam could be starved and Alva determined to retire all his forces to Ghent and Antwerp.[2]   On April 14 William of Orange issued a proclamation from Dillenburg expressing his grief at the miseries suffered from the exactions, outrages, and cruelties inflicted by the Spaniards, and assured the people of his determination to

of Saxony and the landgrave of Hesse were strong partisans of France (*ibid.*, IV, Introd., 25).

The strongest advocate of France for the imperial crown was the elector palatine, who burned with an ambition to "Calvinize the world," and embraced with ardor a project which could not fail to redound to the honor of the Huguenots. The elector of Saxony and the landgrave were less complacent.   The first was a friend of the emperor Maximilian and expressed his indignation at the imperial pretensions of Charles IX.   Even William of Hesse, in spite of his hereditary attachment to the crown of France, returned a guarded reply (*ibid.*, IV, Introd., 28 and 123).

[1] The revolt took place on Easter Sunday, April 6, 1572.   On the whole subject of the revolt of the Netherlands at this time see Janssen, *History of the German People*, VIII, chap. ii; La Gravière, "Les Gueux de Mer," *Revue des deux mondes*, September 15, 1891, p. 347; November, 1891, p. 98; January 15, 1892, p. 389.

[2] See the letter of President Viglius to Hopper in *Arch. de la maison d'Orange-Nassau* III, 415, and *C. S. P. For.*, No. 260, April 19, 1572.

liberate the land from their tyranny. As many towns and ports had already recognized him as their ruler, he urged others to follow their example, pledging his word to use all his power to restore the ancient privileges and liberties of each.[1]

When news of these wondrous deeds reached France, Charles IX's hesitation was swept away by the combined fervor of Louis of Nassau and the admiral. On April 19, the Anglo-French treaty of alliance was signed at Blois.[2]

Du Plessis-Mornay, a young Huguenot gentleman of twenty-three, of marked literary ability and destined to be the intellectual leader of the Protestants in coming years, who had lately traveled through the Netherlands and visited England,[3] in collaboration with the admiral drew up a remarkable memorial advocating French intervention in the Low Countries,[4] which Coligny presented to the King. English and French volunteers soon poured into the land.[5] Louis of Nassau left for Valen-

[1] *Archives de la maison d'Orange-Nassau*, III, 418–19. On the alliance concluded at the Frankfurt Fair see *ibid.*, III, 448. For the whole subject consult Waddington, "La France et les protestants allemands sous les règnes de Charles IX et Henri III," *Revue historique*, XLII, 266 ff.

[2] The treaty of Blois provided for a defensive league between Queen Elizabeth and Charles IX and stipulated the amount of succor by sea or land to be rendered by either party in case of need; if either party were assailed for the cause of religion or under any other privileges and advantages for the pretext, the other was bound to render assistance; a schedule of the number and description of the forces to be mutually furnished, together with their rates of pay was annexed. De Frixa and Montmorency were sent to England to ratify the treaty. A full account of the gorgeous reception of Montmorency will be found in Holinshed and the Account Book of the Master of the Revels. The earl of Lincoln left for France, May 26, 1572. He was instructed to say, if any mention was made of the Alençon marriage, that Elizabeth felt offended by the way she had been treated in the Anjou negotiations and that in any case "the difference in age should make a full stay."

Text of the treaty of Blois in Dumont, *Corps diplomatique*, V, Part I, 211. The letter of the King to Elizabeth after the signature is in *Bulletin de la société du prot. français*, XI, 72.

[3] *Mémoires et correspondance de Du Plessis-Mornay*, I, 36–38 (Paris, 1824).

[4] *Ibid.*, II, 20–39; cf. Whitehead, *Gaspard de Coligny, Admiral of France*. 248. On the authorship of the memoir consult same volume Appendix II.

[5] *C. S. P. For.*, No. 419, Captain Thomas Morgan to Lord Burghley from Flushing, June 16, 1572; Gachard, *Correspondance de Philippe II*, II, 268, Alva to Philip II, July 18, 1572.

ciennes, which had successfully revolted, accompanied by La Noue and Genlis.[1] On May 24, by a stratagem, Genlis secured possession of Mons, one of the most important fortresses to Spain in the Low Countries in the present state of mind that France was in.[2] From this point of vantage he wrote hopefully to Charles IX for more soldiers, a "good minister," a surgeon, some cannon founders, and drugs.[3] While these events were happening on land, on the sea the Zealanders attacked and dispersed the Spanish fleet in the Sluys on June 8, and seized twenty merchantmen under its convoy:[4] and, to the elation of France,[5] far down in the Bay of Biscay the fleet of Flushing three days later scattered another of Spain's armadas.[6] All Holland, Amsterdam and Rotterdam excepted, was lost to Spain.[7] Sir Humphrey Gilbert with 1,200 English and some French and Walloons landed in the Low Countries, on July 10, and captured Sluys and Bruges.[8] Money poured in upon William of Orange, who in June went to Frankfurt to purchase supplies and enlist men.[9] The duke of Alva was in desperate straits. The Walloons everywhere in the army mutinied and deserted, and he was short of munitions.[10]

[1] La Popelinière, XXVII, 108; Fillon Collection, No. 133, Charles IX to the Duke of Longueville, governor of Picardy from Blois, May 3, 1572. Enjoins him to repair the fortifications of Picardy, and to be on guard against the duke of Alva, who was arming under the pretext of repressing the Gueux.

[2] Gachard, *Correspondance de Philippe II*, II, 356 and note 3; *Archives de la maison d'Orange-Nassau*, III, 425–26; *Mém. de la Huguerye*, 105; see La Popelinière's account (XXVII, 107), of the situation of the city. It was the capital of Hainault.

[3] *C. S. P. For.*, No. 406, June 10, 1572, to Torcy.

[4] *Archives de la maison d'Orange-Nassau*, III, 437.

[5] Coll. Godefroy, CCLVIII, No. 8. French dispute with Spain over navigation of the Sluys.

[6] *Archives de la maison d'Orange-Nassau*, III, 441–42.

[7] In *ibid.*, 463–64, 467–68, will be found a list of the principal officers of the prince of Orange and of the towns at his devotion (cf. *C. S. P. For.*, No. 374, July, 1572).

[8] *Ibid.*, Nos. 478, 511, July, 1572.

[9] The estates met at Dordrecht on July 15 (*Archives de la maison d'Orange-Nassau*, III, 447).

[10] He had received his recall and the duke of Medina-Coeli had been sent to succeed him, and at this hour was on the ground urging a policy of moderation (Raumer, I, 202). Yet Alva refused to give up (*Archives de la maison d'Orange-Nassau*, III, 437).

But such successes were too great to last. Louis of Nassau found he could not hope to hold Mons for long with the slender forces at his command and sent Genlis back to France for reinforcements. Charles IX, under pressure from Coligny, provided men and money secretly, but Genlis' relief column was intercepted on July 16 and captured by the duke of Alva.[1] It was only a question of time before Mons surrendered.[2] The blow was a heavy one to France. It mattered little to France that French subjects were killed or taken prisoner during the siege. But it was of tremendous consequence to France that Alva found on Genlis' person a letter written by Charles IX to Louis of Nassau on April 27, 1572, in which the King said that he was resolved as soon as the condition of affairs at home permitted him, to employ the armies of France for the liberation of the Low Countries.[3] Well might Alva's secretary write "I have in my possession a letter of the king of France which would strike you with astonishment if you could see it."[4] Spain possessed indubitable proof at last of French duplicity.

[1] The march of the Spanish army that intercepted Genlis was so accurate as to give rise to the belief that Alva had prior information. It is uncertain. Mendoza, who was with the Spanish army (*Commentaires*, Book VI, chap. vii) seems to confirm the suspicion. His account (chaps. vii–xiii) is very vivid. Only thirty of Genlis' men escaped; the rest were either killed or drowned. On the warnings given to Genlis, see a relation in *Archives curieuses*, VII. There is an unpublished account of Genlis' defeat in F. Fr., 18,587, fol. 541. According to La Huguerye, 125, he was strangled in prison.

[2] It did so on September 19. See a letter of William of Orange to his brother John, September 24, 1572, in *Archives de la maison d'Orange-Nassau*, III, 511. La Noue prophesied the fall of the city when he saw the heights of Jemappes occupied by the troops of Spain (Hauser, *La Noue*, 33).

[3] As late as August 11, 1572, the Prince of Orange was still looking for the coming of the admiral Coligny into the Low Countries (see a letter of his to his brother John, of this date in *Archives de la maison d'Orange-Nassau*, III, 490).

[4] Albornoz to secretary of state Cayas, from Brussels, July 19, 1572 (see Gachard, *Correspondance de Philippe II sur les Pays-Bas*, II, 269). A note of M. Gachard adds: "Cette lettre, datée de St. Leger, le 27 avril 1572, était écrite par Charles IX au comte Louis de Nassau. Il y disait qu'il était détermine, autant que les occasions et la disposition de ses affaires le permettraient à employer les forces que Dieu avait mises en sa main à tirer les Pays-Bas de l'oppression sous laquelle ils gémissaient. Une traduction espagnole de cette lettre existe aux

The capture of Genlis and the knowledge that Spain had penetrated the whole secret of her design, filled the French government
with consternation, though Charles IX affected a show of courage
he did not feel.[1]   That consternation became abject dismay when
it was learned that Elizabeth of England, partially out of reluctance to have war with Spain, more because of fear lest French
foothold in the Low Countries would jeopardize her commercial
ascendency there, repudiated the treaty of alliance.[2]   As one
reviews the months before the massacre one asks just how far
Elizabeth herself may have been responsible for it.   It was she
who, by her tortuous and insincere policy alarmed Charles IX
and Catherine, causing the Flanders expedition to be abandoned;
it was this which caused Coligny to turn upon Catherine in the
King's council, saying, "This war the King renounced.   God
grant he may not find himself involved in another less easy to
renounce."   The line comes straight from Elizabeth surely, but
can be emphasized too strongly.   That some blame must rest
on the English cannot be denied, however.   Did Catherine de
Medici plan the massacre of St. Bartholomew to save herself from
the wrath of the Huguenots?   Or, in her terror did she seek to

Archives de Simancas, *papeles de Estado*, liasse 551." Charles IX. repudiated its
authenticity (see a letter to Mondoucet, French agent in Flanders, dated August 12,
1572, in *Bulletin de la Commission d'hist. de Belgique*, séries II, IV, 342).
The admiral Coligny, without knowing of the incriminating evidence in Alva's
hands after the failure before Mons, urged Charles IX to declare war upon Spain
at once as the shortest and safest way out of the difficulty (Brantôme, *Vie des
grandes capitaines françois*—M'l'admiral de Châtillon).

[1] As late as August 21, France had the hardihood to protest her innocence
of any enterprise in Flanders (Gachard, *Correspondance de Philippe II sur les
Pays-Bas*, II, 271, Philip to Alva, August 2, 1572; *ibid.*, II, 273, Alva to Philip
August 21, 1572.

[2] There is in existence the record of an extremely curious conversation of the
admiral Coligny upon this subject with Henry Middelmore, one of the English
agents in France, in which the latter frankly said: "Of all other thinges we colde
least lyke that France shulde commaunde Flawnders, or bryng it under theyr
obedience, for therein we dyd see so apparawntlye the greatnes of our dainger,
and therefore in no wyse colde suffer it."—Ellis, *Original Letters*, 2d series, III,
6. I find the same thought expressed in a letter of Thomas Parker to one Hogyns,
written from Bruges, June 17, 1572. See Appendix XXIX.

appease the wrath of the Catholic dragon with human lives? Was the massacre of St. Bartholomew the bloody price of Spain's satisfaction?

But there is another element to be considered in any endeavor to unravel the causes of that event. All the art of Catherine de Medici for years past had been expended in an endeavor to maintain control by balancing the parties against one another. At this minute she was insanely jealous of the admiral Coligny, whose political ascendency seemed all the greater because of the conduct of the Protestants who crowded Paris for the coming nuptials, enjoying their superficial popularity with too much arrogance in many cases, and angering the sentiment of the Parisians, the most Catholic populace in France.

The massacre seems primarily due to the jealousy and hatred felt by Catherine de Medici toward Coligny on account of his great ascendency over Charles IX, coupled with panic after the failure of her deliberate attempt to have him murdered, and fear of war with Spain—a fear all the greater because of England's desertion of France in Flanders at this critical moment, lest English commercial ascendency there should suffer.[1] It was a crime of fear, a horrible resource in a difficult emergency; partly a craven attempt to placate Spain for what had been done against her; partly a crime of jealousy. Perhaps jealousy of Coligny was even a stronger motive than fear of Spain. The attempt upon Coligny's life on August 22, would seem to indicate this.[2] Was the general slaughter of the Huguenots the consequence of the failure of this attempt? If the shot of August 22 had killed the admiral, would the massacre have taken place? I think not. The failure to kill the admiral was the immediate occasion of the massacre of St. Bartholomew's Day. If Coligny had been killed then and there, the massacre probably would not have happened.

---

[1] On this last phase see *Correspondance de Catherine de Médicis*, IV, Introd., xlix ff., and Froude, *Hist. of England*, X, 312.

[2] For a particular account see Whitehead, *Gaspard de Coligny, Admiral of France*, 257–64. Two of Lord Burghley's correspondents give accounts (*C. S. P. For.*, Nos. 537, 538, August 22, 1572). See also an interesting extract from the registers of the Bureau of the Ville of Paris in *Archives curieuses*, VII, 211.

The failure to compass the death of the admiral made Catherine frantic with mingled rage and fear lest the Huguenots concentrated in Paris would rise in reprisal. She took council with Guise, Anjou, Madame de Nemours, and Gondi, the Italian bishop of Paris. The resolution of the King, who at first believed that the duke of Guise was the author of the attempted assassination, was beaten down by his mother, and when his fierce instincts were at last aroused, the way was easy. The hatred of Paris could be relied upon to do its worst, under the guidance of the provost who was taken into the plot.[1]

There is no need to detail the history of this famous day. At one-thirty on the morning of August 24 the tocsin sounded from the tower of St. Germain-l'Auxerrois. Coligny was the first victim. From the Louvre the murderous spirit spread to the Ville, to the Cité, to the university quarter. Henry of Navarre and the prince of Condé saved themselves by abjuration. Montgomery escaped on a fleet horse to the south. Estimates of the dead are so different that any positive opinion is impossible. La Popelinière gives 1,000 for Paris, the Tuscan ambassador 3,000, Davila 10,000. Brantôme says nearly 4,000 bodies were thrown into the Seine.

From Paris the massacre spread to the provinces. On August 25 the fury reached Meaux and Troyes; on the 26th La Charité, on the 27th Orleans and Bourges, on the 28th Caen, on the 30th Lyons. Bordeaux and Toulouse followed. At Rouen, Carrouges, the governor, would not obey the King's warrant until doubly convinced, when he retired to his country house and refused to execute it, though he did not have the courage to prevent the massacre, as was the case at Dijon, Limoges, Blois, Nantes.[2]

---

[1] For the order of Marcel, provost of the merchants, immediately before the massacre, see *Arch. cur.*, VII, 212. On the council of August 24, see Cavalli, 85. Charles IX at first denied any responsibility and blamed the Guises. When this proved a dangerous explanation. he asserted the massacre was made to foil a similar plot on the part of the Huguenots.

[2] At Blois not only the Huguenots were not mistreated but the city became a city of refuge (D'Aubigné, III, 344, note 6). The Mayor of Nantes refused to carry out the orders for massacre (*Bulletin de la Soc. du prot. franç.*, I, 59). Hotman was saved from the massacre at Bourges by his students; on the massacre at Troyes see the relation in *Arch. cur.*, VII, 287; and for that at Lyons an article by Puyroche in *Bulletin de la Soc. du prot. franç.*, XVIII, 305, 353, 401; for

There is no reason for doubting that the massacre of St. Bartholomew was unpremeditated. It was not plotted years before, or even many days before. The light of modern investigation[1]

Normandy, *ibid.*, VI, 461; *Revue retrospective*, XII, 142 (Lisieux); on the massacre at Rouen, Floquet, *Hist. du parlement de Normandie*, III, 126 ff.; on the massacre at Bordeaux see *Arch. de la Gironde*, VIII, 337. De Thou, Book LIII, says there were 264 victims. On the massacre at Toulouse see *Bull. de la Soc. du prot. franç.*, August 15, 1886; *Hist. du Languedoc*, V, 639. On the non-execution of the massacre in Burgundy see *Bull. de la Soc. du prot. franç.*, IV, 164, and XIV, 340 (documents). Th reason for this leniency was the nearness of Burgundy to the frontier.

[1] The contemporary literature on the massacre is given by M. Felix Bourquelot, editor of the *Mém. de Claude Haton* in a long note in II, 673–76. Summarized, these opinions are the following: 1. The massacre was done in order to avert a massacre by the Huguenots, after the wounding of Coligny. This was the belief of Marguerite of Navarre (*Mémoires*, ed. Guessard, 264).

2. The massacre was premeditated by Charles IX and his mother from the time of the Bayonne conference.

3. The massacre was intended to be a military stroke, the government preferring to attempt their overthrow in this way rather than by battle on the open field.

Salviati, the papal nuncio, who ought to have known, explicitly denies the rumor that a conspiracy was on foot by the Huguenots. In a dispatch of September 2 (I quote the French translation of Chateaubriand who copied them for the Paris archives) he says: "Cela n'en demeurera pas moins faux en tous points, et ce sera une honte pour qui est à même de connaître quelques choses aux affaires de ce monde de le croire." In reply to the Pope's urgency to extirpate the Protestants, he wrote on September 22: "Je lui fis part de la très grand consolation qu'avaient procuré au Saint Père les succès obtenus dans ce royaume par une grace singulière de Dieu, accordée à toute la Chrétienté sous son pontificat. Je fis connaître le désir qu'avait sa Sainteté, de voir pour la plus grande gloire de Dieu, et le plus grand bien de France, tous les hérétiques extirpés du royaume, et j'ajoutai que dans cette vue le Saint Père estimait que très à propos que l'on revoqua l'édit de pacification." On October 11th, he writes: "Le Saint Père, ai je dit en éprouve une joie infinie, et a ressenti une grande consolation d'apprendre que sa Majesté avait commandé d'écrire qu'elle espérait qu'avant peu la France n'aurait plus d'Huguenots." Cardinal Orsini, who was dispatched as legate from Rome to congratulate Charles IX and to support the exhortations of Salviati, describes his audience with the King on December 19. Orsini assured the King that he had eclipsed the glory of all his house, but urged him to fulfil his promise that not a single Huguenot should be left alive in France: "Se si rigardavva all' objetto della gloria, non potendo niun fatto de suoi antecessori, se rettamente si giudicava, agguagliarsi al glorioso ac veramente incomparabili di sua Maesta, in liberar con tanta prudentia et pietà in un giorno solo il suo regno da cotanta diabolica peste . . . . Esortai . . . . che con essendo servitio ni di Dio, ni di sua Maesta, lasciar fargli nuovo piede a questa maladetta setta, volesse applicare tutto il suo

has proved this to the satisfaction of every unprejudiced historian, whether Protestant or Catholic.   The combination of causes that led to the action; the motives of the principals; the responsibility for the massacre are today known with as much certainty as moral forces having relative and not absolute values can be.   Even unprejudiced contemporaries, La Noue and Henry IV himself, did not believe the massacre to have been premeditated.   A general slaughter of the Protestants was an old idea, but never regarded as a practical one, save by the papacy.   The guilt of the massacre in all its monstrous proportions and consequences rests upon Catherine de Medici first of all.   Fundamentally considered, it was the crime of a tigerishly hateful and essentially cowardly woman's heart.   Catherine was the author and instigator of it. The Guises entered into the plot chiefly to avenge themselves upon the admiral and really had little interest in prosecuting it beyond

pensiero e tutte le fore sue per istirparla affatto, recandosi a memoria quelle che ella haveva fatto scrivere a sua Santità da Monsignor il Nuntio, che infra pochi giorni non sarebbe pi un ugonotto in tutto il suo regno."—Bibliothèque Nationale MSS Ital., 1,272.   The Pope proclaimed a jubilee in honor 'of the massacre.

Subjoined is a list of the leading authors and articles upon this subject.   The most recent consideration which sifts all preceding investigation is that by Whitehead, *Gaspard de Coligny, Admiral of France*, London, 1904, chaps. xv, xvi; Phillipson, "Die römische Curie und die Bartholomaüsnact," *West Europa*, II, 255 ff.; Bague-nault de Puchesse, "La St. Barthélemy: ses origines, son vrai caractère, ses suites," *R. Q. H.*, July–October, 1866; "La premeditation de St. Barthélemy," *R. Q. H.*, XXVII, 272 ff.; Boutaric, "La St. Barthélemy d'après les Archives du Vatican," *Bib. de l'école des Chartes*, sér. III, 3; Theiner, Continuation of Baronius,- I (Salviati's letters); Gandy, "Le massacre de St. Barthèlemy," *Revue hist.*, July, 1879; cf. review in *Bull. de la Soc. prot. français;* Rajna, in *Archivio storico ital.*, sér. V, No. XXIII, January 15, 1899; Michiel et Cavalli, "La Saint-Bar-thélemy devant le sénat de Venise.   Relation des ambassadeurs . . . . traduite et ann. par W. Martin, Paris, 1872; Soldan, *Hist. Taschenbuch*, 1854; G. P. Fisher, "The Massacre of St. Bartholomew," *New Englander*, January, 1880; Loiseleur, "Les nouvelles controverses sur la St. Barthélemy," *Rev. hist.*, XV, 1883, p. 83; "Nouveaux documents sur la St. Barthélemy," *Rev. hist.*, IV, 1877, p. 345; Tamizey de Larroque, "Deux lettres de Charles IX," *R. Q. H.*, III, 1867, p. 567; "La St. Barthélemy, lettres de MM. Baguenault de Puchesse et G. Gandy," *R. Q. H.*, XXVIII, 1880, p. 268; Dareste, "Un incident de l'histoire diplomatique de Charles IX," *Acad. des sc. moral. etc.*, LXXI–II, 1863, p. 183; Laugel, "Coligny " *Revue des deux mondes*, September, 1883, pp. 162–85.

his death.[1] The duke of Anjou and Tavannes were the fanatics. Charles IX was the creature of his mother's malign influence and the victim of his own ferocious temperament which he had long indulged, and to which he now allowed monstrous license. For the rest the massacre of St. Bartholomew was perpetrated by men whose natures were compounded out of religious bigotry, political enmity, personal resentment or mere ruffianism and love of violence. The massacre of St. Bartholomew could not possibly have been of the remotest political benefit to any person. It was both a crime and a blunder. But Catherine de Medici was a ruler whose political conduct was governed by her personal feelings and prejudices. In the crisis in which she was, she had not the acumen to discern, or the courage to dare to follow, the course that lay open before her if she had had eyes to see and an understanding instead of a passionate heart. That course lay toward Italy and not toward the Netherlands. If France had reasserted her claims to Naples and Milan, then in the possession of Philip II, the nation would have been united in a common cause that would have appealed to ancient pride and achievement as well as existing animosity against Spain. England would have had no reason to be jealous, for her hand would have been free in Flanders. Moreover, in Italy France might have looked for support from Tuscany and Ferrara. Switzerland would have supported the enterprise; Venice would have made no opposition and the Emperor, for all his Spanish attachments, could not have done so. With the Turk in the Mediterranean on her side, France could have gone into war with Spain and the Pope without fear and with great promise of success.[2]

[1] The duke of Guise is not so bloody, neither did he kill any man himself but saved divers; he spake openly that for the admiral's death he was glad, for he knew him to be his enemy. But for the rest, the King had put to death such as might have done him very good service (*C. S. P. For.*, No. 584, September, 1572).

[2] Montluc clearly appreciated that this was the case and developed the idea in his *Commentaires*, VI, 231–33. Quite as remarkable are the observations of the Venetian ambassador: *Rel. vén.*, II, 171. Spain anticipated the possibility of a French attempt to recover the Milanais: "The King of Spain being suspicious of the said league has given commission that Italy and Milan be in readiness."— *C. S. P. For.*, No. 120, February 7, 1572, from Venice.

CHAPTER XVI

THE FOURTH CIVIL WAR

The massacre of St. Bartholomew, like a bolt out of a clear sky, precipitated a new storm—the fourth civil war. La Rochelle was the storm center, though Sancerre and Montauban were rocks of safety for the Huguenots of the center and south of France, no less than three thousand Protestants and Politiques of Toulouse finding refuge in the latter place.[1]   When Charles IX's murderous passion was overpast and reason returned, he attempted to avert a new war by offering favorable terms to the Rochellois.[2]   But when the town fortified itself and refused to trust the "favorable" terms offered by Biron and turned toward England for aid, the marshal was commanded to take the city by storm.[3]   The government was heavily embarrassed in its military preparations.   Money was scarce and the rate of interest 15 per cent.[4]   Soldiers of judgment and experience pointed out that without either Swiss or Germans the King could not successfully batter the town, "for Frenchmen were not fit for the keeping of artillery, or to make the body of the 'battle' of footmen," and the Swiss diet refused to let France draw more mercenaries from the Alpine lands.   The King was equally unsuccessful in his endeavor to recruit footmen in Germany.[5]

---

[1] *Hist. du Languedoc*, V, 528, note, 544, note 2.   On the siege of Montauban, see La Bret, *Histoire de Montauban*, 2 vols., 1841.   There is a letter of the marshal Brissac on the resistance in F. Fr., No. 15, 555, fol. 104.

[2] See abstract of Biron's commission in *C. S. P. For.*, November 6, 1572; cf. *Correspondance inédite d'Armand de Gontaut Biron, maréchal de France*, par E. de Barthélemy, Paris, 1874, from the originals at St. Petersburg.

[3] *Coll. des autographes*, 1844, No. 104, Charles IX to the duke of Longueville, November 4, 1572.

[4] *C. S. P. For.*, No. 640, November 13, 1572; cf. No. 637; *Archives de la maison d'Orange-Nassau*, IV, 38–39, letter of Brunynck, secretary to the prince of Orange, to John of Nassau, December, 1572.

[5] *C. S. P. For.*, Nos. 667, 673, §§17–20 (1572).

The enigmatical policy of Elizabeth was also a deterrant in the beginning of the war. While she sent the earl of Worcester into France in January, 1573, to treat of commerce and to dangle the prospect of her marrying Charles IX's youngest brother, the duke of Alençon, before the eyes of the French court,[1] the English queen did not turn a deaf ear to the petition of the Rochellois.[2] If after the massacre there was less fear of strengthening France by giving aid to the Low Countries, on the contrary it became doubly necessary for England not to break with Spain, so that the policy of Queen Elizabeth was a timid and hesitating one.

When England's policy was perceived to be so weak, the government pushed forward its military preparations against the city and the Italian artillery commander, Strozzi, in mid-December, took Marans, not far from La Rochelle, and put the garrison to the sword. But the Rochellois maintained the ramparts against all onslaught. The attacking army, under command of the duke of Anjou, lay in the dike under the curtain of the town walls, but could get no farther. To add to the discomfiture of the Catholics, the King's army was in want of food-stuffs on account of the rising of the country roundabout, especially Poitou and Limousin.[3]

The dearth, however, was more than local. The winter of 1572–73 was again a hard one, and though the spring of 1573 opened early and mild, there came recurrence of cold; so much so that processions were held, imploring the grace of God upon the fields where much of the grain was killed. The ensuing high

---

[1] C. S. P. For., Nos. 683 and 755, Worcester to the Queen, February 5, 1573.

[2] This petition is a remarkable compound of current politics and biblical history. In it the inhabitants of La Rochelle, her "tres obeissains fidelles subjects," beg that she will consider and follow the example of Constantine, who broke off all alliance with his friend Licinius to whom he had given his sister in marriage, on account of his tyranny practiced on the Christians of the East. They remind her also of the evil done by Herod in keeping his rash oath. She ought not therefore to keep the league with those who wish to exterminate her people in Guyenne, which belongs to her, and whose arms she bears. If she will succour them they will willingly expose their lives and goods in order to acknowledge her as their sovereign and natural princess (ibid., No. 682, 1572).

[3] Ibid., No. 800, February 28, 1573; No. 948, May 3, 1573; Chroniques Fontenaisiennes, 166, 167.

prices of grain were made higher owing to the fact that great amounts of it were stored by the dealers against the market. There were bread riots and popular tumults in various localities and many towns fixed a maximum price. This condition of things aggravated the state of war throughout the country. Multitudes of people crowded the towns. These refugees brought their possessions with them, their linen and household goods, their sheep and their cattle, which they were forced to sell for a song in order to buy bread.

The hard times also led to the migration of people from province to province and increased the vagabondage that already existed. The hunger was so great that men and women devoured vegetables, and even grain, raw. In consequence of the lack of food or the way in which it was consumed, suffering and disease ensued. Those who were fortunate enough to possess a garden plot with a few vines or fruits or vegetables were compelled to guard them by night and by day against the spoiler. It was considered an act of charity for those who had fruit trees, after themselves gathering the fruit, to permit those more wretched than they to strip the branches of their leaves and consume them. Paris suffered with the rest of France, for it was impossible to supply the city with food from the Beauce and Picardy and Champagne. Grain was imported from Spain and even from the Barbary coast, the timely arrival of six vessels, on one occasion, saving the capital from the pinch of famine.[1] The "hard times," which lasted more than a year, naturally bore heaviest upon the poorer classes, whose wretched condition contrasted with the luxury and vanity of the wealthier classes, with whom extravagance reached an extreme.[2]

[1] See Claude Haton, II, 710, 711, 717, 718, 722-25, 726, 729, 731. The government sent out inspectors to make an inventory of the grain still available. Much of it was confiscated for the use of the army at an established price, and a maximum price fixed for the sale of the remainder.

[2] Ibid., 715, 716 (see a discourse upon the extreme dearth in France and upon the means to remedy it, in Arch. cur., VI, 423). The dearness of all things, according to the writer, probably Bodin, is the result of the excessive luxury which prevails among the higher classes and the combination made by the merchants to raise prices. He proposes the establishment of public granaries and that the government price be made obligatory for all dealers.

During the winter there was a complete cessation of hostilities before La Rochelle. Not a cannon was discharged all through the months of December, January, and February.[1] In derision of the King's camp, some of the more daring of the Huguenot soldiery strutted about adorned with cards and dice to signify that the King's troops were better gamesters than soldiers.[2] The truth is, Protestant France was not all of one mind to continue the resistance. There were two parties in the Huguenot capital, the irreconcilables, who wanted war to the knife and favored looking to England for support; and a more moderate faction led by that Bayard of the Protestants, the heroic La Noue, who, believing that the great enemy of France and of the Huguenots was Spain,[3] with proper guarantees stood ready to forget and forgive the massacre, so far as it was possible for human memory and feeling to do so, recognizing that that event was a catastrophe to Catholic as well as to Protestant France; that, however monstrous it was as a crime, as a blunder its effects were even more calamitous.

As for the crown, it was even more anxious than the moderate Huguenots to avoid a protracted siege and come to some form of settlement.[4] With this aim Charles IX, through the medium of the duke of Longueville, governor of Picardy, early in October had made overtures to La Noue, who was still in Flanders. After some hesitation La Noue came to Paris where he had a conference with the King and the queen mother. So trusted and so capable was he that Charles IX gave him practically discretionary powers to bring about a settlement, and in the middle of November La Noue went to La Rochelle.

[1] C. S. P. For., No. 800, February 28, 1573.

[2] Ibid., No. 1,000, May 31, No. 1,027, June 9, 1573.

[3] The Politiques hoped to persuade Charles IX to stop the war at home and exact redress from Spain for the massacre in Florida by attacking the Spanish West Indies. Even the duke of Anjou favored this. See Appendix XXX.

[4] La Popelinière, XXI, 214 and 232 bis; C. S. P. For., No. 1,042, Dr. Dale to Lord Burghley, June 16, 1573: "The hearts of all men were being discouraged with the long siege" and the King's heart bled "to see the misery of his people that die for famine by the ways where he rode."

For days the intrepid leader vainly endeavored to secure entrance into the city.[1] Finally, on November 26 he was reluctantly admitted. During the cold and weary weeks of December, January, and February, while besieged and besiegers were lying on their arms upon the walls or in the trenches, La Noue alternately entreated and expostulated, urging the necessity of peace in the face of vilification, the Huguenot minister La Place even calling him "perfide traistre, déserteur de son parti." "The word of the King," said Catherine de Medici, to the deputies of the Reformed on one occasion, "ought to be sufficient for you." "No," replied one of them, "not since St. Bartholomew."[2] Even La Noue's influence could not overcome the radical party in La Rochelle which imprisoned as many as advocated capitulation no matter what the terms might be. At last on March 12, 1573, the brave man gave up hope of persuading the zealot populace and returned to the King's camp. Angry at the failure of these pacific overtures, the government forces redoubled their attacks. On March 22 the royal artillery opened a terrible fire upon the city, more than 1,500 cannon-balls being thrown. On April 7 there was a furious assault, even women fighting on the wall, and the attack was repeated on the 10th, 13th, and 14th, on the last day there being five separate attempts to take the city by storm.

Montgomery, who had been sent to England for assistance,[3] appeared with about seventy ships, and was on the point of giving battle in the bay, when a fleet of forty vessels from the ports of Brittany and Normandy hove in sight. These ships, with what Anjou could muster, made too great a body for Montgomery to

[1] La Rochelle at first refused to let La Noue enter. On the whole matter see Hauser, La Noue, chap. ii.

[2] C. S. P. For., No. 1,547, March 21, 1573; Raumer, II, 265; the marshals Biron and Strozzi, with Pinart, were commissioned for the purpose (Arch. hist. du Poitou, XII, 233). The negotiations may be seen in detail in Loutzchiski, Doc. inédits, 62 ff.

[3] Vie de La Noue, 95; Letter of Charles IX to the duke of Anjou, February 7, 1573, Coll. Lajariette, Paris, 1860, No. 669; Coll. Godefroy, CCLVI, No. 57. At the same time Charles IX wrote in person to Montgomery, trying to lure him from the enterprise he was engaged in. See Appendix XXXI.

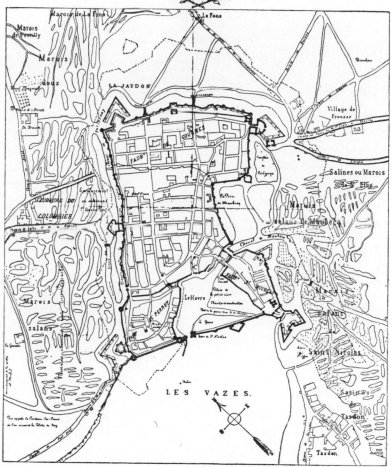

Plan de la Rochelle en M·D·LXXII.

From *Histoire au siège de La Rochelle en 1573*, traduite du Latin de Philippe Cauriana (La Rochelle, 1856).

risk an engagement, and so he retired to Belle-Ile, which was made a Protestant naval base.[1]

Meanwhile, the Swiss in camp had toiled in the trenches and "swamp angel" guns were established in the marshes to batter the port of St. Nicholas. On June 11 the supreme assault on La Rochelle was made and repulsed. The attacking force by an escalade gained possession of the rampart but found a mighty trench before them, so that they were constrained to beat their way along the rampart in the hopes of finding a place to cross it. Those in the camp, seeing their comrades gain the ramparts, cried, "ville gaignée!" But the Rochellois lured the enemy along the wall "and when they were entered set upon them both before and behind with such fury that they were all either slain or hurt, and the rest who were coming to succor the foremost were repulsed with great loss."[2]

After the failure of the great assault, because the soldiery without was so much discouraged by failure, angry for lack of pay,[3] and weakened by losses and disease,[4] the only recourse of the crown was to capitulate with the Rochellois with as much reservation as possible. Villeroy's report on the condition of things before La Rochelle was too convincing to be ignored.[5] In the first week of July, after two days' deliberation, Charles IX signed the terms, although they were not published at once.[6]

The general provisions were that those of La Rochelle should have life, goods, and liberty of conscience and that the town, together with Montauban, Sancerre, and Nîmes should also have "free

[1] C. S. P. Ven., Nos. 540, 541, April 6 and 20, 1573.

[2] Ibid., For., No. 1,050, June 22, 1573; Chroniques fontenaisiennes, 169.

[3] See the series of documents on this head in Coll. Godefroy, CCLVI, Nos. 25, 29, 30, 38, 41–43, 46, 73, 77.

[4] When the army disbanded, it was a frequent sight in the villages to see the wounded or sick being transported in baggage wagons (Claude Haton, II, 737). The villages near La Rochelle where the camp had been established were burned upon the evacuation of the troops "to prevent the plague which began to be hot." —C. S. P. For., No. 1,107, Wilkes to Walsingham, July 31, 1573; cf. No. 1,052, June 25, to the same effect.

[5] C. S. P. For., No. 1,072, Dr. Dale to the Queen, late in June, 1573.

[6] The articles were sent to the Catholic camp on July, 6.

exercise of the religion and find a garrison for themselves." The edict declared that the memory of all things which had happened since the 24th of August should be extinguished; that the Catholic religion was to be established throughout the country, except at the four cities named. Bailiffs and judges ordinary were to see to the decent interment of those who died in the Reformed religion. Those who gave security that they would change their religion should be admitted to the universities, schools, hospitals, without hindrance, and finally that any French Protestant might sell or alienate his goods and retire to any country he pleased, provided it were not to the territory of any princes where war obtained, a provision obviously intended to protect Spain in the Netherlands.[1]

But the fourth war of religion was not yet entirely over. While La Rochelle with 2,000 men daily labored to repair its battered walls, Sancerre was not to be tempted by the terms, and the south of France still held out. The heroic resistance of Sancerre, perched like an eagle's nest on a steep hill above the Loire, is one of the epic stories of the sixteenth century. For nearly eight months (January 3 to August 19, 1573) the city withstood every assault and only succumbed at last when reduced to direst famine. Horses, asses, dogs, cats, rats were all consumed. Soup made of boiled parchment became a luxury. The inhabitants ate "pain de paille haschée et d'ordorze y meslant du fumier de chevaux et tout ce qu'ils pensoient avoir quelque suc." Even the bodies of the dead were disinterred and consumed. When human nature could endure no more, Sancerre threw itself upon the mercy of its conqueror. It was granted liberty of worship and the people spared from massacre and pillage for the price of forty thousand livres; but its mediaeval glory was shorn from it. The splendid clock-tower of the town was destroyed, its ramparts razed.[2]

In spite of the pacification at La Rochelle and the fall of San-

[1] Hist. du Languedoc, V, 543, note; C. S. P. For., No. 1,090, July 11, 1573.

[2] Lery, Histoire mémorable de la ville de Sancerre, contenant les entreprises, buteries, assaux et autres efforts des assiégeans: les résistances, faits magnanimes, la famine extrème et délivrance des assiegez, 1574; Discours de l'extrème famine etc. dont les assiegez de la ville de Sancerre ont été affligez et ont usé environ trois mois, Arch. cur., VIII, 21.

cerre, the Midi still resisted. In Languedoc and Dauphiné the Huguenots were especially strong.[1] Their harvests were garnered into walled towns; their army included 2,000 arquebusiers besides the Huguenot gentry and they were well prepared for further war.[2] On the anniversary of the massacre (August 24, 1573) deputies of all the churches of the south convened at Montauban and took the preliminary steps in the formation of the great Huguenot confederation which in December assumed the direction of the war, the regulation of finances, civil administration, and religious protection.[3]

Languedoc was divided into two governments with Montauban and Nîmes as centers under the authority of the viscounts of Paulin and St. Romain, each assisted and controlled by a council. The councils, in turn, in all important matters were required to consult the local assemblies of Protestants. All these assemblies were elective. The Protestant organization thus constituted an all but full-fledged state within a state, asserting its own power to lay taxes, to administer justice, to carry on war, and to make peace. It was estimated that 20,000 men in these regions were able to bear arms.

In consequence of the continuance of the war in the south the Swiss and the rest of the soldiery not yet licensed were sent from the camp before La Rochelle into Dauphiné and Languedoc. But the government was heavily embarrassed financially and had been compelled to resort to forced loans in Paris and the old shift of mortgaging the revenue until the grant of the clergy was made in

---

[1] C. S. P. For., No. 1,101, July 23, No. 1,107, July 31, 1573. In Languedoc and Dauphiné the Huguenots were strong, and possessed of many towns (see a letter of Louis of Nassau in Archives de la maison d'Orange-Nassau, IV, 75 and the "Names of all the towns in the south of France of which the Huguenot party could be sure of, together with a list of the noblemen attached to the party" in Appendix XXXII).

[2] Vie de La Noue, 99; C. S. P. For., No. 965, May 16, No. 1,095, July 23, 1573. A deputation of Huguenots of Languedoc came to Fontainebleau in September, 1573 (cf. Letter of Schomberg to Louis of Nassau, September 29, 1573, Archives de la maison d'Orange-Nassau, IV, 211 and Appendix 117).

[3] Long, 115, 116. The instrument of government contained 89 articles.

June.[1]   Even then it did not urge war.   Charles IX, jealous of
the Guises and of the military reputation which his brother had
acquired, was again manifesting his hatred of the restraint imposed upon him, and desirous of recovering his independence.

The tendency of France was to return to its earlier policy which
had been interrupted by the massacre.[2]   Charles again inclined
to sustain Holland in its rebellion against Spain,[3] at least under-
handedly.   To strike Spain was at the same time to strike at all
the influences which he hated.   Accordingly France made overtures
anew to the prince of Orange, although it was not without repugnance that William of Orange brought himself to listen to them.[4]
But the voice of policy was stronger than sentiment.[5]   For on

[1] C. S. P. For., Nos. 972, 986, March 20 and 30, 1573.   The collection of these
forced loans was expedited by the presence of Strozzi's men-at-arms and the Scotch
Guard in the Louvre; and two bands of Swiss at St. Cloud.   In this way, Charles
IX was able to collect the money "without danger of commotion," and avoided
that worst of expedients to the crown, the States-General (see particulars in Dr.
Dale's letter to Burghley of January 11, 1573, ibid., No. 1,291).   In June the
assembly of the clergy agreed to furnish the queen mother 200,000 livres and within
three years to redeem 1,800,000 livres' worth of the King's debts.   The clergy made
a great stroke by obtaining the creation of four receivers-general for the collection
of these subsidies, the appointments to which they sold for between 600,000 and
700,000 livres, thus saving themselves that amount in the final (ibid., No. 1,027,
June 9, 1573).   But this relief came too late for the government to continue the
prosecution of the war before La Rochelle.   The capitulation with the Rochellois
was too far advanced to be withdrawn.   Moreover, the crown itself was anxious
to close the war.

[2] Catherine de Medici to Schomberg, September 13, 1572, Arch. de la maison
d'Orange-Nassau, IV, Appendix, No. 13; Weill, 86; Revue retrospective, V, 363.

[3] Nég. Tosc., III, 876.   On July 7 the Tuscan ambassador wrote: "E, se
questo regno si liberassi delle guerre civili, saria facil cosa la rompessi con
Spagna; chè questo, credo, sia il fine di tutti li trattamenti che fa Orange in questo
regno.—Ibid., 883.

[4] Ibid., IV, 108, 109.

[5] In the same month William of Orange dispatched to France the Seigneur
de Lumbres, whose popularity with the King was so great that he even offered to
take him into his service (Archives de la maison d'Orange-Nassau, Introd., p. 21,
and p. 165), and another agent with instructions to treat with the King and the queen
mother (ibid., IV, 119–24, May, 1573).   William stipulated for the preservation
of the rights and privileges of whatever provinces and towns might be conquered
by France, and that in case of open war by France upon Spain, in lieu of an
annual subsidy of 400,000 florins, France should give assistance with men and

December 11, 1572, the famous siege of Haarlem had begun. It was Alva's purpose by the capture of this city to cut the communications between south Holland, where the prince of Orange was, and north Holland.[1]

From Germany the faithful and far-sighted Schomberg earnestly urged the project and so artfully did he fulfil his mission that the elector palatine, the landgrave, and the archbishop of Cologne all espoused it.[2] "The repose of the kingdom, the security of the state, the ruin of the great enemy of France, direct and firm alliance with the princes of Germany, the subversion of all the designs of the house of Austria, and the culmination of your desires, is in the hands of your majesty," he wrote to Catherine on March 23.[3] At last, after months of deliberation and delay, the threads of these tortuous negotiations were all drawn together at a secret interview of Catherine de Medici with Louis of Nassau at Blamont in Lorraine, in December, 1573.[4]

ships of war, besides the sum mentioned, to be paid within two years after the conclusion of peace (ibid., IV, 116–19; cf. the prince of Orange to Louis of Nassau upon the proposed French alliance, June 17, 1573).

[1] Ibid., IV, 33. On May 15, 1573, the prince of Orange concluded a treaty with England, permitting the English to enter the Scheldt in return for which the prince was to be permitted to purchase arms and ammunition and powder in England (Archives de la maison d'Orange-Nassau, IV, 94). For William of Orange's connection with La Rochelle see ibid., 43 and 56. Compare letter of Charles IX to the duke of Anjou, March 18, 1573, complaining of the depredations of the "Wartegeux" on the Norman coast (Coll. Godefroy, CCLVIII, No.49).

[2] Archives de la maison d'Orange-Nassau, IV, 273, 274; Correspondance de Catherine de Médicis, IV, 270, 271, note.

[3] Archives de la maison d'Orange-Nassau, IV, 270 and Appendix 43. Schomberg and Louis of Nassau drew up the articles of the proposed treaty. In Appendix 44 will be found the articles as originally drawn up, and on p. 116 the modified form of them as they were changed by the prince of Orange. The most important change is that whereby the prince altered the word "subjection" as applied to the Netherlands to "protectorate." The further idea is expressed that these negotiations would be fruitless unless the Edict of Pacification were established with full force in France (ibid., IV, 270, 271). On the whole subject of French negotiations in Germany after St. Bartholomew see Waddington, Rev. hist., XLII, 269 ff.

[4] De Thou, VII, 37 (cf. Louis of Nassau's letter to his brother on the subject in Archives de la maison d'Orange-Nassau, IV, 278 ff.). Charles IX was ill at the time and the queen mother went alone to Blamont (ibid., IV, 276, 277; Mém du duc de Bouillon). The Spanish ambassador in France was not unobservant of the

But there was yet another reason why the crown of France was desirous of closing the conflict at home, which goes far to explain the government's willingness to compromise with La Rochelle. The throne of Poland had become vacant upon the death of Sigismund Augustus, the last of the Jagiello house, on July 7, 1572. The crown of Poland was an elective one, the suffrage being in the hands of the diet, composed solely of the two privileged orders. In the factional strife that too often ensued, the deadlock was sometimes broken by the election of an outside prince. This vicious and unnational policy triumphed in 1573. The Emperor, the King of Spain, and France had each a candidate. But Poland had no mind to experience the fate of Bohemia and pass under the suzerainty of the Hapsburgs. Spain, too, in the person of her ambassador, was deprived of a hearing and compelled to make overtures in writing. In this wise the way was cleared for French diplomacy. In the autumn of 1572, Charles IX had been sounded by the Poles as to the candidacy of the duke of Anjou and had intimated the conditions to be expected.[1] On December 19, the secretary of the bishop of Valence, the French agent who had been hastily dispatched to Poland, arrived in Paris, and gave great hope for the election of the duke of Anjou, though the Polish diet had not met yet on account of the plague.[2]

When it convened on April 15, 1573, the dexterous feat was accomplished by the papal legate, Cardinal Commendone, who, for his spiritual master, was hostile to the Emperor for having lately made a three years' truce with the Turks and thus marred the glory of Lepanto, and opposed in principle to the widening

favorable policy of Charles toward the Netherlands and so informed the duke of Alva (*Archives de la maison d'Orange-Nassau*, IV, 132). The peace of La Rochelle was a hard blow to Spain (Languet, *Epist. secr.*, I, 201; St. Goard to Charles IX, July 17, 1573 in *Archives de la maison d'Orange-Nassau*, IV, 164-69). These negotiations of the prince of Orange and his brother with England and France, however, came too late to save Haarlem. On July 12 the unhappy city succumbed. On the 14th the Spaniards entered and began a regular massacre, in which nearly 1,800 persons were either slain with the sword, hanged, or drowned (*ibid.*, IV, 173; cf. a letter of the prince of Orange to Louis of Nassau, giving details of the surrender on July 22, 1573, *ibid.*, 175).

[1] *C. S. P. For.*, No. 686 (1572).   [2] *Ibid.*, No. 673, December 20, 1572.

of Spain's activities anywhere, in view of the supreme struggle of the faith in France and the Low Countries, where the cause of Rome was in sore need of Spanish support. The French envoys[1] then skilfully introduced the name of the duke of Anjou, lauding his Catholic virtues in the ears of a Catholic populace; promising that if elected Henry of Valois would spend all his revenues—how little these were the Poles could not know—in Poland for the benefit of the kingdom; they promised, too, that the prospective king would recover from the Muscovite all the territories whereof the kingdom of Poland had been despoiled in times past, as well as Wallachia from the Turks.[2] The arguments told, and on May 19, 1573, the duke of Anjou was elected king of Poland.

On August 8, 1573, the official deputation of Polish nobles sent to France to notify the duke of Anjou of his election reached Metz, and soon afterward (June 24, St. John's Day) arrived at Paris. They were the advance guard of almost two thousand Polish nobles and gentry who visited the kingdom during this summer. They were all magnificently lodged and entertained in the city at the expense of the crown, or rather at the expense of the people, for a new tax was imposed for purposes of entertainment. The appearance of the Poles struck the French with amazement. They were all tall, handsome men, "speaking Latin down to the very hostlers," but marvelously given to drink and great gourmands. The wine-shops of the capital were almost drunk dry. Two Poles, the saying went, drank more wine and consumed more meat than six Frenchmen.[3]

---

[1] These were Montluc, bishop of Valence, and M. de Rambouillet. The former's speeches (April 10 and 22), are printed in *Mém. de l'estat de France*, II, 147, 224, in a French translation. The original discourses were in Latin. In *Arch. cur.*, IX, 137, is a letter of one of Rambouillet's suite.

[2] See the account of the election in *C. S. P. For.*, No. 1,082, June 5, 1573; cf. Languet, *Epist. secr.*, I, 189; Castelnau, ed. Le Laboureur, III, 298. The news of the duke of Anjou's success was naturally received with greater pleasure in Paris than anywhere else in Europe. Bonfires were lighted and the *Te Deum* sung in honor of his election (*C. S. P. For.*, No. 1,027, June 9, 1573). The clergy, in the assembly of the clergy which took place soon after the news arrived, voted the duke a subsidy of 300,000 crowns (*ibid.*, No. 992).

[3] Claude Haton, II, 734; *Nég. Tosc.*, III, 886, 887.

The honor of the crown of Poland salved the wounded pride of Anjou, still before La Rochelle. But the army murmured so much that a royal mandate was issued making it a misdemeanor to argue or to discuss the Polish election in the streets of Paris, or to discountenance the election of the duke of Anjou to the throne of Poland in written work or speech.[1] Without victory, without pay, without even enough to eat, the soldiers grumbled to the point of mutiny and averred that the government was bribed, and took the Huguenot money in order to provide funds for the King's trip to Poland.[2] Henry dared not openly leave the camp for fear of their rebellion and was compelled to make a feint of going boating in the bay and then effect an escape by sea to Nantes.[3]

Distance lent enchantment to the view. Poland was in a wretched condition through the dissensions of the nobility. The Emperor was angry and talked of stopping the duke *en route*.[4] Lithuania seceded and entered into an alliance with the duke of Prussia, the king of Sweden, and Russia, to overthrow the Polish government.[5] The Hanseatic cities, too, like Dantzig, Riga, and Revel, were very dissatisfied, for it was open knowledge that Poland aspired to the control of their commerce.[6] The Poles

[1] *Nég. Tosc.*, III, 886, 887.   [2] Claude Haton, II, p. 735.

[3] *C. S. P. For.*, No. 1,100, July 23, 1573.

[4] The existence of a plot to kidnap the duke of Anjou in Germany in order to force France to return the Three Bishoprics was suspected by Schomberg (*Archives de la maison d'Orange-Nassau*, IV, Appendix, Nos. 112, 113). The duke was also afraid to go to Poland by way of Germany, fearing to get into difficulties on account of the massacre of St. Bartholomew, which still vividly angered the Protestant princes (*ibid.*, IV, Introd., p. xxvi, and pp. 15, 19, 26, 32). His first thought was to go by way of Venice and Ragusa, through Servia, Bulgaria, and Moldavia (Languet, *Epist. secr.*, I, 197; *Archives de la maison d'Orange-Nassau*, IV, 168, note). The advantage of the ancient alliance between France and Venice at this time would have been great. There was also some thought of his going entirely by sea, and the good offices of England were invoked to protect his journey (Castelnau, ed. Le Laboureur, III, 345). The young prince of Condé had been invited to go along, but excused himself on the ground that he was afraid of being arrested for his father's debts, "being a marvellously great sum."—*C. S. P. For.*, No. 1,245, December 12, 1573.

[5] *Ibid.*, No. 1,097, July 18, 1573, from Frankfurt.

[6] *Ibid.*, No. 1,177, September 20, 1573; *Archives de la maison d'Orange-Nassau,* IV, 295.

themselves soon discovered that their new king was a goose without a golden egg. For the French lawyers found an interpretation of the promise that the French would discharge the debts of the realm to the effect that the promise meant only those arising since the death of the late king. The Polish agents in Paris made wry faces at the finding, but so the agreement was registered by the Parlement of Paris on September 17, 1573.[1] In the same month the duke of Anjou set out for his new kingdom, going via Nancy, Heidelberg, and Frankfurt to Cracow. Metz he avoided because the Emperor, still sullen and still smarting from the loss of the city twenty-one years before (1552), had commanded the imperial commissioners appointed to conduct him, to receive him in Metz as though it were a free city of the empire, which the French naturally refused to permit.

Again the foolish affection of Catherine de Medici for one of her children,[2] again her political fatuity, threw France far off from the course she should have followed. As before the massacre, so now that course was the path to Italy.[3] Instead of narrowing the field of her ambition for her children and concentrating her power, not content with Poland for the duke of Anjou, she even dreamed of the Hapsburg crown for Charles IX,[4] and that of England for Alençon. Schomberg's missions in 1572-73 to Germany[5] were not merely to dispose the German princes in favor of France's projected enterprise in the Netherlands, but also to persuade them, especially the electors of Cologne and the Palatinate, in favor of the French King's imperial ambition. France's policy in Poland[6] and her policy in Germany were two

[1] C. S. P. For., No. 1,168, September 18, 1573.

[2] For Catherine's intense interest in the Polish question, see Vol. IV of her Correspondance, passim, and Arch. de la maison d'Orange-Nassau, IV, 267.

[3] Commentaires et lettres de Montluc, V, 299-306, 309-18, 322-24—a series of remarkable political judgments.

[4] Archives de la maison d'Orange-Nassau, IV, 31; Appendix, No. 69 and p. 96.

[5] Ibid., IV, Appendix, Letters 1-8 refer to Schomberg's mission to Germany in the spring and summer of 1572.

[6] The history of Henry of Anjou's career in Poland has been written at length by the marquis de Noailles, Henri de Valois et la Pologne, Paris, 1867 (see also

parts of one grand design and in a large sense had to stand or fall together. Peace with the Huguenots was an essential element in the forwarding of this project, especially with the Protestant German princes, as Schomberg pointed out.[1]

But there were two great obstacles in the way of advance—German resentment because of the massacre of St. Bartholomew[2] and the counter-diplomacy of Spain.[3] The Guisard-Spanish party at home naturally exerted itself to thwart the prosecution of these designs.[4] Morvilliers warned Charles IX that their continuance would involve France in a war with Spain.[5]

L'Epinois, "La Pologne en 1572," *R. Q. H.,* IV, 1868, p. 266; Bain, "The Polish Interregnum," *English Hist. Review,* IV, 645). In Coll. Godefroy, CCLVI, Nos. 54, 62, 64, 66, 70, 72, is a series of letters dealing with French interest in Poland at this time.

[1] *Archives de la maison d'Orange-Nassau,* IV, Appendix, Nos. 69 and 71.

[2] *Ibid.,* IV, Appendix, No. 17, Schomberg to Catherine de Medici, October 9, 1572. The landgrave bluntly said that twice before such overtures had been made to German princes—in 1567 and 1571—and that civil war and the massacre had followed (*ibid.,* No. 72).

[3] St. Goard to Charles IX, July 9, 1573, *ibid.,* IV, Appendix, No. 66; Schomberg to the duke of Anjou, February 10, 1573; *ibid.,* Appendix, No. 34. The intense Catholic prejudices of the duke of Anjou, now king of Poland, were a serious bar to the progress of Schomberg's negotiations in Germany. He warned the duke not to give the impression of Spanish leanings (Schomberg to the duke of Anjou, October 9, 1572, *ibid.,* IV, Appendix, No. 18), and seems almost to have persuaded him to abandon his intense Catholic-Spanish predilection (*ibid.,* pp. 15, 268). The duke of Anjou is even said to have given Schomberg 100,000 francs. The letter is said to have been burned at the time of the Coconnas conspiracy in order to shield the duke of Alva's son (*ibid.,* IV, 384).

[4] Charles IX to St. Goard, May 10, 1573, regarding a dispatch of the Spanish ambassador to Philip II telling of the negotiations of the King with Louis of Nassau (*ibid.,* IV, Appendix, No. 55).

[5] *Ibid.,* IV, Appendix, No. 51.

CHAPTER XVII •

THE LAST DAYS OF CHARLES IX. THE CONSPIRACY OF THE POLITIQUES

The war in the south, during the months of these negotiations, had gone on in its own course almost unhindered by the government. Many of the men of service had gone with Anjou into Poland and many others, especially the Swiss, were licensed. In consequence the Huguenots made themselves masters of the Rhone, even seizing Avignon, to the great anger of the Pope, who refused to receive Paul de Foix as French ambassador to Rome on the double ground that he was of the Huguenot persuasion and because the French King would not give safe-conduct to troops from Italy to go to Avignon for the purpose of recovering it.[1] After the departure of his brother for Poland, Charles IX weakly took up the Protestant issue again, and he and his mother spent three days at Chantilly with Montmorency in consideration of the course to follow.[2] Deputations from various provinces came to the King to petition immediate reduction of the taxes on account of the exhausted state of the country, but there was a unanimous wish against calling another session of the estates on account of the expense.[3] As an earnest of the King's good intentions, the prince of Condé was made governor of Picardy, an office made vacant by the timely decease of the duke of Longueville, the prince, to the chagrin of the duke of Nevers who was an aspirant for the post, having recovered from the smallpox, with which the duke of Alençon also fell ill.[4] The King had planned to convene deputies of the Huguenots of Languedoc and Dauphiné at least at Compiègne, but fell ill of smallpox[5] and the project came to an

[1] C. S. P. For., Nos. 1,202, 1,286, November 11, 1573, January 2, 1574.

[2] Nég. Tosc., III, 894, December 23, 1573.

[3] Ibid., 891–93, November 5, 1573.

[4] C. S. P. For., Nos. 1,132, 1,138, August 18–22, 1573.

[5] The attack was aggravated by a heavy cold taken while hunting so that Charles IX was compelled for a season to quarter himself in a small inn at

end.[1] To add to embarrassments Paris and Rouen, where the populace were of the opposing religions, entered into war for the restraint
of foodstuffs, Paris stopping all wine passing down the Seine and
Rouen in turn preventing corn from passing up the river to Paris.[2]
The economic condition of the country gave the government great
concern. Hard times and high prices still prevailed and the
measures of the government only irritated things the more, though
some of them were wisely meant. For example, in February,
1574, an edict of the King forbade the circulation of all foreign
silver coin, as well as that which was mutilated or debased. When
the merchants of Troyes learned of this condemnation of all foreign
or cut coin, they sent a deputation to remonstrate with the King,
saying that their town and the county of Champagne as well as
all Lorraine and Burgundy abounded with this money and no
other; and it was not possible to exclude these coins from the
country without entailing ruin, if the edict were enforced. They
further urged that the edict would act as a serious bar to traffic
across the frontier. But the King refused to rescind the ordinance.
In consequence, those familiar with money palmed off the forbidden currency upon the simpler folk, who found to their dismay
that they had been cheated, when the King's officers refused to
accept these coins in payment of taxes. Nevertheless, in the
long run, the action raised the standard of coin in France.[3] Less
wise action was the new sale of offices—those of the *procureurs
du roi*—and it was even suggested that the office of advocate be
made a salable one, but fortunately for the administration of
justice, this was not done.[4]

Vitry. He was not scarred by the pox but he lost flesh alarmingly by reason of the
illness and never recovered his health, and passed into quick consumption (cf.
C. S. P. For, No. 1,229, November 18, 1573, Dr. Dale to Burghley).

[1] *Nég. Tosc.*, III, 891; *R. Q. H.*, XXXIV, 485.

[2] *C. S. P. For.*, No. 1,235, November, 1573.

[3] The écu which formerly had circulated as 57 sous *tournois* went up to 58;
Spanish pistols, which were at 55 rose to 56; testons de France valued at 12 sous
by the edict rose to 12 sous 6 d. *tournois*. Bad coin was driven out of the realm.
Claude Haton, II, 749, 750.

[4] *Ibid.*, 752, 753.

Popular suspicion was also attached to an ordinance commanding the governors of the provinces, through the bailiffs and senechals, to take a census in their localities, giving the name, surname, and employment of all men between the ages of twenty-one and sixty. It was beyond the imagination of the people to know the reason of this action, or to divine what the King meant to do. Some thought that the crown was going to establish a local constabulary for the arrest of the numerous robbers and vagabonds, who, under the guise of war, looted and pillaged the country, and that men would be chosen in each parish like the francs-archers of the days of Louis XII and Francis I. Others thought that the King merely wanted to raise a new army to send into Languedoc where the Huguenots and the Poiltiques were now making common cause together. Others still thought that the device was one for taxing purposes.[1]

Worst of all, however, was an event that happened late in December, 1573, which threatened to make the war general again. This event was the discovery of a plot to overthrow the Protestants in La Rochelle. The King seems to have been innocent of the project, and repudiated the government's part in it. The author of the plot was La Haye, the president of Poitiers, who ingratiated himself with the people of the town and managed to secure some of his accomplices positions in the guard. The gate of the city was to be treacherously opened to a strong force secretly brought up under cover of darkness on the night of December 15. But on the day before, one of the company betrayed the plan to the authorities of the city.[2] Tremendous indignation prevailed in Huguenot circles as a result of this disclosure. English merchants in Rouen, Dieppe, and the Norman ports for a time apprehended local massacres, for Montgomery was known to be in England.[3] In the provinces, from day to day, news came of the doings of the

[1] Claude Haton, II, 760 (1574).

[2] See details in C. S. P. Ven., No. 567, December 30, 1573. The queen mother was accused of planning to take La Rochelle by surprise (Archives de la maison d'Orange-Nassau, IV, 309–11; Nég. Tosc., III, 896).

[3] C. S. P. Ven., Nos. 568, 569, January 22, February 1, 1574.

Huguenots. La Noue was in Lusignan; there were Huguenot movements in Poitou, Limousin, and Guyenne;[1] again it was word from Sedan, the seat of the duke of Bouillon, that there was a suspicious rendezvous of Huguenots there; another time that there were 500 Protestant horse and 1,200 footmen assembled at St. Lô.[2] The government was under apprehension lest suddenly, either at home some danger might assail France, or that abroad, by the actions of Germany and England, material assistance might be given to the Huguenots to carry their designs into effect, for the waters of the Channel and the Bay of Biscay swarmed with privateers.[3] On February 25 the Reformed party issued a famous declaration "printed at Rochelle in diverse languages that the truth of our cause and purpose may be known to all Christians." Finally, news of real material importance came that Montgomery, whom Guitery had joined, had landed near Coutances and marched to Carentan, which surrendered within two days. Since then Montgomery had taken various forts and castles, among them Argentan, and ten pieces of artillery.[4] Charles IX immediately commissioned the sieur de Torcy, lieutenant-general in the government of the Ile-de-France and the viscount of Turenne to treat with him, making promise of favor and protection if he would lay down his arms. But Montgomery replied that the memory of St. Bartholomew was too fresh for him to do so; and for that matter he would have to refer the King's terms to the body of the Reformed, of which he was only a member.[5]

[1] For details of this war see *Chronique des guerres en Poitou, Aunis, Xaintonge et Angoumois de 1574 à 1576.* ed. by Fontenelle de Vaudoré, Paris, 1841.

[2] *C. S. P. For.*, No. 570, February 6, No. 572, February 28; *ibid., Eng.,* No. 1,336, March 8, No. 1,338, March 8, No. 1,357, March 23, No. 1,342, March 15 (1574).

[3] On March 9, 1573, Sir Thomas Smith wrote to Walsingham: "Pirates of all nations infest our seas and under the flag of the prince of Orange or the count of Montgomery, pillage the English and foreigners impartially." (Cf. Walsingham, 392. *C. S. P. Ven.*, No. 575, March 24, 1574.)

[4] Montgomery to Burghley, from Carentan, March 23, 1574 (C. S. P. For., 1351; cf. *C. S. P. Ven.*, No. 576, March 26; Delisle, *Les deux sièges de Valognes en 1562 et 1574*, St. Lô, 1890).

[5] *C. S. P. For.*, No. 1,352. Commission from the King to the sieur de Torcy, etc., dated Bois de Vincennes, March 11, 1574. Montgomery's reply is subjoined,

The Huguenots possessed a hierarchy of religious assemblies which served to unite their forces, through consistories, colloquies, and provincial synods, into a national body. Yet there was not an absolute uniformity in this organization. In the north of France each town maintained its own particular administration, separate and distinct. La Rochelle is a type of this kind and was fiercely jealous of its "franchises and liberties" after the manner of the German cities.[1] In the south, however, these local governments fused to form the great association, which rendered possible the creation of a genuine Huguenot political state. This development was materially aided by the Politiques. For one of the results of the massacre of St. Bartholomew was the crystallization of the liberal Catholic element represented by the marshal Montmorency and his brother, Damville, into a real political party. It was composed of a group of young nobles, ambitious and ill satisfied, with whom politics was of more importance than religion, and who were hostile to the queen mother and to the Guises. Among them were the duke of Alençon, who perhaps dreamed of succeeding his brother, when Henry of Anjou was far away in Poland, for Charles IX's days were evidently numbered; the young princes of Navarre and Condé, who had been driven to espouse Catholicism by terror, the viscount of Turenne and the whole house of Montmorency. Even in the camp before La Rochelle this faction of the Politiques laid its plots, endeavoring to put the fleet under command of the duke of Alençon, and probably upon the advice of the king of Navarre opened intercourse with La Noue.[2] La Noue was persuaded that much

dated March 22; *ibid.*, *Ven.*, No. 577, April 2, 1574. Montgomery must have been in error as to the date of his arrival at Coutances, which he puts on March 11. It must have been earlier. Torcy's commission bears this date. On May 29 the chief of the Huguenots, or rather, Montgomery, wrote to Lord Burghley from Carentan, justifying the taking up arms, and stating what need there is of the favor and protection of the Queen (*ibid.*, *For.*, No. 1,429, May 24, 1574).

[1] Weill, 128, 129.

[2] *Mém. du duc de Bouillon*, 89. The scheme was to deprive the duke of Anjou of the command before La Rochelle and put the duke of Alençon and Henry of Navarre in command both by land and by sea. It failed, though Charles IX seems to have been willing, because Anjou flatly refused to resign (see letter in Appendix XXXIII).

might be gained by the fusion of the Huguenots and the Politiques. The significance of this development must not pass unnoticed. The whole character of the war was ultimately changed by it. La Noue first, and later Damville, became the genius of this alliance. He negotiated with Damville, with Alençon, with Henry of Navarre. He sent Du Plessis-Mornay to England. But his greatest feat of diplomacy was the persuasion of the people of La Rochelle to adopt the new course. It required all the eloquence, all the charm, and all the strategy of a born leader of men to convince the hot-headed and impetuous Rochellois, but he finally succeeded, and the alliance was at last concluded between the Huguenots of religion and the Huguenots of state, the connecting link being the new party of the Politiques.[1]

The Protestants and the Politiques speedily converted theories into practice in the south of France, where their confederation spread over all Languedoc and much of Guyenne. Two towns in each province were appointed as "Confederate towns." Special parlements pronounced upon all law cases which arose between litigants of either group. Liberty of worship was recognized as sacred right and this *de facto* government even undertook the trial and condemnation of the authors of the massacre of 1572.

We get clear intimations of these new political ideas in the literature of the time.

In the last days of Charles IX a political treatise appeared entitled *Du droit des magistrats sur les sujets*, purporting to have been published in Magdeburg, which advanced the thesis that the kingship, although established by God, was a popular institution, and that, if the king were unfaithful to his office, he could be set aside.[2] The *Franco-Gallia* of Hotman proclaimed the sovereignty of the people and the dependency of the crown upon its will. The same idea dominates the *Junius Brutus* of

[1] Forneron, *Histoire des ducs de Guise*, II, 276. On the whole question see De Crue, *Le parti des Politiques au lendemain de la St. Barthélemy*, Paris, 1892; Weill, 133 ff.

[2] Weill, 88, 89. The actual author was Beza.

Hubert Languet. Popular sanction, he says, alone makes the king; election is an inalienable right of the people to whom the king is responsible. A pamphlet inspired by the Montmorencys and called *La France-Turquie* compared Charles IX to the Sultan and accused him of endeavoring to reduce his subjects to eastern servility.

An incident that occurred at this time shows how far the idea of limited monarchy obtained among the Huguenots. In the course of one of the negotiations the prince of Condé was asked to sign a paper for his party. His reply was that he and the king of Navarre "had no other authority in that party than that which they had received with the articles of their election," which did not attribute a monarchical power to them, the party being composed of a great number of the nobility and the third estate, who had given power to them.[1]

Yet there was not complete homogeneity in the new order of things. The Politiques, except high nobles, and the rank and file of the Huguenots represented liberal democratic ideas. But the nobles could not forget their ancient lineage. The *assemblées de généralité*, created in 1573, included the chief members of the nobility, and although the third estate occupied an important place in them, the generals were all nobles.[2] The nobility were not slow to resume their ancient superiority owing to the influence of the king of Navarre, who was not as pliable as the prince of Condé, particularly after the Huguenot alliance with the Politiques.[3]

An enormous amount of provincial spirit had been aroused during the course of the wars. One of the speakers in the *Reveille-matin* speaks of the half-independence of Dauphiné, and points out the strong tendency to re-establish the ancient provincial organization. This theory of the Huguenots was in harmony with their constant assertion that they were restorers of the past, not revolutionists. Feudal traditions were too strong in France to be displaced by this new change. While the bourgeoisie

---

[1] Weill, 132; citing La Huguerye, II, 84.

[2] Weill, 95–97.   [3] *Ibid.*, 133.

formed town groups, the Protestant and Politique nobles appealed to the provincial spirit. By a species of political atavism the régime of the Middle Ages began again to prevail.[1] Every captain considered himself a petty sovereign. When the King ordered Montbrun to respect the majesty of the law, the haughty rejoinder was that arms made men equal in the game of politics. "In time of war when one carries a weapon in his hand and sits in the saddle, the whole world is comrade."

The government accordingly made renewed endeavors to carry on the war. The provost of Paris was authorized on March 30 to make proclamation that all vassals and others in Paris belonging to the ban and arrière-ban, should assemble, fully equipped on April 15; all gendarmes were ordered to repair to the governors and lieutenant-governors of their several provinces, by April 20.[2] Montpensier was sent into Anjou with instructions to do nothing against La Noue, but to keep the passages of the Loire and prevent him from joining with Montgomery. The hope was yet to arrange terms with the Huguenots and for that reason Strozzi, for whom La Noue had been exchanged after Moncontour, and Pinart were sent to La Noue, bearing credentials from Henry of Navarre, and Villeroy dispatched to Languedoc. Simultaneously emissaries were also sent to Sedan, for fear lest the prince of Condé and the duke of Bouillon might conspire with Louis of Nassau. East, west, south, the clouds of war hung over France.[3] In the court intrigue and accusation were rife all this time. In February the duke of Guise feigned, or believed, that he discovered a plot to assassinate him, of which Montmorency was the author.[4]

[1] See Corvière, *L'organisation politique du parti protestant tenu à Millau* (1886).

[2] *C. S. P. For.*, Nos. 1,349, 1,356, March 17 and 30, 1574. There were ten ensigns in every regiment, each of 300 men.

[3] *Ibid.*, No. 1,388, April, 1574. The prince was reputed to have about 6,000 or 7,000 reiters, "French, German, or Swiss."—*Ibid.*, No. 1,433, Wilkes to Walsingham, May 31, 1574.

[4] See details in *ibid.*, No. 1,322, February 16 1574.

The absence of Henry of Anjou at this critical stage filled Catherine with alarm, and strenuous efforts were made to bring about a settlement. A secret agent of the queen mother named Pierre Brisson at this time tried to bribe La Noue by the offer of 10,000 *écus de rente* to retire to England. It must have been a great temptation, for already the intrepid leader was ruined by the war; but his nature was too noble to accept the terms. Charles IX for a season shook himself out of the apathy of mortal illness, while the Huguenots and the Politiques bent every endeavor to perfect their plans during the absence of the heir to the throne in Poland. The scheme was to declare Henry of Anjou deprived of his rights to the crown and to recognize the duke of Alençon as heir-presumptive with the title of lieutenant-general of the kingdom. Elizabeth of England[1] and William of Orange were counted upon for influence and assistance. With this purpose a conspiracy was set on foot much like that attempted at Meaux in 1567. The duke of Alençon and the king of Navarre were to make their escape from court and effect a union with Guitery, chief of the confederates in Normandy. They were then suddenly to seize St. Germain and carry off the King and queen mother. The plot was that the king of Navarre, the duke of Alençon, and some of their gentlemen should go forth from the court on the morning

---

[1] Hume supposes (*Courtships of Queen Elizabeth*, 177) that Elizabeth, knowing that this plot was in progress, again withdrew her permission for an interview with the duke of Alençon. She feared the result if the interview were unsuccessful; she would not allow a public visit under any circumstances, and did not wish a private. The recent expedition against La Rochelle had also angered her subjects, so that now the negotiations were once more apparently at a standstill. But we must not forget her private scheme. Nothing could be more in line with Elizabeth's policy than to promote a family quarrel in the French royal house. That she was well informed of the plot can scarcely be doubted, for March 16, 1574, we find a safe-conduct for Alençon in the foreign papers; and the permission given for him to come to the Queen as soon as he has notified her of his arrival in England. April 1, moreover, Dale wrote to Walsingham, "The Duke has hope in the Queen and feareth much"—there is nothing more to explain the reference. Hume does not explicitly state Elizabeth's connivance and the editor of Hall, Vol. II, does not mention the plot at all (p. xxi); neither does Burlingham in his résumé. It can scarcely be doubted, however, that Elizabeth was actively interested or, at least, informed of its progress.

of this day as if to hunt, and ride toward Mantes, which was a town in the appanage of the duke, and garrisoned by a company of the marshal Montmorency under the command of a brother of Du Plessis-Mornay. The gate was to be opened upon their appearance.[1] March 1, 1574, was the day set for the enterprise, but there was a misunderstanding between the leaders, and unfortunately, as in 1560, there were too many informed of it. Catherine had vague information, and was on her guard. But final failure was due to a false move of Guitery, who arrived upon the scene a day ahead of the appointed time, and with insufficient forces.

Success depended upon Guitery's arriving at the hour of six on the morning of March 1 with 300 gentlemen and some footmen, but on February 27 the wild rumor was spread that there were some 700 or 800 horsemen of the religion seen within three leagues of St. Germain. Everybody made ready for flight "removing of stuff as if they had fled before an enemy." In the morning the march was made in battle array to Paris, Charles being so weak that he could scarcely ride his mule.[2]

At Paris, fearful of going to the Louvre, the King lodged in the house of De Retz in the Faubourg St. Honoré and then went to Bois de Vincennes. Failing in his purpose Guitery sought to cross the Seine at Mantes, probably with the intention of joining La Noue who, having taken Lusignan and other towns in Poitou, as unsuccessfully was endeavoring to cross the Loire to join Guitery.[3] When the first alarm was over, the King and queen mother tried to make light of the episode. But it was a symptom the lesson of which could not be mistaken. It is plain that Charles IX and his mother feared greatly what Alençon might be planning, but he affirmed vigorously that he was only trying to escape from court.[4] When questioned, he disclaimed any treasonable intent

---

[1] *Mém. de madame Mornay*, 74, 75.

[2] De Thou, Book LVII; *Arch. cur.*, VII, 105.

[3] *C. S. P. Ven.*, No. 572, February 28, and *ibid.*, *For.*, Nos. 1,331, 1,336, 1,350, March 2, 8, 22, 1573.

[4] The duke of Alençon and the king of Navarre issued a declaration denying all knowledge of Guitery's enterprise against the King at St. Germain. Tract

or purpose to disturb the kingdom, but admitted his hatred for the court party and his sympathy for the Politiques. In a long harangue the duke accused the King of undue favoritism of his brother, the duke of Anjou. The ground of his reproaches seems to have been pique because of the fact that, while in camp before La Rochelle, affairs of importance were never discussed in his presence.

After the departure of the king of Poland, when he hoped to have more insight into public affairs, he had not been admitted, nor was he able to obtain the dignity and functions which had belonged to his brother. And these facts had lowered his reputation in the court to such an extent that the Guises not only desired to quarrel with him but were continually laboring to effect that result.[1]

Further, Alençon complained

that the king and his mother threw difficulties in the way of his intentions in Flanders; and made use of such well-reasoned arguments that it was clear the case that he put forward had been prepared by persons possessing greater experience and knowledge than his capacity could pretend to have. But he did not reveal any names. He alleged that he would have to remain a poor prince unless by force of arms he could acquire a position whereby he might obtain a sufficient reputation to accomplish a marriage with the queen of England; that in France the authorities and powers enjoyed by his brother, the King of Poland, were not given him, and that what little power he had was only in name, while, on the other hand, the prince of Orange has sought his aid by very large offers and many great promises had also been made to him from Germany and England, and that in the kingdom of France many persons had pledged their word to follow his fortunes everywhere.[2]

The Guisard faction and Biragues, the chancellor, in order to strike Montmorency, who with Damville was the leader of the Politiques, urged a drastic course. At the meeting of the King's council, the chancellor said to the King:

You should take into account the continual fear for your own person, and the imminent ruin which threatens the whole kingdom given you by God, the governor; and these considerations without doubt should move your majesty to follow the example of King Louis XI, your ancestor, who was so renowned in history, and to cause the world to know that while your Majesty is full of clemency, so you can also punish when the occasion demands.[3]

printed at Paris by Frederic Morel, 1574, p. 8; cf. *Lettres de Henri IV*, I, 60; *Mém. de la Huguerye*, I, 182, note 2.

[1] *C. S. P. Ven.*, No. 573, March 10, 1574.

[2] *Ibid.*, No. 574, March 17, 1574.   [3] *Ibid.*

In view of the high estate of those involved, Catherine de Medici, however, refused to follow out this resolute policy. But both princes and Montmorency were kept under surveillance though nominally allowed their liberty. This Scotch verdict of "not proven" was a great disappointment to the Guises who probably are responsible for the "conspiracy" trumped up two weeks later. It was alleged that a plot had been "discovered" against the King and the queen mother which was to have been carried into effect on Easter Day. On April 8, Alençon, Henry of Navarre, and the marshal Montmorency, were together in the castle of Bois de Vincennes when suddenly the gates were shut and double guards set, for there was a rumor of the appearance of strange horsemen in the vicinity. At the same time the gates of Paris were closed and no one was permitted to pass out with any horse or weapon. La Mole, one of the gentlemen attached to Alençon, was suddenly arrested, and with him another gentleman of Alençon's entourage, the count Coconnas. Both were imprisoned in the Conciergerie, and refused converse with the duke. The prince of Navarre, Alençon, and Montmorency, however, still were suffered to go abroad but "with such company as might be masters."[1] Things now rapidly passed from farce to tragedy. Alençon and Navarre would confess nothing,[2] the latter showing "a very bold face without any fear of consequences." The examination was with the purpose of acquiring colorable information from the inquisition of La Mole and Coconnas

[1] C. S. P. For., Nos. 1,377, 1,378, April 10–12, 1574; ibid., Ven., Nos. 580, 581, April 9–10.

[2] But it is not to be doubted that back of the affair was a secret movement of the liberal Huguenots and the Politiques to put Alençon upon the throne in event of the death of Charles IX and so foil the succession of the bigoted Henry of Anjou. Vie de Mornay, 23: Jalluard à Taffin, ministre du St. Evangile, May 8, 1574: "L'emprisonnement du duc d'Alençon, roy de Navarre, mareschal de Montmorenci, et autres, ont apporté non seulement un grand estonnement, mais aussi rompu des grands desseins."—Archives de la maison d'Orange-Nassau, V, 2; cf. IV, 375. Moderate men perceived the value of Alençon as a couterpoise to Henry of Poland (cf. C. S. P. For., No. 1,431, May 25, 1574). On the entire matter see De Crue, "La Molle et Coconat et les négociations du parti des Politiques," Rev. d'hist dip., VI, 1892, p. 375.

in order to implicate the duke of Montmorency. The poor wretches had nothing of the divinity that hedged the princes of the blood and were inquisitorially examined and judicially murdered.[1] The duke of Alençon in vain entreated for the lives of his friends. Charles IX, who was morbid and savage and stricken unto death[2] would only allow that, instead of being executed in public, they should be put to death in prison.[3] On April 30 La Mole and Coconnas were beheaded and quartered.[4]

But for once the ascendency of the queen mother over the King was of good effect. Charles IX was urged to mete out the same penalty to his brother, the marshals Cossé and Montmorency, and Henry of Navarre. If it had not been for powerful intervention this might have been the case.[5] Imagine the astonishment of the world that expressed surprise when Philip II imprisoned his son if such an act had been done! In the ferocious mood now become habitual with the King, such a thing is conceivably possible. But Catherine de Medici spared Henry of Navarre now, as in the massacre of St. Bartholomew, because the Bourbons were needful as a checkmate to the Guises. Such conduct, too, might have driven England and the German Protestant princes into active support of the Huguenots—a considera-

---

[1] *Arch. cur.*, VIII, 127 ff. Among other charges, La Mole was accused of practicing sorcery—"that there should be an image of wax and a strange medal in the chamber of La Mole for some enchantment."—*C. S. P. For.*, No. 1,398, Dr. Dale to Burghley, April 27, 1574.

[2] *Ibid.*, April 22, 1574; No. 1,398, April 27, 1574.

[3] *Ibid.*, *Ven.*, No. 586, May 2, 1574.

[4] *Ibid.*, and *ibid.*, *For.*, No. 1,401, Dale to Burghley, April 30, 1574. The whole process was a mockery of justice. According to another report the King promised "that he would write to the Parlement to delay the proceedings. But the bearer of the letters, on arriving at Paris found the Porte St. Antoine closed. The execution was so much hurried that in a moment they were both executed. It is said this was done by reason of a perfumer relating to the first President what had passed in Court, and that the Queen Mother had obtained their pardon. For which cause they were made to come more quickly from the Conciergerie, the carriage made to journey hastily, and directly they arrived at the place of execution they were executed without the usual proclamations."—*C. S. P. For.*, No 1,403, May 2, 1574.

[5] Claude Haton, II, 765.

tion which had made Catherine hesitate before August 24, 1572. A living dog was better than a dead lion.[1] "The King told that he should bear in mind that while the duke and Navarre were alive, he could do what he pleased, but if they were dead there would be no remedy."[2]

The real motive and animus of the whole cruel affair—the destruction of the Montmorencys by the Guises—was not long in forthcoming. Hitherto the duke had been allowed guarded freedom, even to go hunting. But within a few days after the death of La Mole and Coconnas came word of the capture of Damville, Montmorency's brother, in Languedoc. Immediately the duke of Montmorency and the marshal Cossé were shut up in the Bastille. The ancient and bitter grudge of the Guises against the Montmorency-Châtillon house, half of which had been paid in the murder of the admiral, narrowly missed being sated at this hour. In the blood-thirsty mood in which the King was, the purple of kingship probably would not have protected

[1] C. S. P. Ven., No. 584, April 19, 1574. Both Henry of Navarre and his fellow-prisoner seemed to have believed in these days that if Charles IX should die their own expectation of living would be slender, and their only hope be in corrupting the guard. But they were without money. This is the purport of a cipher dispatch, dated May 22, from Paris and sent to Burghley to be deciphered by him personally. This he actually did, for the draft is in his handwriting (ibid., For., No. 1,422, 1574; cf. No. 1,431. His reply—to Walsingham—was sent three days later (by a slip of the pen he has, however, written "March" instead of May).

[2] C. S. P. For., No. 1,408, Dr. Dale to Burghley, May 5, 1574. See a letter of Emanuel Philibert of Savoy, to Charles IX protesting against the arrest of Montmorency, May 19, 1574, in Coll. Godefroy, CCLVI, No. 92. Elizabeth seems to have interested herself very much in their fate and sent Thomas Leighton to France in their behalf. The face of affairs thus was changed, for to give some credibility to her stories of a happy family, Catherine had to allow the princes more liberty. Besides, Leighton was captain of Guernsey, and could be of great assistance to Montgomery so that he had to be well treated and his desires gratified. The Guises, however, were gaining great influence in court again and in event of the King's death, Alençon expected the Bastille. To escape this he desired money from Elizabeth to bribe his guards and Burghley actually recommended that this course be followed. De Thoré, the youngest of the constable's sons, fled to Cassel for safety (Claude Haton, II, 763 and note). The fury of the Guises pursued him even in Germany (see a letter of one Davis to count John of Nassau, June 7, 1574, in Archives de la maison d'Orange-Nassau, IV, 19, giving some particulars on this head, and one of Schomberg to the same, August 28, at p. 49).

the duke.   But at heart Charles IX and his mother were craven cowards, and the latter, at least, was not wholly lost to prudence.   Fortunately for the duke of Montmorency and for France, the word of Damville's capture was a false report.   He had intercepted the instructions sent to Joyeuse and the governor of Narbonne for his apprehension and taken his precautions. Damville was too great a lion to rouse the anger of, while he was at large, and nothing but treachery could overthrow him, for he was in possession of Beziers, Montpellier, Pasenas, Beaucaire, Boignelles, and Pont St. Esprit, and as leader of the united Politiques and Huguenots of the south, in control of Languedoc, Dauphiné, and Provence.[1]

The great political anxiety he labored under aggravated the condition of Charles IX, whose constitution, undermined by smallpox and his indulgences, had now been attacked by consumption.   He was reduced to skin and bone and so weak that he could not stand and suffered from effusion of blood through the mouth.[2]   But the ferocity of his nature remained unsubdued. The faculty of medicine, the members of which were called in consultation, pronounced the King's condition hopeless.   "I believe you speak truly," was Charles' comment on the verdict. "Draw the curtain down that I may have some rest."[3]   On the

[1] See C. S. P. For., No. 1,417, May 17, 1574; Hist. du Lang., V, 520, note 1.

[2] Yesterday he was more ill-at-ease than ordinarily, and no one entered his room, but at sunrise several gentlemen and priests came in.   The priests performed the service, at which the queen mother was present.   He has been of better countenance since hearing of the execution of De la Mole and Coconnas, and said he hoped to live to see the end of all his conspirators (C. S. P. For., No. 1,403, May 2, 1574).   Early in April, two couriers were dispatched to Poland to warn Henry of Anjou to be ready for any emergency (ibid., Ven., No. 590, May 2, 1574).   Dr. Dale, the English ambassador, reports, under date of May 22: "On the 22d the King fell suddenly sick.   The audience appointed with the ambassador of the duke of Florence was countermanded, the best physicians sent for, and the opinion is that the King is in great danger.   The falling down of blood into his lungs is come to him again, and the physicians gave their opinion that if it should happen again they could not assure him of any hope.   Paris, 22 May, 1574."—C. S. P. For., No. 1,422.

[3] Frémy, Un ambassadeur liberal sous Charles IX et Henri III, 226.   The King actually said : "Tirez moy ma custode," from the Latin word custodire, to protect.   Claude Haton, II, 767, gives an impressive account of the deathbed scene.

night of May 29 a violent hemorrhage foretold the end. The King died on May 30, 1574, at two hours after noon.[1]

The queen mother at once assumed the regency[2] in compliance with one of the last commands of Charles IX, and removed from the Bois de Vincennes to the Louvre, where Alençon and Navarre were kept under close scrutiny, for until the return of Henry from Poland there was great uncertainty as to what might happen. The two were without money to corrupt the guards if so dangerous an expedient were hazarded; the windows of their chamber "grated like a prison."[3] Catherine's policy was to promise redress of grievances and reconciliation of all at the coming of Henry III, who learned of his brother's death at Cracow on June 15.[4] To that end she appealed to La Noue and Damville but the Iron Arm flouted her overtures from his strongholds of Lusignan and Niort, condemning the queen for her treatment of Montmorency,[5] and the imprisonment of Alençon and Henry of Navarre.

The last stage in the eventful career of Montgomery was also reached at this time. He had suddenly left Carentan with about 650 horse, attacked the city of Alençon and then attempted to raise the siege of St. Lô. But Matignon had more forces than he had supposed and drove him into Domfront. After a vigorous defense he yielded the place upon the promise that his life would be spared.

---

[1] *C. S. P. Ven.*, No. 591, May 30, 1574. For other accounts see *Arch. cur.*, VIII, 253, 271. There is a remarkable tract in the State Paper office "giving particulars of the ancestors and birth of Charles IX, the civil wars of his reign, his victories, the massacre of St. Bartholomew, his famous sayings, his wife and daughter, his decrees, his motto, his favorite servant, his master and nurse, his liberality, his sports, his study of music and singing, the fiery spectre seen by him, his breaking the law, his speech in the senate, his amours, his affliction of the ecclesiastics, his study of liberal sciences, his food, drink, and sleep, a prodigy preceding his death, his sickness, his discourse before his death, his death and testament, description of his body and stature."—*C. S. P. For.*, No. 1,628 (1574). The queen of France returned to Vienna and died in a convent in 1592.

[2] Isambert, XIV, 262.

[3] *C. S. P. For.*, No. 1,448, June 10, 1574.

[4] Henry III, to Elizabeth (see Appendix XXXV).

[5] *C. S. P. For.*, Nos. 1,449 and 1,464, *anno* 1574.

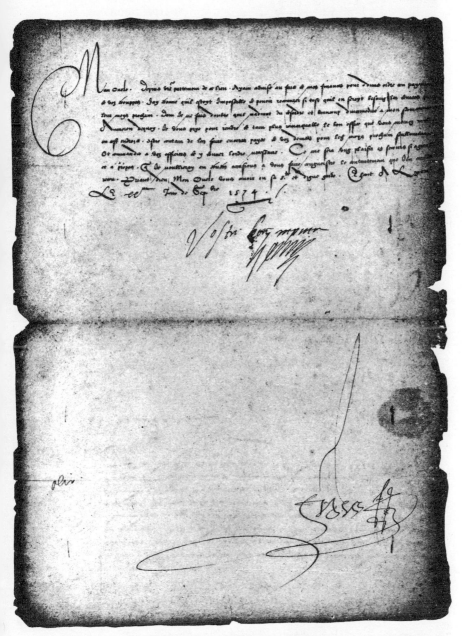

LETTER OF HENRY III OF FRANCE TO THE DUKE OF SAVOY

Relates to the pay of his troops. Written from Lyons, September 20, 1574, within a few days after his arrival in France from Poland. Original owned by the author.

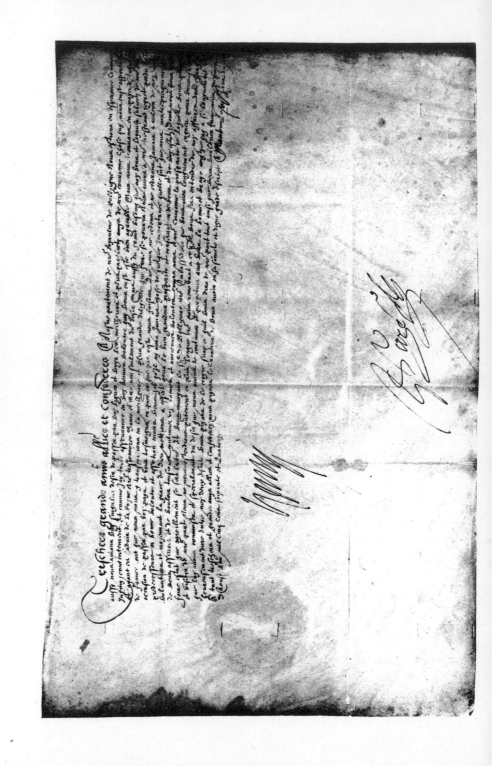

But Catherine de Medici hated him above all men in the earth and had no scruples about inaugurating the reign of Henry III with bloodshed. She refused to honor Matignon's pledge. Montgomery was brought under heavy guard to Paris, being viewed by curious gazers all along the road, and was beheaded and then quartered on June 26, before an enormous crowd of people.

9 Catherine risked a Protestant uprising in order to sate her vengeance upon the man who had slain Henry II. The Venetian ambassador, however, conjectured that there was more of policy than of revenge in the act. "It was certainly more to please the Parisians from whom she hoped to have efficient aid than for any other reason that she had Montgomery put to death."—*C. S. P. Ven.*, No. 588, May 20, No. 597, June, 1574. Matignon was made a marshal of France as his reward (*ibid., For.*, No. 176, June 13, 1575). For particulars of Montgomery's execution see *Arch. cur.*, VIII, 223 ff.; and the *Discours de la mort et execution de Gabriel comte de Montgommery, par arrest de la court, pour les conspirations par luy commises contre le roy*, Lyon: Benoist Rigaud, 1574.

CHAPTER XVIII

HENRY III AND THE POLITIQUES. THE PEACE OF MONSIEUR
(1576)

The attention of Europe was fixed upon France by these events. What was going to happen in the absence of the heir to the throne? Would a frightful wave of retaliatory vengeance for the massacre of St. Bartholomew and the process of Vincennes sweep over the land? These were the questions that were asked, not only everywhere in France, but in many quarters of Europe. The Tuscan ambassador wrote that the châteaux of the Montmorencys were filled with provisions and munitions of war.[1]

The Politiques, as a class, being imbued with Hotman's teachings in the *Franco-Gallia*, inveighed against Catherine for having assumed the regency without consent of the estates. They and the political Huguenots were at one, and demanded searching reform. It was their hope to prevail upon the queen mother to come to a definite agreement before the arrival of Henry III in France, in the expectation that the King upon his arrival would find it expedient to accept it. They demanded the reorganization of justice and the army; they condemned the alienation of the crown lands, increase of the tithe, and the new taxes; they insisted upon an examination of the accounts of those who had managed the public finances and the royal revenue, this investigation to include not only the ministers who had enriched themselves, but also the superintendents of finance from Henry II down to the present time, not excepting the cardinal of Lorraine. They demanded the expulsion of the "foreigners," naming the chancellor Biragues, the marshal de Retz, and the duke of Nevers who were all Italians. They hated the Guises as a foreign house and quasi-German.[2]

It was high time for some sort of settlement. The country

[1] *Nég. Tosc.*, III, 926–27, April 5 and May 11, 1574.
[2] "Tenuti per forastieri e Alemanni."—*Rel. vén.*, II, 228.

was crying out against the thieves and brigands, who frequented the roads in great numbers under the guise of war and pretended to be in the service of the King.[1]

But Catherine refused to deal with any matter of state until the arrival of the King. She showed an almost feverish anxiety for her son's coming, fearing that the duke of Alençon would be put forward for the crown by the Politiques.[2] In Germany, at the same time, the Orange party, with the aid of Schomberg, labored to promote the cause of the Politiques and liberal Hugue-nots, and in September a deputation came from the count palatine to urge the cause of toleration in France.[3] But it was slow and hard work, for as La Noue had bitterly said the year before: "The iron of the German nation was heavy and hard to work; it was silver that made things move."[4] Moreover, the agents of Spain and the Guises were encountered at every turn.

In the meantime Henry III had left Cracow on June 16, running away from his kingdom like a thief in the night,[5] and came home

[1] Claude Haton, II, 778. These bandits were sometimes called "Foruscits" or "Fuorisciti," from the Italian *uscir fuora* (see a letter of the cardinal of Armagnac in *Rev. hist.*, II, 529).

"En 1576 les paysans du Dauphiné s'étant soulevés, entreprirent vainement ce qu'ils ont exécuté plus de deux siècles après cette époque. Ils se rassemblèrent en un corps considérable pour piller et brûler les châteaux, et exterminer les gentils-hommes. Mandalot, à la tête d'une troupe déterminée, dissipa avec promptitude ce rassemblement qu'on appela la ' Ligue des Vilains.' "—*Histoire ou mémoire de ce qui se passa à Lyons pendant la ligue, appelée la Sainte-Union, jusqu'à la reddition de la ville sous l'obeissance du roi Henri IV*, Bibliothèque de Lyon, No. 1,361.

[2] "On taschast de réconcilier par tous moyens les malcontens et principale-ment ceux qui, par le passé, ont eu crédit et autorité en France, qui pourront aug-menter les troubles et soustenir la mauvaise et pernicieuse volonté de ceux qui voudroient invertir l'ancienne et naturelle succession de la couronne de France."—Du Ferrier to Catherine de Medici, June, 1574, in Frémy, *Un ambassadeur liberal sous Charles IX et Henri III*, 235.

[3] Articles proposed by the count palatine's ambassador for a pacification (*C. S. P. For.*, No. 1,556, *anno* 1574). The post was subsidized by the French King by way of Reinhausen, Neustadt, Kaiserslautern, Limbach (near Hamburg), Saarbrück, St. Avold, and Metz (*Archives de la maison d'Orange-Nassau*, V, 49).

[4] *Vie de La Noue*, 87.

[5] The Poles made a hard attempt to prevent Henry from leaving the kingdom. They were dissatisfied that he assumed the title King of France without consulting

by way of Italy, via Venice, where he was extravagantly entertained by the senate,[1] Ferrara (July 29), Mirandola, Mantua,
and Turin, which he left on August 28, and arrived at Lyons on
September 6.[2]   Catherine, who showed great impatience, met him
there (she arrived at Lyons on August 27).   So fearful was she
lest Alençon and Henry of Navarre would escape that the young
princes had traveled in the coach with her.[3]   The procession moved
as if through a hostile country by way of Burgundy and Chalons-
sur-Saône, some of the guard marching in advance, the rest
bringing up the rear.   "Marshal de Retz was always on the wing
of her.   Some of the guard marched two leagues before and some
two leagues after."[4]

Those who were at all optimistic had clung to the belief, until
the development of events shattered their hopes, that Henry III
would endeavor to pacify his subjects, arguing that if he were
inclined to war, he would not have refused the assistance proffered
him in Italy of men and money, and that the French crown could
not further hazard the reduction of the kingdom piecemeal.[5]
Damville had met the King at Turin, having come there under a
safe-conduct of the duke of Savoy, to persuade Henry III to adopt
a conciliatory policy, which he at first inclined to follow.

But the moment he came under the sinister influence of Catherine de Medici, he cast this prudent advice to the winds.   It was

them, and wanted him to govern his new kingdom through ministers chosen from
among them, and to employ himself in military exploits against the Tartars and
Turks (Languet, *Epist. secr.*, I, 121).

[1] Frémy, *Un ambassadeur liberal sous Charles IX et Henri III*, 232.

[2] *C. S. P. For.*, No. 1,543, September 10, 1574.

[3] The duke and his fellow-captives made several efforts to escape, in one of
which Alençon narrowly missed doing so (see the account in *C. S. P. Ven.*, No.
600, July 26, 1574).   In consequence, when Catherine started to meet her son at
Lyons, leaving the government of Paris in care of the Parlement (*ibid.*, No. 1,509,
July 10, 1574), the young princes traveled in the coach with her.   "Her chick-
ens go in coach under her wing, and so she minds to bring them to the King."
—*Ibid., For.*, No. 1,511, Dale to Walsingham, August 9, 1574.

[4] *Ibid.*, No. 1,537, Dale to Sir Thomas Smith and Francis Walsingham,
September 2, 1574, from Lyons.

[5] See the striking comments of the Venetian ambassador, *Rel. vén.*, II, 245, 246.

she who dissuaded him from what was wisely counseled[1] and in advance of his arrival had made military preparations to resume the war by importing Swiss mercenaries and German reiters again.[2] Accordingly, instead of extending the olive branch, the King expressed his determination to wage unremitting war upon the Huguenots and Politiques rather than grant the demands they made. The deputies of La Rochelle who came to Lyons, requesting a surcease of arms, were repulsed by the King and told it was but a scheme of the Huguenots to gain time for preparation. The establishment of three camps was ordered, one in Dauphiné, the second in Provence and Languedoc, and the third in Poitou. At the same time Schomberg and Fregoso were sent into Germany for assistance.[3]

When Henry III definitely resolved to follow out a policy of suppression Damville was summoned to Lyons to answer for his governorship. It was a fatal blunder on the part of the King, for the action of the crown hardened the tentative co-operation of the Protestants and the Politiques into a positive alliance. At Milhau, in August, 1574 the Protestants recognized Damville, while he in turn admitted their leaders into his council. The form of government established at Montauban the year before acquired new strength and greater extent. Provincial and general assemblies were formed without distinction between Protestants and Politiques, upon the basis of mutual toleration; in places where

[1] *Rel. vén.*, II, 245, 246.

[2] *C. S. P. For.*, No. 1,543, September 10, 1574, No. 1,555, September 11, 1574; Thomas Wilkes to Walsingham and Dr. Dale to Sir Thomas Smith and Walsingham. There were 6,500 Swiss at Châlons (*ibid.*, No. 1,537, September 2, 1574). Henry III had sent orders in advance of his coming. commanding that on the 30th of August all the companies of ordinance should retire in garrison and await the orders of the provincial governors. Troops were levied in Picardy, Champagne, Brie, Burgundy, and Lorraine, to prevent the Protestant reiters from gaining entrance into the country and were put under the command of the duke of Guise, Vaudemont, and the marshal Strozzi (Claude Haton, II, 779).

[3] *C. S. P. For.*, No. 1,590, November 4, 1574. The headquarters of the Catholic forces were between Dijon and Langres, but troops patrolled the whole course of the Marne and extended westward to Sens. Artillery was sent up the Seine from Paris. The camp of the horse was fixed near Troyes (Claude Haton, III, 779).

the two creeds obtained each side promised to observe the peace and Damville engaged not to introduce the Catholic religion in any town of which the Huguenots were masters.

The men who took this step justified it by alleging that a foreign faction had acquired control over the sovereign; that it was destroying the kingdom, the nobles, the princes of the blood, and with them the very institutions and civilization of France; and that it was their hope to arrest this process. The programme of the Huguenot-Politique party, in addition to complete religious toleration, insisted upon the abolition of the practice of selling offices, the convocation of the States-General, the reduction of the taxes. In this demand they were supported by the provincial states of Dauphiné, Provence, and Burgundy. The confessional idea was deliberately kept in the background. Men no longer talked of a war of religion, but of a "Guerre du Bien Public" as in the reign of Louis XI.

With the nobles Damville's was a name to conjure with. A large portion of the Catholic nobility, who for a long time had been severely reproached for not seriously opposing the Huguenots, sympathized with his attitude. If the bench and bar of France was strongly attached to the principles of the Catholic religion, the nobility who were hereditary enemies of the legists, whose teachings had for three centuries tended to abridge their feudal rights, out of sheer self-interest, aside from any other motives, now inclined toward the Calvinists. Only radical Calvinists, like Du Plessis-Mornay, opposed the union and were bitter in denunciation of the overtures made by their more moderate brethren, notably La Noue, to Damville and the Politiques.[1]

A royal edict let the Huguenots understand what was to be expected. The King's determination was to clear the valley of the Rhone from Lyons to Avignon with the aid of the Swiss and then to subdue Languedoc on the one side and Dauphiné on the other. Such a plan was more bold than practicable, and Henry was likely to find it too hard to accomplish, especially by winter

[1] De Thou, Book L, chap. xii; *Vie de Mornay*, 23; Coll. Godefroy, CCLIX, No. 2, "Les habitants du diocèse de Montpellier au roi, 4 juin, 1574."

sieges. The Protestants had fortified themselves in Livron on the left bank of the Rhone and at Pouzin across the river, which was inaccessible except by one approach and then only four men could advance abreast.

But there was another matter, the difficulty of which Henry III underestimated, namely the army. The Protestants were so entrenched in their strongholds as to make the use of horsemen against them impracticable. The Swiss were low-class mercenaries, good as ordinary footmen but useless for a siege. Moreover, all of them, reiters and Swiss, were not disposed to move unless they saw their pay in their hands and were utter strangers to discipline, wasting the country "to make a Christian man's heart bleed."[1] In one case the wretched peasantry followed their despoilers to the confines of Lyons and fell upon them in desperation, recovering what had been taken from them. What did the King do? He actually had to punish these wretched subjects of his in order to retain the services of the reiters at all!

Yet the King for a moment showed some of the old fire he displayed at Moncontour and amazed the Protestants by taking Pouzin after three weeks of siege. The victory was marred, though, by the shameful conduct of the Swiss, the reiters, and the Italians in the royal army, who sacked and burned it. Much the same state of things prevailed wherever these riotous plunderers penetrated—in Picardy, in Champagne, in Poitou. But Henry III having reached Avignon, discovered that he was no better off for his success. Meanwhile Damville, with whom the duke of Savoy had honorably dealt, returned from Turin, and reached the vicinity of Montpellier and Beaucaire before the King was aware of it.[2]

When the King sent the cardinal of Bourbon to talk with him, Damville sent back word that he thought the example of his brother "too dangerous to come to court where they who sought the ruin of his house had too much credit,"[3] and advised the King to remove

[1] For other interesting details see *C. S. P. For.*, No. 1,568, September 29, 1574.

[2] Le Laboureur, II, 135.

[3] *C. S. P. For.*, No. 1,584, October 23, 1574.

the strangers within his gates, meaning Biragues and De Retz.[1]
Henry III could accomplish nothing at Avignon and yet knew
not how to get away.   He could not go up-river on account of the
current.   The Huguenots at Livron barred the road on the left
bank; Montbrun was in the hills in Auvergne; La Noue's men
were stopping the King's post daily and Damville controlled Provence and Languedoc; La Haye, King's lieutenant in the sénéchaussée of Poitou seceded to the Politiques.[2]   Vivarais declared
its neutrality and refused to side with King or Politiques.   The
people of Tulle refused to pay taxes either to Catholics or Protestants until overpowered by the latter, and thus the country continued to endure a war which it hated.   Henry truly was in a
plight.   He was without money, too, and could not hope to get
any so far from Paris.   He even feared that the soldiery with him
might be bribed to desert.[3]   To crown the royal anxiety Damville's declaration was so public and so bold that the King feared
that foreign aid would soon be forthcoming in the Protestant service.   The fear was not without ground.   For the marshal actually
proposed to make a league with the Sultan and introduce a Turkish fleet into the harbor of Aigues-Mortes.[4]   Coupled with this
possibility was a projected enterprise against Spain in Franche
Comté in which the Huguenots of Champagne and Burgundy
were interested, but which was primarily the project of the elector
palatine and the prince of Orange.[5]

[1] Schomberg's comment is amusing: "Monsieur le mareschal Damphille
se contint sagement, dont les ennemis de ceste maison s'arrachent la barbe."—
August 28, 1574, in Arch. de la maison d'Orange-Nassau, 49.

[2] Chroniques fontenaisiennes, 228–32; L'Estoile, I, 37; Weill, 137, note 3.

[3] "A little piece of money might win the reiters to join with them of the religion."—C. S. P. For., No. 1,623, December 23, 1574.

[4] Aigues-Mortes was a strong port and the staple of salt for Languedoc, Dauphiné, the Lyonnais, and Burgundy (ibid., No. 17, January 25, 1575).   Dr. Dale
thought that the project was to connive at a Turkish attack in Germany for the
purpose of embarrassing the Catholic princes there (ibid., No. 1,620, December
23, 1574.

[5] The plot was an old one and long in preparation.   See a letter of St. Goard
to the King, May 20, 1573 (Archives de la maison d'Orange-Nassau, IV, Appendix,
No. 59.   The Spanish had been advised by word from Besançon, on April 3, that

It is a significant fact that the war has now lost almost all confessional character and become a factional conflict between the
rival houses of Guise and Montmorency.   Catholicism and political corruption on the one hand were opposed to administrative
reform and religious toleration.   After the creation of the Politique
party, the Huguenots of state had merged with them.   Except
in the case of radical Calvinists and bigoted Catholics, religion
had become a minor issue with the French unless it were artificially
exaggerated.[1]   It was a mortal enmity on either side, and one
which there was slight hope of settling.   The hostility of the Guises
and the Montmorencys was the real seed of the civil war.[2]   It
depended upon the individual in almost every case whether his
participation one way or the other was motived by convictions as
to the public good or by private interests.   The number of those
who directly or indirectly were attached to the warring houses
almost divided the realm between them and the wretched people
were badly treated by both parties.[3]   So widespread and deep
rooted was this mutual enmity throughout France, that the Venetian ambassador, no mean observer, wondered when it would end,
because it was to the interest of each to sustain it.   The King was
a shuttlecock in this game of political battledore.   The ruin of the
crown, instead of being feared by them, was regarded as a possible

those of Geneva and Bern had confederated with the Lutheran cantons and secured the favor of the duke John Casimir, whose purpose was to overcome Besançon
and the free county of Burgundy (cf. letter of De Grantyre, the French agent in the
Grisons, to Bellièvre, April 8, 1573, Coll. Godefroy, CCLVIII, No. 52, and
the letter of Charles IX to Bellièvre, May 9, 1573, ibid., No. 55).   The author of
the plan was a Dr. Butterich, councilor of the elector (Archives de la maison
d'Orange-Nassau, V, 89, 99, 101, 107, 120-3.   The Swiss cantons were also appealed to, but Beza hesitated (ibid., 111).   Spain had secret information of the
plot (ibid., 89).   It finally failed (see a letter of Butterich to John of Nassau,
June 6, 1575, ibid., 214; cf. Languet, Epist. secr., I, Part II, 106, July 11, 1575).

[1] An example of eccentric partisanship is afforded by the duke d'Uzes, who
was a Huguenot, but who for enmity toward Damville joined the King.   Henry
III made him a marshal and left him in chief command when he went to Rheims
(C. S. P. For., No. 1,617, December 23, 1574; No. 13, January 16, 1575).   Bellegarde was also made marshal in this year (ibid., No. 1,570, September 29, 1574).

[2] "Seminario della guerra."—Rel. vén., II, 230.

[3] Claude Haton, I, 782, 783.

way to give their enmity freer rein.   Each party counted not only upon paying its debts, which were enormous, by victory, but in establishing the power of its house more permanently than ever for the future.   While the war cost the King and the country *écus par milliers*, it cost them nothing, at least of their own.   The weakness of the crown was the strength of the rivals.   They fattened on war, for peace deprived them of their authority, their power, and their partisans.   Until one or the other faction was crushed, the hostility was certain to endure, and thus the war seemed doomed to last indefinitely.   If, as the result of fatigue or a truce, a respite was made, the time was brief, and was terminated as soon as one or the other side had accumulated some substance again.   The only remedy for such a state of affairs was to be found in a foreign war, either in Flanders or Italy.[1]

The union of the Huguenots and the Politiques made them very strong, especially in the south.   But on the other hand the duke of Guise received much assistance from Flanders.   When the successor of Alva, Requesens, learned of the death of Charles IX, he had offered the aid of Spanish troops to Catherine de Medici.[2] Although the proffer was declined, the practical result was the same, for owing to lack of pay in the Low Countries, thousands of reiters and Walloon and German footmen flocked across the border in the summer and autumn, where they were welcomed by the duke of Guise, who, somewhere and somehow, found the means to pay them.[3]   But below the stratum of professional soldiers in France there was another class in arms which feudal society was not used to see in such a capacity.   This was the people; not town militia, for town and provincial leagues had made men familiar with them, but the peasantry.   The protracted wars by economically ruining and morally debauching this class had

[1] See the luminous *Relazione del Giovanni Michel*, the Venetian ambassador in France in 1575, ed. Tommaseo, II, 229–33.

[2] *Correspondance de Philippe II sur les Pays-Bas*, III, 105, note, June 15, 1574.

[3] *Ibid.*, 165–66, Requesens to Philip II, September 24, 1574: "Il y a en France beaucoup d'Espagnols qui ont déserté des Pays-Bas; il sont recueillis par M. de Guise et d'autres qui leur font un bon traitement et leur donnent de grosses payes."   M. Gachard has paraphrased the letter.

generated a breed of men who sprang from the soil like the dragon's teeth of Greek fable, men who by observation and practice were used to the matchlock and the sword, brutalized by oppression, long made desperate by burdensome taxes and the wrongs of war.[1]

The weariness of vigil in the depth of winter and overconfidence seem to have relaxed the alertness of Henry III's foes. At any

PIKEMAN AND COLOR-BEARER
(Tortorel and Perissin)

rate, having extorted 50,000 francs from the noblemen and gentlemen in his train in order to pay the soldiery around him, the King, raising the siege of Livron on January 24, 1575, managed to slip through the defiles to Rheims for his coronation. The coronation

[1] "La longa continuazione della guerra, che tutti li paesani che prima erano disarmati e vilissimi, tutti dati all' arte del campo e all' agricoltura, ovvero ad alcuna delle arti mecaniche, adesso sono tutti armati, e talmente essercitati e agguerriti che non si distinguono dalli più veterani soldati; tutti fatti archibugieri eccellentissimi."—" Relazione del Giovanni Michel," *Rel. vén.*, II, 232; cf. Long, 167: "Des violences et des outrages exercés par quelques petits gentilhommes

was a triumph of the Guises. For far from being set back by the death of the cardinal of Lorraine on December 29, at Avignon[1] their star seemed to be higher than before. The cardinal of Guise took the place of his deceased uncle as primate of Rheims; the duke of Guise was grand chamberlain; and the duke of Mayenne and the marquis d'Elbœuf were the chief lay peers. The sole outsider was De Retz who officiated as constable for the occasion. The crowning took place on February 15. Shortly after the event, apparently in a sudden whim of passion, Henry III married Louise de Vaudmont, whose father was uncle of the duke of Lorraine and whose mother had been sister of the unfortunate Egmont. But the marriage was without political significance —indeed the new queen was of so little station that Catherine de Medici, in a letter to Queen Elizabeth, expressed her humiliation at her son's marriage.[2]

The main issues of France, religious toleration and political reform, were now more obscured than ever by the rivalry of

sur des paysans excitèrent la vengeance des villageois voisins, qui, furieux, accoururent en grand nombre. Les provocateurs imprudents se sauvèrent, mais leur maisons furent pillées et saccagées. On voit déjà *la haine du peuple*, poussé au desespoir par les impôts et par les exacteurs, contre les privilegiés. Le peuple, si mal disposé, ne devait pas être provoqué dans son ressentiment. Les defenseurs de la cause commune vont se lever."

[1] The English ambassador gives particulars of the cardinal's death. "The King would needs go in procession with the Battus, who are men that whip themselves as they go as a sort of penance. The cardinal went in this solemn procession well-nigh all the night, and the next day he said mass for a solemnity, wherewith he took a great cold and a continual fever which brought him into a frenzy, wherein he continued divers days. A Jew took upon him to work wonders and gave him a medicine whereby he came to his remembrance for a time. Upon the medicine there did break out certain pustules or spots in his body like the pourpres, whereby some would say he was poisoned. Shortly after he fell into his old frenzy and so died, the 18th day after he first fell sick."—*C. S. P. For.*, No. 1,624, December, 1574.

[2] *Ibid.*, No. 58, March 23, 1575. This letter is not printed in the *Correspondance de Catherine de Médicis*. The Venetian ambassador has a long and interesting character-sketch of the queen in *Rel. vén.*, II, 243. There are several monographs upon this "pure, douce et mélancolique figure" (Galitizin, *Louise de Lorraine reine de France (1553–1601)*; Meaume, *Etude historique sur Louise de Lorraine reine de France (1553–1601)*, Paris, 1882; Baillon, *Histoire de Louise de Lorraine, reine de France, 1553–1601*, Paris, 1884.

the factions around the throne.   The queen mother bore the
Guises greater hatred than before because of their new ascendency
and had little less spleen toward the Montmorencys, but carefully dissimulated and sought on one pretext and another to remove
them from around her son.   For this purpose Bellegarde, who
was an old attaché of the house of Montmorency and owed his
popularity with the King to a handsome face and a well-turned

ARQUEBUSIER
(Tortorel and Perissin)

leg, was made a special ambassador to Poland in order to get him
out of the way.   His comrade on the mission was Elbœuf—an ill-
matched pair indeed.   Their business was to carry 200,000 crowns
of the Paris bourgeois to Poland to bribe the Polish diet not to
elect a successor to the absent Henry.   If the Poles were obdurate,
Elbœuf was to advocate the election of the duke of Ferrara, who
had Guisard blood in his veins.   At the same time Biron and
Matignon were made marshals to counterpoise the influence of
De Retz who forthwith resigned his office and vowed he would
"meddle no more."   There were heart-burnings, also, over the

bestowal of the government of Normandy, vacated by the death of the duke of Bouillon. The duke of Nevers claimed that it had been promised him while in Poland; the duchess of Nemours demanded the post for the duke and declared that Nevers was "a foreigner." Henry III finally sought to compromise by giving the office to his insignificant father-in-law, whereupon the duke of Nevers quit the court in a rage. Squabbles of precedence, too, vexed the King's mind. Montpensier challenged the claims of the Guises to court precedence before the Parlement, and Madame de Nemours therefore quarreled with her daughter. "They were all bent to preparations of war," quaintly wrote Dale to Walsingham, "but these domestic discords do tame them. It is a very hell among them, not one content or in quiet with another, nor mother with son, nor brother with brother, nor mother with daughter."[1]

The state of the finances was deplorable, and Henry resorted to various devices to provide himself with funds. The mission of Elbœuf and Bellegarde to Poland was delayed, while the King implored the Pope, the duke of Savoy, and Venice for the money needed;[2] the pay of the King's household servants was nine months in arrears and the last money wages of his guards had been paid by an assessment levied by the King upon the noblemen and gentlemen of the court. Paris, as usual, was heavily mulcted by a forced loan of 600,000 francs, besides heavy contributions extorted from the foreign merchants there. But the mass of the money had to come from the church lands. A letter-patent in the form of an edict was forced through the Parlement authorizing the alienation of 200,000 livres de rente of the temporalities of the clergy, the King reckoning to raise a million and a half of francs by the process, but few were ready purchasers. In addition to these practices the "parties casuelles" were farmed to a Florentine money-broker named Diaceto for 60,000 francs per month. Henry III resorted to worse expedients than these, though. He sold four seats in his council for 15,000 livres each; forced the collectors of the revenue to anticipate the revenue for a twelve-month and then dis-

---

[1] C. S. P. For., No. 33, March 3, 1575.

[2] The Pope finally advanced a sum upon the security of the crown jewels (C. S. P. For., No. 168, June 6, 1575).

possessed them of their posts after he had deprived them of the profits thereof and sold them to others; and dilapidated the forest domain by selling two trees in each arpent.[1]

The position and conduct of Damville afforded the greatest hope for the future if Henry III could have been made to see things in the right way. Damville himself dominated all Languedoc and Provence; his lieutenant, Montbrun, controlled Dauphiné; Turenne was in possession of Auvergne; the Rochellois had agents at court seeking for a firm settlement of affairs; even the cardinal Bourbon and the duke of Montpensier leaned to the side of the Politiques. In 1575 the existence of the old party of Huguenots, the Huguenots of religion, was practically at an end. Individual radical Calvinists there were in plenty but the Protestant *organization* was that of the political Huguenots.

It was manifest by the spring of 1575 that the prince of Condé and Henry of Navarre on the one hand, and Damville and his brother, together with Alençon, were bound to join hands in the common purpose to establish permanent religious and greater civil liberty in France. "Liberty and reform" was the policy of the hour, if not the watchword. The declaration of the assembly of Milhau in August of the previous year had been the handwriting on the wall—a message which the misguided Henry III obdurately refused to read. On April 25, 1575, that message was repeated in even clearer terms in the form of a manifesto issued by Damville which defined the joint policy of the Politiques and the political Huguenots. It was the declaration of a patriot, and not a partisan, least of all a rebel, who, like Cromwell, found himself compelled to lead a movement for political reform against an obstinate crown that either would not or could not understand the issues.[2]

---

[1] *C. S. P. For.*, Nos. 55, 57, 67, March, 1575. The clergy in Dauphiné protested against the burden laid upon the church there by the King's measure, complaining that its support was not costing the crown a sou there; one of them even had the face to declare that they had more to hope from Damville than from the King (*ibid.*, No. 67, March, 1575).

[2] Declaration et protestation de Henry de Montmorency, seigneur Damville, mareschal de France, gouverneur et lieutenant général pour le Roy en Languedoc. Issued from Nîmes, April 25, 1575. There is an abstract of it in *C. S. P. For.*, No. 106, 1575.

Reading between the lines of the constitution agreed upon at Nîmes, the republican nature of the government therein provided for is noticeable.[1] The right to exercise the sovereign rights of legislation, of justice, of taxation, of making war and peace, of regulating commerce no longer were vested in the King where the Act of Union prevailed, but in a representative body. Languedoc, Provence, and Dauphiné were *de facto* independent of the crown.[2] Supplementary articles of Condé and Damville, and of the Catholics and Protestants of Languedoc, Provence, and Dauphiné demanded (1) that freedom of exercise of religion without distinction be permitted; (2) that the parlements should be composed half of Catholics, and half of Protestants, the latter to be nominated by the prince of Condé; (3) that justice be done upon the authors of the massacre of St. Bartholomew and the forfeit and attainder of the admiral be reversed; (4) that the places at present held by the Huguenots be retained besides Boulogne and La Charité, and that for additional defense the King should give them in each province two out of three towns to be named to him by the prince of Condé; (5) that the King pay 200,000 crowns for expenses of the war; (6) that neither the marshal de Retz, nor the chancellor Biragues should have any part in the negotiations for peace; (7) that the duke of Montmorency and the marshal Cossé should be set at liberty, and their innocence declared in full Parlement "en robe rouge;" (8) that the heirs of those who have been murdered should have their estates returned to them; (9) that the queen of England, the elector palatine, and the dukes of Savoy and Deux-

---

[1] "L'organisation politique de cette Union (Union protestante) fut élaborée dans les assemblées tenues à Milhau, en décembre, 1573, et en juillet, 1574. La base fut l'autonomie des villes, que usurpèrent peu à peu l'administration. La Rochelle et Montauban confièrent l'autorité à des chefs électifs, pris dans la bourgeoisie. En suite ces républiques urbaines se fedérèrent. Il fut décidé que chaque généralité aurait son assemblée et que délégués des généralités formeraient les états généraux de l'Union. Ainsi se constitua au sein du royaume une république fédérative. où l'élément aristocratique ne tarda pas à dominer (Lavisse et Rambaud, *Histoire générale*, V, 147; cf. Cougny, "Le parti républicain sous Henri III," *Mémoires de la Sorbonne*, 1867; Hippeau, "Les idées républicaines sous le règne de Henri III," *Revue des Soc. savant. des départ.*, IVe sér., III.

[2] L'Estoile, I, 3, 38.

ponts should be parties to the peace; (10) that within three months after peace the States-General be assembled to establish good order in France.[1]

For a while there seemed to be a prospect of the King yielding to these demands. He was growing jealous of the influence of the Guises, and began to perceive that coercion was impossible.[2] At the first audience Henry received the deputies graciously, saying he "liked their speech, but their articles were hard." The articles were debated *seriatim* by the King, both with the deputies and with the council. The chief hitch was upon the fourth demand. The King was willing to permit exercise of Protestant worship in *one* town in each bailiwick, *except closed* towns, whereas the deputies demanded freedom of worship in all places *in the suburbs* as provided by the Edict of January. As a matter of prudence, it would seem to have been better policy for the crown to permit worship in the suburbs of all towns rather than exact a provision requiring concentration of the Protestants in one place in each bailiwick; however, the King probably thought Calvinism would be less likely to spread under such a restriction than if the Huguenots enjoyed numerous places of worship.[3] The queen mother sought to persuade Montmorency to use his influence to abate the demands with promise of release from the Bastille as his reward. But the duke replied that "if his imprisonment might do the King pleasure or profit he was content to be there all his life; but to meddle in the peace, or to write of that matter, never understanding their doings, were to make himself guilty in it, and to be thought to make himself to be an instrument to their ruin, and therefore it were ill for him."[4] Thereupon Henry III broke off the negotiations hoping still, as earlier, to be able to separate the Huguenots and the united Catholics.

---

[1] I have availed myself of the synopsis in *C. S. P. For.*, No. 112, May, 1575.

[2] Dr. Junius to the prince of Condé, *Archives de la maison d'Orange-Nassau*, V, 237.

[3] See Dr. Dale's observations in letter to Burghley, May 21, 1575; *C. S. P. For.*, No. 138.

[4] *Ibid.*, No. 121, May 4, 1575. Through the duke of Savoy Henry III seems to have offered to set Montmorency free, provided Damville would deliver up Aigues-Mortes (*ibid.*, No. 168, June 6, 1575).

Events thereafter thickened rapidly.   Narbonne, Perigueux, and Tournon in Lyonnais were taken by the Huguenot-Politique armies.   The last place was got by Damville himself.   Tournon was an especially strong town on the Rhone about three leagues from Valence, with Livron to the south of it.   The capture so discouraged the duke d'Uzes that he requested leave to resign on account of the desertions among his following.[1]   Instead command was given him, "to spoil Languedoc in order to famish them against winter."   But the duke was too wise to obey and Damville was permitted to gather in the harvest without molestation.   For if the King had tried ravaging, the whole country would have risen against him.   St. Jean-d'Angély, Angoulême, and Nérac revolted so far as to expel the garrisons in the town.   In Burgundy, where Tavannes had founded the League of the Holy Spirit, a Politique league was formed.[2]   The narrow escape Damville had at this time from death by poison drew men more than ever to him.   As a climax to the woes of Henry III on July 15, 1575, the Polish diet declared the throne vacant, absolving all from allegiance to him.[3]

The *spontaneous* nature of the rising of the country in the summer of 1575 is an interesting historical phenomenon.   It was by no means confined to the south of France.   In Champagne, the nobles, some of them vassals of Guise, and *peasants* united to fall upon the reiters.   Madame de Guise fled from Joinville in fear of being surprised by a sixteenth-century Jacquerie.   In Brittany there was a similar stir when the King attempted to confiscate the extensive lands of the duke of Rohan upon his death.   Certain things remind one of happenings in the French Revolution.   Many in Champagne left the land and went into the borders of Germany like the "emigrés" after August 4, 1789.   In Paris there were house-to-house visits not unlike those of September, 1793.   There was universal feeling against the reiters.   In Normandy an asso-

---

[1] C. S. P. For., Nos. 114 and 287, anno 1575.

[2] Letter of the duke of Guise to M. de Luxembourg from Châlons, September 3, 1575, Coll. des autographes, 1846, No. 213.   The duke of Guise was anxious for the safety of Langres.

[3] C. S. P. For., No. 235, July 15, 1575, from Cracow.

ciation of gentlemen was formed for the special purpose of protecting the country from them.[1]

The anxiety of the government was all the greater because it was not exactly known what relations existed between the Huguenots and Politiques and the English. The treaty which had obtained between Charles IX and Elizabeth was renewed by the latter on April 1, 1575, and confirmed by Henry III on May 4.[2] But Elizabeth was not the person to be bound by official word. On the Picardy-Flemish border mutual distrust prevailed. In December, 1574, Requesens had advised Philip II of his fear of the renewal of Huguenot activity in the Low Countries, which had been dead since the Genlis disaster,[3] and the garrisons on the frontiers had been increased accordingly. The marriage of Henry III to Louise de Vaudemont gave the Spanish governor great inquietude, for the unfortunate Egmont was her uncle, and Egmont's eldest son, in March, visited his royal cousin of France.[4] Requesens was apprehensive, too, of a marriage between the duke of Alençon and the daughter of William of Orange,[5] and over the fact that the French envoy in Flanders, the sieur de Mondoucet, prudently avoided using the official post, but employed his own couriers in dispatching missives to Paris.[6] "All the neighboring states are actuated by malicious intentions," he wailed to Philip II.

---

[1] C. S. P. For., No. 345, September 13, 1575. In Appendix XXXIV will be found a long account in Latin from the pen of Dr. Dale upon the condition of France at this time.

[2] C. S. P. For., No. 120, anno 1575. Even before leaving Poland Henry III had anxiously written to Elizabeth urging the good offices of his ambassador in England, De la Mothe-Fenelon (see the letter in Appendix XXXV). The articles of peace agreed to during the life of King Charles provided that in the event of the death of one of the contracting parties, that party's successor should be allowed the space of one year to accept or refuse the conditions of peace, the other party being bound by the articles to continue in friendship in the event of the former accepting these articles; the Queen now insisted that, when these articles were first agreed to, the French King was at peace with all his vassals and had by the Edict of January conceded to the Huguenots the free exercise of their religion, and therefore at the present time he was bound to observe all that had been promised (C. S. P. Ven., No. 624, April 24, 1575).

[3] Correspondance de Philippe II, III, 209 and note.

[4] Ibid., 271.   [5] Ibid., 333.   [6] Ibid., 348.

"The French and the English are in correspondence, and both are inspired by the same spirit of hostility against the Catholic religion and against your majesty, as the sole protector thereof."[1]

The arrest of a secretary of Montmorency at Boulogne in March, as he arrived from England, and who admitted he was going to find Damville,[2] coupled with the absence of the prince of Condé and Charles de Meru, the youngest Montmorency, in Germany, so disquieted the King that early in June Schomberg was dispatched across the Rhine to discover what Condé was doing; if he found that levies of cavalry were being made for service in France, he was instructed to enroll 8,000 soldiers for the service of the King.

Schomberg proved a good agent, for he shortly afterward wrote that he believed a secret engagement existed between Queen Elizabeth, some of the German princes, and the enemies of the French King at home; and that Condé, having expended 30,000 crowns, had raised 8,000 cavalry which might be expected to arrive at the frontier by the middle of August, although it was given out, and believed by some, that these reiters were intended for service in the Netherlands.[3]   On the strength of these suspicions, espe-

---

[1] *Correspondance de Philippe II*, III, 319, 320.

[2] *C. S. P. Ven.*, No. 622, March 22, 1575. In Arch. nat., K. 1537, No. 22, is the report of a Spanish spy, written from Calais on March 18, 1575, which confirms the suspicion of English tampering in France. Printed in Appendix XXXVI.

[3] Schomberg's observations were absolutely just, for on July 23, 1575, at Heidelberg, an instrument was signed by Charles Frederick, the elector palatine, Henry, prince of Condé, and Charles de Montmorency, in which the count palatine acknowledged the receipt from the English Queen of 50,000 "crowns of the sun, each crown being of the value of six English shillings sterling," which amount was transferred to "Henri de Bourbon, prince de Condé, chief of those of the religion in France, as well as of those Catholics with them associated" (i. e., the Politiques). Elizabeth's name was to be shielded throughout, the elector assuming entire liability for repayment which was to be made "before the army now levied in Germany for service in France shall depart to France" (see *C. S. P. For.*, No. 254, "The obligation and quittance of the prince of Condé," July 23, 1575, Heidelberg; cf. *ibid.*, *Ven.*, 627; July 12, 1575, the guess of the Venetian ambassador in France). Cf. *ibid.*, No. 633, September 7, 1575. The Venetian ambassador seems to have thought that trouble in Ireland would prevent England from advancing any more to the Huguenots (*ibid.*, No. 631, August 9, 1575). The harvest of 1575 was generally good. But no invading army would enter France before the grain was cut and stacked (cf. *ibid.*).

cially when the duke of Guise sent word in the first week of September that 2,500 reiters had crossed the Rhine, the English ambassador, Dr. Dale, who hitherto had lodged in the Faubourg St. Germain, was advised to remove into the city, ostensibly for his greater security, but really to prevent him from receiving unknown persons secretly at night, as was possible where he resided.[1]

At this juncture, when everything was tense and everybody was on edge, the duke of Alençon managed to make his escape from the court (September 15). While not actually confined, like the duke of Montmorency, he and Henry of Navarre had both been kept under continuous surveillance for months and various efforts made by them to get away had failed. Dismay prevailed at court when the escape was known. The King was "as a man out of courage," and betook himself to extravagant religious demonstration, as before, when at Avignon, "going from church, as though deserted by all his people."[2] He knew that his brother's presence would draw many of the gentry, who were yet hesitating, to the ranks of the Politiques.[3] He had no means to levy an army, nor the resources to sustain it.

In this crisis Catherine de Medici kept the clearest head of all at the court. While she sought to wheedle the runaway prince with smooth words, going as far as Dreux to meet him, detachments were ordered out from Rouen, Orleans, and Chartres to surround him. But Alençon was not to be trapped and rode swiftly

---

[1] *C. S. P. Ven.*, No. 634, September 11, 1575.

[2] *Ibid., For.*, No. 388, October 3, 1575; L'Estoile, *anno* 1575; see the interesting details of Henry III's curious fits of contrition in Frémy, "Henri III, pénitent; étude sur les rapports de ce prince avec diverses confréries et communantés parisiennes," *Bull. du Com. d'hist. et d'archéol. du diocèse de Paris*, 1885.

[3] Claude Haton, II, 780; Walsingham to Burghley, *State Papers, Foreign, Elizabeth*, CV, No. 51, printed in Appendix XXXVII. From Dreux the duke issued a manifesto, September 17, 1575, in which he explained his conduct and complained of the undue taxation and the imposition which the people were suffering in the King's name, declaring that he would take under his protection all the French of the two religions, and demanding the call of the Estates-General for redress of grievances (Claude Haton, II, 781 and note). Alençon styled himself "Gouverneur-général pour le roy et protecteur de la liberté et bien publique de France" (*C. S. P. For.*, No. 365, September, 1575).

off toward the Loire in the hope of falling in with La Noue or the viscount of Turenne. At the same time the duke of Guise was ordered to make a vigorous resistance against the coming of Condé's reiters. But even his army was in a bad state on account of the defection of officers and men, who had gone over to Alençon, so that new troops had to be sent him.[1] Almost all the soldiery in the service of the King was withdrawn from Dauphiné and Languedoc and concentrated in Burgundy and Champagne.[2] Much depended upon the result of the coming battle with the reiters. If the King's troops were beaten, Paris would be in a serious strait between the King's enemies. Already, in consequence of the withdrawal of troops, all Auvergne, Bourbonnais, Nivernais, Gâtinais, and the Beauce were in arms, and the gentlemen of these regions had gone over to the duke of Alençon. Only the vigilance of the garrisons at Orleans and Tours, Moulins and Nevers, enabled the crown to maintain the line of the Loire river.

The reiters attempted to evade Guise and find another way of entrance into France, so that the duke left his artillery in Lorraine and by forced marches went to Sedan, with the intention of giving battle there. But the reiters, about 2,500, under Thoré, avoided an engagement and maneuvered to join a Protestant force of 2,000 Picards, and Guise fell back on Rheims in order to hold the crossing of the Aisne, meantime asking the King for reinforcements which were so slow in coming that the duke was compelled to retire to the Marne. On October 9 he established his headquarters between Château-Thierry and Epernay, near Port-à-Pinson. The encounter took place near Fismes, on the Marne, above Dormans, on October 10. Not more than fifty were killed on either side and the combat did not deter the reiters from continuing their course and crossing the Seine near Nogent-sur-Seine, which they were able to do on account of low water. Their chief loss was of two or three cornets of reiters whom Guise bribed to

---

[1] Claude Haton, II, 784, 785.

[2] Paris furnished the King 4,000 soldiers at its own expense. The new troops were lodged in the faubourgs of St. Germain, St. Marceau, and Notre-Dame des Champs (*ibid.*, 787).

desert. De Thoré owed his easy escape, however, to the serious wound which the duke of Guise sustained. For a bullet struck him in the side of the face, tearing his ear clear away and so mangling the cheek that he was fearfully scarred for the rest of his life and always wore a velvet mask.[1]

The insignificance of the victory of the duke, however, did not deter the King from proclaiming a solemn procession and *Te Deum* in honor of the day. The "victory" also was made the justification of a new tax. On October 12, 1575, by command of the King, the burgesses of Paris assembled in the grand room of the Hôtel-de-Ville where the provost of the merchants, Charron, made known a new demand of the King for aid in the form of a capitation tax upon the burgesses of the city and other places in the *prévôté* of Paris for the payment of 3,000 Swiss, making half of the 6,000 which the King required for defense of the realm, in addition to the sum of 15,000 francs expected for each of the ensuing months.

Once again were the people of Champagne made the victims of the spoiler. All the horses of the poor laborers whom the reiters encountered on the road were forcibly seized, as was also the case in the hostelries where they lodged. A single parish lost thirty horses. The only payment the poor peasantry got was to be beaten for their protests.

For the space of three or four days one might see along the roads and in the villages soldiers all of the time, making for the crossing of the Seine at La Motte de Tilly. Two troopers rode one horse and their presence was hard upon the merchants and the priests, whom they met in the way. The smaller merchants were despoiled of their property, and those known to be wealthy had their riches extorted from them by force, or else were held prisoner until ransomed. To make matters worse, in the wake of the army came a rabble of looters and plunderers, mostly French.[2]

It was obvious that as long as the reiters were in the field, the King could send no force against his brother. He blamed the

---

[1] Claude Haton, II, 788–89; D'Aubigné, Book VII, chap. xix. From this circumstance the duke was often called Le Balafré. (*C. S. P. For.*, No. 450, November 10, 1575.)

[2] Claude Haton, II, 797.

queen mother for everything that had happened, especially for
the escape of Alençon, and Catherine, by way of reply, is said to
have sent him a copy of Commines to read with the advice to emu-
late the policy of his crafty predecessor. But as a contemporary
scornfully observed, Henry of Valois was not Louis XI. What
could be expected from a King who spent his time "going from
abbey to abbey and devising with women."[1]   In sorrow and
anxiety, sustained by the dukes of Montmorency and Montpensier
and the fine old marshal Cossé, Catherine made earnest efforts
to negotiate a truce with the duke of Alençon.

Prefacing his demands by the caution that he could not negotiate finally without Condé or Damville, Alençon demanded surrender of Pont-de-Cé on the Loire, besides La Charité, Bourges,
Angoulême, Niort, Saumur, and Angers for the Huguenots; and
Mezières in Champagne, Langres in Burgundy, or La Fère in
Picardy for the prince of Condé;[2] a large settlement for himself;
a promise that the States-General should be convened for the
Politiques; the crown to pay 200,000 crowns to the Protestant
reiters; the exercise of Calvinist worship in as ample terms as
obtained in 1570 (till more fully provided for in the ultimate articles
of peace); the revolted provinces to remain in arms, except in
the case of mercenaries, it being understood that no acts of hostility
be done and commerce and trade to be free during the interim.
The King's council, when these sweeping terms were laid before
it, advised the King to yield, seeing no way out on account of lack
of means to carry on the war. But Henry III was furious and
threw the articles in the fire. In defiance of the advice of his
friends, who told him to employ what few funds he had in corrupting the reiters with Condé, he sent 30,000 crowns more to Germany
to purchase assistance.

In this strait, money came suddenly, as from heaven. The

[1] C. S. P. For., No. 422, October 29, 1575. The King called these pilgrimages
"nouaines" (cf. ibid., No. 506, Dr. Dale to Lord Burghley, December 20, 1575).

[2] Protestant worship was provisionally authorized in the towns held by the
confederates. Angoulême and Bourges refused to open their gates to Alençon and
so he was offered Cognac and St. Jean-d'Angély instead. The prince of Condé
was refused admittance to Mezières (Claude Haton, II, 805, note).

papal nuncio proffered 100,000 crowns at once and promised 200,000 more, while the Venetian government, in memory of his visit there in the year previous, made him a gift of his jewels that were in pawn. Finally, to crown the King's jubilation at this sudden turn of events, word came from Germany that the reiters hired by Schomberg and Bassompierre were coming "and would not be stayed by the truce." Henry III at once broke off negotiations. The hope was to sever Alençon from the prince of Condé and then, preferably by bribery, by war if necessary, overcome the latter, for Schomberg persuaded the King that this course was practicable. To this end commissioners were sent abroad to levy new taxes.[1] Great ingenuity was shown in the devising of new forms of taxation. In June, 1575, two edicts had been issued, one requiring the fixing of new seals to bolts of woolen cloth and the establishment of a *greffier des tailles* in each parish;[2] the other creating the office of four *arpenteurs* (land commissioners) in each jurisdiction of the realm. The number of notaries was also augmented.[3] In December the King made a pretext of the coming of the reiters to demand a new subsidy from the pliant and obedient people of France, under cover of raising men for the war. Of the Parisians he demanded the sum of 200,000 livres, to pay three thousand Swiss. Another pretext was the repair of the bridge at Charenton, which the Huguenots had broken in 1567.[4] These taxes fell all the more heavily because in addition to the ruin of the country by war, the crops were short throughout the land on account of the dry summer. "The rivers everywhere were so low that in many places one could wade them. Every morning the sun rose and every evening it set red and inflamed."[5]

[1] For details as to this levy, see Claude Haton, II, 804. This tax was laid upon the clergy, as well as others, and called forth a protest from the former, who pleaded an edict issued by Henry III at Avignon shortly after his return from Poland, forbidding the governors to enforce the payment of tailles, munitions, etc., upon the clergy.

[2] Fontanon, IV, 840.

[3] Claude Haton, II, 820.

[4] Paris remonstrated against this *ibid.*, 828 and note 1).

[5] *Ibid.*, 817; L'Estoile, I, 46.

In the meantime, fear prevailed in Paris lest the forces of Damville and the viscount of Turenne would effect a junction with those of the duke of Alençon and the united body march upon Paris, and garrisons were hastily put in Montereau, Corbeil, Charenton, St. Cloud, and St. Denis. The old trenches on both sides of the river were repaired and platforms erected in the fields around the city. Montmartre especially was fortified. The townspeople of the capital as well as villagers from the outside were impressed into the work with picks, shovels, and baskets. Mills were erected within the city, and the city was provisioned. The King issued an edict ordering the peasantry within thirty leagues around the capital to thrash their grain and to store it in fortified towns known to be faithful to the crown, unless they were dwelling within nine leagues of Paris, in which case the grain was to be brought into the city. All the passages of the Loire were guarded. The result of all this was a reign of terror in the Ile-de-France. The soldiery indulged in all sorts of brigandage, so that in sheer desperation the villagers sometimes fired their towns. Provisions were commandeered without recompense. To such outrages were the poor people subjected that the inhabitants of one town, Jogny, begged the commander to have mercy upon them. But instead of so doing, Puygaillard loaded the little deputation with reproaches and had them beaten by the soldiers in the presence of all.[1]

With the memory of the elder prince of Condé's presence before the walls of Paris, and the battle of St. Denis, where the constable Montmorency was killed, the Parisians were willing to labor in the trenches for the safety of Paris. But they were not willing to be taxed further. In a remarkable remonstrance, joined in by the clergy, the Parlement, the Chambre des Comptes, the Cour des Aides, the provost of Paris, and the bourgeois and citizens of every quarter of the city, protest was made against the extortion of 200,-000 livres, which Henry III proposed to raise in this hour of extremity. After reciting that civil discord had prevailed in France since 1560, and that during the space of fifteen years the crown

[1] Claude Haton, II, 806–8.

had obtained 36,000,000 francs from Paris and other towns, and 60,000,000 from the clergy, besides other gifts and subsidies, with little progress to show either in politics or religion, the memorial proceeded to point out some of the causes of this universal corruption in scathing terms:

Simony is openly permitted. Benefices are held by married gentlewomen who employ the revenues far differently to the intention of the founders. The people are left without religious instruction and thus stray from the true religion. There is but little justice to be obtained through the venality of the tribunals, causing their neighbors to hold them in abomination. The number of those holding office is very great and part of them notoriously incapable and the rest poor, being thereby prone to evil actions. Justice is further impeded by the impunity with which murder is committed. Great cruelties and barbarities are committed by the foot soldiers and by the gendarmerie, which does not now consist of gentlemen but of persons of vile condition. Not only by these, but by the soldiers of his guard, is pillage made on the houses of his people, ecclesiastical holdings, and hospitals even in Paris itself, so that the poor cannot obtain common necessaries.[1]

During these weeks Montmorency had earnestly labored in favor of peace, pleading, arguing, expostulating both with his own younger brothers and Alençon. He was as earnestly supported by Catherine de Medici, now converted to a peace policy by the force of events,[2] but both were continually thwarted either by the King's inconstancy or the machinations of the Guises.

The illness of the queen mother—she suffered so much from sciatica that often she was unable to leave her chamber—and the frivolity of the King were a positive advantage to the Guises' policy.

It will be remembered that the fortress of La Fère had been tentatively demanded of the King for the prince of Condé. Henry III had replied offering Doulens in Picardy instead of either La Fère or Peronne, which was later suggested, on the plea that he could not exact obedience from the inhabitants of the latter places. This demand for a border fortress near Flanders was made by the duke of Alençon, in reality to further his own advantage in

---

[1] C. S. P. For., No. 535.

[2] Dr. Dale writes on February 28: "The Guises are nothing privy to the queen mother's doings and she likes as evil of them."—C. S. P. For., No. 634, February 28, 1576.

the Spanish Netherlands, and he took the method of having Condé take title to it as a means of concealing his purpose.

The possible disposal of any border fortress in Picardy in such a way tremendously alarmed the king of Spain and the Guises who concerted to break the peace.[1] This plan is the true origin of the formation of the famous Holy League, which, although it assumed organized form only after the peace of Bergerac (September 17, 1576), nevertheless existed in a tentative state this early, in the combined action of the dukes of Guise, Nemours, Mayenne, and Nevers, Biragues the chancellor, and other satellites of the house of Guise to prevent peace being made on such terms, and to break it in event of its being made.[2] Twice this cabal called upon the King to give battle before all the forces of the opposition were united and twice the queen mother foiled their purpose by securing delay. On February 22 a violent scene took place between her and the council—Henry III was sick—in which Catherine branded those who said her son was a traitor as liars and declared that in spite of opposition "it shall be peace."

The indifference of Henry III to the gravity of the situation and his supreme egotism are remarkable, yet thoroughly in keeping with his character. For hours together he would prate of poetry and philosophy—"de primis causis, de sensu et sensibili and such like questions"—with his favorites, in the retirement of a cabinet, while the realm was going to rack and ruin. The Venetian ambassador describes one of these symposiums with minute care in a dispatch of February 3, 1576.

For the last few days [he says] his Majesty has taken his pleasure by retiring into a small apartment which has no window, and to his apartment

[1] C. S. P. For., No.592, January 1576: "The King of Spain makes the King very great offers to break the peace."

[2] Dr. Dale to Sir Thomas Smith and Walsingham. All the fair promises of the delivery of Bourges and La Charité are like to come to nothing, as may appear by the enclosed letter of Monsieur to the Court of Parliament. There is a secret League between Guise, Nemours, Nevers, Maine, and others of that house, together with the Chancellor, against all that would have any peace, and if it should be made, to begin a sharp war afresh (C. S. P. For., No. 583, anno 1576). From the first Languet was skeptical. He anticipated reaction (Epist. secr., I, Part II, 181, 205).

his Majesty summons four or five youths of the city who follow the profession of poets and light literature, and to meet these people his Majesty invites the Duke of Nevers, the Grand Prior, Biragues, Monseigneur, De Soure, the queen of Navarre, his sister, Madame de Nevers, and the marshal de Retz, all of whom profess to delight in poetry. When they are thus assembled his Majesty orders one of these youths to speak in praise of one of the virtues, exalting it above all the others, and as soon as he has concluded his reasoning each person in turn argues against the proposal which has been made. His Majesty consumes many hours in this exercise, to the small satisfaction of the queen mother and everybody else, who would desire to see in times so calamitous his Majesty attending to his urgent affairs, and not to amusements, which, however praiseworthy at other times, are now from the necessity of the case condemned by all, seeing that the King for this cause fails to be present at his council and there to discuss matters which are of the greatest importance and which having regard to his own position and that of his kingdom can easily be imagined to require attention.[1]

Strange as it may seem, the Guises' determination to continue the war comported with the wishes of some of their enemies—a circumstance which illustrates how singular was the alliance existing between the Huguenots and the Politiques. The religious Huguenots already, in the middle of December, had remonstrated

[1] M. Frémy has published a work in which he makes the bizarre claim that the origin of the Académie française is to be at least remotely ascribed to Henry III (*Les origines de l'Académie française. L'Académie des derniers Valois, 1570-1585*, d'après des documents nouveaux et inédits, 1888. There is a review of it in the *English Hist. Review*, III, 576). Some one has said that "all the Valois kings were either bad or mad." The aphorism would seem to apply to the character of Henry III, in both capacities. He was a mountebank, a roisterer, a dabbler in philosophy, a religious maniac, and a moral pervert. L'Estoile and Lippomano especially abound in allusions or accounts of him (e. g., *Rel. vén.*, II, 237-39). Compare this account with the earlier observations of Suriano, *ibid.*, I, 409, and Davila, VII, 442. On the "mignons," Henry III's favorites, see L'Estoile, I, 142, 143. Henry III's very handwriting manifests his character: "Son écriture semble tout d'abord régulière, mais elle n'est pas formée, les lettres s'alignent sans s'unir, sans se rejoindre, certainement c'est une des écritures les plus difficiles à déchiffrer . . . . C'est l'homme qui s'y révèle l'indolent, l'efféminé monarque qui de son lit écrivait ces lignes à Villeroy: 'J'ay eu le plaisir d'avoir veu vostre mémoire très bien faict comme tout ce qui sort de vostre boutique, mais il fault bien penser, car nous avons besoin de regarder de près à nos affaires. Je seray sitost là que ce seroit peine perdue d'y répondre. Aussi bien suis-je au lit *non malade, non pour poltronner, mais pour me retrouver frais comme la rose.*' "—La Ferrière, *Rapport de St. Pétersbourg*, 27.

against the terms of peace proposed on the ground that the offers made did not promise as much of advantage or security as a continuation of the war. It was argued that the truce would result in greater prejudice to them since the King would still be prepared for war and that if they now let the opportunity pass of establishing their fortune by the aid of the reiters, the result would bring calamity to them.[1] These narrow-minded dissidents looked with ill favor upon the politic course of the duke of Alençon in avoiding the pillage of the towns he took, even of trusting to their loyalty and refraining from putting garrisons in them (some of these towns were Dreux, Romorantin, Thouars, and Loudan), and censured him for his pacific overtures to the Parlement of Paris.[2] Accordingly they hailed with delight the escape of Henry of Navarre (February 5, 1576), and his immediate abjuration[3] of the Catholic faith which he had been forced to confess on St. Bartholomew's Day, and the renewed advance of the reiters into Burgundy and Auvergne and thence across the Loire into Bourbonnais, notwithstanding the fact that these mounted mercenaries "made a terrible spoil with fire and fagots" wherever they went.

The reiters took the road toward Langres, crossed the Seine above Châtillon into Auxerre, making for the passage of the Loire River at La Charité, in order to effect a junction with the duke of Alençon, who was in Berry, not far from Bourges. Champagne and Brie were filled with robbers in the wake of their advance, who, pretending that they were soldiers, plundered the townspeople and robbed wayfarers and travelers. There were regular bands of these freebooters, the members of which were paid regular wages by their captains. But the anarchy in the provinces did not compel the King to stop his dallying with philosophy, or his love for mad-cap pranks. He went off on a Shrovetide frolic in March, "riding about the town to cast eggs and such other disorders," leaving Mayenne to labor with those nobles who refused to be com-

---

[1] See the remonstrance in *C. S. P. For.*, No. 505, December 19, 1575.

[2] *Ibid.*, No. 584, January 9, 1576.

[3] For particulars see Dale's letter to Smith and Walsingham, *ibid.*, No. 605, February 6, 1576; Claude Haton, II, 829.

manded "by a boy that never saw wars and a soldiery whose pay was a whole quarter in arrears."[1] Mayenne made his headquarters at Moulins to prevent the reiters uniting with Alençon and the Huguenots of Poitou and Guyenne. It required all the address of the marshal Biron to restrain the young commander from throwing himself upon them, almost careless of the outcome, for defeat could have been little worse than the daily shrinkage of his army from desertion.[2]

Henry III at first had pretended to make light of the escape of his cousin. But the presence of Henry of Navarre in the field soon had an important influence. It was the one thing needful to complete the organization of the Huguenots, many of whom looked upon the prince of Condé more as a Politique than as one of them. The harmonious working of the two parties opposed to the crown was now possible in greater degree than before. Henry of Navarre, the prince of Condé, the duke of Alençon, and Damville united, were in a position to bring things to a focus. The actual territory controlled by Henry III at this time was little, if any, greater than the ancient Ile-de-France, Burgundy, and Champagne of his ancestors in the twelfth century. The Hugue nots and Politiques so divided the realm among themselves that a map of the kingdom at this time reminds one of that of France in the feudal age. Henry of Navarre had made his headquarters at Saumur and thus was able easily to control Anjou; the allegiance of Guyenne, Béarn, and Poitou was certain; the duke of Alençon was in occupation of the "midlands"—Berry (except Bourges)

---

[1] C. S. P. For., Nos. 614, 625, 662, February 14–22, March 8, 1576. Mayenne, whose marquisate was erected into a duchy on January 1, 1576, had succeeded his brother, the duke of Guise, as chief commander of the royal forces, and advanced toward Lorraine in order to prevent the reiters from joining the enemy. Henry III had sent Biron (he had been made a marshal in the June preceding—ibid., No. 178, June 13, 1575) to them to persuade them not to enter France, representing that a truce had been concluded between the King and the duke of Alençon. But the prince of Condé replied that if the duke had made his peace with the King, he, the prince, had not. Biron failed and La Noue was sent, who likewise was unsuccessful (Claude Haton, II, 824, 825).

[2] C. S. P. For., No. 662, Dale to Smith and Walsingham, March 8, 1576; Claude Haton, II, 832.

and most of Bourbonnais and Nivernais. Young Coligny, who
had succeeded Montbrun, was in Dauphiné, and his fealty to the
religion was unswerving; Damville and his lieutenants controlled
all Languedoc, Provence, and Auvergne; young Montgomery
was in Lower Normandy where English assistance secretly helped
him, while the prince of Condé, backed by the count palatine,
endangered Picardy.

The winning cards were all in the hands of the Huguenots and
the Politiques. Without territory, without funds, with an unpaid
army or hireling mercenaries only, the crown had no other recourse
than to accept the situation and make peace unless Henry III
and the queen mother stooped to the worse humiliation of receiving the support of Philip II. And so it came to pass that while
Paris daily expected to withstand a siege and the faubourgs and
gates were so crowded with those living outside the walls and
refugees from the environs "that a man could scarce enter the
gates for the people, carriages, and cattle,"[1] Henry III signed
the Act of Peace, May 2, 1576.

The peace of 1576, sometimes called the Peace of Monsieur,
from the duke of Alençon's prominent part in its formation, was
the most complete and elaborate charter yet given the Huguenots,
embodying the wisdom that experience had taught. It is to be
noticed that the settlement involved both toleration of the religion
and political reform. The provisions of this composite peace may
be classified under four heads, each of which was an essential element in the late opposition to the crown, viz:—the Huguenots,
Henry of Navarre, the duke of Alençon, the Politiques.

The King granted to the Huguenots public exercise of the
Calvinist religion throughout France except within two leagues
of the court and four leagues of Paris. The Huguenots were
declared eligible to all offices and dignities without discrimination
on account of religion. As a security for the King's justice against
possible abuse of these rights, the crown engaged to establish
mixed parlements, half Catholic, half Protestant, at Poitiers,
Bordeaux, Toulouse, Montpellier, Grenoble, Aix, Dijon, Rheims,

[1] C. S. P. For., No. 740, April 17, 1576.

and Rouen, and a new chamber in the Parlement of Paris with two presidents and eighteen councilors, nine of them Catholic, nine Protestant. Protestant advocates, *procureurs-généraux* and *greffiers* civil and criminal were to be connected with each of these mixed parlements.

For further protection of the Huguenots, eight cautionary towns were to be ceded to them, to wit: Aigues-Mortes and Beaucaire in Languedoc; Périgueux and Le Mas de Verdun in Guyenne; La Rochelle in Poitou; Yssoire in Auvergne; Nions and Serres (château included) in Dauphiné; Cennes "la grande tour et le circuit" in Provence. Additional demands were for general oblivion for all conduct and action by persons of either side; revocation of all decrees, judgments, and proclamations hitherto made; rehabilitation of the memory of Admiral Coligny and restoration of their livings and honors to his children as well as in the cases of Montgomery, Montbrun, Bricquemault, and Cavagnies. No prosecution was to be made with regard to the actions done at St. Germain-en-Laye and Bois de Vincennes.

Two of these provisions were received with great dissatisfaction by the Huguenot deputies and when published were decried by many of the Protestants. The first of them was the prohibition of Protestant worship within the faubourgs of Paris, the act specifically declaring that St. Denis, St. Maur-des-Fosses, Pont-de-Charenton, Bourg-la-Reine and Port de Neuilly were within the prohibited confines. The other one which met with great objection was that touching the security towns.[1] The deputies demanded two towns in every government (there were fourteen governments). But the King would yield only eight, these to be chosen from the towns already in possession of the Huguenots, a proviso which eliminated such important points as Niort, Angoulême, and Cognac. In the case of La Charité and Saumur, over which the longest discussion arose, a compromise was reached by giving them

---

[1] Dr. Dale wrote truly to Lord Burghley saying that the Protestants had "gotten more without any stroke stricken than ever could be had before this time by all the wars, as appears by the note of the provinces that are to be under the government of them and their friends."—*C. S. P. For.*, No. 777, May 11, 1576.

to Alençon in appanage. Long and acrimonious debate was made over this article, and at one stage the negotiations were so nearly broken off that Paris was notified to be prepared for a renewal of the war. The crown's demands in this matter were really not unreasonable, for these eight towns were not included in the number given to Henry of Navarre or the prince of Condé, or in the appanage of the duke of Alençon.[1]

If the demands of the Huguenots were excessive, those of Henry of Navarre were still more sweeping. He not only aimed to live like a king in the future in his own country of Béarn, but sought to commit the crown to the recovery of the kingdom of Navarre as well. All the past claims and grievances of his ancestry were embodied. He demanded: That the King of Navarre command in his government of Guyenne extending from Pilles to Bayonne, in such manner as his ancestors had done; that all captains and governors obey him as the governor and lieutenant-general of the King; that he have the providing of the necessary garrisons; that all his lands and seignories should recognize no other government than he appointed and that all towns and fortresses belonging to him should be at once surrendered; that his right to his kingdom be preserved, and that his subjects should not be taxed for the services of the king of France, according to their ancient immunities; that all gentlemen being his servants, officers, or subjects should come and go and traffic freely through all France without molestation; that his officers and servants should enjoy such privileges as if they served the royal family of France; that he and his heirs should be discharged from the guarantee given by himself and his mother toward the purchases of ecclesiastical property, and for the payment of the reiters; that in view of the fact that the late king had granted 200,000 livres to his mother, the late queen of Navarre, for the celebration of the nuptials of himself and his queen, the King's sister, which has never been paid, and furthermore, because there was also yet due 120,000 livres, arrears of the pension of the late king of Navarre, he prayed the King to deal with him as favorably as he could for payment;

[1] La Popelinière, III, 361.

that if any offices or benefices fell vacant in seignories of the king of Navarre, he should have the nominating and presenting of such persons; that the King would preserve to him in his lands and seignories his privileges and accustomed sources of revenue, such as the *droit de tabellionage* and *de sceaux*.

Having so far required everything that could conceivably be based upon things present, Henry endeavored to revive the ancient claims of his house in a startling fashion. The old feudal spirit of William of Aquitaine and Raymond of Toulouse seems to have been reincarnated in his person at this time. For Henry demanded further that he be recompensed for the 6,000 livres promised in time past, in virtue of the right that Françoise de Bretagne, wife of Aleyne, sieur d'Albret, father of John of Navarre, had had to the duchy of Brittany.[1] But even this was not all, for Henry of Navarre finally made the demand that the pension of 46,000 livres which his grandfather had enjoyed in recompense for the loss of Navarre, from which his great grandfather had been expelled in 1512 by Ferdinand of Aragon, be continued to him, and *that the King of France should promise to help him to recover Navarre!*[2]

In the nature of things, not a tithe of these demands could be granted by the crown, least of all the last. The massacre of St. Bartholomew had proved how perilous it was to try to drive Catholic France into a war with Spain, and France was less ready now than in 1570–72 to join battle with Philip. Perforce Henry of Navarre had to be content with a restoration of things as they were on August 24, 1572.[3]

The duke of Alençon had created for him a position stronger than that of Henry of Navarre. As a prince of the blood and as a Politique he occupied middle ground between the crown and the Huguenots; in consequence, many of the places which neither

---

[1] This claim ran back to the reign of Charles VII; the original amount was 25,000 livres. Louis XI altered it to 6,000 livres, plus the county of Gaure and the town of Fleurance, and this revised form was approved by Charles VIII in 1496 (cf. *C. S. P. For.*, No. 672, §5; May 16, 1576).

[2] Henry of Navarre's memoir is given *in extenso* in *ibid.*, No. 671, May 15, 1576.

[3] La Popelinière, III, 365.

of the chief principals was willing to resign were included in the grant to him. While technically all the territories so concerned were regarded as appanages,[1] it is plain that a distinction may easily be made between the duchies of Alençon, Maine, Anjou, Touraine, and La Roche—which had originally been given him as a prince of the blood—and places like Bourges, Moulins, Loches, Saumur, La Charité, Pont-de-Sel, Amiens, Moulans, and Mantes. These latter possessions were practically a class apart of security cities intrusted by compromise to the duke. This was particularly true of Saumur and La Charité, which insured the Protestants of passage across the lower and upper Loire, and so linked the South with Normandy on the North and the Palatinate and the German Protestant states to the east. Moreover, Moulins in Bourbonnais and Bourges in Berry assured the Protestants of position there, so that the whole left bank of the Loire from Auvergne to Nantes was in their control. Mantes was meant to compensate the Huguenots in the vicinity of Paris for the loss of Charenton.

The King yielded the government of Picardy again to the prince of Condé, but the matter of what town should be his created much heated argument. The prince himself at first stoutly contended for Boulogne, although he did not say that its convenience to England was the chief reason for his desire. But Henry III as stoutly refused. Then Amiens was suggested, and as compromise this city was given to the King's brother. Condé then demanded Peronne. Although the King would have preferred Doulens or even St. Quentin to this concession, he yielded. The only other detail concerning the prince was the obligation to pay his and his father's debts in Germany, which the crown assumed.

Damville did not come in for as much honor as his colleagues, but was far from being ignored. As the chief of the Politiques or "les catholiques associez," as they were defined in the interest of peace, Damville was and remained the leading man in Languedoc. Aside from the retention of Damville in his government, promise was made the Politiques to summon the States-General

---

[1] Maffert, *Les apanages en France du XVI⁰ au XIX⁰ siècle* (1900).

at Blois within six months for the reformation and reorganization of the administration.[1]

It follows as a matter of course that the maintenance and protection of the multitude of social and civil rights that made the web and woof of a civilized society was guaranteed, such as the validity of Protestant marriage, land and property titles, freedom of education, commerce and trade, etc.

A very delicate matter to adjust was the future relation of the electoral count palatine and the duke John Casimir, his son. A secret alliance had existed between the count palatine, England, and the prince of Condé since July, 1575. In November, Alençon and the Politiques joined the alliance. One of the terms of that alliance was that Metz, Toul, and Verdun were to pass to Casimir as the price of his support and both Huguenots and Politiques— at least Alençon—stood pledged to assist him in securing these Three Bishoprics. But it was manifestly impossible to expect the French crown to grant such a cession, nor is it probable, now that peace had come, that any in France looked with amiability upon this article of the contract of Heidelberg. It were too great a humiliation to have this brilliant conquest of 1552 thus passively surrendered. Fortunately it was found possible to placate John Casimir with less distinguished sacrifices. His claims were purchased for an enormous sum of money—or at least the promise of it; no less than two million florins (three million francs), part to be paid in the coming June and the balance at the next two fairs at Frankfurt, in addition to which he received the whole seigneury of Château-Thierry[2]—worth 20,000 francs per annum— a perpetual colonelcy of 4,000 horse, a company of 100 men-at-arms and 12 reitmeisters, all of which was confirmed by Henry III's declaration that he would "repute and esteem the count palatine and Duke Casimir as good neighbors."

[1] Articles du maréchal de Dampville, gouverneur de Languedoc et des Etats du pays, présentés au Roi pour la décharge de la province, May 2, 1576.—Coll. Godefroy, XCIV, No. 21.

[2] Nusse, "La donation du duché de Château-Thierry par le duc d'Alençon à Jean Casimir, comte palatin du Rhin," *Annales de la Société hist. et archéol. de Château-Thierry*, Vol. XI (1875), p. 61.

The terms of the Peace of Monsieur[1] were exceedingly unpopular in Paris, whose citizens had been the heaviest contributors to the expenses of the war thus closed and who had made strenuous military preparations in defense of the capital, and the unpopularity of Henry III was not enhanced in the eyes of the Parisians by the King's repudiation of a part of the *rentes*, the incomes of which were the chief means of support with many.   But when Charron, the provost of the merchants, and the counselor Abot, at the head of a deputation of the foremost citizens of the capital protested against this high-handed action to the King's own face, Henry III with a sneer which carried with it a covert threat rejoined: "Hang a man and he tells no tales."[2]

The camps of the duke of Alençon and the Protestants were broken up when the peace was published.   The soldiery around La Rochelle and in Poitou, Anjou, and Berry, returned home, except some troops which were reserved until it was seen what Casimir and his reiters, who were near Langres, would do.   These marauders, with many French of Champagne and Brie, crossed the Yonne above Sens and arrived in Champagne between May 10 and 11 and remained there for a week, living on the land.   After having sojourned six or seven days between the Seine and the Vauluisant, on the 16th they moved on to a place between Troyes and the village of Mery-sur-Seine, where they remained for fifteen days to the distress of the people and absolutely destroyed

---

[1] The text of the Paix de Monsieur is in Isambert, XIV, 280.   The sources for the history are many.   The correspondence of Dale, the English ambassador in France, and the other English agents, Wilkes and Randolph, in *C. S. P. For.*, 1876, for March, April, and May, is full and detailed (cf. D'Aubigné, Book VIII, chap. xxvii; De Thou, Book LXXII).   La Popelinière, III, 360 ff., gives the text of the treaty and the letters-patent of the King.   The act was registered in Parlement on May 14, 1576, though signed by the King on May 2.

[2] Two days before this scene took place, the newly elected king of Poland Stephen Bathori, prince of Transylvania, had written informing the deposed Valois that he had assumed the Polish crown and desiring to know what Henry would have done with the household stuff he had left behind in Poland (*C. S. P. For.*, No. 789, May 29, 1576).   The Emperor had had numerous partisans, but refused to accept the condition that he fix his residence in Poland (*Epist. secr.*, I, Part II, 143).

the little village of Marigny, which had but two persons left in it. In order to find food they foraged for miles. The peasantry turned their cattle loose or drove them, together with their possessions, into the fortified towns or châteaux. But the gentry were less safe than the peasantry even, for the latter had already been so despoiled that nothing was left to be taken. Out of this frightful state of affairs rose an organized resistance which is very interesting to observe, for the nobility and gentry of the region and the local peasantry, forgetting their class antagonism, made common cause together. Whenever these "vigilance committees" found themselves to be stronger or happened upon stragglers from the main band, they threw themselves upon them; sometimes the victims were bound and cast alive in the river Aube or Seine. Between St. Loup-de-la-Fosse-Gelane and St. Martin-de-Bossenay, a group of ten or twelve reiters were thus set upon and only one escaped. But the vengeance their comrades meted out upon the offenders was terrible, for the troopers, numbering over a hundred horsemen, the next night burned all the villages round about.[1]

Not until September was this scourge removed from the land. By that time they were bought off and were conducted to the frontier by Bassompierre, the Alsatian gentleman in the King's service, who was well rewarded, as he deserved to be, for the accomplishment of the perilous task. But the licensing of the regular troops immediately afterward still prolonged the agony of the province for a season.[2]

The Peace of Monsieur may fittingly be said to have terminated the period of the *religious* wars of France. The dominant issue of the succeeding years of conflict from 1576 to 1598 was not a religious, but a political one. Why permanent peace did not result it is not the work of this volume to narrate. Suffice to say that Spain and Spain's instrument, the Holy League, were to blame for the ensuing years of strife.

The germ of the provincial Catholic leagues had been the desire, on the part of the Catholics of France, to resist the progress

[1] See the vivid details in Claude Haton, II, 834–40, 847, 851, 858.
[2] *Ibid.*, 855–60.

of Calvinism. But in the hands of the French nobles these local leagues, controlled by the aristrocracy and welded into one mighty organization under the leadership of the duke of Guise, backed by Spanish gold, became a new league of the public weal, which, under the cloak of religion revived the feudal ambition of the French nobility to acquire power at the expense of the crown.

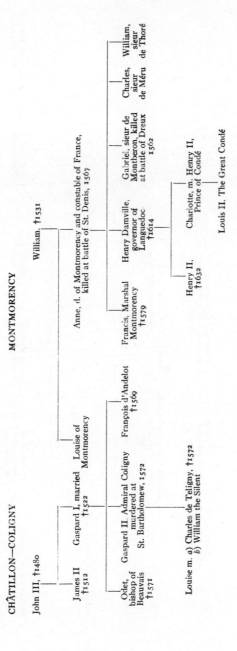

CHÂTILLON—COLIGNY   MONTMORENCY

John III, †1480

William, †1531

James II, †1512   Gaspard I, married Louise of Montmorency, †1522

Anne, d. of Montmorency and constable of France, killed at battle of St. Denis, 1567

Odet, bishop of Beauvais †1571   Gaspard II. Admiral Coligny murdered at St. Bartholomew, 1572   François d'Andelot †1569

Francis, Marshal Montmorency †1579   Henry Damville, governor of Languedoc †1614   Gabriel, sieur de Montberon, killed at battle of Dreux 1562   Charles, sieur de Méru   William, sieur de Thoré

Louise m. a) Charles de Teligny, †1572 b) William the Silent

Henry II, †1632   Charlotte, m. Henry II, Prince of Condé

Louis II. The Great Condé

HOUSE OF LORRAINE AND GUISE

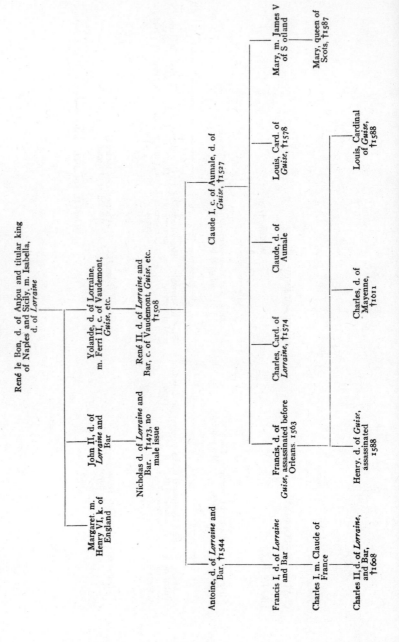

René le Bon, d. of Anjou and titular king of Naples and Sicily, m. Isabella, d. of *Lorraine*

Margaret. m. Henry VI, k. of England

John II, d. of *Lorraine* and Bar

Yolande, d. of Lorraine, m. Ferri II, c. of Vaudemont, *Guise*, etc.

Nicholas d. of *Lorraine* and Bar. †1473, no male issue

René II, d. of *Lorraine* and Bar, c. of Vaudemont, *Guise*, etc. †1508

Antoine, d. of *Lorraine* and Bar, †1544

Claude I, c. of Aumale, d. of *Guise*, †1527

Francis I, d. of *Lorraine* and Bar

Francis, d. of *Guise*, assassinated before Orleans. 1563

Charles, Card. of *Lorraine*, †1574

Claude, d. of Aumale

Louis, Card. of *Guise*, †1578

Mary, m. James V of S otland

Charles I. m. Claude of France

Henry, d. of *Guise*, assassinated 1588

Charles, d. of Mayenne, †1611

Louis, Cardinal of *Guise*, †1588

Mary, queen of Scots, †1587

Charles II, d. of *Lorraine*, and Bar, †1608

HOUSE OF BOURBON
Louis IX, †1270

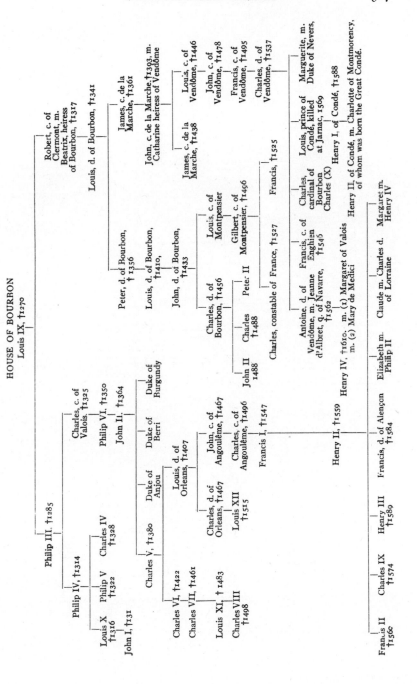

APPENDICES

Appendices

APPENDIX I

[P. 49, n. 2]

STATE PAPERS, FOREIGN

ELIZABETH, VOL. XIII, No. 456

[The Cardinal of Lorraine and Duke of Guise to the Queen-Dowager of Scotland]

Madame nous avons receu votre lettre par ce marinier present porteur et sceu par icelle lestat en quoy sont les affaires de dela *[two pages in cipher]*.

Quant aux nouvelles de deca nous voullons bien que vous sachez que depuis quinze ou vingt jours aucuns malheureux ont essaye icy demectre a fin une conjuration quilz avoient faicte pour tuer le Roy et ne nous y oublyoient [pas][1] tout cela fonde sur la religion dont aucuns des principaulx autheurs [ont este pris] et pugniz. Maiz tant plus nous allons avant et plus trouvons nous [que ceste conspiration] a longue queue ayant este bastie de longue main et appuyee par daucuns gr[andz qui se] sont trouvez bien trompez.   Car nostre Seigneur a bien sceu defendre sa cause.   S'est quasi le mesmes train qui ont prins voz Rebelles mais ilz voulloient commancer par le sang et lespee une autre fois vous en scaurez plus par le menu.   Et pour fin de ceste lettre vous dirons madame que la compaignye faict Dieu mercy tresbonne chere et nous recommandons treshumblement a votre bonne grace, Priant Dieu ma dame vous donner en sante tresbonne et treslongue vye.   De Marmoustre le ix° jour davril 1559.

> *[Signed]*   Voz treshumbles et tresobeissans freres
> C. Car[al] de Lorraine Francoys s[r] de Lorraine.

[Addressed]   A la Royne
> Douairiere et regente Descosse.

[Not endorsed]

[Pencil note by editor]   This is dated "more Gallicano" which commences the year at Easter.   In 1560, Easter day fell on the 14 of April, consequently this letter dated on the 9th would appear to be, as it is dated, in 1559, being in fact 1560.

No. 460

["A portion of the previous letter in French" (Calendar)]

Estant que avecques plus de commodité et de moyen vous navez esté et nestez secourue autant que nous voyons et jugeons trop bien quil seroit neces-saire ce que n'a pas este retardi par faulte de debvoir de soing et de diligence.

---

[1] The words in brackets are faded and are supplied from No. 460.

Car nous en avons cherche . . . .[1] moyenes possibles et mesmes po^r essayer si ceste Royne dangleterre s . . . . addoucir et contenir par quelques remedes qui n'ont . . . . en son endroict, car apres avoir faict du cousté du Roy tout . . . . de penser po^r luy oster la jalousie et le soupcon qu'elle monstre au . . . . nous y avons employe le Roy catholicque tant que par son ambassadeur il luy . . . . quil ne souffriroit pas que elle donnast faveur aux rebelles . . . . aulcune chose au preiudice des droictz et authorite du Roy et de . . . . fille en Escosse.   Depuis y a este envoyé l'evesque de Valence conseillier au . . . . po^r luy rendre raison plus pertinente de l'intention du Roy, et quil ne ch . . . . l'obeissance de ses subiectz, resolu de retirer ses forces apres qu . . . . restablies au bon chemin, tout cela n'a de rien servi si elle n'a . . . . vous avez peu veoir par les articles qu'elle a f . . . . son Ambassadeur si honteux que nous croyons qu'elle sass . . . . nous n'en ferions rien et par ainsy elle passeroit oultre . . . . qui est de la guerre, dont nous veryons peu de moyen de . . . . si ce n'est po^r . . . . refuge l' . . . . de Sieur de Glayon ques^r les . . . . y envoye po^r luy en parler des grosses contz ayant delibere si . . . . obstinee de secourir le Roy de tout ce de luy qu'il vouldra et . . . . a accorde luy bailler gens et vaiss . . . . po^r remettre lobeissance . . . . dont il a este prins au mot.   Et y a este envoye . . . . scavoir de la duchesse de Parme de quel nombre ou . . . . lad. dame charge expresse d'en accommoder le Roy de tout . . . . Cependant Madame nous ne perdons point le temps a faire ad . . . . qui sera dun si bon nombre de vaisseaulx et si bien formy de gens et de toutes choses convenables que nous esperons que lad.   Royne ne ses forces n'auront pas le moyen de les garder de vous secourir tout le p . . . . veryons est qu'elle ne peult estre preste que vers la fin de Iuillet. Mais si ferons nous tout ce que sera possible au monde po^r la mettre plustost a la voyle et ne espargner argent soing ni diligence comme nous nous asseurons que vous croyez bien.   Et neantmoins cherchons nous tous aultres moyens de vous faire secourir de deniers soit de Flandres ou d'ailleurs et aussy ne craindrons nous en adventurer par petites pommes cependant et pour y commencer avons nous advise vous renvoyer . . . . eur dedans vng aultre petit vaisseau que luy avons faict equipper, ne luy . . . . espargne aussy argent car il a eu po^r estre venu icy et le hazard qu'il a douze centz francz que le Roy luy a donnes et trois centz escus po^r son retour.   Avecq luy nous vous envoyons par ung clerc qui l'accompaigne la somme de mille livres et vingt cacques de pouldre menue grevée par ce que nous avons sceu par les lettres des sieurs de la Brosse et Doysell qui vous en avez besoing par dela ce sera pour attendre toutz jours mieulx estantz bien deliberez de . . . . perdre une seule occasion de vous secourir ainsy par le menu au danger . . . . . perdre quelque chose.

Cependant, Madame, il fauldra que de vostre coste vous faciez le mieulx . . . . pourrez et sur tout qu'il soit donné ordre a tenir les places bien . . . .

---

[1] Ellipses indicate places where the MS is faded or creased so as to be illegible.

rnies louant sa ma^te bien fort la defensive sur la quelle les capitaines de dela sont d'advis que vous vous mettiez qui est ung moyen pour avoir la raison de la legerete et mal consyderée entreprise de lad. Royne dont nous esperons que le mal tombera a la fin sur elle et qui Dieu ne laissera impunye la faulte qu'elle faict.

. . . . a este grande consolation au Roy et a toute ceste compaignie d'avoir entendu . . . . les souldatz de dela ayent si bonne volonté, cela nous faict . . . . Dieu qui tout yra mieulx qu'elle ne vouldroit car si led. . . . . gneur Roy catholicque chemine en cecy de bon pied dont il nous asseure il est impossible que la chose ne tourne a sa confusion.

Quant aux nouvelles de ca nous voulons bien que vous scachez que depuis xv ou vingt jo^rs aulcuns malheureux ont essaye icy de mettre a fin une conjuration quilz avoient faicte po^r tuer le Roy et ne nous y oublioient pas. Tout cela fondé sur religion dont aulcuns des principaulx autheurs ont esté pris et punis. Mais tant plus nous allons avant et plus trouvons nous que ceste conspiration a longue queue ayant este bastie de longue main et appuyee par daulcuns grandz qui se sont trouvez bien trompez. Car nostre Seign^r a bien sceu defendre sa cause. Ceste [quasi le mesmes]^1 train qui ont prins voz rebelles, mais ilz vouloient [commancer par le] sang et l'espee. Un autre foys vous en scaurez [plus par le menu] Et po^r fin de ceste lettre.

[Not signed]

[Not addresssed]

[Endorsed]   12 April, 1559^2 (1560) Card. & D of Guise to the queen Dowager whereof another copy was sent to the Q. Ma^te the 3 of Aprill and was dated at Mayremoustier the viij^th of the same.

STATE PAPERS, SCOTLAND

Elizabeth, Vol. III, No. 58.   (Translation.   The parts in italics have been deciphered.)

[The *cardinall of Lor: and duke of Guise to the Quene douag:*]^2

[April 29]

Madame   This bearar hath made verie good diligence to bring us yor lettres wherof we wer verie gladde, for that by the same we understoode yor newes, and the rath^r, for that we had reccyvid none from yo^w, sins the comminge of *Protestant the courrone.* Sins which tyme the *Quene of England* hath ever kept us in allarme to begynne the *warre* and to shew *by all her dealinges that she* had sent to be doinge and sturringe the coles. We beleeve

---

¹ The words in brackets are faded and are supplied from No. 455.   ² The date is in Burghley's hand.   ³ The MS is torn here.

² The reference to the original cipher is "State Papers, Scotland, Elizabeth, Vol. III, No. 82." (This is not signed addressed or endorsed. Pencil note by editor: "See April 29.")

she hath forgotten nothinge, wherby she might thinke to draw anye fruict of her evell disposicion: yf she had fownde thinges in cace to go through wth her businesse. Neverthelesse shee hath gyven us the fairest wordes of the world. *Wherunto the Frenche King hath not so muche trustyd* but that he hathe advertisid the king of Spaine of all that *she hath doon* who having well considered the mater, hath made answer that there is no cause why to disalow his entent specially to go through wth the maters on that side, and that to chastise the Rebelles he will gyve the King, as manye vessells, men, and vitailes, as he will, and so hath writen to the said queene, who knowing that she can hope for nothing of that, that she maketh a rekening of, begynnithe to use oth^r languaige, and causythe her ambassad^r to saye that that she hath done hath ben for none oth^r cause, but for the jalousye she hath of her Realme, and fearinge to be sodaynly taken unwares. So that it seemithe, that she repentethe to have gon so farre furth in the mater. And we beleeve that before theese lettres come to yor handes, yo^w shall have well perceyved, that her intentes ar waxed verye colde. And yf that which she hathe caused to be said by her Ambassado^r be true, yo^w shall have understand all the hole storie, by a man whome the Sr de Sevre the kinges ambassad^r in Englande, hathe sent unto yo^w. Neverthelesse we have thought good to sende yo^w backe againe this said bearar, by the waye of Flandres to advertise yo^w, that we thinke that your Rebelles wilbe farre from their rekeninge, yf they make their accompte of the said Ladyes protection. Or elles there is much dissimulation.

And yet the King knowing after what sorte he must trust Englishemen, leavithe not of, to prepare xxiiij great ships to thintent (yf neede requyre, and that it do appeere, that the sayd Ladye doth contynue her evell disposicion) to gyue ordre wth the same and oth^r forces wch he keepith in a readinesse, to souccour yo^w in such sorte, as he shall have the reason that he requyrethe, of thone and thoth^r.

Yn the meane tyme he hathe sent the busshoppe of Valence, counsello^r in the K^es pryvie counsell, towardes the Queene, to understande plainely her meaninge, and in cace that the same be good, then to come to yo^w wth good and large memorialles, to assaye to appease thinges on that side and to fynde the meanes to wynne tyme.

The thing (Madame,) that greevithe us most, is, that the meanes is hindred and stopped, to soucco^r yow wth money as ofte and as readily as we wold be glad to do, and as yo^w have neede of it. Which we durst not aventure, nor also o^r brother Monsr le Marquis for the evident danger that might happen. But yt cannot be longe before we see some waye open, and yow maye be sure (Madame) that we will not lose one quarter of an houre.

Now (Madame) we must wth yo^w, lament the Evell, that the mater of religion maye bring into a Realme, which hath so gone to worke on this side, that w^thin these xij or xv dayes, there is discouvered a conspiracy, made to kill us bothe. and then to take the King, and gyve him masters and gouvernours to instruct and bring him up in this wretched doctryne. For which pourpose there shuld assemble a great nombre of personnes heerabowtes who ar not w^{th}out the comforte and favour of some great ones. And betwixt the sixth and xv^{th} of this monethe, they shuld execute the same. So that w^{th}out the healpe of God and thintelligences wch we have had from all partes of christendome, and also of some of the conspiratours, that have disclosed it, the matter had taken effect. But God hath provyded heerin for us. The mater being discouvered, and manye beinge prissoners, we hope that the same shall be bowlted out, and so the danger avoyded. Wherof, and how the same shall breake out, yo^w shalbe more particularly advertised heerafter, specially if the waye be freer, then hitherto it hath ben. Yn the meane tyme yo^w shall receyve (if yt please yo^w) our humble commendacions prayeng God &c. Montignac is presently arryved upon the depeche, wherupon ordre shall be taken out of hande.

[*Not signed*]

[*Not addressed*]

[*This and other deciphered letters* (Queen Dowager of Scotland to MM. d'Oysel and de la Brosse 29 [April] and "a private man's letter to d'Oysell" [29 April] 1560) *are written on the same sheets of paper, and are endorsed together:* "The interceptyd lettres discyphred," *and endorsed in Burghley's hand:* "B. 12. Martii. 20. Martii lettres deciphred from France to the Q. dowag."[1]]

APPENDIX II
[P. 98, n. 1]

ARCHIVES NATIONALES,
K. 1,494, PIÈCE NO. 70

[*L'Ambassadeur de France, Mr. de L'Aubespine, évêque de Limoges, au Roi d'Espagne, Philippe II*]

Tolède, 4 avril 1561

[*Suscription*] Au Roy.

[*Au dos, alia manu*] A Su Magestad. Del obispo de Limoges, a IIII° de Abril 1561.

Sire, par ce que la Royne aura peu escrire a Vostre Majesté et Monsieur le Prince d'Evoly aussi, vous aurez entendu l'estat auquel les choses se retrouvoient parmy les Estatz particuliers en France il y a vingt jours par la malice de quelques ungs mal sentans de la foy, lesquelz avoient faict une menée en certaines provinces afin que l'on feist tomber le gouvernement du royaume

---

[1] The Editor's pencil note to the cipher (Scotland ii. 82) is "March 12," but the letter is calendared under [March 20].

en autre main que celuy de la Royne vostre mere, la sentans ferme et constante a n'endurer leurs erreurs et a les punir.   Depuis est arrivé l'un de mes gens avec deux pacquetz de Monsieur de Chantone, lesquelz j'ay faict mectre entre les mains de Sajas.[1]   M'advertissant ladicte dame par le mesme courrier que le Roy de Navarre s'est monstré si conforme en tout ce qu'elle a desiré et peu approuvant la temerité de telles entreprinses, qu'il s'est accommodé pour aussi recevoir quelque lieu et contentemant d'estre seul lieutenant general du Roy vostre bon frere en France soubz ladicte dame, afin que la multitude des autres seigneurs et gouverneurs de tout le royaume n'amenast point la confuzion qui y estoit, que l'on eust quelque adresse, et que, par ce moien aussi il feust plus honnoré et respecté d'ung chascun sans aucune diminution de l'authorité de ladicte dame, laquelle, Sire, demeure chef de toutes choses, ayant les quatre secretaires d'Estat soubz elle, les pacquetz, finances, dons et autres graces avec la personne du Roy, et commande au conseil ainsi que de coustume, tellement que chacun espere, comme aussi faict Sa Majesté et ainsi qu'elle me commande vous dire, Sire, que desormès il y a certaine apparance de toute tranquilité et repos, car ce que dessus est passé, arresté et signé entre eulx et de leurs mains pour articles irrevocables, ayant pour ceste cause mandé aux Estatz qu'ilz eussent à ne penser ne disputter plus sur telz pointz, ains seulement en ce qui concerne le mesnaige du royaume, les reculans et remettans a s'assambler a la fin de l'esté prochain.   Et ce pendant, suivant l'instante requeste du peuple, le Roy vostre bon frere, Sire, partira de Fontainebleau incontinent après ce Quasimodo pour se faire sacrer à Reims dedans le XXe de May, et incontinent après sus le mois de Juing faire son entrée à Paris, d'autant que ces deux actes sollemnelz donnent plus d'authorité et contentement à tous nos subjectz, et que, cela faict, la Royne vostre mère pourra aussi, comme elle desire, plus soigneusement user de la main forte et justice en tout ce qui se presentera.   Ce que dessus, Sire, amandera, s'il vous plaist, en vostre endroit l'opinion mauvaise que nous avions quant je parlay a Monsieur le prince d'Evoly de l'yssue de noz Estatz, lesquelz, par ce remede, sont frustrez de plus rien toucher ne negotier qui concerne le gouvernement.   Me commandant tres expressement la Royne de remercier fort affectionneement Vostre Majesté des bons et roiddes offices desquelz Monsieur de Chantoné a usé près d'elle pendant ces disputz, et asseurant Vostre Majesté que ce luy est obligation telle qu'elle peult faire estat de son amour et affection autant que de sa propre mère, comme de son costé elle se confie tant en sa bonté et amitié que, si l'on eust voulu faire plus de tord a son honneur et preminance, elle eust usé de ce que Dieu a mis.   Sire, soubz vostre obeissance, comme de son meilleur amy, desirant que Vostre Majesté face en semblable estat de tout ce que sera en elle.   Ceulx, Sire, qui avoient tramé ce que dessus pensoient remuer en nostre conseil et autres endroitz les hommes et honneurs à

---

[1] Cayas, secretary to Philip II.

leur guise; mais, par ce moien, ilz sont hors de leurs desseings.   S'estant
Monsieur le prince de Condé contenté d'une declaration qu'on luy a donnée
pour sa justification, à la charge qu'il peust, quant bon luy sembleroit, estre
à la Court près ladicte dame, ainsi qu'il y a esté permis.   Monsieur le connestable a, Sire, faict de bons et saiges offices en cet establissement, me charge-
ant de vous presenter ses tres humbles recomandations, vous requerant,
comme font Leurs Majestez, qu'il vous plaise en sa faveur confirmer en Flandres
une abbaie de dames à l'une de ses parentes que les religieuses desirent fort
depuis le decez de feu madame de Lallain, comme j'éscris à Monsieur le conte
d'Horne.   Ce que, Sire, j'eusse de bouche esté faire entendre à Vostre Majesté;
mais la crainte que j'ay eu de le troubler parmy ces sainctz et devots jours
m'excusera s'il luy plaist, et commandera á Monsieur le pricee d'Evoly qui
cy est, de me faire donner quelque responce sur ceste lettre et sus une precedente
que je vous escrivis il y a deux jours, afin que je puisse faire entendre à la
Royne vostre bonne mère le contentement que recevrez de ce que dessus et
vostre bon conseil.   Quant mon courrier partit, Monsieur le conte d'Heu
avoit desja esté licencié du Roy et de la Royne mère, et suis attendant, Sire,
Monsieur de Montrueil, lieutenant de Monsieur le prince de la Roche-sur-
Yon, lequel arrivera icy dedans quatre ou cinq jours, venant devant pour preparer
ce qu'il sera de besoing et pour aussi visiter la Royne, qui me faict estimer que
ledict seigneur Conte ne sera pas en ceste ville que quatre ou cinq jours après
Quasimodo,[1] dont noz dames ne sont pas contentes, la Royne pour le desir
qu'elle a de reveoir Vostre Majesté plustost, et les autres pour leur interest
particulier.

Sire, je me recommande tres humblement à vostre bonne grâce, priant le
Créateur vous donner entres bonne santé tres heureuse et longue vye.

De Toledo, ce IIIIe d'avril 1561.

Vostre tres humble serviteur
S. DE L'AUBESPINE
E[vesque] de Lymoges

APPENDIX III

[P. 153, n. 1]

STATE PAPERS, FOREIGN

ELIZABETH, VOL. XXXVIII, No. 179

[Letter of the duke of Guise to the cardinal of Lorraine]

[1562, *June* 25]

Extraict de la lettre de Guyse escripte de sa main au cardinal.

Ie vous envoye ce porteur en dilligence pour vous advertir que tout fut
yer accorde.   Et puis vous dire que le commancement est lhonneur de Dieu

[1] On the margin, in the writing of Philip II: "Es menester tener prevenido
lo que se les ha de dar para este tiempo."

service du Roy bien et repoz de ce royaume. Cedit porteur est suffisant et nauront noz chers cardinaulx que part ceste lettre comme aussi nostre mareschal de Brissac qui congnoistra quil y en a qui sont bien loing de leurs desseins. Nostre mere et son frere ne jurent que par la foy quilz nous doibvent et quilz ne veullent plus de conseil que de ceulx que scavez qui vont le bon chemyn. Conclusion la Religion reformee en nous conduisant et tenant bon sen va a baz leaue et les amyraulx mal ce qui est de possible. Toutes noz forces nous demeurent entierement les leurs rompues les billeez rendues sans parler dedictz ne de preches et administracion des sacremens a leur mode. Ces bons seigneurs croiront sil leur plaist cedit porteur de ce quil leur dira de la part de trois de leurs meilleurs amys et bayse la main. De Baugency ce xxve jour de Iuing 1562.

[*No signature*]

[*No address*]

[*Endorsed*] Extraict dune lettre escripte de
la main de mr de Guyse au
Cardinal de Lorraine deXXe
Iuing 1562.

APPENDIX IV
[P. 155, n. 2]

STATE PAPERS, FOREIGN
ELIZABETH, VOL. XXXIX, No. 211, vj
[*Letter of the duke of Aumale to Catherine de Medici*]
[1562, *Iuly* 9]

Madame, je viens presentement de recevoyr la lettre quil vous a pleu mescripre touchant quelques marchandz anglois que lambassadeur de leur Royne vous a faict entendre avoyr este prys par les gens de guerre qui sont icy pres de moy pour le service du Roy et le vostre. Dont encores Madame je navois ouy parler, bien de quelques soldatz anglois qui furent pris y a assez long temps par le sr Dallegre qui voulloient entrer a Rouen et lesquelz tost aprez je feiz renvoyer sinon quelques ungs qui se sont voluntairement mys a vostre service parmy noz bandes vous pourrant asseurer Madame, que tant sen fault que je permecte telles choses Que tout ce que jay en plus grande recommendation, est de les laisser librement et tous les autres estrangers qui sont icy mesmes voz subiectz de quelque religion quilz soient de trafficquer et negotier comme ilz faisoient au paravant ses troubles, sachant trop bien de quelle consequence cella est pour vostre service. Et ne puis penser dou viendroit ceste prise si ce nest par ceulx mesmes de Rouen Dieppe et le Havre qui pillent et prennent indifferemment sur les ungs et les autres sans aucune exception. Toutesfois Madame, je mectray peyne de faire si bien rechercher parmy ses trouppes que sil y en a aucuns qui en ayent quelque chose je la feray delivrer et nen sera perdu ung seul denyer, ainsy que je lay faict entendre a ce present porteur que ledit ambassadeur ma envoye expres.

Madame je prye Dieu vous avoyr en sante et donner tresbonne et longue vye. Au Mesnil devant Ste Catherine le ixe jour de Juillet 1562.

Vostre treshumble et tresobeissant
serviteur et subiect
CLAUDE DE LORAYNE

[*No address*]

[*Endorsed*] 9 Iulii 1562.
The coppye of the duke d'aumalles
letter to the Quene mother.

[*Enclosed in a letter from Throckmorton to the Queen, from Paris, 12 July, 1562 (No. 211)*]

APPENDIX V
[P. 177, n. 3]

STATE PAPERS, FOREIGN
ELIZABETH, VOL. XLVI, No. 973
[Letter of the prince of Condé to the earl of Warwick]

[1562, *December* 14]

Monsr le Conte. Attendant que la commodite se presente plus propre de vous pouvoir voir et diviser privement avecques vous envoiant maintenant ceste depesche en Angleterre je nay voulu oublier a vous ramentevoir le besoing que nous avons de joir en vostre secours, auquel jespere moiennant la grace de Dieu me joindre de brief pour par apres mectre quelque fin a tant de calamitez. Si Monsr le Conte de Montgoumery est de retour avecques quelques forces, je serois bien dadvis se pour nous devancer, vous vous acheminissiez droict a Honnefleur pour plus faciliter le chemin et a lune et a laultre armee. Me recommandant sur ceste esperance a vostre bonne grace je supplieray le Createur vous donner Monsr le Conte avecques sa tressaincte grace ce que plus desirez. Escript au camp de St Arnoul ce xiiije jour de Decembre 1562.

Vostre plus afecsionne et parfayt amy
LOYS DE BOURBON

[*Addressed*] A Monsr
Monsr le Conte de Quarruich.

[*Endorsed in Cecil's hand*] 184 December. Prince of Cond. to the Er. of Warwyk.

APPENDIX VI

[P. 203, n. 2]

STATE PAPERS, DOMESTIC

ELIZABETH, VOL. XXIX, No. 50

[Admiral Clinton to Cecil]

S^r I am sure that yo^w are advertysed of the Appoyntement for New haven I would gladly understand the quenes ma^tes plesure for my farther Servyce. I lefte the Philipp and Mary the Lyon the Sakar and twoo gales wth viij victualers wyth m^r Wynter in the roade of New haven to joyne wth the shipps under his charge for the Dyspayche of the men and such thinges as is to be brought thense and lefte m^r Holstocke to assyste m^r Winter and I wth the Elizabeth Jonas and the Victorie cam hither this evenyng and synse my comyng wth the advyse of m^r vycechamberlen I have dyspaychen a suffycyent nomber of shippes that I founde presentely here to goo to New haven to fetch all thinges thense that is to be brought I cam to New haven yester day at one a cloke in the after none & departyd thense at twoo a clok this morning fyndyng my lord of Warwycke a shippborde redy to departe and at my fyrst coming Edward Horsey came to me wth monser de Lynerols from the Frenche King the quene and the constable as he sayd to vysyt me wth offer of any thing that was their for my comoditie and sayd that the king desyryd me to com on land to hym and their wth he tould me the Appoyntement for New haven.   I sayd to hym that the plage of dedly infexion had don for them that I thynke all the force of France could never a don for yf the mortalitie had not taken a way and consumynyd our Captens & Soldiors in so grete nombers they could never a prevailyd nor a proched so neare the towne yet ys it apparant vnto yo^w the noble coraige of the lorde lyevetenaunt and the valeantnes of his soldiors hath bene shewyd as moch as might be in men having fought agaynst an unsesable plage of pestylence & the whole force of France And as I doo reioyce that my contreymen hath so worthely behavyd them selfes so am I hartely sorry that yor chanse is to recover that towne, and so I desyryd hym to geve my humble thankes to the King the quene & the constable for their corteous mesaige and offer sent to me but I having charge by the quenes Ma^tes comandement my mistres of thes shipps and nombers of men I can not departe from them and so we departyd and afore the comyng of Edward Horsey & the sayd frenshe man to me I not knowyng at that tyme where my L of Warwyk was sent William Drury wth a Trompet to New haven to speke wth my lord from me.   And at his landing the Prynce of Condy & dyverse of the noble men found hym their and usyd hym verey curteosly and offeryd hym a horse to ryde to se the towne and a jentilman to attend on hym and declaryd to hym that my lord of Warwyk was gone to the See and had taken a shipp to departe.   And this moche I thought mete to let yo^w understand prayng yo^w that I may know the quenes Ma^{tes} plesure for my dyspayche hense. Thus I take my leave. From Portesmowth the last of Iuly a° 1563.

[*Signed*] Your assured friend to comand

E. CLYNTON

[*Addressed*] to the right hono^rable
Sr William Cicill Knight
pryncipall Secretare
to the quenes Ma^{ty}.

[*Endorsed*] xxxj. July 1563.
to m^r Secretary from the
L. admyrall.

APPENDIX VII

[P. 253, n. 1]

STATE PAPERS, FOREIGN

ELIZABETH, VOL. LXXVII, No. 846

[*Letter of the prince of Condé to his sister*]

[1565, March]

The copy of the Prynce of Condes letter to his sister the Abbesse of Chelis.[1]

Ma Soeur, lennuy ou je suis de linjure que lon a faict a Monsieur le Cardinal de Lorraine m'a mis au lict, comme vous dira vostre homme, de la fascherie que jay de veoir ainsy traicter les Princes. Qui me faict dire que lunion de noz maisons est plus que necessaire; comme il le peult bien congnoistre a ceste heure, et sil leust plustost faict, il leust tenu en peur et crainte cculx qui nous doibvent obeissance et non par les armes eussent puissance de commande-ment. Surquoy jay faict a ce porteur entendre mon oppinion, et de la facon que mondict seigneur le Cardinal se doibt gouverner. Qui me gardera vous en faire plus longue lettre, hors mir que je veux confesser que si jeusse sceu ce qui cy est passe; jeusse veu lhistoire pour empescher une telle honte et oultraige, qui est plus grand que je nay jamais ouy parler que Prince ayt eu. Je luy suis et seray, tel que je luy ay promis. Et si jeusse este aupres de luy, je luy eusse faict prevue de ma volunte, plus par effect que par parolle. Je vous iray veoir quand le me manderez. Qui sera la fin apres avoir prie Dieu etc.

[*No signature*]

[*No address*]

[*Endorsed in Cecil's hand*] March 1565.
Copy[2] of a letter from the Marischall
Montmorency to the Duke
of Montpensyar
and a letter from the Prince of Conde
to the Abbass of Cheliss.

1 This heading is in another hand.
2 This copy is on the other side of the same sheet of paper.

APPENDIX VIII
[P. 259, n. 1]

STATE PAPERS, FOREIGN
ELIZABETH, VOL. CXI, No. 612

[Montluc's Treason]

[1570, March 27]

Ont deferes avec luy les sieurs de Larride de Mirepoix et Negrepelice

Le sieur de Montluc charge davoir intelligence avec le Roy despaigne pour mettre en ses mains le pais de Guienne de quoy il reste accuse envers le Roy de France et la Royne sa mere par le sieur de Peres en Quercy et son filz le sieur de Marchassetel beau frere du sieur de Crussol qui ont envoye tout expres ung gentilhomme en court a ceste fin instruit de lettres et memoires par lesquelles est porte que le seneschal de Quercy a dit ausdits sieurs de Peres et Marchassetel quil avoit este solicitte de faire mutiner la ville de Montaubain a fin de donner occasion audit de Montluc de la piller se plaignant que ses services nestoient recongneuz mais quil sen vengeroit et plusieurs autres propos sembles quilz veullent maintenir avoir este proferez par ledit de Montluc qui est aussi charge de sestre assemble lieu ung lieu nomme Granale distant quatre lieues de Tholose avec le cardinal Darmaignac et ung seigneur despaigne pour conferer de cest affaire d aultre part que les prelats de Guyenne et Languedoc ont fait certaines assemblees et accorde entre eulx quelques levees de deniers et contribucions necessaires a cest entreprise et ont deputte secrettement levesque de Lodene vers le roy despaigne.

Le sieur de Marchassetel est ung jeune gentilhomme dune maise de xii a xv. mille livres tournois de rente et a fiance nagueres la soeur de Monsieur de Crussol

Le seneschal de Quercy arrivant nagueres en court adverti de ce que dessus se veult purger a levesque de Vallence frere dudit sieur de Montluc disant ne scavoir que cestoit et quon le mettoit a tort en cest affaire. Toutesfoys ledit sieur de Vallence homme collere de son naturel et passionne et laffaire de son frere aisne estant de telle consequence obtient du roy que lesdits seneschal de Quercy et gentilhomme seroient ouis au conseil prive ou le seneschal a nye publicquement ce que dessus Neantmoings le bruit est quen particulier parlant a la royne luy aie dit beaucoup de grandes choses. Le gentilhomme apersevere monstrant sesdites lettres et memoires et quil estoit prest se rendre prisonnier ou submettre a telle autre peine pour soustenir son dire Comme aussi feroient ceulx qui lavoient envoye lesquelz viennent maintenant en court pour maintenir tout le contenu desdites memoires et proposer plusieurs aultres griefs contre ledit de Montluc tel est le bruit la royne apres avoir ouy lesdits seneschal et gentilhomme depesche ung nomme Duplessis varlet de chambre du roy vers ledit sieur de Montluc Pour entendre la veritte lequel de Montluc au lieu de se purger commenca a hault louer ses faicts et services et a se plaindre de la mescognoissance quen avoit le roy et dont pouvoit venir quon soubson de luy et mauvaise oppinion que sestoit tousjours honnestement acquicte des charges quon luy avoit donnees   Bien aict confesse avoir parle a Granale avec le Cardinal Darmagnac mais que cestoit en passant chemin pour aller a Tholose et communicquer avec luy des affaires du roy ou lon dit sestre trouve ou ung nomme Don Pierre de Navarre bastard dalbert evesque de Cominges. Ce quencores est trouve mauvais pour ce que lun et lautre nen ont rien escript au roy ny a la royne. Pourquoy sont mandez en court lesdits de Montluc et Marchassetel pour se representer devant leurs maiestez.

Cest la cause pourquoy le sieur de Montluc a envoye cartel contre tous ses adversaires &c. disant que tous ceulx que vouldront maintenir quil aict intelligence avec le roy despaigne ont menty sauf et excepte les princes du sang et autres ses superieurs ausquelz il doit honneur et reverence quil est prest de les combatre a toutes sortes darmes en quoy il espere ne faire moings de devoir que il navoit que vingt ung ans &c.

[*No signature*]

[*No address*]

[*Endorsed*] 27° Martii. Informacion
contre Monsr de Monluc.

APPENDIX IX

[P. 303, n. 2]

BIBLIOTHEQUE NATIONALE

Fonds français, Ms. no. 3,197, f° 92, recto

[The Cardinal's War]

[2 juillet 1565]

[*Au dos*] Coppie. De Monsr de Salzede à Monsr d'Auzances, du IIe Juillet 1565.

Cause de l'empeschement faict a Monseigneur le Cardinal par le Sr de Salcede.

Monsieur, comme le diable qui ne cerche jamais que de mectre des choses en avant, il est survenu que, estant arrivé Monseigneur le cardinal de Lorraine a Ramberviller, ses officiers m'ont dict aultre commandement de publier et attacher par touttes les villes et chastellenyes la protection et sauvegarde qu'il a recouvert de l'Empereur, le double de laquelle je vous envoye signé et collationné de son chancellyer. Et avec cela, je suis esté adverty de bon lieu certainement qu'il veult et a despeché capitaines pour mettre ès place lesquelles je conserve il y a environ dix ans aux despens du Roy et avec ses soldatz; et veoir à ceste heure ung remuement devant moy avec ceste saulvegarde et¹ une particularité que je sçay je ne suis deliberé de le souffrir que premièrement le Roy et la Royne ou vous (comme les representans) vous n'ayez bien pensé le faict et la consequence que cela peult advenir² pour l'advenir.² Je vous asseure, Monsieur, que je suis bien mary qu'ayant tant

---

¹ For *est*.   ² The original probably has *amener*.

faict de services à Monseigneur le Cardinal et à sa maison, comme tout le monde sçayt bien, il[1] me contraigne pour mon honneur de thumber en sa malle grace. Et quant luy au aultre vouldront mectre quelques particularitez en avant, vous vous bien asseurer avec tous mes seigneurs et amys que je mouray et me coustera ma vye et mon bien que je ne serviray jamais aultre que a monseigneur et et roy, auquel je suis tant tenu. S'il vous plaist de me envoyer la coche de madame d'Auzances[2] par Florymont,[3] je vous envoyeray à Metz en charge ma femme et enffans avec le peu de bien que j'ay en France, pour vous asseurer que je ne feray jamais chose qui ne soit pour le service du Roy, synon pour sa grandeur et authorité. Et, en ce pendant que j'aurai de voz nouvelles, j'entretiendray les choses en l'estat que j'ay deliberé, avec la plus grande modeste que je pouray, sy je ne suis contrainct aultrement. Et sur ce, je me recommande de bien bon cuer a vostre bonne grace et prye Dieu

Monsieur, vous donner tres heureuse et longue vye.

De Vic,[5] ce IIe jour de Juillet. Ainsy signé:

P[o]. DE SALCEDE.

APPENDIX X
[P. 307, n. 7]

STATE PAPERS, DOMESTIC
ELIZABETH, ADDENDA, VOL. XIII, No. 71
[George Poulet to Sir Hugh Poulet]

[1567, April 22]

It may pleas yo[u] to be advertysed that wheras (aswell at my last being wth yowe, as by your severall letters) yowe have geven me specyall charg for then-quyring of such currauntes as might be learned from the frenche partyes, wherin having hetherto desysted, rather for want of convenient matter then of dew remembraunce, I have therefore thought yt my duty wth all convenyent speede to advertise yo[u] of soche newes, as I have benne presently enfourmed of by certeyne of this isle w[ch] came upon Satterday last from Normandy, who have declared that there was a greate rumo[r] of warres, and the newes so cer-tayne as a boy of myne being at Constaunces for the recovery of a grief w[ch] he hath, was hydden by his host the space of one day, and so pryvely wth dyvers others of this Isle conveyed over with all speede. Moreover I under-stand that there were taken up at Constaunces and theraboutes iij[c] soldio[rs] w[ch] ar now in garrisson at Graundville and that there ar viij[xx] soldio[rs] in Shawsey and two greate shippes well appointed. Also that a servaunte of the

[1] *Il* is missing.

[2] M. d'Auzances (or Ausances) was lieutenant of the king in the district of Messin.

[3] Places in Lorraine.

frenche Kinges hath passed alongest the sea coastes of Normandy and hath taken the names of the principall masters and marryners in thos partes. The leke brute of warres and preparacion for the same ys in Bryttayne as I have learned by a barke of Lyme wch came from St Malos and aryved in this Isle upon Sonday last at night, who declareth that they were prevely admonished wth all speede to departe from thens, and that Monsr Martigues governo^r of Bryttayne was appointed to com this present Tusday with a greate company in to the sayd towne of St Malos where greate preparacion was made for the receyving of him and his retynewe. Thes ar the specialst and most credybel yntellygences wch I have as yet lerned from thos partes, the presumpcions wherof as they ar very manyfest and dangeros so can they not be to myche credyted and dylligently prevented, wherefore I have wth all speede sent this bearer unto yo^u wth thes my advertysementes whom I have charged not to slacke his duty in conveyaunce of the same, to thend that yo^u being enfourmed of thes premysses may returne youre pleasure and advise for ower better procedinges in the same, as to yor discrete wysdom may seme most expedyent, beseching yo^u yt may be as briefly as ys possyble. And in this meane tyme I shall not fayle God willing to enforce and make redy the power of this castle and isle for the resisting of all daungers and sudden attemptes wch may be geven by the ennymy to the uttermost of ower power. Although the estate and furnyture of this castle ys not unknowen unto yo^u, yet have I thought good to send herew^{th} enclosed a byll of suche necessaryes as ar specyally wanting in the same. There ys no other speciall matter worthy the certifyeng for this present from this yor charge where all thinges remayne in thaccoustomed good and quyet estate thankes be to God, whom I beseche long to preserve yo^u. From Iersey the xxij^{th} of Aprill 1567.

Yowr most obedyent sonne
GEORGE POULET

[*Addressed*] To his right wurshipfull father
      Sr Hugh Poulet Knight.
[*Endorsed*] 22 April, 1567.
      Mr George Poulett to his father
      Sr Hugh Poulet from Jersey.

APPENDIX XI
[P. 326, n. 3]

STATE PAPERS, FOREIGN
ELIZABETH, VOL. XCIV, No. 1,338
[*Sir Henry Norris to Queen Elizabeth*]

Yt may like yor Maiesty to be advertized . . . . Wryttin at Paris this last of Septemb^r 1567, in haste.

Yt is here reported for truthe that Amyans Abevill and Calleis are takin to the princes beholfe wherof I doubte not by y[r] Ma[ty] is advertized or this. Also they have Lanne [1] Soyzon [2] Abevill Bollein [3] Ameins and so alonge the riuer of Sene which be the best appointid townes of Artillery in Fraunce.

By y[r] highnes most humble and
obedient subiect and servant
HENRY NORREYS

[*Addressed*] To the Quene's most excellent
Maiesty:

[*Endorsed*] 30 September 1567
S[r] H. Norreys to the
Q. Ma[ty].

APPENDIX XII
[P. 334, n. 1]

STATE PAPERS, FOREIGN

ELIZABETH, VOL. XCV, No. 1,457

[*Printed Pamphlet of 6 pages*]

LETTRES DU ROY, | PAR LESQUELLES | IL

ENIOINT DE FAI | RE DILIGENTE PERQUISITION
& RE | CHERCHE DE TOUS LES GENTILS-HOM | MES,
TANT D'VN PARTY QUE D'AUL | TRE, QUI SE SONT
RETIREZ EN LEURS | MAISONS DEPUIS LA
BATAILLE DONN | EE PRES S. DENYS.

A. PARIS,
PAR ROB. ESTIENE IMPRIMEUR DU ROY
M. D. LXVII
AUEC PRIUILEGE AUDICT SEIGNEUR

DE PAR LE ROY.

Nostre amé & | feal, Pource que | nous desirons sça | voir & entendre à | la verité quels Ge | ntils hommes de vo | stre s'y sont retirez depuis | la bataille dernièrement donnee | pres S. Denys, tant ceulx qui e | stoyent en nostre armee, ou ail | leurs pour nostre service, que les | aultres qui ont suyvi le party du | Prince de Condé: |

A ceste cause nous vous | mandons, & tres-expresseement en | joignons, Que incontinent la pre | sente ,receue, vous ayez à faire di | ligente perquisition & recherche | par tout vostredict ressort, de tous | lesdicts Gentils-hommes tant d'un | costé que d'aultre, qui se sont, ain | si que dict est, retirez en leurs mai | sons. Et ceulx que vous trouverez | estants de la Religion pretendue |

---

[1] Laon.   [2] Soissons.   [3] Boulogne.

reformee, lesquels se seront pre | sentez ou Greffe de vostre siege, & | faict les submissions portees par nostre Ordonnance & Declaration | sur ce, qui est de vivre paisible | ment en leurs maisons sans jamais | ung se mouvoir à prendre les armes, | sinon avec nostre exprès comman | dement & lesquels au demeurant | observeront en cela nostredicte | Ordonnance & Declaration, ne | faisants aucun monopole, ne cho | se qui tende à sedition : Vous don | nerez ordre & tiendrez la main | quils soyent maintenus en la joys | sance du contenu en icelle Ordonnance & Declaration, pour vivre | & demeurer doucement en leurs | dictes maisons, sans souffrir ne | permettre qu'il leur soit mesfaict | ne mesdict en corps ne en biens. | Et là où il s'en trouveroit qui feis | sent autrement, vous leur interdi | rez ladicte joyssance, les faisant | punir & chastier selon que vous | sçaurez le cas le requerir.

Et au regard de ceulx desdicts | Gentils-hommes qui seront venus | en nostre armee, ou auront esté | employez ailleurs pour nostre ser | vice & en nostre obeissance, s'e | stans semblablement retirez en | leurs maisons apres la bataille, | vous les manderez venir par de | uers vous, ou bien les advertirez | par lettres, & leur remonstrerez de | nostre part le tout qu'ils font à no | stredict service & à leur honneur | & reputation, n'estant maintenant | heure de nous abandonner en ce | ste occasion : Les exhortant de ve | nir incontinent retrouver nostre | camp & armee, & les asseurant qu'il | ne se presentera paradventure ja | mais occasion où nos bons, fidèl | les & affectionnez subiects puis | sent faire meilleure preuve de | leur bonne volonté & affection en | nostre service, que en ceste cy, & dont nous recevions plus de con | tentement, que nous sçaurons bien | recognoistre envers eulx. Et | au contraire vous leur ferez sça | voir que oultre la juste cause d'in | dignation, que nous aurons alen | contre de ceulx qui y defauldront, | nous ferons proceder au saisisse | ment en nostre main de tous & | chascuns leurs fiefs & tenemens | nobles, pour estre regis par Con | missaires. Mais sur tout ne fail | lez de nous envoyer incontinent | les noms & surnoms, qualitez & | demeurances de tous les dessus | dicts Gentils-hommes de costé & | d'aultre retirez en leursdictes mai | sons. Et vous nous ferez service | tresaggreable. Donné à Paris le douziesme jour de Decembre, | mil cinq cens soixante sept.

[*Signé*]   CHARLES

[*Et au dessous*]   ROBERTET

[*Et sur la superscription est es | cript*]

A nostre ami & fealle le Prevost de | Paris, ou son Lieutenant.

Leves & publiees à son de trompe | & cry public par les carrefours de ce | ste ville de Paris, lieux & places ac | coustumez à faire cris & publications, | par moy Pasquier Rossignol sergent, cri | eur juré pour le Roy ès ville, Prevosté | & Viconté de Paris, accompaigné de | Michel Noiret commis par le Roy pour | trompete esdicts lieux, & d'un aultre | trompete, le dixseptieme iour de Decem | bre, l'an mil cinq cens soixante sept.

ROSSIGNOL

APPENDIX XIII
[P. 352, n. 2]

BIBLIOTECA BARBERINIANA
VATICAN LIBRARY, NO. 5,269, FOLIO 63
[*Discorso sopra gli humori del Regno di Francia, di Mons. Nazaret*]

Quante uolte il Rè Christianissimo ha ricerco Nostro Sig^{re} di danari contanti, ò di permissioni di cauarne somme maggiori, et grossissime dal Clero di Francia, ò di soccorso di gente Italiana, ò di altro aiuto, che si potesse cauare da sua Beatitudine, tante n'è stato in somma compiaciuto, conciosia, che la bontà del Papa, et la prontezza, et uolontà grande, che Sua Santità ha del continuo hauuto d' impiegare ogni sua forza, et autorità a salute di quella Corona, et ad esterminatione degli Heretici gli ha fatto prestare più fede alle promesse, che loro M^{ta}, faceuano a parole del ben futuro che alle uere ragioni di coloro, i quali predicauano il Male, et la corruttione presente, et palpabile tale, secondo essi da mettere per perduto qualunque cosa si donaua ò porgeua per quel aiuto con il medesimo zelo ha proceduto sua Santità nell' aduertire al Re, alla Reina, et alli altri Ministri suoi fideli, et Catholici degl' inganni, et male opere di certi, i quali si uedeua chiaramente, come proponendo fallacie, et usando falsità et tradimenti, cercauano con sommo artificio di leuare l' obedienza al Rè, et corrompere la giustitia, et Religione di quel Regno, come in gran parte è loro riuscito, cosi non ha mancato di mettere qualche uolta in considerazione qualche rimedio per troncare i disegni delli Ugonotti, parendoli, come Papa et Padre commune, che se gli appartenesse di ricordar quello tocca al bene de fideli, et come Vicario di Christo in Terra di doversi intromettere in cosa appartenente all' uffitio suo per quanto concerne il riformare la Chiesa di Dio, cioè renderle in quel Paese la sua debita forma, et dignità essendouene il bisogno, ò la necessità grandissima, mà in parte alcuna non è mai riuscito di far frutto, anzi quando le loro M^{ta} non hanno hauto per fine di ualersi degli aiuti; et autorità del Papa, manco hanno tenuto conto, nè pur mostro di curarsi di corrispondere con quella dimostratione di parole, che ci conuiene ad ubedienti fig^{li} et deuoti a questa Santa Sede; Perciochè all' altre cose, che l'hanno dechiarato, lo fece manifesto, et palpabile, quando dopo la battaglia ultima di Móncontor, essendo il tempo appunto proprio de uenire a dare castigo à chi lo meritaua, come ricordauano i Ministri di Nostro Sig^{re} per parte sua, che era tempo di fare, et ne mostrauano il modo, fu risposto loro dalla Reina propria con parole assai espresse, come il Rè si trouaua in età di autorità, et con forze, et prudenza di saper gouernare lo Stato suo, da sè, senza hauere à pigliare consiglio, nè Legge da Principi esterni. Onde meritamente da quel tempo in quà è parso a Sua Santità di uolere andare un poco più consideratamente, non giudicando che se gli conuenisse di doversi ingenire in cosa d'altri più oltre di quelche fosse grato alli Padroni, sperando pure, che come l' era affirmato, così asseueratamente l'età del Rè con il ualoroso animo suo, et con le prouisioni, che loroM.ta presumeuano di fare più che à bastanza per trouarsi al sicuro in ogni accidente, potessero superare la peruersità de Ribaldi, et ogni altra difficultà.

Hora che dalli intollerabili Capitoli da questa ultima impia pace apparisce tutto il contrario, ueggendosi come restano del tutto oppressi i Cat.ci et gli Ugonotti tanto solleuati, che non si preuagliano in qualche parte: mà che mettano necessità, et in loro soggettione il Rè medesimo.

Non può ne deue sua Beatitudine mancare di tutti quei Uffity, che si appartengono al grado suo per aprire la mente del Rè con modo, che sia cauato dalle tenebre, oue altri cerca di tenerlo, et sia illuminato delle prouisioni, che Sua M.ta può porgere per la salute, et conseruatione dello Stato, et uita di tutti i buoni, che senza pronto, et potente rimedio se ne andranno in perditione, non potendo mai reggersi quel Regno senza buona giustistia, et religione; le quali sono corrottissime con l'Intervento delli Heretici in esse, li quali Heretici non accade dubitare, che hanno sempre hauuta, et hanno tutauia più che mai la principale mira loro fissa alla rouina del Rè et uaglionsi apparentemente di quelle due cose, che sono generalissime per chiunque cerca di distruggere un Dominio, ò una Monarchia, cioè la prima di mettere in diffidenza à chi lo regge quei Prencipi massimamente, che lo possono sostenere, et porgere consigli; et aiuti dà conseruarsi il suo debito imperiò, come si sà, che hanno tanto tempo procurato di conseguire più, et sopra ogni altra cosa li Ugonotti del Rè di Spagna con dar ombra, et metter gelosia, che Sua M.ta Catt.ca et suoi Ministri ancor d' auantaggio fussero sempre per procurare, non che desiderare la divisione della Francia; perchè la bassezza del Rè Christianissimo, redondaua à grandezza del l' altro interpretando perpetuamente, et le parole, et i fatti, che ueniuano da quella parte al peggior senso, il quale argomento, sebene in superficie hauesse del propabile in qualche parte, nondimeno la natura del Rè Cat.co tanto inclinata al bene, et alla quiete, fà conoscere a pieno il contrario, come dimostra pur troppo chiaramente l'occasione, che ha lassato passare, con il non havere con effetto animo di nuocere alla Francia per pensiero di accrescere se stesso; Ma è assai alli Ugonotti di hauere messo Zizania da ogni parte, tanto che l'uno non si fidi dell' altro, sicome hanno cerco, che gli riesca di consequire del Papa, sebene non è uenuto loro fatta, perche Sua Beat.ne per sua troppa bontà pospone ogni altra occasione, hauendo risguardo solo al seruitio di Dio, et al bene di quella Corona et del Rè.

L'altra seconda cosa è di mettere diuisione nel Popolo, che di ciò non accade produrne ragioni, ueggendosi pur troppo per gl' istessi capitoli dell' accordo. E necessaria adunque inanzi ad ogni altra cosa di provare con buone ragioni, come la setta delli Ugonotti con li suoi capi, sono sforzati a tenere in perpetuo la persona del Rè per inimica implacabile, perchè oltre à quello che è detto di sopra l'hanno troppo grauemente offesa, nello Stato nell' honore, et quanto ad essi nella uita sicome testifica quella giornata di Meos, nella quale fu forza a Sua M^ta trottare sino a Parigi nel modo che è notorio.

Molte altre congiure, et conspirationi fatte da essi contra la persona di Sua M^ta et tanti trattati, et ribellioni usate per occuparle le sue Terre, sono palesi, et ṇ'appariscono i processi fatti per le scritture, che furono trovate à Sciantiglione di Coligni, et che offende non perdona, onde considerata la natura loro, non resta dubbio, che come consij di havere macchinato contra alla uita del Suo Sovrano Padrone, et offesolo nell' honore, et nello Stato tante uolte così abbomineuolmente, come è nonsolo palese; ma prouato a chiunque lo uole sapere, non potranno in eterno essere fideli, nè obedienti Vassalli; anzi non staranno mai quieti se non per fraude, et con intentione d' ingannare Sua M^ta quando uegghino le cose in termine, che li habbia da riuscire, et se gli mancarà il modo con l' Armi scoperte, et con congiurationi palesi, come per lo passato; perchè la loro setta hauesse declinato, forse per il danno riceuuto nelle battaglie, che Dio benedetto hà fatto loro perdere, ò perchè dubitino di poter essere oppressi dal ualore, et uirtu, che uede essere nel Rè è non solo uerisimile, ma chiara, et sicura cosa, che procureranno di aiutarsi per ogni uia etia indirettissima, et seguitaranno il lor costume solito, et però non perdoneranno à ueleno, nè ad altra sorte di scelerata uiolenza, come la morte del Marescial di Bordiglione, quella di Monsig^r di Ghisa, et infinite altre simili ci ammaestrano, perchè conosceranno, come niuna uia è più certa di assicurarli ad ogni misfatto, et insieme da conseguire il fine del colorire i loro peruersi dissegni; onde si può fare uera conseguenza, che niuna persona fidele al Rè, et prudente possa, ne debba persuadere Sua M^ta a disarmare, ò à fidarsi in alcun modo poco, ne molto delli ribelli di Christo, et suoi.

Hè che intenda d'huer concordato con essi altrimenti, che con l'intentione, che hebbe già il Rè Luigi XI. il quale considerata l'unione de Grandi contra di se uolse rendersi facile di promettere ogni condittione, benchè iniqua, che da ciascuno l' era chiesta, mà dissipati che hebbe i capi della ribellione, come furono deposte l' armi, incontinente gli troncò tutti, senza indugio, ne risguardo alcuno. Anzi hà da guardarsi Sua M^ta ben diligentemente da tutti coloro i quali con si gran carità gridano pacis bona, et abusando della clemenza, et benignità del Rè, si sforzano d'ingannarlo, commendando questa pace particolare con le lode della pace in genere; perchè con le sue proprie non lo potriano fare: Chi non sà che la pace per se stessa è buona ? Mà chi non sa ancora che Sicary, i Venefici, gli Assassini gli Assassinatori, gli Incendiarij, i Sacrilegij, gli Heretici, et gli huomini senza fede, ne honore meritano punitione, et esterminatione. Chi non sà similmente, che hauer preso per trattata la Roccella per forza Angolem, et tante, et tante altre Città, et Terre in tutti i modi, che l' hauere assediato il suo Rè, che l'abbruciare le Chiese, dar il guasto alle Prouincie, et distruggere, et esterminare, ò ribellare i Popoli è cattiva cosa, et peccato irremediabile. Mà che il liberarsi da si graue indignità, et oppressioni, et che il cauar lo Stato suo, et suoi buoni Vassalli, et se stesso da tale calamità, et miserie, come è la uile, et abbietta seruitù di chiunque si troua sottoposto alle crudeli Tirannide, et rapina de' capi delli Ugonotti, non è esser seuero, et rigido, mà à fare il douere, il dritto, et quelche ricerca la Giustitia; Come può il Rè uolgere gli occhi pieni di quel generoso spirito che hanno mostro i suoi antecessori in tante et si grande Imprese, da i quali ha riceuuto il titolo di Christianissimo, acquistato d' essi per i loro meriti verso la Roccella, et tutto il Paese, che chiamano di conquista, et tolerare di uederselo tolto con i Popoli ribellati, et in tutto alienati dalla sua obedienza, et Religione con le Chiese antichissime, et si eccellenti, et nobili edifitij tutte demolite, la qual cosa auuiene non solo ne Paesi doue hanno pensato d'annidarsi, ma da tutte le parti del Regno, douunque sono passati con l' armi, che se ne uederanno i uestigii per li secoli auuenire, nonchè per li successori nostri, talmente hanno adoperato il ferro, et il foco contro la fede di Christo, et la giurisdittione, et l'autorità Regia.

Si che quando per qualsiuogla mondana ragione pur uolesse Sua M^{ta} scordarsi l'offese si graui fatte alla Corona, à sè, et all' honore, et dignità sua, non può, ne deue posponere quelle, che sono commesse contra Christo, et alla sua legge, et non può mancare di giustitia alli suoi Popoli fideli, et Cat.^{ci} che chieggono pietà, et gridano uendetta, chiari di non douere, nè poter, ne uoler havere mai pace, nè triegua à modo alcuno, sapendo di non potersi mai fidare d'essi, come l'esperienza gli ha dimostro molte uolte a troppo loro gran costo. Però quando uedessero di essere abbandonati, et derelitti dal Rè, et dal Gouerno, piutosto che restare a descrittione di gente si scelerata per fuggire la rapacita, et enormissime crudeltà loro saranno forzati di ricorrere ad ogni ultimo refugio.

Si può dunque proporre in considerazione al Rè qual sia più pietoso uffitio, quanto a Dio, et più glorioso quanto al mondo, hauer fatto un accordo con l' inique, et intollerabili condittioni, che si ueggano con Vassalli, et ribelli reintegrandoli nè beni, et dignità, gradi preminentie, uffitij, et benefitij, cedendoli parte dello Stato proprio, con il lassar loro delle principali Fortezze del suo Regno in diverse Prouincie, pagandoli danari di nuouo, oltre all' assoluerli di quanto hanno rubbato alla Corona, et al Popolo, et quello che importa più di tutto il resto, permetterli il libero esercitio delle loro Heresie, o l' hauere liberato i suoi fideli soggetti, et se la Casa Sua, et il suo Regno, et la Christianità, da si pestifera et perniciosa Canaglia, Bella usanza certo si potrebbe chiamare l'usurpare con la Tirannia, che s'hanno fatto gli Ugonotti, le Città et gli Stati pertinenti alla Corona, saccheggiare et espilare tutte le Prouincie, doue si sono potuti cacciare con ogni sorte di tradimento, et quando non si hà havuto altro refugio, ricorrere alla pace, et al perdono per non restituire quello che si è rubbato, et occupato à forza, et Tirannicamente. Tollerassi, che uno, ò pochi transfugi, infame, si facciano capi di una setta, et senza cagione, ò ragione pur finta, ò apparente; non chè con autorità, et giusto titolo, sotto colore di uolersi fare riformatori dé Preti diformati, et disobedienti, pigliano l'armi contra il Rè, lo minacciano, faccino le battaglie seco, lo mettino nelle necessità, doue Sua M[ta], è stata, et si truoua tuttauia, et li diano le leggi piutosto, che castigare chi lo merita, et reintegrare la giustitia, et la Religione nel suo Dominio, senza le quali due cose mai si uisse, nè si potrà uiuere rettamente in alcun luogo.

Anzi è troppo chiara cosa, come questo male non corretto: mà così trasandato andarà augumentando si ogni giorno maggiormente di sorte, che si habbia da mutare Imperio, come si uede che desiderano, et procurano con ogni diligenza gli Ugonotti che segua. E adunque la pace, cosi fatta pericolosa, et dannosa, come si è dimostro, sicome al punir li malfattori sarà sempre trouato necessario, honesto, et utile. Bisogna hora poi considerare, posto, che si debba fare se il Rè hà il modo da reintegrarsi nel suo prestino Stato, et autorità, et obedienza, et di ciò forse si potrebbe uenire in certa cognitione col misurare qual sia più il numero de Cat[ci] ò quello degli Ugonotti, qual siano maggiori, et più gagliarde le forze, et armi de ribelli, ò quelle del Rè, quale delle due parti habbia più facile il modo da cauare gente forastiera, et sia meglio appoggiata d'amicitie de Prencipi Potentati, et de danari.

Et in fine secondo tali propositioni farne la conseguentia, per due Ugonotti, che siano nel Regno, si ode calcolare, che si ha da contraporre più di otto Cat.[ci] gli ribelli hanno perduto nelle battaglie oltre alla reputatione, et la quantità degli huomini molti Capi grandi, che haueuano come il Prencipe di Condè, Dandalotto, et tanti altri, talmente che non accade far paragone dell'armi sue a quelle del Rè, essi sono senza denari, et non possono così a loro posta più cauare nuoui soccorsi d'Alemagna, et Sua M[ta] ne ha da sborsare ad essi a millione, et può hauer Reistri, Suizzari, Italiani, et Spagnuoli quanto li piace, et purchè uolesse sarebbe aiutato da tutta la Christianità, et quello che importa non meno di tutto il Resto, ha ad arbitrio, et disposition sua la giustitia, con la quale sola non è dubbio, che sarebbe bastante de regolare il tutto.

Sono accettate queste ragioni perchè non si può negare, Ma si risponde, che la Nobiltà di Francia, che è quella dalla quale depende il Popolo, totalmente è corrotta per la maggior parte, et da questo procede tutto il male, che la grandezza del Rè proprio in ogni tempo è stata principalmente per il seguito, et obedienza de i Nobili, et mancandogli essi Sua M[ta] resterebbe debolissima, et allegano le battaglie guadagnate per diuina dispositione, che non si sono poi proseguite, nè cauatone quel frutto, che si speraua, et douenasi. Onde si uà imprimendo nell'animo di Sua M[ta] che per quel verso mai si potrà uedere il fine, et che però manco mal sia essere ricorso all'accordo in quei modi, che si è potuto, perchè il tempo farà ben lui. Le quali fallacie sono troppo palpabili, toccandosi con mano, et uedendosi con l'occhio chiaramente doue stà la magagna: percioche il Re uorrà recarsi la mente al petto, e redursi a memoria delle cagioni, perchè non fù seguitata la Vittoria dopo la battaglia di San Dionigi, et perchè si diede tempo tante, et tante settimane alli Ribelli di riunirsi, et stabilirsi nelloro capo, et non si uolse mai obedire d'andare a cauarli da Monteri, o Faulnona, come sa chiunque si trouò, che si poteua fare senza alcun pericolo, et perchè a Craton in Campagna, quando si segui- tauano li Ribelli non si uolse combatterli, nè manco andarli appresso da uicino, ò tagliargli i passi, come è palese, che si poteua per non impedirgli la congiuntione con il soccorso, che ueniua loro di Germania, conoscerà mani- festamente Sua M^{ta} di essere stata tradita, et sa da chi, et lo proua da far punire i malfattori per giustitia, ma non è stata consigliata da uenirne mai all' esecutione, perchè Sua M^{ta} non hà uoluto consigliarsi con altri, che con coloro che la tradiscono. Veggasi quel che seguì poi con l'altra pace fatta con mira, et intentione di dare la stretta alli capi di quella maledetta setta, dopo che hauessero deposte l' armi, et reso le Fortezze; acciochè con tal mezo si conseguisca l' intento, che si deue hauere senza tanto sangue per non de- bilitare le forze proprie. Ma i traditori, che dauano il Consiglio, o almeno erano partecipi di esso, seppero guidare le cose in modo, et si lasciò uscire la uolpe dalla tana, et portò il caso, che appunto quelli di cui altri si fidaua più, et che haueua l'ordine di fare l' essecutione, auuertissero si a tempo i Ribelli, che furono i primi a repigliare l' armi, et uscirne di Noyrs, et con- seruaronsi la Roccella, et hebbero in ordine di poter pigliare Angoslen per forza, prima che le forze del Re fossero unite esse da opponesseli, che anco questo, come il resto uiene procedette tutto dalli traditori tiranti adrieto le prouisioni Regie per dar tempo a complici di lauorare, Placque pur poi a Dio, che miracolosamente fosse ammazzato, il Prencipe di Condè, et disfatto parte delle genti di Moners, ma non si seguitò, come si poteua doueua, et conueniuasi. Venne ancora il Duco di Dupponti, che si poteua combatterlo, et uincerlo al sicuro, et non si fece per le cagioni, che si seppero, et pure non ci si prouidde.

Fu seguitato, et verso Limoges si hebbero diuerse occasioni di romperlo senza alcun risico, et non fù esseguito per la colpa di chi n' impediua la essecutione con l'autorità, che haueua nell' essercito Regio; acciochè si lasciasse se unire col Coligni, anzi fù procurato con buona cura di guardare l' Essercito Regio in forma, et in siti, che la fame, et gli stenti l' hauessero a fare sbandare, dando andito, commodità, et aiuto à ribelli di godere il Paese, et d'impatronirsi de' magazzeni, de uittouaglie munitioni, et artigliarie preparate da alcune persone, che si era troppo apparentemente ueduto, che erano colpeuoli, in ciò si uenne al paragone, come questi tali scellerati traditori erano di più autorità, essi appresso le loro Maestà, che qualunque recordaua la salute, et il seruitio di esse, come riusci similmente quando si era fatta deliberatione de Suizzeri, et Italiani, così all' ingrosso, che il Re auesse facoltà di farsi la ragione con l' armi à malgrado de Francesi, che la seruiuano male, i quali misero sù Monsr Duca d'Angiù che la impregnò, come cosa che offendesse la dignità, et honor proprio di Sua Altezza, conoscendo chiaramente, che l' intenteone de chi gouernaua, et consigliaua Sua M^{ta} non era uolta ad altro fine, che fargli inimici, ouero diffidenti tutti gli altri Prencipi, et in somma priuarlo di tutti gli aiuti esterni.

Le difficoltà, che furono interposte, per consumar tempo nell' andare al soccorso di Poiters, sono anco loro ben note, perchè ùhebbero da interuenire diuersi capi, che andarono con le genti Italiane, finalmente, come Piacque a Dio seguì la battaglia di Moncontor, dopo la quale il Rè medesimo sa, come fù tenuto a bada sotto San Giouanni d'Angelin, nè si uolse mai mandare parte della Cauallaria, non che tutto l'Essercito dietro alli Ribelli rotti, et in fuga, di sorte che non era possibile, che si riunissero, se non se gli fusse lasciato in preda le migliori, et più opulenti Prouincie di Francia per accrescere loro il seguito de Padroni, et lasciarli reinferscare, et rimettere insieme. Dalle quali cose si ode, che il Rè medesimo hà scorto qualche cosa, che gli ha fatto nausea. Ma essendo Sua M^{ta} attorniata di gente, che lo cerca d'ingannare, et tradire per ogni uerso, ella non può discernere i Lacci, che gli sono tesi ne i pericoli doue si troua, però e da cercare di far la molto ben capace delle sopradette cose, mostrandoli, che es non si lieua da torno quei ribaldi, che cercauano così grandi artificij di rouinarla, ella si prouocherà l' ira di Dio, ne douerà più sperare nella sua diuina misericordia, che così miracolosamente l' ha sostenuto, et protetto fino al presente, ma restarà in preda di coloro, che non hanno altra mira, che di fare andare in precipitio la Sua Corona.

Di sopra e fatto mentione di alcuni particolari dè più sostantiali, accioche accadendosi si sappiano addurre per essempio al Rè, alla persona del quale pare, che si debba far capo direttamente, et parlare a Sua M^{ta} senza maschera, perchè certo non se gli può far maggior benefitio, che id storarli le orecchie, et aprirgli occhi, et la mente per farli bene intendere liberamente, come non resta, che da lei medesima, se non uorrà porre rimedio a tanti mali, à quali tutti può prouedere facilmente, con punire quelli, che nominatamente si daranno in una lista, et degli altri, che gli paia, che lo meritino, secondo il riscontro, che trouarà su le scritture cauate da Casa Coligni, et ancora, che alli ribelli di Christo, et suoi, che hanno fatto tutte, et si grandi, et inaudite sceleratezze, secondo l' opinione di alcuni, non accade considerare di guardar Fede ò promessa fatta, nondimeno si può fare di castigare solo quelli, che hanno tradito, mentre seruiuano nel campo, ò nel Consiglio regio, che fia senza alcun dubio a bastanza.

Hassi d' auuertire ancora il Rè, come fin che Sua M^{ta} se n' è ita presso alle grida, et è stata con effetti del tutto Ingannata, ella può esser scusata appresso Dio, et al Mondo, ma dopo che saranno scoperte le magagne, et rappresentatole la uerità, et il modo di non star più in preda, et alla descrittione de' traditori se non ci può: uederà la colpa di tutti i male, si ridurranno sopra le sue spalle, et restarà abbandonata da Sua Diuina M^{ta} appresso della quale più non uarranno i prieghi, et oratione del Papa, et de gli buoni, et fedeli, che forse hanno giouato più di ogni altro aiuto humano a sostenerla. Vedesi, che gli Heredi uanno cercando sottilmente a qualunque occasione di fare che il Rè offenda Dio per prouocargli il suo giusto sdegno, mettendogli inanzi con la sua pelosa carità di conseruarsi l' amicitia del Turco di usurpare i benj Ecc[ci]. et fino a mettersi a fare nuove Imprese fuora del Regno col mezo delle loro Armi, la qual ultima cosa non è incredibile in alcun mode se già il Re non uolesse darsi loro in preda del tutto, perciochè quando quell' armi si uoltassero contra qualunque si sia stato di Prencipe Catholico Nostro Sig[re] non potrebbe mancare di far quanto si appartiene al debito dell' offitio suo, senza risguardo d' altra mondana consideratione, trattandosi della gloria dj Dio, et conseruatione della Sua Santa Legge, nel qual caso Sua Beatitudine sarebbe forzata di procurare con la medesima caldezza di souuenire, et aiutare altri contra gli Heretici, che ha fatto con il Rè Cat[co]. et con Venettiani, la qual Lega si hà da ricercare, che sia uolta contra gli Heretici, et Infedeli, piutosto, che altroue.

Sopra la competenza, et gara de grandi, si possono dir moltj particolari in uoie, che sarià troppo lunga cosa mettere in scrittura, basta, che tutto seruono a negare la debita obedienza al Padrone, et al uoler portar l' armi con le quali s' impedisce la giustitia, et fino a tanto che il Re non punisce a qualche uno de buoni, che lo meriti, perchè altri non preuarichi poi in modo, che una parte, et l' altre si chiarisca per effetto, come Sua M[ta] uuole conseruarsi la superiorità, che se gli conuiene, mai sarà libera da queste molestie, et sempre si starà in preda di ogni uno.

E. uerisimile, che la Reina ami più di tutti gli altri lo Stato, et la uita del Re et l' unione, et conseruatione de gli altri suoi Figliuoli, essendo essa prudente quanto si sa, et hauendo tanta cognitione delli humori, quanta le ha fatta imparare la lunga amministratione del Gouerno, che ella ha hauuto, però non si può dubitare, che Sua M[ta] per ambitione di conseruarsi l' autorità preuarichi in parte alcuna di quel che deue, ma la proua ci ammonisce troppo, che da lei non si può aspettare quelle esecutioni, che ha mostro al Duca d'Alua in Fiandra, che basta a stabilire le solleuationi, et ribellione, perchè il sesso non gli lo promette, et anco in uerità di essere scusata, essendo stata Forastiera, et senza appoggio di potersi reggere secondo lei in simili casi, bisognando delle cotai deliberationi persona di gran cuore, et che habbia oltre l' autorità l' attitudine di fare con le mani proprie, quando l' occasioni lo ricerchi, però con la M[ta] della Reina, non pare che accada pensare di poter profittare per tal uerso, si che il trattarne con essa non si deue hauere per opportuno, et anco di questo si potrebbe pigliar Conseglio sul luogo per gouernarsene secondo che giudicassero meglio quelli che si sà, che sono buoni, et ueri Cat[ci] et che non hanno più mira alle passioni particolari per il desiderio di hauer maggior partecipatione nel Gouerno, che al seruitio, et ben publico.

Intorno alle quali cose è ben necessario, che chi sarà impiegato habbia molta prattica, et gran prudenza da saper usare la descrittione essendoci bisogno di somma consideratione, percioche quando si trouasse tanto in preda a chi gl' Inganna, che altri si disperasse di poter illuminarlo, et che si restasse ben chiaro di non douer cauar Frutto dalla persona di Sua M^{ta} sarebbe da uoltarsi forse ad altra strada, cioè uerso quei Prencipi, et grandi, che si conseruano Catholici, et che restano essosi et esclusi dal Re, et dal gouerno, et priui di autorità, et reputatione, i'quali se haueranno un capo dependente dal Papa del quale sappino di potersi fidare, sono atti a uolersene, et con il mezo della sua autorità far tale unione d' arme di Cat^{ci} in quel Regno, che il Re sia forzato a riconoscersi del suo errore, perchè la maggior parte delle Prouincie di quel Regno sono sotto il gouerno de Prencipe, o Sig^{re} Cat^{co}. ciascuno de quali saprà, et potrà ridurre le associationi, che furono incominciate con i loro Capi minori, et mediocri, et supremi da ualersi dell' arme, nel modo stesso, che hanno sempre usato gli Ugonotti, et con esse dare adosso a gli Ugonotti da ogni parte per estinguerne la prima razza, che anco sopra ciò in uoce si può esprimere uarie cose, le quali sarebbono noiose a mettere in scritto, et a tal proposito si può ridarre a memoria quello che loro M^{ta} mandarono ad offerire al Papa per sicurtà della loro rissolutione di non uolere mancare subbito, che potessero liberare quel Regno dalla Heresia, cioè di capitulare espressamente, che a detti Gouernatori delle Prouincie se le usurpassero in caso di tal mancamento.

L' abbandonare questa causa non è secondo la bontà, et pietà di Nostro Sig^{re} nè a ragion di Stato conciosiache non si prouedendo è da dubitare, et da tener per certo, che gli Ugonotti anderanno sependo, et cercando d' impatronirsi se gli riusci sse à fatto del Regno per procedere poi anco più oltre con imprese esterne, et forse hanno dissegno col mettere su il Re a nuoue Imprese di conseguir l' una, et l' altra Impresa in un medesimo tempo col far morire il Re, et li Fratelli, et altri grandi, che potessero per uia di congiure, et di tradimenti preualersi dell' entrata della Corona, et del Clero a sostenere solo l' Imprese cominciate in compagnia del Re, la qual consideratione, sebene paresse lontana non è da gettarsi dopo lè spalle; anzi è consentaneo alla ragione di permeditarsi, et fare con la prudenza quei rimedy, che sono giudicati più conuenienti.

Frà quali s' intenda il mandare al Re, et alli Cat^{ci}. una persona sola, o due, una diretta a Sua M^{ta}. et l' altra alli Cat^{ci}. che si riferisca, et obedisca al principale.

Forse non sarebbe inconueniente di mandare anco uerso il Re Cat^{co}. persona ben confidente, et sincera et rissoluta, che potesse cauare Sua M^{ta} Cat^{ca}. de Generali, parlandogli con buona intelligenza delli humori prefati di Francia, et mostrandogli quanto sia il pericolo, che portano gli Stati di Fiandra, si perchè con il tempo diuentando Heretica la Francia, quelli Stati infetti di già non si potranno a modo alcuno conseruare da Sua M^{ta}. Cat^{ca} quali remedij ella presume di farci, et sapere, accioche si potesse disponere, et pensare se con i Vinetiani et altri Prencipi si potesse fare simili offitij per tastarli il polso douendo essi presumere, che sempre, che fusse mosso guerra alli Stati del Re di Spagna a loro non rincrescesse di potersi aiutare della Lega fatta, ma necessario, non che opportuno, in ogni caso pare il far prouisione quà de danari, de quali Sua Beat^{ne}. ha a ualersi grossamente, si per aiutare quelle cose, come per diffendere Italia, et il resto della Christianità dalle forze di questa scelerata setta. Et perchè le deliberationi di tanta importanza, nella quale si tratta della salute del Regno, et della conseruatione della Santa Sede, et della Christianità si hanno da fare con matura consideratione, si potrebbe per auentura discernere meglio qual partito fosse da pigliare prima, o poi, et come, et fino a qual termine udendone il parere di quelle persone, che paressero, et fussero giudicate intelligenti, et confidenti. Quanto alle richieste fatte adesso dal Re, la risposta fatta da N^{ro} Sig^{re} sopra la dispensa del Duca di Ghisa, et della Prencipessa di Portiano, non può essere più giusta, ma è facile a temperarla col mandare la dispensa del tutto spedita per chi andasse, accioche si uaglia di darla, o non appalesarla, secondo, che trouerà, che sia più a proposito per li humori; Conciosiache se si conclude affatto il Matrimonio di Portogallo, come è da stimare, che sia il disegno, chi sa che Madama Margherita non diuentasse moglie del Duca di Ghisa, piutosto che del Prencipe di Nauarra. Et circa il permettere che gli Ugonotti possino habitare sicuramente nella Città, et Contado di Auignone, non parche accada stare in dubbio, che Sua Santità, non lo può, ne deue concedere, ma di restituire i loro beni, et lasciarli contrattare, perchè ne sgombrano, si può ben forse hauerci consideratione, se con questa gratia fatta al Re si uedesse di accomodare con Sua M^{ta} qualche una delle cose più sostantiali, et anco ciò pare, che bisogni rimettere alla descrittione, et prudenza di chi si uolesse mandare, il quale deue hauere per massima, che sempre, che il Re uoglia essere così impio, che si risolua di fare quello, che può per leuare al Papa, et alla Santa Sede quello Stato, non ci è rimedio a diffendersi, ne essendo Auignone troppo circondato dalle sue forze, però conuiene auitarsi di conseruarselo, come si è fatto per l' adietro in tutti i tempi con l' autorità, et beneuolenza, et fauore del Re, al quale se può rimostrare che N^{ro} Sig^{re}. non uuole, ne intende tenere con l' armi perturbato il suo Regno, mà solo tanta guardia nella Città, et Terre, che ui sono, che basti a non lasciarle rubbare per tradimento a quattro di quei scalzi Ugonotti, come ne sono state tolte tante a Sua M^{ta}.

Douendo questa scrittura seruire solo per informatione delli humori di quel Regno, non pare, che accade farla ordinata, ne limitata, però sarà fatta, come si è potuto all' imprescia &c.

APPENDIX XIV
[P. 354, n. 1]

STATE PAPERS, FOREIGN
Elizabeth, Vol. XCVII, No. 1,711
[Printed pamphlet of 6 pages]

[Title page]

ESTABLISSE
ment de la Fraternite
des Catholicques de Chaalon sur
Saone erigée à l'honneur
du Benoist Sainct
Esprit en l'an
1568

[Woodcut representing the Holy Trinity]
Au Nom de Dieu
Amen

Nous soubscritz bien | acertenez que la sain | cte Eglise Catholique | ne peut faillir, errer, ny | vaciller en l'observan | ce de la pure, sincere | & vraye volonté de Iesu-Christ nostre | souvérain Dieu, comme estant co | lumne & fermeté de verité, qui est, & | doit estre de consequent fondée & esta | blie sur la doctrine des Prophetes, des | Evangelistes, & des Apostres. Dont Je | su-christ mesme est la maistresse Pierre | angulaire qui a voulu le sainct Esprit | demeurer à iamais tant que le monde | sera monde eternellement avec sadicte | Eglise Catholique. Dont n'est à croy | re, comme nous ne croyons que | Dieu ayt permis son peuple Chre | stien vivant soubz ladite Eglise, estre | par aveuglement en erreur, & idolatrie | par l'espace de mil cinq cens & plus | d'ans. Soit par les celebrations de la sain | cte Messe, assistance du peuple & cere | monies d'icelle, entretenue par tant de | sainctz & grandz personages en scavoir, | religion, saincte vie, martyrisés pour le | nom de Dieu, Confesseurs vivans austere | ment en toute parfaicte doctrine, Vier | ges, que autres bons fidelles d'icele Egli | se catholique. Par l'approba-tion de la | quelle (non autrement) nous avons pure | credence des sainctes escritures, du Viel | & Nouueau Testament, donc d'icelle | lon ne se doit devoyer, retirer, ny demen | tir en maniere, que ce soit, sans blasphe | me, erreur, & damnation. Mais doit lon | par l'ayde supplication, & prieres à | Dieu, & illumination de son S. Esprit | estre fermes & stables, reiectant tous flots | des persuasions de nouvelle doctrine, | soubs quelconque pretexte quelle puis | se estre suggerée.

A ceste consideration par in | tention Chrestienne soubs la divine puis |- sance & espoir par l'inflammation du | benoist S. Esprit d'estre maintenus & | conservez en nos consciences, en l'union, | mansuetude, crainte, & obeis-sance d'icel | le Eglise catholique, à l'imitation de la | maiesté du Roy nostre sire, & soubs sa | protection & bon plaisir, desirans nous | efforcer de luy

rendre & rapporter sub | mission & prompte obeissance, en tou | tes les choses,
que nous voyons, & sca | vons estre observées, selon la saincte vo | lonté de
Dieu, au salut eternel de nos | ames, par sadicte maiesté royale & ses | tresex-
cellens predecesseurs, qui ont ve | scu & sont decedez puis l'heure qu'ilz | ont
estez oinctz & sacrez de la celeste | unction par le mystere de la saincte Mes | se
dont ilz remportent le nom de tres | chrestiens. |

Nous avons soubz ledict bon vou | loir & plaisir du Roy faict entre nous
& | pour tous autres Catholiques qui ad | ioindre se vouldront une fraternité
qui | s'appellera Confrairie & société des Ca | tholicques. En laquelle sera
esleu un | Prieur pour luy obeir es choses & en | droicts concernans les poincts
dessusdicts | circonstances & deppendances à mesme | fin sera chascun dimanche
a noz fraiz | celebree une Messe du Benoist sainct | Esprit en l'eglise de
nostre dame des Car | mes de Chaalon & aultres iours qui sera | avisé par
ledict Prieur ou seront tenuz | d'assister ceulx qui seront appellez pour | ladicte
assemblee en bonne & louable de | votion & continuer en prieres qu'il plaise |
à nostre pere celeste conserver sa dicte | Eglise & la purger de toutes pertur-
ba | tions & remettre icelle en une seule foy & | donner prosperité a nostre
Roy en tous | ses affaires & luy prolonger la vie a la gloi | re & sanctification
du nom de Dieu à l'avan | cement & manutention de la religion Ca | tholique
& courone de France & sil adve | noit (que Dieu ne vueille) que quelques |
uns par une effrenee volonté entreprins | sent contre l'intention de sa dicte
maie | sté d'user d'emotions, iniures, detractions | contre ladicte religion
Catholique, vio | lences sacrileges, invasions, conventicules, | à l'effect des-
susdict, batteries, meurtres, | pilleries d'Eglise, rouptures d'aultelz | images,
croix, & choses dediees au servi | ce divin. Promettons y resister par tous |
deux moyens tant par promptz advertis | semens aux superieurs & iusques
à sa di | cte maiesté que aultrement comme il sera | de besoin. Et si les
effortz estoyent si pe | tulentz qu'ilz requissent prompt empe | schement:
Promettons y tenir par une | unanimité la main & faire tout ce que | par nos
superieurs sera ordonné pour la | manutention de ladicte religion, resister |
aux entreprinses contraires. Et au cas | qu'il advint que Dieu ne vueille que
les | persones de sa maiesté & de messieurs | ses freres qui maintiennent &
maintien | dront nostredicte religion & Corone fus | sent oppressees de sorte
que ne sceussions | avoir advertissemens de leurs volontez. | Promettons
rendre toute obeissance au | general chef qui sera esleu sur la presen | te
société. En tesmoin desquelles cho | ses susdictes & pour l'observance &
ac | complissement d'icelles, Nous les avons | tous soubsignez & marquez
de noz | seings & marques accoustumez audict | Chaalon, le dimanche vingt-
cinquiesme | iour du mois d'Avril l'an mil cinq cens | soixante huict.

Comme Secretaires esleus en ladicte fraternité & par ordonnance du superieur en icelle.

LAMBERT.

[1] BELYE.

[Not endorsed]

[1] This letter is printed V. and is altered in ink to B.

APPENDIX XV
[P. 354, n. 4]
STATE PAPERS, FOREIGN
ELIZABETH, VOL. C, No. 1,862
[Catholic League in Maine]

Nous soubsignez confederez et alliez par saincte et divine alliance pour la continuation et maintention de lhonneur souverain deu a notre Dieu le createur et aux commandementz & ordonnances de la saincte eglise catholique apostolique & romaine et pour la maintention de lestat du Roy treschrestien et trescatholique, notre souverain prince esleu & a nous baille par la grace et providence divine pour notre chef & souverain terrien debateur & conservateur de lad. eglise catholique & romaine et des sainctz decretz & concilles dicelle, et de lobeissance que nous et tous ses bons subiectz luy devons et a noz seigneurs ses freres aussi treschrestiens & trescatholiques, repoz de son Royaume & de tout son peuple Et afin de maintenir lad. eglise et religion catholique apostolique & romaine pour obvier par tous moyens licites raisonnables et permis de Dieu aux damnees entreprinses machinations et conspirations que Sathan a mys es cueurs daucuns malheureux qui ont tendu & tendent par tout lesd. artz dyaboliques de non seulement imminer mais du tout subvertir lad. religion catholique apostolique & romaine et lestat & auctorite du Roy notre bon souverain catholique et treschrestien Prince & legitime defenseur dicelle et de nosd. srs ses freres, et pour tenir moyennant layde de Dieu et le consentement & accord de leurs mates tout le peuple en repoz Pour servir a Dieu & a notre mere saincte eglise et rendre lobeissance deue a leurs Mates, faire obeir la justice tant de ses courtz de parlementz que autres ses juges magistratz, Promettons et jurons vivre et mourir en lad. religion catholique apostolique & Romaine et lobeissance deue ausd. Mates et a leur justice Nous promettons aussi & jurons ensemble toute obeissance service et ayde et de noz personnes & biens pour empescher & courir sus avec leurs auctoritez contre tous perturbateurs innovateurs et contrevenantz a lad. religion; en estats desd. mates & a leurs sainctz & catholiques edictz & ordonnances divines & polytiques et de nous secourir les ungs les autres aux effectz susd. par tous moyens contre tous rebelles heretiques sectaires de la nouvelle religion en quelque lieu quilz soient & qui en sont suspectz ou nadherentz a notre party et tendans a fins contraires. Le tout jusques a la mort inclusivement. Le xje Iuillet 1568.

Depuis ces presentes signees par la noblesse mercredy dernier elles furent signees en cahier distinct toutesfois en mesme livre par les presbytres. Et vendredy portees par lesd. presbytres auturs estat Et y ont soubsigne les eschevins & procureurs de la ville plusieurs des officiers du Roy et des bourgeois avec menasses a ceulx qui nont voulu signer destre tenuz suspectz. Et par

la conference quils ont eue tous ensemble, la noblesse sest chargee du reigle-
ment pour assembler et dresser les gens de guerre et ceulx qui peuvent porter
les armes et dadviser et eslire les chefz pour leur commune.   Et les presbytres
et le tiers estat sen sont de tout submys a la noblesse.   Ils font signer & jurer
par les bourgades aux procureurs & plus apparentz des parroisses.

   Lesgail sest faict en la ville du Mans pour la solde des harquebuziers a
cheval pour mons[r] le seneschal de Maine Et ayant a son arrivee trouve les
portes assez mal gardies a faict publier la garde avec injunction des peynes.

[*Not signed*]

   [*Endorsed*] Copie de lassociation faicte | par les provinces.

STATE PAPERS, FOREIGN
ELIZABETH, VOL. C, No. 1,863

   Cest le Roole de la saincte union contenant quarante rooles en
   parchemin cestluy compris.

Nous soubsignez confederez & alliez par saincte et divine aliance es Duché
Canton et Conté du Maine, pour la continution et manutention de l'honneur
deu a Dieu notre createur, de ses sainctz comandementz, et ordonnances de
la saincte Eglise catholicque, apostolicque et Romaine: Et pour la manutention de lestat du Roy treschrestien et trescatholicque notre Souverain
Prince, esleu et a nous baille par la grace et providence divine pour notre
Chef et Souverain terrien dominateur et conservate[r] de lad. saincte Eglise
Catholicque, Apostolicque et Romaine, et des sainctz decretz et conciles
d'icelle, et de lobeyssance que nous et tous ses bons subiectz luy debuons,
et a tous nos Seigneurs ses freres aussy treschrestiens et trescatholicques
Princes, repos de son Royaume, et de tout son peuple: Et afin de maintenir
lad. s[te] eglise et Religion catholicque, Apostolique et Romaine, po[r] obvier
par tous moyens licites raisonnables et permis de Dieu, aux damnees entreprinses, machinations et conspirations que Sathan a mises es cueurs d'aucuns
malheureux qui ont tendu et tendent par tous artz diaboliques de non seulement imminuer mais du tout subvertir lad. Religion catholique; Prince treschrestien et legitime defenseur, et de nosd. Sieurs ses freres.   Et pour tenir
moyennant layde de Dieu, consentement et accord de leurs maiestez, tout le
peuple en repos pour servir a Dieu et rendre lobeyssance deue a leursd[es] maiestes, faire obeyr la justice, tant de ses Cours de parlement que aultres des
juges et magistratz.   Promettons et jurons vivre et mourir en lad[e] Religion
Catholique Apostolique et Romaine et obeyssance deue ausd[es] Maiestes Aus-
quelles Maiestez et Iustice nous promettons et jurons toute obeyssance, secours,
et ayde, et de nos personnes empescher et courir sus, aveq leurs authoritez,
a tous perturbateurs, innovateurs, et contrevenants a lad. Religion, et Estatz
desd[es] Maiestez, et a leurs sainctz et catholiques Edictz, et ordonnances divines
et politiques: Et nous secourir les uns les autres aux effectz susd[es] par tous

moyens contre tous rebelles, heretiques, sectaires tendantz a fin contraires Le tout jusques a la mort inclusivement.　Faict et arresté au Mans lunz^me jour de Iullet 1568.

[*Not signed*]

[*Endorsed in Cecil's hand*]

　　　Copy of a Conspyracion by | vow, in France by the | Catholicques ag. the contraryes.

APPENDIX XVI

[P. 359, n. 1]

STATE PAPERS, DOMESTIC

Elizabeth, Vol. XLVII, No. 72

[Walsingham to Cecil]

S^r . . . .

Notw^thstandynge my frend doothe assure me that he is advertysed by sooche as he doothe imploye in that behalfe, that ther wer of late certeyne lodged in Sowthewerke whoe nowe are departed, whos clos keping of them selves gave great cause of suspytion of no dyrect meanynge.　At this p^rsent s^r I am requested by him to advertyce you that in taulke that passed of late betwene the new come Cardynaule and him, towching the undyrect dealynges of the Cardynaule of Loreyne emongest other thinges he shewed him that thre of late were sent by the sayde Car. of Loreyne to exequte the lewde practyce in the searche wherof yt pleasethe you to imploye us two of the partyes, he thus descrybed them unto him as followethe.　The one to be of natyon an englysheman, of complexion sangwine, his beard read, and cot (as commonly they terme yt marchesetto) of vysage leane, of stature hye.　The other of natyon an Italyan, of complexion cholerycke and swarte, his bearde of leeke hue, and cot, of vysage full faced, of stature and proportyon lowe, and sooche as commonly we tearme a trubbe.　After I had herde the descryptyon of them I declared unto him that alreadye ye were advertysed of the leeke and that you towld me that thos descryptyons were so generayle, as they myght as well towche the innocent as the gyltye.　I further towlde him (as of my selfe) that the Cardynall Shatyllglion myght use this as a meane to make his ennemye the more odyowse to this estate.　To the fyrst he replyed, that the rather he had cause to be iealowse of thos descryptyons, for that he knewe an Inglysheman of leeke descryptyon, havinge the Italyan tonge verry well, and the Frenche reasonably well, that passed to and fro betwene the pope and the Card. of L. and also the seyde partye resorted myche to the noble man that at that tyme was lodged in my frendes howse; and therfor the rather he seyde he was leeke to be imployed in so lewd a practyce.　To the seconde he seyd that he hath had so good exsperyence of the synceryte and dyrect dealynge of the howse of Shatiglion as he knowethe assuredly that they woold not seeke by so undyrect a meane to make any man odyowse: And saythe he further to assure you, that sooche a practyce may be in hande: I knowe by letters that I sawe by a secret meane wrytten from Roome unto the bysshop of Viterbo, abowt syxe years passed, in the tyme of B. Francys (of late memorye) the leeke practyce was in hande the cavse also I knowe whie yt tooke no place, and therof can advertyce m^r Secretarye when yt shall please him to deal wth me in that behalfe. Besides to provoke me to wryte he added further, that he understood by sooche as he imployed in searche at Sowthewerk that one of thos whom they holde for suspected shoold have a redd berde, wth the rest of the merks aboverecyted: and therfor for that he is not to be fownde in Sowthewerke, he dowbtethe he may be repeyred to the coorte: wherfor he desyerethe you most earnestly, that ther may be some appoynted by you fytt for the purpose to have regarde in that behalfe. Thus levinge any further to troble your honor I commyt you to God. From London the xvth of September a° 1568.

Y^r honors to commaunde
Fra: Walsyngham

[*Addressed*] To the right Honorable Sr William
      Cicill principall Secretarye and
      one of her Ma^{tes} privie counsell
    At the
          Court.

[*Endorsed*] 15 fbr, 1568.
      Mr Francis Walsingham to
      my m^r

APPENDIX XVII

[P. 375, n. 2]

STATE PAPERS, FOREIGN

Elizabeth, Vol. CX, No. 533

[News from La Rochelle]

Monsieur l'Amiral escript du commencement du moys de Ianvier, que larmee de Messeigneurs les Princes se trouve fort gaillarde et plus saine quelle n'a esté depuis ung an, et estime quele changement d'air a esté ung des moyens, dont Dieu s'est servy pour faire cesser les maladies qui y ont regné jusques a lors. Lad. armee estoit au port de s^{te}. Marie a trois lieues d'Agen et tenoit tout le bord de la riviere de la Garonne depuis les portes d'Agen jusqs pardela Marmande et du long de la riviere du Loth jusqs a Villeneufve ou y a de petites villes mais riches & abondantes de toutes choses necessaires a une armee, et desquelles on tire quelques finances.

Mon: le Conte de Montgommery est de l'autre bord de la riviere de la Garonne tenant tout le pais de la jusqs en Bearn et jusques a Lengon, et au hault de la riviere jusqs a Haultvillar qui de son coste amasse le plus de finances quil peut. Il ny a point dennemys qui facent teste, ou donnent empeschemt Ilz se tiennent clos & couverts dedans les villes et laissent la campaigne libre aux dictzs^{rs} Princes. Mons. le Mar^{al} Danville se tient a Tholose, et mons^r de Montluc a Agen. Ilz ont des forces mais separees & mal unies de voluntez et de lieux. Le Sr de la Vallette avoit este envoyé pour les rassembler et s'essayer de faire plus que lesditz Srs Danville et Montluc mais il s'en est retourné sans rien faire.

Monsr de Pilles et ceux qui estoient dedans St Iehan sont venuz au camp bien sains et gaillards, ayans soubstenu le siege tant que les pouldres ont duré & faict actes aussy belliqueux & magnanimes qui se sount faictz de notre cage en siege de ville.

Il avoit este faict ung pont a batteaux sur lad. riviere de la Garonne sur lequel hommes, chivaux charettes et artillerie avoient passé huyt jo^{rs} durant, mais tant par la rive des eaux que par la faulte dung qui estoit alle prendre ung moulin des ennemys po^r lamener aud. port de Ste Marie. lad. moulin luy est eschappe et a choque et rompu led. pont. Si est ce quon y a depuis donne tel ordre quon ne laisse de passer.

Il y a plus^{rs} advertissements quil y a quatre mil Espaignolz a la frontiere d'Lespaigne & que le Prince Daulphin s'en va les trouver avec une troupe de cavalerie po^r le^r faire escorte.

Mr de Lavauguyon est venu entre les deux rivieres de la Dordogne et du Loth avec vingt cornettes de cavalerie pour tenir les passages desdictes rivieres. doubtant que Messrs les Princes les veillent repasser, mais cela na empesché le Sr de Pilles de passer le Loth, et saprocher desdictes cornettes, esperant les reveoir de plus pres en brief.

Les reistres des dictz seigneurs Princes ont receu ung payement, et son, si bien satisfaictz et contens que jamais ne fut veu une plus obeissante nationt Ilz sont partie dela la riviere auec M. le Conte de Montgommery et partie decha, ne faisans difficulte de se separer et recevoir le commandant de tous ceux quil est ordonné et d'aller en tous lieux ou il le^r est commande.

Mons. le Conte de Mansfeld faict infiniz bons offices tous les jo^{rs},esquelz il monstre ung zele a ceste cause avec une magnanimité, de laquelle il ne cede a person quelconques. Et ne fault doubter que Dieu ne layt envoyé pour ung tresgrand bien et necessaire comme aussy le Conte Ludovic de Nassau prince tresvertueux et fort advisé.

Quand a la negotiation de la paix, les admis de la Rochelle portent que ung moys durant le Roy et la Royne ont souvent envoye devers la Royne de Navarre pour l'exhorter a entendre au bien de la paix et haster les deputez, lesquelz ont longuement differé a cause des difficultez qui ont este mises en avant tant po^r le peu de seurete quon trouvoit aux passeportz qui estoient envoyez de la partie de le^{rs} majestez, que po^r la distance du lieu, ou le pourparte de lad. paix estoit assigné et ordonné, qui est la ville d'Angiers, en laquelle a Co^{rt} se retrouve a present.

Finalement leurs majestes ont renvoyé autres passeportz, et depesché le s^r du Croq le^r m^e d'hostel, pour conduire lesdictz deputez, lesquelz furent nomez au conseil tenu a la Rochelle le xme de Ianvier, ascavoir, les s^{rs} de Beauvoir la Nocle lieutenant de feu Mons. d'Andelot, Cargeoy gentilhomme de Bretaigne, Compain chancelier et la Chassetiere Brodeau secretaire de la Royne de Navarre. Le Sr de Theligny est aussy des deputez, mais avec sauf conduit pour et retourner quand bon luy semblera et besoing sera, pour raporter no^{les} de lad. negotiation a lad. Dame Royne et a Messeigneurs les Princes et Mons. l'Amiral selon les occurrences.

Et encore qu il semble que le Roy desire la paix et quon ayt advis quil la veult faire a quelque pris que ce soit, si est ce que pour le peu de foy et seurete quon a esprouve par deux foys en celle qui a este faute, on est resolu de la faire a ce coup avec laide de Dieu bonne, asseuree et inviolable. Et a ceste fin on a baille aux dictz deputez ung pouvoir si restraint quilz ne peuvent rien conclure sans premier avoir ladvis de lad. dame Royne desdicts Srs Princes et dud. Sr Amiral, et jusqs a ce quil ayt este par les susdictz dame Princes et S^{rs} arreste. Ce qui ne se fera sans pallablement avoir surce le conseil et deliberation de nos confederez et de ceux qui nous ont favorise, aide et secouru en ceste cause comme il est raisonable, et a fin de pouvoir mieux asseurer lad. paix; esperans que en y procedant de ceste facon et establissant le pur service de Dieu par dessus toutes choses il honora les actions de ceux qui y seront employez.

Au reste la charge desdictz deputez consiste en trois points ascavoir la liberte des consciences et exercice de la Religion sans distinction de lieux ou personnes. La seurete & protection de nos vies et personnes & la restitution de biens honne^{urs} charges, estatz et dignites.

Ceux qui sont hors de ce Roy^{me} quon a resolu dadvertir premier que de conclure aucune chose sur le traicte et pourparte de la paix sont dune pt les princes D'allemaigne et mesmes monsie^r le Prince d'Aurenge, et dautre pt Monsie^r Le Car^{al} de Chastillon par ce quil y a eu si estroictes promesses et obligations faictes par ceux qui ont en pouvoirs de Messeu^{rs} les Princes, quil a este trouvé raisonable de ne rien faire sans le commun advis de tous ceux qui sont participans en ceste cause et qui lont favorisee.

Le Baron de la garde se vante desja si la paix se conclut de faire ung voyage en Escosse avec ses galeres.

[*Not signed*]

[*Not addressed*]

[*Endorsed in Cecil's hand*] Ianvar 1569

Extract of letters from Rochelle &c.

APPENDIX XVIII

[P. 387, n. 1]

STATE PAPERS, FOREIGN

ELIZABETH, VOL. CVIII, No. 359

Catherine de Medici to the duke of Anjou

[1569, September 10]

Extraict de la lettre de la Royne escritte de sa propre main a Monseigneur le Duc du dix^me Sep^re Dclxix escritte au Plessis les Tours.

Mon filz, Sanger irent tout a ceste heure darriver de vostre frere par lequel nous a mande la bonne et utile nouvelle de l heureux desassiegement de Poittiers avec ung tresgrand honeur de mons^r de Guise et de tous ceulx qui y estoient pour le grand et notable service quilz ont fait a Dieu au roy et a ce royaume et de vostre frere de les avoir si bien secouruz qen faisant semblant dassieger Chastellerault et de donner ung faulx assault il a fait a quil vouloit et pourquoy le roy lavoit envoye et a ceste heure il regardera de mettre peine dabreger toute ceste guerre que avec layde de Dieu il mettra bien tost le repoz en ce royaume et me semble que jamais ny eust plus doccacion de remercier Dieu et le continuer de prier a fin quil nous mette hors de tant de maulx.

[*No address*]   [*No signature*]

[*Endorsed*] Copie de la lettre de la Royne a Monseigneur le Duc.

APPENDIX XIX

[P. 389, n. 4]

STATE PAPERS, FOREIGN

ELIZABETH, VOLUME CIX, No. 444

[*Norris to Cecil*]

Right honorable . . . . The Admirall hathe lately written to the Cap^en of la Charite that praise be givin to Gode he maye now joyne wth the vicountes at his pleas^r & that he hadd forces sufficient to make hedd to his Ennemis, Praying the Governo^r to loke carefully to the places on the frontiers & provide all thinges necessarie for the commyng of Monsr de Lizy, withe the Armey of Allemagnes whiche puttithe these in great feare & use all meanes to treat a Peax that possibly the can . . . . Wrytten at Tours thise 19th of December 1569 . . . .   Yo^r honours ever assuride to commaunde

HENRY NORREYS

[*Addressed*] to the Right Honorable Sr William Cisill Knight principall Secretarie to the Quene's most Excellent Maiestie & of hir highnes preavy Cownsell.

[*Endorsed*] 19 xbr 1569
Sr Henry Norreys to my m^r
from Tours.

APPENDIX XX

[P. 392, n. 2]

STATE PAPERS, FOREIGN

ELIZABETH, VOL. CXI, No. 580

Double de la responce faicte par le Roy aux ar^{cles} presentez a sa Ma^{te} par les deputez de la Roine de Navarre.

Le Roy ayant entendu ce qui luy a este exposé de la part des deputez de la Roine de Navarre des Princes de Navarre de Conde Srs Gentils-hommes & autres de toutes qualitez qui sont avec eulx *les treshumbles requestes* faictes a sa Ma^{te} de leur donner la paix avec les seuretez qui sont en son pouvoir pour les faire jouir du benefice dicelle. Ensemble les submissions qui luy ont este faictes de luy rendre lobeissance & fidelité quilz lui doibvent Sadite Ma^{te} pour la *singuliere affection quelle a tousjours* portée a la Roine de Navarre Princes de Navarre & de Conde pour la proximité de sang dont ilz luy appartiennent Le desir quelle a de la conservacion de ses subgectz *speciallement de sa noblesse* pour monstrer a eulx & a tous les dessusditz son affection & clemence paternelle & royalle envers eulx et la volunté quelle a de voir ses subgectz ensemble revinz soubz son obeissance & son royaulme en repos de troubles qui y sont de present leur a accordé pour parvenir a une bonne syncere & entiere pacification desditz troubles les choses qui sensuyvent.

Car les treshumbles req^{tes} presentees a sa Ma^{te} de la part de la Royne de Navarre et de Messeigneurs les Princes il est manifeste que le but de lad. dame et desd. Seigneurs Princes n'est et ne fut onques d'oster au Roy sa couronne comme ilz ont esté calumniez, mais d'entretenir le vray pur et libre service de Dieu, come le Roy suyvant la req^{te} des estatz la accordé a tous ses subgectz.

Nous sommes persuadez de la bonne affection que sa Ma^{te} a portee a la Roine de Navarre et a Messieurs les Princes au paravant que ceulx qui aujourdhuy soubz le nom du Roy oppriment le Royaulme eussent chassé d'aupres de sa personne tous ses meilleurs et plus loyaux conseillers et mesmes qu'au paravant ces dernieres troubles nonobstant les fausses accusations calumnies et im-postures dont on avoit charge lad. Dame Roine et Messieurs les Princes, ce neantmoins n'avoient tant sceu faire ceulx de Guyse que de faire oublier a sa Ma^{te} son bon naturel, tellement que personne na doubté si sa Ma^{te} se fust conduicte selon sa bonne inclination que sa bonne affection ne se fust tousjours monstree en leur endroict et eussent este traictez comme bons et prochains parens loyaulx subgectz et tresobeissans serviteurs. Toutesfois il est cogneu notoirement que par les mauvaises praticques desquelles ont usé ceulx qui sont aupres de sa Ma^{te} lad. dame Messieurs les Princes, les Srs Gentilshommes et autres estans a leur suyte ont este beaucoup plus cruellement traictez que les poures Chrestiens qui tombent entre les mains des Turcqs et Infidelles.

Ceulx de Guise ont assez faict de preuve de la bonne affection quilz ont a la conservation des subgectz de sa Ma^te, quand par les secrettes Intelligences quilz ont avec la maison Despaigne et speciallement avec le Duc d'Albe depuis huict ans en ca ils ont faict mourir la meilleure partie de la noblesse et autres subgectz de lune et lautre religion et mesmement les plus loyaulx & affectionnez au service de sa Ma^te.   Et quant a aymer la noblesse il est certain que ce sont ceulx qui la haissent et craignent le plus et apres eux les gens de lettres comme ceulx qui naturellement sont ennemys de la tyrannie, et de lusurpation quilz ont voulu faire de la couronne et en particulier des comtez d'Aniou et de Provence, et que ne promections jamais lalienation de la souveraincté de Bar, que ceulx de Guise ont essaie de praticquer depuis la mort du Roy Henry plus^rs fois et on scait encores ce quilz ont faict dernierement.   Et quant au repos public il est certain que la paix et le Cardinal de Lorraine ne peuvent loger en ung mesme royaulme.

Premierement que la memoire de toutes choses passées demeurera esteincte & supprimée comme de choses non jamais advenues Quil ne sera loizible ne permis en quelque temps ne pour quelque occasion que ce soit den faire jamais mention ne procés en quelque court jurisdiction que ce soit ne ailleurs, et a ceste fin sera imposé silence a ses procureurs generaulx en toutes ses courtz de parlemens & leurs substitudz, sera aussy defendu a toutes personnes princes d'en renouveller la memoire ny en faire reproche sur peine destre puniz comme infracteurs de paix & perturbateurs du repos public.

Semblables choses nous ont este promises deux foix mais les courtz de parlemens et autres juges inferieures n'ont laisse de faire mourir ceulx quilz ont peu apprehender, le peuple a massacre par tout ou ils a esté le plus fort, les assassinats ont este tous publics, de justice ils ny en a point eu les injures plus grandes que jamais ce mot de rebelle a este familier en la bouche des Gouverneurs des Provinces et singulierement des soubz Gouverneurs dont la France est infectée, et consequemment des pctis, partant pour effectuer ceste promesse est de besoing que sa Ma^te pourveoie a la justice et a son prive conseil comme elle seulle le peult et doibt faire autrement ces promesses sont trappes et pieges.

Que tous arrestz sentences jugemens & procedures faictes en quelque Court et devant quelques juges que ce soit durant les presens troubles & aux precedens pour raison des choses passees durant ou a cause desditz troubles a lencontre des dessusditz ou aucuns deceulx seront mis a neant cassez & revoquez.

Il nest rien si naturel que tous affaires soyent dissoutes par le moyen quel les ont este assemblees et partant est de besoing que les courtz qui ont faict la playe facent la guarison donnans arrestz et sentences contraires a leurs premiers arrestz et sentences, aillent en personne despendre les effigiez et ossemens

des executez ou en effigie ou apres leur mort pour le moins en semblable sol-
lemnité quilz les ont executez comme il fut faict a Rouen en la personne des
seigneurs de Harcourt et de Granville Et quant a ceulx qui ont este executez
de faict que punition exemplaire soit faicte des Iuges qui ont este autheurs
de telles sentences mesmes contre le vouloir et intention du Roy et que les
heritiers des defunctz prennent leurs interestz sur les biens desd. criminelz.

> Quilz ou aucuns d'eulx ne pourront jamais estre recerchez pour
> raison des praticques ou intelligences quilz pourront auoir eves avec
> Princes Potentatz Communautez ou personnes privees estrangeres
> ny a cause des traictez ou contractz quilz pourroient avoir faictz
> ou passez avec eulx pour raison des choses concernans lesdictz
> troubles & dependances diceulx dont le Roy les a entierement des-
> chargez et leur en baillera toutes tres & seuretez qui seront a ceste
> fin necessaires en la meilleure & plus autentique forme que faire se
> pourra.

Ce scroit a ceulx de Guise a prendre lettres d'abolition pour avoir eu
secrettes praticques avec les antiens ennemys de la couronne, les avoir mis
dedans le Royaulme pour parvenir a leur damnable desseing dusurper le
Royaulme et au contraire ceulx qui en une extreme necessité ont eu recours
a leurs antiens amys et confederez pour secouer ce joug et maintenir le Roy
et la Couronne meritent toutes sortes de louanges et de recognoissance pour
leur grande valleur & pour tant de pertes.

> Que par le benefice de ceste paix tous les dessusditz seront remis
> & reintegrez en leurs honneurs & biens pour diceulx jouir eulx leurs
> enfans heritiers successeurs ou ayans cause paisiblement et sans
> aucun empeschement.

Cest article ne peult avoir lieu si ce que est dict cy dessus sur lar^{cle} 3 nest
execute. Item puis que ceulx qui ont tué de sang froid Monseigneur le Prince
de Condé et contre la loy de la guerre. Ceulx qui ont emprisonne Monsieur
d'Andelot et ce trahistre qui a tué le s^r de Mouy ont este hault esleuez et
renumirez Messieurs leurs enfans ne peuvent estre remis en leurs honneurs
sinon que punition exemplaire soit faicte de si pernicieux hommes de leurs
complices & adherens que si Dieu mesmes a desja faict la vangeance d'aucuns
(comme il la faict) si leur memoire nest condamne.

> Et pour gratifier particulierement lesditz Princes & ceulx de la
> noblesse qui auront estatz charges & pensions de sadite Ma^{te} le Roy
> les remectra en sesditz estatz charges et pensions pour en jouir ainsy
> comme dessus est dit.

Cest article ne tend qu'a diviser les grands davec les petis pour les opprimer
les ungs apres les autres.

> Et quant au faict de la religion le Roy, leur permectra de demeurer
> & vivre paisiblement dedans son Royaulme en entiere liberté de

leur conscience sans estre recerchez en leurs maisons ny les abstreindre a faire chose pour le regard de ladite religion contre leur volunté Et encores pour plus grande seureté sadite Ma^{te} leur accordera deux villes lesquelles le s^r de Biron leur nommera, dedans lesquelles ilz pourront faire tout ce que bon leur semblera et quilz vouldront sans estre recerchez. Et neantmoins en chascune desdites villes sadite Ma^{te} aura ung Gentilhomme capable & ydoine pour avoir loeil a ce quil ne soit faict chose qui contrevienne a son auctorité & repos de son Royaulme et qui mainctienne ung chacun en paix et repos Ne voulant sadite Ma^{te} quil y ayt au reste de tout son Roiaulme aucun ministre ne quil soit faict autre exercice de religion que de la sienne.

Dautant que cest ar^{cle} est le noud de la matiere il est aussy captieux en toutes ses parties.

Premierement il est couché si a propos quon ne scavoit recueillir sil s'entend seulement des Princes et de la noblesse oubien generallement de tous Et on scait comment on sest servy par cydevant de telles facons de parler.

Secondement il y a de la contradiction manifeste en ce quil est dict expres, quil y aura entiere liberté de conscience et neantmoins quil ny aura point de ministres en France.

Tiercement de limpossibilité, car quelle peut estre la liberté de la conscience ou il n'y a point dexercice de religion? Le Cardinal de Lorraine pense que liberte de conscience et stupidite de conscience soit ung. Or la liberte de conscience est en la liberté de la foy qui est en Christ comment se peut engendrer entretenir et augmenter la foy que par la parolle delaquelle estans privez il ne reste aucune liberté. Le Cardinal se trompe en ce quil pense que la liberté gise a avoir congé de n'aller point a la Messe, de n'aller point aux pardons et choses semblables, mais la liberte de la conscience ne gist point a ne point faire ce qui est mauvais, mais a faire ce qui est bon. La verite dict qui oyt ma parolle et qui la mect en effect est bien heureux. Il sensuyt doncq que qui ne loyt point est malheureux Il ne dit point qui ne va point a la Messe. En somme notre liberte nest point composee de negatives, mais fondee sur propositions affirmatives quil fault faire. Item si le Cardinal ne peut comprendre quelle est ceste liberté des Chrestiens, comme il ne peult ne luy ne quiconques soit en ce monde sil n'est regendre denhault, au moins peult il bien entendre que quand nous n'avons moyen de contracter mariages, baptizer les enfans, et enterrer noz mortz que nous n'avons aucune liberté en noz consciences, mainctenant quil me dise comment (ayans en horre^r les actes de la papauté) nous pouvons faire ces choses estans privez du ministere de la parolle de Dieu, et consequemment de pasteurs legitimes, mais il semble que nous sommes comme luy cest adire que la religion ne nous est que jeu et que nous serions contentz que tous le monde vinst en Atheisme comme il est certain que si cest ar^{cle} avoit lieu avant peu de temps la France seroit pleine de Payens ct en peu de temps il seroit a craindre comme desja il est de trop, que ce mauvais conseil ne fust dommageable a ceulx qui l'ont donné et mesmes a tout lestat en general.

Quartement, cest ar^{cle} est ung piege pour attrapper tous ceulx qu'on vouldra exposer a la mercy dung juge de village, car jusques on sestendra ceste liberté? Si ung homme prie soir et matin ou a quelque autre heure du jour, on dire quil aura faict acte de ministere comme on trouvera desja assez de gens condamnez voire a la mort et executez pour avoir prie Dieu, si on chante ung pseaume en sa maison ou en sa bouticque on en sera recerché car on dira comme il a esté desja souvent juge que cest autre exercice que de la religion du Roy cest adire de ceulx qui sont prez de sa personne qui toutesfois nen ont point du tout. Si on lit en la bible ou en quelque bon livure si ung maistre apprend a ung enfant a lire dedans ung nouveau testament, si on luy apprend son oraison en francoys on sera en peine. Brief, accorder aux hommes une telle liberté de conscience est autant comme qui osteroit les fers a ung homme et neantmoins on luy osteroit aussy tous les moyens de recouvrer pain et vin et le laisseroit en mourir de faim.

Finallement quant aux villes qui nommera le Sr de Biron, on verra quils nommera ou des bicocques ou sil nomme de bonnes villes que ce sera pour praticquer de les aliener de la cause commune soubz lumbre de quelque promesse; mais quoy quil y ayt, comment se peult accorder que dedans ces villes on fera ce quon vouldra, et quil y ayt ung Gentilhomme qui y commande, il est aise a juger que mectre ung homme de Commandement dedans une place, cest lavoir a se devotion toutesfois et quantes et quand cela ne sera point, quest ce que deux villes en France quelques grandes et fortes quelles puissent estre les forces estans une fois rompues et divisees, et mesmes en ung si grand Royaulme quelle commodite pourroient apporter deux villes a ceulx qui en seroient infiniment eslougnez, mais le but de tout cela est faictes comme en lan 1568, et on vous traictera aussy de mesmes.

Et quant aux offices de justice finances & autres inferieurs actendu que depuis la privation faicte diceulx par decretz & ordonnances de justice suyvant les edictz du Roy autres ont esté pourveuz en leurs placcs et sont aujourdhuy en exercice diceulx. Que largent qui en est provenu a este despendu & emploie pour soustenir les fraiz de la guerre le Roy ne les peut aucunement restituer ne retracter lexecution de ses edictz pour ce regard Actendu mesmes les grandes plainctes & demandes que font ceulx du clerge de sondict Royaulme & autres ses subgectz catholiques pour avoir reparation du dommage par eulx souffert tant en leurs biens qu'en la desmolition des eglises et maisons du patrimoine dicelles par tous les endroictz de sondit royaulme a lencontre de ceulx qui ont faict lesdites demolitions & dommages Ausquelz ne pourroit justement desnier de faire droict &

justice a lencontre de ceulx contre lesquelz ilz vouldroient pretendre sil falloit entrer en cognoissance de cause et reparation des dommages souffertz dune part & dautre.

Il ne s'est jamais veu et ne se peult faire sinon par une tirannie extreme (ce que nous n'estimons pas que sa Ma^te face jamais) qu'en France les officiers n'ayant forfaict soient deposez de leur charge, si que quand les Roys lont voulu procurer les particuliers ont tousjours en droict gaigne leur cause contre les Roys mesmes.   Et quant a largent dispensé il y a assez de moyens recouvrer argent par la vendition des biens temporelz des ecclesiastiques Car puisque nous ne sommes point autheurs des troubles, ains deffendeurs en necessité extreme, que ceulx qui se pouvoient bien passer de la guerre et vivre en paix, en leurs maisons, puis quilz ont tant desiré la guerre quilz ne cornoyent entre chose doibvent aussy en porter la folle enchere comme encores silz ne nous font autre raison nous esperons que Dieu la nous fera et en briefe Que si il estoit question d'entrer en compensation il se trouvera que nous avons souffert infinies pertes plus que les autheurs des troubles, en quoy quil y ayt tant de gens et bien meurdriz par des juges et officiers massacrez par le peuple depuis la derniere pacification tant de femmes violees par les gens de guerre et mesmes des plus remarquez qui cela surpasse toute perte & que toutes fois nous esperons que Dieu ne laissera pour impuny quoy que les vivans en rien ne regardans point aux jugemens quil en a desja faictz sur les plus mauvais d'entreulx qui se jouoient ainsy de son Nom de Ma^te glorieuse.

Voulant sadite Ma^te pour lobservation des choses susdites avec toute bonne foy & syncerité leur bailler toutes leurs seuretez qui sont en son pouvoir et quilz luy vouldront honnestement & raisonnablement requerir lesquelles seuretez le Roy fera esmolloguer & passer par ses courtz de parlemens & autres juges quil appartiendra.

Les bons subgectz (telz que nous sommes) n'ont point acoustumé de demander les formes de seuretez cest a sa Ma^te de nous les donner bonnes et asseurees, et puis quil na este en sa puissance de nous garder sa foy il nous donnera sil luy plaist les moyens de nous garentir contre ceulx qui la vouldroient enfraindre en notre endroict, et quant a ses courtz de parlemens nous ne pensons pas que pendant quelles serons composees de telles gens quelles sont quil nous garde foy et administre justice veu quilz sont noz parties formelles.

Veut et entend sadite Ma^te que les dessusditz reciproquement pour luy rendre la fidele obeissance quilz luy doibvent ayent a se departir de toute alliance, confederation, et association quilz, ont avec les Princes Potentatz ou Communautez estrangeres hors du Roiaulme pareillement de toutes intelligences praticques & associations quilz ont dedans & dehors icelluy.

Quilz ne feront aucunes assemblées contribution ne cullettes de deniers sans expresse permission du Roy declarée par ses lettres patentes.

Quant a ces deux ar^{cles} sa Ma^{te} scait que nous n'avons rien promis que nous n'ayons tenu ce que nous ferons encores la paix estant bien asseurer.

Quentieront & feront sortir hors sondit Roiaulme dedans ung moys apres la conclusion de ladite Pacification par le chemin qui leur sera prescript par sadite Ma^{te} sans foulle ne oppression de ses subgectz tous estrangers estans a leur service, et conviendront avec eux de leur paiement a leurs propres coustz & despens. Et a ceste fin leur donnera le Roy telle permission quil sera besoing pour entr'eulx leuer les sommes qui leur seront necessaires.

Cest ar^{cle} est impossible en toutes ses parties, car les estrangers ne pouvent en ung mois se retirer, ilz ne peuvent ny ne doibvent sortir par le chemin qui leur sera prescript sinon quilz veulent se precipiter eulx mesmes a leur mort, ce que nous ne leur conseilleront jamais, plustost choisirons nous de mourir avec eulx. Et davantage ilz sont assez fortz pour se faire voye par ou bon leur semblera. Si nous promectons que les subgectz de sa Ma^{te} ne soient point foullez cest une trappe, car nestant aucunement en notre puissance de laccomplir ceulx de Guise diront que nous avons rompu la paix. Il ne nous est non plus possible de les paier de noz deniers particuliers car la cruauté de noz ennemys nous a osté tous les moyens que nous avions au paravant et mesmes dedans ung mois une telle cuillette ne sa pourroit faire et quand elle le seroit il nous souvient comment nous fusmes traictez a Auxerre et qui est le pis les particuliers ne vouldront contribuer, se souvenans bien comme ilz ont esté traictez pour avoir contribué aux troubles precedens suyvant les tres patentes de sa Ma^{te}.

Laisseront aussy les armes et separeront toutes leurs autres forces tant de pied que de cheval par mer & par terre se retireront chacun en leurs maisons qon bon leur semblera incontinent apres la conclusion de ladite paix pour la ou ilz seront vivre paisiblement.

Les seuretez de la paix estans bonnes se departiront voluntairement des armees, mais ilz se ressentent de plus de dix mil hommes des leurs qui ont esté cruellement meurdriz aux dernières troubles obeissans a ung semblable article que cestuy   Partant il est necessaire que sa Ma^{te} y pourveoie.

Remectront entre les mains du Roy ou de ceulx quil commectra les villes chasteaux & places quilz detiennent pour le present et en feront sortir les forces quilz y ont y déllaissant semblablement lartillerie & autres munitions qui sont en icelles, au pouvoir de ceulx qu'ordonnera sadite Ma^{te}.

Et generallement restitueront de bonne foy a sadite Ma^{te} ou a ceulx quil commectra toutes les choses a elle appartenantes qui se trouveront encores en nature soit es villes & places quilz tiennent ou autres lieux quilz soient ou par mer ou par terre. Faict a Angiers le iiij^e jour de Feburier 1570. Ainsy signe CHARLES et au dessoubz DE LAUBESPINE.

Quant a ces deux ar^{cles} la paix estant asseuree feront ce quilz promectront. Toutesfois lexperience a monstre a Orleans, Auxerre, Autun, Vallence, Montpellier et autres villes comment sil ne plaist a sa Ma^{te} de pourveoir a lestat de gouverneurs de gens dautre humeur que ceulx qui ont este commis au gouvernement des places depuis les secondes troubles il seroit beaucoup plus expedient aux poures habitans des villes de mourir vaillamment a la breche que de voir devant leurs yeulx les horribles meschancetez quilz ont veues, et qui sont telles que nous avons honte seullement de les nommer.

[*Not signed*]

[*Endorsed in Burghley's hand*] 8 Martii 1569 (1570).
Respons to the articles of the
fr. K^{es} answer to the Q. of
Navarrs Deputees.

APPENDIX XXI
[P. 396, n. 2]

STATE PAPERS, FOREIGN
ELIZABETH, VOL. CXV, No. 990

Distribution des gouvernementz d'aulcunes Provences en France dernièrement faict par les Protestantz et Premierement

Le Segneur de Montbrun general pour le pais de daulphine et Provence,

Monser de St Romain general pour le duche de Nismes, Montpellier. Mande, Vivaretz, Uses, et le puis avec 600 livres en pention per chascun moys 200 harquebusiers et trois cornettes de Cavallerie.

Le vicounte de Paulin pour les duches d'alby, Castres, St Pol, Carcassonne, Narbonne, Bessiers, Aix et Lodesve.

Le Sr de Serignac Montauban et tout le pais bas, Quercy, Agenois, diocese de Thoulouse, Rioux, La Nur Mereboix et Albert.

Le Cap: de Guynieres pour les dioceses de Palmes Costrance Comiges, et toute la counte de Foix.

Le Baron darroy les pais de Ricaon, Besomiris, Cascogne et Armignac.

Le Viconte de Pimal toute la seneschalce d'avergne.

Le Visconte de Gordon Loyer et le hault guibry Limosin et leurs adjacentes.

Laissant lentier sang aux Srs de la Noe et de Montgomery des affaires qui concerneront la Rochelle lesquieux pourvoieront de choses aux gouvernementz des paix de Guienne, Poictou, Torenne, Le Meine, Bourgoigne Bretaigne, Normandie et autres adjacentes.

A este en oultre ordonne par l'assemblee generalle desdits protestantz que chascun desdict chefs comandiria en son departement quilz prendrent tous les deniers du Roy. Item tous les revenus des ecclesiastiques cotiseront de gre ceulx de la Religion selon l'exigence des affaires, et les Catholiques de gre ou de force, et contrainderont le solvable pour insolvable.

[Not signed]

[*Endorsed*] Distribution de provences
par les protestans.

APPENDIX XXII

[P. 399, n. 1]

ITINERAIRE DE MONTGOMERY EN GASCOGNE

Pendant L'Annee 1569[1]

8 juin. Quitte Nontron, nanti des pleins pouvoirs de la reine de Navarre (France protestante).

21 juin. Arrive à Castres et y organise l'expédition du Béarn.

27 juillet. Part de Castres à midi pour se rendre en Béarn (Mémoires de Jacques Gaches. Lettre de Montgomery à Jeanne d'Albret).

28 juillet. Occupe Mazères, en Foix, et traverse l'Ariège (Mémoires de J. Gaches.)

Il franchit l'Ariège probablement au pont d'Auterive, puis le Salat. Il était le i[er] août à Montbrun; le 2, ayant passé sans encombre la Garonne au pont de Miramont (Courteault, *Blaise de Montluc*, p. 544).

2 août. Pille Saint-Gaudens (Durier, Huguenots en Bigorre).

5 et 6 août. Traverse la plaine de Tarbes et loge à Pontac, le 6 au soir (*ibid.;* Bordenave, *Histoire de Béarn*, p. 259).

7 août. Passe le Gave à Coarraze (Bordenave, *loc. cit.*).

9 août. Entre à Navarrenx (Lettre du 11 août).

11 août. Quitte Navarrenx et arrive sous les murs d'Orthez vers midi (Bordenave, p. 266; Lettre du 11 août).

12–14 août. Assiège Orthez.

15 août. Signe la capitulation.

16 août. Occupe la ville, où il a une entrevue avec le comte de Gramont (Bordenave, p. 276).

18–19 août. Prend Artix et fait massacrer les frères mineurs du couvent (*ibid.*, p. 280).

22 août. Fait rendre des actions de grace à Pau (*ibid.*, p. 280).

23 août. Séjourne à Pau (Lettre à Jeanne d'Albret).

24–29 août. Oleron, Mauleon de Soule.

30 août. Entre en Bigorre, par le Vic-Bilh.

31 août. Traverse Maubourguet.

[1] From Communay, *Les huguenots dans le Béarn et la Navarre*, p. 175.
The italicized portions are further details which I have added.—J. W. T.

1er septembre. S'empare de Tarbes et met tout à feu et à sang (Durier, Huguenots en Bigorre).

2–4 septembre. A Tarbes.

5 septembre. Quitte cette ville (Lettre à Jeanne d'Albret), pour aller en Chalosse (Bordenave, p. 286).

6 septembre. Occupe et rançonne Marciac (Lettre).[1]

7 septembre. Entre à Aire-sur-Adour (Lettre).

11 septembre. A Grenade-sur-Adour (Lettre).[2]

12–18 septembre. Capitulation de Sainte Sever (Bordenave, p. 287) *et Mont de Marsan vers Montault et Mugron delà l'Adour* (Courteault p. 553 n. 2).

19 septembre. Traverse Amou (*ibid*).[3]

20–28 septembre. A *Orthèz* (Courteault, p. 555). Va à Navarrens, ou il ordonne l'exécution de Bassillon, gouverneur de cette ville.

28 septembre. Arrive à Salies de Béarn (Lettre).[4]

1–6 octobre. Séjourne à Salies, où il réorganise la justice.

10 octobre. Ouvre le synode de Lescar et part pour la Bigorre.

13 octobre. Occupe Betplan (Huguenots en Bigorre).

14–17 octobre. Etablit son camp à Lahitole (*ibid.*).

18 octobre. Quitte Lahitole et se dirige vers Marciac (*ibid.*).

21 octobre. Arrive à Nogaro (Lettre), qu'il pille et brûle (Huguenots en Bigorre).

22 octobre. Traverse Eauze (Comment.).

3 novembre. Occupe Condom (Huguenots en Bigorre), d'où il écrit aux consuls d'Auch.

3–17 novembre. Fait des courses dans l'Armagnac; menace Auch et Lombez; ravage Samatan (*ibid.*).

17 novembre. Rentre à Condom (Dupleix), d'où il écrit aux consuls de Bagnères (Huguenots en Bigorre).

Décembre. Faict sa jonction avec l'armée des princes.

APPENDIX XXIII

[P. 402, n. 1]

ARCHIVES NATIONALES

K 1,515, PIÈCE No. 23 A

[Montauben, janvier 1570.]

[*Au dos*] Proclamation des Rebelles de France.

De par Messeigneurs les Princes de Navarre et de Condé.

Il est tres expressement commandé et enjoinct a tous gentilzhommes, capitaines, soldatz faisans profession de la religion reformée non enrollés

---

[1] Cf. Courteault, p. 553 n. 2.

[2] Cf. *Les huguenots en Béarn*, p. 64.   [3] *Ibid.*, pp. 65, 68.   [4] *Ibid.*, p. 68.

soubz les enseignes et compaignies retenues pour la garde et deffence des villes tenues soubz l'obeyssance du Roy et desdictz Sieurs Princes, de in continent et sans delay se rendre en leur armée pour y estre employez au service de Dieu et du Roy sellon leur degré et quallité, et ce, sur peyne d'estre tenuz pour ennemys de la cause de Dieu et de la religion. Enjoinct aux gouverneurs des villes ou ilz seront sans expresse licence desdictz Srs Princes, d'iceulx faire vuyder et desloger promptement, deffendre leur estre baillé logis ne vivres et les soldatz desvalizés et desgradés de leurs armes et chevaulx. Sy ont lesdictz Sieurs Princes estroictement deffendu et inhibé a toutz capitaines, soldatz et aultres estans de la presente armée de brusler, desmolir ny ruyner aulcuns chasteaulx, maisons ne ediffices apartenans aux gentilzhommes de quelque religion qu'ilz soyent, ne aussy des paisans et peuble estans ez bourez et villages du plat pais. Et d'aultant que les Courtz de Parlement et aultres officiers de la justice et conseil des villes, principalement ceulx de la ville de Tholouze se sont renduz, par une hayne trop cruelle et incapable, refracteurs, voyre directement oppozés à la publication et entretenement de la pacification dernierement establye en ce royaulme, jusques à faire mourir inhumainement et ignominieusement le Sieur Rappin, maistre d'hostel du Sieur feu prince de Condé, nostre tres chere et tres amé oncle et tres honnoré seigneur et pere, contre toute foy et seureté publique a luy octroyée tant par le edict de pacification que par expres sauf conduict et passeport a luy baillés especiallement par Sa Majesté aux fins d'apporter et faire publyer ledict edict de la pacification; oultre le cruel meurtre contre les loix et debvoirs de la guerre commis en la personne du baron de Castelnau et aultres gentilzhommes, capitaines et soldatz prins en guerre durant les troubles. Lesdictz Sieurs Princes, pour reprimer et faire cesser de leur pouvoir telles inhumanitez non ouyes entre les plus barbares nations de la terre, et, par le chastiment des perturbateurs de la paix et foy publicque, parvenir à quelque tranquillité stable entre ceulx qui desirent la seureté et conservation de cest Estat et coronne de France, ont habandonné en proye, pillage et feu toutes maisons, ediffices, bestail, meubles, danrées et biens quelzquonques qui se trouveront appartenir aux presidents conseilliers de ladicte Court de Parlement de Tholouze et aultres lieux, justiciers et administrateurs et generallement officiers de ladicte ville, pappistes ou atteistes; et pour cest effect permis aux capitaines, soldatz et aultres quelzconques estans en ceste armée uzer de tous lesdictz actes d'hostillité à l'endroict des dessusdictz. Deffendant tres expressement mesfaire en aulcune façon, ains conserver de tout leur pouvoir les maisons et biens appartenans à ceulx qui font profession de la religion reformée, de quelque qualité ou condition qu'ilz soyent   Et, affin que nul ne puisse ignorer lesdictes deffences et provision, ensemble les causes et occasions d'icelle, ont volu ces presentes estre cryées a cry publicque tant en la ville de Montauban que en la presente armée.

Faict à Montauban, au mois de janvier mil cinq cens soixante dix.

APPENDIX XXIV
[P. 412, n. 2]

ARCHIVES NATIONALES
K 1,515, PIÈCE No. 68

[11 mars 1570.]

[*Au dos, propria manu*] Lo que se dixo de parte de los Principes de Bearne y Conde a Biron.

Dicho y pronunciado a los XI de março, a tres horas despues de mediodia, delante de Mos^res los Principes y Almirante, gentileshombres y cabeças de lex-ercito de los dichos Señores Principes.

Mos de la Caçe ha dicho a Mos de Biron que tenia mandamiento de todos los Señores y gentileshombres del exercito para dezirle:

Que, como ellos loan infinitamente a Dios por la gracia que ha hecho al Rey de le tocar el coraçon e inclinarle a la paz tan necessaria, assi davan muy humildes gracias a Su Magestad de la buena voluntad que tenia de les estender sus braçocs y abraçallos como buenos y fieles subditos, mas, porque estiman y creen que la privacion de los exercicios de la religion es para ellos mas dura muerte que ninguna que se les pudiesse dar, supplican muy humilmente a Su Magestad les otorgue un medio con que acquieten sus consciencias para con Dios, al qual si se mostrassen desleales, Su Magestad no podria esperar que ellos le fuessen muy fieles, porque quien no es fiel á Dios no lo puede ser á los hombres, que no es libertad de consciencia estar sin palabra de Dios, sino una insoportable servidumbre, que si huvieran consentido de vivir en esta licencia llamandola libertad de consciencia, Su Magestad con razon devria tomar resolucion de no se fiar jamas dellos y de no los tener jamas en estima de hombres de bien.

Que Dios dize que sobre nosotros ha embiado la muerte, es a saber que cien muertes nos vienen mas a cuenta que alexarnos voluntariamente del derecho camino de la vida eterna.

En lo demas dize que ellos havian (con muy grande desplazer suyo) sido forçados por muchas causas de emplear sus vidas por defender a los que avian sido sus defensores, cosa que no les devia ser imputada a mal, ni delante de Dios, ni delante de los hombres, sino solo a aquellos que contra justicia y contra las leyes han siempre oprimido sus consciencias y sus honrras y sus vidas. Al presente, dessearian por quanto su dever les obliga, podellos emplear en el servicio de Su Magestad y cumplimiento de su Estado, en pre-juyzio de aquellos que se reyan de sus miserias comunes y esperavan dello provecho.

Por el particular de Mos^r de Biron, el dize que todos sentian una grande obligacion para con el, por la buena intencion que mostrava al acrescenta-miento del reposo publico, que si fuesse en su mano de le poder mostrar quanto lo estimavan, el veria en lo que tenian y estimavan aquellos que, como el, no dependian de alguna particularidad, mas de la sola voluntad del Rey y de la consideracion de la utilidad publica; que el Rey no podia hazer election de señor de su Corte mas agradable a toda la compañia ni mas proprio para la execucion divina entan sancta impressa, en la qual rogava a Dios le llegasse a effecto, de manera que ellos viessen presto un buen fin que fuesse a gloria de Dios y contentamiento de Su Magestad y reposo de sus consciencias y alegria de todos sus subditos.

Finalmente le dixo que ellos quedavan persuadidos que, como el avia valerosamente aventurado su vida en campaña por les hazer mucho mal sin razon, agora con razon el emplearia sus officios y buenos medios para les procurar el bien que desseavan, sin el qual podian menos passar que sin el pan que comian ordinariamente.

A loqual Mos de Biron respondio lo mas sabia y graciosamente que fue possible, dandoles siempre seguridad del desseo que Su Magestad tenia de hazer paz, y representandoles el alegria que ternia de representar a Su Magestad las buenas razones que el les avia oydo, y hazerle testimonio del buen proposito en que todos en general y en particular estavan de querer dar a Su Magestad la obediencia que le era devida, y que este era solo el medio por el qual podia Su Magestad ser vencido. En fin, el uso de muy honestos agradescimientos, y assi mismo dio seguridad de emplear sus buenos officios en un negocio que el creya havia de causar tanta utilidad al Rey y a sus subditos.[1]

APPENDIX XXV

[P. 413, n. 1]

STATE PAPERS, FOREIGN

ELIZABETH, VOL. CXII, No. 693, j

[Extraict des Lettres du S^r card^{al} de Lorraine]

Quant a la paix discessum est re infesta, qui nous faict esperer bien. Et se reassemblent a cest heure tant de grandes personnaiges mesmes messieurs de Conseil de Paris. Chacun y fera & dira son opinion et oyra parler le Roy ainy chacun en pourra dire a cueur ouverts. Les offres que leur auroent este faictez cestoient les villes de la Rochelle Sancerre & Montauban usque ad biennium ut civitates refugii sans tenir offices ny benefices. Et que les haultz justiciers & plains fiefs de haubert en Normandie ne seroient empesches ny recherches faisant dedans leurs maisons & ceulx presant tantum tout ce que

---

[1] The above document was sent by Biron to M. de Fourquevaux, French ambassador in Spain. There is an extract from the letter of Biron to Forquevaux translated into Spanish, same carton (K. 1,515), pièce No. 69. Biron's letter is dated March 17, 1570, from Narbonne.

bon leur sembleroient en leur religion alibi nusquam itaque ilz ont demande temps de deliberer & feront respons dedans six sepmaines. Ce Chateaubriant ce iiij^e May 1570.

[*Enclosed in a letter by Sir Henry Norris to Sir William Cecil from Paris, May 24, 1570*]

APPENDIX XXVI
[P. 417, n. 3]
ARCHIVES NATIONALES
K. 1,515, PICÈE No. 118

[*Au dos, alia manu*] Copia de carta del Nuncio a Su Magestad. De Madrid al Escurial, a 26 de Junio 1570.

Para escrivir a Francia, como se hizo. Lo de Mos. de Fox.

Copia di una lettera, che il Nuntio scrisse a S. M^{ta} Cat^{ca}.]

Mi è doluto assai intendere che V. M^{ta} Cat^{ca} senta qualche indispositione di stomaco, il che deve ser residuo de la incomodità del camino. Il Signor Dio la mantenga sana longamente, con ogni contento et felicita.

Per le ultime lettere d'Italia ch'io trovai in Madrid, quali sono di 17 de maggio, S. S^{tà} mi avvisa d'havere inteso che la Regina di Francia sta in animo di far cancelliere di quel regno di Francia Monsr di Foys, hora Imbasciatore in Venetia. Et perche questo homo, oltre l'essere indiciato grandemente nel Santo Offitio de la Inquisitione di Roma e parente e dependente da quella buona donna chiamata la Regina di Navarra, et è persona superba, inquieta di spirito, amica di novita et discordia, et di piu si tiene offeso da Sua Santità per non havere consentito ch' egli vadi a Roma, et credo il medesimo sia con V. M^{tà} por una causa simile di non haverlo accettato in Spagna; queste cause, dico, et altre che Sua Santita considera, gli da gran sospetto che, se questo homo fosse posto in tale administratione, la quale può infinitamente in quel regno, come nel Cancellier passato s' è veduto per esperientia, non cercarebbe altro che di unire le voluntà de queste due donne, et non solo, favorendo la parte ugonota, travagliare le cose di Francia (pur troppo travagliate), ma anchora quelle de li circunvicini, maxime nelli Stati ecclesiastici e di V. M^{tà} Cat.^{ca}, non solo per vendetta de la offesa, et per l' odio che a l' uno et l' altro verisimilmente porta, ma anchora per la propria inclinatione sua. Onde Sua Beatitudine, facendo sopra cio quello che puo per la sua parte, desidera e ne prega V. M^{tà} a volere similmente cercare ogni via di impedire tale elettione. et quando non si possi altro, si degni scrivere a l'Imbasciatore, et vedendo passar inanti tal cosa, si unisca con il Nuntio, et insieme si lassino intendere apertamente dalla Regina che Sua Beatitudine et S. M^{tà} Cat^{ca} haveranno per male ch' ella dia uno officio di tanta importantia in mano di persona tale il che non deve fare, si ella desidera di essere tenuta fautrice de la fede cattolica desiderosa de la grandezza et quiete del Re suo figliuo lo et della unione e^t

bene de la Christianità. Spera Sua Santità che, con questo rimedio si possi obviare a quello inconveniente, peroche la Regina prefata mostra pure di havere qualche consideratione in simili attioni di non far cosa che possi con ragione dispiacere a Sua Santita et a V. M^{tà}. Et perche da una parte questo negotio ricerca presta provisione, et da l'altra non è honesto che in questo tempo io dia perturbatione a V. M^{tà} con la mia presentia, ho voluto communicarla con il Cardinale, et scrivere a V. M^{tà} Cat^{ca} la presente, supplicandola humilmente si degni farmi dare quella grata risposta che comandara ch' io scriva a Sua Beatitudine sopra questa materia. Et, basando reverentemente le regali mani a V. M^{ta}, prego N. S^{r}. Dio la concervi longamente felice.

Di Madrid, li 26 di Guigno 1570.

APPENDIX XXVII
[P. 422, n. 1]

STATE PAPERS, FOREIGN
ELIZABETH, VOL. CXV, No. 937,

[*The Vidame de Charters to Marshal Montmorency*]

Monseigneur, j'ay receu une lettre quil vous a pleu m'escripre pour responce a ce que vous avois escript par monsieur de Saragosse. Iay congneu que pensiez que je fusses encores au lieu dont vous avois escript. Si jeuse pense que ma presente y eust este requise j'euse differé tant quil vous eust pleu le me faire entendre Mais il vous estoit fort aise a penser que si lon prenoit goust par deça a ceste negociation elle seroit adressee a monsieur le cardinal de Chastillon, ou a l'ambassadeur du roy. On seroit envoye quelqu'ng des francoys favoris. Quand a moy ie n'ay pretendu en cest affaire que le service du roy et de la couronne de France, et si les affaires succedoient comme je y voy une telle espoirance et asseurance sil estoit poursuivy diligemment. Le contentement que je desire ne me pouroit fuir. Il est vray que je serois fort marry si jamais j'oyois dire que par faulte de diligence cest affaire fust demoure imparfaict, aussy seroit ce ung domage public oultre le particullier du prince au quel les premiers fruicts en appartiennent. Monsieur une lettre que jay receue de mons^{r} de Saragosse me faict entrer en soupçon et craincte que en atendant entre deux personnes qui ne se sont jamais veues qui ostera prenner le bonnet il ne se mette quelqung entre deux qui face perdre l'occasion de contracter une grande amitie & fort utille a la France, la quelle estant perdue sensuyviroit le dommage et le regret (mais en vain). Je suis bien asseure que larcheduc d'Austriche ne sendormira pas et ne laisera perdre l'occassion qui se presente a une assemblee des estatz qui se vont tenyr voire les previendra sil peult ne perdra pas une heure, que pendant quil voyt que la royne est en deffiance et doubte pour les affaires de la royne D'escosse et des differens quelle a avec le roy D'espaigne et quilz voyoient que l'empereur avent en pouppe, et quil faict des mariages telz quil scavroit souhaiter. Il ne se serve de l'occassion & faveur du temps et pendant que les amis simulez paistront la jeunesse animeuse et la rempliront de grande espoirance, luy prometant par adventure des plus grandes choses (combien quelles ne soient pas aysees a trouver, et pour moy je ne les scay pas ilz prendront cest 'advantage sur la partye et renforceront leur grandeur de la puissance et faveur d'un royaulme qui nest point petit Et vous ose bien dire quil y a de la part de ceux en qui gist la resolucion de cest affaire une grande inclinacion et une grande consideracion de long service de cest ancyen serviteur et de la subjection et humiliacion quil a monstree de la quelle vous scavez que le sexe se delecte. Ausy est ce leur façon de regner la quelle toutes veulent exercer, tant plus les roynes. Il ne fault penser que les dificultes pour la religion puissent engendrer quelques difficultez aux capitulacions qui facent plus de retardement. Car je scay par la bouche de la dame et ausy par ceux qui ont sceu toute ceste negotiacion passee, et par ung qui y a este employe qui ne parle pour metre le beau devers elle nestant de ses subjects mais estranger, que la charte blanche luy a este donnee. Et sest contente l'Archeduc pour le faict de la religion de si peu que cella se doibt estimer pour rien. Davantage la consideracion de lage qui est plus vivill et meur donne ung beau lustre aux persuasions et jugement de ceux qui tendent de ce costé la. Avec ses advantages du long service et age convenable, je crains que ceux qui tiennent le party contraire ne persuadent avec aparence a cause du trop long silence ou froide poursuite quil y aye du contemnement ou de la froideur en ceux de la France estant chose propre au sexe de faire plus de choses par despit que par amour est a craindre quel la froideur de ceste part ne soit cause de l'eschauffer et faire haster plus quelle ne fairoit si nestoit pour se faire regretter apres a loisir par ceulx qui se seroient portez trop froidement en son endroit Larticle de la lettre du gentilhomme qui vous porta ma lettre (qui me faict craindre que en voulant traicter de la part de la France avec fort grand respect et par adventure prendre l'honneur devers nous l'affaire nen sera pire) est quil dict que si lon estoit asseure par deça de la bonne volonte de ceux de dela la mer on y pouroit entendre ce qui me semble estrange de vouloir qu'une ville se rende avant quelle soit sommee. Il me semble que cest beaucoup quelle parlamente, sans avoir ouyr parler le canon. Et nest par peu de chose qu'estant sa principalle defence de la difference de laage et de linconstance de la jeunesse, et la crainte destre dicy a quelques anees, peu aymes et mesprisee et en danger de veoir de ses yeulx aymer dautres, lon luy a faict abandonner ceste contre escarppe et le corrider tellement que lon peult veoir au pied de la muraille que je vous asseure nest point veue de flans. Des particularitez et moyens que lon a tenue en ses approches jusques la jen ay dice quelque chose a ce gentilhomme qui est fort affectionne a cest affaire en faveur du bien de la France. Et dabondant en hayne de la grandeur qui se voit preparer a la maison d Autriche si elle s'impatronize de ce royaume, tellement quil nest a craindre si non que la tradiuite ne donne loisir a ceux

qui de long temps ont faict deseing de se saisir de ce pais de venyr au bout de
leur intencions lesquelles sont fort favorablement receues, et croy quils jouyront
en bref si leurs conseilz ne sont troublez par une diuersion & par obiect nouveau
plus desirable que celuy qui ce presente Ce qui me semble estre indubitable-
ment en la jeunesse d'un prince qui a la reputacion dauoir le sens meur devant
les ans et ausi courageux et dausy grande espoirance que prince ne soit ne de
lage des hommes.   Monsieur vous scavez trop bien combien la maisson d'Au
triche seroit agrandie sur la maison de France si elle estoit renforcee de ce
royaume.   Et ny a point de doubte quelle ne donnast pour tousjours par cy
apres la loy a la France et est chose seure quelle contraindroit le roy a rompre
la paix quil a donnee a ses subiectz.   Davantage si par ce mariage nest donne
satisfaction au grand coeur de monsr frere du roy pour loccuper et luy donner
matiere de faire plus grandz deseingz   Il ne fault point doubter que tous ceux
qui prennent la couleur et pretexte de la religion pour advancer les moiens de la
divission et ruyne de la France afin d'agrandir la maison d'Autriche ne proposent
a monsieur duc danjou quelques mariages qui sera au despens de la couronne de
France si la bonne nature et amitie dentre les freres ne resiste a leur malicieux
deseingz.   Mais il ne sen scauroit proposer du quel se doive espoirer plus de grandeur, non seulement a luy mais a toute la maison de France en gaignant le dessus
sur la maison d Autriche, la quelle veult soubz couverture & douceur du mariage du roy faire avaller ceste curee & gaigner ung royaume sans ce quil luy soit
donne empeschement et ne fault point doubter que si le mariage de larcheduc
se faict quil ne soit en peu de temps mieulx obey que na este le roy Philippe
et ce moiennant le danger de la religion et leur sera aise de nous donner la loy
ou pour le mains de nous faire redoubler la ruyne de la France par division
et guerre civille.   Au contraire si ce bien est resceue pour noz princes il y
aura bien de quoy rendre la pareille a ceux qui ont dresse tous leurs conseilz
a procurer que la France se ruynast par une guerre civile   Voyans que par
guerres ouvertes jamais ilz n'auroient peu paruenir a leur intencion.   Pour
amour du mal quilz ont faict monsr pouroit iustement avec forces du roy
faveur dangleterre et moiens du prince dorenge avoir la confiscacion de la
Flandre par droict de feodalite pour felonnie commise.   Et ausy la maison
d Autriche qui se bastit lempire hereditaire et la monarchie se trouveroit en
ung instant deux freres roys ausy puissans lun que lautre pour contrepois
de son ambition liggnez avec les princes protestans de lallemaigne et auroient
les deux freres plus de part en lempire que ceux qui se veulent atribuer par
la ruyne des anciennes maisons de la Germanye come de la maison de Saxe
et des princes palatins qui sont amateurs de la couronne de France.   Le
partage de monsieur d allencon seroit aise a trouver en la duche de Millan
auec la faueur de lallemaigne, des Suises ausy et des princes Italliens devotieux
de la France Et si besoing estoit por le recouvrement du royaume de Naples,
la faver du Turc se trouveroit par apres ung a propos.   Monsr il ma semble
que cela est si aparent, et si facille a persuader que puis que vous en aurez

une fois ouvert la bouche il ny faudra plus autre·soliciteur que le roy mesmes qui peult veoir par ce moyen son royaume luy demourer uny ses freres partagez Sa force telle et si grande quil ne poura estre offence ny commande par menasses qui contraigñent faire la guerre a ses subiects pour complaire a ceux qui sont envieux de sa grandeur et n'ont peu trouver moyen de la diminuer que par elle mesmes. Lors ce pouroit faire une legue parfaicte entre noz princes & les protestans de la Germanie & les suisses De ceste facon ung grand plaisir viendroit a la royne de veoir tous ses enfans roys Lors leglisse galicane pouroit sexempter des erreurs de leglisse Romayne comme elle a faict plusieurs fois le temps passe, lors se pouroit faire ung concille general au quel les erreurs introduictes par lambition et advarice ce leglisse romayne ne seroient favorisses et confirmees par praticques et corruptions, et en la France l'allemaigne et langleterre s'introduiroient une ordre et pollice de religion et unite de doctrine que toutes les autres provinces de la cristiente seroient contraintes dembrasser et finiroient les differens des subiectz avec leurs princes desquelles Sathan se sert pour la destruction de la Christeente et pour donner loisir au turc d'usurper pendant que les princes Chrestiens s'amussent a defendre les supersticions du Pape et maintenyr sa grande^r.

Monseigneur je me recommande treshumblement a votre bonne grace et vous suplie de rechef me departir de votre faveur et conseil touchant comment je me doibs gouverner a escripre a leurs ma^{tes} ou non: Monsr je prie Dieu vous donner tresheureuse et treslongue vye. De la Ferte ce ——^{1} jour doctobre 1570

[Not signed]

[Not addressed]

[Endorsed in Cecil's hand] Octob. 1570.

The vidam of Chartres to the Marshall Montmorency.

[Enclosed by Sir Henry Norreys to Cecil, 4 November, 1570.][2]

APPENDIX XXVIII

[P. 426, n. 3]

STATE PAPERS, FOREIGN

ELIZABETH, VOL. CXVIII, No. 1,174

[Marshal Montmorency to Cecil]

Monsr jay este tresaise davoir entendu tant par la lettre que mauez escripte du xxij^e du passe, que par le s^r du Pui present porteur le desir qui vous avez de veoir bien tost affectuer ce qui a este miz en avant pour estraindre une

[1] A space is left blank to the MS.

[2] This letter of Sir Henry Norris is a draft originally intended to be sent to the Queen, with the terms of address altered throughout—*your highness* altered to *your honour*, etc.

bonne & ferme alliance, entre ces deux royaumes, ayant par votre prudence & longue experience de lestat & cours des affaires, passez & presens tresbien cogneu combien cella seroyt en ce temps, non seullement convenable Mais aussi necessaire, pour le bien seurette & grandeur de lun & de lautre, a quoy de ma part je ne fauldray de tenir la main de tout mon pouvoir et de my employer syncerement, de cueur & daffection Vous priant a ceste cause Monsr, que desormays avec une bonne Intelligence & correspondance, que pour cest effect nous aurons ensemble Nous mections peine de vaincre les difficultez & rompre les obstacles.   Que aucuns y mectent tous les jours, artificieusement, de sorte que au plustost, avecques votre bon ayde, nous y puissyons veoir lheureux suites, que nous desirons.   Qui tourne (avec occasion, de raisonable tantement dune part & dautre, au repoz unyon & grandeur de ces deux couronnes, et a la confuzion de ceux qui sefforcent d empescher ung si bon euvre ce que masseurant, que vous vouldrez faire et cheminer en ce faict avec votre Integritte acoustumee, je ne mestandray plus avant en ce propoz.   Si ce nest pour vous prier de creoire ced. porteur, de ce quil vous dira de ma part, come moy mesmes   Qui surce me recomanderan tresaffectueus^t a votre bonne s^r Priant Dieu vous donner Monsr en parfaicte sante bonne & longue vye.   De Gaillon le xxv^e jour de May 1571.

[Signed]   Votre obeissant et parfaict amy
MONTMORENCY

[Addressed] A Monsr
            Monsr de Burghley.

[Endorsed] 20 May 1571
            Montmorency to my L.

APPENDIX XXIX
[P. 448, n. 2]

STATE PAPERS, DOMESTIC
ADDENDA, ELIZABETH, VOL. XXI, No. 58
[French-English Alliance, 1572]

Good m^r Hoggyns . . . .We allso here of a gret lege made wth France wch y₃ thowghte that thereby the Frenche pretendith some further feche to serve there tourne: God of his goodnesse kepe the noble yle of Inglande to lyve wthout givynge ower much credith to forren fryndshipe.   Here ys gret preparation as ever I sawe for wth in this xx dayes there wyll be x thousant horsmen & fyfty thousant fotmen: lykewyse by se 80. saylle of men of warre.   Don Jhon de Austria ys come wth his galles to Genova & the Venecians goith outwarde agaynst the tourke who hath augmentyd there forces.   The deuke of Savoye armyth for the Kynge 8000 fottemen and as it ys sayd commyth hym sellf in parson.   Flushynge saluted the deuk de Medina cely very vyle at his com-

mynge & burnte iij shipes of marchantes onlye by treson of a Floshynge verlet
that came out of Spayne wth them & toke apon hym to led them in to the port
of Sleuce & set then on grond hym sellf wente his waye yet the daye after the
wynd beynge very good the rest of the deuks armey housted vp saylle, and in
dyspite of the toune of Flushynge passed to the Raynykyns wth out hurt more
then one gonner slayne The portyngall flyte of this contry lyke fallse trayters
strok ancker before Flushynge wch ys lyk that many thereby ar undone. The
gensys tok off the iij shyppes that wer bornet xxvj. spaynyardes & in the toune
honge them. Lykewyse the Spayniardes aboute xv. dayes past toke xxx
frenche horsmen commynge to Monsse amonge wch as yt ys sayd the sone of
monsir Mongomvrey was one who offerryd for his ransome 5000 crounes he
& the rest his compaynyons wer hanged at Flyford vj. dayes past so that here
ys no favor but hangynge on both sydes. Our cuntrymen & wemen as my
lade of Northumberland lieth at Maklynge & so doth m^r Daykeres where not
many dayes past [two] of my l. Setones sones wer lyk to have byn slayne in
the tumolte wch standeth yet but in a mamerynge yet nowe they begyne to
come coler & to obbey the maigestrates. The pore erle of Westmarland lieth
at Lovayne & so doth my lade Hungerford my old knyght & otheres . . . .
Thoughe I begone, wryte I pray you to me & send yor letters to my l. to Brugys
& in so doynge I wyll wryt to you wekelye from the campe of our occurrance,
in hast wryten this present tewsdaye the xvij of Iune at Brugys 1572.

Yo^r lovynge frende
Thomas Parker

[*Addressed*] To his lovyng fryend m^r Robert
    Hoggyns at m^r Edmunde Hoggyns
    his house in Mylke Streete give
    thes. At London.
[*Endorsed*] 17 Iunii 1572.
    m^r Tho. Parker to m^r
    Hogans from Brugis.

APPENDIX XXX

[P. 457, n. 3]

BIBLIOTHEQUE DE L'INSTITUT, COLLECTION GODEFROY

Vol. 256, fo. 71, recto (no. 39 du catalogue)

[Le duc d'Anjou à Charles IX.]

[La Guerche, 19 janvier 1573.]

[*Suscription, au dos*] Au Roy, Monseigneur et frere.

[*Au dos, alia manu*] Monseigneur, de XIXe janvier 1573.

Monseigneur, par la depesche que je vous fiz hyer, je vous ay adverty
que le Sr de Biron m'avoit escript que, quand toutes les compaignyes de gens

de pied françoyses dont nous avons faict estat seroient la, après avoir demeuré dix ou douze jours aux tranchées, il n'en scauroit rester plus hault de six mil hommes, et qu'il estoit necessaire d'en avoir plus grand nombre.   Sur quoy j'avois advisé d'envoyer devers Monsr l'amyral pour avoir quarante enseignes de celles qui sont auprès de luy.   Et estant presentement, venu devers moy le Sr de Beaulieu Ruzé, que le Sr de Biron m'a depesché expres, tant pour aucunes particularitez que j'ay donné charge au Sr de Lanconne (que j'envoye devers vous) vous dire, que pour m'advertir, encores que les forces y soient si petites qu'elles sont, qu'ilz estoient neanmoins d'adviz que je ne laissasse pas de m'acheminer au camp.   Ce que j'ay resolu de faire et de partir demain de ce lieu, pour m'en aller a Châtellerault et de la à Poictiers.   Et cependant je renvoye ledict Ruzé devers ledict Sr de Biron pour me revenir trouver en chemin, et me rapporter au vray ce que sera survenu depuis.   Et ay depesché incontinant ung courrier devers ledict Sr Amyral, pour faire partir tout aussy tost lesdictes quarante enseignes, ou ce qu'il me pourra envoyer, et qu'il les face embarquer à Moyssac, d'ou elles peulvent venir par eaue, jusques à La Rochelle, luy ayant mandé les lieux par ou elles auront a passer et par mesmes moien audict S^r admiral et de Montferrant de pourveoir qu'il y ait des batteaulx et estappes des vivres.   Et ne veoy aucune chose qui puisse apporter retardement a vostre service, que de n'avoir les deniers, pour pouvoir faire faire monstre a mon arrivée au camp, principallement aux gens de pied, d'autant qu'il est a craindre que, n'estans poinct payez et s'asseurans que je ferois porter argent avec moy (comme je l'avois promis a celles de vostre garde et du capitaine Gadz), ilz se desbendent et que le nombre que je m'attendz y estre n'y soit poinct.   Je vous supplie tres humblement, Monseigneur, de commander que l'on regarde de cercher tous les moyens dont l'on se pourra adviser pour m'envoyer les troys cens mil livres que je debvois avoir avant mon partement de la Court.

Au demeurant, Monseigneur, j'ay receu la lettre qu'il vous a pleu m'escripre du XIIIe de ce moys, et veu par le contenu d'icelle comme vous avez resolu deux poinctz.   Le premier, de la suppression de tous offices qui vacqueront, pour congnoistre la grand charge que cela apporte à vous et à voz subgectz, pour les gaiges qu'il leur fault payer.   Et l'autre, que vous avez commandé qu'il ne soit depesché cy apres aucun office ou benefice dont il vous sera baillé memoire ou placet, que troys moys apres que vous verrez les roolles qui en seront faictz, pour les departir à ceulx qui font service, principallement en ce camp auprès de moy.   Ce que je ne fauldray leur faire entendre, suivant ce qu'il vous plaist me mander.   J'ay aussy veu le memoire que vous a esté baillé de ce que l'on vous propose pour la conqueste que vous pouvez faire à l'Yndie avec peu de despence, laquelle je ne puis trouver que très bonne, lorsque vous serez en paix et que voz affaires le pourront permectre, y estans les richesses et commoditez portées par ledict memoire.   Vous sçavez combien telles entreprises et conquestes ont apporté de proffict au feu Empereur et

Roy Catholique, pour le grand nombre d'or qu'il a tiré et tire ordinairement du Peyrou, tellement que, sans cela, il n'eust eu moyen d'entretenir et soldoyer les armées et forces qu'il a entretenues jusques à present, qui me faict vous conseiller (soubz vostre meilleur adviz) de ne laisser poinct perdre ceste occasion, quand vous congnoistrez qu'elle pourra estre mise a execution. Presentement, j'ay eu nouvelles que le Sr Paul Emille a tant faict que ceulx de La Rochelle qui le detiennent prisonnier l'ont mis à rançon pour mil escruz, dont aulcuns de ses amys ont respondu pour luy. Laquelle somme il n'a aucun moyen de fournir, si ce n'est de vostre liberalité, grace et speciale faveur, laquelle je vous supplie vouloir estendre en luy pour cest effect, et luy faire paroistre la souvenance que vous avez tousjours eu de ceulx qui vous font service. Aussy, Monseigneur, j'ay esté adverty que l'estat de viceneschal de la Haulte et Basse Marche, qui est ès terres de mon apennaige est a present vacant par mort, la disposition et provision duquel neanmoins vous appartient. A ceste cause, je vous supplie encores le vouloir accorder aux Sieurs de Villequier, pour lesquelz je vous en faictz requeste, et commander que la depesche et provision soit faicte en leur faveur au nom de tel personnaige suffisant et cappable qu'ilz nommeront et non autrement. Sur ce je supplieray le Createur vous donner,

Monseigneur, en tres bonne santé, très longue et très heureuse vie.

Escript à la Guierche, le XIXme jour de janvier 1573.

[*Propria manu*] Vostre tres humble et tres obeissant frere et subget.

HENRY

[Original]

APPENDIX XXXI
[P. 458, n. 3]

STATE PAPERS, FOREIGN
ELIZABETH, VOL. CXXVI, No. 419
[*Charles IX to Montgomery*]

Monsr le Conte j'ay este bien ayse d'entendre par le sr de St Iehan votre frere la bonne volunte en laquelle il vous trouva de vous contenir doulcement par dela et sans entreprendre ou favoriser aucune chose qui soit contre le bien de mon service, qui est ce que je desire de vous, et me semble que ne scauriez mieulx faire pour votre honner & advantaige, ayant pour ceste cause advise vous envoyer le sr de Chasteauneuf present porteur expres pour vous dire & asseurer que vous comportant d . . . .[1] je vous feray conserver en tout ce qui vous touchera il vous maintiendray ainsy que mes autres bons & loyaulx subjects comme vous entenderez plus particullieremt dud. Sr de

---

[1] The MS is torn here.

Chasteauneuf Sur lequel me remectant du surplus dont je vous prie le croire, je priray Dieu Monsr le Conte vous avoir en sa s^{te} & digne garde. Escript a Paris le ixme jo^r de feurier 1573.

[Signed]   CHARLES
PINART

Monsr le Conte, j'ay faict desgaiger
votre vaisselle de trois cens escuz, et
ay commande au tresor^r de mon eschiequer
la garde po^r la vous faire rendre
comme je luy ay ordonne.[1]

[Addressed] Monsr le Conte de Montgommery.

[Endorsed in Burghley's hand]
9 Februar, 1572. (Sic.)
fr. Kyng to the Count
Montgomery by Chasteaunevff.

APPENDIX XXXII
[P. 461, n. 1]

STATE PAPERS, FOREIGN
ELIZABETH, VOL. CXXI, No. 1,428

Liste des villes des quelles ceuex de la relligion sasseurent en France.

*Monsr le Prince de
Conde et Monsr de
Rohan y
commaundent*

En Xainctongne, La Rochelle
St Jehan, St Angely ou commaunde Monsr de St Mosmes.
Roian, Port de Mer
Pons
Bouteville, et quelques Chasteaux

*Monsr de St Geniez,
Monsr de Longe*

Sur la Riviere de Dordonne
Bergirac imprenable
St Foy
Chastillon
Pinnoymant &c. Et sur disces il ny a presques pas un Papiste, ny mesme en tout le Pays.

[1] The postscript is in the same hand as the king's signature.

Monsʳ de Madailham,
Le Baron de Beauville

Sur le Riviere du Lot
Villeneufve d'Agenois
Clerac.
Sᵗ Linerade.

Monsʳ de Turène

En Perigort, Perigueux Ville Capitale et Plusieurs Chasteaux
Montflanquin

Monsʳ de Chappes,
Lieutenan: le Baron
d'Uzac, &c.,

Figiac
Bellie
Puynirol ⎫
Tournon ⎬ ces trois sont imprenables; et sont au R. de N.
Lanzarte ⎭
Turene ave toutes les terres de Monsieur de Turene en Lymosin.
Briene la gagliarde.
Usurstie. qui sont des meilleures: Toutes les surd. places sont bien accom-
    modees et sont toutes deçe la Riviere de Garonne.

Monsʳ le Baron de
Luzignian, Monsʳ
de Fauaz

Sur la Garonne au bord de deca sont
Agen ville Capitale d'Agenois grande et riche
La Reolle, Lonne ville, dont le Chasteau est imprenable; et sur le Rivage
    dela sont
Lengon
Millau
Le mas de Verdoun &c.

Le Roy de Navar
parce que c'est son
patrimonie y a
partout Portien
de les plus affectionez

Entre le Garonne et le pays de Bearn nous tenons
Leystoure ville Episcopale richen et imprenable patrimonie de R. de N.
Mauvesin
Fleurance
Cauze, bonne et forte ville
Nerac
Castel Jalouz

Balas ville riche, episcopale

Le mont de Marsan; forte

Tout le conte de Bigorces et les pays de Marsan, Tarsan Gavardan

Tarbe ⎫

Aire ⎬ villes episcopales

La principaute de Bearn

La basse Navarre

Le Pays des basques, a quoy on a donne tiel ordre que nouristant la paix il
ne si changera rien.

Au contrarie de puis la paix Grenade Beaumont et Verdun villes ont reconut
le Roy de Navarre p^r governeur et se sont mises soubz sa protection et
tous les jours si la paix tient quelque peu si en mettra de nouvelles. M.
L. Amirall a assiege Beaumont a cause de cela ou il a este tresbien battu.

M. le Vicount
de Terides

Pays de Quercy nous tenons

Montauban imprenable et une des belles villes de guerre du monde.

M. la Vicount
de Gourdon

Figeac capitale de Haut Quercy

Caussade

Realville

St Antonin

Villemur &c. en ces villes tout le peuple est de la religion.

Vicont
de Paulini

Au pays de Rourgue.

Millaut ville episcopale

Vabres ville episcopale

Creissel et autres en grand nombre fortes d'assietes dont nous ne scavons le
nom. Le peuple aussi est de fort longtemps de la religion et sont en
tous ces pays des relliques des vieux.

Le Baron de
Audon

En Languedoc, toute la Conte de Foix qui tient depuis les montz Pirenees
jusques aux portes de Thoulouse Patrimonie du R. de N. en icelle sont

Pasmicas ville forte peuplee, presque de la religion episcopale.

Foix ville et chasteu imprenable.

Sa Verdan

Mazores

Le Carla

Le mas d'Azil, toutes riches et imprenables. Et ceste derniere se faict une quantite purniable de Saltpetre pour muner tout le pays de poudre.

Le baron de
Monbardies

En Lauraignais partie du bas Languedoc sont

Puylaurens

Revel

Soureze

St Paul

Cramain &c.

Castres ville episcopale imprenable

L'Isle d . . . .[1] et plusieurs autres en la montagne.

[1] A space is left blank in the MS.

M. de Chastilon,
M. de Thore,
M. de St Romain, &c.

Au hout Languedoc, y en a infinies, les plus notables sont

Monpelier

Nismes

Aiguesmortes

Lunel

Aimargnes

Marsilargnes

Sommieres

Uzez

Auz

Aleth

Lodeve la pluspart episcopale

Tout le Pays de Vivarez; et le Pays de Sevènes.

M. de [L] Ediguieres

En Daulphine nous tenons tout le haut Pays, et du bas pays presque toutes les villes . . . .[1] quatre ou cinq. Gap et Dis villes principales sont a nous et cinq cens gentilihomines tous de la religion entre les quels y a tresbon ordre.

Le Baron d'Alemagne

En Provence nous avons quelques bonnes villes, entre autres Seine, le grand Tour, et tout le meilleur du Conte de Venisse, appartenant au Pope à cause d'Avignon.

Le Roy de Navarre ces places fournies de garnissons necessaires tant de pied que de cheval, peut sans sortir de Guienne mettre huict mil hommes de

[1] A space is left blank in the MS.

pied en campagne et mille gentilihomines et fournir l'equippage de six canons et deux couleurines &c. et quand il sera joinct avec les forces de Languedoc (car le Daulphine a le Rhosne entredeux) il poura faire estat de 10000 hommes de pied 2000 chevaux des meilleurs qui se virent jamais en France, et 10 canons, quatre couleurines et la pouldre et munitions et equipage d'iceux.

Pour les affaires de la guerre en son conseil il est assisté de Mr de Meru. Monsieur de Turene qui a esgarde sur la Perigort et Lymosin en sa absence. Mr de la Nouë chef et superintendant de sa maison.

M^r de viconte de Terride, Baron de Serignac, vieux Capitaine.

M^r de St Geniez, vieux Capitaine et homme de bon entendement.

M^r le Baron de Lusignan. Gouverneur de Agenois.

Mr de Fontralles, M^r le Baron d' Audon.

Mr de Guitry qui sont tous des meilleurs Cap: de France.

Pour le mainement des negogiations, outre les susd. il est assiste de Mr de Grateinx son Chauncelier, M^r des Aginz President et M^r des Requestes et plus^{rs} autres de mesme reing.

Outre ceux y y a plusieurs Princes, Seignurs, Vicontes, et Barons affectes de tout temps au party de la religion. Toutesfois je les ay lieu voulu mettre icy croire ilz me sont vennues en memorie.

Le R. de N.	Le Baron de Mombardices
M' le P. de Conde	Le Vicount de Lalant
M. de Rohan	Le Baron de Montanhils
M. de Nemours	Le Baron de Monlieu
M. de Laval	Le Baron de la Rochalais
M de Rochebernard son frere	Le Prince de Chalais
M. de Meru	M. de Mouy
M. de Thore	M. de la Forse gendre de M. de Biron
M. de Turene	Le Vicont de Chasteauneuf
M. de Chastillon	Le Baron de Piersebuffiere
M. de Clermont	Le Baron de Salignac
M. de la Noué	Le Baron de Beinac
M. de S. Genie et ses freres	Le Baron de Bresolles
M. le Viconte de Tirrede	Le Vicont de Paulini
M. de St. Romain	Le Vicont de Panart
Le Baron de Fontrailles	Le Vicont de Gourdon
Le Baron de Ardon	Le Vicont de Arpajon
Le Baron de Senegaz	Le Baron de Cabrere
Le Baron de Mirambeau	M. de Ediguires
M. de Languillier	M. de Guitry
Le Baron de Verac	Le Baron de Longa
Le Vic: de Savailhan	M. de Campagnac
Le Baron de S. Gehniz	M. de Boesse

M. de Montguiron	Le Baron de Beauville
Le Baron de Montandie	Le Baron de Reine
Le Baron de Luzignan	Le Baron de Vercillac
M. de Bonevall	Le Baron de S. Nauphan
M. de Ussac	Le Baron de S. Arlaye
Le Vicont de Rochouart	Le Vicont de Meherin
Le Baron de Almagne	Le Vicont de Belsane et autres.

Tous les desus nommes sont en Guienne et de Guienne ou Languedoc ou pr le moins ont porte les armes a ceste dernier guerre. Quant aux autres Seigneurs et Capitaines des autres Provinces de France qui ont pareille ulcouse[?] et la monsteront au besoing, ascavoir es provinces assises deca la Riviere de Loure, ilz sont sans comparison en plus grand nombre pour respost des lieux ou ilz sont; nous ne les avons point nommés pas ce quilz ont attendu une armée de Reistres present s'y jettes, attendant la quelle ilz se sont le mieux quilz ont peu compertes en leurs maisons.

[*Not signed*]

[*Endorsed*] Les villes des quelles ceux de la
Religion s'asseurent en France.

APPENDIX XXXIII
[P. 474, n. 2]
BIBLIOTHEQUE D L'INSTITUT, COLLECTION GODEFROY
VOL. 256, FO. 83 RECTO, NO. 45 DU CATALOGUE
[*Le duc d'Anjou à Charles IX*][1]

[Camp devant La Rochelle, 17 février 1573].[2]

Monseigneur. Par le jeune Seguier que j'ay depesché depuis deux jours devers Vostre Majesté, elle aura entendu comme j'estois sur le poinct envoyer devers icelle le Sr de Bourrique, l'un de mes maistres d'hostelz, pour la sattisfaire de tout ce que je pouvois avoir à luy faire entendre de l'estat de ceste armée. Suivant ce, je l'ay presantement faict partir si bien instruict de touttes choses que je ne doubte qu'il ne luy en sçache rendre très bon compte. Me restera à supplier, comme je fais très humblement, Vostre Majesté le voulloir en ce qu'il vous dira de ma part oyr avec la mesme foy et creance dont elle a tousjours voullu m'honnorer. J'ay veu ce qu'il luy a pleu me mander par sa depesche du XIme de ce mois sur la proposition que aucuns avoient faicte de donner la charge de vostre armée de mer à mon frere Monsr le Duc et au Roy de Navarre chose que je rejectay aussi tost pour les mesmes considéra-

---

[1] See the subscription and the notice of receipt at the end of the despatch.

[2] Although the Catalogue has the date February 18 it is a mistake; the document has very clearly 17th.

tions, que Vostredicte Majesté a bien sceu prendre, et n'estois pour le permectre en aucune sorte, de maniere que Vostredicte Majesté demourera,
s'il luy plaist, en repos de ce cousté la.

Monseigneur, je supplie le Createur donner à Vostredicte Majesté en
très bonne santé et prosperité tres longue et tres heureuse vye.

Escript au camp devant La Rochelle, le XVIIme jour de febvrier 1573.

Monseigneur, j'ay veu par les dernieres depesches qui vous sont venues
d'Angleterre de S^r de La Mothe Fenellon, la demonstration que ceulx de vos
subiectz qui sont refugiez par dela font de procurer de leur part l'entier repos
de vostre royaume avec ceulx de leur religion.   Chose qui me semble estre
très avantageuse au bien de vostre service, et que, pour l'effect de leur bonne
intention, il vous plaise leur bailler touttes les seuretez necessaires pour venir
par deça.   Estant ceste voye, si elle peult proffiter, beaucoup plus aisée et
seure que celle de la force, outre le moien que ce vous seroit de conserver
beaucoup de voz bons subjectz et serviteurs et soulaiger d'autant vostre bourse.[1]

[*Propria manu*] Vostre treshumble et tres obeissant frere et subget

HENRY.

[*Au dos*, Suscription] Au Roy, Monseigneur et frere.

[*Au dos, alia manu*] Monseigneur, du XVIIme febrier.   Mr de Bourricques.

[Original]

APPENDIX XXXIV
[P. 503, n. 1]

STATE PAPERS, FOREIGN

ELIZABETH, VOL. CXXXIV, No. 186, iij

[*Dr. Valentine Dale to Lord Burghley*]

Es eo tempore quo proximè ad te scripsi nullum fuit mihi prorsus tempus
animi laxandi, ita fui partim itineribus partim multis gravibus & impeditis
rebus administrandis distractus, nec satis etiam nunc scio an mihi liceat aliqua
intermissione frui ut de liberioribus ac amœnioribus studiis possim aliquantisper
cogitare   Neque verò tuam nunc volo sive tarditatem sive negligentiam in scrib-
endo accusare nulla est enim mihi remissæ erga me tuæ amicitiæ vel minima
suspitio.   Ut scias igitur quid rerum hic agatur Nunquam tanta animorum
consentione ad pacem conspiratum est nec unquam tamen magis diversis studiis
de pacis conditionibus ineundis actum est Coguntur enim planè jam omnes
longo & ancipiti bello fessi & ad inopiam atque egestatem usque redacti
necessario nunc tandem ac serio de pace cogitare.   Neque enim aut æris
alieni quo infinito premuntur dissolvendi ratio est, nec sumptus qui sunt

---

[1] The postscript it found thus, between the date and the signature.

apud istos profusissimi diutius sustinere possunt.   Vectigalia autem ac ceteri reditus regii aut oppignorata aut distracta sunt ut annui regis proventus ne ad erogationes quidem domesticas satis sufficiant.   Vident igitur omnes si bellum gerendum sit, infinita contributione opus esse, cum nullæ sint principis ad bellum gerendum facultates, & omnis qua opus sit regi pecunia ab aliis sumenda aut potius extorquenda sit.   Homines autem nobiles per quos bellum precipuè geritur quorum amplissimæ sunt facultates (nam hi pæne soli prædia possident & vicena aut tricena aut etiam centena plerique millia aureorum nummum habent annua) Hi quantam alicunde pecuniam corradere possunt eam prodige & profuse ilico profundunt, nulla est enim eis cura rei familiaris, sed tanqam in diem viventes quibus opus habent rebus quantivis comparant eam quam habent pecuniam negligentes & quam non habent quibusvis rationibus vel quamvis cum jactura conquirentes.   Solent autem illis ut plurimum belli presertim tempore sumptus a rege subministrari.   Nunc autem quum videant nihil esse regi, quod det, corpora sua periculis libenter non subjiciunt, inviti autem hoc presertim tempore ad bellum non adiguntur, itaque fit ut qui ferè uni pro principe soliti sint decertare hi bellum in primis detrectent.   Plebs autem rustica inops semper est atque egena, non enim ut nostri improvidos reperiunt prediorum dominos, a quibus prerogata quadam modica pecunia exili reditu conductis agris, ad magnas opes perveniant, sed aut Coloni partiarii agrum magno labore parvo autem cum compendio colunt, aut justum fructuum precium pendunt.   Hoc verò tempore vastationibus populationibus & direptionibus ita sunt expilati, ut nec bos ad arandum nec frumentum ad sementes faciendas supersit: tantum abest ut illorum pecunia bellum geri possit.   Reliqua sunt oppida que sanè sunt multa & cives certe ditissimi Nam que magna ut scis nostris est trium millium coronatorum pecunia, apud istos ducentorum aut trecentorum millium exiguè sunt facultates, & qui urbes incolunt soli aut sub pignoribus & hypothecis nobilium proventus possident, aut eorum facultates fœnere exhauriunt.   Inter istos autem cives opifices non nomino, quorum infinitus est numerus qui admodum difficulter victum magnis laboribus in urbibus querunt non enim in agris locus illis est ubi se ac suos tenuiter colendis agris aut pecore pascendo, ut nostri faciunt, alant.   Itaque in urbis quisque proximas se confert, ubi officinas instituunt & vitam labore producunt. Multo minus inter cives numerandi sunt hi, qui passim in viis scatent omnibus oratoriis preceptis ac artibus instructi quo hominum mentes ad elemosinam & commiserationem permoveant.   Neque etiam bonos illos viros hic nomino, quorum magnus est numerus qui se fratres dici volunt, quamvis inter se odiis plusquam fraternis dissideant quos ego planè eos esse existimo quos Chaucerus noster ex loco illo parum honesto sese proripere scribit. qui nugas ac nenias venditando in eam authoritatem pervenerunt.   Ut æquum existiment rogari potius sese quam rogare: tanquam viri omnibus virtutibus excellentes ad quorum pedes bona nostra projicere debeamus, quanquam illorum pæne jam explosa est disciplina ab illis quorum novum est ancupium qui se Jesuistas appellant, & perfecti volunt esse, juxta illud. Estote perfecti sicut ego sum, inter quos Darbesherus noster non est minimus apostolorum si noster dicendus est qui & nos & seipsum deservit & aliam vitam alios mores sequitur, illi autem quos dixi Cives qui tantum opibus valent, clientelis miseorum opificum in quos imperium habent & suis divitiis freti, pecuniam sibi imperari non patiuntur, sciunt enim neminem esse qui eos cogere possit, cum rex parum fisus nobilibus, tutelam urbium arma, machinas, bellicas, mœnia, & quicquid est roboris illis commiserit, rogati autem immensas & crebras priores pensitationes & tributa causantur itaque pauxillulam tandem aliquam pecuniam prout nec causa postulat tanquam ab invitis quasi vi sibi exprimi patiuntur. Jam Episcopi Abbates & alii quibus opima sunt sacerdotia cum videant omnium oculos in se ac bona sua esse conjectos nec aliquam aliam esse rationem conficiende pecuniæ nisi quæ ex eorum bonis & prediis distrahendis redigatur. Quis erit (inquiunt) tandem nostri expilandi finis si bellum adhuc duret An non sex decimas annuas fructuum nostrorum pensitamus. Vix annus adhuc est quod octingenta millia francorum que sunt centena millia librarum nostrarum in profectionem Polonicam dedimus jamque nos urgent Questores regii ad solutionem unius millionis & dimidiæ francorum, que summa est quingentorum millium coronatorum gallicorum, quos rex approbante pontifice nobis extorquet: cujus pecuniæ solvendæ rationem nullam adhuc habemus. Non tametsi pontifex ad rem tam piam nempe ad bellum intestinum alendum, predia ecclesiastica ad eum summam venire permiserit, emptores tamen non reperiuntur, coguntque nos officiales & ministri regii pecuniam quam non habemus, nostro periculo representare: recepturos aliquando ex distractione bonorum, si qui tandem reperiantur, qui tam dubio jure litem futuram presenti pecunia velint comparare. non enim ignotæ sunt artes pontificiæ: Veniet namque facile tempus cum Pontifex iste aut successor aliquis ejus restitutionem in integrum pro ecclesia non sine dirarum etiam imprecatione a se impetrari facillime patiatur, nulla habita eorum ratione qui in bona ecclesiastica pecuniam impenderunt. Itaque eo ventum est ut hi quorum causa bellum hoc geritur & qui evangelicos plurimum oderunt hi nunc pacem maximè expetant, & quemvis Dei cultum potius permittant, quam se indies argento emungi patiantur imò quidvis inquiunt potius in malam rem doceant Hugonoti, neque enim magis ab illis quam ab istis possumus expilari Nec est illorum non inepta sanè oratio. Jam homines miseri qui sedibus pulsi patria carent, inopes vagantur, quibus insidiæ undique tenduntur, supplicia & mortes intentantur, qui deserti ab omnibus, perpetuas excubias ad sese tuendos agunt hi pacem si unqam antehac nunc certè fessi ac defatigati miserè cupiunt, ut aliquis tandem sit laborum finis & patria terra quiescere liceat. Nemo est igitur qui non uno ore pacem affectet, ad pacem oculos, animum & omnes cogitationes convertat. Quin & Pontifex ipse sibi timens & veritus quem res nec sit habitura exitum,

& precipuè de comitatu Avinionensi sollicitus, alios non lacessitos esse malit, quam de suis rebus in periculum venire: sperans futurum ut rex intermisso bello integris viribus eos facile opprimat, quos nunc lacerato regno satis vexare non possit. Ex qua re factum est, ut sermonibus hominum certa pax facta, & negocium prorsus transactum esse diceretur, & ea fama per uniuersum orbem sparsa sit, pacem jam manibus teneri. Sed cum de pacis conditionibus agi ceptum est, longe fuerunt alie hominum voluntates, longè alius rei exitus. Nam quibus antea sua facilitate impositum est, ne in idem discrimen inciderent Evangelicæ libertati & saluti sue presidiis, urbibus ac rebus aliis que ad vitam tuendam pertinent sibi consulere voluerunt, nec se aliorum fidei committendos esse censuerunt quin rebus omnibus integris arma sumere possent, ut si non melior at saltem non deterior istis pactionibus illorum conditio fieret. Alii contra qui spe miseros illos homines devorarant & sibi occasionem egregiam oblatam existimabant, incautos homines vafricia & insidiis prorsus opprimendi, cum viderent non esse locum dolis quin potius futurum ut Evangelium propagaretur, nec esse in illorum potestate, ut istis conditionibus homines Evangelici exterminarentur, quidvis potius faciendum esse suadebant, quam locum illis dari quos extinctos esse cupiunt, hi & se & sua omnia regi offerunt, & quoduis discrimen subeundum esse censent. Itaque nunc Pontifex bellum alioqui formidans pecuniam mutuam satis amplam u(l)troneus offert: (sibi tamen satis callide pignoribus cavens) ut regis animum a pacis cogitatione avertat. Sunt etiam alii viri providi & rebus suis prospicientes, qui sciunt vetus illud esse, mobilia esse gallorum ingenia ad suscipiendum bellum (neque enim in tanta penuria & tantes difficultatibus de aliis perturbandis desinunt cogitare, nec istis unquam aut voluntas aut pecunia ad alios vexandos deest) qui ista penitius perspiciunt & sibi prudenter cavent, hi frigidam suffundunt, pristinam gloriam nominis gallici commemorantes, & ignominiam ob oculos ponentes, si tale dedecus subeatur ut quasi victi manus tendere, & leges jam non dare sed accipere cogantur, futurum ut tempore vires regia crescant, alii contra vel simultatibus solvantur, vel insidiis opprimantur, vel premiis & pollicitationibus separentur, qua ex re fiet aliquando ut rex victor stirpem illam hominum prorsus exterminet, & ecclesiæ Romane vindex eternam sibi famam ad posteros transmittat. Hic ego si tibi que fuerint postulata, que responsa, que argumenta in utramque partem adducta, qua constantia permansum sit in petitis, quibus artibus Evangelicorum legati tentati sint, quibus intercessoribus res tractata sit, historiam tibi non epistolam scriberem nolo tamen tibi ignotum esse egregiam fuisse in hac re Helvetiorum protestantium operam, ego autem quod potui porro ut est apud comicum nostrum. His igitur rebus effectum est ut post multas & longas de pace disceptationes incertiores simus multo quam dudum, pacem enim facere noluit bellum autem gerere non possunt.

Cum ista superiora aliquot dies scripta apud me haberem, nec describendi esset ocium accepi tandem tuas vicesimo quarto Maii scriptas, ex quibus intelligo esse etiam apud vos fidefragos, ut tuo verbo utar, nam fœdifragos usquam gentium reperiri non est fas dicere, itaque nactus ocium te istis quibuscunque carere nolui, nec si tibi sit cordi ullum laborem recusabo, quin priores etiam meas queas tu le amisisse tantopere quereris descriptas ad te mittam. Vale & nostros omnes meo nomine diligenter saluta nam eos de mea salute sollicitos esse scio. Lutietie Parisiorum ultimo Junii 1575.

Tui amantissimus

V. D.

[*Not addressed*]

[*Endorsed*] Ult°. Junii[1] 1575

    Mr D. Dale to m l.

    from Paris.

[*In Burghley's hand* a lettre wrytten in latin concerning the state of France.

APPENDIX XXXV

[P. 503, n. 2]

STATE PAPERS, FOREIGN

Elizabeth, Vol. CXXXI, No. 895

[*Henry III to Queen Elizabeth*]

Treshaulte tresexellente, et trespuissante princesse Nostre treschere et tresamee bonne seur et cousine ayant entendu le trespas ces jours passez advenu du feu Roy nostre trecher s^r et frere nous en avons receu ung tresgrand regret enuy & desplaisir pour la singulliere affection et fraternelle amitie quil nous a tousjours portee et demonstrée par tous bons offices. Et aussy pour la perte grande qui en demeure generallement a toute la Chrestiente, et a nous particullierement, qui luy avions tant dobligation comme nous avons encores en sa memoire, pour tant d'honneurs et de faveurs quil luy a pleu tousjours nous departir de son vivant. Ce que saichant que les princes ses voisins auront pareillement porte avec douleur, et mesmement vous, avec qui il avoit et a tousjours eu si bonne & parfaicte amitye, voisinaige et intelligence. Nous avons pense estre bien convenable a l'amitye mutuelle qui est aussy entre nous noz Royaumes et pais de nous en condoulloir avec vous, comme nous faisons par la presente en attendant qu'estant arrivé en nostre Royaume de France (ainsy que nous l'esperons bien tost avec layde de Dieu) nous puissions nous acquicter plus dignement de cest office. Voullans bien vous dire & asseurer cependant que si vous avez congneu le feu Roy notred. S^r et frere desireulx de conserver la bonne et sincere amitye voisinance et intel-

---

[1] Altered in Burghley's hand from *1° Julii*.

ligence que vous aviez ensemble, vous n'en debuez pas moings attendre & esperer de nous son successeur a la corone de France Ne voullant seullement continuer en lad. amitye, mais la fortifier asseurer et augmenter par tous honnorables & dignes offices que doibuent les princes amis les ungz aux autres ainsy qu'avons donne charge au s^r de la Mothe Fennelon vous faire entendre que vous prions recevoir et avoir agreable aupres de vous pour y estre notre conseiller et ambassadeur resident, tout ainsy quil estoit du feu roy nostre feu S^r et frere Et ne pouvons aussy trouver que tresbon l'exercice quil a faict de ladicte legation de puis ledict decedz advenu, tant suivant les tres de feu notred. S^r & frere que celles de la Royne nostre treshonnoree dame et mere qui en avoit tout pouvoir et a laquelle nous envoyons presentement le nostre le plus ample quil nous est possible.   Saichant combien elle merite de cested. corone, et combien elle sest aussy tousjours rendue affectionnée au bien de nous tous ses enfens, et des affaires et prosperite de notred. Royaulme, vous priant croire ledict s^r de la Mothe de ce quil vous dire sur tout ce que dessus et y adjouster foy comme feriez a nous mesmes Qui prions Dieu treshaulte tresexellente et trespuissante princesse Nostre treschere et tresamee bonne seur et cousine vous avoir en sa tressainte et tresdigne garde.   Escript a Cracovye le xv^{ne} jour de Juing 1574.

[Signed]   Vostre bon frere et cousin

HENRY
Warsevicz

[Addressed]   A treshaulte tresexcellenle et
                trespuissante princesse Nostre
                treschere et tresamee bonne
                seur & cousine la Royne
                D'Angleterre.

[Endorsed]   June xvth 1574.
                From the K. of Polonia to her Matie.   Dated at Cracovia.
                He condolethe the deathe of the K. his brother offreth and
                requireth lyke contynewance of amitie as was betwene her and
                his brother Desiereth her Matie to accept Mon^{sr} de la Mothe
                for his Ambassadeur.

APPENDIX XXXVI

[P. 504, n. 2]

ARCHIVES NATIONALES

K. 1,537, PIECE NO. 22

]Report of a Spanish Spy about Calais (Deciphered)]

[*Au dos*] Descifrado.

Avisos de Cales à XVIII° de Março 1575

[*En tete*] Avisos de Cales à XVIII° de Março 1575

Quiero dezir el runrun que anda entre estos Franceses, no porque me passe por el pensamiento que deva ser assi, pero en secreto se dize que el Rey de Francia anda tramando para yr sobre los Estados, ó tomarlos, y que su her, mano se casa con hija del Principe, y otros muchos casamientos que se hazen- y que se haze armada en toda Francia para ello, y oy ha llegado aqui aquel Embaxador con treynta cavallos, que va á la Reyna de Inglaterra, y viene de Paris, y assi mismo se aguarda (segun se dize) el que esta en Brusselas, para yr tambien a la dicha Inglaterra. De suerte que no se sabe otro sino esto, que, como digo, se dize en secreto, y en partes que nos lo han dicho. Plegue a Dios que nos guarde dello, que bien creo si suspection dello huviesse, lo sabria el Embaxador que esta en Paris y lo advertiria a essa Bolsa, pues importa. Aunque, como digo, no creo nada dello, y no he querido dexar de escrivirlo en esta, para que se tenga aviso dello, sin que se entienda, pues no se suffre dezir.

APPENDIX XXXVII

[P. 505, n. 3]

STATE PAPERS, DOMESTIC

ELIZABETH, VOL. CV. NO. 51

[*Walsingham to Lord Burghley*]

My verry good L. I send your L. sooche letters as I receyved from owre Imb. dyrectid unto you by the wch yt may appeare unto you that Q. mother had some intentyon under the cullore of a Parle w^t her sonne to have intrapped him. I thinke the gentleman hathe to good exsperyence of her to truste her (thowghe nature myght somewhat move him therin) I longe to heare that he were past the Ryvere of Loyre: for before that tyme I shall be greatly jealouse of his savetye. Her ma^t was perswaded under the cullor of scooryng the seas to have set owt two of her shipps to have receyved him yf being not well as-systed he shoold be forced to flye but she can not be drawen to yelde therto. This daye ther came letters from the justyces of Devonshire that the seconde of this monethe ther arryved on ther cost 48 sayle of Spanyshe men of warre whoe desyered herborrowynge but were denyed for that they had no passeporte of her mat. Notwtstandyng they suffered the Admyrall and vyceadmirall to come in to the porte of Darmouthe: wher as the gentlemen advertyce yt is thowght they wyll lande some treasvre to be conveyed by lande unto London The rest of the ships are gon towardes Dunkyrke. The Generall of them is Don Petro de Baldis whoe maryed Petro Malendas daughter. The arryvall of this armye makethe me greatly to dowbt the P. of Oranges well doinge: whoe alreadye seamethe to be in verry harde case. I praye God owre merchauntes fynde them good neyghebowres. Owt of the northe we have hearde nothing laetly And so having nothing ells to advertyce I commyt your L. to Goods good kepyng most humbly takyng my leave. At Rycot the vjth of Octobre 1575.

Yr L. to commavnde

FRA: WALSYNGHAM

[Addressed] To the right honorable
my vearie good Lord the
L. treasurer.

[Endorsed] 6. Octob. 1575.
Mr Secret: Walsingham
the Spanish flete in
the west.

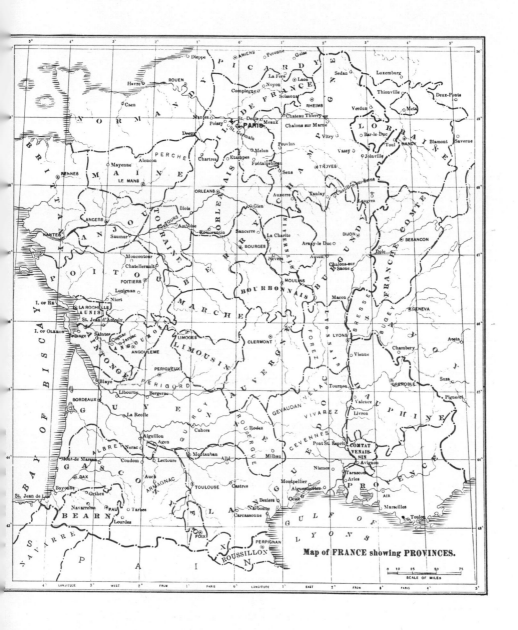

Map of FRANCE showing PROVINCES.

SCALE OF MILES
0   10   25   50   75

INDEX

INDEX

Abbeville, riot at, 133.

Acuna, Don Juan de, mission of, to Savoy, 308.

Adresse, baron des, Huguenot chieftain in Dauphiné, 147; prince of Condé thinks of joining, 153; lieutenant of, in Provence, 395.

Agde, court at, 252.

Agen, riot at, 133, 134; Catholic league of, 215, 225, 254; Montluc thinks of retiring to, 403; Montluc fortifies, 406.

Aides, 82.

Aigues Mortes, Damville introduces Turkish fleet into, 492.

Aix, association of Provence formed at, 214, 225; court at, 251.

Alava, Spanish ambassador in France: theft of cipher of, 266, 317, n. 6; exceeds instructions in threatening war, 266, n.; charges Catherine de Medici with duplicity 315; protests against overtures for peace, 417; incident with Tavannes, 418, 419; haughty reply of Charles IX to, 441.

Albanian troops with Alva, 307, 310.

Albi, 395, 405, 406. *See also* Viscounts.

Albret, Jeanne d', queen of Navarre, wife of Antoine of Bourbon and mother of Henry IV: mentioned, 120; Antoine of Bourbon quarrels with, 132; demand for banishment of, by Spanish ambassador, 133; consideration shown, 239; plot of Montluc and Spain to kidnap, 260; excommunicated, 261; maintains court preacher to anger of Catholics, 288; mobilizes troops in Béarn, 307; territories of, 350; crushes Catholic League at St. Palais, 355; crosses Garonne River "under the nose of Montluc," 368, n.; pawns her jewels, 378; directs foreign negotiations with Huguenots, 379; negotiations of government with, 391–93.

Alençon, François, duke of, youngest brother of Charles IX: governor of Paris, 358; marriage negotiations with Queen Elizabeth, 430 ff.; character and appearance of, 432; Hugue-

not-Politique plot to recognize, as heir apparent, 477, 478; complaint of, to Charles IX, 479; arrested, 480; escape of, 505; revolt of provinces to, 506; terms demanded of Henry III, 508; privileges of, in Peace of Monsieur, 519, 520.

Alessandria de la Paille, Alva at, 311.

Alexander VI, bull of, 300.

Allny, secretary sent to confer about peace, 344.

Alsace, Baron Bolwiller of, 301.

Alva, duke of, proxy for Philip II at marriage of Elizabeth of Valois, 3; suspected of urging inquisition in France, 12; favors repressive policy of Henry II, 117; upon commerce of Low Countries, 163; purposes to have Havre put in hands of Philip II for mediation between France and England, 198; advises fortification of Gravelines, 267, 268; instructions at Bayonne, 273; advises execution of Huguenot leaders, 274; relations with Catherine de Medici at Bayonne, 277; influence over duke of Montpensier, 304; Philip II determines to send, to Netherlands, 305; march of, through Savoy, Franche Comté, and Lorraine, 305–11; sails from Cartagena and arrives at Genoa, 309; arrives at Brussels, 312; and the Gueux, 314; arrests Egmont and Hoorne, 318; opinion of, of cardinal of Lorraine, 336, n.; appealed to by cardinal of Lorraine, 336, 337; offers aid to Catherine of Medici, 338; suggests coming in person to relief of French crown, 338; instructions to, 351; protests against Huguenot activity in Flanders, 360; defeats Louis of Nassau at Jemmingen, 361; executes Egmont and Hoorne, 361; offer of aid accepted by France, 380; Jeanne d'Albret protests against, 393; tyranny of, in the Netherlands, 441; revolt of Flushing and Middelburg against, 444; determines to retire his forces into Ghent and Antwerp, 444; desperate straits of, 446; intercepts Genlis' relief column, 447.

DATE DUE

APR 24 '67		
DEC 9 '6		
MAR 24 '68		
APR 12 '69		
MAR 26 '70		
FEB 20 '7		
OCT 28 '7		
FEB 3 '72		
MAR 2 5 '74		
FE 21 '79		
FE 1 8 '80		
OCT 2 1 '8		
OCT 14 '8		
GAYLORD		PRINTED IN U.S.A.